POSTCOLONIALISM
IN AFRICAN BIBLICAL INTERPRETATIONS

WITHDRAWN FROM
THE LIBRARY

UNIVERSITY OF
WINCHESTER

D1615681

KA 0387641 1

Society of Biblical Literature

Global Perspectives on Biblical Scholarship

Number 13

POSTCOLONIAL PERSPECTIVES
IN AFRICAN BIBLICAL INTERPRETATIONS

POSTCOLONIAL PERSPECTIVES
IN AFRICAN BIBLICAL INTERPRETATIONS

Edited by

Musa W. Dube, Andrew M. Mbuvi, and Dora Mbuwayesango

Society of Biblical Literature
Atlanta

UNIVERSITY OF WINCHESTER
LIBRARY

UNIVERSITY OF WINCHESTER

03876411   220.6

DuB

POSTCOLONIAL PERSPECTIVES
IN AFRICAN BIBLICAL INTERPRETATIONS

Copyright © 2012 by the Society of Biblical Literature

All rights reserved. No part of this work may be reproduced or transmitted in any form or by any means, electronic or mechanical, including photocopying and recording, or by means of any information storage or retrieval system, except as may be expressly permitted by the 1976 Copyright Act or in writing from the publisher. Requests for permission should be addressed in writing to the Rights and Permissions Office, Society of Biblical Literature, 825 Houston Mill Road, Atlanta, GA 30333-0399, USA.

"Race, Scripture, and Colonialism: Olaudah Equiano's Narrative of Biblical Origins" appeared originally as "Colonialism, Biblical World-Making, and Temporalities in Olaudah Equiano's Interesting Narrative," by Sylvester A. Johnson. *Church History*, Volume 77, Issue 04 (2008), pp. 1003–1024. Copyright © 2008 American Society of Church History. Reprinted with the permission of Cambridge University Press.

Library of Congress Cataloging-in-Publication Data

Postcolonial perspectives in African biblical interpretations / edited by Musa W. Dube, Andrew M. Mbuvi, and Dora R. Mbuwayesango.
    p.   cm. — (Society of Biblical Literature global perspectives on biblical scholarship ; no. 13)
Includes bibliographical references and indexes.
ISBN 978-1-58983-636-5 (paper binding : alk. paper) — ISBN 978-1-58983-637-2 (electronic format)
    1. Bible—Postcolonial criticism—Africa. 2. Postcolonial theology—Africa. 3. Theology—Africa. I. Dube Shomanah, Musa W., 1964– II. Mbuvi, Andrew Mutua. III. Mbuwayesango, Dora R.
BS511.3.P68 2012
220.6096—dc23   2012006437

Printed on acid-free, recycled paper
conforming to ANSI/NISO Z39.48-1992 (R1997) and ISO 9706:1994
standards for paper permanence.

This volume is dedicated to the memory of Rev. Dr. Justin Ukpong, (b. Dec. 26, 1940–d. Dec. 16, 2011). Eminent New Testament scholar, first Vice Chancellor of Veritas University, Nigeria, and a pioneering member of the African Biblical Hermeneutics Section in SBL.

CONTENTS

Abbreviations

AACC	All Africa Conference of Churches
AJB	*American Journal of Bioethics*
AJBS	*African Journal of Biblical Studies*
ANTC	Abingdon New Testament Commentary
AS	*African Studies*
ATJ	*African Theological Journal*
ATS	Acta Theologica Supplementum
BAS	Biblical Archaeology Society
BCTSAA	*Bulletin for Contextual Theology in Southern Africa and Africa*
Bib	*Biblica*
BibInt	*Biblical Interpretation*
BIS	Biblical Interpretation Series
BNHS	*Bulletin: News for the Human Sciences*
BOTSA	*Bulletin for Old Testament Studies in Africa*
BR	*Biblical Research*
BSASAW	Bible Studies for African-South African Women
BT	*The Bible Translator*
BTh	*Black Theology*
BTB	*Biblical Theology Bulletin*
CASAS	Centre for Advanced Studies of African Society
CBQ	*Catholic Biblical Quarterly*
CC	*Cross Currents*
ChCr	*Christianity and Crisis*
CHSHMC	Center for Hermeneutical Studies in Hellenistic and Modern Culture
CH	*Church History*
CI	*Critical Inquiry*
CL	*Christianity and Literature*
CM	*Challenge Magazine*
CSJLCS	Critical Studies in Jewish Literature, Culture, and Society
EAEP	East African Education Publishers
ECS	*Eighteenth-Century Studies*
ExpTim	*Expository Times*
FFNT	*Foundations and Facets: New Testament*
FT	*Feminist Theology*

FTS	Feminist Theology Series
GBOT	*Ghana Bulletin of Theology*
GPBS	Global Perspectives on Biblical Scholarship
GT	*Grace and Truth*
HRRC	*Human Resource Research Centre*
HTR	*Harvard Theological Review*
IBMR	*The International Bulletin of Missionary Research*
ILJ	*Indiana Law Journal*
Int	*Interpretation*
IRM	*International Review of Mission*
JAAS	*Journal of Asian and African Studies*
JACT	*Journal of African Christian Theology*
JAH	*Journal of African History*
JAPS	*Journal of African Policy Studies*
JBL	*Journal of Biblical Literature*
JCPS	*Journal of Commonwealth and Postcolonial Studies*
JCT	*Journal of Constructive Theology*
JETS	*Journal of the Evangelical Theological Society*
JFM	*Journal of Family Ministry*
JFSR	*Journal of Feminist Studies in Religion*
JRA	*Journal of Religion in Africa*
JRE	*Journal of Religious Ethics*
JRT	*Journal of Religious Thought*
JSNT	*Journal for the Study of the New Testament*
JSNTSup	Journal for the Study of the New Testament Supplement Series
JSOT	*Journal for the Study of the Old Testament*
JSOTSup	Journal for the Study of the Old Testament Supplement Series
JTSA	*Journal of Theology for Southern Africa*
LT	*Living Tradition*
MF	*Ministerial Formation*
MFS	*Modern Fiction Studies*
MJT	*Melanesian Journal of Theology*
NCR	*The New Centennial Review*
NedGTT	*Ned. Geref. Teologiese Tydskrif*
Neot	*Neotestamentica*
NICOT	New International Commentary on the Old Testament
NIGTC	New International Greek Testament Commentary
NAOTS	*Newsletter on African Old Testament Scholarship*
NovR	*Nova Religio*
NRSV	New Revised Standard Version
NT	*Notes on Translation*
NTS	*New Testament Studies*
OTE	*Old Testament Essays*
OTL	Old Testament Library
PL J.	*Migne, Patrologia latina*

PMLA	*Proceedings of the Modern Language Association of America*
RAL	*Research in African Literatures*
RB	*Revue Biblique*
ResQ	*Restoration Quarterly*
RevExp	*Review and Expositor*
RIL	*Religion and Intellectual Life*
RL	*Religion and Literature*
RT	*Religion and Theology*
SBL	Society of Biblical Literature
SBLASP	Society of Biblical Literature Abstracts and Seminar Papers
SBLDS SBL	Society of Biblical Literature Dissertation Series
SC	*Social Compass*
SCP	Studies in Classical Philology
SJOT	*Scandinavian Journal of the Old Testament*
SHE	*Studia Historiae Ecclesiasticae*
SNTSMS	Society for New Testament Studies Monograph Series
SPS	Sacra Pagina Series
SWC	*Studies in World Christianity*
SZBUI	Studien Zur Befreiung Und Interkilturalitat
TCCE	*Theologies and Cultures: Church and Empire*
TCS	*Theory, Culture, and Society*
TPI	Trinity Press International
TTran	*The Translator: Studies in Intercultural Communication*
TSe	*Theology and Sexuality*
ThViat	*Theologia Viatorium*
USQR	*Union Seminary Quarterly Review*

ACKNOWLEDGMENTS

The editors would like to thank a number of people who made this volume possible. First, we want to thank some members of the steering committee of the African Biblical Hermeneutics section at the Society of Biblical Literature, between 2004 and 2010—Justin Upkong and Gerald West—who oversaw the sessions that gave us these papers. Second, we want to recognize all the contributors for their enthusiastic participation in this project and for making every effort to get their essays in on time and in good form. Much of the editorial work was done during the time when Musa W. Dube was on sabbatical. We would like to thank the institutions that hosted Dube, Union Theological Seminary in New York and University of Bamberg in Germany, for providing both the space and resources that contributed to this publication. We would also like to thank Dr. MonaLisa Covington at Shaw University for helping out with the indices. Leigh Andersen and Kathie Klein at SBL have been wonderful to work with throughout the process of getting the manuscript from a collection of working drafts to the completed final product.

Introduction

The Scramble for Africa as the Biblical Scramble for Africa: Postcolonial Perspectives

Musa W. Dube

Space, whether one refers to a geographical terrain, a physical abode, a body, or an imagined place or community, is a site for the interrogation of geometries of power, of how these relations of power are secured, and also of how they may be unmasked. How then might biblical scholars take *our spaces* seriously?[1]

Centuries of the Scramble for Africa

Recent research indicates that 470 million Christians live in sub-Saharan Africa and that one in every five Christians in the world lives in Africa.[2] The same research indicates that biblical faith is expressed alongside other faiths—alongside four hundred million Muslims, mostly in upper Africa, though not exclusively so, and the uncounted number of adherents to African Indigenous Religions, who, more often than not, subscribe to both Christian and Islamic faith. North African Christianity can be linked to the biblical myth of Mary and Joseph's sojourn to Egypt, where baby Jesus finds security against Herod's unwelcoming designs (Matt 2). It could also be linked to the Lukan theological history of the early church, which records the story of an Ethiopian who was converted and baptized by Peter (Acts 8:26–40). Historically, Christianity in North Africa is as old as the early church. The latter gave us the prevailing Egyptian Coptic church and the Ethiopian Orthodox church and a whole line of celebrated church fathers such as Origen of Alexandra, Tertullian, and Augustine of Hippo. While North African Christianity was the earliest, sub-Saharan Christianity is now the most thriving. The history of the latter covers five centuries. The Bible has been read within precolonial, colonial, struggle-for-independence, postindependence, neocolonial and

---

1. Abraham Smith, "Taking Spaces Seriously: The Politics of Space and the Future of Western Biblical Studies," in *Transforming Graduate Biblical Studies,* ed. Elisabeth Schüssler Fiorenza and Kent Harold Richards (Atlanta: SBL, 2010), 64.

2. See The Pew Forum on Religion and Public Life's Web site report, "Tolerance and Tension: Islam and Christianity in Sub-Saharan Africa," April 15, 2010.

globalization contexts. The articles in this volume interpret the Bible through and
with this postcolonial history. Through critical evaluations of previously offered
theories and themes and through the introduction of new themes, this volume
presents African biblical interpretation through a postcolonial lens. As used here,
African Christianity refers to multiple and various practices, movements, and interpretations of biblical texts across the massive continent and also through various times, denominations, countries, genders, races, classes, ethnic groups, cultural beliefs, and interest groups.

The history of Christianity in sub-Saharan Africa can be traced to the earliest
traders with Africa in such areas as the Gold Coast (modern-day Ghana), Central
Africa, the Monomotapa Empire, through contacts with Portuguese and Dutch
traders in the Cape of Good Hope. This particular stage did not necessarily include colonization of lands but was characterized by its slave trade, which has
given us the current African diaspora communities in the Americas, the Caribbean, and Europe. It was not until the modern European imperial movements of
the eighteenth to nineteenth century that a more forceful agenda was undertaken
to Christianize sub-Saharan Africa. One thinks here of legendary figures such as
David Livingstone (1813–73), a missionary who set out to "open" the continent to
the three Cs: Christianity, commerce, and civilization.[3] To be specific, "to open up"
the continent for Western Christianity, commerce, and civilization.

In this extremely gendered colonial language, the African continent was being
penetrated by the West, its male subjugator, and inseminated with Western seed to
give birth to the Westernized African. David Livingstone died in the African continent in a relentless pursuit of this agenda. He was buried with the kings of England—in Westminster Abbey—in recognition of his service to the mother of all
empires—the British Empire. But African people supposedly insisted that David
Livingstone's heart should be buried in the continent. One cannot help but wonder
if the heart of Livingstone, buried in the African soil, is the little leaven that leavens
the whole flour, or is it an incurable virus that wreaks havoc in our bodies? Was
this wrench bloody heart, disembodied and buried in African soil, perhaps, an attempt to arrest Livingstone's reckless agenda of the three Cs?

David Livingstone's dream to open Africa for Western Christianity, commerce,
and civilization did not die with him. Henry M. Stanley, a naturalized American,
who was commissioned to find David Livingstone and who was inspired by Livingstone, returned to the continent to "explore the rivers and lakes of central Africa."
He recorded his exploration in a book, *Through the Dark Continent*, published
in 1877. He published another volume in 1890 entitled *In Darkest Africa: Quest,
Rescue, and Retreat of Emin Governor of Equitima*. His agenda was a continuation
of David Livingstone's. Nonetheless, these two men were but a drop in the ocean
compared to the many Western missionaries and traders who worked in various

3. See J. H. Worcester Jr., *David Livingstone: First to Cross Africa with the Gospel* (Chicago: Moody, 1990).

African sites, often preceding the colonization of the native people they served or following colonization. It was not unusual, however, for missionaries such as John Mackenzie to call for the colonization of native people.[4]

While the likes of Livingstone, Stanley, and Mackenzie worked at a period when colonization was random, irregular, and often had disinterested mother countries, the end of the nineteenth century was a colonial "climax." Each Western colonial power was poised to grab and own every available piece of Africa. There was such high competition and tension between colonial powers that it necessitated regulation to avoid a war. The situation led to the infamous Berlin Conference of 1884–85, which sought a more agreeable way of partitioning the African continent among Western colonial powers. This was the so-called Scramble for Africa.

African communities and their lands were, of course, neither consulted nor invited to the Berlin Conference. The participants were Western European powers, traders, and their missionaries. Africa, surrounded by numerous suitors, did not have the choice to choose a suitor nor to refuse one. This was not a love story. The history speaks for itself. The modern history of the Western colonization of Africa was a violent process of taking Africa by force. It was indeed a gang rape, so to speak. The essays in this volume amply demonstrate that the trauma of this history is not just an archive of the past, but a continuing story. We bear the wounds of the "Scramble for Africa" upon our bodies and lands.

In just about two centuries, Christianity has assumed a stronghold in the African continent while coexisting with African Indigenous Religions, Islam, and other religions. Has the heart of David Livingstone become a mustard seed? The throbbing and boisterous pulse of contemporary African Christianity/ies is seemingly causing discomfort in the Western world, which finds African Christianity conservative, perhaps mirroring the missionary teachings that sought to uproot African people completely from their religious beliefs by teaching the strictest biblical adherence, or reflecting the contemporary charismatic/Pentecostal movements, or both. Tinyiko Maluleke asks if this was perhaps an experiment that went wrong. Could it be a historical backfire?[5] Perhaps! But the perceived conservative character of African Christianity depends on reducing diversity into sameness, as depicted by Western scholars and researchers, mirroring the colonial habit of refusing Others their own voices as well as the tendency to characterize the Other as an uncivilized savage.[6]

---

4. See Anthony Dachs, *Papers of John Mackenzie* (Johannesburg: Witwatersrand University Press, 1975). John Mackenzie, a missionary who served in southern Africa over a long time, openly advocated the colonization of natives, as his letters amply demonstrate.

5. Tinyiko Maluleke, "Of Africanised Bees and Africanised Churches: Ten Theses on African Christianity," *Missionalia* 38, no. 3 (2010): 369–79.

6. See Phillip Jenkins, *The New Faces of Christianity: Believing the Bible in the Global South* (Oxford: Oxford University Press, 2006), who sets out to prove the conservativeness of global south Christianities. In the process we are all lumped into one category of sameness, namely that of conservative Bible readers and Christians.

The writing is on the wall. In sub-Saharan Africa, biblical interpretation, its institutions, and readers will always be related to modern colonial history, for *the Scramble for Africa was the Scramble for Africa through the Bible*. As we shall observe, the scramble to get Africa back from the colonial clutches was and still is waged through the Bible (yet the Bible is not the only viable weapon).[7] That the Scramble for Africa was a scramble through the Bible is therefore an interpretation crux.

The interpretation of the Bible, as attested by the chapters in this volume, is firmly framed within the African historical context. This scramble did not end with Westerners' sharing of the body of Africa among themselves. It was followed by Africans' scramble to get Africa back from the colonizers in a history that is known as the struggle for independence, which ranged from after World War II to the recent postapartheid era. The Scramble for Africa continues today in the post-independence era. The neoliberal economy known as globalization is the scramble of former colonial powers, in the company of new rising global powers, to have free access to global markets and cheap labor, without necessarily granting the same rights to all countries. In short, biblical interpretation in the sub-Saharan Africa cannot be separated from politics, economics and cultural identity, of the past and present. Biblical interpretation in the African continent is thus intimately locked in the framework of scramble for land, struggle for economic justice and struggle for cultural survival. Biblical interpretation remains wedged between Western and African history of colonialism, struggle for independence, post-independence and the globalization era. Biblical interpretation in Africa is the site of struggle as the essays in this volume amply demonstrate.

While modern Christianity in sub-Saharan Africa can be held to be two to five centuries old academic biblical interpretation does not have a longer history. Ironically, the colonial missionary agenda was thoroughly educational. Schools were introduced to educate and bring up Bible readers—literacy itself was introduced to promote bible translation, interpretation, conversion and training of preachers. One would expect that African biblical scholars in the sub-Saharan region would be numerous, but history is unfortunately not generous. To my knowledge black sub-Saharan biblical scholars constitute a handful of individuals, just slightly above thirty. An earlier generation also constitutes a handful of individuals, who were often oscillated between church leadership, ecumenical movements, and the academy, in the likes of Kwesi Dickson, John Mbiti, John Pobee, and Mercy Oduyoye.

This ironic situation may be attributed to the fact that initial colonial churches anticipated a relationship of dependence or one that was informed by colonial racism, where African believers were not expected to do their own thinking or to

---

7. See Diane M. Stewart, *Three Eyes for the Journey: African Dimensions of the Jamaican Religious Experience* (Oxford: Oxford University Press, 2005), who documents how enslaved Africans in Jamaica used African Indigenous Religions as part of their resistance.

provide independent leadership. The immense volume of African Christians (470 million) is thus adversely correlated to its biblical scholars and theologians. This phenomenon in itself risks maintaining colonial relations, where research, thinking and theories of interpretation of the Bible remain generated by the former colonial "mother countries" while formerly colonized Christian countries, like children, continue to eat from their mother's hand. Nowhere is this more evident than in the wholesale transfer of popular American evangelicalism into African via TV programming, whose producers do not even make the effort to erase the locally irrelevant 800 numbers from the screens. Hearing and nurturing the voices of African biblical scholars, both sub-Saharan and North African, is thus imperative.

This volume of academic writers thus follows upon the earlier generation of scholars such as John Mbiti, a New Testament scholar (*New Testament Eschatology in an African Background*), who ended up working primarily in African Indigenous Religions; Kwesi Dickson, whose books include *Biblical Revelation and African Beliefs* (1969); *Uncompleted Mission: Christianity and Exclusivism* (1984) and John Pobee whose books included, *Towards an African Theology* (1979) and *Persecution and Martyrdom in the Theology of Paul* (1985). These scholars were trained mostly to serve in the church, used their training for academic ends and made it their agenda to bring in African Indigenous Religions, which were (and still are) often excluded from the colonially-founded academic programs. It goes without saying that the church being patriarchal, the voices of trained African women biblical scholars would even be scarcer. It was thus quite ground breaking when Mercy A. Oduyoye published her *Hearing and Knowing: Theological Reflections on Christianity in Africa* (1986) and set on the road to find and nurture other African women studying religion, thereby launching the Circle of Concerned African Women Theologians in 1989. Some of biblical interpretation books that came from the Circle include: *Other Ways of Reading; African Women and the Bible* (2001); *Grant Me Justice; HIV/AIDS and Gender Readings of the Bible* (2004). In recent time, a second generation of African Biblical scholars has attempted to register their presence in collective volumes such as *Semeia 73: Reading With: An Exploration of the Interface between Critical and Ordinary Readings of the Bible* (1996); *The Bible in Africa: Transactions, Trajectories and Trends* (2000); *Reading the Bible in the Global Village* (2001); *Bible Translation and African Languages* (2004). In addition many contributors have individually published a number of books and numerous articles in various journals and books. One consistent factor is that all writers engage with the empire in their own different ways: in specific times, forms and geography, as the eight sections of this book ably demonstrate. This volume builds upon these efforts and takes the African history of colonial contact into consideration, beginning with North-Atlantic slavery to the Post-Apartheid and globalisation era. It embraces the multifaceted contexts of "reading," the prolonged context of struggle for justice and the hybridity of biblical interpretation in Africa, for the Bible coexists with African Indigenous Religions, Islam and other religions.

From the recent academic history, this volume comes out of papers that were presented in the "African Biblical Hermeneutics" Sections at the Society of Biblical Literature (SBL) Annual Meetings. The African Biblical Hermeneutics sessions were a product of an earlier bigger group on "The Bible in Africa, Asia, the Caribbean and Latin America," which ran during the 1990s to the early 2000s. Gradually the group had mobilized more scholars from these various regions. It also became clear that the group straddled too many worlds, hence, when its lifespan came to an end, various groups were formed to continue to investigate independently biblical interpretation in Africa, Asia, the Caribbean, and Latin America. Because during this time there was also an organised movement for encouraging minorities in biblical studies, the newly formed groups collaborated with their diaspora communities and investigated biblical interpretations among African Americans, Asian Americans and Hispanics. As Two-Thirds World scholars of the Bible interacted and collaborated in these spaces, the centrality of the modern empire to their work became evident, ushering the postcolonial framework of reading the Bible. The gurus of this movement include, among others, Fernando F. Segovia, R. S. Sugirtharajah, Vincent Wimbush, Gale Yee, Gerald West, Justin Ukpong and Kwok Pui Lan. The founding members of the African Biblical Hermeneutics Section were Dora Mubwayesango, Justin Ukpong, Musa W. Dube and Gerald O. West. This particular volume comes from this history. With few exceptions, it presents papers that were first presented in SBL in the African Biblical Hermeneutics, between 2004 and 2010.

EVALUATIONS OF AFRICAN FEMINIST/GENDER-BASED BIBLICAL INTERPRETATIONS

To begin with the cover, it features two *adinkra* symbols from Ghana: *sankofa* (meaning "go back and take it") and *Nyamedua* ("the tree of God"). According to Mercy A. Oduyoye *Sankofa* is a symbol that encourages "a critical appropriation of one's heritage," while *Nyamedua* is a symbol that represents the "traditional altar to the Supreme Being, the constant presence of God."[8] The combination of these symbols on the cover communicates the agenda of this volume; namely; to critically examine the interaction of biblical texts with African people and their cultures, within the postcolonial framework. It also highlights that biblical texts are read with and through frameworks of African Indigenous Religions in various countries and contexts. At the same time, as this volume amply demonstrates, the *sankofa* act is a critical appropriation of history and all traditions.

Accordingly, the first section, featuring feminist/gender-based biblical interpretations begins with my article "*Talitha Cum* Hermeneutics of Liberation" which takes us right back to the heritage of Kimpa Vita of 1684–1706. Kimpa Vita, a

---

8. See Elisabeth Amoah, ed., *Poems of Mercy Amba Oduyoye* (Accra: Sam-Woode, 2001) 47, 68.

former indigenous doctor (*nganga*) converted to Catholic Christianity, later proclaimed that she was a spirit medium, possessed by the spirit of Saint Anthony. On this state, she began to propound a decolonizing perspective about the Bible. She contextualized biblical places to her land (Bethlehem was in Sao Salvador) and biblical characters as black (Jesus, Mary and his disciples were black). In an outright rejection of colonizing Christian symbols she called for the de-installation of white portraits of Jesus, Mary and the disciples, while insisting that God shall restore the colonially disgraced land of Congo. Although just twenty years of age, when she began her proclamation, she received a massive following, for she spoke to the concerns of her people. This caused panic among the powers that be, who decided to silence her by burning her, together with her child, on a stake for allegedly preaching heresy. Hers was a typical example of a discourse of resistance, a decolonizing reading of the Bible, and a scramble to regain her land by re-reading the text for decolonisation. Reviewing the biblical interpretations of contemporary African women readers, M. A. Oduyoye, M. Masenya, M. W. Dube and T. Okure, within the story of Kimpa Vita, the chapter highlights that their reading practices continue her legacy, for *sankofa* acts involved going forth between African Indigenous Religions and Biblical religion to propound an oppositional postcolonial feminist reading of both faith traditions. The struggle continues.

Elivered Nasambu-Mulongo's chapter is a very close analysis of Madipoane (Ngwana' Mphahlele) Masenya's African biblical scholarship. Born and raised in apartheid South Africa, where black people were structurally reduced to nothing, Masenya has distinguished herself as one of the very few African women who have written widely on African woman's interpretation of the Bible. Her published works have appeared in numerous journals, commentaries, books and edited volumes, covering several books of the Hebrew Bible such as Proverbs, Job, Esther, Ruth and the Prophets. Nasambu-Mulongo's evaluation highlights that Masenya has not only contributed to biblical interpretation, she has also significantly contributed by formulating a theory of reading; namely, *Bosadi* (womanhood) hermeneutics, drawn from Northern Sotho and the post-apartheid context. In a world where most methods and theories of reading the Bible are Eurocentric, Masenya's formulation of *Bosadi* hermeneutics are a significant way of decolonizing biblical scholarship. By drawing on her *Bosadi* hermeneutics from Northern Sotho cultures, Masenya performs a critical *sankofa* act; namely, that in the African continent the Bible exists with and through African cultures, a position that is subversive to the colonial Christianity's attempt to annihilate the later.

In her chapter, "Hanging Out With Rahab," Lynne Darden highlights that African postcolonial history and biblical interpretation have diaspora communities. Part of the Scramble for Africa included enslavement that constitutes most of people of African descent outside the continent. Naming Dube's interpretive lens as "Rahab's Hermeneutic," Darden holds that Rahab, the sex worker was virtually located in the borderland of her city, living in the middle; in between continuity and discontinuity, which allowed her to skillfully negotiate with the invaders of her land. Darden brings Dube's Rahab's hermeneutic to dialogue with womanist biblical reading, using the case of Cheryl Kirk Duggan. In so doing, Darden becomes the go between, who calls for a conversation between postcolonial hermeneutic in the continent and people of African descent in the diaspora. Undoubtedly more conversations and bridges are critically needed between African scholars of the Bible on the continent and the diaspora. The importance of Darden article therefore cannot be overemphasised.[9]

Decolonizing Biblical Interpretation in and with Creative Writing

The second section of this volume is on reading postcolonial biblical interpretations in and with creative writing. The families of creative literature examined for biblical interpretation stretches from earliest contact zones to current global contexts. Biblical interpretations are drawn from colonial anti-slavery diasporic narratives (Sylvester Johnson); missionary travel narratives (Gerald West); letters of the first 'literate' sub-Saharan African Christians (Sam Tshehla); the earliest African novels written during the organized struggle for liberation and in the post-independence era (Andrew Mbuvi) and historical novels that recapture the historical colonial contact zone (Hans van Deventer). In all the categories of literature investigated in this section, more work still needs to be done. As pointed above, African academic biblical scholars have been hard to come by, but this section underlines that when investigated from other sources of literature, African biblical interpretations have been abundant from the very earliest colonial contact zones.

Johnson's chapter represents an analysis of diasporic writing from people of African descent who had been subjected to slavery. Equiano (1745–1797) captured in West Africa as a small boy and sold into slavery, renamed Gustavus Vassa, bought his freedom and became central to the abolitionist movement in the UK. His autobiography, *The Interesting Life of Olaudah Equiano or Gustavus Vassa the African*, played a crucial role in the abolitionist movement. Johnson's analysis of Equiano's biography finds an intense decolonizing engagement with biblical texts. Equiano reads the Biblical tradition in comparison with his Ibgo traditional religions showing many similarities; re-reads racist biblical commentaries; and constructs a re-reading that traces and links his Igbo origins with biblical Jewish ancestors. Given that enslavement of African people was often based on colonial discourse that constructed African people as ahistorical and godless, Equiano's *sankofa* act is a decolonizing reading which sets out to dispute the colonial discourse by claiming divinity and history from both his Igbo and biblical traditions. Equaino's oppositional reading of the Bible thus assumes a stance of hybridity; uses the master's

---

9. See Hugh R. Page, ed., *The Africana Bible: Reading Israel's Scriptures from Africa and the African Diaspora* (Minneapolis: Fortress, 2010), which represents an encouraging collaboration between African American and African biblical scholars.

tools to bring down his house and demonstrates how all interpretations are rhetorical constructions for particular ends.

Gerald West takes us back to one of the earliest missionary travel narratives in South Africa, recounting their encounters with indigenous black South Africans. The case study he uses is represented by Queen Mmahutu of the Batlhaping. Biblical interpretation between the colonial missionaries and the indigenous early readers is radically different. While colonial missionaries opened and read the Bible, the indigenous people brought their own questions to the Bible and engaged it in their own terms, from the very beginning. This leads West to point out that, "the Bible would not always speak as the ones who carried it anticipated." Since colonial context was a writing moment, for an essential part of colonizing the Other included describing them in detail in endless letters, reports, documentations, travel narratives and diaries, African scholars in different countries need to begin to investigate indigenous biblical interpretation in the earliest contact-zone encounters.

Sam Tshelha's chapter gives us a third level of colonial encounter and the voices of the colonized. He analyses letters from educated Basotho, which means they were mostly Christians who were educated in mission schools, but because their cultural worlds were still intact, they maintained a critical posture towards biblical texts. In Botswana P. Mgadla and S. C. Volz collection of *Words of Batswana: Letters to Mahoko a Becwana 1883–1896* has been recently published in 2006. My reading of the latter resonates with West's findings; namely, that earliest sub-Saharan Christian readers of the Bible in colonial contexts brought their own questions and were quite oppositional to missionary teaching.[10] It suffices to say more research is needed in this type of literature from various countries and ethnic groups, where missionaries pitched their tents. Further, in both collections, the missionary writing and native letters, a conscious decolonising and suspicious reading is needed, for the missionary had significant control on presenting issues from their perspective and controlling the native voices that got heard, since the publishing houses and papers belonged to the mission centers. Tshetla's chapter is particularly significant in pointing us to a research archive that is yet to be sufficiently investigated by African biblical and literary scholars.

Mbuvi's chapter gives us a fourth level of native biblical interpretations in a postcolonial history of the continent. This level represents a generation of those who were more educated thus writing longer works, novels. In this category there is, perhaps, a latitude of freedom to speak more oppositional than we might find from earlier letters sent to missionary newspapers, for their writing and interpretations are informed by a particular historical context in the postcolonial plot; namely, the struggle for independence. Be that as it may, most creative writers of this time were largely graduates of mission schools, who could embrace, reject or collaborate with missionary biblical teaching. Mbuvi's chapter investigates the case

---

10. See my unpublished paper "Exegeting the Darkness: Reading the Botswana Colonial Bible," presented in Atlanta, SBL Annual Meeting, 2010.

of Ngũgĩ wa Thiongo, one of the scholars whose name stands high among post-colonial theorists in the world; and Bessie Head (1937–1986) a renowned South African woman writer in exile, who lived and died in Botswana. A child of a bi-racial couple, Bessie's mother, who lived in Apartheid South Africa, was sent to a mental hospital for her liaison with a black man to give birth secretly. Bessie's background makes her writing sensitive to all forms of ethnic discriminations that she observes among Batswana and constructs a narrative of ethnic-coexistence than discrimination.

Baptized and educated in Christian mission schools, like Kimpa Vita, Ngũgĩ was renamed James—a name that he discarded as his thinking became decolonial-ist. Similarly, while he first wrote in English at a later stage as part of decoloniz-ing his own thinking and practice grew—Ngũgĩ stopped writing in English and started writing in his native language, Gikuyu. Needless to say, this was a radical *sankofa* act! In his earliest novels Ngũgĩ explicitly uses biblical stories, to critically engage the empire during the colonial times. Later, writing in the post-indepen-dence time, dealing with independence disappointments, Ngũgĩ remained with biblical texts and themes as part of his language. Mbuvi's analysis of Ngũgĩ biblical interpretations highlights that his perspective was changing, just as he was chang-ing from Western Christian names and languages, to a more radicalized view of the Bible. This is captured by the titles of his novels such as *A Grain of Wheat* and *The Devil of the Cross*. Mbuvi's chapter has taken a big bite by analyzing the works of these two authors, for each of them has produced a literary canon. Nonetheless the analysis of Ngũgĩ wa Thiong'o's work provides an evident case of using the Bible in the scramble to get African lands from colonizers as well as insisting on African Indigenous Religions. In the work of these authors, engaging the empire and the Bible is not peripheral, but central to the agenda of their writing.

The last chapter in this section, features (Hans) van Deventer's analysis of a South African novel published in 2005. The novel's setting is in the late-eighteenth- and nineteenth-century Cape Colony South Africa, featuring well known histori-cal missionaries of the time (James Read, Van der Kemp and Moffat). It features a Khoi-Khoi man, whose indigenous beliefs attach a significant religious mean-ing to the Praying Mantis. The main character of the novel, Cupido Cockroach, is perhaps by indication of his last name destined to be something we wish to doom away; but something which has the tenacity to come back, by its tendency of ensuring that at its death it leaves behind a batch of eggs to re-hatch and thus resurrect against what seems to be its final decimation. Cupido's journey from his Khoi-Khoi traditional beliefs to embracing the biblical religion would entail continuous experiences of dying to his culture, which is required by his new bibli-cal faith, and the simultaneous tenacity of his indigenous religious beliefs' refusal to disappear. The three women in his life—his mother, first wife (Anna), and the second wife (Kartyn)—become the continual reminder of his indigenous faith and voice of reason in analyzing the racial disempowerment that he faces as a black indigenous missionary.

Cockroach is finally dismissed from his missionary job for supposedly failing to do his work, but this act in itself is a mark of victory for his indigenous faith given that the death of a cockroach is accompanied by birth of other cockroaches in bigger numbers. Indeed the natural sciences place the praying mantis and the cockroach in the same family, which puts a major twist on how we should read the protagonist's journey. It also makes Deventer title for this chapter, "God in Africa: lost and found; lost again and found anew" the most appropriate in describing the tenacity of indigenous cultures even as they embrace and intermingle with the death-dealing colonial biblical religions. Cockroach's journey into biblical faith would, like in the Kimpa Vita story, entail moving back and forth between the two belief systems. Deventer's chapter also connects with Gerald West's chapter, not only for addressing the same historical colonial context and analyzing the introduction of the Bible in colonial settings, but also in the role of native women characters. Both chapters are noted for featuring native women as the oppositional characters who even if they accept the Bible and its Christian faith, do so critically, in their own terms and without forgoing their indigenous beliefs.

Colonized Bibles: Re-Reading the Colonial Bible and Constructing Decolonizing Translation Practices

Section four features re-readings of colonial translations and discusses what could constitute decolonized biblical translations. As these chapters amply demonstrate, not only was colonial ideology packed in colonial travel narratives, missionary reports, letters and other descriptions of the Other, it also found its way to the colonial Bible translations. I accidently came upon this phenomenon in 1995 when I discovered that in the Setswana Wookey Bible of 1908 the word Badimo (ancestors) was used to translate demons! So literally Jesus in the colonial Setswana Bible goes around casting out Ancestors instead of demons. I was shocked to the bones: not only were we a colonized people, even our divine powers had been subjugated to the same. Yet missionary translations were not only colonizing Bibles that sought to dispense with African indigenous beliefs, they were also a patriarchalizing discourse, for the gender neutral African names of God took on a full patriarchal garment. These discoveries led me towards investigating the Setswana colonial Bible translations and to attempt an Africa-wide project of re-reading of colonial Bible translations with the Circle of Concerned African Women Theologians. This effort was frustrated by lack of sufficiently trained biblical scholars, leading to only two articles, where a continent wide volume was originally sought.[11] Consequently, in

---

11. See Musa W. Dube, *Other Ways of Reading: African Women and the Bible* (Atlanta: SBL, 2001). Dora Mbuwayesango, "How Local Divine Powers Were Suppressed: A Case of Mwari of the Shona," 63–77, and Seratwa Ntloedibe-Kuswani, "Translating the Divine: The Case of Modimo in the Setswana Bible," 78–100, were the only papers that were submitted.

one of the African Biblical Hermeneutics sbl sessions we featured the question of re-reading colonial Bibles, which gave birth to the chapters in this section.

Gosnell Yorke, a Caribbean person of African descent from St. Kitts-Nevis, opens this section. Yorke is not only a biblical scholar but has actually served as a translation consultant in the region of Southern Africa and writes from experience. His article lays a broad history of Bible translation in the African continent into three stages: First, the north African translations that included the Septuagint in Alexandria, the Coptic and Ethiopian Geʿez translations, which occurred centuries earlier, but did not have much impact on sub-Saharan Africa; Second, missionary translations that occurred in the context of the modern imperial context in the pre-independence era. Yorke pays much attention to missionary translations, highlighting how they were informed by the colonial context. Bible translation was a mission-driven agenda in an imperial age, which was often carried out according to various competing mission bodies. Third, the contemporary (modern) translations that begins to involve African people as Bible scholars, translators and consultants.

Yorke discusses the structures and translation houses that were established to control and facilitate translation according to Western established theories of the likes of Eugene Nida. Although the third stage supposedly features native translators, the latter operate within the established structures, theories and patronage of the former colonial masters. Indeed Yorke points out that there are some sites where translation is still largely in the hands of outsiders, despite the active involvement of indigenous mother-tongues speakers. Yorke calls for Afrocentric translations, which would, among other things, highlight African presence within the Bible, decolonize the available colonial Bibles that are still in use; equalize the power relations of native translators and consultants who are, more often than not, outsiders; and, in my view, depatriarchalize the translations by being faithful to gender-neutral African languages. However, Yorke acknowledges that economic power; the politics of gate-keeping; the lack of sufficiently trained biblical and linguistic native scholars; and the Western hermeneutical hegemony will continue to be a challenge in the quest for an Afrocentric approach to biblical translations. Realizing these challenges, in the days when Yorke was a translation consultant in Botswana, he ensured that he invited University of Botswana based mother-tongue biblical and linguistics scholars to be actively involved in the ongoing translation project. Yorke's approach indicates that it is not always about lack of trained scholars, but rather there is an agenda to control translation for particular ends.

Enerst M. Ezeogu's chapter perhaps best illustrates most of the challenges discussed by Yorke in contemporary bible translation projects. Using the case study of the Igbo Catholic Bible in Nigeria, Ezeogu outlines factors that impact a biblical translation in contemporary African settings under three categories. First, there are

This was followed up by Gosnell Yorke and Peter M. Renju, eds., *Bible Translation and African Languages* (Nairobi: Acton, 2004), written by translation consultants.

extra-textual issues which include administrative and monetary matters. Second, there are source-textual matters, which include deciding on source texts used for translation, translating gender, number and race. Third, there are receptor-textual factors, which include the various dialects in most African languages and reviewing colonial translations that tended to use loan words as well as confronting the multi-layered colonial legacy of being caught in between Latinized (following the Catholic tradition) and anglicized words (following the British colonial language). The last category illustrates the challenges confronted by contemporary natives in reviewing colonial bible traditions that have more than a century among faith communities. How should decolonizing reviews proceed without raising objections from attached receptor communities? How can completely new translations be undertaken where economic constraints are a factor? Due to lack of biblical scholars, Ezeogu highlights that contemporary translations that depend on English biblical translations, instead of Greek and Hebrew, end up importing embedded Western cultural assumptions.

Lovemore Togarasei's chapter presents a re-reading of the Shona colonial Bible translations and an investigation on "subsequent improvements" for possible decolonizing practices. Building on Dora Mubwayesango's earlier analysis of the Shona Bible, which focused on gender and the naming of God, Togarasei's re-reading of the Shona colonial Bible for imperial ideology asks how the various Shona dialects, were handled and how the Shona cosmology and spirituality was handled, using the case study of 1 Pet 4:3. According to Togarasei, the Shona missionary translators were incompetent in both languages—biblical and native languages. Togarasei places his discussion of the Shona Bible in the colonial context. He highlights that following Cecil John Rhodes in 1890, various missionary bodies divided the country among themselves (the scramble for Zimbabwe) and often gave themselves huge tracts of land. These included London Missionary Society, Apostolic Faith Mission, Catholic Church, Methodist Church, Anglican Church, Dutch Reformed Church and the Lutheran Evangelical Church. Zimbabwe has long been a highly colonized land. Indeed the scramble for Zimbabwe continues! Accordingly the Shona Bible translation was a process that was negotiated between the different mission bodies over time given that Shona language had five dialects, occupied by different missionary bodies. Togarasei focuses his investigation of colonial ideology on the translation of the word, "banqueting" in 1 Pet 4:3, which is listed among the vices to be avoided by readers. In the Shona colonial Bible translation the word was rendered *mabira*. Amongst the Shona, *mabira* is a central ritual used to communicate with ancestors on all issues affecting the family and community. Much like the Setswana colonial Bible translation that rendered ancestors as demons, the translation of *mabira* into a vice that must be avoided, demonized Shona culture and sought to distance indigenous readers from their own beliefs system. Togarasei's investigation of contemporary native speaker translators indicates that efforts were made to decolonize the Shona Bible through a review. Contemporary native translators have replaced *mabira* with *kuraradza*, which means a drinking party, not an ancestor veneration ritual. They have also made attempts to avoid loaned words (anglicised Shona words). But, as other cases have attested, readers, however, remain attached to the colonial Shona Bible, for they "still believe that the Union Shona Bible is *the* Bible."[12]

Elelwani B. Farisani's essay gives us a window into the history of Bible translation into Tshivenda, one of the eleven languages of South Africa. Discussing translation ideology, he quotes that at the 1998 launch of a revised version it was held that the translation "will empower the church of Christ to conquer the country for Christ," thereby highlighting that translation is still carried out under colonising ideology of conquest. Yet as Farisani underlines the translated Bible also empowers indigenous people to make their own interpretations, which may be different from the conquest agenda propounded by translation houses. In various stages, Farisani evaluates the history of TshiVenda, discusses some translation theories and revisits the colonial translation of 1936, using the case of 1 Kings 21:1–16. Like Yorke and Ezeogu, Farisani highlights challenges that face Bible translations projects in the African continent.

Overall, this section highlights significant research areas for African biblical scholarship, which current and future biblical students, must seriously consider. First, the reading of colonial biblical translations and their ideologies needs to be investigated and exposed. These chapters and the few published elsewhere, indicate that we have barely begun. Second, since these colonial translations have been read from the colonial times for more than a century, the impact on specific cultures needs to be studied and evaluated. One good example here is the gendering of African names of God into male gender, where they were largely neutral. Third, the new revised versions also need to be studied for the changes they make and what they maintain. Fourth, the study of colonial Bibles and their revised versions should contribute to new theories of translation. Data from the colonial translations indicates that theoretical claims of faithfulness to the original texts are not only untrue, they are also outright colonizing practices. New theories that will seek to respect both the so-called "source text" and the "receptor cultures" are imperative. The current claim of preserving the source text, a posture that is often used to annihilate Other cultures, is a perfect colonizing tool. Fifth, African biblical scholarship needs to commit itself to producing more biblical scholars, to be able to carry out translations and revisions from their very own mother tongue speakers.

Lastly, this section has major pedagogical implications for biblical studies as a whole. It is a standard practice to subject postgraduate students to learning two

12. I had the same findings with Batswana readings just as Aloo Mojola had similar findings with the Swahili readers. See Musa W. Dube, "Consuming a Cultural Bomb: Translating Badimo into Demons in the Setswana Bible," *JSNT* 73 (1999): 33–59; and Aloo O. Mojola, "Postcolonial Translation Theory and the Swahili Bible," in *Bible Translation and African Languages,* ed. Gosnell Yorke and Peter Renju (Nairobi: Acton, 2004), 77–104.

other European languages such as French, German and Spanish. For African students, who through colonization have already been instructed in languages of their former colonizers, this practice is often just another painful layer of colonization, for it serves to drive us even away from our languages and cultures and adds nothing to our scholarship. The pedagogical implications of this section are that African biblical students need to study, instead their own languages as part of doing biblical studies. African biblical students should be able to choose two African languages that were first used to translate the Bible in their regions. This shift will not only serve well in the re-reading of colonial Bibles, it will also build a significant profile of scholars who are equipped to assist with current biblical translations and revisions in their countries.

SCRAMBLING FOR THE LAND: READING THE LAND AND THE BIBLE

The three chapters in this section focus on land in the text and in the postcolonial contexts. Although colonialism which involved geographical spaces has largely subsided worldwide, land remains central to the postcolonial discourse. This is primary because the former colonized lands bear the marks and scars of this history, and many times the wounds are still bleeding, physically and psychologically. And so are its inhabitants. The Scramble for Africa continues as a historical reality and interpretation crux for African biblical scholars. While wars of independence were fought and won, it was mostly the political leadership that changed while economic and cultural power remained in the hands of the former colonizer. Just how the struggle for economic liberation must be wedged in the postcolonial era is a vital question. Land ownership, in many former colonies, best represents the *a luta continua* of this unfinished agenda in the postcolonial historical archives of resistance.

As the chapters of Robert Wafawanaka and Themba Mafico highlight, examining the acquisition, characterisation, use, and ownership of land in the text and history is thus central. Their focus underlines the unfinished business of economic independence from former colonizers. Both authors are natives of Zimbabwe, a country which in recent decades has highlighted how the struggle for independence continues because the empowerment of the dispossessed indigenous people remains an outstanding agenda. I am closely intertwined with the colonial story of Zimbabwe, since my parents were forced to move to Botswana after their land was declared a white man's farm. My parents had two choices: to move to dry, arid reserves designated for natives, or remain and become servants of their new land owner. Perhaps in resistance, or disbelief, my parents chose to remain, but the consequences of their new servanthood status soon became evident when their private property ownership was restricted. My parents then chose to move to Botswana, where we still live in the land-related series of Zimbabwean dispersion. While it is more than a half century since my parents moved, Zimbabwean natives face the same dilemma today, since the struggle for independence did not deliver the land back to the hands of the dispossessed people. My father, at 90, still yearns to find the grave of his mother.

As Wafanaka points out, "At independence in 1980, 97% of Black Zimbabweans owned 45million acres of poor land while 3% of whites owned 51million acres of mostly fertile land, more than half of the country." Where must the disposed indigenous people of settler colonies go? And what court of justice will hear their cases? The question of how was land acquired, used, owned and characterised in both biblical and African cultures, is thus a reading that these chapters investigate as they confront the colonial history that marks both the land of Zimbabwe and its people.[13] This indeed is linked to the historical fact that biblical stories were central to modern colonisation in Zimbabwe and many other areas. As Togarasei's chapter on biblical translation in Zimbabwe highlights, not only were native Zimbabweans moved into particular reserves, they were also given various missionaries to accompany their land and cultural dispossession. Just how one should re-read the biblical text for economic empowerment of the dispossessed is the focus of Wafawanaka and Mafico as they point us to the postcolonial history of Zimbabwe.

Robert Wafula's follows closely on this land quest, by examining the Abraham and Lot stories, concerning movement in search for land and settlement. Wafula's chapter proceeds by exploring the recently published *African Biblical Commentary* (henceforth *ABC*), an evangelical/charismatic sponsored work, whose contributors had "to sign an Association of Evangelicals in Africa statement of faith." This underscores that *ABC* contents had to comply to the demands of its sponsors. Wafula, frames his analysis within a postcolonial framework by discussing Edward Said's research on Orientalism as a colonial discourse of subordinating the Other through consistent binary oppositions that represent the other as lacking. Wafula further discusses postcolonial frameworks provided by Homi Bhabha and Spivack, which point to the colonial contact zone as also characterised by gendered discourse and fluidity, which goes beyond the binary oppositions to include a third space of hybridity. Wafula then draws from Elisabeth Schüssler Fiorenza's call for ethics of reading and Musa W. Dube's postcolonial feminist reading of the text. Applying these frameworks to the ABC reading of the Abraham-Lot circle of

---

13. Although Stephen Moore in his chapter "A Modest Manifesto for New Testament Literary Criticism: How to Interface with a Literary Studies Field That Is Postliterary, Post-theoretical, and Postmethodological," featured in his book *The Bible in Theory and Postcritical Essays* (Atlanta: SBL, 2010), 368–69, says "postcolonial studies has yielded remarkable little in the way of readily identifiable methodologies" and while he cites Edward Said for "only" yielding the overly general strategy of "contrapuntal reading," I believe the latter holds the potential to open the Pandora's box in biblical studies that Moore has long yearned for. When applied, as attested by Wafawanka article on land, biblical studies will hardly be recognizable from its neat antiquarian boundaries. Rather, contrapuntal biblical studies will be read with thousands of world histories, untouched archives, cultures, structures, and contemporary contexts. If biblical studies applies contrapuntal reading, the Pandora's box would be nothing less than a tsunami on the current form of naïveté of biblical studies.

stories, Wafula finds the *ABC* commentator oblivious of the ideologies peddled by the text. According to Wafula, the *ABC* fails to read Abraham's story within its larger ideological agenda that had already assigned his "seed" to Canaan, a land with indigenous natives. [14]

AFROCENTRIC BIBLICAL INTERPRETATIONS: "UNTHINKING EUROCENTRISM"

In their book *Unthinking Eurocentricism: Multicultralism and the Media*, Ella Shohat and Robert Stam highlight that colonial discourse has thoroughly informed academic paradigms, by situating the West (Europe, North America) as the center of knowledge production to maintain the ideology of superiority and the suppression of the Other. This discourse which they name as Eurocentric presents Western history, philosophies, theories, methods, texts, stories; culture and structures as the epitome of knowledge production and all that is best. Holding that "Eurocentrism is the discursive residue or precipitate of colonialism, the process by which European powers reached positions of economic, military, political and cultural hegemony in much of Asia, Africa, and the Americas," [15] Shohat and Stam, point out that the Eurocentric discourse is multi-faceted; including that it

> projects a linear historical trajectory leading from classical Greece (constructed as "pure," "western," and "democratic") to imperial Rome and then to metropolitan capitals of Europe and US.... Eurocentricism attributes to the "West" an inherent progress toward democratic institution ... elides non-European democratic traditions, while obscuring the manipulations embedded in Western formal democracy and masking the West's part in subverting democracies abroad.... In sum Eurocentrism sanitizes Western history while patronizing and even demonizing the non-West, it thinks of itself in terms of its noblest achievements—science progress, humanism—but of the non-West in terms of its deficiencies real or imagined.[16]

Obviously mainstream academic biblical studies and theology is steeped in Eurocentric perspectives. It wades deep in the oceans of Eurocentricism, far from the shores of redemption and unashamedly so. As attested by its terms of analysis and knowledge production, they are primarily drawn from Greek culture, hence the discipline speaks of "exegesis," "eisegesis," "hermeneutics," "ekklesia," "soteriology," "kyriarchy," "democratic," "theology," "androcentric;" "rhetoric," and the Greco-Roman context as the privileged history upon which academic biblical interpre-

---

14. See Randall C. Bailey, "They're Nothing but Incestuous Bastards: The Polemical Use of Sex and Sexuality," in *Reading from This Place*, vol. 1: *Social Location in the US*, ed. Fernando F. Segovia and Mary Ann Tolbert (Minneapolis: Augsburg Fortress, 1995), 121–38.

15. Ella Shohat and Robert Stam, *Unthinking Eurocentrism: Multiculralism and the Media* (New York: Routledge, 1994), 15.

16. Ibid., 2–3.

tation must occur. Every time we say hermeneutics, we are evoking Hermes the messenger to the Greek gods.[17]

Take these Eurocentric paradigms away, biblical scholars will not know what to do. Give biblical scholars a reading from Other worldviews, they dismiss it as unscholarly. Myopia reigns! In addition to requiring postgraduate students to learn two more European languages, for philosophy and theory, biblical studies draws from its Western thinkers such as Plato, Aristotle, Hegel, Kant, Nietzsche, Heidegger,[18] Karl Marx, Michel Foucault, Derrida, Lacan, French Feminists to mention a few. A few other non-Western thinkers, such as Edward Said, Gaytri Spivack, Homi Bhabha and Ngũgĩ wa Thiongo, have recently made entrance in Biblical studies. But they are only a drop in the ocean, paddled by a few scholars, who are swimming against the tide. Biblical studies is still largely steeped in Eurocentricism, projecting Greece as "where it all started."[19] Those of us who come from former colonies drink our fill, as we inevitably become colonized by the terms of the discipline. I confess I have taken a full baptism and I am still drowning in the Eurocentric epistemologies, although not without a struggle.

The three essays in this section make efforts to displace the Eurocentric biblical studies, by positing other ways and places of reading. African Americans, living in the belly of Eurocentrism, have long strived to highlight other ways of producing knowledge, by highlighting Egypt as another place instead of a singular focus on Greece. According to Shohat and Stam, "Afrocentric discourse posits Africa, and especially Egypt, as a site of origins."[20] Ezeogu's chapter is an exercise in Afrocentric interpretation in which standard tools of biblical "exegesis" are used to highlight aspects of the text that are of special interest to people of African descent. The chapter submits the thesis available in Matthew 1 in which Mary and her son Jesus, were known to be Africans of Egyptian origin resident in Galilee. According to Ezeogu, this tradition created difficulties for Jews of Matthew's time in accepting Jesus as their Messiah, since a Messiah was expected to be a Hebrew of Davidic line. Matthew, therefore, retells the story in such a way as to portray Jesus as a son of Abraham of the bloodline of David. Ezeogu holds that Matthew's makeover leaves many gaps. The chapter thus identifies these historical and narrative gaps and shows how the thesis of the African origin of Mary and Jesus fills them.

David Adamo's Chapter offers a critique of Eurocentric engagement with the Psalms. The chapter summarizes main methodological approaches used, high-

---

17. Henry L. Gates, *The Signifying Monkey: A Theory of African-American Literary Criticism* (Oxford: Oxford University Press, 1988), has posited another messenger of Gods, Eshu, instead of the usual culprit, Hermes.

18. See Shawn Kelley, *Racialising Jesus: Race, Ideology, and the Formation of Modern Biblical Scholarship* (Routledge: New York, 2002), whose book traces racism among the foremost thinkers of European philosophy and how it has influenced biblical scholarship.

19. Shohat and Stam, *Eurocentricism*, 55–58.

20. Ibid., 56.

lighting that they are predominantly Eurocentric. Arguing that the dominant models of reading Psalms in the scholarship at large and among African scholars are Eurocentric, Adamo seeks to shift the centre and point to multiple Other centres. He challenges the existing Eurocentric dominance and provides a number of alternative approaches that have emerged from and are consonant with African cultures and traditions, especially from Nigeria.

Madipoane Masenya's article is another example of reading from many other centres and worldviews in knowledge production. Using her *Bosadi* perspective, Masenya performs a critical *sankofa* act. Masenya calls on both Badimo (Ancestors) and Modimo (God) and draws from the Northern Sotho storytelling traditions, proverbial philosophy, sayings and worldview to read Job's Lament. Masenya situates her reading in Sepedi language, given that the language itself is the cradle of a cultural worldview. Instead of just Greek and Hebrew centred worldviews and Eurocentric philosophies and theories, Masenya's article has many italicised Sotho-Pedi words, phrases, sayings and proverbs, immediately sending the message to the reader that she reads from many Other centres as well. Using the character of Mmanape, a woman who carried a child in her womb for nine months, successfully delivered and raised a boy-child for twenty-six years and even gained patriarchal approval for mothering a boy child, she experiences a tragedy: her son dies in a car accident. In this storytelling, Masenya takes us deep into the worldview of mothering, birthing and burying. It is the art of going deep into the waters of Mother Earth and only to return the child back into deep soils of Mother Earth.

How does a grieved mother find healing? And here comes Job: a man who experienced massive loss of all his daughters, property and health. Mmanape a Northern Sotho woman comes to journey with Job, in search for healing. Surely Job has seen the worst, he did not only loose one child, he lost all of them. Here in Job's story a grieved mother must indeed find the road towards healing. But what does Mmanape find in Job's lament? Job curses the day he was born and blames his mother's womb that brought him to this life. This is shocking for Mmanape. Mothers are blamed for pain and death. What about mothers who are grieved: Do they only have themselves to blame? In short, Mmanape finds no comfort in Job's misogynist lament. In this chapter, Masenya has given us one of the most intense and original reading of Job's lament from a Bosadi perspective, using the worldview of Northern Sotho and her biblical training.

John David Ekem investigates the European and Ghananian translations and interpretations of the phrase "*ton arton hemon ton epiousion*," which is located within the Matthean and Lucan versions of 'The Lord's Prayer.' He argues that from a Ghanaian hermeneutical perspective, the question of 'economic survival' and the need to strive for moral and economic excellence should play a crucial role in the interpretation of the text. Ekem's chapter evaluates all the possible interpretational options and argues that it would be most appropriate to interpret, "*ton arton hemon ton epiousion*" as a reference to the supply of "needs necessary for our existence." This interpretation is not only supported by some Early Church Fathers, it is also meaningful to Ghanaian target audiences. In making this argument, namely, that meaning should be driven by the context and needs of the readers; Ekem is challenging the fiercely guarded translation theories that privilege the original text over against the so-called receptor communities, their languages and their needs.

<h2 style="text-align:center">BIBLICAL INTERPRETATION FOR RECONSTRUCTION</h2>

The colonial times were characterised by the re-reading the Exodus narrative for liberation in the struggle for independence. The colonized's reading sought to take away Exodus from the colonizers, who regarded themselves as divinely chosen races that had the right to dispossess the indigenous people of their lands. Instead they re-read Exodus for their liberation, positioning themselves as the oppressed, exploited and enslaved, whose cry has reached God's ear and eye.[21] But in the 1980s and early 1990s most wars for liberation in the continent ended characterised by the arrival of new nations such as Zimbabwe, Namibia and South Africa. Apartheid had finally crumbled, somewhat. Moreover, the global context was also characterised by the end of the cold war. It was a time of great hope, just before the disappointments became evident.

A theology of reconstruction and its reading of Ezra–Nehemiah emerged from this context: gone, it was assumed, are the revolutionary wars and now was the time to rebuild from the colonial devastation. But much as this textual shift is proposed, both books feature the coming in of some groups into a land that is already occupied by others. The crux of the matter is how to share the economic cake, the land, and to coexist with each other and the land in a relationship of liberating interdependence. In reconstruction reading as well, it is clear that the historical Scramble for Africa was not only the Scramble for Africa through the Bible, but also that the scramble to get back some pieces of Africa, by those who lost it, is still wedged through the Bible.

Elelwani B. Farisani's chapter gives us highlights of the earliest proponents of reconstruction theology by evaluating the works of Charles Villa-Vicencio, Jesse Mugambi and Andre Karamanga. Given the new context of post-independence, the proponents underlined the need to shift from liberation metaphors and scriptures, such as Exodus, to a new language of thinking and working through

---

21. See Robert A. Warrior, "Canaanites, Cowboys, and Indians: Conquest, and Liberation Theology Today," *ChrCr* 49 (1989): 261–65, who has highlighted that for dispossessed natives of settler colonies the Exodus narrative is historically and ideologically oppressive and does not work for liberation purposes. Indeed as the attempt to employ Ezra–Nehemiah for postliberation context points to the same challenge, we need to take Warrior's suggestion that we must look elsewhere, instead of confining ourselves to the same biblical texts that legitimized our oppression.

the Ezra–Nehemiah paradigm of rebuilding. A new day had dawned and hope reigned. Farisani interrogates these scholars' reading of the Ezra–Nehemiah and finds insufficient engagement with the chosen scriptures and lack of problematizing its ideology. In particular, their reading of Ezra–Nehemiah does not sufficiently problematize how the text empowers the returning exiles over the *am haaretz* and its exclusivist ideology, which required the divorce of foreign wives. For Farisani, Ezra–Nehemiah text must be read against the grain, fully identifying its oppressive ideology.

Coming from Zimbabwe, a country that fully embodies the hopes and disappointments of post-independence, Wafawanaka revisits the interpretation of Ezra–Nehemiah for reconstruction. In the colonial Zimbabwe, the indigenous were exiled within their own country by being moved to some reserves, which were arid, crowded and infertile areas. Independence should have meant returning to their lands and beginning the process of reconstruction. But as Wafawanka's earlier chapter points out, when the Lancaster Conference of 1980 was signed the country was given political independence while land remained in the hands of settler colonizers. The Zimbabwean government, with the help of former colonizer, was supposed to buy the land and redistribute it, a process that was only partially fulfilled, leading to the ceasing of the land by force and further devastation of people and the land. Getting back the land, has been a long protracted and devastating struggle, for those who took the land, although initially foreigners are now Zimbabweans and they are not volunteering to share it.

The Scramble for Africa is thus not just history, it is a living story that continues to play itself out on our lives. A reading of Ezra–Nehemiah for reconstruction from a Zimbabwean perspective is complicated but necessary. Clearly, it would challenge Farisani's position that those who remained in the land were necessarily oppressed by the returning exiles. Wafawanaka proceeds by placing Ezra–Nehemiah within the Deutronomistic history that associated Israel's subjugation by foreign nations with sin. He argues that the returning exiles adopted a survival posture, which involved expelling foreign wives. While Wafawanaka underlines that reconstruction is vital, he problematizes the identity politics of the Ezra–Nehemiah, pointing out that colonial ideology thrives by strategies that divides and stratifies people, leading to postcolonial explosions such as the Rwanda genocide of the 1990s.

Gerrie Snyman's chapter uses collective memory of South Africa as a hermeneutical framework to read Ezra–Nehemiah. One particular collective memory in South Africa is the theological justification of apartheid. The collective memories of the 'victims' of apartheid have drawn attention to the issue of subjectivity, urging the perpetrators to take stock of their own reading practices. Ezra's sending away of the strange women and children and Nehemiah's separation of the people from strangers echo the apartheid regime's policy of separate development. Synman's chapter strives to elucidate the role of collective memory as a hermeneutical framework for a bible-reading community struggling to come to terms with its perpetrator legacy and seeking to participate in constructing a new social order guided by a human rights framework. It asks the following question: In what way does an apartheid collective memory allow a perpetrator community to employ Ezra and Nehemiah in his or her own everyday reconstruction of society? In problematizing the ideology of Ezra–Nehemiah of resettlement, Synman is consistent with both Farisani and Wafawanaka. In short, these chapters amply demonstrate that given that the Scramble for Africa was a scramble through the Bible, this history will always remain an interpretation crux in reading biblical texts in the African contexts.

Social Engagement and Biblical Interpretations

In the African continent where the struggle for justice and empowerment still continues, the role and place of scholars becomes an ethical issue. Should a scholar ignore the struggles of the communities and maintain conversation only with other scholars? How should one situate their scholarship in the community for social transformation? The three chapters in this section give us three case studies. The first chapter, by Sarojini Nadar, investigates the work of Gerald O. West, who for over two decades has promoted socially-engaged scholarship. Her chapter critically explores the ideological, academic and socio-political implications of the model of social engagement developed by West. Nadar's analysis examines three focus areas: motivation, method and representation. She explores and interrogates West's methods by asking vital questions concerning the functions and responsibilities of both the faith communities and intellectual engagements. She questions how the communities are subsequently represented by the intellectuals. In conclusion, Nadar holds that collaboration between scholars and community is vital, however, the challenge which remains for organic intellectuals is to use the opportunities, which they have been given through their privileged access to education, to empower those in the community who have been structurally denied opportunities.

Emmanuel Katongole examines Musa W. Dube's work with HIV&AIDS as one example of a social-engaged scholarship. Because HIV&AIDS has interrupted our world and our lives in such radical ways, Katongole holds that we must allow it to interrupt our scholarship radically as well. For Katongole, allowing this interruption leads us to question our existing paradigms, it calls for the adoption of new methodologies and approaches. Even more importantly, it calls us back to the discipline of dreaming news visions in relation to our bodies, sexuality, family life, the church, and the world. HIV&AIDS an epidemic that was scientifically discovered in the early 1980s, has in just three decades, claimed more thirty million people worldwide, two-thirds of those in Africa. Dube who describes HIV&AIDS as an epidemic within other social epidemics, named this tragedy as a context of doing scholarship under a paradigm of shattered dreams. For Katongole, the challenge is how to embrace HIV&AIDS not only as threat, but to see it as a *kairos,* that is, as a moment of truth and a unique opportunity that forces us to dream and inhabit dreams of God's new creation. Katongole sees Dube's work with HIV&AIDS as a positive challenge, for it presents a model of embodied and embodying herme- neutics of life within the academy. However, Katongole suggests that Dube needs to pay more attention to the notion and practice of lament in the Bible. Biblical lament is not a mode of wading in one's own helplessness, but a posture of naming prevailing social injustice and protesting its unacceptability, thereby calling for transformation and living hope.

While Nadar and Katongole examine scholars' social-engagement with their communities, Alice Yafeh-Deigh's reading of Luke 10:38–42 seeks to highlight the liberative power of silent agency for Cameroonian women. The chapter seeks to offer *one* of the many potential readings of the story within the context of a postco- lonial Afro-feminist-womanist biblical hermeneutics. Yafeh-Deigh's postcolonial Afro-feminist-womanist approach takes the concerns of disadvantaged, marginal- ized grassroots women as the starting point of analysis and seeks to discern ways in which this story, that is not written with contemporary Cameroonian women's experience in mind, can be critically recontextualized and hermeneutically appro- priated within the context of their own lived experiences. Yafeh-Deigh's working premise is that the passage is about Mary's subversive choice and the evaluation of that choice by Martha and Jesus. She holds that Mary creates and enables a unique kind of agency, namely silent resistance. For Yafeh-Deigh, Jesus' consent to and his affirmation of Mary's subversive decision in Luke 10:42 forces the reader to reas- sess the meaning of agency, especially in contemporary contexts where silence, influenced by Eurocentric ideals, is often seen as a symbol of passivity and dis- empowerment. This space that Mary silently intrudes and creates is, according to Yafeh-Deigh, a space that is pregnant with possibilities for Cameroonian women's struggle for liberation and empowerment. Mary's silent agency, she argues, could not only be an empowering strategy for contemporary women in rural commu- nities, it could also be a tool for liberation that effectively challenges established gender roles assigned to men and women.

EMBODIMENT AND BIBLICAL INTERPRETATION IN THE HIV&AIDS CONTEXT

The last section focuses on embodiment, HIV&AIDS and biblical interpretation. In the colonial discourse and postcolonial contexts the body is a central ideologi- cal construct. Enslaved, racialised, gendered, sexualised, violated, lynched, starv- ing, dead, unburied, ghosts and resurrection bodies of resistance characterise the postcolonial history. Malebogo Kgalemang's reading of Mark's passion narrative, from a postcolonial feminist perspective, begins with the gruesome bloody body of the crucified Jesus and its function in modern colonial contexts. The colonial discourse through a hymn teaches the colonized Other to accept their suffering, by displaying the violated body of Jesus as salvific. Kgalemang's chapter gives a close reading of Mark 14–16. The first section examines the scope of postcolonial feminist criticism of the Bible while the second part is the application. Kgalemang's postcolonial feminist interpretation of Mark's passion narrative takes into full cognizance the patriarchal and the imperial context that produced the crucifixion, the role of local politics, its collusion with empire, and the role of women in the narrative. Holding that Markan resistance does not make sense outside the imperial context and outside the politics of gender, Kgalemang concludes that Mark is a colonized patriarchal writer, one who is constituted by the very same ideological principles he calls into critical questioning.

Jeremy Punt's chapter focuses on Pauline bodies and South African bodies. He highlights the intersection of power, body and biblical interpretation, arguing that a focus on the body in contexts of vulnerability foregrounds its interplay with power. Punt holds that while in South Africa there is a pronounced awareness of the material body and its needs, this contrasts with Christian theological tendency of undermining the body. Consequently, Punt interrogates the characterisation of the body in the New Testament, focusing on Pauline letters. Punt finds that in the Pauline traditions the body is central, for Paul frequently invoked the body, using it as the leading metaphor in his letters.

Thus Punt argues that Paul's theological approach and perception was informed by his engagement with bodiliness. Holding that the wide-ranging Pauline discourse on the body is imbued with power concerns, Punt shows the link between body and power in different configurations of various kinds in Paul's letters. For Punt, this reading has three advantages: it allows for rehabilitation of an important concept in Pauline thought; it signals a new epistemology of the body in which contextual nature of the body is taken seriously and the body is understood as a site of revelation. Obviously the centering of the body is vital given the recent wars on sexual orientation debates, characterised by the Anglican communion and among some African governments, and the HIV&AIDS context that has ravaged the continent in the past three decades.

The last chapter in the book highlights African biblical interpretations in the HIV&AIDS context.[22] In this article, I outline several frameworks that informed response to HIV&AIDS: These included the medical, religio-moral, human-rights psychological and social justice perspectives. The question in such contexts for biblical scholars is: How can our reading participate in the healing of communities and relationships in social-injustice driven epidemic? As used here, social injustice refers to a whole range of structural oppressions (e.g., poverty, gender oppression, homophobia, racism, age-based discrimination, exploitative capitalist neo-liberal economic structures etc) covering various marginalized groups such People Living With HIV&AIDS, blacks, women, widows, children, gay people, sex workers, drug addicts, the physically challenged, among others. The chapter gives a rough sketch of some emerging biblical interpretations on reading the Bible in the HIV&AIDS

---

22. This paper was first presented as a keynote address for the Southeastern Commission on the Study of Religion (SECSOR), Atlanta, 2008.

context. In conclusion, I highlight some of the methodological issues raised by HIV&AIDS for biblical studies; namely, that biblical studies should also utilize social-science based fieldwork methods given that it is a text that is read in the social contexts and informs attitudes and practices of individuals and communities.

Works Cited

Amoah, Elisabeth, ed. *Poems of Mercy Amba Oduyoye*. Accra: Sam-Woode, 2001.

Dachs, Anthony. *Papers of John Mackenzie*. Johannesburg: Witwatersrand University Press, 1975.

Dickson, Kwesi. *Biblical Revelation and African Beliefs*. Maryknoll, NY: Orbis, 1969.

———. *Uncompleted Mission: Christianity and Exclusivism*. Maryknoll, NY: Orbis, 1984.

Dube, Musa W. "Consuming A Cultural Bomb: Translating *Badimo* into Demons in the Setswana Bible." *JSNT* 73 (1999): 33–59.

———. "Exegeting the Darkness: Reading the Botswana Colonial Bible." Presented in Atlanta, SBL Annual Meeting, 2010.

———, ed. *Other Ways of Reading: African Women and the Bible*. Atlanta: SBL, 2001.

Dube Musa W., and Gerald West, eds. *The Bible in Africa: Transactions, Trajectories, and Trends*. Leiden: Brill, 2000.

Dube, Musa, and Musimbi Kanyoro. *Grant Me Justice: HIV/AIDS and Gender Readings of the Bible*. Pietermaritzburg: Cluster; Maryknoll, NY: Orbis, 2004.

Fiorenza, Elisabeth Schüssler, and Kent Harold Richards, eds. *Transforming Graduate Biblical Studies*. Atlanta: SBL, 2010.

Gates, Henry L. *The Signifying Monkey: A Theory of African-American Literary Criticism*. Oxford: Oxford University Press, 1988.

Jenkins, Phillip. *The New Faces of Christianity: Believing the Bible in the Global South*. Oxford: Oxford University Press, 2006.

Kelley, Shawn. *Racialising Jesus: Race, Ideology, and the Formation of Modern Biblical Scholarship*. Routledge: New York, 2002.

Maluleke, Tinyiko. "Of Africanised Bees and Africanised Churches: Ten Theses on African Christianity," *Missionalia* 38, no. 3 (2010): 369–79.

Mbiti, John S. *New Testament Eschatology in an African Background*. Cambridge: Cambridge University Press, 1972.

Mgadla, P. T., and S. C. Volz, trans. and ed. *Words of Batswana: Letters to "Mahoko A Becwana," 1883–1896*. Cape Town: Van Riebeeck Society, 2006.

Moore, Stephen. *The Bible in Theory and Postcritical Essays*. Atlanta: SBL, 2010.

Oduyoye, Mercy A. *Hearing and Knowing: Theological Reflections on Christianity in Africa*. Maryknoll, NY: Orbis, 1986.

Page, Hugh R., ed. *The Africana Bible: Reading Israel's Scriptures from Africa and the African Diaspora*. Minneapolis: Fortress, 2010.

Pew Forum. "Tolerance and Tension: Islam and Christianity in Sub-Saharan Africa," April 15, 2010.

Pobee, John. *Toward an African Theology*. Nashville: Abingdon, 1979.

———. *Persecution and Martydom in the Theology of Paul*. Sheffield: Contiuum, 1985.

Segovia, Fernando F., and Mary Ann Tolbert, eds. *Reading from this Place*, vol. 1: *Social Location in the United States*. Minneapolis: Augsburg Fortress, 1995.

Shohat, Ella, and Robert Stam, *Unthinking Eurocentrism: Multiculturalism and the Media*. New York: Routledge, 1994.

Stewart, Diane M. *Three Eyes for the Journey: African Dimensions of the Jamaican Religious Experience*. Oxford: Oxford University Press, 2005.

Ukpong, Justin, et al. *Reading the Bible in the Global Village*. Cape Town: GPBS; Atlanta: SBL, 2001.

Warrior, Robert A. "Canaanites, Cowboys, and Indians: Conquest, and Liberation Theology Today." *ChCr* 49 (1989): 261–65.

West, Gerald, and Musa W. Dube, eds. " 'Reading With': An Exploration of the Interface between Critical and Ordinary Readings of the Bible. African Overtures," *Semeia* 73 (1996).

Worcester Jr., J. H. *David Livingstone: First to Cross Africa with the Gospel*. Chicago: Moody Press, 1990.

Yorke, Gosnell, and Peter Renju. *Bible Translation and African Languages*. Nairobi: Acton, 2004.

1. Evaluations: African Feminist/Gender-Based Biblical Interpretations

TALITHA CUM HERMENEUTICS OF LIBERATION: SOME AFRICAN WOMEN'S WAYS OF READING THE BIBLE

Musa W. Dube

THE LEGACY OF KIMPA VITA/DONA BEATRICE (1682–1706)

Sub-Saharan African women's academic biblical readings are possibly less than thirty years old. However, sub-Saharan African women's biblical interpretations go as far back as the time when the Bible came to co-exist with sub-Saharan African cultures, people and lands.[1] I particularly want to recall the story of Kimpa Vita, a Congolese woman who was renamed Dona Beatrice after her Christian baptism.[2] Kimpa Vita was an African Christian woman in colonial times, when the biblical readers of that time and place operated within the colonial ideology and practice of domination of other cultures, lands, people and minds.[3] Kimpa Vita was therefore a colonized African Christian woman, who together with the rest of her people was subjugated to foreign rule, religion, culture, economics, and taught to despise all that represented the cosmology of her people.[4]

Through her faith, Kimpa Vita crossed cultural boundaries and the power worlds of the colonized and the colonizer.[5] This was highly dramatized by the fact

1. North African Christianity was as old as Christianity itself. Perhaps the birth narrative of Matthew captures this by underlining that after his birth Jesus fled and sought political asylum in Egypt until such a time when Herod was no longer alive.

2. For further information see John K. Thornton, *The Congolese Saint Anthony: Dona Beatriz Kimpa Vita and the Antonian Movement, 1684–1706* (New York: Cambridge University Press, 1998).

3. See V. Y. Mudimbe, *The Invention of Africa: Gnosis, Philosophy, and the Order of Knowledge* (Indianapolis: Indiana University Press, 1988), for an extensive analysis of the colonization of Congo and the construction of space in colonial times.

4. See Barbara Kingsolver, *The Poisonwood Bible: A Novel* (San Francisco: Harper Perennial, 1998), a recent narrativation of the colonization of Congo. Joseph Conrad, *Heart of Darkness* (1902; Harper and Brothers, 1910), is the classical colonial narrative construction of the same.

5. For further readings on boundaries and boundary crossing, please see Avtar Brah, "Diaspora, Border, and Transnational Identities," in *Feminist Postcolonial Theory: A Reader,* ed. R. Lewis and Sara Mills (New York: Routledge, 2004); Homi Bhabha, *Location of Cul-*

that she was renamed, "Dona Beatrice." She embraced the agenda of the colonizer
by accepting Christianization; allowing herself to enter another cultural world,
one that bid her to despise her Congolese being. By renaming her, the colonial
church symbolized that she had accepted the gospel of conversion, 'civilization'
and rejection her Congolese identity. Baptism is a Christian ritual that symbolizes
dying and rising with Christ. In African colonial contexts, however, it took further
meaning. It also symbolized dying to one's African culture and rising to Western civilization. Assuming a new Christian name, and discarding one's so-called
pagan name, came to underline that one has been buried to their African cosmology and had now risen with Christ, to live a Christianized and civilized/European
lifestyle.

This missionary assumption was, perhaps, not the experience of Kimpa Vita/
Dona Beatrice. Despite this border crossing, this seemingly betrayal of her culture,
the selling out to the colonizer—we do well *not* to think of Kimpa Vita as one who
had bought, "a one way ticket" into the colonizer's agenda. As the story of her
revolt will highlight, Kimpa Vita is, perhaps, better seen as one who had "bought
a life time round ticket." That is, she had a ticket that allowed her to keep crossing
boundaries, going to and from one world to another.[6] Each time the footmarks of
her crisscrossing painted the other world with the colors of another world, until the
paint of her crisscrossing could not go unnoticed. One can very well say the Christianized and "civilized" Kimpa Vita answered to the name Dona Beatrice when
she was in her Congolese African world and she answered to the name Kimpa Vita
when she was in the colonial church space. With all this crisscrossing, one can say
she began to mix up her old and new names—at times becoming Kimpa Dona,
and other times becoming Vita Beatrice, on others, becoming Vita Dona, and still
in other times becoming Kimpa Beatrice. In so doing, she was mixing the supposedly separated and opposed worlds of the colonized and the colonizer. Kimpa Vita
was bound to loose any sense of these boundaries. It was not long before Kimpa
Vita/Dona Beatrice's true colors were discovered. That is, while she was supposedly dead to her Congolese world, she was discovered to be wearing and weaving
a new multi-colored coat of boundary crossing—in that highly unequal world of
the colonized and the colonizer of her time.

To use Leticia Guardiola's words, Kimpa Vita had "played a chameleon, cheat-

ture (New York: Routledge, 1994); Gloria Anzandula, *Borderlands: La Frontera the New
Mestiza* (San Francisco: Aunt Lute Books, 1987); and Alison Blunt and Gilian Rose, eds.,
Writing Women and Space: Colonial and Postcolonial Geographies (New York: Gilford Press,
1994).

6. In biblical studies, the work of Leticia Guardiola best articulates the hermeneutics of
boundary crossing. See "Borderless Women and Borderless Texts: A Cultural Reading of
Matthew 15:21–28," *Semeia* 78 (1997): 69–81; "Border-Crossing and Its Redemptive Power
in John: A Cultural Reading of Jesus and the *Accused*," in *John and Postcolonialism: Travel,
Space, and Power,* ed. Musa W. Dube and Jeffrey Staley (Sheffield: Sheffield Academic Press,
2002).

ing the system,"[7] but somewhere she must have forgotten to wear the right colors in the right place. Thus Kimpa Vita/Dona Beatrice began to talk her walk. She began to prophesy, calling into being a new world.

> Kimpa Vita proclaimed that the Spirit of St Anthony had taken possession of her.[8] Empowered by the Spirit, Kimpa Vita's preaching became a powerful protest against the Catholic Church and the colonial government. She wanted all the crosses, crucifixes, and images of Christ to be destroyed because, as she said, they were just as good as the old fetishes. She proclaimed that God will restore the subjugated kingdom of Kongo. Vita held that Christ came into the world as an African in Sao Salvador[9] and that he had black apostles.[10] . . . With this radically subversive proclamation for both the colonial church and government, Kimpa Vita was recognized as a dangerous thinker. She was thus condemned to death and was burnt at the stake in 1706.[11]

Through her proclamation, Kimpa Vita was re-writing and re-telling the Christian script in a colonial space. To the colonial missionaries Kimpa Vita's proclamation was a shocking revelation for one who had supposedly bought a one way ticket into the world of colonial conversion and civilization. Colonial missionaries were shocked to discover that she had a dangerous lifetime return ticket that brought black paint into a white colonial church space—one that was filled with a white-blue eyed blond Jesus; Mary the mother of Jesus; male disciplines and apostles. Worse, Kimpa Vita was not only journeying to and fro and mixing colors; she also refused to embrace the unequal inclusion that was served to her Congolese people. She realized that the divine images of power were as white as the colonizers themselves—legitimating and feeding each other; and serving to suppress the colonized black people of Congo. Kimpa Vita/ Dona Beatrice with her lifetime round ticket, her crisscrossing foot marks had brought black paint into the white colonial church, repainting Jesus, his disciples and his mother as black and reasserting that this black Jesus will restore the kingdom of Congo. Clearly, Kimpa Vita had not died to her Congolese world when she accepted Colonial Christian conversion, "civilization" and a new name, Dona Beatrice.

By assuming this position in her proclamation, Kimpa Vita/Dona Beatrice:

- First, revealed herself not as a dead and buried colonized African Christian woman who was now renamed, Dona Beatrice. Rather, she was

---

7. Ibid.

8. Saint Anthony was "a popular Catholic saint and miracle worker."

9. This was by then the colonial capital of Congo, which she apparently renamed Bethlehem.

10. Kimpa Vita is held to have told her followers that "Jesus, Mary, and other Christian saints were really Kongolese."

11. Musa W. Dube, "Readings of the *Semoya*: Batswana Women Interpretations of Matt. 15:21–28," *Semeia* 73 (1996): 111–29, 113.

Kimpa Vita of the resurrection power, who rises and returns with her suppressed African and black identity. Resurrection is the power to come back against powers of annihilation and the powers of colonial domination. It is the art of insisting on the right to be alive and to live freely.

- Second, through her proclamation, she was calling for the redefinition of the colors of the power, in the divine and political space of the colonial Congo. By repainting Jesus with black colors and insisting on the restoration of the kingdom of Congo, Kimpa Vita was insisting on the empowerment of the black colonized people of Congo. She was calling for decolonization. It is notable that she claimed that Jesus and his apostles/disciples were black Congolese and called for the pulling down of all the white images in the church. This would create a situation where the black Christ would be embodied by the black people of Congo. A black Christ would identify with the colonized Congolese and their struggle for liberation. Kimpa Vita's talk was challenging whiteness and its colonizing ideology both at the spiritual and political levels.

- Third, by painting Jesus and his disciples/apostles black, Kimpa Vita was articulating an African Christology of resistance. The Jewish Jesus and his apostles were now black Congolese Africans. Moreover, the black Jesus, unlike the white one, supported the restoration of the colonized kingdom of Congo. This new Jesus much like her is a "border crosser," who does not endorse the colonization of the other. The baptized Dona Beatrice has emerged with a new body—the black body of Jesus. She is, according to the African theological thinking, inculturated, a term that means that one simultaneously inhabits the biblical and Africa cultural world without privileging one world over the other. Her blackening of Jesus is a postcolonial African Christology that seeks liberating interdependence of cultures, rather than exclusiveness or the domination of one by the other, and certainly not the unequal inclusion of colonial conversion.

- Fourth, by claiming that the spirit that moved her was the spirit of St Anthony, not that of Jesus or that of the Trinity, in many ways Kimpa Vita/Dona Beatrice, did three important things: first, she shifted and neutralized the focus from Jesus, who in the colonial space was one of the outstanding instruments of colonization. The status of Jesus as single intermediary rendered the African community of ancestors, who are considered the intermediaries between God and the living, as irrelevant. Claiming the spirit of St Anthony is thus a way of revaluing the many living voices of the dead who continue to inspire and inform the living, according to the African cosmology. Second, by claiming to be informed by the "spirit," Kimpa Vita was opening an oral canon, which would become a subversive text that refused to be tied to the written biblical text. This spirit canon would be an asset to African women's empowerment in the highly male Christian church and canon.[12] As many researchers of AICs indicate, African women have risen to become church founders, prophets, bishops, faith-healers etc, often claiming that the spirit has authorized them to assume these positions of authority in the society. The Spirit canon subverts the patriarchal biblical texts, becoming an oral canon that empowers women and men. Third, as a woman, Kimpa Vita/Dona Beatrice is empowered by a spirit that allows her to speak and to challenge colonial church ideology and the colonial state. In so doing, she transgresses the gender divide that relegated most women to the periphery of power. She at once embodies the oppositional space of crisscrossing genders, races, religions, class, cultures and texts. In this crisscrossing Kimpa Vita calls into being the space of multiple boundary crossing: a state of traveling to and from the guarded boundaries of the colonized and the colonizer and between other guarded social boundaries.

As the story tells us, Kimpa Vita and her subversive text did not escape the colonial missionaries policing of boundaries—for the challenge it was positing to the highly unequal world of that time. It did not escape the missionaries' ears that she was challenging both the colonial church and state and calling into being a highly inculturated space: a hybrid space of cultural intimacy. She was quickly marked as a heretic and was martyred on stake in 1706.

Her martyrdom was a second death attempt, given that the first attempt was made through burial by baptism and renaming her in order to eliminate her African identity. But what will happen now, would the spirit of Kimpa Vita arise again? Would she keep on rising against the oppressive structures of colonialism and colonizing Christianity? Would she continue to rise and cultivate a new inculturated space of cultural kissing, which empowers men and women; white and blacks; Christians and non-Christian—all people? Historically, Kimpa Vita is held to be the founder of AICs.[13] These are churches that sought to resist colonization of their countries and colonizing Christian practices.[14] As I have said elsewhere,

---

12. See Dube, "*Semoya*," for further elaboration on the Spirit canon and its uses among women of the AICs.

13. Following closely in the identity of their founder, AICs are well documented for what has been termed, in colonial language, "syncretistic." Some good books on the history of AICs include G. M. Sundkler, *Bantu Prophets in South Africa* (London, 1961); Inus Daneel, *The Quest for Belonging: Introduction to the a Study on African Independent Churches* (Mambo: Gweru, 1987).

14. According to Norbert C. Brockman, "Kimpa Vita (Dona Beatrice) c. 1682–1706: The Antonian Movement Congo/Democratic Republic of Congo/Angola," "The Antonian movement, which Kimpa started, outlasted her. . . . Her ideas remained among the peas-

The centrality of women in AICs could not be ended with the crucifixion of Kimpa Vita. A line of other women have ever since heard and responded to the word of the Spirit of God to serve as church founders, leaders, prophets, and faith healers. Outstanding among these are Ma Nku, Grace Tshabalala, Alice Lenshina, and Mai Chaza, who became founders and leaders of massive AICs movements in this [last] century.[15]

In other words, it is my contention that Kimpa Vita's spirit and vision is repeatedly resurrected. It is my contention that her spirit dwells not only among the AICs women and men leaders, but also among many African academic biblical readers of today. I therefore want to highlight what I call the "*Talitha cum*" African women's biblical hermeneutics of reading by briefly highlighting the practices of four African women: Mercy A. Oduyoye; Madipoane Masenya, Musa W. Dube and Teresa Okure. *Talitha Cum* hermeneutics refers to the art of living in the resurrection space: the art of continually rising against the powers of death—the powers of patriarchy, the powers of colonial oppression and exploitation, the powers that produce and perpetuate poverty, disease and all forms of exclusion and dehumanization. Walking in the legacy of Kimpa Vita, African women's *talitha cum* hermeneutics are ways of living and insisting on staying alive; even where one confronts oppressive powers that crushes, one dares to rise. Before I turn to discuss the above four women, I need to briefly elaborate on the source of naming, that is, *Talitha cum*, African women's (biblical) hermeneutics of life.

RESURRECTION POWER: *TALITHA CUM* HERMENEUTICS OF LIFE

As used here the term, *talitha cum* is drawn from the Markan story of Mark 5: 21–43. In the story, Jesus is thronged by a huge crowd when a synagogue leader, Jairus, comes pleading: "my daughter is at the point of death, come lay hands on her so that she may be healed and live." Jesus begins to walk with Jairus to his house to attend to the dying child. His emergency journey gets high jacked by a bleeding woman, seeking healing from her 12 year bleeding. Meanwhile the daughter dies. Jesus insists on walking with Jairus to attend to the dead girl. He arrives at the house of Jairus and goes to the place where she is sleeping and says to her, "*talitha cum*," which means, "little girl, I say wake up." She wakes up and starts walking around, to the utter amazement of the mourning crowd. In this essay, I have decided to use the term *talitha cum*, drawn from Mark 5:21–43, to frame African women's practice for several reasons:

First, it is a story that has captured the imaginations of African women theolo-

---

ants, appearing in various messianic cults until, two centuries later, it took new form in the preaching of Simon Kimbangu" (http://www.gospelcom.net/dacd/stories/congo/kimpa).

15. Dube, "*Semoya*," 113.

gians, inspiring a number of articles,[16] books,[17] performances[18] and practices. (This author is particularly addicted to the story and finds her way to the story too many times). Its centrality became evident at the launching of the Circle of Concerned African Women Theologians in 1989, when the two books from this historical meeting were named after this story. The first book was named *The Will to Arise: Women, Tradition, and the Church in Africa* and the second was *Talitha Qumi.*

Second, the story is popular because it represents the struggles of African women against colonial powers and patriarchal oppression—with the highly desired results of liberation and life. In the story, the discourse of colonial resistance is underlined by assigning the number twelve to both the dying daughter and the bleeding woman, thereby suggesting that Israel is a sick dying daughter; a bleeding woman who has endlessly sought for healing, which is finally delivered by Jesus. This reading for national liberation is further underlined by the beginning of the chapter where Jesus meets a man who is heavily possessed by demons and lives among the tombs. The demons that possess the man are apparently "a Legion," that is, a term evocative of the Roman imperial guard that is assigned to this region. The guard is representative of the Roman Empire.

Legion trembles before Jesus, suggesting that he is confronted by a different and decolonizing power. Jesus casts out the Legion into a herd of pigs, which then run and get drowned in the sea. In all the stories of the demon possessed man, the bleeding woman and the dying daughter, Jesus is presented as liberator from colonial occupation, which, according to the story, it is as a situation of living in deadly ill-health, so much so that one basically, comes to dwell with the dead, hurting himself. For African women, the story thus highlights the impact of colonial domination; affirms their struggles against international exploitation, from colonial times, to neo-colonial and global village era.

---

16. See Teresa Okure, "The Will to Arise: Reflections 8:40–56," in *The Will to Arise: Women, Tradition, and the Church in Africa,* ed. M. A. Oduyoye and M. Kanyoro (New York: Orbis, 1992), 221–30; Dube, "*Talitha Cum*! Calling the Girl-Child and Women to Life in the HIV/AIDS and the Globalization Era," in *African Women, HIV/AIDS, and Faith Communities,* ed. Isabel Phiri et al. (Pietermaritzburg: Cluster, 2003) 71–93; Dube, "*Talitha Cum*: A Postcolonial Feminist and HIV&AIDS Reading of Mark 5: 21–43," in *Grant Me Justice: HIV/AIDS and Gender Readings of the Bible,* ed. Musa W. Dube and Musimbi R. A. Kanyoro (New York: Orbis, 2004).

17. African women's books named after this story of rising include M. A Oduyoye and M. Kanyoro, eds., *The Will to Arise: Women, Tradition, and the Church in Africa* (New York: Orbis, 1992); idem, Talitha Qumi: *1989 Conference Proceedings* (Ibadan: Day Star Press, 1990); Nyambura Njoroge and Musa W. Dube, eds., *Talitha Cumi! Theologies of African Women* (Pietermaritzburg: Cluster, 2001).

18. See Dube, "Fifty-Years of Bleeding: A Storytelling Feminist Reading of Mark 5:24–43," in her *Other Ways of Reading: African Women and the Bible* (Atlanta: SBL, 2000), 50–62; and idem, "Twenty-Two Years of Bleeding and Still the Princess Sings," in Dube and Kanyoro, *Grant Me Justice,* 186–200.

Third, the story provides for gender empowerment. First, by using women's bodies to symbolize the state of a colonized nation, the story perhaps also succeeds to communicate that in colonized settings women are likely to suffer more given their prevailing gender oppression.[19] The story, however, not only exposes exacerbated gender oppression, it also provides for gender empowerment. That is, a bleeding woman, whose health status makes her further distanced from the public space and empowerment within patriarchal system, takes it upon herself to seek and get empowerment. She reaches for the garment of Jesus with the full intention of getting healing and does so without asking any permission from Jesus. In so doing, she appropriates for herself the right to healing. (Healing here refers to healing from colonial, patriarchal, physical oppression—basically all that is oppressive). Jesus only gets to know when power leaves his body. When Jesus discovers it, he searches and finds her. Yet, without rebuke, he pronounces, "Daughter, your faith has healed you, go in peace." The story, therefore, provides a framework for women's agency, insisting that oppressed women (and nations) have the right to search and reach for their own empowerment against all that oppresses and exploits them—and there is no need to ask permission from those in power. That is, disempowered women and nations must make it their duty to seek for healing. Gladly, in this story, Jesus is characterized as one who supports their search for liberation and healing from all forms of oppression.

Lastly, this story is magnetic to African women, since it seems to embody the arts of hope, healing, resurrection and liberation. Where one walks too close to death and co-habits with the dead (the demon possessed man/the young girl), where one lives for too long in ill-health and suffering (the bleeding woman), one can actually be healed. One can resurrect from death and return to life. Hope is sustained for those who are internationally oppressed; those who are oppressed due to gender and physical ill-health. According to this story, liberation is a divine right that is in fact attainable. Death is denied its power as one can actually resurrect, just as the demon possessed man and the dead girl were liberated from the clutches of death. He also stands in contrast to the colonizing employment of his figure as single intermediary by the colonizers.

Talitha cum African women's hermeneutics is therefore the practice of living daily in confrontation with international oppression of the past and present; gender oppression of the past and present, physical wounds of the past and present: a confrontation of sickness and death, which must give way to healing. Healing here is a concept that includes the healing of international relations, class, race, ethnic, age, spiritual, environmental, gender relations, national relations and physical bodies of individuals and communities that get sickened when relations are not

---

19. See Dube, "*Talitha Cum*! A Postcolonial Feminist and HIV&AIDS Reading of Mark 5:21–43," 123–28, where the point of gender and empowerment is closely interrogated.

well.[20] The story of the bleeding woman, the sick daughter and Kimpa Vita thus embody that liberatory energy and vision that empowers African women to live in the resurrection power from the ever unending death dealing oppressive forces that invade the continent and their lives. Let us now look at the individual examples of the above tabulated women in their given order and how they articulate their *talitha cum* hermeneutics.

MERCY A. ODUYOYE: IN-CULTURATED FEMINIST HERMENEUTICS

Mercy A. Oduyoye is not trained as a biblical scholar yet she is the most illustrious African theologian of the continent. Her star lies not only in her publications. Above all, it lies in her historical effort to establish the Circle of Concerned of African Women Theologians, which is now a vibrant Pan African association of academic women in religion and theology. The Circle has a membership of about six hundred women, who mobilize each other regionally, nationally and continentally to research, think, write and publish theological material in search of the resurrection space of life from international exploitation, gender, class, ethnic, national, environmental and age oppression—all that keeps Africa and the African people as a whole suppressed. Mercy has published a number of books including *Introducing African Women Theology; Daughters of Anowa: African Women and Patriarchy; Beads and Strands: Reflections of an African Woman Christianity in Africa.*[21]

How then does Oduyoye embody the legacy of Kimpa Vita? How does she articulate *talitha cum* hermeneutics? Oduyoye's work is much too extensive to be adequately and fairly treated within the limits of this essay. I wish to use two brief examples: One is her acknowledgment of the coexistence of multiple scriptures in the African context and second her use of them. In her chapter "Jesus Saves," Oduyoye points out that

> The religious background of these studies is the primal religion of Africa and Judaism. What we in Africa have traditionally believed of God and the transcendent order has shaped our Christianity. But that is only part of the story. Islam strides shoulder to shoulder with Christianity in Africa... Religious maturity, traditional hospitality to the stranger and the sacredness of blood ties have enabled the adherents of these faiths to accept the other's right to exist and in the family to share each other's festivals.[22]

---

20. See "Divining Ruth for International Relations," in Dube, *Other Ways of Reading*, 179–95, where I make a more detailed analysis of the link between relationships and health.

21. Mercy A. Oduyoye, *Beads and Strands: Reflections of an African Woman on Christianity in Africa* (New York: Orbis, 2004); idem, *Introducing African Women Theology* (Cleveland: Pilgrim Press, 2001); idem, *Daughters of Anowa: African Women and Patriarchy* (Maryknoll, NY: Orbis, 1995).

22. Oduyoye, *Beads*.

In an article co-authored with Elizabeth Amoah, "Christ for African Women,"[23] Oduyoye demonstrates this historical crisscrossing tradition of Kimpa Vita in the service of resurrection. Oduyoye and Amoah hold that "most Christians refer to Scripture as meaning the Hebrew Bible and its Christian supplement, the New Testament, but we would like to start with a reference to the "unwritten Scripture" of the Fante of Ghana."[24] In their construction of African woman's Christology, Amoah and Oduyoye insist that "all human communities have their stories of persons whose individual acts have lasting effects on the destiny and ethos of the whole group. Such people are remembered in stories."[25] Living between the Hebrew, Christian, Fante and women's stories/scriptures, Amoah and Oduyoye begin to construct their Fante feminist Christology in this way:

> When the Fante were journeying to their present home in Southern Ghana, they crossed vast tracts of waterless plains and they thirsted. Such an agony of a people on the move, but their leader Eku, the matriarch, did not despair. She spurred them on . . . they came to a place they could settle in peace and prosperity. They then came to a pool of water. Having suffered much treachery on their journey, none dared to salve the parched throat with the water, invitingly before them. It could have been poisoned by their enemies. Matriarch Eku took her life into her hands, drank from the pool, and gave to her dog to drink. The people waited. They peered at the woman and her dog with glazed eyes. Neither human nor animal had suffered from drinking water of the pool. All fell to and drank their fill, shouting Eku *Aso* (Eku has tasted) . . . Eku has tasted on our behalf. We can now drink without fear.[26]

In this article, which begins by recognizing other scriptures and other Christ figures, Amoah and Oduyoye do a number of other things: they return to the Christian Testament; review African male constructions of Christology; assess Christological titles of non-academic women faith leaders; and assess "Africa's business," that is, the existing "life-denying forces." They conclude that "Jesus of Nazareth, by counter cultural relations he established with women, has become for us the Christ, the anointed one who liberates the companion, friend, teacher, and true Child of Women. . . . Jesus is Christ—truly woman, yet truly divine, for only God is the truly Compassionate One."[27]

Here the story of the matriarch Eku has merged with the story of Jesus as well as the stories of African women in search for liberation. They go on to conclude that, "*An African woman perceives and accepts Christ as a woman and as an African*".[28]

23. Mery A. Oduyoye and Virginia Fabella, eds., *With Passion and Compassion: Third World Women Doing Theology* (Maryknoll, NY: Orbis, 1988).

24. Ibid., 35.

25. Ibid., 36.

26. Ibid.

27. Ibid., 44.

28. Ibid. (emphasis added).

Here Christology crosses boundaries of texts, cultures, gender and colonizing Christian perspectives and paints Jesus in many colors and genders in search of *Talitha cum*—the resurrection from the "life-denying forces." No doubt the crucified Kimpa Vita of 1706 is alive in the hermeneutics of Oduyoye!

Masenya Madipoane: *Bosadi* Hermeneutics

Madipoane Masenya, is the first black South African woman Hebrew Bible scholar. She has published numerous articles in journals and books and written a book entitled *How Worthy Is the Woman of Worth.*[29] Her embodiment of Kimpa Vita's legacy and efforts to articulate *talitha cum* hermeneutics, in the historically exclusive, exploitative and oppressive context of apartheid South Africa, is best articulated in what she calls *Bosadi* hermeneutics. According to Masenya, *bosadi* perspective investigates what ideal womanhood should be for "an African-South African woman Bible Reader."[30] Masenya's description of *bosadi* highlights that it is a concept drawn from Northern Sotho tradition that seeks to look critically at both the Sotho and biblical traditions in search for liberating perspectives.[31]

In her article, "Esther in Northern Sotho Stories: African South African Women's Commentary,"[32] demonstrates her crisscrossing of boundaries by reading both from the biblical stories and Sotho oral stories and proverbs. At times she compares these narratives, while at other times; she uses them to illuminate one another, thereby demonstrating a blackened and expanded canon, which goes beyond the written biblical text. This expanded canon certainly resists the colonial missionary dismissal of African cultures, by revaluing the oratures (oral literature) of Sotho people.

It might be worth pointing out that another black South African woman, Gloria Plaatjie, also demonstrates this tendency to expand what constitutes scripture. In her article "Toward a Post-apartheid Black Feminist Reading of the Bible: The Case of Luke 2:36–38,"[33] Plaatjie insists on reading with and from non-academic women Bible readers, thus upholding the authority of Kimpa Vita's space of discernment and resistance. Plaatjie also insists that what is authoritative, what is redemptive and what is empowering for black South African women who were the worst victims of apartheid South Africa, is not just to read the Bible—a book that was instrumental in shaping the apartheid ideology; rather, it is also to read

---

29. Madipoane Masenya (ngwana' Mphahlele), *How Worthy Is the Woman of Worth? Rereading Proverbs 31:10–31 in African-South Africa* (New York: Peter Lang, 2004).

30. Masenya, "A Bosadi (Womanhood) Reading of Proverbs 31:10–31," in Dube, *Other Ways of Reading*, 148.

31. For further elaboration see Masenya, "Proverbs 31:10–31 in a South African Context: A Reading for Liberation of African (Northern Sotho) Women," *Semeia* 78 (1998): 55–68.

32. Dube, *Other Ways of Reading*, 27–49.

33. Ibid., 114–44.

UNIVERSITY OF WINCHESTER LIBRARY

the Bible with and in the light of the current South African constitution. According to Plaatjie,

> The constitution of post-apartheid South Africa is that country's biggest achieve-
> ment, for it recognizes the racial and gender equality of all South Africans. . . for
> Black South African women who sacrificed all other interests and focused on
> fighting against apartheid, the constitution of post-apartheid South Africa is in
> everyway a central and authoritative text. It carries sacred status for it symbolizes
> what black people fought and struggled for: *justice and dignity for all.*[34] (Emphasis
> added)

Musa W. Dube: Postcolonial Feminist Biblical Hermeneutics

The present writer also stands within the legacy of Kimpa Vita and *talitha cum*
hermeneutics in her work, which is mostly characterized as postcolonial feminist
interpretation of the Bible. This perspective is best articulated in her book *Postcolonial Feminist Biblical Interpretation* and other articles. According to Dube,

> Postcolonial readings of the Bible must seek to decolonize the biblical text, its
> interpretations, its readers, its institutions, as well as seeking ways of reading for
> liberating interdependence. Liberating dependence here entails a twofold will-
> ingness on the part of readers: first, to propound biblical readings that decolonize
> imperialistic tendencies and other narrative designs; second, to propound read-
> ings that seek to highlight the biblical texts and Jesus as undoubtedly important
> cultures, which are nonetheless, not above all, but among the many important
> cultures of the world.[35]

This agenda, upholds the Kimpa Vita vision of a round ticket approach to cultural worlds, which resists the colonialist approach of hierarchy and binary oppositions. The elaboration of Dube's work simultaneously seeks to resist gender
and all forms of oppression through seeking to cultivate a framework of liberating
interdependence.

The *talitha cum* edge of Dube's hermeneutics has recently been highlighted by
her focus on the global crisis of HIV&AIDS epidemic, which she describes as an epidemic driven by social injustice.[36] In this area, Dube has recently edited volumes
such as *HIV/AIDS and the Curriculum: Methods of Mainstreaming HIV/AIDS in
Theological Programs* and *Grant Me Justice: HIV/AIDS and Gender Readings of the
Bible.* Given that HIV&AIDS is a global crisis that calls for global action, Dube argues that "in a world where 21 million people have died in 21 years and 40 million

---

34. Ibid., 116.

35. Dube, "Savior of the World but Not of This World: A Post-colonial Reading of the
Spatial Construction in John," in *The Postcolonial Bible,* ed. R. S. Sugirtharajah (Sheffield:
Sheffield Academic Press, 1998), 118–35, 133.

36. See Donald Messer, ed., *Breaking the Conspiracy of Silence: Christian Churches and
the Global AIDS Crisis* (Minneapolis: Fortress Press, 2004).

are infected, we [scholars] have to realize that our highest call is to become prophets of life."[37] In her latest reading of Mark 5:21–43, from "A Postcolonial Feminist
and HIV&AIDS Perspectives" Dube asks: "How can New Testament readers and
Christians stand in the narratives of postcolonial, feminist and HIV&AIDS search
for justice and healing the world. . . ?"[38] She goes on to say, "[W]hile I have no formula to give, what I definitely know is that this is a fitting duty for all of us who live
in the HIV&AIDS era to read for healing and liberation. . . ."[39] According to Dube,
"one must struggle with how they can take the challenging role of calling *talitha
cum* to the dying and the dead in the age of HIV&AIDS epidemic."[40]

TERESA OKURE: HERMENEUTICS OF LIFE

The questions posed by Dube are perhaps better addressed by Teresa Okure's biblical hermeneutics of life. Okure, the first New Testament woman scholar in Africa,
has written numerous articles and published or edited a number of books including *To Cast Fire Upon the Earth: Bible and Mission Collaborating in Today's Multicultural Global Context* (Pietermaritzburg: Cluster, 2000), *The Johannine Approach
to Mission: A Contextual Study of John 4:1–42* (Tübingen: Mohr, 1988), and co-
edited *Global Bible Commentary* (Nashville: Abingdon Press, 2004). In her article
"First Was the Life, Not the Book," Teresa Okure holds that

> Life as the starting point and abiding context of hermeneutics is not only impor-
> tant; it is the reality that imposes itself. Emerging and liberative trends in biblical
> studies (Third World, women's feminist, womanist, reader-response hermeneu-
> tics and inculturation) require that readers address their life situations as part of
> interpreting scripture. The biblical works themselves are records of people who
> struggled to understand the meaning of their life in relation to God.[41]

Okure insists that the whole Bible should be seen as an attestation of people seeking to understand and live their lives in their situation and in relation to God.
The writers of Genesis only wrote as they reflected on life itself, just as the rest
of the books in Hebrew Bible were written from their own life situation. Teresa
Okure insists that "the story of the Bible is therefore about life and life holds the
key to comprehending it."[42] It is on these bases that she entitled one of her articles
as, "First was the life and not the book." In an earlier essay, "Reading from This
Place: Some Prospects and Problems," Okure is very emphatic about the implica-

---

37. Dube, "The Prophetic Method in the New Testament," in *HIV/AIDS and the Curriculum: Methods of Mainstreaming HIV/AIDS in Theological Programmes* (Geneva: WCC,
2003), 43–58, 43.
38. Messer, *Breaking*, 137.
39. Ibid.
40. Ibid., 138.
41. Okure, *Cast Fire*, 196–97.
42. Ibid., 194.

tions of her proposal for the ethics reading. Okure holds that with a life-centered hermeneutic, "[I]t becomes possible to discern those interpretations that are in accordance with the one will and intention of God, which is to give and promote life in all its fullness (John 10:10). She goes on to say, "[A]ny interpretation that fails to do this becomes suspect and should be regarded as inauthentic."[43] The life-centered hermeneutics, in other words, are grounded not only on God as the creator of life, but also on God as the author of a good life. The biblical texts are but a fraction of human testimonies of grappling with living the God-given life. For Okure, therefore, the authenticity of any interpretation should be measured by its capacity to promote and support life—qualitative life, life as God meant it to be for all members of the earth communities.

In conclusion, the various proposed methods of African women theologians stand in the legacy of Kimpa Vita's resurrection. That is, the power to resist and rise from death-dealing powers of oppression, suppression and exploitation; the art of insisting on life and quality life. This often entails resisting colonizing and patriarchal ideologies in biblical and African oral canons as well as constructing a space of liberating interdependence between cultures, genders, ethnicities, races, sexualities, religions, nations, cultural worlds, and the environment. Teresa Okure's proposal for a hermeneutics of life, her assertion that *"first was the life, not the book"* radically extends the canonical boundaries of what we read and why we read. In short, Okure re-inscribes *life as the scripture* that we ought to read and therefore to be in the business of maintaining its quality against all the death dealing forces and the social injustices that often trivialize the lives of many. This seems to me, the best summary of the *talitha cum* hermeneutics of reading in the resurrection space for life.

43. T. Okure, "Reading from this Place: Some Problems and Prospects," in *Reading from this Place*, vol. 1: *Social Location and Biblical Interpretation in the United States*, ed. Fernando Segovia and Mary Ann Tolbert (Minneapolis: Fortress Press, 1995), 52–66, 57.

BOSADI: MADIPOANE (NGWANA' MPHAHLELE) MASENYA'S CONTRIBUTION TO AFRICAN WOMEN'S BIBLICAL HERMENEUTICS

Elivered Nasambu-Mulongo

The name Madipoane (Ngwana' Mphahlele) Masenya is increasingly becoming synonymous with *Bosadi* (womanhood) approach to biblical studies. *Bosadi* approach is a postcolonial, postapartheid biblical scholarship that challenges existing scholarship to establish a proper link with its readers in their various unique sociocultural, religious, and political contexts. For over twenty-five years, Masenya has been developing *Bosadi* approach with the aim of accommodating the perspectives and experiences of African–South African women faced with postapartheid and postcolonial issues. Masenya sees loopholes in traditional methods' ability to address the context of an African–South African woman. The present Essay discusses the contributions of Prof. Madipoane Masenya's *Bosadi* interpretation of scripture. The paper looks at how the *Bosadi* approach rereads biblical texts to address issues such as poverty, sexism, racism, foreignness, classism, family, suffering and HIV/AIDS, and African cultures. The paper mentions some appraisal from other scholars. This essay aims to show that *Bosadi* approach is a worthy alternative interpretative approach to African women's interpretation of scripture.

A *BOSADI* (WOMANHOOD) APPROACH

Masenya's words below resonate with her interests in biblical studies. Masenya defines her scholarly interest as *Bosadi* interpretation of biblical texts.[1]

---

1. Madipoane Masenya, "Their Hermeneutics Was Strange! Ours Is a Necessity! Rereading Vashti as African–South African Women," in*Her Master's Tools? Feminist Challenges to Historical-Critical Interpretations*, ed. C. Van der Stichele and T. Penner (GPBS; Atlanta: SBL, 2005), 183; J. T. Brown, *Setswana English Dictionary* (Johannesburg: Pula Press, 1979), 217. Masenya defines "Bosadi" as "a woman," "married woman," or "wife." It should be observed, however, that in her most recent published Ph.D. dissertation, Masenya has showed dissatisfaction with this phrase. She uses the phrase "women liberationist approach" and observes in the footnote that she is still developing an appropriate way of naming her scholarship. See also her *How Worthy Is the Woman of Worth? Rereading Proverbs 31:10–31 in African-South Africa* (New York: Peter Lang, 2004), 9–12.

Given the past history of marginalization as Africans and as women in South Africa, a history in which we were defined, a history in which even what belonged to us, for example, the rich heritage of our African culture, was defined for us, a history which resulted in an identity crisis, there is a need to reclaim what legitimately belongs to us. There is need to re-define and rename ourselves. To call ourselves in our own names and say it in our own voices.[2]

Bosadi approach is an African woman's de-centering of scholarship that departs from dominant readings by locating itself within a unique reading community. The reading community is the "*Bosadi* women" or "African–South African women" or "Northern Sotho women."[3] *Bosadi* reading takes into account the essence of the sociocultural, faith experiences and perspectives of African–South African women readers.

It should be pointed out that Masenya's scholarly undertakings are informed and shaped by her own background and upbringing. A renowned contemporary senior scholar in biblical studies and African women's discourses, Professor Masenya is South African by birth. She traces her journey into biblical studies back to her patriarchal church and theological educational upbringing in apartheid and colonial South Africa. In both "Redefining Ourselves: A Bosadi (Womanhood) Approach,"[4] and "Is White South African Old Testament Scholarship African?,"[5] Masenya gives her readers the glimpse of her social, political, spiritual and scholarly context. She grew up in apartheid South Africa where different racial groups were designed in such a way that blacks lived mainly in poor unfertile rural areas, received Bantu (Black) education, Bantu (Black) Christianity and Bantu (Black) theology, all of which did not prepare scholars to challenge apartheid or demand contextual theologies. All her theology professors in an all black seminary were white males. The few Black scholars also interpreted scripture with Western eyes and failed to confront androcentrism but instead normalized it[6] Masenya blames Western oriented biblical studies and silencing of those who used alternative methods for the failure of Black scholars to confront these prejudices in read-

---

2. Madipoane (Ngwana' Mphahlele) Masenya, "Redefining Ourselves: A Bosadi (Womanhood) Approach," *OTE* 10, no. 3 (1997): 439.

3. Brown, *Dictionary*, 217; Masenya, "A Bosadi (Womanhood) Reading of Genesis 16," *OTE* 11, no. 2 (1998): 277; idem, "Their Hermeneutics was Strange!" 183. Masenya observes that the word *bosadi* that is used to describe womanhood also refers to a woman's private parts, and she applies the term to a number of South African tribes because of their familiarity with the word *bosadi*. It is my assumption that in her discussion of the texts, she combines all meanings for the term *bosadi*, thus, "women," "married," "woman", "wife," and "woman's private parts."

4. Masenya, "Redefining," 439–48.

5. Madipoane Masenya, "Is White South African Old Testament Scholarship African?" *BOTSA* 12 (2002): 3–8.

6. Masenya, "Redefining," 439–40.

ing.[7] And despite these biblical studies taking place within Africa, African contexts were largely marginalized.[8]

Masenya sets clear similarities and differences with other methods of interpretation. She sees limitations in historical critical methods because of their emphasis on the pastness of the Bible in its original setting and claims of objectivity and universality of reading.[9] Like African male biblical scholars,[10] Masenya considers the importance of African culture and contextual issues such as the context of the reader within a postcolonial African continent.[11] However, she departs from these readings by addressing the prevailing androcentricism and sexism in both the African culture and biblical texts. *Bosadi* approach particularly looks at the impacts of African culture, mainly their positive and negative impacts on the postcolonial and postapartheid African–South African woman.[12] Like Western feminism, *Bosadi* approach addresses sexism in the Bible and in the history of interpretation.[13] However, *Bosadi*, takes a unique turn by addressing the history of colonial, racist and missionary readings of biblical texts, which Western feminism has been complacent with. Like womanist interpretations, *Bosadi* approach interrogates racism and classism in biblical texts but within a specific context and social location, namely South Africa.[14] *Bosadi* approach, like African feminist biblical scholarship

---

7. Masenya, "Their Hermeneutics!" 184–85; idem, *How Worthy?* 19.

8. Masenya, "Redefining," 439–40; idem, "White South African," 3–8.

9. Masenya, *How Worthy?* 18–19; James Barr, *Holy Scripture: Canon, Authority, Criticism* (Philadelphia: Westminster, 1983), 28.

10. Itumeleng J. Mosala, *Biblical Hermeneutics and Black Theology* (Grand Rapids: Eerdmans, 1989), 3, 121,169; Masenya, *How Worthy?* 3. Black Theology as made clear in Mosala's presentation, as in the Bosadi approach, addresses issues of class and oppression based on race. Having been founded on liberation grounds, Black Theology focuses on retrieving the voices and experiences of black people in South Africa with a purpose of empowering them with hope. However, Black Theology in Masenya's analysis did not seriously address androcentricim both in biblical texts and within Africa culture.

11. Masenya, *How Worthy?* 9.

12. Ibid., 53–54. In Masenya's understanding, African feminism in the Continent does not aggressively pursue the issues of androcentricity in African culture and biblical texts while their different colonial orientations imply that they are not faced with issues of classism and racism as those found in South Africa, Namibia, and Zimbabwe. This alone makes the idea of African feminist interpretation a limited term that does not apply equally to the experiences of African women on the Continent.

13. Ibid., 4. Masenya is in agreement with white feminism's sociocritical theory in its suspicion of androcentric biblical texts. Masenya, however, differs with white feminism by focusing on sexism both in biblical texts, African culture, and elsewhere as well as classism.

14. Masenya, "A Bosadi (Womanhood) Reading of Proverbs 31:10–31," in *Other Ways of Reading: African Women and the Bible*, ed. Musa W. Dube (Atlanta: SBL, 2001), 147–48. *Bosadi* approach is similar to womanist biblical scholarship in addressing racism, classism, and sexism. The difference lies in their different social locations, historical orientations, and emphases so that womanist interpretations are based in North America and address

acknowledges androcentricism in African culture but African feminism, in Masenya's view, fails to criticize the impact of missionaries in biblical interpretation. She also thinks that African feminist biblical studies are irrelevant to postapartheid Southern Africa countries facing unique problems such as classism.[15]

For Masenya therefore, the failure of existing scholarship to address the position of an African South African woman has to do with the conception of those very methods. [16] She engages both the theory and practice of historical critical methods while showing their limitations. In her magnum opus, *How Worthy is the Woman of Worth? Rereading Proverbs 31:10–31 in African-South Africa,* Masenya's reading of the acrostic poem of Prov 31:31–31 shows the limitations of traditional methods in addressing women at the margins. Placing the issue of family at the center of reading, Masenya dates Prov 31:31–31 in the early postexilic period, around the sixth century B.C.E., because of the value the text places on the family in a reindustrialized world. Traditional scholarship dates the text at the end of the postexilic period, an understanding that advantages elite industrialized reading.[17] Masenya takes on the scholarly disputed term *'eseth chayil* that is often translated as "good-", "perfect-" or "capable-" woman.[18] Traditional scholarship views the woman of Prov 31:10–31 as a hardworking, ingenious and unselfish woman that today's woman and mother ought to emulate.[19] Masenya chooses the title "woman of worth" as a suitable title to represent the woman of Prov 31:10–31.

At issue is whether the woman of Prov 31:10–31 is liberated and independent or subordinated. According to Masenya, like the African–South African woman, the woman of virtue in Prov 31:10–31 is endowed with ability and focus to the traditional mode of family although working under the shadow of her husband. This description does not represent the modern disrupted family. Similarly, the woman of Proverbs, being from a reindustrialized world was not a woman of means as claimed by Western feminists.[20] The *'eseth chayil* of both the Bible and Sotho culture is a reindustrialized woman who has the family at heart and works hard although under the umbrella of her husband. For Masenya, the *'eseth chayil* of Prov 31:10–31 challenges African men and whites in South Africa to take on the duties of *'eseth chayil* as well.

---

racism, sexism, and classism associated with the history of slavery that plugged them from their homeland. *Bosadi* approach on the other hand addresses racism, sexism, and classism associated with the history of colonialism, apartheid, and missionary enterprises within the South African location and context. *Bosadi* equally takes seriously the location within African culture and the significance of family.

15. Masenya, *How Worthy?* 53.

16. Masenya, "White South African?" 3–8.

17. Masenya, *How Worthy?* 69–80.

18. Carol R. Fontaine, "Proverbs," in *Women's Bible Commentary with Apocrypha*, ed. Carol A. Newsom and Sharon H. Ringe (exp. ed.; Atlanta: Westminster John Knox, 1998), 160.

19. T. McCreesh, "Wisdom as Wife: Proverbs 31:10–31," *RB* 92 (1985): 25–46.

20. Fontaine, "Proverbs," 160.

Essentially, Masenya's analysis of the woman of worth in Prov 31:10–31 brings to light the unappreciated work of the North Sotho woman. Masenya's liberative reading questions both the text, the history of interpretation of the woman, and Northern Sotho cultural failure to appreciate the woman of virtue while reviving the strengths of selflessness and hard work in this woman.

Bosadi reading of the story of Queen Vashti in the Hebrew text of Esther highlights the limitations of traditional methods in addressing women who find themselves as foreigners in their own country. According to the traditional reading of the book of Esther, Queen Vashti, the wife of king Ahasuerus who is replaced by Esther was deposed for failing to obey King Ahasuerus' request that she shows off her beauty as she was an exceptionally beautiful wife, Hebrew *towb mar'eh* (Esther 1:11). Traditionally, Vashti's presence at the beginning of the text is seen as thwarting the presence of Esther while her disposal is seen as an important turning point for the Jewish people. The narrative in the book of Esther is presented in the context of Jews living in a foreign land. What is disconcerting about these androcentric reading is that it has continued to shape the African woman across culture and class and further influenced the Church's teachings that portray Esther as a representative of a good wife as opposed to Vashti.[21]Masenya locates the story of Queen Vashti within South Africa under the apartheid regime. In Masenya's observation, Like an African- South African woman, Vashti was in exile in her own home country and was doubly powerless in a patriarchal cultural setting that did not legitimate women's power despite her capabilities.

Nevertheless, this interpretation is far from insinuating that Masenya is unable to see the value of historical critical methods. She recognizes that traditional methods' emphasis on the meaning of the text in its own age frees exegesis from dogmatic framework in which the Bible was interpreted in the past. Secondly, it affords insight into biblical times and especially, the growth process that the biblical text underwent.[22] She is however uneasy when focus remains with the texts rather than the reading community. She also seems to recognize the significance of the Bible to its original readers, and she is aware that reading the Bible's original context enlightens her own understanding of the biblical woman. It also helps her in the construction of an alternative *Bosadi* approach. Therefore, Masenya utilizes the method's understanding of the pastiness of the Bible in constructing the sociopolitical situation of the African–South African woman, and, in so doing, she prioritizes the reader while bringing the same texts to bear on the sociocultural, economic, and political situation of an African–South African woman.

Black theology which preceded African feminism in the continent was considered a liberation approach addressing issues such as class and oppression based

---

21. Masenya, "Their Hermeneutics!" 188. Masenya shares the story of a pastors' wives group whose readings of the text of Esther concluded that Esther is a good wife as opposed to Vashti.

22. Masenya, *How Worthy?* 19.

on race. Having been founded on liberation grounds, Black Theology focused on retrieving the voices and experiences of black people in South Africa with the purpose of empowering them with hope.[23] However, While Black theology adequately addressed the oppressed; this same theology in Masenya's analysis did not seriously address androcentricism both in biblical texts and within Africa culture, a culture that was sexist and patriarchal even before colonialism and apartheid.[24] Masenya is concerned with areas where African culture was sexist placing value on men and boys more than women and girls, hence making both women and girls to feel inferior within their own cultures and contexts[25].

To retrieve the images of women and girls in Africa South Africa, Masenya uses story telling methods to retell the stories in such a way that even historically contested and overly patriarchal stories become powerful tools that represent and empower the African–South African woman and girl child.[26] In the book of Esther, Masenya compares the status of women and girls by both African culture and the Bible using the story of Esther in the book of Esther and North Sotho cultural stories with the aim of showing some positive aspects. In the theme of the Orphan, the North Sotho story shows that within difficult circumstances, orphan boys are expected to fend for women even if those women are older and mature than them. The story of Esther on the other hand while narrated from the perspective of men and with male characters such as Mordecai overshadowing Esther, has some good values for North Sotho women. Esther's determination to survive despite her age, gender and foreignness in the Persian court provides a good example of how women can be persistent in seeking for their own survival despite their marginalized status within patriarchal cultures.[27] Masenya uses the same comparative approach in the androcentric text of Psalm 127:3–5 to address the issue of family, in particular the text's emphasis on fatherhood through procreation of many sons. She observes that these are egotistical issues that are overemphasized at the expense of land, women and the quality of life of those children.

In the same vein, women become valued only as mothers of those sons.[28] Noting prominence of a big family for both African and ancient Israelite culture, Masenya observes that women and earth become victims of exploitation within patriarchy that sees little significance in them. Masenya unveils the patriarchal

---

23. Mosala, *Biblical Hermeneutics*, 3, 121, 169; Masenya, *How Worthy?* 3.

24. Masenya, "Struggling to Find 'Africa' in South Africa: The Bosadi (Womanhood) Approach to the Bible," *SBL Forum* 3, no. 5 (June 2005).

25. Madipoane (Ngwana' Mphahlele) Masenya, "An Ecobosadi Reading of Psalm 127," in *The Earth Stories in the Psalms and the Prophets*, ed. N. Habel (Sheffield: Sheffield Academic Press. 2001), 109–22; Masenya, "Esther and Northern Sotho Stories: An African–South African Woman's Commentary," in Dube, *Other Ways of Reading*, 27–31.

26. Madipoane Masenya, "Esther and Northern Sotho Stories: An African–South African Woman's Commentary," in Dube, *Other Ways of Reading*, 27–31.

27. Ibid., 35.

28. Masenya, "Ecobosadi," 118–20.

and hierarchical nature of both the Psalm's presentation of the idea of procreation and family, seeing its equivalence with postapartheid postcolonial African-South Africa culture. She observes that the Hebrew plural noun, *banim* ought to refer to both boys and girls. She also articulates that women are like earth because both are marginalized and abused. She therefore questions the validity of the androcentric interpretation of the text to a Mosadi woman. Masenya finds redeemable aspects for women in this androcentrtic text and encourages women readers to read the text by siding with mother earth.

Masenya's analysis of the story of Esther shows that even very androcentric biblical stories have redeemable aspects. Her oral narration of the story further introduces the power of language when biblical stories are allowed to speak to the postcolonial and postapartheid receiving community in their own tongue for the first time. Equally unique is her address of family size using Psalm 127, an issue that remains a taboo among most African communities even if the quality of life for many African children today remains unacceptable.

Clearly, Masenya's *Bosadi* approach is aware that both the Bible and African culture can be irredeemably patriarchal because of their subjugation of women. To engage the patriarchal nature of African culture and that of the Bible and missionary interpretations, Masenya uses what feminists have called a hermeneutics of proclamation that urges telling the truth about accountability, sin and redemption. Addressing HIV/AIDS, Masenya takes issue with the fact that African male perpetrators of the disease are culturally socialized through proverbs and sayings to believe that all women belong to them. This understanding coupled with today's "false prophets" helps the spread of AIDS. In Masenya's comprehension, the church should borrow a leave from the Hebrew Bible's "independent Prophets" in asserting their role in the fight against AIDS. Even so, Masenya acknowledges that prophets such as Hosea, whose metaphor of marriage to a whore is compared to Israel's relationship with Yahweh, nevertheless, do not offer good examples of prophetic messages to today's victims. Most importantly, Masenya's suggestion of dramatization of biblical Prophetic books through Jeremiah's yoke (Jeremiah 27:19), Isaiah's nakedness (Isaiah 20) and Ezekiel's wall (Ezekiel 12), texts that addresses Israel's unfaithfulness, shows that Masenya is interested in the church's ability to disrupt the thinking and or metaphysical buildup underlying patriarchal cultures that privilege men's sexuality and excuses their violence against women.

Masenya's *Bosadi* interpretation in a way aims at a feminist hermeneutical turn. She learned over the years that the context of an African–South African woman is different from other women's contexts, a situation that prompted her to reformulate her hermeneutical discourse over time.[29] This hermeneutical shift obviously calls for Masenya's engagement with biblical texts by being wary of the traditional themes and history of interpretation already imprinted in the understanding of those texts in order to bring to light the realities of African–South African women.

---

29. Masenya, "Struggling to Find 'Africa.'"

This is well reflected in her use of biblical role models where she utilizes a herme-neutic of suspicion that goes beyond simply questioning the status of women in the Bible. She is keen to look at these women's oppression but also their race, eth-nicity, class and context. This way, she engages the reader with the focus on some ignored aspects of biblical women's stories and experiences that are of significance to her approach.

Masenya's reading of the story of Sarah and Hagar in Gen 16 exposes the re-alities of postapartheid South Africa, where women from different races live to-gether and where power; surrogate motherhood and foreignness are realities. Tra-ditional readings have placed less emphasis on the position of Hagar as a foreign woman in Sarah's household.[30] Instead, Hagar has by tradition been portrayed as a slave, a rebellious, controlling, and uncontrollable woman.[31] Traditional read-ings have also focused more on the issue of an heir for Abraham.[32] Readers have therefore tended to identify themselves with Abraham and Sarah because of their roles as patriarchs and founders of Israel's faith so that Abraham and Sarah have rarely been faulted for Hagar's plight. In fact through these readings, scholars have tended to sympathize with Sarah's actions towards Hagar and even found them acceptable.[33]

Masenya first takes issue with the missing Hebrew noun *ama* (a slave) in the text and contents that Hagar was a *shipha* (a handmaid) or *hva* (a wife/woman) and that she came to Abraham to play the role of surrogate motherhood, an idea that highlights both foreignness and the world that places significance on sur-rogate motherhood.[34] She notes that compared to Sarah, Hagar was economically powerless. This is evidenced in the morality of Sarah's words and actions towards Hagar. Hagar's foreignness as a woman in Abraham and Sarah's house presents a feminist problem of a marginalized woman while Sarah's barrenness provides a feminist agenda of sexism. Nevertheless, the harsh reaction of Sarah to Hagar within the same predicaments of serving the patriarch Abraham shows the power of patriarchy, and how race and class negatively affect women's ability to forge

---

30. Masenya, "Genesis 16," 272–74.

31. L. J. Wood, *Genesis: A Study Guide* (Grand Rapids: Zondervan, 1975), 72; E. A. Speiser, *Genesis* (AB; Garden City, NY: Doubleday, 1962), 121; Gerhard von Rad, *Genesis: A Commentary* (London: SCM, 1963), 189.

32. Claus Westermann, "Sarah and Hagar: Flight and Promise of A Son," in *Genesis 12–36: A Continental Commentary,* trans. John J. Scullion (Minneapolis: Augsburg For-tress, 1985); John Skinner, "The Flight of Hagar and the Birth of Ishmail," in *A Critical and Exegetical Commentary on Genesis* (Edinburgh: T&T Clark, 1969), 5; Ephraim Avigdor Speiser, *Anchor Bible,* vol. 1: *Genesis: Introduction, Translation, and Notes* (New York, NY: Doubleday), 121.

33. Von Rad, *Genesis,* 86–87; Wood, *Genesis,* 71; Victor P. Hamilton, *The Book of Genesis 1–17* (NICOT; Grand Rapids: Eerdmans, 1990), 444.

34. Speiser, *Anchor,* 121; von Rad, *Genesis,* 189; Masenya, "Genesis 16," 280–81.

the same goals.[35] In Masenya's estimation, like Hagar, African–South African women have been suppressed to poverty and economic powerlessness compared to their White counterparts who are privileged economically.[36] What's important in Masenya's analysis here is that her social location in South Africa allows her to pay attention to the character of Hagar as opposed to traditional feminist liberationist interpretation that emphasized only Hagar's role.[37] This way, Masenya also manages to show that the failure of Sarah and Hagar to forge unity in the face of patriarchy due to the racial and economic imbalance between them is a challenge to the prejudices embedded in feminist readings of suspicion that fail to recognize the struggle of marginalized women in the presence of racism and classism in all institutions.

Masenya's reading of the book of Ruth from the *Bosadi* approach on the other hand highlights success and empowerment when women create unity and their own survival within patriarchal structures regardless of race and class. Here, she departs from dominant readings by interpreting Naomi's words to both her daughters in law, "Go back to your father's house," (Ruth 1:9) and to Ruth, "I will seek rest for you" (Ruth 3:1) to suggest that the security of a wife in Israel was founded in the house of her husband and not fellow women. Likewise, women without their own male children were fated for poverty.[38] Masenya observes that Ruth decided to clutch to Naomi because Ruth wanted some economic freedom while Naomi's loss was that of the death of men in her household.[39] This idea echoes in Athalia Brenner's assertion that Ruth's foreignness and low class status were an obstacle to her full integration into Israel.[40] Masenya's reading privileges Ruth and Naomi's status of survival, a persuasive critique of women with unique experience of surviving without husbands through slavery, apartheid and other circumstances and is indicative of the diverse lenses through which women appropriate biblical

35. Masenya, "Genesis 16," 280.

36. Ibid., 281; See also S. J. Teubal, *Hagar the Egyptian: The Lost Tradition of the Matriarchs* (San Francisco: HarperCollins, 1990). Masenya agrees with Teubal that Hagar was Sarah's handmaid, which is an accurate prediction as is evidenced in the fact that it is Sarah who suggested and handed over Hagar to her husband, Abraham (16:3).

37. Susan Niditch, "Genesis," in Newsom and Ringe, *Women's Commentary*, 20. The title that Niditch gives to her work, "Hagar: Mothering a Hero," is evidence of Western feminist concerns with Hagar's hero child and not Hagar herself as a person.

38. Masenya, "Struggling with Poverty/Emptiness: Rereading the Naomi-Ruth Story in African-South Africa," *JTSA* 20 (2004): 46–59.

39. Amy-Jill Levine, "Ruth," in Newsom and Ringe, *Women's Commentary*, 86. Levine observes that Naomi considered marriage as the only source of security while Ruth's decision to stay with her mother implies that Naomi considered marriage as the only source of security.

40. Athalya Brenner, "Ruth as a Foreign Worker and the Politics of Exogamy," in *A Feminist Companion to Ruth and Esther*, ed. A. Brenner (Sheffield: Sheffield Academic Press, 1999), 158–62.

material.[41] *Bosadi* reading of Ruth/Naomi story not only shows the difference in women's readings but also opens the readers' eyes to the lives of those who have been shortchanged in reading and practices of the Bible.[42] Masenya's reading also shows how the powerless survive and further debunks the myth that marginalized and suppressed women of different races are without agency.

And being aware of the overly patriarchal nature of biblical texts and their sympathies for men, Masenya formulates her own female characters in her feminist approach to stories. In "Between Unjust Suffering and the 'Silent' God: Job and HIV Suffers in South Africa," Masenya uses an otherwise male story of Job and his friends to address the issue of suffering and HIV/AIDS and their implications on female victims. This she does in an empowering way while also challenging the ideological notion that wisdom can only be found in men. Without divorcing traditional biblical characters in the story of Job, Masenya identifies four African–South African female fictional characters to represent Job and his three friends; Eliphaz, Bildad and Zophar. Mmalehu, an HIV positive devout Christian woman represents the character of the faithful Job in the Bible who suffers unjustly. Masenya then retells the story of the character of Job and his dialogues with the friends regarding the reason for Job's suffering.[43] Like Job's friends who held to the traditional understanding that suffering is caused by sin, Mmalehu's friends operate within a Christian worldview that informs them that Christians cannot suffer from AIDS unless they have sinned against God. In spite of several similarities between Job and Mmalehu, Mmalehu as a woman is dispossessed, yet, reminiscent of her friends who seem to view her case differently; she has the audacity to remain a believer in God. In Masenya's analysis, the talk of friends in good faith even if it is insufficient still helps victim recovery. Masenya encourages the victims' ability to persevere in faith, repudiate those who do not share in their agony and be open to God in the face of suffering.

Masenya's reading encourages HIV positive Christian women in Africa-South Africa without a voice to tell their own stories in their own language without allowing patriarchal beliefs within Christianity and popular culture to disrupt their courage and openness to God and in so doing reclaim the book of Job for them-

---

41. Scott C. Williamson, "But Ruth Clung to Her," *JFM* 18, no. 2 (2004): 90–91.

42. Levine, "Ruth," 86–87.

43. Masenya, "Between Unjust Suffering and the 'Silent' God: Job and HIV Sufferers in South Africa," *Missionalia* 29, no. 2 (2001): 188–99. Masenya admits that she goes against the traditional Western scholarly approaches in using the book of Job to address the issue of women and HIV/AIDS in Africa-South African context. She places the story in a retelling mode where four fictional female characters replace Job and his friends and retell the dialogues by assuming the speeches in the dialogues of Job. Like the friends of Job, these women's understanding is that people suffer because they have sinned. Mmalehu in Masenya represents the person of Job.

selves.[44] *Bosadi* reading here manages to disrupt the worldview of Christianity by speaking to the doubly oppressed African–South African women AIDS victims in a way that helps their own self-transformation.

SCHOLARS' APPRAISAL OF *BOSADI* APPROACH

Masenya's *Bosadi* approach to biblical texts takes into consideration several issues that are significant to an African–South African woman. These analyses, although concrete in many ways nevertheless have met criticisms from some biblical scholars who think *Bosadi* is an inadequate approach to biblical studies. Masenya's comparative reading of some biblical texts alongside African culture has some scholars alleging that *Bosadi* is not different from African inculturation, a method of interpretation that compares African cultures and those of the Bible. Referring to Masenya's analysis of Prov 31:10–31, Gloria Kehilwe Plaatjie argues that the difference between Masenya's bosadi and the inculturation method, is that Masenya adds gender concerns to the latter.[45] Plaatjie is particularly apprehensive of Masenya's conclusion about the Psalm, when Masenya observes that African–South African women exemplify the woman of Proverbs and that this hard work attitude should be the pursuit of all. According to Plaatjie, Masenya's interpretation shows that she "fails to question the structural forces at work that allow certain workers to reap fruits of their labor while others remain poor."[46]

Masenya has responded to this criticism by arguing that Plaatjie has in mind Masenya's earlier works that excludes her later much developed *Bosadi* approach. She observes that unlike traditional African and Black theologies, *Bosadi* deals with texts and cultures critically and is not blinded to the realities of the political situation of African- South African peoples.[47]

For a postapartheid postcolonial African scholar like Masenya, inculturation method is important in creating a link between the bible and the reading community in their various historical, political, religious and social contexts. Inculturation is not the sole approach to biblical studies by African scholars.[48] Masenya admits that there are similarities between *Bosadi* and African inculturation hermeneutics, especially African interpretative techniques that take seriously the context of the reader; constructs texts under consideration and recognizes the strong interaction between African culture and the Christian faith.[49] Indeed inculturation has

---

44. Ibid., 195–97. The Bible also shows that there was serious punishment for the women victims while, for men, the issue was only serious if it involved a married woman.

45. Gloria Kehilwe Plaatjie, "Toward a Post-Apartheid Black Feminist Reading of the Bible: A Case of Luke 2:36–38," in Dube, *Other Ways of Reading*, 114–42.

46. Masenya, "Struggling to Find 'Africa,'" http://sbl-site.org/publications/article.aspx?articleId=402.

47. Ibid.

48. Justin S. Ukpong, "Rereading the Bible with African Eyes," *JTSA* 19 (1995): 3–14.

49. Masenya, *How Worthy?* 9–12.

been a successful method in dealing with theological and biblical issues in Africa
for a while now. Proverbs 31:10–31 is however a particularly problematic text for
cultures that expect more from women and little from men for being men. Bosadi interpretation of the woman of Prov 31:10–31 tends to dispose bosadi as a
scholarship that is short of recognizing the potential crisis in the African culture,
history of interpretation and colonial missionary emphases of this text. This possible vulnerability shows that inculturation may limit scholar's ability to question
the multifaceted nature of patriarchy both in culture and the biblical text under
consideration.

Plaatjie also claims that *Bosadi* approach is elitist and that Masenya reads neither with nor from non-academic Northern Sotho women. Plaatjie notes that
Masenya chooses to speak for North Sotho women, placing them at the level of
subalterns who cannot speak . . . all these from the comfort of academic halls.[50]
Masenya counters this claim, by stating that she is neither interested in scientific
nor literary readings of the Bible that leave the believer's life untouched, rather, she
is concerned with people who believe in the Bible as the word of God and that her
role is to make the marginalized person the main hermeneutical focus.

Plaatjie's claim may be exaggerated given that Masenya herself is writing as a
native of South Africa and belonging to the people she identifies as readers of
Bosadi approach. Masenya has noted that the people she writes for collectively
understand the meaning of *Bosadi*. She has a shared experience of life as a Black
girl growing up within rural South Africa and receiving Black education, Black
theology and Black Christianity. This makes her an insider and not an outsider.

Tinyiko Maluleke faults Masenya by accusing her of being preoccupied with
ethnic concerns. Maluleke argues:

> It is my reticence that Masenya's proposal although not always argued well and
> often well misunderstood, blazes a new trail and holds great potential for future
> African hermeneutics. Unlike many critiques of Masenya, my reticence about
> bosadi has little to do with ethnic tenor, bosadi is no more "ethnic" than Alice
> Walker's womanism or Oduyoye's bold and otherwise presposterous declaration
> that all African women are "daughters of Anowa", an Akan woman. It is inad-
> equate and ineffectual to engage Masenya at this level.[51]

Masenya has responded to Maluleke's accusation by accusing Maluleke of reading
Bosadi from non-African eyes. She observes that the use of the word "bosadi" is
deliberate since it is well-understood among several Northern Sotho settings and
other Southern African languages although different words are used for it. Masenya has clearly taken a while to construct a *Bosadi* approach to biblical studies;

50. As quoted by Masenya, http://sbl-site.org/publications/article.aspx?articleId=402,
downloaded 23 June 2011

51. As quoted by Masenya, http://sbl-site.org/publications/article.aspx?articleId=402,
downloaded 23 June 2011.

this is evidence that "bosadi" may be a limited term in reference to the people she is writing for.

Reacting to Masenya's article "Is White South African Old Testament Scholarship African?" Innocent Himbaza has particularly attacked Masenya's understanding of context in reading.[52] Himbaza raises the issue of the significance of traditional approach to scripture in the name of four windows, which he observes are critical in reading a biblical text. He remarks that the four, including the one on context can be studied irrespective of one's location. Himbaza also notes that the reader's context forms only one window of reading and that one cannot originate the meaning of a text, history of biblical authors, textual evidence or reception of the author's interpretations. Masenya counters this by emphasizing that the question "Is White South African Old Testament Scholarship African?" was in reference to the history and practice of Old Testament studies in South Africa as opposed to Hebrew Bible studies in general. She also says her question was based on her own experience of this scholarship.

Masenya's response to Himbaza shows that in her understanding, historical critical methods are called "white scholarship," within the South African context. Certainly, there remains a general assumption that white scholarship (historical critical methods), and indeed biblical studies in general are the business of white men and the West. Western churches and institutions remain the main source of funding and supervising African biblical scholarship both within and outside the continent. Accordingly, Western donors and institutions are committed to selecting, excluding and domesticating their ideal African scholars who disseminate historical critical methods and their accompanying ideologies due to non critical training and funding these African scholars receive. Regrettably, these approaches, which have little concern for Africa, are normally studied as ends in themselves, and that's how African biblical scholars remain consumers of western biblical methodologies and hermeneutical frameworks with no agenda for Africa.[53]

Bosadi approach acknowledges the contexts under which books were produced. Masenya has a problem with white scholarship and historical critical methods because these approaches allow the meaning of a text to remain in the past with no relevance to the reader. The text has many windows of reading, but the context of the reader is particularly important, which Masenya labors to show in her *Bosadi* approach. Masenya's is stating that African Christians do not need biblical studies cooked from outside their contexts because the methods used are irrelevant.

Of course the issue of context can be complex in certain texts that may be doubly patriarchal. For example, the theory of prophetic theology was successfully used in addressing apartheid in South Africa.[54] Masenya uses the same theory to

---

52. Innocent Himbaza, "La Recherche Scientifique et la Contextualisation de la Bible," *BOSTA* 14 (2002): 2–7.

53. Masenya, "A Response to Himbaza and Holter," *BOTSA* 13 (2002): 9–12.

54. In 1985, an anonymous South African group of theologians developed the "Kai-

address HIV/AIDS victims in South Africa. The problem is that unlike the context of apartheid, the sociocultural makeup of people targeted with prophetic theology are male who have been privileged with culture that allows them multiple sexual partners in an increasingly pluralistic world. Such people may even find consolation in some patriarchal Prophetic books like that of Hosea, which portray the woman negatively in an unfaithful marriage.

Examples of the patriarchal book of Hosea show that contextual theology that simply compares the cultures of the Bible and those of Africa may not be adequate in addressing serious issues such as HIV/AIDS. Hosea is not necessarily an irredeemably patriarchal book; however, a prophetic theology that addresses AIDS sufferers with this book in mind should use a postcolonial feminist critical eye that takes into consideration the text, its history of reading, victims and perpetrators, those in authority as well as cultures that promote sexual freedom for men and not women. Such a reading should begin by asking questions concerning Yahweh's words and actions, the nature of the names Hosea gives his children, punishment offered to the mother and the role of innocent children in this marriage.[55] In so doing, women victims who live under the leadership of church leaders who believe in the sexist nature of African culture and the Bible seek for their own freedom through the text. Likewise, women who are accused of witchcraft when their husbands die of HIV/AIDS feel empowered by both the Bible as the word of God and challenge patriarchal culture that marginalizes them while at the same time helping a more applicable text to the reader that does not show irredeemable androcentricism

Some readers may hesitate to use *Bosadi* approach's folk tales to compare African–South African and biblical cultures. Folk Tales which may not necessarily have taken place in history can as well compromise with the concept of scriptural authority. Also, some African Feminists may be disappointed with Masenya's readings that do not go far enough in recognizing the ideology of patriarchy in biblical texts. Masenya downplays the problem of divinity in feminist theology by saying that feminists are not interested in issues regarding the language of God even if she acknowledges that her own African male student was surprised to learn that God could be a woman.[56] It is puzzling considering that there were such concepts within African traditional religions including the existence of female goddesses in a number of African cultures. Even if the language of God is beyond description, given the pronouns used in the Bible that designate God as "he," an interpretative decision that takes seriously the African cultural understanding of God can

---

ros Document," which was a critique of state and church theology for their inaction on apartheid in South Africa and advocated for a prophetic theology that addressed suffering, liberation, and hope for the oppressed. This document, based on black theology, was successful in addressing apartheid as well as the church's theological role

55. Gale A. Yee, "Hosea," in Newsom and Ringe, *Women's Commentary*, 207–12.

56. Masenya, *How Worthy?* 40–41.

still illumine the concept of God and perhaps help with some of the irredeemable patriarchal texts. Given that such images of God, Jesus and Mary have come to be associated with whiteness and blue eyes, there is need for an African Women's biblical hermeneutics that does justice to the persons of the divinity by addressing this patriarchal complexity surrounding the nature of God. These images should be revived and bring interpretation to a closer appreciation by African–South African women. Masenya's failure to analyze critically these issues may be a result of her ambivalent position in viewing the bible as the word of God and desire to interpret it for the South African woman.

The book of Ruth in particular exposes *Bosadi* limitations in questioning patriarchy. Masenya observes that the story of Ruth and Naomi demonstrate that the security of a woman can only be found in men. This assertion can be seen to endorse patriarchy and a betrayal of the cause of African woman who have endured and even died of violence in the hands of their spouses because of the belief that women can only be valued or find security with men through marriage. And in this era of HIV/AIDS in Africa, which Masenya herself devotes her works selflessly to in regards to the victims; it is obvious that men play a key role as perpetrators through the culture that advantages them to have multiple sexual partners. Masenya's cultural retrieval of the persons of Naomi and Ruth within the African–South African culture disadvantages her own purpose of resisting cultural underpinnings behind both the biblical text and African–South African culture of today. The tossing of the coin at the gates is typical of African customs of men competing to inherit the widow after the death of her husband. Masenya's interpretation can therefore potentially be a loophole in the very hermeneutics that purports to unearth stories and experiences of African–South African women. Like Musimbi Kanyoro, Masenya reads Ruth and Naomi according to African cultural expectations and fails to interrogate the real ideologies embedded in the text.[57] Ruth is not just an androcentric text; it is highly patriarchal and colonial at best. It needs a highly charged postcolonial reading that is liberative.

CONCLUSION

The preceding has been an examination of the contributions of Prof. Madipoane Masenya's *Bosadi* approach to biblical studies. We have looked at the meaning and practice of *Bosadi* approach and especially how *Bosadi* approach allows a scholar to address different issues within the African South African context, most of which cannot be addressed using traditional methods. We have also looked at how

---

57. Musimbi R. A. Kanyoro, "Biblical Hermeneutics: Ancient Palestine and the Contemporary World," *RevExp* 94, no. 3 (1997): 372. Kanyoro, who follows inculturation methods, reads Ruth as an example of a good daughter-in-law who accepted the marriage within the dictates of Kenyan culture and tradition, where a woman marries in the family and not to an individual man.

other scholars view *Bosadi*. I have included my own understanding as well. While the work of other African feminist biblical scholars such as Theresa Okure, Musa Dube and Musimbi Kanyoro among others cannot be underestimated, the very concept of *Bosadi* interpretation is a brilliant opening to African feminist biblical scholarship in their different and unique socio political, religious and historical circumstances as African women in the continent. This exercise has shown that *Bosadi* approach is a discourse of assertion that has finally delivered to African women a tool in biblical scholarship and interpretation.

Bosadi understanding of the social location of a reader provides a way forward to African feminists to move in identifying their own discourses within their own unique social, political economic and historical contexts. It reminds of the rich historical values and sources of knowledge endowed to African women, which they ought to utilize and warns against potential domineering theories of patriarchy, racism and classism as well as African women's own absence on the discoursing table. Masenya's concerns for the sociopolitical situation of South Africa is evidence that she breathes fresh scholarship by unveiling the veil from biblical scholarship and allowing it to speak to African–South African women for the first time. By doing this, she demonstrates that it is possible to use different interpretative methodologies to arrive at the meaning of a text for the readers of today.

Bosadi uses inculturation methods that helps show the similarities between biblical and African world views. As a Christian and African South African female scholar, inculturation becomes a powerful tool that helps in redeeming an African Southern African woman where both the Bible and *Bosadi* culture are patriarchal. A *Bosadi* use of folktales unveils subordinated but otherwise unknown rich knowledge of African–South African women; prove that these women are the real owners of the Bible and that the Bible is their story. By using the folktales, Masenya recognizes and documents the untold stories and experiences of African women from all over the continent. She enables neglected African women's stories and experiences to gain their entry into the pages of academic biblical discourses to change if not offer alternative ways of reading. By locating herself within a postcolonial and postapartheid South Africa, Masenya is declaring that colonial and apartheid histories are part of Africa and African women's biblical interpretations do injustice to the womenfolk by not recognizing these facts in their approaches.

Masenya's analysis of biblical texts in light of her context shows us that patriarchy is a complicated ideology that is constructed in the culture, writing, reading, history and practice of texts. Readings from a postcolonial postapartheid and missionary perspective within the African–South African location have to dig deeper in unearthing patriarchy and how it penetrates the thinking of both the perpetrators and their victims.

Bosadi opens yet another space in the already available interpretative methods as well as challenging readings of representation in subordinating the voice of the subaltern, who can no longer play an inferior role. Masenya's *Bosadi* approach no doubt shows its worth as an applicable method to the study of biblical studies considering the wider issues that it addresses.

Works Cited

Achtemier, Paul J., gen. ed. *HarperCollins Bible Dictionary.* 2nd ed. San Francisco: Harper and Row, 1996.

Ashcroft, Bill, Gareth Grifiths, and Helen Tiffin, eds., *The Post Colonial Studies Reader.* London: Routledge, 1995.

Ateek, N. A., and M. Prior, eds. *Holy Land—Hollow Jubilee: God, Justice, and the Palestinians.* London: Melisende, 1999.

Barr, James. *Holy Scripture: Canon, Authority, Criticism.* Philadelphia: Westminster, 1983.

Bird, Phyllis A., Katharine Doob Sakenfeld, and Sharon H. Ringe, eds. "Reading the Bible as Women: Perspectives from Africa, Asia, and Latin America," *Semeia* 78 (1997): 11–165.

Brenner, Athalya, ed. *A Feminist Companion to Ruth and Esther.* 2nd ser.; Sheffield: Sheffield Academic Press, 1999.

Brown, J. T. *Setswana English Dictionary.* Johannesburg: Pula Press, 1997.

Dube, Musa W. *HIV/AIDS and the Curriculum: Methods of Integrating HIV/AIDS in Theological Programmes.* Geneva: WCC, 2003.

———. *Other Ways of Reading: African Women and the Bible.* Atlanta: SBL 2001.

Getui, M. N., K. Holter, and V. Zinkutatire. *Interpreting the Old Testament in Africa: Papers from the International Symposium on Africa and the Old Testament in Nairobi.* Nairobi: Acton, 2001.

Habel, N. *The Earth Stories in the Psalms and the Prophets.* Sheffield: Sheffield Academic Press, 2001.

Hamilton, Victor P. *The Book of Genesis 1–17.* NICOT; Grand Rapids: Eerdmans, 1990.

Himbaza, Innocent. "La Recherche Scientifique et la Contextualisation de la Bible," *BOTSA* 13 (2002): 2–7.

Holter, Knut. "Is It Necessary to Be Black?" *BOTSA* 13 (2002): 7–8.

———. *Old Testament Research for Africa: A Critical Analysis and Annotated of African Old Testament Dissertations, 1967–2000.* New York: Peter Lang, 2003.

Kanyoro, Musimbi R. A. "Biblical Hermeneutics: Ancient Palestine and the Contemporary World," *RevExp* 94, no. 3 (1997): 363–77.

McCreesh, T. "Wisdom as Wife; Proverbs 31:10–31," *RB* 92 (1985): 25–46.

Mlilo, Luke, and Nathanael Soede, eds. *Doing Theology and Philosophy in the African Context.* Denktraditionen im Dialog. SZBUI 17; Berlin: IKO-Verlag, 2004.

Mosala, Itumeleng J. *Biblical Hermeneutics and Black Theology.* Grand Rapids: Eerdmans, 1989.

Newsom, Carol A., and Sharon H. Ringe, eds. *Women's Bible Commentary with Apocrypha.* Exp. ed. Louseville: Westminster John Knox, 1998.

Patte, Daniel, gen. ed. *Global Bible Commentary.* Nashville: Abingdon, 2004.

Phiri, Isabel, A., B. Haddad, and M. Masenya (ngwana'Mphahlele), eds. *African Women, HIV/AIDS, and Faith Communities.* Pietermaritzburg: Cluster, 2003.

Skinner, John. *A Critical and Exegetical Commentary on Genesis.* Edinburgh: T&T Clark, 1969.

Speckman, M. T., and L. T. Kaufmann. *Towards an Agenda for Contextual Theology: Essays in Honour of Albert Nolan*. Pietermaritzburg: Cluster, 2001.

Speiser, Ephraim Avigdor. *Genesis: Introduction, Translation, and Notes*. AB 1. New York, NY: Doubleday, 1962.

Snyman, Gerrie. "Being Haunted by the Past: A Response to Prof. Jesse N. K. Mugambi." *BOTSA* 14 (2002): 13–16.

———. "Social Identity and South African Biblical Hermeneutics: A Struggle against Prejudice?" *JTSA* 121 (2005): 34–55.

———. " 'Who Has the Moral Right to Speak?' A Reflection on a Discourse within Old Testament Studies." *OTE* 15, no. 3 (2002): 799–820.

Vander Stichele, C., and Todd Penner, eds. *Her Master's Tools? Feminist and Postcolonial Engagements of Historical-Critical Discourse*. GPBS; Atlanta: SBL, 2005.

von Rad, Gerhard. *Genesis: A Commentary*. London: SCM, 1963.

Wood, L. J. *Genesis: A Study Guide*. Grand Rapids: Zondervan, 1975.

Westermann, Claus. *Genesis 12–36: A Continental Commentary*. Trans. John J. Scullion. Minneapolis: Augsburg Fortress, 1985.

Williams, Delores S. *Sisters in the Wilderness: The Challenge of Womanist God-Talk*. Maryknoll, NY: Orbis, 1993.

Williamson, Scott C. "But Ruth Clung to Her." *JFM* 18, no. 2 (2004): 90–95.

Select Masenya Bibliography

Masenya, Madipoane (Ngwana' Mphahlele). "Between Unjust Suffering and the "Silent" God: Job and HIV/AIDS Sufferers in South Africa." *Missionalia* 29, no. 2 (2001): 186–99.

———. "The Bible and Prophecy in African–South African Pentecostal Churches." *Missionalia* (2005): 35–45.

———. "The Bible, HIV/AIDS, and African/South African Women: A Bosadi Approach." *SHE* 31, no. 1 (2005): 187–201.

———. ". . . But You Shall Let Every Girl Live": Reading Exodus 1:1–2:10 the Bosadi (Womanhood) Way." *OTE* 15, no. 1 (2002): 99–112.

———. *How Worthy Is the Woman of Worth? Rereading Proverbs 31:10–31 in African-South Africa*. Peter Lang: New York, 2004.

———. "Is White South African Old Testament Scholarship African?" *BOTSA* 12 (2002): 3–8.

———. "Liberation with Us? Re-reading the Book of Exodus in a Post-Apartheid South Africa." *AJBS* 19, no. 2 (2003): 51–69.

———. "The Optimism of the Wise in Africa and in Israel: How Helpful in the Time of HIV/AIDS?" *OTE* 18, no. 2 (2005): 296–308.

———. "A Response to Himbaza and Holter." *BOTSA* 13 (2002): 9–12.

———. "Sacrificing Female Bodies at the Altar of Male Privilege: A Bosadi Reading of Judges 19." *ThViat* 27, no. 1 (2003): 98–122.

———. "A Small Herb Increases Itself (Impact) by a Strong Odor: Reimagining Vashti in Esther 1 in an African–South African Context." *OTE* 16, no. 2 (2003): 332–42.

———. "Struggling to Find 'Africa' in South Africa: The Bosadi (Womanhood) Approach to the Bible." *SBL Forum* 3, no. 5 (June 2005). http://www.sbl-site.org/publications/article.aspx?ArticleId=402.

———. "Struggling with Poverty/Emptiness: Rereading the Naomi-Ruth Story in African-South Africa." *JTSA* 120 (2004): 46–59.

———. "Teaching Western-Oriented Old Testament Studies to African Students: An Exercise in Wisdom or in Folly?" *OTE* 17, no. 3 (2004): 455–69.

Madipoane (Ngwana' Mphahlele) Masenya. "African Womanist Hermeneutics: A Suppressed Voice from South Africa Speaks." *JFSR* 11, no. 1 (1995): 147–55.

———. "The Bible and Women: Black Feminist Hermeneutics." *Scriptura* 54 (1995): 189–201.

———. "Biblical Authority and the Authority of Women's Experiences: Whither Way?" *Scriptura* 70, no. 3 (1999): 229–40.

———. "A Bosadi (Womanhood) Reading of Genesis 16." *OTE* 11, no. 2 (1998): 71–287.

———. "An Ecobosadi Reading of Psalm 127." Pages 109–22 in *The Earth Stories in the Psalms and the Prophets*, ed. N. Habel. Sheffield: Sheffield Academic Press, 2001.

———. "A Feminist Perspective on Theology with Particular Reference to Black Feminist Theology." *Scriptura* 49 (1994): 64–74.

———. "Freedom in Bondage: Black Feminist Hermeneutics." *NedGTT* 1 (1995): 115–23.

———. "Making the Context of African–South African Women a Hermeneutical Focus in Theological Education." In *National Initiative for the Contextualisation of Theological Education*, 2000.

———. "A Mosadi Reading of Prov. 31:10–31." *NAOTS* (1999): 2–6.

———. "The Naomi-Ruth Story from an African–South African Woman's Perspective Ngwetši (Bride)." *JFSR* 14, no. 2 (1998): 81–90.

———. "A Northern Sotho Marriage Setting: A Weal or a Woe? Focus on Some Feminist/Womanist Principles." *ThViat* 21 (1994): 29–56.

———. "Proverbs 31:10–31 in a South African Context: A Reading for the Liberation of African (Northern Sotho) Women." *Semeia* 78 (1997): 55–68.

———. "Reading the Bible the Bosadi (Womanhood) Way." *BCTSAA* 4, no. 2 (1997): 15–16.

———. "Redefining Ourselves: A Bosadi (Womanhood) Approach." *OTE* 10, no. 3 (1997): 439–48.

———. "What Differences Do African Contexts Make for English Bible Translations?" *OTE* 14, no. 2 (2001): 281–96.

———. "Wisdom Meets Wisdom: Selected Old Testament Proverbs Contextualised in a Northern Sotho Setting." *NedGTT* 1 (1994): 15–23.

———. "A Woman Reads Proverbs, 10–11." *BNHS* 3, no. 1 (1996): 10–11.

Masenya, Mmodipoane (Ngwana 'Mphahlele), and C. Landman. *Their Story Is Ours: Biblical Women and Us*. BSASAW; Pretoria: Powell Bible Centre, 1997.

Masenya, Mmodipoane (Ngwana 'Mphahlele), Isapel Phiri, and B. Hadad, eds. *African Women, HIV/AIDS, and Faith Communities*. Pietermaritzburg: Cluster, 2003.

Masenya, Mmodipoane (Ngwana 'Mphahlele), P. Gundani, T. Maluleke, and I. Phiri, "The State of Theological Education in Southern Africa: Issues and Concerns." *MF* (2002): 67–75.

Hanging Out with Rahab: An Examination of Musa Dube's Hermeneutical Approach with a Postcolonial Touch

Lynne Darden

I never felt closer to her than now. I mean Rahab the sex worker of Jericho, I have been (and I still am) in her house. I have thought her thoughts. I have laughed with Rahab's laughter. I have cried with Rahab's tears, until I realized that maybe I will just have to hang my tears to dry.

—Musa W. Dube[1]

Rahab the prostitute is literally located on the borderlands of Jericho. Joshua 2:15b relates that her residence is actually on the city wall: "for her house was on the outer side of the city wall and she resided within the wall itself" (NRSV). Ironically, it is the dwelling in a house that is located in-between the walls of society, that Rahab and her entire family and "all that belong to them" (Josh 2:13) were miraculously saved from annihilation after the walls of Jericho came "a tumblin' down." Their survival is credited to Rahab's keen negotiation skills with the two young men that Joshua sent out to spy out the territory, particularly the land of Jericho (Josh 2:1). The spies were open to her negotiations because she had saved them from the king of Jericho who was aware of their entrance into the land and who, in fact, had commanded Rahab to turn them over to him (Josh 2:4–6). Instead, she chose to disobey the commands of her king and had taken them up to the roof and hid them under stalks of flax until the coast was clear for them to escape. Under the cover of darkness, she lowered them down by a rope through her window (Josh 2:15a). For her action on the behalf of these foreign infiltrators, she requested of them that when the Israelite tribes, led by Joshua and the priests, invaded Jericho that they remember what she did and to reciprocate her deed by ensuring her family's survival and "all that belong to them" (Josh 2:13).

---

1. Musa W Dube, "Rahab Is Hanging Out a Red Ribbon: One African Woman's Perspective on the Future of Feminist New Testament Scholarship," in *Feminist New Testament Studies: Global and Future Perspectives,* ed. Kathleen O'Brien Wicker, Althea Spencer Miller, and Musa W. Dube (Religion/Culture/Critique series; New York: Palgrave Macmillan, 2005), 177–203.

Rahab was familiar with being in the middle, with living in-between continuity and discontinuity, acceptance and rejection, life and death, and dream and
nightmare. This phenomenon of being both in and out, gives us a clear glimpse
into the mystique and power of Rahab. Her skills of negotiation infiltrate, influence and inform the Israelites, her eventual colonizers, and eventually the blood
of the colonized Rahab, blood that is "almost the same but not quite" like Joshua
and his tribes, will flow through the veins of the kings of Israel, and by extension,
her blood, the blood of Jericho, will flow through the veins of, arguably, the most
influential figure in Western culture—Jesus Christ.

Rahab Hermeneutics

Musa Dube's interpretive point of departure is what I term a "Rahab hermeneutic"—a cultural-critical, feminist, framework whose infiltration into the biblical
guild has made it possible for an increased number of "two-third world feminist"
including postcolonial-womanist scholars,[2] to reside with her "in the walls" of
the biblical field. Dube's Rahab reading prism has helped spearhead a reading
strategy that privileges marginal social locations, and in so doing, questions the
motives of the production of an entrenched patriarchal historical critical paradigm that has dominated the biblical guild since the nineteenth century. This is a
radical and therefore risky position that exposes the field to "other" ways of interpreting the biblical texts that intentionally interrogates the sociopolitical praxis
of the status quo. This fresh reading framework questions the traditional claim
that only by the rigorous application of the various methods that comprise the
historical critical paradigm—source criticism, form criticism, tradition criticism,
textual criticism, philology, and so on—is a meaning reproduced that is univocal
and value-free.[3]

This very learned and extensively detailed analysis, however, is accused by
cultural critics, including Dube, of never explicitly venturing beyond the horizon of the original audience.[4] In addition, the paradigm has been charged with
being limited to discerning the Western and patriarchal theological meaning

----

2. Postcolonial-womanist biblical scholars are African American women who focus on
a fusion of postcolonial theory and womanist biblical hermeneutics as a framework for
interpreting biblical texts.

3. Fernando F. Segovia, "And They Began to Speak in Tongues," in *Reading from this
Place*, vol. 1: *Social Location and Biblical Interpretation in North American Perspective*, ed.
Fernando F. Segovia and Mary Tolbert (Minneapolis: Augsburg Fortress, 1994), 11. Musa
Dube's work falls under the wider rubric of the cultural studies paradigm laid out in this
essay. Also see "Cultural Studies and Contemporary Biblical Criticism: Ideological Criti-
cism as Mode of Discourse," in *Reading from this Place: Social Location and Biblical Inter-
pretation in Global Perspective,* ed. Fernando F. Segovia and Mary Tolbert (Minneapolis:
Augsburg Fortress, 1995), 1–11.

4. Ibid.

embedded in the text and intentionally silencing the possible complex political agendas, concerns and issues that lurk in the shadow of the text's message.[5] It is for this reason that the claim of an objective historical criticism in its early stage could be argued as being actually a masked or camouflaged subjectivity that reflected the worldview of primarily Western male scholars/theologians. This camouflaged subjectivity was greatly informed by Frederich Schleierm-acher's philosophical hermeneutics, an Enlightenment influenced contribution to biblical studies that was far more reaching than one might assume.[6] Schlei-ermacher's main distinction was the suggestion that interpretation is an "art of understanding", an act of living, feeling and intuiting being human. Accord-ing to Schleiermacher only by "deadening ourselves" can the re-constructed composition take place. He also suggested the ability to intuit the mind of an-other because there is a commonality, an affinity, between the author and the interpreter.[7]

A "Rahab hermeneutic" unmasks the historical critical reproduction of mean-ing by revealing: (1) we can never "deaden ourselves" in order to "transform our-selves into another person" because, (2) we live in the world of the present, not the past and, (3) we bring to the text certain preconceptions and presuppositions, and furthermore, (4) these preconceptions/presuppositions are a condition of our par-ticular cultural and social location, therefore, (5) it is inevitable that the cultural/ social location will inform the production of meaning that the historical critic has selected to expound upon, and, (6) historical interpreters can, at best, merely

---

5. Though this is truer of the early stage of the paradigm in the nineteenth century than of historical criticism today.

6. According to Herman Waetjen, "Schleiermacher's hermeneutics of reproduction fostered the progression of historical consciousness and promoted the somewhat earlier development of historical criticism and its application to the biblical texts." See Herman C. Waetjen, "Social Location and the Hermeneutical Mode of Integration," in *Reading from this Place: Social Location and Biblical Interpretation in North American Perspective*, ed. Fernando F. Segovia and Mary Tolbert (Minneapolis: Augsburg Fortress, 1994), 77. Also see Anthony C. Thiselton, *New Horizons in Hermeneutics: The Theory and Practice of Trans-forming Biblical Reading* (Grand Rapids: Zondervan, 1992), 204.

7. Central to Schleiermacher's theory is the linguistic nature of communication in gen-eral. There is no understanding without language. Language falls into a combination of gen-eral patterns—grammatical (the objective aspect) and psychological (the subjective aspect). The principle upon which Schleiermacher's articulation rests is that of the hermeneutic circle. Understanding is circular. The circle as a whole defines the individual part, and the parts together form the circle. It is within this circular, dialectical relationship between the whole and the parts that meaning emerges. Therefore, the hermeneutical circle requires an attempt on the part of the interpreter to position himself or herself with the author and, at the same time, to distance himself/herself from the author in order to make new sense of the text or utterance in the context of the linguistic system.

reconstruct the *possibilities* of the ancient writer's preconceptions/presuppositions *and* only by way of a contemporary historical mediation.[8]

A "Rahab hermeneutic" emphasizes the interrelationship between the text and—in the words of Fernando F. Segovia—"real, flesh-and-blood readers."[9] The explicit focus on feminism and cultural criticism, including postcolonialism shifts the gaze of the scholar toward a very different approach to interpretation with its own mode of discourse and theoretical spectrum and away from the exclusive gaze of Western male clerics.

A Rahab hermeneutic approaches interpretation with the understanding that any text that has been separated from its original context and subsequently has become part of a universal tradition requires integration into the reader's contemporary situation. This hermeneutical approach suggests that biblical interpretation is a reading activity that involves living in the present as well as reading the past. It considers that the present context as well as the context of the past must necessarily factor in when constructing meaning. Thus, the particular meaning uncovered will be directly related to a contemporary reality that is in "partnership" or "solidarity" with the ancient text. In this way, the ancient biblical text is thrust forward into another reality that is culture-specific and/or gender-specific to the interpreter. This re-casting of the text is indicative of its capacity to satisfy individual and communal yearning for a communication with the Divine. Therefore, for a Rahab hermeneutic, the historical mediation that interprets text is based on a direct application of contemporary life. Following the suggestion of postcolonial biblical critics, this approach assumes that imperialism-colonialism is not simply a system of economic and military control, but perhaps more importantly, it is a systematic cultural penetration/domination that subjugates psychologically and intellectually. And, because the objective of a Rahab hermeneutic is an enhanced understanding of the work scripture does in negotiating the uneven relationship of domination/subjection, both in antiquity as well as in contemporary society, this reading approaches the text with the assumption that imperial-colonial practices are encoded in the biblical text.

R. S. Surgirtharjah, a prominent scholar of postcolonial biblical criticism points out, the postcolonial biblical critic operates explicitly within the context of cultural domination. He states:

> Postcolonial biblical criticism makes clear that biblical studies can no longer be confined to the history of textual traditions but needs to extend its scope to include issues of domination, western expansion and its ideological manifestations as central forces in defining biblical scholarship.[10]

---

8. This is exactly how the ancient writers constructed meaning. For instance, the authors of the gospel narratives shaped Jesus' activity around their own immediate imperial context in relation to their community's experience of imperial domination.

9. Segovia, "And They Began," 1.

10. R. S. Sugirtharajah, *Postcolonial Criticism and Biblical Interpretation* (Oxford: Oxford University Press, 2002), 74–75.

In other words, it must be hermeneutically suspected that an ideological bias informs the production of meaning by traditional historical biblical scholars and this suspicion must always be consciously taken into consideration.[11] With this in mind, R. S. Sugirtharajah suggests that a postcolonial biblical hermeneutic explicitly identifies four codes that are embodied in the narrative—hegemonic, professional, negotiated and oppositional.[12]

The hegemonic code functions to legitimate the dominant values and ideological interests of the ruling class. It tends to embrace colonial models and patriarchal practices. The professional code is concerned with preserving, centralizing and interpreting laws, traditions and customs. The negotiated code is concerned with how an event or experience is interpreted to meet new theological/ideological situations. The oppositional code is the voice of the group on the margins that locates their place in the discourse in spite of the text being produced by those who have vested interests. By diligently seeking out these codes that are embodied in the text, the postcolonial biblical scholar presents a more multilevel meaning than that traditional historical biblical scholar. Operating under a feminist-postcolonial framework that also entails applying an intense critical gaze on contemporary patriarchal and imperialistic/neoimperialistic practices and procedures, Musa Dube's hermeneutical approach exposes how these practices/procedures are embodied in the biblical text. Her interpretive process operates under the assumption that patriarchy and colonialism are systematic cultural penetrations of domination.

Dube's *Postcolonial Feminist Interpretation of the Bible* is an illustration of her Rahab hermeneutical approach. Through a close literary reading of Matthew, particularly Matthew 15:21–28, Dube highlights the imperial symbolism that is interwoven throughout the text, including Jesus' tendency to "exorcise" the native demons he comes in contact with on his many travels throughout foreign lands. In Matthew 15:21–28, Dube portrays the Syro-Phoenician woman and her daughter as types of the land in order to set up a "decolonization" of the narrative.[13] Gazing through a feminist lens, Dube symbolizes Jesus' healing of the daughter with the Western world's entrance into her homeland, Africa, under the modern guise of "progress." That is to say, Jesus' actions are read metaphorically as Western Christian invasion and conquest. Dube claims that the Syro-Phoenician woman symbolizes pre-modern, non-progressive Africa that is incapable of providing either physical or spiritual sustenance for her own people symbolized by the (absent) daughter.

---

11. The active application of a hermeneutic of suspicion is still vitally necessary even in this era of biblical studies since the early historical-critical method remains entrenched in the conservative graduate programs in American universities, which continue to hold dominant positions in academia.

12. Sugirtharajah borrowed and revised these terms from Stuart Hall, the British cultural critic, who applied these terms to his analysis of how televisual discourse operates. See *Postcolonial Criticism*, 75.

13. Dube, *Postcolonial Feminist,* 118–21.

Dube's point of departure in this interpretation of Matt 15 is, in fact, the gene-alogy of Jesus Christ listed in Matt 1. For Dube, the intertextual recall of Rahab, signifies the colonizer's desire to enter and domestic the land of Canaan. She claims that "through the character of Rahab, the ideology of presenting the tar-geted groups like women who require and beseech domination is reasserted in the articulation of mission."[14] The use of Rahab also serves to reinforce and naturalize the subjugation of women in societies in which these narratives are used. Presup-posing that most of our canonized texts were born in a world of persistent impe-rial and patriarchal settings, her objective in this interpretation is to perform a postcolonial feminist reading that exposes the power relation in the construction of mission, empire, gender and race. As part of her of postcolonial strategy, Dube asks four basic questions to determine whether the Matthean text has an imperial-izing context: (1) does the Matthean text have a clear stance against the political imperialism of the time? (2) does the Matthean text encourage travel to distant and inhabited lands and how does it justify itself? (3) how does the Matthean text construct difference: is there dialogue and liberating interdependence, or is there condemnation and replacement of all that is foreign? (4) does the Matthean text employ gender and divine representations to construct relationships of subordina-tion and domination?[15] Through the close reading of Matt 15:21–28, Dube brings her Rahab reading prism to bear upon the pericope and interprets the passage as a type-scene land possession.

RAHAB HERMENEUTIC INFLUENCED BY THE SPIRIT
OF THE AFRICAN INDEPENDENT CHURCH (AIC)

The empowering works of the women of the African Independent Church (AIC) serve as the foundation of a Rahab hermeneutic. The group of Churches began as a protest movement against the white-male- only leadership in the missionary-founded churches of the nineteenth century.[16] African women have always played a central role in these churches as founders, prophets, bishops and archbishops and have been instrumental in envisioning a religion that reflected the African struggle for liberation from colonialism, capitalism, racism and cultural chauvin-ism.[17] It is against this historical background of political protest, a search for cul-tural liberation through the integration of biblical views with African religious views, and an experience of God's spirit empowering both women and men of various races that the interpretive practices of the AIC churches should be under-stood. Their approach should be seen not only as a mode of political resistance, but also a demonstrated will to cultivate a space for liberation.

---

14. Ibid., 121.
15. Ibid., 129.
16. Ibid., 184.
17. Ibid.

Womanist Critique of a Rahab Hermenuetic

Womanist biblical interpretation is also grounded in a contemporary contextual departure. That is to say, like Rahab, womanist scholars also reside "on the wall", dwelling between continuity and discontinuity, acceptance and rejection, of dream and nightmare. It is this location, in-between the borders, where womanist scholars also admonish, challenge and subvert the dominant ethos. Womanist biblical scholars are advocates for liberation whose overall objectives are: (1) to expose and confront oppressive ideological interpretations, (2) to recover the presence of the other in the biblical texts, and (3) to articulate liberation from a history of dominant interpretations that have been instrumental in the oppression of African Americans. In addition, womanist scholars question the essentialist belief that all African Americans are in need of liberation from an overtly oppressive Eurocentric society since (1) greater numbers of African Americans are moving into positions of political and economic power since the 1990s; and (2) therefore, the dimensions of sociopolitical oppression are becoming more complex and more subtle. Therefore, because of these shifts in the nation's demographics, more complex readings of the biblical narratives must be produced that addresses more fully the dilemmas, issues and concerns of the community. Therefore, womanist scholars re-frame a Rahab hermeneutical approach for a wider and more complex set of conflicts within the community itself as an added dimension. The need for a Rahab hermeneutic to not only challenge and provoke the dominant patriarchal and imperialistic elements of mainstream society, but also to provoke the African American community to be ware of its own co-optation to the oppressive elements of society in its cultural negotiations, and to better represent the "double consciousness" of the twenty-first century African American citizen is an important objective. A more complex Rahab hermeneutic will increase its focus on exploring the community's unreflective appropriation of the oppressive elements of an increasingly neo-imperial, capitalistic, global society.

I suggest that Cheryl Kirk-Duggan employs a womanist version of a Rahab hermeneutic in her essay "Let My People Go! Threads of Exodus in African American Narratives" in *Yet with a Steady Beat: Contemporary U.S. Afrocentric Biblical Interpretation* edited by Randall Bailey. In this essay, Kirk-Duggan challenges the view of the exodus narrative as a quest for liberation. For her the oppression-liberation paradigm does not adequately inform the African American community. She claims that "it is much easier to deal with the concept of a chosen people and to cheerfully disregard the matter of manifest destiny and the vast complexities of how class and diversity plays out within the book of Exodus."[18] She urges us to be mindful not only of the two-edged nature of the texts, but also, I would suggest, of one's own am-

---

18. Cheryl Kirk-Duggan, "Let My People Go! Threads of Exodus in African American Narratives," in *Yet with a Steady Beat: U.S. Afrocentric Biblical Interpretation,* ed. Randall C. Bailey (Atlanta: SBL, 2000), 123–43.

bivalent identity when examining the ambiguities and paradoxes within the bible. Kirk-Duggan states that "although the warrior-God tradition inspired social movements and freedom they are themselves violent and antithetical to peace and social justice."[19] She explores Lorraine Hansberry's *A Raisin in the Sun* as a contemporary Exodus narrative depicting the yearning of a deprived community's aspirations of realizing the American dream and highlights the complexity of the struggle for attaining that goal as the family prepares for its exodus out of the inner-city into the suburbs. Individual family members respond to the tension of liberation in different ways as they wait for God to appear in the mail for in this version of the biblical narrative God is an insurance check. Both Walter Lee and Beneatha (whose name is a pun on lower class), like Aaron and Miriam, have their own selfish views about the money. We begin to wonder if the hopeful place of dreams has actually become a place of bondage, as Hansberry reveals to us each of the characters flaws based on their individual desires of attaining the American dream.

In the same essay, she examines the music of Sweet Honey in the Rock, an a capella women's group that sings songs of protest and resistance to oppression. She sees their songs as embodying the spirit of Exodus. The song "More Than a Paycheck" is an indictment against the freedom to bring environmental illnesses, disease, injury, and stress to our families in the name of money, and "Battle for My Life" urges us to be free enough to see the problems of the human condition.[20]

She writes in the last stanza of her poem that opens her essay:

> Kicking Back
> Busted out of bondage
> Talking and living
> In the midst of Exodus
> Where is our Reed Sea?
> Our Mount Sinai?
> What are we free to do, to be?
> Free not to be?
> Who is our Moses?
> Our Pharaoh?
> Our Yochebed and Miriam?
> Who are We?: Them?
> Is There an Us?
> Who is our God?
> Let my People Go![21]

Cheryl Kirk-Duggan's essay is an example of how a womanist interpretation reframes a Rahab reading prism to provoke her own community to be acutely aware of its own contradictions.

---

19. Ibid., 130.
20. Ibid., 139.
21. Ibid., 123.

CONCLUSION

Rahab's request that "you will spare my father and mother, my brothers and sisters, and all who belong to them, and deliver our lives from death" (2:13) implies that her family owned slaves and, therefore, Rahab might not be the deprived, marginalized, weak, inferior woman that we often portray her as. She schemes like an elitist who is only interested in preserving her family's wealth and position. As an elite member of society, we would be remiss not to question her actions of betrayal against her own people, her disobedience of the commands of her king, in favor of foreigners who were on a mission of conquest and annihilation justified by the claim of being the "the chosen people." There is the nagging possibility that Rahab, the harlot, who exists in-between the walls of Jericho moved men around like chess pieces for selfish gain. She is indeed a master of the technique of camouflage. But you might ask, "What choice did she have?" She chose the lesser of two evils—colonization over annihilation. After all, she infiltrated Joshua's culture and somehow made it her own, for she not only survives, but thrives within it. She is transformed from a "deviant sexual other" to an accepted tribal member, becoming an ancestor to a king of the Israelite nation. Yes, this is true. Yet, she must have always remembered the sacrifices, the hard decisions that had to be made as she weighed her options and always had to be careful that her strategic infiltration did not morph into a full-blown appropriation of the colonizer's culture.

WORKS CITED

Bailey, Randall, ed. *Yet with a Steady Beat: U.S. Afrocentric Biblical Interpretation*. Atlanta: SBL, 2000.

Dube, Musa W. *Postcolonial Feminist Interpretation of the Bible*, Danvers MA.: Chalice, 2000.

———. "Rahab Is Hanging Out a Red Ribbon: One African Woman's Perspective on the Future of Feminist New Testament Scholarship." In *Feminist New Testament Studies: Global and Future Perspectives*, ed. Kathleen O'Brien Wicker, Althea Spencer Miller, and Musa W. Dube. Religion/Culture/Critique series. New York: Palgrave Macmillan, 2005.

Segovia, Fernando F., and Mary Tolbert. *Reading from this Place: Social Location and Biblical Interpretation in North American Perspective*. Vol. 1. Minneapolis: Augsburg Fortress, 1994.

———. *Reading from this Place: Social Location and Biblical Interpretation in Global Perspective*. Vol. 2. Minneapolis: Augsburg Fortress, 1995.

Sugirtharajah, R. S. *Postcolonial Criticism and Biblical Interpretation*. Oxford: Oxford University Press, 2002.

Thiselton, Anthony C. *New Horizons in Hermeneutics: The Theory and Practice of Transforming Biblical Reading*. Grand Rapids: Zondervan, 1992.

Wicker, Kathleen O'Brien, Althea Spencer Miller, and Musa W. Dube. *Feminist New Testament Studies: Global and Future Perspectives*. Religion/Culture/Critique series. New York: Palgrave Macmillan, 2005.

2. BIBLICAL INTERPRETATION IN AND THROUGH CREATIVE WRITING

Race, Scripture, and Colonialism:
Olaudah Equiano's Narrative of Biblical Origins

Sylvester A. Johnson

The autobiography of Olaudah Equiano (1745–1797) offers an unusual portrait of the dynamic relationship between scripture and colonialism. In 1789 Equiano, who also went by the name Gustavus Vassa, related his experience of slavery to support abolitionism in Britain in the form of a best-selling, two-volume autobiography entitled *The Interesting Narrative of the Life of Olaudah Equiano, or Gustavus Vassa, the African, Written by Himself.*[1] This essay examines Equiano's claims about African origins in his autobiography. I argue that Africa's supposed invisibility to history was a foundational problem for Equiano that urges a postcolonial analysis, one that reveals how Equiano crafted his own image of Africa to parry the imperial dehumanization of Africans. Equiano's intriguing agency is nevertheless complicated by the numerous pitfalls of his biblical strategy.

Equiano's Narrative of Jewish Origins

In the first chapter of his *Interesting Narrative*, Equiano discusses religion among the Igbo nation of West Africa. He reminisces about his childhood and provides accounts of divination and medical knowledge. Quite remarkably, Equiano alludes to similarities between Igbo religion and ancient Jewish religion—these include taboos against touching corpses to avoid ritual contamination, civil adjudication based on *lex talionis*, and attention toward cleanliness through ritual washing. It is the latter portion of this chapter that reveals Equiano's governing intention behind relating anecdotes to describe Igbo religion.

> . . . Here I cannot forbear suggesting what has long struck me very forcibly, namely, the strong analogy which even by this sketch, imperfect as it is, appears

---

1. Equiano published nine editions of his autobiography and eventually switched to a single-volume presentation to enhance the book's marketability. For a detailed history of Equiano's publishing (and the definitive biography of Equiano), see Vincent Carretta, *Equiano, the African: The Biography of a Self-Made Man* (Athens and London: University of Georgia Press, 2005), especially chap. 12.

to prevail in the manners and customs of my countrymen, and those of the Jews, before they reached the Land of Promise, and particularly the patriarchs, while they were yet in that pastoral state which is described in Genesis—an analogy which alone would induce me to think that the one people has sprung from the other.[2]

At this point, Equiano weaves into his discussion the biblical commentaries of John Gill (1697–1771), John Brown (1722–1787), and Arthur Bedford (d. 1745). He cites these writers in order to present as their confirmation of his casual impression what is actually a well scripted, thoughtfully orchestrated argument designed to persuade the reader that the Igbo are derived from biblical, specifically Jewish ancestors—Abraham and Keturah. In his autobiography, in other words, these commentators seem to confirm "what has long struck" him as more than coincidental similarities between the Igbo and the Jews. A careful study of Equiano's sources, however, reveals that *none* of these commentators actually claim that Africans are descendants of ancient Jews; the claim is Equiano's exclusively.[3] The degree to which Equiano handles his sources to derive an interpretation uniquely his own is evident from the generally positive light in which he discusses Igbo religion, in contrast to the demeaning perspective of his commentary sources. Not only does Equiano ignore his commentators' characterization of Africans as "wicked" and "miserable," but he also sanctifies Igbo religion through erecting a genealogy that is biblical in origin and Jewish in nature. Igbo religion is derived through revealed religion—if not the gospel, then certainly the Torah.

This closer inspection of Equiano's sources in biblical commentary readily reveals what is at once impressive and tragic. Equiano is working with the writings of theologians who revile Hamites, in keeping with a long history of biblical representation, and these Hamites are said to be the ancestors of blacks. Even more pressing is the problem of historical consciousness conjured by these writers, especially Bedford—Africa lies beyond the realm of history. West Africa, however, is the darling of Equiano's childhood memories. As he claims in his 'interesting narrative,' this was his birthplace, the land of the Igbo. In this context, Equiano's audacious manipulation of these commentators—he pieces together the excesses of glosses and footnotes—becomes a means of circumnavigating entirely the Hamitic myth of African origins and instantiating the Igbo within the realm of Israelite identity—the Igbo are descended from the chosen people and, despite being in the heart of a non-historical land, their roots lie at the center of biblical history.

Equiano's narrative has garnered considerable attention from several scholars. Adam Potkay argues that the overriding framework in Equiano's narrative

---

2. Olaudah Equiano, *The Interesting Narrative of the Life of Olaudah Equiano, or Gustavus Vassa, the African: Written by Himself*, 2nd ed. (London: T. Wilkins, 1789), 1:25.

3. John Brown, *A Dictionary of the Holy Bible* (Edinburgh: John Gray and Gavin Alston, 1769), 16, 573.

presents his life as an adumbration of Christian salvation history.[4] Potkay offers a crucial corrective when he surmises that many scholars have imprudently ignored or grossly misinterpreted Equiano's relationship with Christianity by claiming that Equiano never truly accepted the religion of his conquerors.[5] But he is too quick to dismiss the imperial meanings and the context of violent conquest that enabled Equiano's sense of being 'rescued' from Africa.[6] The work of Joanna Brooks is also relevant here.[7] Brooks' historical study of early modern African literature (Diasporan, that is) charts in a compelling way the rise of complex tropes at the hands of these authors whose representational discourse indexes thoughtful, critical resistance to the colonial array of racist, dehumanizing assumptions about blacks.[8] However, like Potkay, Brooks fails to identify any problems that might have emerged from the colonizing, religious context of these writers.[9] Wilson Jeremiah Moses and Henry Louis Gates also lend important insights into the imperatives of colonial representation in Equiano's *Narrative*. Moses suggests, for instance, Equiano's was a colonial Christian consciousness that demanded a particular knowledge about Africa and blackness that was demeaning, alienating, and haunting. Gates' now classic treatment of the "Talking Book trope," likewise, is especially relevant here for understanding what was at stake for African authors such as Equiano. Equiano portends a mastery of literacy, notes Gates, in an effort to represent the black as a "member of the human community."[10] This signification of literary humanness was necessitated by the domain assumption of black racial

---

4. Adam Potkay, "History, Oratory, and God in Equiano's *Interesting Narrative*," *ECS* 34, no. 4 (2001): 601–14.

5. Ibid. Also see Adam Potkay and Sandra Burr, eds., *Black Atlantic Writers of the Eighteenth Century: Living the New Exodus in England and the Americas* (New York: St. Martin's Press, 1995).

6. Potkay, "History, Oratory, and God in Equiano's *Interesting Narrative*," 602, 612 n. 10. Potkay seems not to have examined Equiano's commentary sources. Had he done so, he would have realized that Equiano does subvert considerably the colonizing claims of his sources.

7. The classic treatment of this hybridity is that by Paul Gilroy, *The Black Atlantic: Modernity and Double Consciousness* (Cambridge: Harvard University Press, 1993).

8. Joanna Brooks, *American Lazarus: Religion and the Rise of African-American and Native American Literatures* (New York: Oxford University Press, 2003), 33–35.

9. Jonathan Edwards, *History of the Work of Redemption*, in *The Works of President Edwards* (1817; repr., New York: Burt Franklin, 1968), 5:221–222. As Brooks notes, George Whitefield owned slaves and used their labor ensure the profitability of an orphanage he owned. For an excellent study of Whitefield's shift from abolitionism to slaveholding and public advocacy of slavery, see Stephen Stein, "George Whitefield on Slavery: Some New Evidence," *CH* 42, no. 2 (1973): 243–56, esp. 244–45.

10. Henry Louis Gates, Jr., *The Signifying Monkey: A Theory of Afro-American Literary Criticism* (New York: Oxford University Press, 1988), 128.

inferiority touted by influential contemporaries of Equiano such as David Hume, Georg W. F. Hegel, and Immanuel Kant.[11]

COLONIALISM, TEMPORALITIES, AND THE REFRACTIVE SUBALTERN

Any assessment of Christianity's forceful role in Equiano's biography should consider this underside of Equiano's conversion and the harrowing meanings of race and geography constituted through relations of conquest and white Christian domination. Otherwise, one risks representing colonialism as a sublime experience for peoples (however gainfully they might be positioned within European power structures and enamored of evangelical religion) who are members of a race targeted for enslavement, genocide, and subjugation.[12] It is, in fact, precisely in the complex of meanings about *temporalities* and *geographies* that one finds the most forceful imperatives behind Equiano's engagement with biblical narrative to establish his putative relationship between the "Eboan nation" and the Jews.

The racialized geography that emerged under European conquest over the Americas, Africa, and the "Orient" fundamentally relied on a synthesis of temporal and spatial (geographical and cartographical) methods that transformed human populations into colonial subjects by ordering them as people of a different time (the backward races of primitivist discourse) and of particular lands (black Africa). In this way, Africa as a geographical and racial space was temporally reduced to a history-less simulacrum. The more explicitly religious dimension of this process is visible in what Kathleen Biddick has described as the thoroughgoing construction of a historical consciousness that displaced European Jews from contemporary society into the ancient world. The Christian "typological imaginary," Biddick explains, imposed a temporality of identitarian time ("that was then, this is now") through which Christianity superseded Judaism. This temporal order of things was a hegemonic means of encoding the contemporary world as an exclusively Christian era (*anno domini*). As Biddick explains by examining 'medieval' Christianity, Christian supersession was not a one-time event limited to early Christian history. Rather, this style of imagining history perpetually evolved and was reinvented through more complex, expansive means. The result was a deadening process that repeatedly transformed contemporary Jews into living relics of a by-gone era who, under the Christian gaze, signified biblical times and biblical peoples past, and by this means established a Christian and modern present, in which Jews had no rightful place.[13]

---

11. Ibid., 141, 153.

12. Equiano rather explicitly frames his enslavement and eventual Christianization as a fortunate event, one for which he is deeply grateful because it effected his deliverance from a continent of spiritual darkness; in other words, he had escaped eternal damnation.

13. Kathleen Biddick, *The Typological Imaginary: Circumcision, Technology, History* (Philadelphia: University of Pennsylvania Press, 2003). Biddick explains how Christian car-

In like fashion, Charles H. Long has noted the startling efficacy of colonial tem-poralities in the making-through-conquest of the Atlantic world. Long urgently observes that the roots of modern knowledge and Enlightenment representation are firmly grounded in the colonial contacts afforded through imperial conquest in the Atlantic world and in the 'Orient'—encounters with the "empirical other." Colonialism also situated those designated as 'primitives' as the elemental loci for studying religion as a *genus*.[14] By erecting categories of Oriental (the East), primi-tive (Africans and Native Americans), and modern (Europeans) subjectivities, an evolutionary logic of teleology, articulated through theories about the origin of religion, achieved the same subjugating structures of temporality that Biddick identifies in the Christian typological imaginary.[15]

Examining the overtures of black religious data such as Equiano's in this way requires one to reject primitivism and colonial temporalities as a means of inter-preting African subjectivity in the Atlantic world. Otherwise, accepting a colonial framework requires one to conclude that blacks can never be located within the realm of the '*now*' that is but only beyond the boundaries of modernity, striking up deep contrast as primitives. Rather than embrace the enchantment of this coloniz-ing temporality, Long proposes that black subjectivity itself must be recognized as a productive site for examining the meaning of modernity and conceiving a non-historical temporality.[16]

Long's assessment is paralleled in Homi Bhabha's explanation of the potential

tography was a technology that literally erased Jews from space and represented the *topos* of Europe as a Christian land devoid of contemporary Jews.

14. See, for instance, Jonathan Z. Smith, *Imagining Religion: From Babylon to Jonestown* (Chicago: University of Chicago Press, 1982), xi; Michel Foucault, *The Archaeology of Knowledge*, trans. A. M. Sheridan Smith (London: Tavistock, 1972); Charles H. Long, "Re-ligion, Discourse, and Hermeneutics: New Approaches in the Study of Religion," in Ma-thieu E. Courville, ed., *The Next Step in Studying Religion: A Graduate's Guide* (Continuum International, 2007), 183–97.

15. See Vincent L. Wimbush's introduction to his edited *African Americans and the Bible: Sacred Texts and Social Textures* (New York: Continuum, 2000); and idem, *Theoriz-ing Scriptures: New Critical Orientations to a Cultural Phenomenon* (New Brunswick: Rut-gers University Press, 2008). Wimbush has compellingly argued for applying methods of cultural history to understand how scriptures have been deployed to refashion the world symbolically (world-making), particularly as a means of ordering relations of power, effect-ing human destruction, negotiating social suffering, and constituting psychological modes, especially in the recent centuries.

16. See Charles H. Long, *Significations: Signs, Symbols, and Images in the Interpretation of Religion* (Aurora, CO: Davies Group, 1986), 85–87; "Religion, Discourse, and Herme-neutics," 195–97; "Bodies in Time and the Healing of Spaces: Religion, Temporalities, and Health," in *Faith, Health, and Healing in African American Life*, ed. Stephanie Y. Mitchem and Emilie M. Townes (New York: Praeger, 2008); and especially his "African American Religion in the United States of America: An Interpretative Essay," *NovR* 7, no. 1 (2003): 23–25. Long crystallizes a reading of black bodies as coeval with and incorporating modern

for subaltern subjects to disrupt modernity's fictive articulation of time and space. Bhabha explains the spatial distancing, the perspective formed through recession from "the event," that achieves the vista of modernity—*viz.*, looking back to the Enlightenment *qua* event in order to see modernity, which has superseded a Dark Age. Modernity is constituted through "the enunciation" achieved in the very act of gazing back toward the event (for Bhabha and Long, the Enlightenment; for Biddick, the emergence of Christendom and expulsion of Jews). The enunciation thereby constructs and animates the semblance of modernity, of the "now" that can never be identified with "what was then." Bhabha makes clear that the discourse of modernity masks subjectivity (of Europe and, more precisely, the West) as an era or epoch (identitarian time—the now that is, modernity). But of course the epoch cannot subsume 'primitive' peoples; because modernity is *not really* an era so much as it is *an effect of the subjectivity* of Western conquerors (this is why *modern* and *primitive* peoples can encounter each other in real time without recourse to time travel—otherwise no primitives would still be alive in the modern period but would be extinct). Modernity, thus, denies coevalness between the one and the other.[17] Bhabha, furthermore, also proffers as evidentiary analysis the false promise of "the event"—modernity brings civility. What it portends is fictive.[18]

Equiano's narrative refracts the white light of Christianity's knowledge about Africa into a colorful array of complications and distills the particulate matter of colonial ruptures precisely because of his liminality. He demonstrates the disjuncture that Homi Bhabha refers to as "deformations" and "time lags." Equiano, writing from his British home in the metropole, resided within the geography and temporal space of Christendom. But unlike his fellow European Christians, Equiano is not from Christendom; he is from 'heathendom.' And unlike the English commentators populating his footnotes, Equiano cannot so easily elide the fault lines beneath his gesture of incorporating a non-biblical Africa into Christianity's temporal and geographical knowledge-world. He is forced, in fact, to employ these fault lines and fissures as footholds and leverage points to pry open a portal of entry into the colonizing, identitarian history of a Christian, colonial world. Equiano is located at a critical point at which this means of relegating—of ordering and assigning—peoples (here as racial and religious types) to a temporal status became wed to the exigencies of empire whose colonizing reach was global.

Through this imperial process was born the Atlantic world, and in this world, the many peoples of Africa and the Americas were located—conscientiously put in

subjectivity, thus serving as data that become efficacious for theorizing the contemporary world.

17. Biddick, *Typological Imaginary*, 22–23.

18. Homi Bhabha, *The Location of Culture* (London: Routledge, 1994), 236–55. Bhabha foregrounds the relationship between modernity and violence in a manner that recalls Hannah Arendt's classic thesis in *The Origins of Totalitarianism* (New York: Harcourt, 1951), and that parallels the recent work of Irene Silverblatt, *Modern Inquisitions: Peru and the Colonial Origins of the Civilized World* (Durham, NC: Duke University Press, 2004).

their place—beyond the boundaries of the temporal center. They were people without clear ties to the historical purview of biblical thinking, without obvious linkage to the sphere of "human history." Europe's colonial conquest over Africa and the Americas, in this way, emerged through well-practiced techniques of scriptural world-making and modernizing historiographies (secularized supersession), the genealogical trail of which points up a prototypical primitivism (representing contemporary Jews as pre-modern and ancient) that would be elaborated and rarified when applied throughout the Atlantic world. Africa, according to this framework, was without history. Africans, unlike Jews, were stuck not *within* ancient history but *behind* a cordon of historylessness that marked off a Dark Continent *devoid* of historical agency. What is forced to the surface in the "deformations" and "lags" is the cost of Equiano's location as a colonized entity whose perspicacity awakens him to the daunting task of forging an "African" subjectivity. It becomes evident that European colonialism forced upon the conquered and conquerors alike a style of thinking about Africa that legitimized European conquest and African destruction.

Three issues emerge as apparent in consideration of such a history of power. First, it is imperative to take seriously the centuries of human destruction that have occurred in a mechanistic, rational fashion because of colonial knowledge about peoples whose humanity has been obscured.[19] Second, it is instructive to recognize that these Africans, particularly one such as Olaudah Equiano, perceived this problem of African representation and responded to it through the strictures of slavery, race, and empire. Equiano began with the condition of explaining the Igbo nation as a people whose origins necessarily lay outside of Africa. This was the common means whereby colonial frameworks represented Africa as ahistorical, and it was with this problem Equiano was left to contend.[20] Third, the problem of the strategic destruction of African religions is critical in Equiano's Christianization experience. What Wilson Jeremiah Moses has examined as the "Fortunate Fall" thesis—African Christians believed enslavement was ultimately good because it saved them from an unchristian plight in Africa—conditions Equiano's worldview, inspiring his missionary zeal.[21] There can be no question that Christianity's foray into Africa was predicated on the genocidal eradication of African religions.

---

19. Lewis Gordon has aptly examined the routine, mechanistic nature of dehumanization within colonialism in *Fanon and the Crisis of European Man: An Essay on Philosophy and the Human Sciences* (New York and London: Routledge, 1995). His analysis of modernity as a colonial problem of historical consciousness is the most theoretically astute.

20. Philip S. Zachernuk has examined this problem in the work of Nigeria's black intelligentsia under colonialism. See his *Colonial Subjects: An African Intelligentsia and Atlantic Ideas* (Charlottesville: University of Virginia Press, 2000).

21. This assessment of life in Africa as a one leading to eternal doom—assuming no intervention from Christian missionaries—compelled African Christians to express gratitude for having been enslaved because, according to Christian theology of the afterlife, any cruelty and suffering involved paled in comparison to the eternal torment they would have

CONCLUSION: AFRICAN SUBJECTIVITY AND THE SPECTER OF COLONIALISM

Equiano does not cleanly subvert colonial paradigms in some revolutionary gesture. It is nevertheless imperative to recognize that every attempt to subvert global mechanisms of conquest must emerge as a less-than-purist enterprise forced into compromise or delimited by the exigencies of the status quo. This is why it would be inadequate merely to gainsay Equiano's hampered resistance to colonial representations of Africa, given his success in emerging from total domination as a slave to enterprising agency as an independently wealthy abolitionist author. It is on this very score that one should consider Vincent Carretta's contention that Equiano was actually born in the Carolinas of North America. Carretta elaborately proffers that Equiano conscientiously and strategically reinvented himself as one born in Ibgo-land to create his own version of knowledge about Africa and to manufacture an African subjectivity. For if Carretta is right, then Equiano was pioneering not only because he asserted that Africa was historical but also because he deployed a native African identity in his autobiographical act of self-representation. When he did so, he succeeded in negating the social death through natal alienation that attends the institution of slavery.[22] Despite the fact that slavery has functioned throughout human history to dissolve the ancestral linkages of slaves, Equiano has for centuries existed in the minds and memory of his readers not as Equiano the Negro or black American (read as ethnically rootless) but as *Equiano the African*, a member of the Igbo nation. The point here is that Equiano not only rejected the dimensions of biblical colonialism that rendered Africans as ahistorical Hamites, but he did so as a means to crafting an *African* identity, thereby defying the social death that would come to characterize the representation of those black slaves born in the Americas.

We must conclude that Equiano was not parroting biblical commentators but manipulating them to his own ends. His story of enslavement and freedom capitalized on the body of meanings in biblical commentary in order to circumnavigate the trend of designating Africans as descendants of Ham. In the end, Equiano is still trying to find himself in the Bible as one who has been conquered by the logics of colonial Christianity, but he does so on his own terms. That Equiano was heir to a history of scripturalizing the world—remaking it to conform to biblical characterizations—should not hide from us the fact that he also, in turn, bequeathed to Atlantic readers complicated meanings about slavery, Africa, scripture, and the prerogative of invention within the context of colonial violence. His autobiography did more than any other single text to galvanize British sentiment against the

---

suffered had they continued an unchristian life in Africa. Wilson Moses compares this idea in a number of early modern African writers. See Moses, *The Wings of Ethiopia: Studies in African-American Life and Letters* (Ames: Iowa State University Press, 1990), 146–51.

22. See Orlando Patterson, *Slavery and Social Death: A Comparative Study* (Cambridge: Harvard University Press, 1992).

slave trade. And thus, his representation of Africa, audacious assertion of African identity, and strategic foray into a stream of canonical history reveal his capacity, albeit compromised, as a forceful interpreter of race and scriptures and as a willful inventor of Africa ably positioned within the intricate process of biblical world-making.[23]

Works Cited

Arendt, Hannah. *The Origins of Totalitarianism*. New York: Harcourt, 1951.

Bhabha, Homi. *The Location of Culture*. London and New York: Routledge, 1994.

Biddick, Kathleen. *The Typological Imaginary: Circumcision, Technology, History*. Philadelphia: University of Pennsylvania Press, 2003.

Brooks, Joanna. *American Lazarus: Religion and the Rise of African-American and Native American Literatures*. New York: Oxford University Press, 2003.

Brown, John. *A Dictionary of the Holy Bible*. Edinburgh: John Gray and Gavin Alston, 1769.

Carretta, Vincent. *Equiano, the African: The Biography of a Self-Made Man*. Athens and London: University of Georgia Press, 2005.

Courville, Mathieu E. *The Next Step in Studying Religion: A Graduate's Guide*. New York: Continuum, 2007.

Edwards, Jonathan. *The Works of President Edwards*, 1817; repr., New York: Burt Franklin, 1968.

Equiano, Olaudah. *The Interesting Narrative of the Life of Olaudah Equiano, or Gustavus Vassa, the African: Written by Himself*. 2nd ed. London: T. Wilkins, 1789.

Foucault, Michel. *The Archaeology of Knowledge*. Trans. A. M. Sheridan Smith. London: Tavistock, 1972.

Gates, Jr., Henry Louis. *The Signifying Monkey: A Theory of Afro-American Literary Criticism*. New York: Oxford University Press, 1988.

Gilroy, Paul. *The Black Atlantic: Modernity and Double Consciousness*. Cambridge:Harvard University Press, 1993.

Gordon, Lewis. *Fanon and the Crisis of European Man: An Essay on Philosophy and the Human Sciences*. New York and London: Routledge, 1995.

Long, Charles H. "African American Religion in the United States of America: An Interpretative Essay." *NovR* 7, no. 1 (2003): 23–25.

———. *Significations: Signs, Symbols, and Images in the Interpretation of Religion*. Aurora, CO: Davies Group, 1986.

Mitchem Stephanie Y., and Emilie M. Townes, eds. *Faith, Health, and Healing in African American Life*. New York: Praeger, 2008.

---

23. Especially pertinent here is Philip Zachernuk's argument that the construction of Africa was practiced no less by African writers than by European colonial authors. Zachernuk identifies Edward Said's critique of representing the Orient as a clear signal to take seriously the inventive nature of colonial discourse, whether generated by colonizers or the colonized (Zachernuk, *Colonial Subjects*, 32, 33). See Edward W. Said, *Orientalism* (New York: Vintage Books, 1979).

Moses, Wilson. *The Wings of Ethiopia: Studies in African-American Life and Letters*. Ames: Iowa State University Press, 1990.

Patterson, Orlando. *Slavery and Social Death: A Comparative Study*. Cambridge: Harvard University Press, 1992.

Potkay, Adam. "History, Oratory, and God in Equiano's Interesting Narrative." *ECS* 34, no. 4 (2001): 601–14.

Potkay, Adam, and Sandra Burr, eds. *Black Atlantic Writers of the Eighteenth Century: Living the New Exodus in England and the Americas*. New York: St. Martin's Press, 1995.

Silverblatt, Irene. *Modern Inquisitions: Peru and the Colonial Origins of the Civilized World*. Durham, NC: Duke University Press, 2004.

Smith, Jonathan Z. *Imagining Religion: From Babylon to Jonestown*. Chicago: University of Chicago Press, 1982.

Stein, Stephen. "George Whitefield on Slavery: Some New Evidence." *CH* 42, no. 2 (1973): 243–56.

Wimbush, Vincent L., ed. *African Americans and the Bible: Sacred Texts and Social Textures*. New York: Continuum, 2000.

———. *Theorizing Scriptures: New Critical Orientations to a Cultural Phenomenon*. New Brunswick: Rutgers University Press, 2008.

Zachernuk, Philip S. *Colonial Subjects: An African Intelligentsia and Atlantic Ideas*. Charlottesville: University of Virginia Press, 2000.

Indigenous Biblical Hermeneutics: Voicing Continuity and Distinctiveness

Gerald West

For this chapter, I have drawn on a number of strands of African biblical scholarship, hoping that there will be resonances with work that is being done in First Nations/Native American contexts. I have grounded my analysis of indigenous hermeneutics in a specific case study of a local African indigenous community's engagement with the Bible, both as an illustration of indigenous hermeneutics, and, more importantly, as a site from which to theorise indigenous hermeneutics. Central to indigenous hermeneutics, this essay will argue, is a recognition of both continuity with the Christian tradition and a distinctive contribution to the identity of "the gospel."

I will use three biblical quotations to frame my essay; each one offering an angle of indigenous biblical interpretation.

"What Therefore You Worship as Unknown, This I Proclaim to You" (Acts 17:23)

Unlike Athens, Africans already knew the God the missionaries came to proclaim. This is the starting point for African Christianity and for its indigenous biblical and theological hermeneutics. Indeed, the irony of the missionary encounter was that the missionaries had to first ask local Africans what name they used for 'God' before they then proclaimed this 'God' to them, but now as the 'new' Christian 'God'!

The missionaries, of course, were usually entirely dependent on local Africans for translation between European languages and African languages and between European religio-cultural concepts and categories and African religio-cultural concepts and categories. And, of course, there was often considerable miscommunication and misrecognition in the process,[1] sometimes accidental and sometimes

I gratefully acknowledge the financial support of the National Research Foundation toward this research. I dedicate this paper to the memory of the late Kwame Bediako; may his legacy live on, and may Cassie, the young Makah Native American girl with whom I danced the Rabbit, and her people, who shared their lives with me when I was among them

wilful, for these early encounters between missionaries and indigenous Africans were encounters characterized by shifting relations of power. In Africa, missionaries were invariably the vanguard of empire and colonialism, whether they intended to take on this role or not, and while the earliest encounters were usually under the control of the local African clans, the situation soon changed as various colonial forces followed swiftly on the heels of the missionaries.[2]

Notwithstanding the misunderstandings in the early communication between Africans and European missionaries, local African peoples were drawn to elements of what the missionaries had to offer. In Africa, the major attraction of the missionaries was their access to trade goods and trade routes; a related factor which forged links between indigenous Africans and missionaries was the potential of protection the missionaries offered because of their access to guns and to colonial forces; and related to both was the "the mystical qualities attributed to them."[3] On the rapidly changing frontier that was colonialism in Africa, African peoples took careful note of the forms of power the missionaries had access to, appropriating them within their own religio-cultural worldview.[4]

Among the items of power the missionaries brought with them was the Bible. From the way missionaries, and others, used the Bible while they were among African communities, it was apparent to anyone who was watching, and local Africans were rigorously attentive to any and every missionary activity,[5] that the Bible had significant power. For example, when the explorer William Burchell visited the Tlhaping people of Southern Africa in July 1812, he brought a Bible with him, and though he was not a missionary, he did on one particular day use the Bible in a manner that would have made it clear that the Bible had substantial power.

Burchell's public use of the Bible is sparked by his decision to discipline one of his employees. Van Roye, one of Burchell's hired "Hottentots," had consistently shown disrespect and open defiance to Burchell, refusing to obey legitimate orders.

---

sharing the paper on which this essay is based, appropriate the legacy of their ancestors and together with them articulate their own appropriations of the Bible.

1. Jean Comaroff and John L. Comaroff, *Of Revelation and Revolution: Christianity, Colonialism, and Consciousness in South Africa* (Chicago: University of Chicago Press, 1991), 1:179.

2. Gerald O. West, "Shifting Perspectives on the Comparative Paradigm in (South) African Biblical Scholarship," *RT* 12, no. 1 (2005): 48–72.

3. Comaroff and Comaroff, *Revelation and Revolution*, 1:179.

4. Jean Comaroff, *Body of Power, Spirit of Resistance: The Culture and History of a South African People* (Chicago: University of Chicago Press, 1985), 197.

5. See, for example, William J. Burchell, *Travels in the Interior of Southern Africa*, with a new introduction by A. Gordon-Brown (London: Longman, Hurst, Rees, Orme, Brown, and Green, 1824; repr., Cape Town: C. Struik, 1967), 2:390; Gerald O. West, "Early Encounters with the Bible among the Batlhaping: Historical and Hermeneutical Signs," *BibInt* 12 (2004): 251–81.

It became therefore unavoidable, to take serious notice of his conduct; and I immediately ordered all my men to be present at the waggons, and declared that it was now my intention to punish his disobedience; but that I would first hear, in the presence of all, what he had to say in his defence.[6]

Among those present, besides Burchell's immediate party, were the Chief of the Tlhaping, Mothibi, and the Tlhaping leadership, paying careful attention to what was about to take place (2:468). As they watch, Burchell conducts a formal trial of Van Roye. Having laid out his pistols and sword on the chest in his wagon, "to impress more strongly on my people the serious nature of the affair" (2:468), Burchell says, he then "produced a Dutch Testament, and as Van Roye could read tolerably well, I bade him take notice what book it was" (2:470). "With some formality," Burchell uses the Bible, in order to, administer "the usual *oath* to relate the truth." However, the prevarications of Van Roye push him to expound on the oath-taking ritual just enacted:

Seeing this, I admonished him of the dreadful crime which he would commit by uttering a falsity at the moment when he called God to witness his veracity: I explained to him in the most solemn and impressive manner, the respect which he as a Christian ought to show to that book; and that it was better he should at once condemn himself by confessing his fault in the presence of his companions, than by prevarication and wilful misrepresentation, pronounce his own condemnation in the presence of God, to whom all our actions and thoughts were known. (2:470)

Sensing that these admonitions had "had their proper effect upon him" and that "a few words more would decide him to confess that he was blameable" (2:470), Burchell reiterates his use of the Bible as symbol by asking Van Roye to once again "lay his hand on the book," but this time only "after repeating to him the substance of several passages in the New Testament" (2:471). This use of the Bible, as an tactile object of power and a text of power, had the desired effect, and Van Roye confessed that his conduct had not been "influenced by the spirit of obedience which that book taught and commanded a servant to show to a master" (2:471).

His own men, Burchell writes in his journal, "had received a useful lesson" (2:471), but what lesson had Mothibi and the Tlhaping learned? Unusually, Burchell is so consumed with establishing his authority among this own men that he neglects to comment on the impact of this incident on those sitting "at a little distance," those "whose whole attention was fixed on" the proceedings. Those who sat silently watching would have had their initial assessments of the Bible confirmed. They would have seen the Bible used both as a closed object of power and as an opened object with particular things to say. As a closed object the Bible could be used by someone who controlled it to compel others to speak the truth and do their bidding; as an opened object the Bible contained knowledge that was of use

---

6. Burchell, *Travels*, 2:468. The following in-text citations are to Burchell's work.

in a context of contestation. The Bible, it would seem, shared certain features with the sword and the pistol. Clearly these and a whole host of connections of ideas were set in motion by Burchell's use of the Bible. The Bible was now one more idea/object with which the Tlhaping had to transact, and transact they would, for this was clearly a significant item/object of power. Furthermore, whatever the associations and collocations of these signs in the perceptions of the Tlhaping, and my analysis is suggestive rather than definitive, they would have formed the foundation of their biblical interpretation for when next they encountered the Bible.[7]

Some years later the Tlhaping were to encounter the Bible again, this time in the hands of missionaries. John Campbell, a director of the London Missionary Society, had been commissioned and sent to the Cape in 1812 in order "to survey the progress and prospects of mission work in the interior."[8] Campbell made his way from mission post to mission post in the Colony, and when he came to Klaarwater, which was then some distance north of the boundary of the Cape Colony—though the boundary was to follow him some years later (in 1825) almost as far as Klaarwater—he heard that Chief Mothibi of the Tlhaping people, a hundred miles further to the north, had (allegedly) expressed some interest in receiving missionaries.[9] With barely a pause in Klaarwater, spending no more than a week there, Campbell and his party set off for Dithakong ("Lattakoo"), then the capital of Chief Mothibi, on 15 June 1813 and arrived on 24 June.

Having waited for a number of days for Chief Mothibi of the Tlhaping to return to his city, Dithakong, Campbell and his associates had become frustrated. The Tlhaping leadership had refused to allow them to "instruct the people." So, while they waited for Mothibi's return, they proposed to visit a large village further to the north. Learning of this, Mmahutu, senior wife of Mothibi, visited their tent on 30 June and said that she "was averse" to their "going any where till Mateebe came," and that at the very least they should leave part of their wagons and party behind if they did go, being fully aware that they would be too fearful to venture forth without their full complement. Entering into a process of negotiation, and using her reluctance to have them leave as a lever, the missionaries tell her that they would never have thought of leaving Dithakong "even for a day before Mateebe's return" had they "been permitted to instruct the people; but that having nothing to do," they wished to visit that village and hunt. However, being in control of their immediate situation, Mmahutu insisted they remain. Having been persuaded by Mmahutu, the missionaries then "endeavoured to convey some information" to her.[10]

---

7. Vincent L. Wimbush, "Reading Texts through Worlds, Worlds through Texts," *Semeia* 62 (1993): 129–40, here 131.

8. John Campbell, *Travels in South Africa: Undertaken at the Request of the Missionary Society* (3rd ed. correct. ed.; London: Black, Parry, 1815; repr., Cape Town: C. Struik, 1974), 178.

9. Ibid.

10. Ibid., 199.

What follows is a remarkable exchange, capturing as it does the Bible as iconic object of power and aural text of power. Campbell records this encounter with the Bible as follows:

> We explained to her the nature of a letter, by means of which a person could convey his thoughts to a friend at a distance. Mr. A. showed her one he had received from his wife, by which he knew every thing that had happened at Klaar Water for two days after he left it. This information highly entertained her, especially when told that A. Kok, who brought it, knew nothing of what it contained, which we explained by telling her the use of sealing wax. The bible being on the table gave occasion to explain the nature and use of a book, particularly of that book—how it informed us of God, who made all things; and of the beginning of all things, which seemed to astonish her, and many a look was directed towards the bible.[11]

Here the missionaries draw Mmahutu's attention to the power of the letter in at least two respects. First, an object like this can re-present "every thing" that happened in a place in a person's absence. Second, an object like this can be made to hide its message from the bearer and reveal its contents only to the intended receiver. Turning from the letter, to a quite different genre of text (from the perspective of the missionaries), the Bible, but here conflated with the letter (from the perspective of Mmahutu), the missionaries use the interest generated in their exposition of the letter to return to their preoccupation with the contents of the Bible, particularly the matter of origins.

In a letter written to a friend, Mr David Langton, some days later (July 27), Campbell explains more fully what took place during this encounter in their tent. Following Mmahutu's "astonished" looks at the Bible, "Mr Read's eye caught a verse very suitable to our situation in the page that was lying open, viz. Math. 4–16."[12] What Mmahutu would have heard is this: "The people which sat in darkness saw great light; and to them which sat in the region and shadow of death light is sprung up." To which she responded by asking, "'Will people who are dead, rise up again?' 'Is God under the earth, or where is he?'."[13] Her question is not self-evident from the context provided by Campbell's letter or journal entry, indicating that her questions had their own internal "African" logic. Her questions do not seem to deal directly with the passage read. The passage clearly makes sense to the missionaries, being made to bear the full weight of English missionary images of Africa.[14] However, such allusions are probably absent from Mmahutu's hearing of this sentence from the Bible. Whatever she hears, and it may be the word "death", prompts here to bring her own questions to the text/missionaries. Perhaps prior missionary talk of the resurrection had disturbed her, for there is evidence that missionary talk of

---

11. Ibid.

12. J. Campbell, Klaar Water, 27 July 1813 (CWM. Africa. South Africa. Incoming Correspondence. Box 5–2–D).

13. Campbell, *Travels*, 199.

14. Comaroff and Comaroff, *Revelation and Revolution*, 1:86–125.

people rising from the dead worried southern African clans who feared that their slain enemies might arise.[15] Whatever the indigenous logic of her questions, what is clear is that Mmahutu brings her own questions to the Bible.

Already, we see emerging evidence from this very early encounter of recognition that the Bible is both an iconic object of power and an aural text which communicates. What is also clear is that the Bible is both power and knowledge for those who control it. Further, we see signs that it is beginning to be prised from the hands of the missionaries by indigenous questions. Finally, there is even a suggestion that the bearer of the Bible, like the bearer of the letter, might not fully know the power and knowledge it contains. Perhaps the missionaries are not fully in control of this object of strange power—the Bible—they carry; perhaps others—the Tlhaping—might access its mysterious power?

"HOW IS IT THAT WE HEAR IN OUR OWN LANGUAGES
THE WONDERS OF GOD?" (ACTS 2:8)

This quotation from the Bible is used by a significant strand in African Theology to affirm, first, that Africans already knew God before the missionaries came to proclaim God, and second, that, in the words of the Ghanian theologian, the late Kwame Bediako, it is "not that historical circumstances [important as these may be] have made Christianity an unavoidable factor in African life, but rather that the African experience of the Christian faith can be seen to be fully coherent with the religious quests in African life."[16] Bediako then goes on to say, that "Once this point is granted, then it becomes evident that the happenings on the day of Pentecost, as recounted in the second chapter of the *Acts of the Apostles* . . . give an important Biblical and theological warrant for taking seriously the vernacular languages in which people everywhere hear the wonders of God."[17]

Because, as the missionaries to Southern Africa also recognized, "divine speech is vernacular,"[18] it would not be long before the missionaries to the Tlhaping concentrated their efforts on translation. During the visit of Campbell in 1813 it was already clear that translation of the Bible was a central concern.[19] The missionary Robert Moffat's arrival in 1821 gave substance to Campbell's promise to Mothibi

---

15. Robert Moffat, *Missionary Labours and Scenes in Southern Africa* (London; repr., New York: John Snow; repr., Johnson Reprint Corporation, 1842; repr., 1969), 403–5; John L. Comaroff and Jean Comaroff, *Of Revelation and Revolution: The Dialectics of Modernity on a South African Frontier* (Chicago: University of Chicago Press, 1997), 2:342.

16. Kwame Bediako, *Christianity in Africa: The Renewal of a Non-Western Religion* (Edinburgh: Edinburgh University; Maryknoll, NY: Orbis, 1995), 60.

17. Ibid.

18. Ibid.

19. Campbell, *Travels*, 192.

that the Bible would be translated into their own language.[20] A London Missionary Society visitor to Kuruman in 1849 comments in a letter that "Mr. Moffat's time seems mainly occupied in translation of the scriptures."[21]

Moffat held that "the simple reading and study of the Bible alone will convert the world"; the task of the missionary, therefore, was "to gain for it [the Bible] admission and attention, and then let it speak for itself."[22] Implicit in Moffat's project to produce a translation of the Bible in the language of the Tlhaping were two assumptions, first, that translation could indeed take place, that the most vital and sacred matters were translatable, and second, that, though Moffat was disparaging about the linguistic and theological competence of the Tlhaping themselves, he did not question the potential of their language to bear the meanings that the Bible and the Christian faith (and European civilization) might demand of it.[23]

While Moffat, like most of the missionaries, was a product of the prejudices of his people, his translation project did allow Africans to engage with the Bible on their own terms. The Bible would "speak for itself", but like the letter Campbell showed to Mmahutu, the Bible would not always speak as the ones who carried it anticipated.

Moffat himself had minimal theological education,[24] and like many other missionaries readily assumed that the Bible had a self-evident message. However, once translated into the African vernacular the Bible has shown a quite remarkable capacity to find its own voice, even when translated by missionaries like Moffat who had very deliberate ideological agendas and imprecise mastery of the language they were translating into.

Because the Bible was produced by and its texts located within what Bediako refers to as "a primal world-view" there was a substantial resonance between large parts of the Bible and the primal world-views of Africans.[25] Drawing on Harold Turner's characterisation of a primal world-view—including a recognition that humanity has a kinship with nature, a recognition of humanity's finitude and creaturehood, a recognition of a spiritual world of powers and beings more powerful than humanity, a recognition that humanity can enter into relationships with the spiritual world, a recognition that there is continuity between this life and the afterlife, and a recognition that there is no boundary between the physical and the spiritual—Bediako argues that Africans shared a phenomenological relationship with the biblical world-view.

20. Ibid., 208–9.

21. Cited in Comaroff and Comaroff, *Revelation and Revolution*, 1:214.

22. Moffat, *Missionary Labours*, 618.

23. Comaroff and Comaroff, *Revelation and Revolution*, 1:217.

24. Ibid., 1:82–83, Steve de Gruchy, "The Alleged Political Conservatism of Robert Moffat," in *The London Missionary Society in Southern Africa: Historical Essays in Celebration of the Bicentenary of the LMS in Southern Africa, 1799–1999*, ed. John W. de Gruchy (Cape Town: David Philip, 1999), 17–36.

25. Bediako, *Christianity*, 91–108.

UNIVERSITY OF WINCHESTER
LIBRARY

And while some African theologians have argued that this primal world-view was primarily preparatory, preparing Africans for Christianity, others like Bediako have argued that this primal world-view was also constitutive of African Christianity. John Mbiti, for example, made a distinction between 'Christianity', which "results from the encounter of the Gospel with any given local society" and so is always indigenous and culture-bound, on the one hand, and the Gospel, which is "God-given, eternal and does not change," on the other.[26] "We can add nothing to the Gospel, for it is an eternal gift of God," writes Mbiti.[27] In other words, for Mbiti 'the gospel' apprehended by Africans is substantially the same as that transmitted by the missionaries.[28] For Bediako and another African theologian, Lamin Sanneh, the contribution of the African soil is more distinctive. While not disputing significant continuity between what the missionaries proclaimed and what Africans appropriated, Sanneh asserts that "the God of the Bible had preceded the missionary into the receptor-culture—so the missionary needs to discover Him in the new culture."[29] In other words, for Sanneh 'the gospel' is not fully understood until African voices (and others) have spoken.

"YOU HAVE HEARD THAT IT WAS SAID . . . , BUT I SAY YOU . . ." (MATTHEW 5:27–28)

Because, argues Lamin Sanneh, "language is the intimate, articulate expression of culture," the missionary adoption of the vernacular "was tantamount to adopting indigenous cultural criteria for the message, a piece of radical indigenization far greater than the standard portrayal of mission as Western cultural imperialism."[30] In a detailed and wide-ranging argument, which roots itself in a theological exegesis of the Pauline mission to the Gentiles, Sanneh sees "translation as a fundamental concession to the vernacular, and an inevitable weakening of the forces of uniformity and centralization." "Furthermore," says Sanneh,

> I see translation as introducing a dynamic and pluralist factor into questions of the essence of the religion. Thus if we ask the question about the essence of Christianity, whatever the final answer, we would be forced to reckon with what the fresh medium reveals to us in feedback. It may thus happen that our own earlier understanding of the message will be challenged and even overturned by the force of the new experience. Translation would consequently help to bring us

---

26. Ibid., 117.

27. John S. Mbiti, "Christianity and Traditional Religions in Africa," *IRM* 59, no. 236 (1970): 438.

28. Bediako, *Christianity*, 118.

29. Lamin Sanneh, "The Horizontal and the Vertical in Mission: An African Perspective," *IBMR* 7, no. 4 (1983): 165–71, 166.

30. Lamin Sanneh, *Translating the Message: The Missionary Impact on Culture* (Maryknoll, NY: Orbis, 1989), 3.

to new ways of viewing the world, commencing a process of revitalization that reaches into both the personal and cultural spheres.[31]

Sanneh is making an important point here. But before I come to that point, let me recapitulate the elements of indigenous hermeneutics we have discerned so far. First, and I reiterate this because it is fundamental to indigenous hermeneutics, is that "God speaks to men and women—always in the vernacular."[32] Second, and again I draw on Bediako's formulation, "The single most important element for building . . . an indigenous Christian tradition is . . . the Scriptures in the vernacular language of a people." Bediako stresses this point, for though he acknowledges the abundance of theological literature that shapes the missionary Christian tradition, none of this represents "local or indigenous reflection on the original sources of Christian revelation, as received in the local contexts."[33] Third, the Bible is inherently translatable, in both a narrow technical sense and in a more profound theological sense. Fourth, "the message" proclaimed by the missionaries does bear some resemblance to and share some continuity with 'the message' received in translation by Africans. As Sanneh says, "The gospel is potentially capable of transcending the cultural [and ideological] inhibitions of the translator and taking root in fresh soil."[34] And fifth, and I will belabor this point, the very act of turning to another people's language in order to translate the Bible revitalizes that language and the culture within which it subsists, thereby enabling that culture and its people to articulate for themselves what the Bible says.

I want to dwell for a moment on this fifth element in indigenous hermeneutics because it is so often suppressed in the eagerness to affirm the fourth element. Our very use of phrases like "the gospel," which even Sanneh uses, tends to imply that the Bible says the same thing to each and every people, that its central message is clear and in continuity with what was proclaimed it to us. This kind of affirmation, however, is often predicated on the substantive denigration of and damage done to African culture by European missionaries, and the subsequent establishment of European forms of Christianity on African soil. By "European forms of Christianity" I do not only mean its institutional forms but also its theological forms. African Christianity, and other forms of indigenous Christianity, do stand in continuity with the historically dominant forms of Christianity, but what the fifth element in indigenous hermeneutics wants to emphasise is the agency of Africans as they engage with the Bible and Christianity and so their own distinctive apprehensions of their message, both in terms of the content of the gospel, but more significantly in "the shape" of the gospel.[35]

---

31. Ibid., 53.
32. Bediako, *Christianity*, 60.
33. Ibid., 62.
34. Sanneh, *Translating*, 53.
35. Albert Nolan, *God in South Africa: The Challenge of the Gospel* (Cape Town: David Philip, 1988), 14–17.

Sanneh expresses this difference clearly in the above quotation. There are two dimensions to this fifth element. The first dimension is the revitalization of indigenous religion and culture. This occurs when the technical process of translation pushes indigenous respondents to re-examine their culture in order to assist the translators with appropriate language with which to translate biblical texts. This re-turn to local culture, a culture that has often been told by missionaries and other 'civilizing' forces that it is inadequate at best and demonic at worst, revitalizes the culture, as local respondents in the translation process reclaim aspects of their culture in order to provide a language for translation that is true to both the biblical text and their culture. And because there is so much resonance between African religion and culture and the religion and culture of biblical communities and the texts they produced,[36] this revitalization is substantial.

The second dimension is the potential of the receptor culture to now add their own voice to the voices of the many other communities of faith that have interpreted the Bible before them. If God really does speak the vernacular, then what is it that God is saying as understood by this new community of faith? The very act of making the Bible available in the language of the indigenous people causes it to slip from or be prised from the grasp of the missionaries who brought it, as Mmahutu, Chief Mothibi's wife recognized. "If hearers of the Word of God in their own languages may then be presumed to respond in their own terms", argues Bediako, "this is another way of saying that it is not others' but their own questions which they would bring to the Bible, taking from it what they would consider to be *its* answers to their questions."[37] To put it provocatively, what 'the gospel' is yet to be determined, for not all indigenous voices have yet been heard speaking for themselves.

This, I would argue, is the challenge that faces indigenous hermeneutics. Not so much how our understandings of the Bible resonates and remains in continuity with what indigenous communities have received, but in what ways indigenous voices have something different and distinctive to say about what 'the Bible says.' As Sanneh says, "It may thus happen that our own earlier understanding of the message will be challenged and even overturned by the force of the new experience."[38]

CONCLUSION

As we have seen, then, translation as a technical and theological construct provides the potential for the revitalization of both the biblical message and receptor culture. From the beginning of the Tlhaping encounter with the Bible there was something

36. Gillian M. Bediako, *Primal Religion and the Bible: William Robertson Smith and His Heritage* (Sheffield: Sheffield Academic Press, 1997).

37. Bediako, *Christianity*, 63.

38. Sanneh, *Translating*, 53.

about the Bible that drew their attention. First, it was the Bible as an iconic object of indeterminate power; second, it was an aural word that resonated with their world, at least partially; and third, once translated and read by themselves, it was a source of cultural revitalization and a message which went well beyond the imaginations of those who brought it among them. As Bediako says, translation enabled the Bible to become "an independent yardstick by which to test, and sometimes to reject, what Western missionaries taught and practised" and in so doing "provided the basis for developing new, indigenous forms of Christianity."[39]

This kind of analysis of indigenous hermeneutics calls forth a descriptive and then a constructive task. The descriptive task is to describe and document what actually happens with the Bible among indigenous peoples.[40] We will find, no doubt, as Sanneh has said (see above), a dynamic and pluralist Christianity, whose essence is yet to be determined by indigenous voices. The church and even academics have tended to be prescriptive, expounding and explaining what ought to be rather than what is. What awaits us is a more descriptive task.

Once we have a whole array of detailed descriptive case studies, we can then begin the constructive task of providing theological shape to how the Bible is actually appropriated among indigenous peoples, and then bringing these theological resources into dialogue with and placing them alongside the dominant public theology of our churches.[41]

Indigenous biblical and theological hermeneutics begins with the God who is already known and who speaks vernacular. When the Bible and the Christian faith, having already been interpreted and appropriated by others, is brought among indigenous peoples, there is a resonance, at the iconic, aural, and textual levels. Notwithstanding the other socio-political factors that accompany the arrival of the Bible among indigenous communities, these resonances are an important factor in the translation and appropriation of the Bible. But the very process of translation, at both a technical and a theoretical level, requires a return to the local culture in order to find appropriate translation language, which in turn activates and facilitates local ownership of what the Word of God is saying to them. Local ownership of the Bible enables indigenous communities to bring their own questions to the scriptures and to hear both the familiar—what others have said God has said—and the unfamiliar—what in particular God is saying to them and through them to others. Indigenous hermeneutics acknowledges continuity with others and insists on the distinctiveness of its own voice.

---

39. Kwame Bediako, "Epilogue," in *On Their Way Rejoincing: The History and Role of the Bible in Africa*, ed. Ype Schaaf (Carlisle, England: Paternoster Press, 1994), 243–54, 246.

40. Gerald O. West, "The Open and Closed Bible: The Bible in African Theologies," in *African Christian Theologies in Transformation*, ed. Ernst M. Conradie (Stellenbosch: EFSA, 2004), 162–80.

41. Gerald O. West, "Articulating, Owning, and Mainstreaming Local Theologies: The Contribution of Contextual Bible Study," *JTSA* 122 (2005): 23–35.

WORKS CITED

Bediako, Gillian M. *Primal Religion and the Bible: William Robertson Smith and His Heritage*. Sheffield: Sheffield Academic Press, 1997.

Bediako, Kwame. *Christianity in Africa: The Renewal of a Non-Western Religion*. Edinburgh: Edinburgh University; Maryknoll, NY: Orbis, 1995.

Burchell, William J. *Travels in the Interior of Southern Africa*. With a new introduction by A. Gordon-Brown. Vol. 2. London: Longman, Hurst, Rees, Orme, Brown, and Green, 1824. Reprint, Cape Town: C. Struik, 1967.

Campbell, John. *Travels in South Africa: Undertaken at the Request of the Missionary Society*. 3rd ed. corrected ed. London: Black, Parry & Co., 1815. Reprint, 1974, Cape Town: C. Struik.

Comaroff, Jean. *Body of Power, Spirit of Resistance: The Culture and History of a South African People*. Chicago: University of Chicago Press, 1985.

Comaroff, Jean, and John L. Comaroff. *Of Revelation and Revolution: Christianity, Colonialism, and Consciousness in South Africa*. Vol. 1. Chicago: University of Chicago Press, 1991.

———. *Of Revelation and Revolution: The Dialectics of Modernity on a South African Frontier*. Vol. 2. Chicago: University of Chicago Press, 1997.

Conradie, Ernst M., ed. *African Christian Theologies in Transformation*. Stellenbosch, South Africa: EFSA, 2004.

de Gruchy, John W. *The London Missionary Society in Southern Africa: Historical Essays in Celebration of the Bicentenary of the LMS in Southern Africa, 1799–1999*, 17–36. Cape Town: David Philip, 1999.

Mbiti, John S. "Christianity and Traditional Religions in Africa." *IRM* 59, no. 236 (1970): 438.

Moffat, Robert. *Missionary Labours and Scenes in Southern Africa*. London: John Snow, 1842. Reprint, New York: Johnson Reprint Corporation, 1969.

Nolan, Albert. *God in South Africa: The Challenge of the Gospel*. Cape Town: David Philip, 1988.

Sanneh, Lamin, "The Horizontal and the Vertical in Mission: An African Perspective," *IBMR* 7, no. 4 (1983): 165–71.

Sanneh, Lamin. *Translating the Message: The Missionary Impact on Culture*. Maryknoll, NY: Orbis, 1989.

Schaaf, Ype, ed. *On Their Way Rejoicing: The History and Role of the Bible in Africa*. Carlisle, England: Paternoster, 1994.

West, Gerald O., "Articulating, Owning, and Mainstreaming Local Theologies: The Contribution of Contextual Bible Study." *JTSA* 122 (2005): 23–35.

———. "Early Encounters with the Bible among the Batlhaping: Historical and Hermeneutical Signs." *BibInt* 12 (2004): 251–81.

———. "Shifting Perspectives on the Comparative Paradigm in (South) African Biblical Scholarship." *RT* 12, no. 1 (2005): 48–72.

Wimbush, Vincent L. "Reading Texts through Worlds, Worlds through Texts." *Semeia* 62 (1993): 129–40.

Uncelebrated Readers of the Bible:
The Illustrative Case of Early Basotho Christians

Sam Tshehla

> It is the responsibility of African biblical scholars to affirm both the relevance of
> the Gospel and the validity of the cultural and religious heritage of African peo-
> ples. Without affirmation of both, Christianity cannot take root in Africa. . . .[1]

The above excerpt comes from a recent reflection by Jesse Mugambi around the
challenges facing African scholars working within the field of biblical hermeneutics. It is not his modesty in limiting the discussion to African Christianity and/or
African scholarship that is primarily alluring; the insights he shares are of universal import in their own right[2] as well as on account of Africa's growing centrality to
Christian faith in the twenty-first century.[3] Neither is his sentiment set apart by its
prescriptive tone; African Christian scholarship is so often shoddily characterised
by dogmatic lists of do's and don'ts concocted by well-meaning authors who, for
the most part, function as apologists for inherited doctrines.[4] Mugambi's eloquent
elucidation of the historical marginalisation of African interpreters is impressive as

---

1. J. N. K. Mugambi, "Challenges to African Scholars in Biblical Hermeneutics," in *Text
and Context in New Testament Hermeneutics*, ed. J. N. K. Mugambi and Johannes A. Smit
(Nairobi: Acton, 2004), 6–21.

2. Mugambi, "Challenges," 14: "All biblical hermeneutics is necessarily contextual, from
the perspective of those who conduct it. If the Bible is claimed to be universal, the claim
arises from an imperialistic or globalistic ideology. If it is interpreted parochially, the emphasis on particularity of context is often a reaction against globalizing tendencies on the
part of the powers that be."

3. There obtains a near consensus today regarding the centrality of the southern peoples
to world Christianity. See Lamin Sanneh, *Whose Religion Is Christianity? The Gospel beyond
the West* (Grand Rapids: Eerdmans, 2003), for a recent, insightful, and sympathetic review.

4. Anyone who is familiar with writings by Africans will concur that evidence for this
observation abounds. However, adducing one or two examples here will do more harm
than good to those singled out. Perhaps reference to my own exploits in this regard will
suffice: Tshehla, "Philippians 3:7–11 and African Biblical Exegesis: A Reflection," *JACT* 6,
no. 1 (June 2003): 24–30, esp. 28.

it highlights the many historical factors that prompt the need for context-sensitive intellectual exertion in environments like Africa where redress is inescapable.[5]

However, the most outstanding aspect of the above excerpt is the requisite balancing act which it foregrounds.[6] Mugambi refreshingly urges the concurrent affirmation of two fundamental and complementary realities: the Gospel contextualised *and* Africa's cultural-religious heritage affirmed as being equally central to the consequential establishment of Christianity in Africa. Starting with the Gospel is inevitable because it is in their capacity as Christians that African biblical scholars pursue the recovery of their African religio-cultural heritage.[7] And the issue is not so much that African Christians are existentially alienated from their African identity. The issue is that, from an intellectual perspective, their African identity and their Christian identity are not quite eloquently integrated. There obtains some hindrance to the intellectual accession to the experienced reality that the Christ of the Gospel, far from desiring to uproot us from our proud heritage, in fact seeks to bring us home to our true African selves. Africans need to believe that Jesus Christ offers this promise *in him* with no hidden proselytizing agenda.[8]

---

5. Mugambi, "Challenges," 8. The reader of Mugambi's chapter will be impressed by the acute historical depth plus the breadth of scholarly insight which the author displays as he traces connections between seemingly unrelated events. For instance he perspicuously, albeit in passing, traces "the problem of denying African identity in church history" to the "fourth century of the Christian era" in variance from the usual suspect, namely, modern missions commencing in the eighteenth century. He insists, "Despite the prominence and constructive role accorded to Africa and Africans in the Bible, imperial power since Constantine has relegated Africa to the periphery of social influence."

6. The quest for balance, which is a central trait of African philosophy, quite often gets unwarrantably sacrificed when zeal overtakes reason as a motivation for theological reflection. But, as Stephen B. Reid reminds us, absence of balance is indicative of the alienation of the intellectual from his/her organic connections, his/her roots ("Endangered Reading: The African-American Scholar between Text and People," *CC* 44, no. 4 [1994/95]: 476).

7. Kwame Bediako has driven this point home in his incisive reviews of first-generation African theologians and detractors, primarily in his *Theology and Identity: The Impact of Culture upon Christian Thought in the Second Century and in Modern Africa* (Oxford: Regnum, 1992) and subsequently in *Christianity in Africa: The Renewal of a Non-Western Religion* (Edinburgh: Edinburgh University Press, 1995). From the angle of biblical scholarship, this question has been usefully tackled as being at once a matter of both the Bible's impact on Africa and Africa's impact on the Bible. "By placing these two sentences alongside each other we can speak of the encounter between Africa and the Bible as 'a transaction'" (Gerald O. West, "Mapping African Biblical Interpretation: A Tentative Sketch," in *The Bible in Africa*, ed. G. O. West and Musa W. Dube [Leiden: Brill, 2000], 29).

8. Andrew Walls, "Of Ivory Towers and Ashrams: Some Reflections on Theological Scholarship in Africa," *JACT* 3, no. 1 (2000): 1–4. As Andrew Walls eloquently puts it, "In fact, nowadays, if you want to study Africa, you have to know something about Christianity. But it is equally true that if you want to know something about Christianity, you must know something about Africa. . . . Christianity is fundamentally about conversion, about human

He achieved the same feat when he encountered Nathanael (John 1:43–51).[9] Philip has failed as a missionary for as long as the Jesus he presents to Nathanael is unable or unwilling to affirm Nathanael's religio-cultural identity as the starting point of their engagement. And Nathanael will remain an unsettled Christian for as long as he is uncertain of how Jesus Christ truly feels about him and his religio-cultural identity. The beloved evangelist narrates another story where those to whom the Samaritan woman had borne witness were subsequently empowered by their own encounter with the Messiah (John 4:39–42). It was critical for them to encounter him for themselves, that is, beyond the exciting claims which the missionary had made. Jesus would have lost a great harvest had he declined the invitation they extended to him to suspend his plans and spend a significant amount of time with them.[10] Judean-Samaritan politics notwithstanding, the Samaritan converts were more than eager to indulge a genuinely interested Jesus in relation to their true identity and deepest aspirations.

In spite of African hospitality, African Christians have by and large been instructed to live on only the claims made by the western missionary.[11] This tradition persists regardless of the direct and more persuasive connection with the saviour that Africans have shown themselves to possess. In practically every nook, African religions overtly anticipated the arrival of the Gospel and, when it finally arrived, welcomed it with open arms. This is the positive basis for the niggling yearning that African Christians have for an authentic integration between Gospel and African-ness, for their own unmitigated encounter with the Jesus of the Gospel. The ensuing presentation continues attempts to satisfy this longing for that time when African Christians will hear Jesus genuinely affirming them in their own tongues and contexts;[12] this is being done with African readers of the Bible

---

life turned towards Christ. . . . The conversion of African culture is the task of turning to Christ what is already there."

9. All biblical references and/or quotations come from the New Revised Standard Version.

10. Craig S Keener, *The IVP Bible Background Commentary: New Testament* (Downers Grove, IL: InterVarsity Press, 1993), 274: "For Jesus to lodge there, eating Samaritan food and teaching Samaritans (v. 40) would be roughly equivalent to defying segregation in the United States during the 1950s or apartheid in South Africa in the 1980s—shocking, extremely difficult, somewhat dangerous."

11. Mugambi, "Challenges," 6–7. Yet it is still usual to come across Christians opining that the African's mastery of the gospel will inevitably lead to a syncretism, to a watering down of Jesus Christ. In Mugambi's own words, "African Christians, it has often been assumed, cannot and ought not—even if they could—interpret the Bible from the perspective of their own cultural and religious heritage. . . . Through missionary strategy and theological pedagogy, African Christians have been denied what might be called the right to 'ecclesial self-determination.' "

12. Choan Seng Song, "From Indigenous Stories to Indigenous Culture to Indigenous Christian Theology: Case of Taiwan," *TCCE* 2, no. 1 (2005): 101–20. This longing is not unique to Africa. Speaking to his Taiwanese context, he urges quite strongly that: "For theo-

in mind, and nineteenth century Basotho[13] converts are treated as an instructive example.

The balance rhetoric which we emphasize tampers tendencies toward extremism. Our commitment remains one of hearing the word of God just as happened at Pentecost according to Acts 2:6, 11. In contrast to the globalizing thrust of modern biblical scholarship, this contribution reminds that God continues to work through foolish, weak and despised vessels. This persistent work of God was modelled through missionary endeavours to render God's word in African tongues despite the overriding de-Africanization project. The implication for present purposes is simple: the discipline of biblical hermeneutics continues to miss out if, in alignment with the powers that be, it pays little regard to the languages and unrestrained biblical-engagement heritages of peoples of the margins.

GOD SPEAKS FLUENT SESOTHO

"Has not God made foolish the wisdom of the world?" (1 Cor. 1:20)

According to the critical *Essays on Religion and Culture among Basotho 1800–1900* copublished in 2001 by Basotho scholars L. B. B. J. Machobane and T. L. Manyeli, nineteenth-century mission work among the Basotho was characterised in general by an explicit drive to eradicate the Basotho's backward culture.

> In the main the missionary or West European cosmic view . . . conditioned those early purveyors of the Gospel to view Basotho culture and religion as grossly negative. They concluded that Basotho culture and religion were inferior to their own, apprehending Christianity as a European cultural property. Hence they jus-

---

logical reconstruction to be possible, we must set ourselves free from the theological cul-de-sac inherited from Western churches and theological systems, starting our theological efforts with the lives of our people and histories of our nation. . . . I would even go so far as to suggest to you: Forget your Ernst Troeltsch, your Karl Barth, your Paul Tillich. But Jesus you must not forget. . . . If these theologians have, with a varied degree of success, tried to make sense of Jesus within Europe and North America, what prevents us from doing our utmost to explore the meaning of Jesus and what he said and did for us here in Taiwan and in Asia in the past, at present and for the future?" (102).

13. Mosebi Damane and P. B. Sanders, eds., *Lithoko: Sotho Praise-Poems* (Oxford: Clarendon 1974), xiv. A reasonable summary of the otherwise complex story around the identity of the Basotho is that "Africans who now live in Lesotho and the neighbouring areas of the Republic of South Africa generally refer to themselves as *Basotho*. Among historians they have often been referred to as the Basuto, or the Basutos, and among anthropologists as the Southern Sotho, in order to distinguish them from the Northern and Western Sotho, although these divisions were not very marked until the second half of the nineteenth century."

tified dismantling [Basotho culture and religion]. In the process, they destroyed a great deal of Basotho way of life that was not even in conflict with Christianity.[14]

Conflating gospel and culture—instead of keeping them in creative tension in the interest of balance—could thus be said to have been the Achilles' heel of the modern missionary enterprise. With the benefit of hindsight, the truth of Heb 1:1–2 ("Long ago God spoke to our ancestors in many and various ways by the prophets, but in these last days he has spoken to us by a Son . . .") appears to have eluded these ardent servants of Christ. Our elaborate decrying of this history is to a real extent inspired by fears that a great deal of our heritage has been lost in the intervening period. There is no doubt that there was a rich heritage that met the blessed feet of those who proclaimed the Gospel in these parts a couple of centuries ago.[15] In spite of their findings, Machobane and Manyeli do in fact come to the same conclusion that "a study of customs reveals *a confident vein of elementary forms* that obtain in the dispersal and regrouping periods. The vulnerability of this *consistent vein* of religious manifestations, of course, lies in the absence of a 'literary' fall back."[16] The difficult question that remains concerns how much of this heritage might have been destroyed at the encounter.

Clearly engaging in the sort of balancing act which this essay urges, and notwithstanding Christianity's emergence as initially an offshoot of Judaism,[17] the writer of the Epistle to the Hebrews submits that the advent of God's ultimate revelation in the Son need not nullify God's previous dealings with humanity. To a limited degree, the Epistle's appeal to Africans is explained by its author's unique

---

14. L. B. B. J. Machobane and T. L. Manyeli, *Essays on Religion and Culture among Basotho, 1800–1900* (Lesotho: Mazenod, 2001), 3.

15. John S. Mbiti, *Introduction to African Religion* (London: Heinemann, 1991), 2: "Africa has a very rich heritage of what past generations of African peoples thought, did, experienced and passed on to their children. This heritage forms a long line which links African forefathers and mothers with their descendants who now feel proud of it."

16. T. L. Manyeli, "The Authentic Religious Form of Basotho," in Machobane and Manyeli, *Essays*, 102–26, 105 (italics mine).

17. Dudzirai Chimeri, "Interpreting Jesus from an African Context: A Critical Review of the Evidence from Zimbabwe," *JACT* 6, no. 2 (Dec 2003): 28–32 [29]: "The early Christians felt that Jesus was the fulfilment of Israel's hopes and that his significance could not be expressed adequately without pulling in all available categories provided by Jesus' own Jewish faith. . . . Many of the apologetic weapons employed by the early Christians were appropriated from Judaism. The Christian canon is an expanded Jewish canon. . . . As the gospel passed into the Hellenistic context, the same dynamic of cultural appropriation of Jesus applied there also. . . . [However,] [w]ith regard to theology, concepts and practices of ministry, ethics, liturgy and spirituality, African churches are still in a kind of Euro-American 'biblical' captivity. With respect to critical scholarship, Euro-America is still regarded as the epistemological centre of the world. Hence the dire need for African scholarship to evaluate critically the received Western traditions, to develop a contextual focus, and to reconstruct its heritage."

comprehension of matters pertaining to inculturation.[18] Not only does Hebrews affirm the *Son* to be God's final communication (thus relegating precursors to the status of mere shadows), the Epistle also indubitably affirms the cultural and religious *heritage* of the Hebrews (God has always spoken to our predecessors even before the advent of the Son!). Without awareness and memory of God's previous engagements with our predecessors, how might we be able to relate to God? Without awareness and memory, the heritage is in jeopardy even while it survives.

This awareness and memory can be credited for the emergence of African Instituted Churches (AICs). The latter became safe spaces wherein Africans could encounter and engage the God of their forebears in their own tongues, times and cultural garb. Conversely, within Christian Africa, but "except in the African instituted churches, the validity of the African cultural and religious heritage as the social foundation of African Christian ecclesial life is denied."[19] In other words, the founders of AICs were persons who discerned that God had little to say unless God could speak to them in their own tongues, within their own cultural contexts, in sanctuaries of their own choosing, most of which are natural and unadorned. There is credible precedence therefore in regard to what it does mean to concretely affirm the validity of the African cultural and religious heritage.[20]

The question that then remains is whether African Christians are persuaded that African cultural and religious heritage represents a valid socio-spiritual foundation of African Christianity. What do nineteenth century Basotho converts teach us in this regard, and how is the Bible featured? The following observations derive from time spent alongside nineteenth century Basotho neoliterates who comprised the primary interlocutors for my doctoral study.[21] Except for sporadic handwritten manuscripts here and there, or translated contributions to French or English publications, the earliest writings by the Basotho are preserved in Sesotho by the mission newspaper known as *Leselinyana la Lesotho* (*The Little Light of Lesotho*). This Sesotho-medium newspaper was launched in November 1863 by Paris Evangelical Missionaries. It continues to be published to date, now run entirely by the Basotho. The founding editor of the newspaper consciously and laudably en-

---

18. Whether an African is reflecting on the subject of sacrifice or ancestors or priesthood or persecution and so on, s/he is so at home in Hebrews as indeed Kwame Bediako's *Jesus in African Culture: A Ghanaian Perspective* (Accra: Asempa, 1990) demonstrates.

19. Mugambi, "Challenges," 8.

20. Sympathetic studies need to be undertaken that will investigate more specifically the implications of the reality that more and more learned Africans are openly joining these formations as well as that more and more of their ministers are acquiring formal theological training. There is much room for mutual learning here between AICs and mission church African adherents.

21. The study has since been completed. It is entitled "Leselinyana La Lesotho and Basotho Biblical Appropriation between 1863 and 1883" (Ph.D. thesis, University of KwaZulu-Natal, 2009).

couraged Basotho contributions from the onset, thereby facilitating our relatively reliable access to the mind and parlance of early Basotho Christians.

WHAT PRECISELY ARE WE BASOTHO CHRISTIANS SUPPOSED TO BE?

Armed with literacy which was based significantly on the Bible, one of the pressing questions which early Basotho Christians faced concerned how they were supposed to imagine themselves. In the charged missionary environment where distinctions were flagrant between converts and heathen, missionaries and catechists, chiefs and commoners, literate and ignorant, backsliders and the faithful, how were Basotho Christians situated? This question the missionaries were not able to tackle head on; for, as some of them did laudably recognize, the shaping of the Basotho Christian identity was primarily the responsibility of the Basotho believers as such.[22] And rightfully so, nineteenth century Basotho took up the question and created space for some contemplation of what their Christian identity entailed.

The concept which presented itself most forcefully was that of *majakane* (singular *lejakane*). This term applied only to native Christians in general and never to the European missionaries working among them. For this reason its negative connotations were palpable to some Basotho Christians while for others it bore the promise of an authentic indigenous label. One baffled Mosotho Christian ignited matters in the January 1879 issue of *Leselinyana* as follows:

> To my beloved white missionaries, to the catechists, and to the members of Lesotho congregations, greetings! Enlighten me please. I am confused by the word I often hear on the lips of all Christians; they regularly speak of "We Majakane" or such. Why not say "We Christians"? How does that term come to replace "Christians"? I thought that we Christians are sworn to the name of Christ and not to some *Lejakane*. [Written November 1878]

By including every category of Christians, Joas Akime affirms the right enjoyed by all believers of engaging in critical reflection on matters pertaining to the faith. More than merely being courteous, he genuinely expects and invites all stake-

---

22. *Leselinyana*'s editor's attempt in this connection is instructive of the extent to which they could go and no further. In "To the Readers" (*Leselinyana*, October 1872), Adolphe Mabille invited those Basotho whom he hoped were mature and conscientious enough to undertake the task of clarifying what it means to be Basotho Christians. "This concerns especially those who are experienced in sensibly spreading God's word, namely, catechists and schoolmasters." He urged them to compose two-way fictional evangelistic conversations between believing and unbelieving Basotho around the implications of the Gospel as well as around the nature of *majakane*. "Or respond to those who have incorrigibly given themselves over to being Satan's property. Or those who wish to go where their forebears have gone, for they cannot bear the thought of being separated from them. We shall be expecting these compositions until December. Two European missionaries will choose the best two essays. First prize will be £1 . . ."

holders to respond to the question of the exact nature of the identity of Basotho Christians. But since the European missionaries were exempt from the label, their contribution would not carry the same weight as those who along with Akime "are sworn to the name of Christ." Akime's "we" is quite potent and layered indeed.[23]

How did we come to be identified with *lejakane*, he asks, and what has *lejakane* to do with Christ? Basically, what do we, as Basotho Christians, gain from being identified with this concept over and above our natural and universally shared identification with the Christ? Is Christ not adequate as the figure with which we are to be identified along with Christians everywhere? However the issue is eventually resolved, the initiative of these native Christians needs to be acknowledged and celebrated; for they took upon their own shoulders the responsibility of clarifying what their adoptive identity entailed.

Several probable but irreconcilable explanations can be distilled from the replies that Basotho Christians consequently offered. These were debated vigorously among the Basotho, albeit under the watchful eye of their European teachers who at the time carefully controlled what went into print.[24] In a nutshell, and since pleading ignorance was out of the question among learned persons, the strong contenders were: (*a*) the term was meant by unbelievers for ridicule but it actually bodes well for Christians, or (*b*) the concept describes the transitory earthly state and role of Christians and is therefore a fitting label, (*c*) in a tortuous manner, the concept is adapted from the Boer-language's *diakens* (deacons).

You Bear a Stigma of Non-authenticity

For the first group of Basotho believers, being dubbed *majakane* is attractive only because it recalls the experience of the earliest Christians and thus renders Basotho Christians their mirror reflection. In the first century, the earliest associations of the disciples with the term 'Christians' were supposed to be derogative or, at best, discriminatory.[25] Along similar lines, nineteenth century Basotho Christians were labelled *majakane* by their detractors.[26] What exactly the detractors had in

---

23. There appears to be a hidden, perhaps sarcastic reference to 1 Cor. 1:10–13.

24. For instance, "We have received a letter by Alfred B. Moletsane. He refutes claims regarding the imprisonment of the Bataung in the [Cape] Colony. If that is so, we are happy. But we cannot publish his letter since it contains many offensive words not fit to be uttered by one who desires to have his sentiments read and appreciated by all people. If his letter was not rude towards the chiefs and *majakane*, we would have published it" (Editor, *Leselinyana*, May 1874).

25. Paul Mumo Kisau. "The Acts of the Apostles," in *Africa Bible Commentary*, Tokunboh Adeyemo, gen. ed. (Grand Rapids: Zondervan; Nairobi: Word Alive, 2006), 1297–348 [1321].

26. Hermann Dieterlen, *Leselinyana*, September 1883. The accusation ran something like, "You *majakane* [Basotho believers], you are no longer Basotho. You are now a different people; you have deserted initiation rituals, you have deserted your forefathers' customs,

mind by this term remains unclear; David Mosikoane[27] is convinced that *jakane* is an ancient word whose meaning will naturally be hidden to the younger generations. What is very clear however is the strain that such an identification was supposed to impose on those who bore it.[28] In both instances, the association is meant to ridicule, to draw unfavourable attention to the folly of those who are implicated. Yet in both instances, God has turned what was intended for harm into an affirming thing in the manner that only God can.

Greatest difficulty for this position was presented by the possible linkage of the label with a certain missionary by the name of Johannes van der Kemp. The Xhosa people among whom he laboured nicknamed him *Yinkanna* and so the unbelievers dubbed his disciples *mayinkanna*.[29] This appellation the Basotho then corrupted to *majakane*. Identifying ourselves with a fellow-follower of Jesus Christ, however effective he had been among us, presented grave difficulties for especially the European missionaries.[30]

Christians cannot adopt names of their mentors in the faith in place of Christ. It was Jesus himself who according to Matthew (chap. 23) had issued the sanction that there should be no exaltation of human beings among fellow-disciples. What is more, this *jakane* name is not authentically a Sesotho concept since it came with the Basotho exiles who converted while living among the Xhosa where they had taken refuge during the *Lifaqane*.[31] It is therefore grossly inadequate as a tool for self-understanding among Basotho Christians, unless there is more to the term than initially meets the eye.

We Gladly Bear the Stigma of Migrant Labourers

> I find the name likeable, it is quite appropriate. We certainly are *jakile* [in the employ of] the King of kings, and much more than that. What is more, down here is not our home, *re jakile feela* [we are mere migrant labourers]. We have our

and have instead learnt customs from other nations. You are renegades; you have separated yourselves from other Basotho. Christianity is destroying the nation."

27. *Leselinyana*, March 1879.

28. See Sepetla Setsomi Molapo, "Majakane: The Emergence of a Nineteenth-Century Non-initiation Basotho Identity and the Interaction of Basotho Culture and Missionary Christianity (M.A. diss., University of the Witwatersrand, 2003).

29. A similar, though less charged, development had occurred among the Basotho. The disciples of Samuel Rolland were affectionately dubbed *maroellane*.

30. See, e.g., Hamilton Moore Dyke, *Leselinyana*, March 1879.

31. Molapo, *Majakane*, 70: "The etymology of the word *Majakane* suggests therefore that the returning Basotho Christian exiles may not necessarily have referred to themselves by that name but that the name *Majakane* was rather used by Basotho non-converts to refer to their converted counterparts. It was this word, *Majakane*, that Basotho within *naha ya Basotho* (the kingdom of Basotho) were to use to designate Basotho who would convert to the Protestant Christian message of the PEMS missionaries. . . . It speaks of a process of Basotho self-repositioning within an emerging world of missionary Christianity in the 19th century Cape Colony."

> true home. This is not mockery. . . The heathen may have intended the name *ma-jakane* to be a disgrace when they gave it to us, but in fact it signifies the nearness of our redemption. We see also Caiaphus correctly observing matters without realising it . . . (John 11:49–51)[32]

Perhaps the concept *majakane* is appropriate if it is taken as a noun derived from the verb *ho jaka*, meaning to be a migrant labourer. Indeed the unbelievers may have meant to ridicule us, but like Caiaphus and several other characters encountered in the Bible, they were prophesying that which is in fact true about us Christians. Furthermore, the Basotho unbelievers may have meant to stress the temporary and displaced state of Basotho Christians. That is, the impressionable Basotho converts are merely going through an unnatural yet perhaps necessary stage of adaptation to a powerful encroachment. Once they realise the futility of the labour to which they have been deceptively conscripted, they will in due course return to their senses, to the ways of their forebears.

Whereas the unbelievers' judgment is harsh, the believers should appreciate that there is more to the concept than the unbelievers understand. Basotho Christians need to understand their state of *ho jaka* on earth, they are here for only a while and only to gather sufficient rewards.[33] People to whom the light has shone have come to appreciate that their home and destiny lie outside the present world; they have come to realize that God has placed them on earth to work at bringing others to the light. They are servants and temporary labourers in a foreign land and the term *majakane* constantly reminds them of the urgency of their task. Some of the allusions here would include John 4:34–38; 9:3–5; Matt 5:13–16; 2 Cor 5:1–10.

We All Are Servants

> Well, as far as I know, it comes from the Boer-language like many other words we use. In that language *Yakans* appears to mean *an elder of a congregation* . . . [Written at] Morija, 15 January 1879.[34]

The idea of servants is further attested by some Basotho who regard the etymology of *jakane* to be *diakens* (deacons). Moshabesha's explanation was not far-fetched to one who appreciated how the Sesotho language works. Nevertheless, what is most interesting about this interpretation is the suggestion that all Christians, regardless of background or rank, be regarded deacons. It is appealing to see every Christian as a servant whether or not they hold some church office. Yet it is bound to get confusing when some are deacons because of office while all are deacons.

Given these permutations, it makes sense that the term *majakane* was not able

---

32. Maputsoe, *Leselinyana*, February 1879.

33. Some Christians objected to this understanding of the term, for example, Jeremia Mokoena (*Leselinyana*, March 1879), who objected to the insinuation that God treats us as hirelings whereas, in fact, we are God's children and heirs of heaven. For that reason Mokoena dislikes the tag.

34. Neftali Nasone Moshabesha, *Leselinyana*, February 1879.

to cling to Basotho Christians. In a nutshell, the name did not take root probably because, as the preceding review discloses, it possessed no 'spiritual' attributes to contribute to the theological career of Sesotho Christianity. Instead, all it offered were inconclusive stories. Any casual inquiries today among the Basotho as to what *majakane* means will confirm the reality that, in spite of its potentially exciting connotations, the concept died a natural death. Very few Basotho Christians would object to the singing of one of their favourite hymns: *Re bafeti mo lefatšeng* (We are passers by on this earth). Any Mosotho Christian who has read the Gospels will appreciate that we are indeed hirelings working in God's vineyard (e.g., Matt 20). There is no shortage of hymns with this motif too in the Basotho's *Lifela tsa Sione le tsa Bojaki* (Hymns of Zion and of Sojourn).

Yet all Basotho Christians would wonder why they should be associated with some missionary who worked among the Xhosa. However, with the demise of *majakane*, Basotho Christians have remained with no concept that galvanizes them to think of and pursue a uniquely Sesotho Christianity. So the question what exactly are Basotho Christians supposed to look like remains unanswerable. Nevertheless, we are still able to glean a few lessons from nineteenth century Basotho engagements with the Bible and with their faith in Jesus Christ.

WHAT WISE BUILDERS THEY WERE!

It has emerged from the foregoing cursory look at early Basotho reflections that the Bible was one of the cornerstones of their existence. From direct citations to the more preferred allusions, biblical idiom pervades their self-understanding as well as their demeanour. This was facilitated in large measure by the missionaries' conscious emphasis of the saving value of the word of God. Consequently the complete Sesotho New Testament was in circulation a mere two decades from the time missions began in Lesotho; the entire Bible followed suit some two decades thereafter. But this receptivity to the Bible was also due to the high premium which Basotho attach to the efficacy of a superior's utterance.[35] That the Bible should serve as the chief agent of the Basotho's appropriation of literacy was thus inevitable. They genuinely came to believe that "The human spirit will not find assistance or fulfilment through the things of this world; it is only through God's word, which is the Bible."[36]

But it was *Lentsoe la Molimo* rather than 'God's word' as such. Seeing it written down and capable of dependably shrinking physical distance only underscored

---

35. The Basotho have many sayings relating to the non-negotiable authority of a chief's utterance. For example, *morena ha a tene molupo* (a chief is never wrong) or *ntsoe la morena le aheloa lesaka* (a chief's word is to be rallied around and expedited).

36. Filemone Mattheuse, *Leselinyana*, January 1878. Compare with Rapetloane's strong assertion that "God's word is the medicine" that cured Lesotho's wars and related distresses in *Leselinyana*'s very first issue (November 1863). Basotho adulations of the Bible can be multiplied ad infinitum.

Sesotho's capacity to reliably relay even the divine message regardless of who was the messenger. That God spoke Sesotho so profoundly and understood matters that only the cultured among the Basotho appreciate meant that they would gladly share their literacy skills with those who did not possess it, that no aspect of their lives could remain untouched by God's word. There was no room to distinguish between Christian contributions and general or secular debates. Evangelism, praying, teaching literacy, teaching Bible, sociopolitical commentary, all proceeded together from their pens as from their lives. Indeed all that qualified contributions to *Leselinyana* was their being written in Sesotho and not whether, when and where the author was baptized.[37]

It was with immense pride therefore that none less than King Moshoeshoe declared the Sesotho Bible to be the Basotho's ultimate *moruti* (missionary-teacher). Moshoeshoe went on to caution that it is up to the reader to choose either to hear the words or to fixate on the imperfections embedded in written texts.[38] The God who in times past spoke mainly orally has in these last days spoken to the Basotho through pen and paper. God spoke Sesotho then and this fact remains true even after the advent of literacy; and the Sesotho Bible guarantees this all on its own.[39]

---

37. It is vital to keep in mind that the earliest literate Basotho would have acquired literacy in mission schools. Many of them became school teachers cum missionaries to various outposts across southern Africa. Some did become disillusioned with Christian faith and did not become shy in making their qualms known, albeit in a manner that did not alienate the editor.

38. Thomas Arbousset, *Missionary Excursion into the Blue Mountains: Being an Account of King Moshoeshoe's Expedition from Thaba-Bosiu to the Sources of Malibamatšo River in the Year 1840*, ed. and trans. David Ambrose and Albert Brutsch (Lesotho: Morija Archives, 1840 [1991]). As one of these earliest messengers among the Basotho recalls: "Moshoeshoe began a long conversation with me about Sesotho. 'My language is nevertheless very beautiful', said the chief unaffectedly. 'We are only beginning to realise this since we have seen it written down. Thanks to the little books of the missionaries, it will not be altered: there it is written; oh!, your paper; that paper organises everything well.' At this, I burst out laughing, listening to the chief, pointing out to him that there was no dearth of blots on this paper he so much admired. He replied that he had also noticed it; but that these blots 'could be washed with the soap of learning'. (Laughter) 'The stains in a cloth are not the cloth itself', he continued, 'and then I only see words that are being changed because they are Setlhaping words. My language remains my language on paper. If that paper came from some remote corner of the Maloti, and if it arrived by itself at Thaba-Bosiu, it would be recognised as a Mosotho, and we would ask if it had not been written by one of the subjects of Mokoteli'" (101–2).

39. Arbousset, *Missionary Excursion*, 102: "It is two summers since my men and I opened our eyes to the light of the Gospel. It leads us a long way. Even if you and I and your colleagues all disappeared, and even if nobody any longer knew what had become of us, the news that you have brought into the country would remain. My people will never forget it. In this respect, part of your work is done: my children carry a *moruti* [missionary/pastor] in their travelling bag wherever they go."

Because the Bible is not a stand-in for the European missionaries but rather—as God's word in fact—precedes them, its availability renders them more or less redundant. In other words, Cephas wrote himself out of the picture by carefully narrating to Mark all he remembered of the days when the earthly Jesus was discipling him. The European missionaries indeed wrote themselves off the script through their participation in the translation of the Bible into Sesotho. This is an important insight that nineteenth century Basotho communicate to us; namely, God who in past times spoke in various ways among the Basotho, now speaks through the translated pages of the evolving Sesotho Bible. Yet it would be incorrect to presume the textual communication of God to have supplanted all the other forms.[40]

Now that we appreciate that an over-literal definition of literature is a cop-out in the African context, all that remains is celebration of the confident consistent African vein of religious and Christian heritage that has persisted in spite of us. Celebration is called for, not for its own sake, but for the benefit of twenty-first century Christianity. African Christians need to know, celebrate and learn from the transactions enacted by their respective ancestors. In a nutshell, we are being called to contribute to the literary fallback which this heritage so longs for.

Put differently, how will they be celebrated if they remain unknown? How will they be known if they are never spoken or written about? How will they be cited if the agenda excludes the issues that mattered to them? How will the agenda be apposite if it continues to be set elsewhere?

Conclusion

This essay has attempted to demonstrate the urgent need for African biblical hermeneutics to engender a creative critical tension between the African religio-cultural heritage on the one hand and African apprehension of the Gospel on the other. The either/or situation can no longer be sustained; both the continent and the world need African Christians to meaningfully engage these two factors. This is imperative for we are implicated in the message we proclaim. Consequently, those who take the time to critically reflect on the content and manner of their proclamation stand a better chance of being more effective than those who merely perpetuate what they have received.

---

40. As is often the case, biblical scholarship needs to catch up with literary studies. "We have reached a stage, in our study of African literature, when it is no longer polite, in academic circles, to raise an eyebrow when mention is made of the existence of literatures—and other arts—in the non-literate Africa of pre-missionary, pre-colonial days. This is, of course, partly due to the enlightened view held in our day, that verbal art is verbal art, whether it is written or oral. What to call this art then becomes a technicality, and our enlightenment—nay, our *liberation*—leads us, in turn, to liberate the term 'literature' from its erstwhile over-literal definition, and by common consensus 'literature' comes to be used of all verbal art" (Daniel P. Kunene, *Heroic Poetry of the Basotho* [Oxford: Clarendon, 1971], xi).

Several points emerged from the positive evaluation of the evidence. First, the Bible speaks not of events and persons that are strange to us. The historical distance that characterises much of modern biblical studies does not dominate the landscape. There is immediacy and accessibility of the word of God in the Bible. God, who spoke to Basotho ancestors via various media before the advent of the Bible, has in fact now come much closer through the Bible. Indeed, now that Basotho possess the Bible, they need no other interpreter of God's will. The Bible, as it were, stands in continuity with the prophets that God used among the Basotho in former times.

Second, the experience of Moshoeshoe with the Bible affirms the reality that the word of God is not restricted to only some special persons. Moshoeshoe was illiterate, and unconverted, yet he cited from the Bible with ease. He was not a self-confessing Christian, yet he debated biblical themes fervently and with insight.[41] Indeed he went so far as to appropriate some biblical images to his relationship with the Basotho as well as with the European missionaries. He unashamedly contributed to the development of both Sesotho and the Sesotho Bible. The Basotho experience with the Bible thus eschews tendencies toward exclusivism and groupism.

Third, the word of God is not limited to the written. The Bible is to be subjected to a variety of uses as long as the ends justify the means. Not only are sentiments appropriable, but even the written text is negotiable.

It is evident even from this cursory review that ancient Basotho converts to Christian faith were no less perceptive and insightful than their teachers or their descendants. They assimilated as much from their European friends as they deemed profitable. They anticipated and laid solid though unappreciated foundations for much that subsequent Basotho Christian generations would have to deal with. They read the Sesotho Bible very much as Jesus read the Hebrew Bible according to the testimony of the Greek Bible.

Patently, neglect of ways and words by means of which God spoke to the Africans of yore will continue to deprive modern biblical thought of irreplaceable insights and so hamper the development of the discipline.

---

41. "Moshoeshoe . . . would not convert. Realising only too well the strong opposition . . . from the 'traditionalists,' his conversion would likely have split the nation and destroyed his ability to govern it. Well-versed in the Biblical teachings, Moshoeshoe had gradually formed *his own* understanding of Christianity. . . . Moshoeshoe's 'natural tendencies and his turn of mind have always inclined him to think that the interpretation of the matters contained in the Bible ought to vary according to peoples, circumstances, temperaments'" (Stephen J. Gill, *A Short History of Lesotho* [Morija Museum and Archives, 1993], 93, citing Eugene Casalis).

WORKS CITED

Adeyemo, Tokunboh, gen. ed. *Africa Bible Commentary*. Grand Rapids: Zondervan; Nairobi: WordAlive, 2006.

Arbousset, Thomas. *Missionary Excursion into the Blue Mountains: Being an Account of King Moshoeshoe's Expedition from Thaba-Bosiu to the Sources of Malibamatšo River in the Year 1840*. Ed. and trans. David Ambrose and Albert Brutsch. Lesotho: Morija Archives, 1840 (1991).

Bediako, Kwame. *Christianity in Africa: The Renewal of a Non-Western Religion*. Edinburgh: Edinburgh University Press, 1995.

———. *Jesus in African Culture: A Ghanaian Perspective*. Accra: Asempa, 1990.

———. *Theology and Identity: The Impact of Culture upon Christian Thought in the Second Century and in Modern Africa*. Oxford: Regnum, 1992.

Chimeri, Dudzirai. "Interpreting Jesus from an African Context: A Critical Review of the Evidence from Zimbabwe." *JACT* 6, no. 2 (2003): 28–32.

Gill, Stephen J. *A Short History of Lesotho*. Morija Museum and Archives, 1993.

Keener, Craig S. *The IVP Bible Background Commentary: New Testament*. Downers Grove, IL: InterVarsity Press, 1993.

Kunene, Daniel P. *Heroic Poetry of the Basotho*. Oxford: Clarendon, 1971.

Machobane, L. B. B. J., and T. L. Manyeli. *Essays on Religion and Culture among Basotho, 1800–1900*. Lesotho: Mazenod, 2001.

Mbiti, John S. *Introduction to African Religion*. London: Heinemann, 1991.

Molapo, Sepetla Setsomi. "Majakane: The Emergence of a Nineteenth-Century Non-initiation Basotho Identity and the Interaction of Basotho Culture and Missionary Christianity." M.A. diss., University of the Witwatersrand, 2003.

Mosebi, Damane, and P. B. Sanders, eds. *Lithoko: Sotho Praise-Poems*. Oxford: Clarendon, 1974.

Mugambi, J. N. K., and Johannes A. Smit. *Text and Context in New Testament Hermeneutics*. Nairobi: Acton, 2004.

Reid, Stephen B. "Endangered Reading: The African-American Scholar between Text and People." *CC* 44, no. 4 (1994/95).

Sanneh, Lamin. *Whose Religion Is Christianity? The Gospel beyond the West*. Grand Rapids: Eerdmans, 2003.

Song, Choan Seng. "From Indigenous Stories to Indigenous Culture to Indigenous Christian Theology: Case of Taiwan." *TCCE* 2, no. 1 (2005): 101–20.

Tshehla, Maarman Samuel. "Philippians 3:7–11 and African Biblical Exegesis: A Reflection." *JACT* 6, no. 1 (2003): 24–30.

Walls, Andrew F., "Of Ivory Towers and Ashrams: Some Reflections on Theological Scholarship in Africa." *JACT* 3, no. 1 (2000): 1–4.

West, Gerald O., and Musa W. Dube, eds. *The Bible in Africa*. Leiden: Brill, 2000.

Beyond Ecclesial Confines:
The Bible in the African Novels of Ngũgĩ wa Thiong'o (Kenya) and Bessie Head (Bostwana/SA)

Andrew M. Mbuvi

My interest in African novels stems from my early exposure to this genre as part of the English curriculum while going through high school in Kenya. I have since come to learn that African novels, for the last four or five decade of their existence as a body of literature (represented by, but not limited to, the highly influential Heinemann African Writers Series) have become the staple of a lot of the African high school curricula, which expose students to this stimulating form of writing.[1] Only later in life, as I reread these novels, was there recognition of the pervasive engagement of the Bible and Christianity by most of the African novelists I read. And now, as a biblical scholar, my curiosity has been peaked and so my continuing research, part of which is contained in this chapter, was born. My interest is not only to probe this group of writings for their religious tropes, but to investigate the possibility that they provide legitimate, and some times challenging, socially engaged alternative biblical visions from those espoused in traditional ecclesial readings.

In particular, the novels of celebrated Kenyan novelist Ngũgĩ wa Thiong'o and the increasingly posthumously recognized works of the late Botswana (via South Africa) author Bessie Head, form two fairly distinct appropriations of biblical elements, texts, allusions, and imagery, prompting my current interest in a comparative evaluation of some of their writings. Ngũgĩ's explicit use of the biblical texts (as seen in such titles as *A Grain of Wheat* from the Gospel of John 12:24—"Truly, truly, I say to you, unless a grain of wheat falls into the earth and dies, it remains alone; but if it dies, it bears much fruit" [RSV]) and Heads much more muted and nuanced constructions like her image of "a god who walks with no shoes" in *When Rain Clouds Gather*, make for an intriguing investigation. Both writers provide,

---

1. See Phaswane Mpe, "The Role of the Heinemann African Writers Series in the Development and Promotion of African Literature," *AS* 58, no. 1 (1999): 105–23; Adewale Maja-Pearce, "In Pursuit of Excellence: Thirty Years of the Heinemann African Writers' Series," *RAL* 23, no. 4 (1992): 125–32; Becky Clarke, "The African Writers Series: Celebrating Forty Years of Publishing Distinction," *RAL* 34, no. 2 (2003): 163–74.

glimpses into an interaction with biblical texts, teachings and values that not only critique the form of Christian "myth" and experience that formed the basis for Colonialism and apartheid, respectively, but also provide a vision of hope for transformation in postcolonial and post-apartheid humanity.[2]

While at some point in his life Ngũgĩ identified readily with the Christian faith,[3] Bessie Head is more ambiguous even though she does recognize her writing as one of service to humanity and God.[4] Certainly, her persistent and forceful insistence on the value and sacredness of human life, justice, love and equality, draws one to contemplate seriously about the implications of the Christian doctrine of incarnation.[5] Gleaning at whatever aspects of her writing that scholars have contested as having biographical elements, it is clear that a missionary education was part of Head's upbringing, just as it was for Ngũgĩ. However, it only seemed to compound her struggle with the demons of "Christian" apartheid South Africa and its devaluation of nonwhite human life which, as a victim herself, she had first hand experience. Both writers, in a sense, battle the same demons—Western "Christian" civilization and its claim to a "manifest destiny" of divine appointment as "God's representative on earth" that fueled the subjugation of the peoples of Africa.

A Pervasive Use of the Bible in Ngũgĩ wa Thiong'o's Writings

Ngũgĩ's writings have been classified as straddling two phases—the first was when he still wrote in English (the imperialist's language) and the second was when he switched to writing in his mother tongue Gĩkũyũ. One can also talk of two phases—Ngũgĩ writing as a self-identified Christian (earlier phase) and as a self-

2. Ngũgĩ's earlier phase is represented by his first three novels—*Weep Not, Child* (London: Heinemann, 1964), *The River Between* (London: Heinemann, 1965), and *A Grain of Wheat* (London: Heinemann, 1967)—while subsequent writings, including *Petals of Blood* (New York: Penguin, 1977), *Thaitani Mũtharabainĩ (Devil on the Cross)* (London: Heinemann, 1982), with Ngũgĩ wa Mĩriĩ, *Ngahĩĩka Ndeenda (I Will Marry When I Want)* (London: Heinemann, 1982), *Detained* (London: Heinemann, 1980), *Matigari* (London: Heinemann, 1987), and *Mũrogi wa Kagõgõ (Wizard of the Crow)* (New York: Pantheon, 2006), represent the latter phase.

3. Katebaliirwe-Amooti wa Irumba, "Ngũgĩ wa Thiongo's Literary Production: A Materialist Critique" (Ph.D. diss., University of Sussex, 1980).

4. David Maughan Brown, "*Matigari* and the Rehabilitation of the Religion," *RAL* 22 (1991): 173–80; and Randolph Vigne, ed., *A Gesture of Belonging: Letters from Bessie Head, 1965-1979* (London: Heinemann; and Portsmouth, NH: SA Writers, 1991), 132.

5. I am not making any claims about Bessie Head's religious affiliations, and I am not aware of any point during her writing career that she identified herself with Christianity or any other religion. But her earlier upbringing was at least partly in Christian mission schools and in foster homes where Christianity was practiced. Her later inclination toward Eastern religions has prompted some to speculate that she may have entertained Buddhist ideas on a religious level. My intention is simply to scrutinize the themes that dominate her writings and to tease out elements that may reflect a certain Christian religious attentiveness.

identified non-Christian (he drops his Christian name, James).[6] Ngũgĩ conceded that his first two novels in particular were written at a time when he considered himself "deeply Christian" and in them he sought to "remove the central Christian doctrine from the dress of the Western culture, and seeing how this might be grafted on to the central beliefs of our people."[7] In the first three novels Ngũgĩ posits a juxtaposition of the Christianized community with the traditional community that has resisted conversion to Christianity.

In this portrayal, Christianity is not adversarial to African cultures and traditions but virtually balanced competing phenomenon—non-Christian Makuyu and the Christian Kameno in *The River Between*, form the two sides of the river valley. In *A Grain of Wheat*, the Christian concept of individual sacrifice for the sake of the community provides the premise of Mugo's story. It does not however, disentangle the complexity of the sense of his betrayal of Kihika (a messiah–type figure) the freedom fighter who also saw his life in light of the sacrifice of the individual for the sake of the salvation. In *Weep Not, Child* it seems to be the anticipation of Njoroge that identification with Christianity would lead to a hopeful future both for himself and for the community. These sentiments are shared by Waiyaki who at the end of *The River Between* (*The Black Messiah* was Ngũgĩ's original working title for the book) sums up his thoughts:

> For Waiyaki knew that not all the ways of the white man were bad. Even his religion was not essentially bad. Some good, some truth shone through it. But the religion the faith needed washing, cleaning away the dirt, leaving only the eternal. And the eternal that was the truth needed to be reconciled with the traditions of the people. A people's tradition could not be swept away overnight. That way lay disintegration. Such a tribe would have no root, for a people's roots were in their traditions going back to the past, the very beginning Gikuyu and Mumbi. A religion that took no count of a people's way of life, a religion that did not recognize spots of beauty and truths in their way of life, was useless. It would not satisfy. It would not be a living experience, a source of life and vitality. It would only maim a man's soul, making him fanatically cling to whatever promised security, otherwise he would be lost. Perhaps that was what was wrong with Joshua. He had

---

6. Such works like Hugh Dinwiddy, "Biblical Usage and Abusage in Kenyan Writing," *JRA* 19, no. 1 (1989): 27–47, to me fail to capture the complexity of the on goings in Ngũgĩ's thought by positing a simple binary for analyzing the Christian versus non-Christian aspects in Ngũgĩ's works. Ngũgĩ's statement "I am no longer a Christian" has to be scrutinized in light of Ngũgĩ's own criticism of a colonial Christianity (and its expression among postcolonial African elite) that did not embrace his Gikuyu culture and also remained inconsistent with the social concerns exemplified in the Bible itself. Yet Ngũgĩ's posited alternative can be characterized more like a form of "Christian socialism" than the Marxism he claims to have converted to in his later writings. See Lupenga Mphande, "Ngũgĩ and the World of Christianity: A Dialectic," *JAAS* 39, no. 5 (2004): 357–78.

7. Edgar Wright, ed. *The Critical Evaluation of African Literature* (London: Heinemann, 1982), 97.

clothed himself with a religion decorated and smeared with everything *white*. He renounced his past and cut himself away from those life-giving traditions of the tribe.[8]

With this same attitude, the death of Gĩkũyũ traditions at the altar of Western education seems to be permissible for Ngũgĩ:

> Circumcision of women was not important as a physical operation. It was what it did inside a person. It could not be stopped overnight. Patience and, above all, education were needed. If the white man's religion made you abandon a custom and then it did not give you something else of equal value, you became lost. An attempt at resolution of the conflict would only kill you, as it did Muthoni.[9]

River Honia that separates the conflicting hill sides seems to embody this dual sense so that while it divides, it also connects the two valleys. As a source of life for both communities, its continuous flowing throb is articulated in terms of an unknown song that quotes Hab 2:14: "*They shall not hurt nor destroy in all my holy mountains, for the earth shall be full of the knowledge of the Lord, as the waters cover the sea.*" Like white man's religion the river both unites and divides and it comes down to how one interprets that reality. Yet it remains a positive and hopeful rendition of the Christian message stripped of its stifling Western garb.

Land and identity are so closely entwined that a people are not a people without land.[10] A landless people are a people without identity and devoid of divine favor. As Oliver Lovesey points out, Ngũgĩ's novels' "geographical specificity and attention to landscape" are less the result of literary influence than from the sacred values associated with a particular soil.[11] The fight for *wĩyathi*—land inheritance (the ancestral land that is taken over by the colonialist)—in Ngũgĩ's writings resonates with Israel's yearning in the prophetic books for its ancestral land especially in light of the exile in Babylon (e.g., Neh 1:1–10—*WNC* 64). Ngũgĩ, no doubt, envisions this parallel when he makes the central focus of his writings also about land and its rightful ownership that is divinely ordained.[12]

In *Weep Not Child*, Ngotho's ancestral land had been taken away from his family and he had to work the same land as an employee of the "new owner," the Brit-

---

8. Ngũgĩ, *River Between*, 141.

9. Ibid., 142.

10. Ngũgĩ, "Literature and Society," 22, referencing Franz Fanon's *Wretched of the Earth*, writes: "For a colonized people, Fanon has written, the most essential value, because the most concrete is first and foremost the land. People want to control their soil, their land, the fruits of their labour power acting on nature; to control their history made by their collective struggle with their natural and social environment" (Eddah Gachukia and Kichuma Akivaga, eds., *Teaching of African Literature in Schools* [Nairobi: KLB, 1978], 1:1–29).

11. Oliver Lovesey, "Ngũgĩ wa Thiong'o's Postnation: The Cultural Geographies of Colonial, Neocolonial, and Postnational Space," *MFS* 48, no. 1 (2002): 139–68.

12. This is clearly reflected in Ngotho versus Howlands in *Weep Not Child*.

ish settler Mr. Howlands. For both men the land was sacred but for very different reasons:

> Mr. Howlands "seemed to worship the soil. . . . Both men admired this *shamba* [farm]. For Ngotho felt responsible for whatever happened to this land. He owed it to the dead, the living and the unborn of his line, to keep guard over this *shamba*. Mr. Howlands always felt a certain amount of victory whenever he walked through it all. He alone was responsible for taming this unoccupied wilderness."[13]

For Ngotho, staying in the land, even essentially as a "slave" (a *muhoi* is a landless squatter!), meant staying connected with his people and their heritage. For Mr. Howlands, owning it meant mastering the "wilderness" and making it a "garden of Eden."[14] For the former, a spiritual/ancestral reason, for the latter a spiritual/colonial mandate, in biblical terms!

For this reason, while land serves as the motivation of the revolt against the colonialists, Christian imagery provides a language that drives the freedom fighters.[15] For Ngugi, embracing Christianity did not mean capitulation to colonial subjugation. As such, Kihika, perceiving himself as "Moses," one chosen by god to lead his people to freedom from colonial repression, underlines in his Bible the passage from Exod 8:1: "And the LORD spake unto Moses, go unto Pharaoh, and say unto him, thus saith the LORD, 'Let my people go.' " In like manner, the protagonist Mugo in *A Grain of Wheat* answers to the voice in the dark that addresses him as "Moses" by responding "Here I am, Lord!" (164). Subsequently, Kihika, in an apparent interpretation of 1 John 3:16 intones:

> Had Christ's death a meaning for the children of Israel? In Kenya we want a death that will change things, that is to say, we want a true sacrifice. . . . I die for you die for me. We become a sacrifice for one another. So I can say that you, Karanja are Christ. I am Christ. Everybody who takes the Oath of Unity to change things in Kenya is a Christ.[16]

From *Ngahīīka Ndeenda* (*I will Marry when I Want*) onwards, one notices a shifting in Ngũgĩ's attitude towards the use of Christian language and imagery, with such reversal of biblical characters as Jezebel for protagonists.[17] Increased critique

---

13. Ngũgĩ, *Weep Not Child*, 31.

14. Dinwiddy, "Usage," 35, notes that it was issues of land that took Jomo Kenyatta to London.

15. Arthur Shatto Gakwandi, *The Novel and Contemporary Experiences in Africa* (London: Heinemann, 1977), 128–29 (112).

16. Ngũgĩ, *A Grain of Wheat*, 83.

17. The biblical Jezebel is known for her bloody reign and idolatry in Israel in the OT (1 Kings 16:31; 18–21; 2 Kings 9) while in the NT Jezebel is equated with the ruthless Roman Empire (also called Babylon) in Rev 2:24.

of Christianity places the gun and the Bible at the centre of imperialism but tries
to carefully distinguish religion from God.

Gĩcaamba explains:

> And how does religion come into it?
> Religion is not the same thing as God.
> All the religions that now sit on us
> were brought here by the whites.
> And even today the Catholic religion
> is still called the Romans Catholic Church.
> P.C.E.A. belongs to the Scottish protestants.
> The Anglican Church belongs to the English.
> The Orthodox belongs to the Greeks.
> The Baptist belongs to the Americans.
> There are many more religions
> which have been brought here by imperialists from America,
> and which tell us we should give them a tenth of all that we
> produce.
> Where does the ten percent go?
> To America.
> Then they send back to us ten shillings
> taken from the tenth portion we sent them,
> and they tell us:
> This is American aid to your local churches.
> And we give them a standing ovation.[18]

Accordingly, in subsequent writings, the Christian meta-narrative forms the basis
of the critique of society in a more complex utilization of Christian symbols. For
example, the cross, the symbol of Christian salvation, is reconstituted as the image
of the false hopes of socio-political salvation of the postcolonial government in
Kenya, in *Devil on the Cross*. If Jesus' death on the cross was salvific, the death and
resurrection of the devil (rebirth of colonial tendencies in postindependence Kenyan rulers) brought only further death and suffering and not salvation. According to Mphande, "by employing Christianity in terms of its orality, prophecy and
style, Ngũgĩ's aim is thus to use Christianity through its own imagery to expose it
as a capitalist arm."[19]

The novel *Petals of Blood* is an interpretation of Rev 6:1–8, about the four horsemen of the apocalypse in light of the "judgment" that befalls the common people
of the fictitious village of Ilmorog. It is set in the period of waning optimism in
a post-independent Kenya governed by corrupt postcolonial African rulers. The
protagonist Munira, the teacher, embracing Christianity while in jail as a murder

---

18. Ngũgĩ, *I Will Marry When I Want*, 56–57. Note the identity of "Christian denominations" as "religions." This may be Ngũgĩ's deliberate move to reflect people's confused state
because of the competing Christian denominations or groups for converts in Kenya.

19. Mphande, "Ngũgĩ," 369.

suspect and perhaps alluding to Rev 6:1–8, proclaims that the country's current unfortunate state is mere fulfillment of divine prophecy: "They trusted too much in the wisdom of this world: they would not open the book of God to see that these things had been prophesied a long time ago." (42)

The parable of the talents in Matt 25:14–30 is turned into a parody of the last judgment, "wherein the much praised servants of the lord and guardian of his property are transposed into the fat cats of Kenya business men."[20] With this excessive satire comes a new set of "beatitudes" that govern the new "Kingdom of Earthly Wiles."[21] In post-independent Kenya it is the rich, corrupt and the unscrupulous that are getting richer and powerful, without working for it, while the peasants and workers, who work their hands to the bone, can barely survive.[22] With attainment of independence came not the anticipated Paradise and welfare for all the citizens, but instead continued terror now unleashed by the neo-colonial African rulers on any who sought to challenge their autocratic rule.

The story revolves around an "exodus" event that brings the villagers to the city in search of help for the drought from their government representative, the Member of Parliament, captioned in the different title of the sections in the book which when read together state "Walking . . . Toward Bethlehem . . . to be Born Again." An apt summation of the changing sense of Ngũgĩ's earlier optimism is captured in Karega, one of the main character's reflection on the news of his mother's death, while he sat in jail for organizing a strike of workers:

> His mother had worked all her life breaking the skin of the earth for a propertied few: what difference did it make if they were black or brown? Their capacity to drink that blood and the sweat of the many was not diminished by any kinship of skin or language or region! Although she insisted on her immediate rights, she never complained much believing that maybe God would later put everything right. But she now died without God putting anything right.[23]

Some level of optimism in Ngũgĩ's writings returns with the novel *Matigari* where the title itself ("remnant") is an allusion to the OT motif of remnants who were the focus of God's favor following the Assyrian and Babylonian exiles in the prophetic books of the Hebrew Bible. The novel has also been understood as an allegorical interpretation of Luke 24:14 where the Christ-like eponymous protagonist serves "holy communion" in jail, ultimately dies and resurrects, and leaves with a promise for an eschatological return (vii–viii).[24] This has prompted one critic to claim that in *Matigari* we move from individual characters as biblical "Moses" and "Christ"

20. Dinwiddy, "Usage," 42.
21. Ibid., 82.
22. Mphande, "Ngũgĩ," 369.
23. Ngũgĩ, *Petals of Blood*, 343.
24. John A. Anonby, "Grim Present, Glorious Future: Millennial Implications in the Novels of Ngũgĩ Wa Thiong'o," in *Faith in the Millennium*, ed. Stanley E. Porter, Michael A. Hayes and David Tombs (Sheffield: Sheffield Academic Press, 2001), 383.

to the entire novel being something akin to a "Gospel according to Ngũgĩ."[25] If this is the case, then the Gospel Ngũgĩ espouses approaches that which is enigmatically described by Jesus in Matt 11:12—"From the days of John the Baptist until now the kingdom of heaven has suffered violence, and men of violence take it by force."

While recognizing the need for sacrifice, there is yet hope held out that redemptive changes would happen in this life. This trend continues in his most recent political satire novel, *Mũrogi wa Kagõgõ* (*Wizard of the Crow*) it is the tower of Babel in Gen 11 that provides the background of the "Marching to Heaven" building that the sycophants of the "Ruler" want to build in his honor. Inevitably, as I have pointed out elsewhere, Ngũgĩ cannot seem to extricate himself from the hold of Christianity.[26] In his writings the Christian story forms the premise for not just parts of all of his novels (as in the first three) but is the basic framework for entire works such as *Matigari* where the Jesus/ Moses like protagonist is a mystery messianic figure with supernatural powers.

In fact, this very question of Ngũgĩ's engagement with Christianity is the point of an article by Lupenga Mphande who points out that while Ngũgĩ may consider himself of a Marxist persuasion, his novels fail to steer clear of a Christian meta-narrative because his effort to "expose [Christianity] as a capitalist arm of exploitation" does not take cognizance of the fact that the religious has residual persistence.[27]

> Ngũgĩ like many African Marxists does not seem to have resolved these dilemmas in this writing—how can you say that Christianity/religion is the opium of the people, and then turn around and make your own Jesuses to whom people must turn?[28]

The fact is, the very essence of what Ngũgĩ presents as his core desire—justice for the peasantry, equitable distribution of property and wealth, socio-politico-economic balance—need not be anti-Christian. These very concerns are essential in biblical ethics seem to be partly the reason Ngũgĩ cannot seem to find another premise on which to articulate them. Indeed, one could ask how the concern for justice and fairness for the poor, if it is simply Marxian for Ngũgĩ, differs from the Christian teachings on justice and fairness such as those in James 1:27; 2:5–7.[29]

25. Ibid.
26. Andrew Mbuvi, "African Novels: An Unlikely Resource for a Socially Engaged Biblical Interpretation?" *SBL Forum* (2006) http://www.sbl-site.org/publications/article.aspx ?articleId=527. See also Mphande, "Ngũgĩ," 357–78.
27. Mphande, "Ngũgĩ," 369.
28. Ibid., 376.
29. Cf. James 1:27; 2:5–7: "Religion that is pure and undefiled before God and the Father is this: to visit orphans and widows in their affliction, and to keep oneself unstained from the world" and "Listen, my beloved brethren. Has not God chosen those who are poor in the world to be rich in faith and heirs of the kingdom which he has promised to those who love him?"

NUANCED AND SUBTLE BIBLICAL ALLUSIONS, IMAGERY, AND ECHOES IN BESSIE HEAD

Head was stubbornly reluctant to accept the viability of political consciousness and resistance in her work, yet it is hard to see the reality of her writing outside of the themes of prejudice (racialism/racism), tribalism, exile, slavery, poverty, power and religion.[30] While espousing a clear hope for a universe filled with justice, love, forgiveness and laughter, Head is not coy in criticizing the apartheid system of her native South Africa that classified her as less than human. On the other hand, she perceived in her writings the reality that even African political systems exemplified these same vestiges of evil where demonic human control over other humans is perceived to breed violence, destruction and death. Head's life seemed to embody this reality as her escape from the overt racism in South Africa did not resolve ostracism as a foreigner and as a half-caste ("coloured") within the village of Serowe in Botswana.

For both Ngũgĩ and Head, while missionary portrayals vary from their being as inhumane as any other cadre of humanity (see especially *A Question of Power* and *A Grain of Wheat*) to being the epitome of humane ideals, these complex images never explicitly seem to be embodied in one person. This is the one aspect of stereotyping that may be banal in Head's work. Thankfully, it plays no major roles in the larger structure of the writings. If it is even marginally autobiographical in *A Question of Power*, Bessie's experience with missionaries at the mission school might not have been pleasant at all. The statement of the sister that informs Elizabeth about her deranged and asylumed mother, though questioned on its autobiographical authenticity, may reflect a painful moment in Head's tender age.[31] On the other hand, Margaret Cardmore, the missionary wife in *Maru* presents a balancing counterpoint that allows for a measure of reprieve in the overall missionary image in Head's oeuvre.

> Masarwa is the equivalent of "nigger," a term of contempt which means, obliquely, a low, filthy nation. True enough the woman who gave birth to a child on the outskirts of the remote village had the same thin Masarwa stick legs. . . . She had died during the night but the child was still alive. . . . When no one wanted to bury a dead body, they called the missionaries: not that the missionaries really liked to be involved with mankind, but they had been known to go into queer

---

30. See her *When Rain Clouds Gather* (New York: Simon and Schuster, 1968); *Maru* (London: Victor Gollancz, 1971); *A Question of Power* (London: Davis-Poynter, 1973).

31. Head, *A Question of Power*, 16: "The principle of the mission school was a tall, thin, gaunt, incredibly cruel woman. She was the last, possibly, of the kind who had heard 'the call' from Jesus and come out to save the heathen. . . . She said: 'Your mother was insane. If you are not careful you'll get insane like your mother. Your mother was a white woman. They had to lock her up, as she was having a child by the native stable boy, who was a native'" (Cecil Abrahams, ed., *The Tragic Life: Bessie Head and Literature in Southern Africa* [Africa World Press, 1990]).

places because of their occupation. . . . They had a church, a school and a hospital in the village, all founded by a series of missionaries. At that time the church and the school were run by a man and his wife. There is little to say about the man because he was naturally dull and stupid, only people never noticed because he was a priest and mercifully remained silent for hours on end.[32]

Margaret Cardmore the missionary that adopts a *Basarwa*[33] ("Bushman" child— "In Botswana they say: Zebras, Lions, Buffalo and Bushmen live in the Kalahari Desert. . . . Of all things that are said of oppressed people, the worst things are said and done to the Bushmen." (11) By fellow Africans (and white people) she is on the one hand described not as one with the kindness of heart but simply one with an over-abundance of common sense (13). On the other hand, she was the one person that not only adopts an outcast, but loves and breathes into her the sense of being a citizen of the universe. She scribbles in her notepad of the child's mother "She looks like a Goddess," (15) a striking contrast of expression in comparison with the surrounding African communities that regard the Basarwa as less than human. For Cadmore senior, the missionary, this member of lowest of the peoples and an "oddity of human race" radiates divine image. It is in the "least of these" that Jesus proclaimed the divine resides (Matt 25:40).

It is only at going to mission school that the younger Margaret Cardmore "slowly became aware that something was wrong with her relationship to the world" (17) Rather curiously named after the adoptive missionary "mother," the younger Margaret did not fit into the prejudiced norms of racial profiling—a *Mosarwa*, with English names and academically brilliant, who could pass for a Coloured but is determined to unashamedly identify as a *Mosarwa* teacher in a community full of *Masarwa* slaves. It is painful—from the childrens' abused to the victim of the Maru's plot—even with its hopeful ending. While a product of the missionaries, the young Margaret Cardmore is not a replica of the older and in fact seems to embody opposing attitudes even to her more influential "mother" figure.(88) "The young girl had no confusion of heart, only the experience of being permanently unwanted by society in general."[34]

The eponymous hero, Maru, also deconstructs the image of the power-hungry tribal chief who, typically like chief Matenge in *When Rain Clouds Gather*, would rather die than be subject to the people's wishes. Maru is willing to give up the trappings of power to lead a life of exile and ordinary existence because of the woman he loves. "When the people of Dilepe village heard about the marriage of Maru they began to talk about him as if he had died."[35] Yet it goes on to explain

32. Head, *A Question of Power*, 12.
33. Masarwa is derogatory grouping people with things. It is possible Head deliberately uses this instead of the more characteristic Basarwa, to drive home the dehumanization of the Khoisan people.
34. Head, *Maru*, 94.
35. Ibid., 126.

that what had happened to Maru was not death but rather a new beginning for one who lived by the ideals of the "standard of the soul."

In the end Maru's master-plan to get married to Margaret Caldmore involves him getting Moleka his now estranged friend, to marry Dikeledi (Maru's sister). Maru gives up what everyone else considers to be the epitome of existence, as the heir to the chieftaincy of Dilepe village, and relocates to a distant land in order to marry the Mosarwa with whom he had fallen in love. "They knew noting about the standards of the soul, and since Maru only lived by those standards they had never been able to make a place for him in their society." "When the people of Dilepe village heard about the marriage of Maru, they began to talk about him as if he had died."[36] In essence Maru chose societal death over love, which brought new life not only to himself but to Margaret who had virtually died of heart break on hearing Moleka was marrying Dikeledi. It also brought life to the Basarwa community who felt the breath of fresh air of equality and humanity.

The very aspect of Head's refusal here to deal directly with racism and instead to subsume it under the larger umbrella of prejudice allows her to critique not only the colonial enterprise but also the postcolonial African reality. She intones elsewhere that the Batswana blacks were "no different from the Boer. They are blind in their racialism and cruelty and they are not different from the white man."[37] Inevitably it is easy to see how these stories are then perceived to have universal appeal. It makes the equality of humans a central theme in her writings—a theme that is central to the biblical story of creation in Genesis. It is even more intriguing when we note that human characters are given divine dimensions so that the divine and the human are entwined in a complex maze. This is also reflected in Ngũgĩ who exclaims in liberation theological terms that "The voice of the people is truly the voice of God."[38]

The biblical story shares this eschatological vision in its description of God creating humans in the image of the divine (Gen 1–2). Somehow there are vestiges of the divine within humanity that allow humans to hope and foresee a better future and with a more pleasant reality. Head describes this as "a world apart from petty human hatreds and petty human social codes and values where the human soul roamed free in all its splendor and glory. No barriers of race or creed or tribe hindered its activity" (67).[39] Apostle Paul describes it as a world where there is "no Jew or Gentile, male or female, slave or free" (Gal 3:28).

This world is only attainable when, like Maru does, the long held societal dictates are challenged and exposed for their dehumanization of the oppressed and demonization of the oppressor. It comes at a price—Maru had to give up the wealth,

---

36. Ibid.

37. Coreen *Brown*, *The Creative Vision of Bessie Head* (Madison, NJ: Fairleigh Dickinson University Press; London: Associated University Press, 2003), 204–5.

38. Ngũgĩ, *Petals of Blood*, 126.

39. Head, *Maru*, 67.

lifestyle, and power of a village chief-elect to become a commoner, a vagabond and an exile who, for all intends and purposes, becomes "dead" to his people. Such imagery rings true for Christian conversion in some situations in Africa or in such socio-religious worlds as the Islamic communities where families pronounce dead any converts to Christianity. Being "dead to the world" is the way that the apostle describes it in Col 2:20—"Since you died with Christ to the basic principles of this world, why, as though you still belonged to it, do you submit to its rules?" (NIV).

The category of the "kings of the souls" walks these worlds of Head, in their "ragged clothes of filthy beggars." (67) It is hard not to entertain the imagery of a poor Jesus of Nazareth with this description, especially when read in light of Mma Millipede's erudite exegesis of Matt 12:42/Lk 11:31 in *When Rain Clouds Gather*:

> Then came a God who was greater than Solomon, but he walked around with no shoes, in rough cloth, wandering up and down the dusty footpaths in the hot sun, with no bed on which to rest his head. And all that the followers of this God could do was to chronicle, in minute detail, the wonder and marvel of his wisdom. There are two such destinies which faced Africa—that of the followers of Solomon and that of a man with no shoes. But the man with no shoes had been bypassed, scorned and ridiculed while the Solomons stalked the land in their Golden Chevrolets.... The Solomons made the most noise in the world, hopping from one international conference to another, bowing and scraping to the left and to the right. But the God with no shoes continued to live where he always had—in the small brown birds of the bush, in the dusty footpaths, and in the expressions of thin old men in tattered cloths.... All things were mixed up because there were too many Solomons and too many men with no shoes and no one could be certain who would win in the end, except the man with no shoes was too hungry to stand in the parade these days.[40]

The human is often described in terms of the divine, and Coreen Brown understands this as the epitome of Christianity in Head's writings in which the missionary, perhaps as a representation of the apartheid system, cannot fully embody the Christian message:

> However, because Mma-Millipede is, unlike the missionaries, portrayed as someone whose "words match [her] deeds," what she provides is an account of Christianity that puts its faith in God who is a loving protector of all.... Head is using Mma- Millipede's Christian philosophy to define an ideal world, a society that emphasizes human community.[41]

One can see then that Head's refusal to overtly confront issues does not mean that she was avoiding them. On the contrary, she is stealthily putting on a frontal attack on their very foundations. In the same manner, her lack of transparent reference to the Bible does not mean its values and aspirations are missing from her works.

---

40. Head, *When Rain Clouds Gather*, 182.
41. Brown, *Vision*, 68.

While exile, for example, is the product of a violent extraction and isolation from home, roots and heritage—the familiar—in Head's novels, it positively throws one into a new community, a new home. It does for Makhaya who must negotiate and deal with his own ego to become a part of a community of exiles which becomes a real "home" in his eventual marriage to Paulina (Brown 38).[42] Elizabeth in *A Question of Power* finds healing in her connection to her land of exile with the end of the novel having her stretching her hand on to the land as "a gesture of belonging" (206).

<h2 style="text-align:center">NGŪGĪ AND HEAD ON SOME BIBLICAL THEMES</h2>

After highlighting Ngugi's and Head's engagement with biblical elements, it may be useful to focus on select theological topics to see how they have been addressed in their novels.

Eschatology and the Apocalypse

Both Head and Ngugi have been characterized as apocalyptic writers. Ngūgī's works are said to be prophetic histories infused with apocalyptic elements.[43] Even in a recent response to a BBC interview on the postelection violence in his homeland Kenya, Ngūgī himself shares this perspective when he elaborates that, "Writers must sometimes feel like the Greek prophetess Cassandra, gifted to see the future but fated not to be believed. What is unfolding in Kenya could as well have been lifted from my novel *Wizard of the Crow* where the ruling party and the opposition parities engaged in Western-sponsored democracy become mirror images of one another in their absurdity and indifference to the poor."[44]

In *Devil on the Cross*, the prognosis for the fate of the devil (the colonialist) is a crucifixion, pointedly after "three days" (cf. Lk 11:29), by resuscitation as a new breed of neocolonialists. *Petals of Blood's* appropriation of the riders of the apocalypse envisions a postcolonial Kenya that awakens to the gruesome reality of continued poverty, disease, and death in the hands of neocolonialist rulers, who, for Ngūgī, simply spell the arrival of the judgment of the four horsemen of the apocalypse (Rev 6). One of the protagonists, Karega, constantly searches for the basis of the "New World" (2 Pet 3:13; Rev 21:1) that idealizes the peasant life, and social-politico-economic justice (305). *Matigari*, written several years before the South African eradication of apartheid, somehow presages the "Reconcilia-

---

42. Ibid., 38, 69: "This seems apt: while Head's other heroes and heroines show that they have long ceased to believe in the reality of an actual utopia informed by a Christian philosophy, Makhaya still hovers on the brink. And to embody Makhaya's beliefs, Head creates an embryonic, new society, one in which natural instincts become synonymous with Christian humanism in a world ahead of profane social systems."

43. Lovesey, "Horn," 158. Cf. Dinwiddy, "Usage," 44.

44. BBC World, "Ngugi Laments Kenya Violence," http://news.bbc.co.uk/2/hi/africa/718 0946.stml.

tion and Truth Commission of South Africa," when he sets up the commission for Truth and Justice to expose the crimes that have been committed by "John Boys" (African neo-colonialists).

Head's apocalyptic vision counterbalances the nightmares in her writings. As Brown explains, allowing for the envisioning of hope in a utopian existence, "The apocalyptic vision, with its stress on the importance of nature, is the antithesis to a world in which the social is reduced to a manifestation to all that is corrupt, destructive, and oppressive."[45] The apocalyptic vision thus creates alternate worlds into which the chaos of the real world can be escaped, but also in which healing effected therein ultimately permeates into the real world.

As Elizabeth emerges from a torturous torment of mental instability at the end of the intensely psychological novel *A Question of Power*, it is described in terms of Ps 23: "David's song arose in her heart once more, but this time infinitely more powerful and secure: 'I have been through the valley of the shadow of death, but I fear no evil. I shall dwell in the house of the Lord forever.'" As song of victory but also a song of hope that looks to the divine presence as a source of life and renewal and healing. This is the triumph over evil that seems to characterize the utopian eschatological vision that runs through Head's books.

> The concept of the infinite and eternal in the apocalyptic vision is not the eternal life of the Christian redemption, but the infinity and eternity of the natural world with its recurring cycles within which man has his place. It is within this place that the divine will become human; human divine and man will become holy to man.[46]

Arrival at this place of solace and peace seems to be the central element of journeys (literal and figurative) of the characters in her novels.

Head states regarding her writings: "My books are about choices and the constant attempt of avoiding the sources of power. These are the choices which have been essential to me as a writer, and sometimes I put the question to myself if these are the choices that Africa is faced with."[47] Yet this is not achievable simply with any human ability but must needs be the product of divine intervention—an intervention of the power of good over that of evil. This is a restoration of the ideal which echoes the experience of the Babylonian king Nebuchadnezzar who only finds restitution following his recognition of the sovereignty of the God of Israel (Dan 4).

Land and Exile

Land is crucial for both Head and Ngũgĩ. For Head, exile for her homeland forces her to dig her roots deep into her new exile home in a way perhaps it would have

45. Brown, *Vision*, 40.
46. Ibid., 38.
47. Ibid., 231.

not been possible at home. For Ngũgĩ, being exiled from one's own sacred land, without being exiled from the country, is just as devastating. Ngũgĩ repeats the following sentiment in virtually all his writings (this one from Gĩcaamba in *I Will Marry When I Want*, 56–57):

> When the British imperialists came here in 1895,
> all the missionaries of all the churches
> held the Bible in the left hand
> and the gun in the right hand.
> The white man wanted us
> to be drunk with religion
> while he,
> in the meantime,
> was mapping and grabbing our land. . .
> completely cripple our mind with religion!

Ngũgĩ's privileging of the sacredness of land seems to reflect the intersection of the sacred land within the sacredness of the Bible, God's promise of land to Israel (Exod 12:25; Deut 6:3). Similarly, the Gĩkũyũ viewed their land as given by *Ngai* (God) who resides in Mount Kenya. Stealing it from the people by the white settlers is then perceived as a confrontation between the Bible (biblical God) and the Gĩkũyũ God. To fight for the land was to fight for a sacred right to own it. Yet it is intriguing that in the correlations that Ngũgĩ draws from the Hebrew scripture characters like Moses seek to ascertain this very claim of divine ownership of land for the Gĩkũyũ. In essence, for Ngũgĩ, the support for the Gikuyu land ownership by the same Bible that white men used to hoodwink the Kenyans would justify the Gĩkũyũ and not the white man. Ngũgĩ thus uses the Bible to disarm any divine claim that may be made by the white man to own any of the Kenyan land.

For Head's *When Rain Clouds Gather*, portrayal of the land in cooperation with humanity for sustenance harks back to an idealized Eden, in spite of the obvious harshness of the Botswana climate. For Gilbert, Makhaya and the community of exiles in Golema Mmidi the land is the common denominator that joins them to each other. It is the place that God "has set aside to bring all his favorite people together" for indeed "there was not anything that he would not do for a village like Golema Mmidi." (187)

Makhaya is an exile among exiles in the village of Golema Mmidi, an "Eden-like place for the dispossessed," and must reconcile with his egocentrism to find peace with life in that community.[48] Marriage to Paulina Sebeso in the end is only after his coming to terms with his restlessness and homelessness.

Makhaya's transformation is described in language reminiscent of spiritual conversion when it states that Gilbert (the agriculturalist with whom Makhaya

---

48. Maxine Sample, "Space: An Experiential Perspective. Bessie Head's *When Rain Clouds Gather*," in *Critical Essays on Bessie Head,* ed. Maxine Sample (Westport, CT: Praeger, 2003), 25–45 (38).

worked) "had found a new convert to his faith" (101).[49] Gilbert himself is an "exile" from the bourgeoisie lifestyle of his England home where "you could not tell friend from foe" (102) and finds "home" in this unfriendly land with its droughts and famines. These challenges somehow give the drive for him to connect with the land and eventually connect himself with the community in his marriage to Maria.

Both men find completion in marriage to women within the exile community and in their friendship that cuts across racial lines. Paradoxically, Makhaya's healing happens to come partly from a white person after his anger and hatred were kindled by the whites' torture in apartheid South Africa. It is triggered by Gilbert's confession to Makhaya of his sense of vulnerability in his relationship to Maria.

> This odd little confession warmed Makhaya's heart to the man. There might have been so many things that could have stood up as a barrier between a possible friendship, like Makhaya's background and his distrust and dislike of white people. Instead, he found himself confronted by a big man who allowed himself to be bullied by a small woman.[50]

As Fielding describes it, "Besides forming a trinity that restores Makhaya's faith while helping him to reconnect to humanity, Dinorego, Mma-Millipede, and Gilbert also become Makhaya's family—father, mother, and brother" (21). For Ngũgĩ, the "Holy" Trinity is made up of "the worker, the peasant and the patriot" who will bring salvation for the community versus the other Holy Trinity, "the Bible, the Coin and the Gun" (POB 88, 230). Ngũgĩ confronts what he perceives as Western conceptualization with his own reconceptualizations that undermines those of the colonizer.

Death and Hope

For Ngũgĩ, more than Head, the concept of sacrificial death for the sake of the community seems to recur prominently in such characters as Kihika, Muthoni and Matigari. However, even the tragic death of Paulina's son in Head's When Rain Clouds Gather, who is appropriately named Isaac, seems to be a premise for hope and a sacrificial death akin to the Akedah of the biblical Isaac (Gen 22). Makhaya having been the one that found the dead boy's bones finds peaceful reconciliation within himself with his past and resolves to settle in Golema Mmidi, hoping for a fruitful future in marriage to Paulina. As Sample concludes, "The spaces that we see in When Rain Clouds Gather are spaces for healing, sanctuary, growth, affirmation and transcendence."[51]

---

49. Maureen Fielding, "Agriculture and Healing: Transforming Space, Transforming Trauma in Bessie Head's When Rain Clouds Gather," in Maxine Sample, Critical Essays, 11–24 (19), describes it as product of "the trinity of Gilbert, Dinorego and Mma-Millipede who have restored Makhaya's faith."

50. Head, When Rain Clouds Gather, 33.

51. Sample, "Essays," 42.

Brown, maintains that ". . . for Head, the abolition of power must be a priority: love as an appositional quality is offered in its place."[52] And since this love cannot be experienced in the abstract, it has to be epitomized in human to human relationship. So, for Head, it is in this realm that the essence of the divine is to be found since there cannot be simply some abstract God up there. . . it has to be a God fully enmeshed in the dust of the earth and in the filth of humanity. "God is people. There is nothing up there. It's all down here," Elizabeth concludes in *A Question of Power* (109).[53]

CONCLUSION

Head's optimism for the ability of human love, care, and justice to overcome evil, prejudice and hatred is driven by an undergirding recognition that these human traits and values are the essential qualities that define the divine.[54] That is why there is the eagerness to have the commingling of the human and the divine in her writings. The disclaimer by Ngũgĩ to simply use the Bible in his work, even when he has ceased to believe in its divine inspiration, does not preclude the fact that he engages in an interpretive enterprise of the biblical text. His Marxist claim to write for and from the perspective of the common *mwnanachi* (citizen), forces him to relate to the Kenyan masses' engagement with the Christianity in their daily lives.

When Ngũgĩ's vile character, the Anglican priest father Jerrod Brown (formerly Kamau), interprets the miraculous healing of the beggar by Peter and John in Acts 3 as a demonstration that "the Bible is . . . clearly against a life of idleness and begging" (148) in response to a parishioner's request for help, it is clearly to the reader that Ngũgĩ expects one to recognize this as an illegitimate interpretation of the biblical text. As his name change to the anglicized Jerrod Brown suggests, he simply apes his "masters," the British missionaries, whose authoritative ecclesial role he now assumes in the independent Kenya.

And while he may claim not to, Ngũgĩ inevitably is giving his own interpretation since he expects the reader to perceive that indeed the Gospel message, if read aright, would be to take care of the beggars. And how different is this from the Gospel message that Jesus teaches especially in the beatitudes (Matt 5–7)? Indeed one cannot but agree with William F. Purcell that what we have here is a matter of contested translations (and interpretations) of the Bible.[55]

---

52. Brown, Vision, 50.

53. I may be overstating the case here, but this has profound affinity to the Johannine teaching on incarnation and a corresponding affirmation of such biblical texts as 1 John 4:7–8: "Beloved, let us love one another; for love is of God, and he who loves is born of God and knows God. He who does not love does not know God; for God is love."

54. Romans 12:20: "On the contrary: 'If your enemy is hungry, feed him; if he is thirsty, give him something to drink. In doing this, you will heap burning coals on his head.'"

55. William F. Purcell, "Contested Translations: The Gospel versus Foreign Missionaries in John Munonye's *Obi*," *CL* 54, no. 1 (2004): 15–29.

In a similar vein to Hjamil A. Martinez-Vasquez's terminology, Head and Ngũgĩ engage in a resistance of the present that fashions an imagined future with "transformative potential."[56] This is made possible by the flexibility of the novel as their chosen medium of expression. And to do so, the Bible provides a key component in the discourse that engages the potential for transformation of society for the better.[57] Whether they acknowledge it or not, Head and Ngũgĩ tread a path that intersects at their desire for human justice, love, freedom, and hope. These human aspirations flounder in human hands, demanding divine intervention that streams from the biblical imagery of the apocalyptic insistence. This is true not only of Head and Ngũgĩ but of a broad swath of African novelists in whose works, as Gakwandi points out, "The demand for freedom, social justice and equality runs through."[58]

Works Cited

Abrahams, Cecil, ed. *The Tragic Life: Bessie Head and Literature in Southern Africa*. Africa World Press, 1990.

BBC World, "Ngũgĩ laments Kenya violence," http://news.bbc.co.uk/2/hi/africa/7180946.stm.

Brown, Coreen. *The Creative Vision of Bessie Head*. Madison, NJ: Fairleigh Dickinson University Press; London: Associated University Press, 2003.

Brown, David Maughan. "*Matigari* and the Rehabilitation of the Religion." *RAL* 22 (1991): 173–80.

Clarke, Becky. "The African Writers Series: Celebrating Forty Years of Publishing Distinction." *RAL* 34, no. 2 (2003): 163–74.

Dinwiddy, Hugh. "Biblical Usage and Abusage in Kenyan Writing." *JRA* 19, no. 1 (1989): 27–47.

---

56. Hjamil A. Martínez-Vázquez, "Breaking the Established Scaffold: Imagination as a Resource in the Development of Biblical Interpretation," in Caroline Vander Stichele and Todd Penner, *Her Master's Tools? Feminist and Postcolonial Engagements of Historical-Critical Discourse* (GPBS 9; Atlanta: Society of Biblical Literature, 2005), 71–91.

57. Justin S. Ukpong et al., *Reading the Bible in the Global Village* (Atlanta: SBL, 2002), 16, echoes these concerns when discussing incultaration hermeneutics: " 'Personal conditioning' has to do with the how the subjectivity of the reader is constructed, and involves world view, gender, and factors that are *economic, religious, social, political* and *racial*. Every form of conditioning has both positive and negative effects depending on whether or not they constitute liberative or oppressive practices."

58. Gakwandi, *Novel*, 7. Gakwandi notes that African novels have been conveniently classified into three categories: the South African novel with its focus on racism and the ills of apartheid, the Anglophone novel and its focus on the tensions of the coexistence of the Western and the African traditions, and the Francophone novels which tend to emphasize African identity contra the French notion of *assimilation*. Of course, Bessie Head's works refuses to be confined to this categorization as it rises above those parameters to address elemental concerns of human love and prejudice.

Gachukia, Eddah, and Kichuma Akivaga, eds. *Teaching of African Literature in Schools.* Vol 1. Nairobi: Kenya Literature Bureau, 1978.

Gakwandi, Arthur Shatto. *The Novel and Contemporary Experiences in Africa.* London: Heinemann, 1977.

Gallagher, Susan VanZanten. "Reading and Faith in a Global Community." *CL* 54, no. 3 (2005): 323–40.

Head, Bessie. *Maru.* London: Victor Gollancz, 1971.

———. *A Question of Power.* London: Davis-Poynter, 1973.

———. *When Rain Clouds Gather.* New York: Simon and Schuster, 1968.

Irumba, Katebaliirwe-Amooti wa. "Ngũgĩ wa Thiongo's Literary Production: A Materailist Critique." Ph.D. diss., University of Sussex, 1980.

Maja-Pearce, Adewale, "In Pursuit of Excellence: Thirty Years of the Heinemann African Writers' Series." *RAL* 23, no. 4 (1992): 125–32.

Mpe, Phaswane. "The Role of the Heinemann African Writers Series in the Development and Promotion of African Literature." *AS* 58, no. 1 (1999): 105–23.

Mphande, Lupenga. "Ngũgĩ and the World of Christianity: A Dialectic." *JAAS* 39, no. 5 (2004): 357–78.

Oliver, Lovesey. "Ngũgĩ wa Thiongo's Postnation: The Cultural Geographies of Colonial, Neocolonial, and Postnational Space." *MFS* 48, no. 1 (2002): 139–68.

Porter, Stanley E., Michael A. Hayes, and David Tombs, eds. *Faith in the Millennium.* Sheffield: Sheffield Academic Press, 2001.

Purcell, William F. "Contested Translations: The Gospel versus Foreign Missionaries in John Munonye's *Obi.*" *CL* 54, no. 1 (2004): 15–29.

Sample, Maxine, ed. *Critical Essays on Bessie Head.* Westport, CT, and London: Praeger, 2003.

Stichele, Caroline Vander, and Todd Penner, eds. *Her Master's Tools? Feminist and Postcolonial Engagements of Historical-Critical Discourse.* GPBS 9. Atlanta: Society of Biblical Literature, 2005.

Ukpong, Justin S., et al., eds. *Reading the Bible in the Global Village: Cape Town.* GPBS. Atlanta: Society of Biblical Literature, 2002.

Vigne, Randolph, ed. *A Gesture of Belonging: Letters from Bessie Head, 1965–1979.* London: Heinemann; Portsmouth, NH: SA Writers, 1991.

Wa Thiong'o, Ngũgĩ. *Detained.* London: Heinemann ,1980.

———. *A Grain of Wheat.* London: Heinemann, 1967.

———. *Matigari.* London: Heinemann, 1987.

———. *Mũrogi wa Kagõgõ* (*Wizard of the Crow*). New York: Pantheon, 2006.

———. *Petals of Blood.* New York: Penguin, 1977.

———. *The River Between.* London: Heinemann, 1965.

———. *Thaitani Mũtharabainĩ* (*Devil on the Cross*). London: Heinemann, 1982.

———. *Weep Not, Child.* London: Heinemann, 1964.

Wa Thiong'o, Ngũgĩ, and Ngũgĩ wa Mĩrĩĩ. *Ngahĩĩka Ndeenda* (*I Will Marry When I Want*). London: Heinemann, 1982.

Wright, Edgar, ed. *The Critical Evaluation of African Literature.* London: Heinemann, 1982.

God in Africa, Lost and Found, Lost Again, and Found Anew: The Bible in André Brink's *Praying Mantis*

H. J. M. (Hans) van Deventer

Literature and the Bible in Africa

In his novel *Praying Mantis*,[1] the acclaimed South African author, André Brink, gives a vivid account of the clash between cultures and belief-systems on the African continent. The novel, with a distinct picaresque slant, introduces the reader to a historical figure named Cupido Cockroach, who is the protagonist in the story. The novel is set in the Cape Colony at the southern tip of Africa during the early nineteenth-century—a time when this colony was mostly under British rule. The plot centers on the conversion of Cupido, a Khoi-Khoi man, to the Christian faith. This came as a result of the endeavors of the London Missionary Society. He becomes the first missionary of color in the Colony, but at his isolated outpost he realizes that Christianity is unable to bridge the cultural and racial divides created by the colonial authorities. This essay investigates the way in which the novel portrays the understanding and use of the Bible from an indigenous African perspective, as well as from a European perspective. It seeks to highlight the role social context plays in the interpretation of (religious) texts.

First, we should explore the relation between general literature and the Bible in the context of the African continent. In order to do so, the complexity imbedded in terms such as "literature," "Bible," and "African context" is highlighted by referring to a few extreme positions. The Bible holds an important place in the hearts of many people in Africa. However, the ways it is used, read and understood often do not resonate with the manner in which this is done in other parts of the world. In fact, in recent times these distinct "African" ways of transacting with the Bible have become the focus of scholarly attention.[2] When dealing with the way in which the Bible is used in African literature, one also has to take notice of what is labeled

---

1. André Brink, *Praying Mantis* (London: Vintage, 2006).
2. See Gerald O. West and Musa W. Dube, eds., *The Bible in Africa: Transactions, Trajectories, and Trends* (Leiden: Brill, 2001). This volume provides illuminating examples of the nature and diversity reflected in the study of the Bible in Africa.

"African Biblical Hermeneutics." This notion, as well as the concept "African Literature" is briefly discussed.

In emotive language Charles E. Nnolim refers to African literature as "literature of lamentation" embodying "a strong sense of loss: loss of our dignity; loss of our culture and tradition; loss of our religion, loss of our land; loss of our very humanity."[3] This description of a very real *experience* cuts to the core of a central theme manifested in African literature in the post World War II era. If we accept Thomas A. Hale's proposal of adding a diachronic perspective to African literature, we acknowledge that also geographical boundaries and not only modern-day socio-political experiences, can be used as measure for what constitutes African literature.[4] Such proposals open the way for ancient Egyptian hieroglyphic orthography and its influence on writing in other parts of Africa to be severed from the traditional Middle Eastern context and placed squarely in an African context. This notion of African Literature expands the term beyond recent history and seeks to support Africa's claim to rightfully share in a global cultural heritage. This line of thought should be kept in check, though, as the possibility of Afrocentrism fabricating fictitious claims in this regard is real.[5] Although running the risk of over-simplification one can label these two approaches as representative of a minimalist and a "maximalist" viewpoint.

The minimalist seeks to identify a unique experience as *the* valid element in adding the epithet "African" to literature. This experience is located in a very specific socio-historical milieu, namely that of colonial oppression and the need to rediscover an own identity in the wake of the liberty gained in recent decades. In this sense African literature voices the injustices of the past—indeed, the loss that was suffered at the hands of the colonizers. This goes beyond a mere description of the sense of loss but also works towards the rediscovery of a unique identity. In this sense African literature wants to reclaim what was lost during the period of colonization.

The problem with a minimalist approach is that it can be subjected to the same criticism that applies to the approach the colonizers used so effectively, namely that of exclusion. The unique non-Modernist (and essentially non-Western) idea of inclusion, of giving space to other voices, of celebrating commonalities in spite of more obvious differences, encountered by the imperial powers on the African soil, was exploited. What had been the strength of African thought was turned into a weakness at the hands of the colonizers. Thus, it is difficult to imagine how unique African voices can be recovered if the process is steered by the idea of

---

3. Charles E. Nnolim, "African Literature in the Twenty-first Century: Challenges for Writers and Critics," in *New Directions in African Literature,* ed. E. N. Emenyonu (Oxford: James Currey, 2006), 1.

4. Thomas A. Hale, "Bursting at the Seams: New Dimensions for African Literature in the Twenty-first Century," in Emenyonu, *New Directions,* 10–21.

5. See Mary R. Lefkowitz, *Not Out of Africa: How Afrocentrism Became an Excuse to Teach Myth as History* (New York: Basic Books, 1996).

exclusion as reflected in the minimalist approach. Another problem that presents itself is that this approach limits the scope of African literature in the long run. After the injustices have been described, suggestions towards a new identity made and in the process healing facilitated, then what? When the last wound inflicted by colonial powers has healed, should that also close the possibility for African literature? Surely, this cannot be the case.

On the other hand, including everything ever written on African soil under the rubric "African literature" as suggested by the maximalist approach constitutes the other extreme. A first criticism of this position is that African literature cannot be limited to written texts. For the most part of their history, African societies embraced an oral tradition. It will definitely demonstrate a cultural (colonial?) bias to exclude oral tradition from "African literature." Furthermore, not all texts written on the African continent had the benefit of local communities in mind. Especially during the colonial period many texts originating on African soil were written for an upper-class European community. These texts include travel and missionary reports and, although written on the African continent, address European concerns.

Between these minimalist and maximalist approaches there surely is enough middle ground to define African Literature. Once more at the risk of over simplification I propose that African Literature includes all discourses (oral and written) originating from African soil that epitomize uniquely African experiences and relate these experiences to African and universal concerns and communities. This definition seeks inclusion and excludes only those texts that by their very nature want to be included elsewhere.[6]

We encounter a similar duality when turning our attention to the understanding of the Bible in Africa, otherwise referred to as African Biblical Hermeneutics. A glance over the surprisingly large amount of material available under this rubric makes it clear that a universal definition in this regard will be hard to find.[7] On one end of the spectrum there are those who seemingly link the notion of African Biblical Hermeneutics to ethnicity. Hence, John S. Mbiti defines African theologians as those "who belong to a particular ethnic group."[8] He does concede, however, that the recent history of Africa—with specific reference to the ethnic cleansing in Rwanda in 1994—indicates that ethnicity in Africa is in fact often part of the problem. All over the African continent, ethnic (and other) minorities are at the mercy of the majority and the people this majority elected to occupy positions of power.

6. See Rand Bishop, *African Literature, African Critics: The Forming of Critical Standards, 1847–1966* (New York: Greenwood Press, 1988), for a related debate on the dominant use of Western forms of criticism when dealing with African literature.

7. See the extensive bibliography compiled by Grant LeMarquand, "A Bibliography of the Bible in Africa," in West and Dube, *The Bible in Africa*, 642–62.

8. John S. Mbiti, "African Theology," in *Initiation into Theology: The Rich Variety of Theology and Hermeneutics,* ed. Simon Maimela and Adrio König (Pretoria: Van Schaik, 1998), 141.

At the other end of the spectrum there are theologians in Africa who contest the very notion of African Biblical Hermeneutics. Apparently oblivious to how culturally entrenched and bias "universal" modes of scholarship are, the idea of doing something uniquely African is easily brushed aside. In these quarters it is claimed that Western scholarship—for no other form of scholarship exits—holds the only key to unlock the doors to new fields of knowledge.[9] In the same vein we should recall that when the feminist movement entered the hallways of academe during the seventies of the previous century—especially faculties of religion and theology—this development was also frowned upon. It took almost two decades for influential biblical scholars to recognize the contributions made by this movement, and, at the same time realize how excluding white male "scholarship" had become due to the fact that it never questioned its own presuppositions.[10] To be sure, not yet all white male scholars share these sentiments.[11] With feminism drawn into the fray, it should be added that above and beyond the similarities between feminism, African theology and post-colonial theory—all being informed by a shared experience of marginalisation—there is also a marked difference to be noted. Unlike African and post-colonial theology that seek to reclaim the authentic voices once had, feminist and womanist approaches stake claims to positions *not* held in the past.

African Biblical Hermeneutics, then, recognizes the fact that knowledge is not produced in a vacuum, or in an objective manner. As an academic quest for meaning it is able to house all who approach the biblical text with their own unique experiences. Among others African biblical hermeneutics wants to uncover reading practices that exclude certain (African) voices *and* argues why they should be heard. It is a hermeneutic that seeks to empower the powerless by allowing their unique contributions, which originate from unique locations, to count as legitimate, while at the same time arguing why they are indeed legitimate.

Keeping this landscape of diverse opinions in mind, themes and motives from Brink's novel, which was produced on African soil and relates to the use of the Bible in an African context, will be investigated for their relevance to the issue of literature and the Bible in Africa.

---

9. See, for instance, Christo Lombaard, "The Relevance of Old Testament Science in/for Africa: Two False Pieties and Focused Scholarship," *OTE* 19 (2006): 144–55.

10. Daniel Patte, *Ethics of Biblical Interpretation: A Reevaluation* (Louisville: Westminster John Knox, 1995).

11. Robert P. Carroll, "(South) Africa, Bible, Criticism: Rhetorics of a Visit," in West and Dube, *The Bible in Africa*, 187–88 n. 3.

Background to Brink's Novel

In this section an overview of the novel's plot is given, and reference is made to a few methodological considerations related to the question of finding features in the novel that resonate with African biblical hermeneutics.

In *Praying mantis*, the story is set during late eighteenth, early nineteenth-century in the Cape colony at the southern end of the African continent. This dating coincides with what historians refer to as the third period of governance by the Dutch East India Company (DEIC) over this part of the world. The period was marked by tension between a number of colonists and the DEIC due to what was perceived as the Company's failure to protect the colonists who moved further into the interior of the continent.[12] Towards the end of the eighteenth-century, and following on the Prince of Orange's flight to England due to a pro-French party laying claim to the Netherlands, England agreed to occupy the Cape Colony from 1795–1803. In 1803 the Cape was returned to the Batavian Republic, but in the wake of Napoleon's wars the English, in 1806, again occupied the region for strategic reasons. The Peace of Vienna, signed in 1815, formally placed the Cape under British control.

The title of the novel refers to a well-known insect (*Mantis Religiosa*). The Afrikaans title (*Bidsprinkaan*)[13] mirrors the novel's distinct religious slant by employing a higher language register that refers to the act of praying (*bid*), instead of the more common word *Hottentotsgot* used for this insect. *Hottentot* and its cruder derivative *Hotnot* became degrading terms among colonists to refer to Khoi people. The title of the novel is indicative of the symbolic importance attached to this insect in the Khoi-Khoi religious system. The Afrikaans novel also carries a subtitle "'n ware storie" (a true story) that lacks in the English version. The Afrikaans subtitle is reminiscent of the words spoken by a character in Chinua Achebe's novel *Things Fall Apart*. Achebe's novel is divided into three parts and deals with the clash between Western and West African cultures spearheaded by a clash of religions. The words referred to in the subtitle are uttered after stories about sightings of white people began circulating among the West African communities where Achebe's novel is set. One of the characters mentions his previous disbelief in the stories about white people whereupon another, Uchendu, then says: "There is no story that is not true."[14]

Brink's novel, like the one by Achebe, is divided into three parts, but it also reflects a definite picaresque mode of movement "from exclusion to attempted in-

---

12. J. W. Hofmeyr and G. J. Pillay, eds., *A History of Christianity in South Africa* (Pretoria: HAUM Tertiary, 1994), 4.

13. Brink writes his novels simultaneously in both English and Afrikaans. The latter is an indigenous language which developed from Dutch; according to the 2001 census, 13.3 percent of the South African population speak Afrikaans as their first language. This makes it the third-largest language in South Africa after isiZulu and isiXhosa.

14. Chinua Achebe, *Things Fall Apart* (1958; repr., Oxford: Heinemann, 1986), 101.

clusion and back to exclusion."[15] Other picaresque motives in the novel include: an un-heroic protagonist on an eternal journey; the unusual birth of the protagonist; and the ejection motif. In the first part of *Praying Mantis* the narrator introduces Cupido Cockroach. He is the son of a "housemaid" working for a white (colonist) farmer. Cupido is in close contact with *Heitsi-Eibib*, the ancestral hero in his religion. Thus, he is a gifted hunter. He grabs the opportunity to join a lone trader, Ziervogel, on his wagon to explore the world. Ziervogel introduces him to another religion (Christianity). Cupido then meets Anna, who becomes his wife, and decides to bid the road farewell. Eventually they settle in the town of Graaff-Reinet where, against his wife's wishes, he converts to Christianity.

The second part of the novel, narrated by the missionary James Read in the first person, sees Cupido and Anna relocating together with Missionaries Van der Kemp and Read to Bethelsdorp. After the immense setback of Anna's death, Cupido joins the missionaries on another journey. They set out to visit outposts beyond the borders of the colony. During the trip Cupido's zeal for his new religion leads to him being recommended to the office of missionary. This engraved his name in the history of Christianity in South Africa as the first missionary of color.[16] In the third part of the book Cupido is called to serve as minister to the roaming Kora people at one of the outposts they visited earlier. Receiving only promises of a regular income and supplies he is left to his own devices. The congregation steadily dwindles until not a single soul is left. Only now, and after many pleas, he finally receives a visit from a neighboring white missionary, the well-known Robert Moffat. He informs Cupido of his dismissal as missionary in service of the LMS. While reverting back to some of the Khoi-Khoi religious practices Cupido sets off on a new journey.

The novel also exhibits clear characteristics of a post-colonial text. The setting in the eastern part of the Cape Colony at the beginning of the nineteenth-century, as well the roots of the main character, a Khoi-Khoi man, reflects the "in-between" state often related to post-colonial texts.[17] We should also note that Van der Kemp's mission station was situated in an area separating white farmers from the Xhosa people. Here the Khoi-Khoi found a safe space between the Whites and the Xhosa. In the words of Van der Kemp in the novel:

> There is no sense, and no justice, in trying to force them [the Khoi-Khoi] into subservience to the colonists whose only wish is to enslave them. Nor can they expect

---

15. Ulrich Wicks, "The Nature of Picaresque Narrative: A Modal Approach," *PMLA* 89, no. 2 (1974): 240–49.

16. Richard Elphick and Rodney Davenport, eds., *Christianity in South Africa. A Political, Social, and Cultural History* (Oxford: James Currey, 1997), 35; Elizabeth Isichei, *A History of Christianity in Africa* (Grand Rapids: Eerdmans, 1995), 107.

17. Rasiah S. Sugirtharajah, *Postcolonial Criticism and Biblical Interpretation* (Oxford: Oxford University Press, 2003), 22–23.

any justice in an allegiance with the Xhosa, who see no use for them except as buffers to absorb the pressure of whites set on expanding their own territory.[18]

This liminal space finds embodiment in Cupido Cockroach. Throughout the novel the question of loss and/or belonging is addressed from various angles. Cupido is the character that moves from the safe and secure environment into the unknown. In the end he champions over those characters who remained within their fixed boundaries. Cupido crosses boundaries and in the end does not find a home in any single place. His journey always continues.

The reader is also introduced to two different, though related, belief systems that were indigenous to this part of the African continent during the late eighteenth-century. The roots of these beliefs systems stretch back for centuries. The Khoi-Khoi belief system involved a world in which good and evil were seen as competing with each other. The supreme god, *Tsui Goab*, protected life and community and also controlled the environment, especially rainfall. One of the founding heroes in this belief system is *Heitsi-Eibib* who had direct access to the supreme god. He assumed many forms and was able to reincarnate himself. His many graves were marked by heaps of stones, constantly contributed to by people passing by in order to secure their success as herders or hunters. The evil god, *Guanab*, opposed these good forces and caused among others illness and death.[19]

Cupido's first wife, Anna, hailed from the San people who venerated *Kaggen* as supreme Being. Evil in this world, which was caused by the spirits of the dead, was combated through *shamans* (medicine people). Religious celebrations were characterized by ritual dances and chanting with people going into trace-like states. In such a state supernatural potency could enter a person. Some scholars believe that the San rock paintings, which can still be seen in isolated parts of South Africa, represent the experiences of *shamans* during trances. An animal frequently appearing in these paintings is the Eland and it is believed to have been a central religious symbol among the San.[20]

Turning our attention now to describing the use of the Bible in this novel, we should realize that a single theoretical model guiding the reader to locate allusions to the Bible in a novel does not exist. If the statement by David Lyle Jeffrey in the preface to one of the standard works in this field is correct, namely, "for literature in the English-speaking world no text has continued to exert a more formative influence than the Bible,"[21] then it seems as if biblical references and allusions lay

18. Brink, *Praying Mantis*, 138.
19. Hofmeyr and Pillay, *A History of Christianity*, xviii–xix.
20. Ibid., xvi–xviii.
21. David Lyle Jeffrey, ed., *A Dictionary of Biblical Tradition in English Literature* (DBTEL; Grand Rapids: Eerdmans, 1992), xi.

UNIVERSITY OF WINCHESTER
LIBRARY

strewn about in many literary works—ready for the picking.[22] The alphabetically arranged entries in this wide-ranging volume can be grouped together in the following six categories: biblical proper nouns; common nouns; concepts; common quotations or allusions, parables; and familiar terms in Greek, Hebrew and Latin. Each entry is discussed as regards its history of interpretation—beginning with the Bible itself, through the exegetical tradition all the way down to references in English literature. The work does not aim to be comprehensive in any way, but traces only "significant strands in literary development."[23] The investigation in the present essay links up with two of the categories used Jeffrey's work, namely "concepts" (also derived from exegetical and theological formulations) and "common quotations or allusions." Brink's text, due to its subject matter, is especially rich in the latter. This essay focuses primarily on these, but considers biblical "concepts" where they illuminate the plot.

A different approach to the subject is followed by David Jasper and Stephen Prickett, who focus on well-known biblical texts and trace the use of, or allusions to these texts by selected authors.[24] Extensive citations of relevant biblical texts are provided, followed by interpretive comments, but no commentary is supplied on the selected authors' use of these texts. In this sense their work is truly "a reader" as stated in its subtitle and serves as a guide to those embarking on the journey of discovering the Bible in literature. With these methodological comments made, we now turn to the main focus of this contribution.

The Bible in Praying Mantis

In this section the argument follows the three part division of the novel, with reference to the caption given for each section of the novel.

Koup to Kamdeboo[25]

The first reference to the Bible found in the novel occurs when, in the first chapter, the narrator traces Cupido's familial roots to a successful hunting expedition by a group of farmers into the Northern Cape during the mid-eighteenth-century. Concluding a list of wild animals that were shot the reader is informed that "eight Bushmen" were caught "to be tamed as field labourers."[26] On their way back to civilization a number of Hottentots were also "persuaded" to join this group of

---

22. Peter S. Hawkins, "Lost and Found: The Bible and its Literary Afterlife," *RL* 36, no. 1 (2004): 1–14, on the other hand, reminds us by way of illustration that the use of the Bible by contemporary authors is in fact difficult to detect and even harder to evaluate.

23. Jeffrey, *Dictionary*, xi.

24. David Jasper and Stephen Prickett, *The Bible and Literature: A Reader* (Oxford: Blackwell, 1999).

25. These traditional regional names for parts of southern Africa reflect the physical journey of the protagonist in the first part of the novel.

26. Brink, *Praying Mantis*, 5.

farmers. Among these people we find Cupido's unnamed mother. Here the biblical allusion is not to a specific text, but to what Jeffrey describes as a "concept," namely punishment.[27] Hence, Cupido's mother is duly punished "according to the Word of God" for her "unfortunate tendency to abscond."[28]

Hidden among the many references to the Khoi-Khoi religious sphere in chapters two and three there is a peculiar reference to Isa 11:6–9 abbreviated to the commonly recognized "a lion and a lamb lying together."[29] This idyllic picture is revealed in one of the visions that Cupido's mother sees and also includes two further unlikely scenes, namely "a goose suckling a hartebeest kid" and "a leopard tending a brood of chickens." The vision concludes with a distinct allusion to the Khoi-Khoi religious realm in the reference "an eland and a praying mantis mating."[30]

The theme of religious indigenization is apparent in chapter four when the young Cupido is occasionally introduced to the after dinner prayers in the household of the farmer where his mother works as a "housemaid" (14). He does not understand a lot, except that based on his mother's explanation, he is able to forge a link between Jesus and *Heitsi-Eibib*, the hero in his religion, since they both died and were resurrected (15). In chapter five, when Cupido realizes what power the written word holds, he also notices the link between this "strong magic" and the religion of the white people (22).

In the process of the protagonist familiarizing himself with another religion, the novel cautiously points to marked differences in religious systems. As a result, in chapter six, a snake is viewed as sustaining life (25)—a stark contrast to the role the snake fulfils in most biblical texts (e.g., Gen 3). However, in the very same chapter the prohibition to name the mythic figure and Great Hunter, *Heitsi-Eibib*, "in front of strangers" (28) again has a familiar ring to it (see Exod 20:7).

The first part of the novel that centers on Cupido's pre-Christian life hinges on the death of the farmer whilst hunting and the disappearance of his mother. Cupido's introduction to the Christian faith is advanced by a wandering trader who arrives on the farm with two wagon loads of goods, including quite a number of religious artifacts (the Afrikaans text includes among these *Statebybels*—the of-

---

27. Jeffrey, *Dictionary*, xii. Interestingly enough this concept (i.e., "punishment") did not get listed in *DBTEL*—the closest to this idea is a short entry on *Lex Taliones*. In a theologically orientated dictionary this concept is discussed at length by Moshe Greenberg, "Crimes and Punishment," in *Interpreter's Dictionary of the Bible*, ed. G. A. Buttrick (Nashville: Abingdon, 1962), 733–44.

28. Brink, *Praying Mantis*, 5.

29. Ibid., 12. This phrase is of course not from the book of Isaiah, but is known from the Anglican hymnal, no. 597. Isaiah 11:6–7 reads: "The wolf also shall dwell with the lamb, and the leopard shall lie down with the kid; and the calf and the young lion and the fatling together; and a little child shall lead them. And the cow and the bear shall feed; their young ones shall lie down together: and the lion shall eat straw like the ox" (KJV).

30. Brink, *Praying Mantis*, 12. Subsequent in-text page references are to *Praying Mantis*.

ficial Dutch Bible of the period—but it is not mentioned in the English text). The trader, Zervaas Ziervogel, informs the people on the farm that "he is a servant of the Lord of Hosts, sent to spread the Gospel in the interior of this heathen land" (40). This lay preacher displays characteristics of the great Old Testament figures of Moses (40) and Elijah (41).[31] He administers the sacrament to all the un-baptized white children on the farm, and fascinates Cupido with his stories about imaginary journeys—journeys that took him to various biblical places (47–48)

A variety of biblical allusions are introduced towards the end of chapter nine and in chapter ten. In this way the reader is being prepared for the next phase in Cupido's life, namely taking to the road with Servaas Ziervogel. These include the well-known citation "Get thee gone, Satan" (Matt. 4:10) (48) when Ziervogel confronts his own desires towards the farmer's widow, while at the same time "trying to sound out God's feelings about it all" (48). In chapter ten an ironic allusion to God's providence occurs as Ziervogel breaks the news of his departure with a reference to Eccl 3:1–8 in the phrase "a time for coming and a time for going" (53).

Towards the end of chapter ten, whilst on the road, the reader is informed that Ziervogel continues telling stories "mostly from the Bible, but freely embroidered from memory and imagination" (57). To these Cupido responds with the stories his mother told him. However, his captivation with the "Holy Writ" is fuelled by his companion's readings beside the fire at night—"he is enthralled by the mere sound of the words" (58). After Ziervogel's repeated encouragement that Cupido "should become preacher" he has to face a dilemma: should he "shake off" the world of *Heitsi-Eibib* and enter the world of the book? He answers Ziervogel's invitation by saying that he is a (mere) "*Hottentot*," thus electing to stay within the confines of his own religion.

However, his dilemma is worsened after meeting his future wife on a farm where he decides to settle while Ziervogel continues his journeys. Anna Vigilant is a woman who was caught by white people when she was very young. Cupido "becomes more and more confused" when she adds her own stories of the San religion to what his mother told him about the Khoi-Khoi religion and the stories of Ziervogel about the trinity in Christianity. He thus asks: "What should a man believe in, what is the truth?" (76). The narrator also informs the reader of Anna's supernatural powers in an episode that clearly alludes to the story of the ten plagues (Exod 10–11). The death of the farmer's eldest son leads to the release of Cupido and Anna, who settle in the small town of Graaff-Reinet. Here they are introduced to a more established form of Christianity when emissaries of the London Missionary Society arrive. Henceforth more allusions to the biblical text occur (e.g., "war and rumours of war" in Matt 24:6) (83).

At first the tension between Christianity and other belief systems is upheld. Anna warns Cupido not to get involved with the clash brewing in town regarding the "white man's church" (90). She claims it "is much better to let every man

---

31. In the Afrikaans text this is even more explicit with a reference to "man of God."

believe what he wants." However, when Cupido learns about wine that is to be had (a reference to Holy Communion) he is determined to attend a church service. An old man explains the wine to be the blood of the white man's "Tsui-Goab, the one they call Jesus" (91). During the service the tension between the Khoi-Khoi members of the congregation and the whites are reflected in their respective uses of the biblical text when Pss 134 and 74 are sung by the two groups. The words are indicative of tension in the congregation that is fuelled by racial difference. Missionary Van der Kemp, a Moses-like figure with shining face (Exod 34:29), is able to resolve the situation. To Van der Kemp, who is vehemently opposed to the way in which the white settlers act in church, Cupido finds himself drawn. This white man reiterates the earlier words of Ziervogel: "If you really want to you could become a reverend yourself" (100). During their first meeting Cupido hears from Van der Kemp the essence of the Christian gospel: "I told you that we are all slaves of sin. But in the blood of our Lord Jesus Christ we can all be washed clean from sin, freed by his infinite mercy" (100).

After this initial meeting Cupido signs up for catechism. The syllabus includes the following well-known biblical stories: Adam, Eve and the serpent, Noah and the ark, Daniel in the lion's den, Jonah and the whale, David and Goliath, Jesus and the miracles of changing water into wine, healing the sick and resurrecting Lazarus, as well as his crucifixion and resurrection. During the first class Reverend Van der Kemp transports Cupido with his words to another world—"a flood of the purest light" (104). In this scene there are quotations from Ps 103, for example, "wings of an eagle" (104), and "Praise the Lord, o my soul" (105). The last quote forms part of the formulary for the Holy Communion in the Reformed tradition. These words find a complement towards the end of this chapter, which concludes the first section of the book, when the formulary for the Holy Baptism is quoted (108). The occasion is the baptism of Cupido and this event almost leads to his death (109–10).

In the first part of the novel biblical concepts are alluded to, and biblical quotations are placed in the context of other religions to indicate both differences and similarities between belief systems. Where biblical quotations occur in the context of the Christian belief system they either fulfill an entertaining (ironic) function, where for instance the Bible is manipulated to justify a character's selfish actions, or to stress the fact that the Bible is used to promote (racial) divisions in a believing community. Lastly, the biblical references testify to a theological scheme (dogma) by referring to the sacraments. This development in the use of the Bible traces the progression of the main character from an outsider to the Christian religion, to becoming seemingly an insider.

The Reverend James Read

The narrative content of this section of the novel lends itself to many biblical allusions. The reader meets the missionary James Read as a first person narrator who continues the story of Cupido Cockroach after his baptism. Here, the focus of this contribution falls on those allusions that build on themes introduced in the first part of the novel as well as on the development of new themes. Occasional biblical allusions outside these parameters will not be discussed.

The first character the reader meets is at the time of his "writing" the disgraced and no-longer-reverend Read. He picks up on some of the religious issues already raised. At the outset he comments on the notion of getting God on one's side when he says: "Does the soul ever know its own blind reasoning? Where does the inscrutable will of God end and the stubborn self begin?" (114). In the first section of the novel this idea was mooted in a comical way when Ziervogel used a reference to the divine providence to have his way with the widow on whose farm Cupido stayed (53). In the second part on the novel divine providence is introduced as a serious matter.

The description of Cupido given at the outset of this section is of a person totally captivated by his (violent) zeal in the service of the Lord. This is seen in (1) his physical harassment of people who do not want to be baptized, as well as (2) his vehement destruction of cairns erected by the Khoi-Khoi people. He does not heed to the missionaries' gentle reprimands that his actions are "extreme and unnecessary" (123). A third manner in which he expresses his zeal is to substitute the Khoi-Khoi celebrations that coincide with the sighting of the new and full moons with the singing of Christian psalms (124).

The missionaries' references to the biblical text in this section bespeak either their personal trust (e.g., a reference to Ps 24 in the case of Van der Kemp) (139), or their personal anxiety (e.g., a reference to Ps 130 in the case of Read) (140). Read later on relates the death of Van der Kemp to the words in 2 Sam 3:38 ('a great man fallen') and confesses that the words of the "Holy Writ" are of little comfort (177). When the missionaries' attempts fail to bring the white farmers to justice, Read feels that they have failed the Khoi-Khoi people, giving them stones instead of bread (Matt 7:9) (182). He does, however, still cite the Word (2 Cor 4:7) in order to subdue his fleshly desires (200).

In this section the character of Anna, Cupido's wife, is developed in more detail. Mimicking the response of Cupido to Ziervogel's Bible narratives in the first part of the novel, she and Read engage in "trading stories" (141). Each Bible story that he tells is answered by a story from the religious sphere of the Khoi-Khoi. At first she holds on to her traditional convictions and elects not to be baptized. But later on, and with reference to the decision of Ruth ("I must go where he go" [sic]), she decides to get baptized (142). She argues that the missionaries took her husband away from her and by being baptized she hopes to be able to reclaim him.

What is apparent from Cupido's use of the Bible in this section is that it mirrors the promotion of self-interest introduced in the first part of the book. In order to rebuke a gang of armed Khoi-Khoi for an attack on the mission settlement, Cupido "translates" Rev. Read's address of peace into a fire-and-brimstone sermon concluding with the stern warning from Heb 10:31—"It is a fearful thing to fall into the hands of the living God" (150). In what serves as an indication that he has internalized what is viewed as a superior culture, he uses its religious book as a weapon to scare the very people with whom he shares a common culture. This forceful misuse of scripture is almost immediately followed by a racially motivated interpretation of Gen 10. White farmers are pictured as voicing their dismay about the teaching the Khoi-Khoi people receive at the mission station. To their minds the education was wasted on the Khoi-Khoi "being the offspring of Canaan, son of Ham, they had been cursed with perpetual servitude to the whites elected by God" (152). This blatantly racist interpretation begs the question: can *any* understanding of a religious text that lays claim to exclusivity or superiority ever be "correct"?

The mission station founded in the eastern part of the Cape Colony was called Bethelsdorp, thus a reference to the biblical character Jacob is to be expected. The first such reference is to Gen 35:2 where Jacob instructs his family to remove the "strange gods" from their midst. The novel portrays it somewhat differently. The reference to "strange gods" is placed in the context of Jacob's initial renaming of Luz (Gen 28:19) "when he was salvaged from the strange gods in whose midst he dwelled" (153). This is followed by a reference to Cupido's "permanent limp" that he obtained during the skirmish with the Khoi-Khoi (154). The reader notes the way in which the character Cupido resembles Jacob.

In the same context a conversation takes places between Read and Cupido. It is prompted by the maltreatment Cupido received at the hands of a farmer whilst collecting ingredients for soap that Anna makes. The conversation touches on the "Kingdom of God," a "reward in heaven" and links Rev. Read to St. Paul by means of reference to a "dazzling light" that stands in opposition to "a kind of darkness" Read finds in himself (155–56). The incident with the farmer leads to the first glimpse offered of Cupido's "theology" when a verbal communication with God is recorded (157–58). Later in the novel his communication with God will take on a written form.

The novel follows recorded historical events and describes attempts by the missionaries to bring white farmers accused of grave atrocities against the Khoi-Khoi to justice. The circuit court introduced after the second British occupation of the Cape Colony (1806) was dubbed the 'Black Circuit' due to "the many charges of maltreatment of Khoi-Khoi laborers raised by the missionaries Van der Kemp and Read from their mission station in Bethelsdorp."[32] However, very few convictions were made in these cases (176–83). The reasons given were mostly lack of evidence, but one will not be wrong in suspecting lack of justice as well. In the novel it is during this period that both Van der Kemp and Anna die. In her farewell to Cupido she reminds him that although he is a man of God, he is still a *Hottentot* (178). With her death the last voice in the narrative reminding Cupido of his religious roots becomes silent. Her silence elicits a forceful letter from Cupido to God, accusing him of this time making "a bad mistake" (179).

---

32. Hermann Giliomee, *The Afrikaners: Biography of a People* (Charlottesville: University of Virginia Press, 2003), 83.

The reader is informed, however, that his preoccupation with the Word became more and more intense and that it went hand in hand with a growing boldness in explicating this Word. These explications, like those of Ziervogel earlier, became new "works of literature in their own right" (183). While on yet another wagon journey, this time to the Cape to supply transport for Rev. John Campbell of the LMS to inspect their mission, Cupido finds ample opportunity to practice his preaching talents. Ironically, it is on this journey that he also learns about the death of Ziervogel, his first travelling partner. The next journey in the novel is one that Campbell, Read and Cupido undertake to inspect other mission outposts.

Cupido's spiritual link with his former religion becomes evident in episodes involving a small mantis and a whirlwind (203–5). During this journey Cupido's two hour long sermon on a farm persuades Campbell to recommend him as missionary in service of the LMS. Soon he is called to one of the outposts they visited on their journey. When Read expresses his reservations about the call, Cupido answers from Acts 16:9–10 interpreting this call as coming "from God Himself" (207–8). Cupido's only hint of fear stems from the mantis episode, expressing the fact that the symbols from his earlier belief system still lurk beneath the surface. After conquering his fear by viewing the episode as a test from God (208) and asking for a new Bible (because he ate the first Bible he received—see Ezek 3:1–3), Cupido sets off, accompanied by Read, to fulfill his calling. En route another bad omen transpires when the mirror Ziervogel gave to Cupido is shattered—a mishap that almost breaks him as well.

The second part of the book ends with Cupido, now stationed at Dithakong, again writing a letter to God after a scuffle with Rev. Anderson at Klaarwater. He informs God (and the reader) that he has taken a second wife to assist him. While quoting extensively from the somewhat contrasting passages on marriage in 1 Cor 7:8–9 and Gen 1–2 respectively, he rationalizes his decision to get married by recalling God's words in Genesis that it is not good for a man to be alone. In any case, he reasons, God knows better than Paul (216).

Dithakong

At first glance, the last section of the book represents a tragic downward spiral in the life of the missionary Cupido Cockroach. At the onset of his tenure at Dithakong he recalls the words of his first wife, Anna, concerning religion. In the first chapter of this section Cupido contrasts the Khoi-Khoi creation myth with the biblical creation stories (221–22). It begins to dawn on him that when it comes to religion there are more than one possibility, although he still defends his current calling against the accusations from Katryn, his second wife. Like Anna she is a realist and sees only a bleak future for them. Cupido replies to her doubts with a biblical notion that God is (again) testing them (223).

The direct quotations from the Bible in this chapter on the one hand strengthen his hope in his mother's prophecy about his life (Deut 32:10–11, Ezek 17:3). On the other hand biblical references are clustered together to defend his actions against the doubts raised by Katryn when he slaughters their last lamb for a party of hunt-ers passing by (Matt 5:43, Eccl 11:1, Gen 22:8, Luke 18:22). As the missionary he reads a portion from Scripture before the group eats—an act that earns him their respect for the forceful way in which he carries it out. After the luscious dinner, however, he is transported again to the time of his youth through the stories of the hunters (228).

In the second chapter Cupido undertakes his own journey to spread the word to a people whose language he cannot even speak. His claim that heavenly tongues of fire will help them understand (Acts 2:3) is met by sarcasm from Katryn (210). However, the theme of rediscovering his religious roots is continued as he no longer breaks down the cairns they pass (233). His congregation at Dithakong becomes drastically smaller as people begin to leave during the periods of his absence.

As the situation worsens, and there is no sign of their promised provisions, the Bible remains a source for rationalizing the circumstances and bringing comfort (Deut 8:3; Ps 121:1)—at least to Cupido. Katryn's remark that "the Word won't give us food and clothes" is countered by Cupido's reference to Matt 26:41: "Watch and pray, that ye enter not into temptation" (238). Lamenting the fact that a let-ter of possible rescue was lost to *sarês* Cupido cites from the book of Job ("The Lord giveth and the Lord taketh away"—Job 1:21). His wife, Katryn, mirrors the wife of Job, asking: "How can you go on believing?" (241). The rest of the episode reflects the sentiments already voiced by his first wife, namely that the reason for their situation and the lack of support is the fact that they are not white. Katryn remarks, "Their God is white" (243).

Cupido becomes more and more isolated as Katryn does not accompany him on his journeys any longer and his congregation is dwindling further. In the end everyone abandons him—even his wife and children. At this stage Rev. Moffat arrives to confirm his suspicions about what he perceives to be Cupido's incompe-tence. The text confirms the reservations that Cupido's wives have raised all along: the trouble, in fact, is that Cupido is not white. His Scripture reading and forceful preaching of days gone by had become "meaningless phrases" (263). His last letter to God, written on his last piece of paper, combines allusions to biblical themes with references to the Khoi-Khoi religion. He has reached the "the End of the Word" (271). The last chapter of this section and the book confirms that "He has gone beyond words" (272). No biblical reference occurs in this chapter. The W/ word is silenced, but a new journey calls when a mule cart driven by a man called *Arend* (Eagle) takes Cupido away. Here the novel also closes.

An Interpretation of Use of the Bible in *Praying Mantis*

Following the same three part division of the novel used above, this part of the paper attempts to interpret the use of the Bible in the novel. In this it goes beyond the mere description of biblical concepts and allusions that characterize the stan-dard works cited above.

Koup to Kamdeboo

An implicit interpretation of the Bible occurs the very first time that this religious text is mentioned. Significantly it is in the context of punishing a "laborer" that the misuse of the "Word of God" to lend authority to the humiliating actions of the colonists is explicitly noted. The ambivalent nature of the biblical text in the colonial setting is immediately captured. The text proclaiming the gospel of freedom is used to curbed the freedom of those who are viewed as inferior, "indolent and dirty" (4).

The combination of different religious metaphors in chapter three, where Christian and Khoi-Khoi notions of eschatological peace are cited in the same context, opens a theme in the novel claiming that an inclusive approach to religion is closer to the truth than an exclusive one. This theme is continued in the characters of Cupido's wives, it is also realized by the missionary Read and in the end enacted by Cupido himself.

The novel is unambiguous in its insistence that people learn by relating phenomena to their frames of reference. The "fluid religiosity" of the Khoi-Khoi gives further impetus to their incorporation of symbols from other cultures.[33] The connection that Cupido makes between Jesus and *Heitsi-Eibib* in chapter four serves as testimony thereof. The Bible as *text* and the fascination with this unknown phenomenon in oral culture is introduced in chapter five. Cupido is captured by the yearning to be able to write. When merging diverse religious phenomena clashes are bound to occur, as is illustrated by the life-giving role of the snake in guarding the scarce water resources (25). On the other hand different religions also share commonalities, as is made clear with regard to the reverence for the name of *Heitsi-Eibib*.

The introduction of Ziervogel changes the course of the narrative and of Cupido's life. The emphasis now falls on the role stories play in the processes through which religions become inculcated. Initially the references to the Bible are playful and bear testimony to people's misuse of religion to satisfy their own needs. Later Cupido has to face the dilemma of choosing between the worlds of *Heitsi-Eibib* and the Book. At that stage he still chooses the first. His reply to Ziervogel's encouragement to become a preacher can be read as an indication of the sense of inferiority that an unjust and racially defined system has instilled in him, or it may be regarded as a testimony to his clinging to a traditional belief. The latter interpretation is borne out by the fact that *en route* with Ziervogel he continues adding stones to every "cairn erected for the god" and offers sacrifices to the serpents residing in the water sources that they pass by (58).

Ziervogel's departure and Anna's arrival leads to further confusion in the mind

---

33. Elizabeth Elbourne and Robert Ross, "Combating Spiritual and Social Bondage: Early Missions in the Cape Colony," in *Christianity in South Africa: A Political, Social, and Cultural History,* ed. Richard Elphick and Rodney Davenport (Oxford: James Currey, 1997), 31–50.

of Cupido. The narrator carefully establishes a sense of unease also in the mind of the reader with an allusion to the ten plagues (80). Surely, the reader stands to reason, Anna's way of securing freedom for her and Cupido is fiction. The "true story" is the biblical one. The reader experiences the same question as Cupido: "Can different religions lay claim to similar miracles?"

The allusions to the Bible increase when the story line picks up events in Graaff-Reinet where the missionaries Van der Kemp and Read work among the Khoi-Khoi people. This prepares the reader for the second part of the book where Read is the first person narrator. However, the first section of the book does not conclude without reiterating the tension between and within belief systems. The tension *between* these are highlighted by the attempt to incorporate new and old beliefs, here exemplified by an old man's equation of *Tsui-Goab* and Jesus. The tension *within* is captured by the racial divide in the congregation and each group laying claim to Scripture in support of their point of view. The Khoi sing from Ps 134 "Behold, bless ye the Lord, *all* ye servants of the Lord, which by night stand in the house of the Lord" (note the inclusive nature). The whites respond with Ps 74: "Thine enemies roar in the midst of thy congregation" (excluding some of those inside the congregation by referring to them as enemies).

The word that Cupido found so captivating can also be a source of division. To be sure, at this stage he is oblivious to this fact: he sings together with the Khoi-Khoi, but instead of the psalm he sings a rain song for *Heitsi-Eibib*, thus highlighting the difference between and not within religious communities. The latter he would come to experience only later in the novel. The meeting with Van der Kemp and his use of a cleansing metaphor establishes a further life-altering event for Cupido. He seizes the idea of becoming "white" but rightly understands the idea to transcend skin color—a notion Anna is skeptical about (101).

The catechism class has a huge impact on Cupido. While the words of Van der Kemp are the "purest light" to Cupido, Anna sees him as "a dark man" speaking dangerous words (105). The quote from Ps 103 and the formulary for the Holy Baptism refer to the sacraments in the Reformed tradition and represents Cupido's conversion from one belief system to another. In this act Anna does not follow his lead. She has reservations about giving up her belief system and the possibility of ascribing to more than one such system. Although Cupido sees room for all three belief systems, Anna warns that the Christians one day will force him to make a decision for one or the other. As it turns out he needs very little encouragement be baptized. The "old" Cupido drowns (almost in actual fact!) in the Sunday's river and the "new" person whom the reader will meet in the second part of the book is a vehement disciple of the Christian God.

The use of the Bible in the first section of the novel portrays the way in which the main character loses his (traditional) belief as he becomes more and more enthralled by the written stories in the Bible. Embracing a reading culture opens up the religious world associated with that culture. What is left behind is an oral religious world, but one including similar stories. Cupido's life altering decision as seen through the eyes of someone within the newly adopted culture and religion becomes the subject matter of the second section of the novel.

The Reverend James Read

The picture painted of Cupido's zeal for the Lord at the onset of the second section of the novel is in some ways typical of new converts to religious movements. As such it presents a picture of religion that borders on the absurd. However, the narrator soon informs us that in their actions both Cupido and Van der Kemp were driven by a "ferocious sense of pride . . . derived from unwavering faith" (125).

Cupido's use of the Bible after the Khoi-Khoi attack on the mission station demonstrates the way in which religion and more specifically a religious text is (mis)used to favor the individual's own position. The juxtaposition of this event vis-à-vis the unfounded claim by the white farmers to be God's elected people contributes to the tension evoked by Read's initial remarks at the onset of this section of the novel, namely "Does the soul ever know its own blind reasoning" (114).

The establishment of the mission at Bethelsdorp and the link between Cupido and the biblical patriarch Jacob also set the scene for one of the theologically laden parts of the novel. Amidst references to the kingdom of God as portrayed in the gospels and the significance that Cupido provides to Read's own sense of being, a contrast between the two characters is evident. Read ironically tries to rationalize the gospel by postponing answers to difficult issues to the hereafter. Cupido, by contrast, focuses on the here and now, the existential. Referring to the needs of the Khoi-Khoi he remarks: "[w]hat they are suffering . . . is in the body . . . We go hungry. We need help" (156). His outcry to God is based on the injustice that prohibits people from carving out their own reality. What he seeks is immediate divine retribution enacted upon the white farmers for their injustices. This of cause begs the question: if religion is focused only on the hereafter, does it have any meaning in the present?

This line of thought is exemplified by Cupido's intense response to the death of his wife. Nevertheless, his zeal for God continues. In a scene reminiscent of the calling of Ezekiel Cupido actually eats the Word of God. This act is meant to enable him to understand the word. Once the word becomes part of his body, no one will be able to take it away from him.

Through his preaching on the road, Cupido continues the voice of Ziervogel who died at the hands of the Xhosa. From his letters it is clear that the voice of his mother (and Anna—though she is not explicitly mentioned) still resonates in him. He persists in breaking down the cairns of *Heitsi-Eibib*, but now with a sense of sorrow, thinking about his mother. He mentions his zeal for the Lord, *as well as* for *Tsui Goab* (193). During the journey with Campbell and Read this intrinsic ambiguity manifests itself through his old fear of an indoor mantis and a whirlwind.

An explicit example of biblical interpretation is found in Cupido's answer to Read's doubts following his call to Klaarwater. Here again, a biblical text is understood in such a way to justify one's actions, decisions and desires. Indeed, the soul does not know its own blind reasoning. Interestingly enough it is an omen from the Khoi-Khoi religion (the mantis) that casts a shadow over his new venture. The omen of the broken mirror extracts the following self reflection from Cupido: "I was in that mirror . . . [n]ow I left myself behind" (211). His most treasured possession is shattered. He approaches his new future without a thing from his previous life. All he has is a new Bible. Will this word be enough to sustain him in his new surroundings?

While Read takes comfort in the fact that Cupido has the Word with him at his new location in the middle of nowhere, Cupido finds comfort in a new wife. This decision, he feels, should be explained to God. Facing situations where more than one outcome is possible, it is not difficult to find backing in a religious text for any eventual decision. In late twentieth-century literary theory this phenomenon was explained by considering the role of the reader in creating meaning.

Dithakong

Cupido's situation at Dithakong calls for interpretation. The only meaning he can ascribe to the desperate state of affairs is that God is testing them. However, he also draws on his mother's words to find comfort. This comfort, located in his pre-Christian life, is interwoven with and supported by biblical references. Biblical support is also mustered for his illogical decision to share their only lamb when a well-to-do hunting party passes by. The Bible functions as support for images and ideas from his earlier life, while at the same time it is used to transcend the harsh situation he now has to face. This duality is developed further in the last part of the novel.

The ruthless reality of bringing the word to a people whose words he cannot understand is again foiled by a biblical reference. The Bible serves as a screen to blur a harsh reality. His earlier zeal becomes more tempered as he dreams about an eagle that will carry him away, fulfilling his mother's prophecy.

Amidst a situation that becomes more and more hopeless due to no reply to Cupido's letters written on a rapidly diminishing supply of paper ("There isn't much left between him and ultimate silence") (238), he suddenly receives a letter. This word from another world that could possibility alleviate their situation is blown away by a whirlwind—that ominous sign from his previous belief system. Slowly a movement beyond words is set in motion.

In a next episode where Katryn sees through to the heart of the matter, namely that it is a question of race, Cupido does not answer from the Holy Writ. He draws on the "symbolic word," the sacrament of baptism, in his defense. Thus he remarks, just before his family also leaves him: "Maybe the word is not enough anymore" (251). With Moffat's visit this becomes abundantly clear—Cupido's zeal for the word is lost, and with it the word itself. Even the symbolic word of the sacrament of the Holy Communion becomes a synthesis between the Khoi-Khoi and Christian religions (267). The last letter he writes takes this issue even further. What is offered is more than a synthesis—it is a next step in an evolutionary process: from the flesh to the word to going beyond the word, albeit that he does not know how (271). The last chapter confirms the acknowledgment of the unknown.

"Where beyond? Impossible to tell" (272). It is not a return to the past. His last act at Dithakong, re-erecting the cairn he once destroyed, is meant to give the past its rightful place in his life. To let things be the way they were before he came. What lies ahead involves something beyond the past and the present. This is reflected in the disappearance of the praying mantis from the cart. "But they do not need him anymore" (275).

Concluding Remarks

This novel presents the reader with a picture of how Christianity was introduced to the southern part of Africa in the eighteenth-century. The use and misuse of the Bible in the hands of the Europeans is mimicked by new converts to this foreign and exclusive belief system. The Bible as *written* word had a huge impact on oral communities. In the end, however, the novel hints at something beyond the letter: something to be found perhaps in a synthesis of the letter and the creative African spirit. Brink has succeeded not only in creating a text that reflects the basic tenets of African literature, but also in reflecting the manner in which the Bible is understood in this context.

Perhaps the ending of the book is the embryonic manifestation of Nnolim's vision for a new Africa.[34] In what better way can her creative horizon be widened than "invading Europe" with that which she has always had: her traditions, cultures, religions, and stories. But, at the same time, traditions and stories reshaped in the context of colonialization in order to go beyond, to invent a future—to bring from Africa "always something new."

Works Cited

Achebe, Chinua. *Things Fall Apart*. 1958. Repr., Oxford: Heinemann, 1986.

Bishop, Rand. *African Literature, African Critics. The Forming of Critical Standards, 1847–1966*. New York: Greenwood, 1988.

Brink, André. *Praying Mantis*. London: Vintage, 2006.

Buttrick, George Arthur, ed. *The Interpreter's Dictionary of the Bible*. Nashville: Abingdon, 1962.

Elphick, Richard, and Rodney Davenport, eds. *Christianity in South Africa: A Political, Social, and Cultural History*. Oxford: James Currey, 1997.

Emenyonu, Ernst N. *New Directions in African Literature*. Oxford: James Currey, 2006.

Giliomee, Hermann. *The Afrikaners: Biography of a People*. Charlottesville: University of Virginia Press, 2003.

Hawkins, Peter S., "Lost and Found: The Bible and its Literary Afterlife." *RL* 36, no. 1 (2004): 1–14.

---

34. Cf. Nnolim, "African Literature," 9.

Hofmeyr J. W., and G. J. Pillay, eds. *A History of Christianity in South Africa*. Pretoria: HAUM Tertiary, 1994.

Isichei, Elizabeth. *A History of Christianity in Africa*. Grand Rapids: Eerdmans, 1995.

Jasper, David, and Stephen Prickett. *The Bible and Literature: A Reader*. Oxford: Blackwell, 1999.

Jeffrey, David Lyle, ed. *A Dictionary of Biblical Tradition in English Literature*. Grand Rapids: Eerdmans, 1992.

Lefkowitz, Mary R. *Not Out of Africa. How Afrocentrism Became an Excuse to Teach Myth as History*. New York: Basic Books, 1996.

Lombaard, Christo, "The Relevance of Old Testament Science in/for Africa: Two False Pieties and Focused Scholarship." *OTE* 19, no. 1 (2006): 144–55.

Maimela, Simon, and Adrio König, eds. *Initiation into Theology: The Rich Variety of Theology and Hermeneutics*. Pretoria: Van Schaik, 1998.

Patte, Daniel. *Ethics of Biblical Interpretation: A Reevaluation*. Louisville: Westminster John Knox, 1995.

Sugirtharajah, Rasiah S. *Postcolonial Criticism and Biblical Interpretation*. Oxford: Oxford University Press, 2003.

West, Gerald O., and Musa W. Dube, eds. *The Bible in Africa: Transactions, Trajectories, and Trends*. Leiden: Brill, 2001.

Wicks, Ulrich. "The Nature of Picaresque Narrative: A Modal Approach." *PMLA* 89, no. 2 (1974): 240–49.

3. COLONIZED BIBLES:
RE-READING THE COLONIAL TRANSLATED BIBLES

BIBLE TRANSLATION IN AFRICA:
AN AFROCENTRIC INTERROGATION OF THE TASK

Gosnell L. Yorke

INTRODUCTION

At the outset, a caveat is in order: (1) the sheer size and shape of the continent (being more than twice the size of the continental United States);[1] and (2) the linguistic and cultural complexity of the continent (having about one-third of the world's six thousand or so languages) both conspire against us to make our discussion less than entirely exhaustive in scale and scope.[2] In addition, less attention will be devoted to the precise technical and academic aspects of the challenging exercise of Bible translation and more so on matters having to do with the overall *modus operandi* characterizing what African churches in general rightly regard, perhaps, as a sacred ministry. Also, we will look at the issue from both a historical and a contemporary perspective. In essence, an attempt will be made to engage in an Afrocentric *interrogation* of the whole translation tradition on the continent.

Interrogation, as a word, is one which seems to be cropping up everywhere in a discussion of a continent preoccupied with its postcolonial and post-apartheid dispensation, and rightly so. Two examples, perhaps, should suffice: (1) Gikuyu in his African reading of Gen 2–3; and (2) Molefe Kete Asante in his somewhat revisionist reading of African history.[3] This preoccupation with interrogation tends to manifest itself in the realms of politics, economics, academia, and elsewhere—especially in an increasingly globalized world.

Informing the discussion will also be the author's decade-long, field-based, practical experience as a Translation Consultant (TC) with the United Bible Societies (UBS) in Africa—based, at the time, in South Africa but serving mostly

---

1. Paul Bohannan and Phillip Curtin, *Africa and Africans* (3rd ed.; Project Heights, IL: Waveland Press, 1988), 19.

2. See G. Yorke and P. Renju, eds., *Bible Translation and African Languages* (Nairobi, Kenya: Acton, 2004).

3. Samuel Gikuyu, "The Tree of the Knowledge of Good and Evil: An African Reading of Genesis 2–3," *BOTSA* 1 (2003): 11–17; and Molefe Kete Asante, *The History of Africa: The Quest for Eternal Harmony* (New York: Routledge, 2006).

in Angola, Mozambique, Guinea-Bissau, Botswana and Zimbabwe. This meant interacting with former UBS TCs and other colleagues from across the continent, in addition to the numerous African translators in so-called Anglophone, Francophone, Lusophone, and even Hispanophone Africa.[4]

And given the nature of that prolonged field-based, practical experience, we will, perforce, especially in the latter stages of the presentation, be emphasizing the ongoing work of UBS rather than that of other Bible translation agencies which are also working in Africa such as the Summer Institute of Linguistics (SIL) International.

THE THREE PHASES OF BIBLE TRANSLATION IN AFRICA: A BRIEF HISTORICAL OVERVIEW

Origins

The *fons et origo* (source and origin) of Bible translation in Africa goes back to Alexandria/Egypt involving the Greek translation of the Hebrew Bible and other cognate writings. Reference is here being made to the whole Septuagint (LXX) translational tradition and trajectory.[5] This trajectory encompasses the Latin Vulgate, the Coptic translation in Egypt, and the Geʿez or Ethiopic translation in Ethiopia.[6]

Both the Coptic and Ethiopian Orthodox versions have had a less extensive influence on the continent. The Coptic version continues to be used mainly within the liturgical circles of the Coptic Church as does the Ethiopic version in the Ethiopian Orthodox Church. However, neither has been translated into other African languages. Mention should also be made, *en passant,* of the fact that the Ethiopian Orthodox Church has a canon of eighty-one books—fifty-four falling within the Old Testament/Hebrew Bible and twenty-seven within the New Testament.[7]

Missionary Era

The next phase in Bible translation in Africa can be called the missionary era in which foreign missionaries usually benefitted from the socio-political and colonial arrangements and protection made possible by their home countries in the host countries. In the words of Spickard and Cragg, for example, "The scope of

---

4. See E. R. Wendland et al., "Translator Training in Africa," *BT: Practical Papers* 57 (2006): 58–78.

5. See, for example, H. Ausloos et al., *Translating a Translation: The LXX and Its Modern Translations in the Context of Early Judaism* (Louvain: Peeters, 2008).

6. See G. A. Mikre-Selassie, "Early Translation of the Bible into Ethiopic/Geʿez," in Yorke and Renju, *Bible Translation*, 25–39.

7. See P. A. Noss, "Traditions of Scripture Translation: A Pan-African Overview," in Yorke and Renju, *Bible Translation*, 11.

European and North American missionary activity in the nineteenth century was extraordinary. Wherever empire went, there too went missionaries."[8]

Between the first two periods, there was approximately one millennium during which very little translation activity occurred in Africa—except in Arabic especially between the ninth and thirteenth centuries C.E. This was a time which corresponded roughly with the rise and spread of Islam across North Africa while in Europe, it was the time of the emergence of the Renaissance, the Reformation and the invention of movable type by Gutenberg in Germany. In fact, the first book ever to be printed in the West was the Bible itself in Latin.[9]

In addition, the missionary era of Bible translation in Africa coincided with the increasing importance attached to local languages throughout Europe, the spreading influence of the Renaissance there, and the ease with which books could be printed in mass quantities. Further, explorers, spearheaded by the Portuguese, began circling the globe; merchants sought new routes to Asia and expanding markets in the Americas; and European nations, generally, began to engage in empire construction. It is during this period in which we witness the birth of what became known as the whole "Missionary Movement." And it is this emergence to which Molefe Kete Asante refers in his juxtaposition of the "missionary, the merchant and the mercenary."[10]

It is this confluence of forces, also captured in the three Cs of Commerce, Civilization, and Christianity, which helped to precipitate Europe's cultural diffusion throughout the so-called New World—including Africa.[11] In this regard, Ali Mazrui, in his inimitable and provocative way, also writes:

> God, Gold and Glory! Captured in a slogan, these are the three basic imperatives in the history of cultural diffusion. Why do men [sic] burst forth from their boundaries in search of new horizons? They are inspired either by a search for religious fulfillment (the God Standard) or by a yearning for economic realization (the Gold Standard) or by that passion for renown (the quest for Glory).[12]

It is during this second or missionary phase of Bible translation in Africa that we also witness the beginning, in 1804, of the British and Foreign Bible Society (BFBS) whose primary mission was to provide Bibles where they were needed in the languages of the people. The BFBS's vision was missiological, continental, and

8. P. R. Spickard and K. M. Cragg, *How Everyday Believers Experienced Their World: A Global History of Christians* (Grand Rapids: Baker, 1998), 301.

9. Ibid.

10. Asante, *The History of Africa*, 209–21.

11. A. Edoho, "NGOs as Strategic Mechanisms for Achieving Sustainable Development in Africa," *JAPS* 11 (2005): 29. In Edoho's opinion, for instance, "the role of foreign NGOs in African 'development' represents a continuity of the work of their precursors, the missionaries and voluntary organizations that cooperated in Europe's colonization and control of Africa."

12. A. Mazrui, *Cultural Forces in World Politics* (London: James Currey, 1999), 29.

inter-confessional in scope, spawning Bible Society work both in Ethiopia in 1812 and in South Africa in 1820.

It is also during this BFBS period in which we encounter the not-so-highly educated self-taught lay translator in the person of Robert Moffat (1795–1883), the Scotsman, Presbyterian and gardener. Moffat was sent to South Africa by the London Missionary Society in 1817 and, initially, worked among the Hottenots and later among Batswana in Kuruman in what is today Botswana. Mention can also be made of the more educated missionary and translator in the person of Johann Ludwig Krapf (1810–81), a German Lutheran minister who was sent to Ethiopia in 1837 by the Anglican Church Missionary Society and who ended up working throughout much of East Africa, eventually exerting a major influence on the later development of the three different African language families, namely, Ethiosemitic with Amharic and Ge'ez; Cushitic with Oromo; and Bantu with Kiduruma, Kikamba and Kiswahili.[13] A missionary like Cardinal Charles Lavigerie (1825–92) also merits passing mention. He was the founder of the Orders of the so-called "White Fathers" and the "White Sisters," and was a French Roman Catholic who worked mostly in North Africa and who later became Archbishop of both Algiers in Algeria and Carthage in Libya.[14]

During the greater part of the missionary era, missionaries to Africa also sought to learn foreign languages, created orthographies for those languages, and then translated Scriptural products such as catechisms and later Bibles into some of those languages.[15]

Modern Era

The third phase of Bible translation in Africa, which Noss chooses to refer to as the "modern era," is the phase in which someone like Eugene Nida, the Baptist minister and linguist *par excellence,* gets featured. Initially, Nida worked with SIL International and later with the American Bible Society (ABS) which was established in 1816. In fact, Nida has had such a profound influence on this modern phase of Bible translation that not only is his name mentioned in most works devoted to contemporary translation studies, a relatively recent academic discipline, but also at the ABS itself, based in New York City. ABS has now created an Institute in his name.

It was Nida who incorporated developments in linguistics and communication theory into the whole translation task. His translational approach, usually

13. For Kiswahili in East Africa, see A. Mojola, *God Speaks in Our Own Languages: Bible Translation in East Africa, 1844–1998—A General Survey* (Nairobi; Dodoma, Tanzania; and Kampala, Uganda: Bible Societies of Kenya, Tanzania, and Uganda, 2000).

14. Also see Musa Dube, "Consuming a Colonial Cultural Bomb: Translating Badimo into 'Demons' in the Setswana Bible (Matthew 8.28–34; 15.22; 10.8)," *JNTS* 21 (1999): 33–58.

15. Sinfree Makoni, Nkonko Kamwangamalu, *Language and Institutions in Africa* (Cape Town: CASAS, 2000).

captured in the expression, functional or dynamic equivalence, as opposed to the more literalistic formal equivalent approach, places an emphasis on the three meaning-enhancing criteria of faithfulness to the original languages of Scripture, and both clarity and naturalness in the mother-tongue or receptor language itself.

Throughout this period, translators have also benefited (and continue to do so) from various Bible translation workshops held from time to time and of various durations. In addition, the drafts of manuscripts are professionally examined by both linguists and biblical exegetes before they are ever published by the national Bible Society in question.

On a broader scale, the modern or contemporary phase or era of Bible translation in Africa coincided with the era of independence of a number of African countries from colonial control. Beginning in 1957 with Ghana's independence, and especially in 1960, referred to as the *annus mirabilis* by Guy Arnold,[16] African countries gained their independence from their colonial masters in increasing numbers. And at roughly the same time, African churches increasingly assumed independence from their founding missions in Europe and North America.

This somewhat greater sense of autonomy was demonstrated in the establishment of more and more Bible Societies within Africa itself. For example, in 1961 the Bible Society of South Africa was recognized as a separate entity from the BFBS which had nurtured it and, in the same year, the Bible Society for West Africa, based in Nigeria, was formed. Soon after, Bible Societies were opened in other newly independent African countries like Botswana, Cameroon, Ghana, Kenya, Sierra Leone, Tanzania, Zambia and Zimbabwe, to name only a few. Today, there are about 34 such Bible Entities called Societies or Offices depending on their level of economic maturity and ability to support and sustain themselves, independent of outside funding.

In this modern era, more and more African translators, as competent mother-tongue speakers, are being trained to be better translators and more and more African scholars, trained as biblical scholars and/or linguists, are assuming more and more of the responsibility for the whole translation task. It is to UBS's credit, itself officially founded in May 1946, that a cadre of highly trained TCs, both African and non-African, can now be found throughout Africa and serving the various Bible Societies and/or Offices there.

As pointed out earlier, the Bible Society movement was inter-confessional or ecumenical from its very inception. However, it soon became a primarily Protestant phenomenon particularly throughout the nineteenth and twentieth centuries. Nevertheless, following Vatican II in the 1960s, there was a dramatic swing back to interconfessionality. In 1968, for example, UBS and the Vatican signed an agreement, later revised in 1987, in which the two entities pledged to work together. The document is called, "Guidelines for Interconfessional Cooperation in Translating the Bible." And since then, interconfessional Bibles have been published in African

---

16. Guy Arnold, *Africa: A Modern History* (London: Atlantic Books, 2005).

languages like Chichewa in Malawi, Gbaya in Cameroon, and Kiswahili in both Tanzania and Kenya.

Mention should also be made of the fact that the two eras, the missionary and the modern, still overlap or co-exist to some extent; and that they both have as their foci sub-Saharan or tropical Africa. There are cases, for instance, where the foreign-born, non-African missionary is fully in charge of the process with or without the active involvement of one or more national language informers–such as was the case in Guinea-Bissau where the Bible has been translated into Crioulo, a Portuguese-based creole; or the ongoing translation of the Bible there into some of the indigenous languages like Papel, Manjakos and a cross-border language called Balanta—it being spoken in Portugeuse-speaking Guinea-Bissau, French-speaking Senegal, and even a bit of it in English-speaking, The Gambia.

Then there is the current scenario involving the competent mother-tongue African translator and the foreign European or North American TC—one in which the African translator, although s/he is trained and tasked to do the actual translation on a day-to-day basis and is being paid by the national Bible Society, does so under the watchful eye of the European or American TC. This is still true, not only of Africa south of the Sahara Desert and north of the Limpopo River, but also of South Africa itself and "its satellites," namely, Lesotho and Swaziland.

It is against this backdrop, of a continent now in its postcolonial phase, that we find Ngũgĩ wa Thiongo's question and concern quite apropos: He writes:

> I was horrified when I returned [from the University of Leeds, England] to Kenya in 1967, to find that the department of English as organized [at the University of Nairobi] was still organized on the basis that Europe was the centre of the universe. Europe, the centre of our imagination? . . .The basic question was: from what base did African peoples look at the world? Eurocentrism or Afrocentrism?[17]

Alvarez and Vidal; Hatim and Mason; Venuti; Surgirtharajah; Bassnet and Trivedi and others,[18] in their studies in translation and cross-cultural communication, are insisting that translating in a postcolonial mode should be characterized not only by an ideological suspicion but should act as a means of self-affirmation as well. Scholars in translation studies are as sensitive as ever, and rightly so, to the pivotal role which translation plays in helping to shape culture and identity. Sanneh and Badiako, for example, have argued that there is a clear correlation between the translation of the Bible into indigenous African languages and the cultural renais-

---

17. Ngũgĩ wa Thiongo, *Moving the Centre: The Struggle for Cultural Freedoms* (Nairobi: East Africa Educational Publishers, 1993) 8.

18. See R. Alvarez and M. Vidal, eds., *Translation, Power, Subversion* (Cleveland: Multilingual Matters, 1996); B. Hatim and I. Mason, *The Translator as Communicator* (New York: Routledge, 1997); L. Venuti, ed., "Translator and Minority," *TTran* 4 (1998); R. S. Sugirtharajah, *The Postcolonial Bible* (Sheffield: Sheffield Academic Press, 1998); S. Bassnett and H. Trivedi, eds., *Postcolonial Translation* (New York: Routledge, 1999). See also Timothy Wilt, ed., *Bible Translation: Frames of Reference* (Manchester, England: St. Jerome, 2003).

sance which we see at work in the rapidly proliferating African Independent, Initiated, Instituted, International or Indigenous Churches.[19]

Perhaps, for explicable historical and other reasons, the modern phase of Bible
translation in postcolonial Africa is still very much set in what might still be regarded as the "Eurocentric" mode; still being done in the "Eurocentric paradigm"
in that not enough emphasis is being placed on lifting the profile and amplifying
the voice of Africa, Africans and Africana generally–that which we find in the
original languages of Scripture, to wit, Aramaic, Hebrew and Greek. There seems
to be a need for a greater "frontshifting" of things African than that which we find
in Bibles currently available in the various African languages, some of which have
already been mentioned. Typically, such African translations are done under the
lexical and hermeneutical influence of various Western versions.

AN AFROCENTRIC INTERROGATION OF BIBLE TRANSLATION IN AFRICA

To provide some justification for such an interrogation, here are just a few examples by way of illustration. They are drawn from both the Old Testament/Hebrew
Bible and the New Testament. And since African translators are expected to con-
sult resources like Bible commentaries, books and other scholarly helps in their
work, mention will also be made of such resources in passing. In terms of the Hebrew Bible or the *Tanakh*, we will fix and focus our attention briefly on the Torah
or the Law, and the *Nebi'im* or the Prophets—not on the *Ketubim* or the Writings.
That is, only the two first sections of the *Tanakh* will fall within our purview.

The Torah

In Gen 2:10–14, for example, mention is made of four rivers, namely, the Pishon, the Gihon, the Hiddekel, and the Euphrates. What is quite noticeable in most
Western translations (be it in Dutch, English, French, German, Spanish or whatever), is that Hiddekel, associated with Euphrates in Mesopotamia, is correctly
substituted for the Tigris—thus making the text clearer for both modern reader
and hearer (see Dan 10:4).

Also noticeable in such translations is the fact that the same translational logic
is not applied when it comes to the proper identification of the Pishon and the
Gihon rivers. Unlike their treatment of Hiddekel, there seems to be a questionable
hesitation in identifying these two rivers with the Blue and the White Nile respectively. Among others, Albright was of the view that the two "unknown" rivers
before us are in fact the two branches of the Nile.[20] Moreover, it is quite instructive

---

19. L. Sanneh, *Translating the Message: The Missionary Impact on Culture* (Maryknoll,
NY: Orbis, 1989); K. Bediako, "The Doctrine of Christ and the Significance of Vernacular
Terminology," *IBMR* (1998): 109–11.

20. See G. Yorke, "Bible Translation in Africa: An Afrocentric Perspective," *BT: Technical
Papers* 52 (2000): 120. Those translators and commentators who have substituted Hiddekel

that the only other place where the Pishon and the Gihon are juxtaposed, is in the deuterocanonical text of Sirach or Eccelsiasticus (24:25). And there, Davidson was of the opinion that they point to the two branches of the Nile.[21] At a more linguistic level, it is also instructive to note that in contemporary Ethiopic or Geʻez, an Ethiosemitic language akin to Hebrew, the lexical item for the Nile is Geon—thus providing a linguistic echo of the Hebrew word itself.[22]

When this was pointed out to a group of African translators during a Workshop in Ngaoundere in northern Cameroon some years ago (encompassing translators from Benin, Camerooon and Chad), it was not in the least surprising that there was a spontaneous and quite audible "grunt" of delight coming from them and born of pleasant surprise.[23] At that instant, the African translators experienced a moment of intellectual enlightenment and even psychological empowerment in that they were made to see and sense that their continent is featured in Genesis, the "Book of Beginnings"—rather than made to feel that Africa was an afterthought in God's mind and mission as was unwittingly communicated in the nineteenth and the twentieth centuries by some of the Western missionaries to the continent.

The Nebi'im

In Isa 1:18 (and to disambiguate it), the text, perhaps, should be translated or at least explained in a note to mean "as leprous as snow" rather than "as white as snow"—thus giving the false impression that the simile is positive in its connotation. Instead, and harking back to Exod 4:6 and Num 12:10, it is reminiscent of Miriam being made "white as snow" or leprous-like as a result of her racially induced discountenancing of Moses' marriage to the Ethiopian woman. And in Jer 13:23, another text which has been touched and tarnished by what some might perceive as the racist pathology of the West, translators and commentators (who have tended overwhelmingly to be both Caucasian and male) would have us believe that to posses the dark skin of the Ethiopian (African) is to be frowned upon. To the contrary, the point in drawing the analogy between the leopard and the Ethiopian (African) is really this: just as the leopard has no desire to change his spots (why would it—the spots are the basis of its eye-catching beauty) so is there no desire on the part of the Ethiopian to change his/her skin—again, why would s/he want or wish to do so since his/her skin is as beautiful as ever?[24]

---

for Tigris include *Tanakh: The Holy Scriptures* (Philadelphia: Jewish Publication Society); James B. Boice, *Genesis: An Expositional Commentary—Volume 1* (Grand Rapids: Baker Books); and Gordon J. Wenham, *Genesis 1–15 in Word Biblical Commentary* (Waco, TX: Thomas Nelson, 1987).

21. I. Davidson, *Cambridge Bible Commentary* (Cambridge: Cambridge University Press, 1974), ad loc.

22. For more, see G. Yorke, "Bible Translation in Africa: An Afrocentric Perspective," *BT: Technical Papers* 52 (2000): 113–23.

23. Ibid.

24. And to make the point as clearly as possible, especially in the absence of the Hebrew

The punch line then comes after the pair of rhetorical questions has been posed to the effect that just as there is no wish or desire felt by either leopard or Ethiopian to change either spots or skin, so is there no desire on Israel's part to change from her sinful ways and, for that very reason, God's judgment is both soon and certain. And finally: Zeph 1:1 identifies the longest genealogical line among the prophets and one which was grounded in Zephaniah's African (Cush) and royal ancestry. Perhaps not surprisingly, Baker, in conceding that the prophet was of African descent, goes on to opine that he was "a negro" and one who must have been a slave in the service of the temple![25]

The New Testament

As for the New Testament, 1 Pet 5:8 is, perhaps, instructive. Query: is the devil being made to roar like a lion seeking whom he may devour? Or should the text be better translated so as to point to a "growling" lion instead? It seems that the participle in question (ὠρυόμενος) can better be translated and interpreted as follows: "the devil is like a *growling* lion sneaking up on, and seeking to devour us." Lions do not roar when they are stalking their prey. If they did, they would never get a catch and, instead, scare the prospective prey away and, in the process, certainly die from starvation! It takes the eye and ear of an African translator, one who is familiar with lion behavior and wildlife generally on his/her continent, to pick up that nuance and to do so somewhat naturally.

FROM PRODUCT TO PROCESS

An Afrocentric interrogation of the Bible translation task has implications not only for the end product but for the very process itself. In time, the *modus operandi* ought to change as well. There should, in time, be a replicating of the "Western model" in which both biblical scholar/linguist and competent mother-tongue speaker, are one and the same person, as is the case with the ongoing international and electronically driven English Net Bible translation project.[26]

We must concede, however, that there are still some real and perplexing challenges which are generated both from without and from within the continent itself—challenges which serve to decelerate its overall development. A sample list would at least include the following:

---

word יכל (translated in English as "can") at the beginning of the verse, the better translation of what is really a rhetorical question commencing with the hiphil imperfect is not "Can the leopard or the Ethiopian change his spots or skin?" respectively but "would they want or wish to do so?" since, after all, they are quite happy the way they are already!

25. Ibid. See also Randall C. Bailey, "Beyond Identification: The Use of Africans in Old Testament Poetry and Narratives," in *Stony the Road We Trod: African American Biblical Interpretation,* ed. Cain Hope Felder (Minneapolis: Fortress Press, 1991), 165, and G. Yorke, "Biblical Hermeneutics: An Afrocentric Perspective," *JRT* 52 (1995): 1–13.

26. See www.netbible.com.

1. Economic dependency in that there still seems to be an overdependence of the continent on the "monied West" for financial support—including in the area of Bible translation. Of course, such overdependence is historically explicable in that, to a large extent, Europe succeeded in underdeveloping Africa by raping and robbing it of its natural resources or, putting it perhaps more accurately, Africa succeeded in overdeveloping Europe.[27]

2. Then there is the "politics of gate-keeping" in that there still seem to be some exclusionary strategies of Western gate-keepers and subtle and not so subtle forms of political resistance to change with a commensurate loss of control. The experience of the All Africa Conference of Churches is somewhat instructive. Meeting in Ethiopia some years ago, there was a call for a temporary moratorium on Western missionary influence and involvement in the life of the church in Africa. This call was meant to give the African church a bit of "breathing space" so as to assume a more self-sufficient stance. Surprisingly, the fiercest opposition came not from the Africans themselves but from the Western missionaries! This suggests that there are those for whom the whole pathology of overdependency, be it in Africa or elsewhere, is generally of greater benefit to the aid-givers than to the aid-recipients themselves.

3. Still needed is a greater critical mass of African biblical scholars, linguists and translators. However, there is an emerging cadre of such scholars as reflected, for example, at the first pan-African conference hosted by the University of KwaZulu Natal in South Africa in September 2005. This conference was an interdisciplinary and international conference which attracted a pan-African group of such scholars—including some Europe-based scholars as well. And before that, there was the first SNTS (*Studiorum Novi Testamenti Societas*/Society for New Testament Studies)-sponsored post-conference at the University of Pretoria, South Africa, in August 1999.[28]

4. Not to be overlooked is the linguistic challenge. As already mentioned, Africa boasts about two thousand indigenous languages. Only about 150 have complete Bibles in them. In addition, there are the various cross-border linguistic complications induced by the arbitrary carv-

27. See W. Rodney, *How Europe Underdeveloped Africa* (Dar-es-Salaam, Tanzania: Tanzania Publishing House, 1976); and G. Yorke, "Maintaining Excellence amidst a Call for Greater African and Caribbean Academic Collaboration," in *The Nineteenth Norma H. Darlington Founders' Day Lecture* (Kingston, Jamaica: Shortwood Teachers' College, 2009).

28. See full report in G. Yorke, "Bible Interpretation and Translation in Africa: University of KwaZulu-Natal, Pietermaritzburg," *BOTSA* (2006): 3–5.

ing up or balkanization of the continent by Europe during the Berlin Conference (1884–1886). The matter of the dialectal variations within the same African language which, in one country, can be heavily influenced by English; in another, by French; and in still a third, by Portuguese, further complicates the linguistic environment. And in such situations, attempts at the unionization of the language are fraught with political and other complexities.

CONCLUSION

In closing, much of what we have discussed can best be captured, perhaps, in the Portuguese sentence, to wit: *a Guerra acabou mas a Luta continua* ("the war is over but the struggle continues"). By this is meant that, with the advent of democracy in 1994 to the Republic of South Africa, Africa as a continent might well have entered its post-colonial and post-apartheid phase.[29] Similarly, we are suggesting that Africa might well have procured its political independence as a continent as reflected, for example, in the morphing of the OAU (Organization of African Unity) into the AU (African Union) in 2002. However, the continent is still held captive by various and varied factors and forces not the least of which include the ideological stranglehold and hermeneutical hegemony still enjoyed by the powerful West—a stranglehold and a hegemony which we still find expressing themselves in the realm of Bible translation in terms of both product and process.

This therefore makes an Afrocentric interrogation of the task all the more pressing and necessary—an interrogation which resonates with the valid concerns and deeply held convictions of Afro-scholars like Ngũgĩ wa Thiong'o, Molefe Kete Asante and a myriad of others. A larger Afro-vision, in my considered opinion, however, is the need for a pan-African, African diasporic and multidisciplinary team of reputable biblical scholars, linguists, poets and others, women and men, all of whom have some credibility in one confessing Afro-Anglo-Christian community or other. And with such a broad-based and richly diverse group of competent colleagues, we should then challenge ourselves to embark on the production of a more "Afro-friendly" translation of the Bible as a whole.

This venture will undoubtedly be a multi-year translation project which ought to be supported and sustained, at least partially, by sources of Afro-funding. Such a call is entirely consonant with a much earlier one, to wit, that which came from Edward Blyden, an Afro-West Indian-born former Presbyterian, statesman, diplo-

---

29. G. Yorke, "Hearing the Politics of Peace in Ephesians: A Proposal from an African Postcolonial Perspective," *JSNT* 30 (2007): 113–27. Also see J. Punt, "Sex and Gender, and Liminality in Biblical Texts: Venturing into Postcolonial, Queer Biblical Interpretation," *Neot* 41 (2007): 382–98.

mat, educator and naturalized Liberian citizen who lived and worked in the nineteenth century.[30]

WORKS CITED

Alvarez, R. and M. Vidal, eds. *Translation, Power, Subversion*. Cleveland: Multilingual Matters, 1996.
Arnold, Guy. *Africa: A Modern History*. London: Atlantic Books, 2005.
Asante, Molefe Kete. *The History of Africa: The Quest for Eternal Harmony*. New York: Routledge, 2006.
Ausloos, H., et al. *Translating a Translation: The LXX and Its Modern Translations in the Context of Early Judaism*. Louvain: Peeters, 2008.
Bassnett, S., and H. Trivedi, eds. *Postcolonial Translation*. New York: Routledge, 1999.
Bediako, K., "The Doctrine of Christ and the Significance of Vernacular Terminology." *IBMR* (1998): 109–11.
Bohannan, Paul, and Philip Curtin. *Africa and Africans*. 3rd ed. Prospect Heights, IL: Waveland, 1988.
Boice, J. M. *Genesis: An Expositional Commentary*. Vol. 1. Grand Rapids: Baker, 1982.
Davidson, I. *Cambridge Bible Commentary*. Cambridge: Cambridge University Press, 1974.
Edoho, A. "NGOs as Strategic Mechanisms for Achieving Sustainable Development in Africa." *JAPS* 11 (2005): 29–48.
Felder, Cain Hope, ed. *Stony the Road We Trod: African American Biblical Interpretation*. Minneapolis: Fortress, 1991.
Gikuyu, Samuel. "The Tree of the Knowledge of Good and Evil: An African Reading of Genesis 2–3." *BOTSA* 1 (2003): 11–17.
Hatim, B., and I. Mason. *The Translator as Communicator*. New York: Routledge, 1997.
Makoni, Sinfree, and Nkonko Kamwangamalu. *Language and Institutions in Africa*. Cape Town: CASAS, 2000.
Mazrui, A. *Cultural Forces in World Politics*. London: James Currey, 1999.
Mojola, A. *God Speaks in Our Own Languages: Bible Translation in East Africa, 1844–1998—A General Survey*. Nairobi, Kenya; Dodoma, Tanzania; and Kampala, Uganda: Bible Societies of Kenya, Tanzania, and Uganda, 2000.
Punt, J. "Sex and Gender, and Liminality in Biblical Texts: Venturing into Postcolonial, Queer Biblical Interpretation." *Neot* 41 (2007): 382–98.
Rodney, W. *How Europe Underdeveloped Africa*. Dar-e-Salaam, Tanzania: Tanzania Publishing House, 1976.
Sanneh, L. *Translating the Message: The Missionary Impact on Culture*. Maryknoll, NY: Orbis, 1989.

---

30. G. Yorke, "Bible Translation in Africa and Her Anglophone Diaspora: A Postcolonialist Agenda," *BTh* 2 (2004): 162. See also idem, "It's Not Just an American Thing," in *African Americans and the Bible: Sacred Texts and Social Textures,* ed. Vincent Wimbush (New York: Continuum, 2001); Randall C. Bailey, "Beyond Identification: The Use of Africans in Old Testament Poetry and Narratives," in Felders, *Stony the Road We Trod*, 165; and G. Yorke, "Biblical Hermeneutics: An Afrocentric Perspective," *JRT* 52 (1995): 1–13.

Spickard, P. R., and K. M. Cragg. *How Everyday Believers Experienced their World: A Global History of Christians*. Grand Rapids, MI: Baker, 1998.

Sugirtharajah, R. S. *The Postcolonial Bible*. Sheffield: Sheffield Academic Press, 1998.

Tanakh: The Holy Scriptures. Philadelphia: Jewish Publication Society, 1985.

Venuti, L., ed. "Translator and Minority." *TTran* 4 (1998): 135–390.

wa Thiong'o, Ngũgĩ . *Moving the Centre: The Struggle for Cultural Freedom*. Nairobi: East Africa Educational Publishers, 1993.

Wendland, E. R., et al. "Translator Training in Africa," *BT: Practical Papers* 57 (2006): 58–78.

Wenham, G.J. *Genesis 1–15 in Word Biblical Commentary*. Waco, TX: Thomas Nelson, 1987.

Wilt, Timothy, ed. *Bible Translation: Frames of Reference*. Manchester, England: St. Jerome, 2003.

Wimbush, V., ed. *African Americans and the Bible: Sacred Texts and Social Textures*. New York: Continuum, 2001.

Yorke, G. "Bible Interpretation and Translation in Africa: University of KwaZulu-Natal, Pietermaritzburg." *BOTSA* (2006): 3–5.

———. "Bible Translation in Africa: An Afrocentric Perspective." *BT: Technical Papers* 52 (2000): 113–23.

———. "Bible Translation in Africa and Her Anglophone Diaspora: A Postcolonialist Agenda." *BTh* 2 (2004): 153–66.

———. "Biblical Hermeneutics: An Afrocentric Perspective." *JRT* 52 (1995): 1–13.

———. "Hearing the Politics of Peace in Ephesians: A Proposal from an African Postcolonial Perspective." *JSNT* 30 (2007): 113–27.

———. "Maintaining Excellence Amidst a Call for Greater Caribbean and African Academic Collaboration." *The Nineteenth Norma H. Darlington Founders' Day Lecture*. Kingston, Jamaica: Shortwood Teachers' College Publishers, 2009.

Yorke, G., and P. Renju. *Bible Translation and African Languages*. Nairobi: Acton, 2004.

The Politics of Bible Translation in Africa: The Case of the Igbo Catholic Bible

Ernest M. Ezeogu

When I told a friend that I was working on the politics of Bible translating to the Igbo Catholic Bible, he was excited. He understood that I was going to get the scoop on the political wranglings among Igbo speaking Catholic bishops, priests and faithful surrounding the Igbo Catholic Bible project. Such disagreements, if they did take place, would fall within the scope of this study. But when we talk of the politics of Bible translation in biblical scholarship, we mean a whole lot more than such behavior of church leaders and actors that we usually describe as "playing politics." By the politics of Bible translation we mean all the aspects of Bible translation that are determined by external human factors as opposed to the factors that are dictated by the text itself. We mean such decisions that affect Bible translation which are made not because the text necessarily so demands but in the interest of the community (Greek: *polis* = city). The community here could be the cultural-linguistic community, the ecclesial community, the academic community, but most importantly, the target reading community.

Factors that come under the politics of Bible translation can be located in the areas of linguistics and hermeneutics, personal relationship, technology, funding, marketing, and reader-support services. These are factors that affect Bible translations everywhere. In Africa, however, they assume especially challenging proportions on account of the sociocultural situation in which we find ourselves. This essay will try, within a limited scope, to highlight some of the more remarkable of these challenges, using the Igbo Catholic Bible as a test case. We shall present our findings under three broad headings: extra-textual factors, source-textual factors, receptor-textual factors

Extra-Textual Factors

Administrative Interests

Few people wake up one day and start translating the Bible. Usually a Bible translation is commissioned by an authoritative body that sponsors the project. In the case of the Igbo Catholic Bible, the decision to produce the translation was taken by the Igbo speaking Catholic bishops of Nigeria in their meeting in Onitsha on 5 February 1991. The commissioning body spells out what kind of translation they want. In the case of the Igbo Catholic Bible, the bishops wanted an Igbo Bible that is suitable for Catholic liturgical use. Given the fact that there were some non-Catholic Igbo Bibles already in circulation, including a common translation of the New Testament, this statement means at least five things with regard to the translation.

First, it means that the translation will follow the Catholic canon of forty-six and not the Protestant canon of thirty-nine books of the Old Testament. Secondly, it means that the order of the books of the Old Testament, and the numbering of the Psalms, will have to follow the traditional Catholic order in the Vulgate, which follows the Septuagint rather than the Masoretic Text. Thirdly, it means that the translation will have to include "necessary and sufficient explanatory notes" as required by Catholic Church law.[1] Fourthly, it means that where there are textual variants, the translators should follow the variant in the official Catholic Bible, namely, the Vulgate or one of its modern English incarnations, such as the Jerusalem Bible or the New American Bible.

Finally, it means that the translation will have to be approved "by the Apostolic See or the Episcopal Conference" as demanded by the same Catholic Church law (Canon 825 §1). Since it is a version to be used for readings in sacred worship, the translation would have to avoid shocking and explicit language, especially in reference to human sexuality. This means that the tone adopted in the NRSV translation of Gen 4:1, "Adam *knew* Eve his wife, and she conceived and bore Cain" will be preferable to that in the NJB, "The man *had intercourse* with his wife Eve, and she conceived and gave birth to Cain."

Money Matters

Translating and publishing the Bible is costly business. According to a mural hanging in the lobby of the Bible Society of Nigeria building in Lagos, a full translation of the Bible into an African language takes twelve years and thirty million naira, that is, about two hundred thousand United States dollars. Translators are forced to cut corners when a translation project is undertaken in a condition of urgency and scarcity of fund. This was the case with the Igbo Catholic Bible.

Firstly, The Igbo speaking Catholic bishops who commissioned the translation wanted it completed as soon as possible. They instructed the translators to avoid translating from the original languages if that was going to delay the work. At the time of commissioning the translation, individual dioceses and parishes were doing their own *ad hoc* translations of the weekly and daily readings and publishing them in weekly Sunday bulletins. Some bishops were so impatient that they even suggested to the translation committee to simply assemble these random translations done by untrained personnel, edit them where necessary, bind them

---

1. *Code of Canon Law,* 1983, Canon 825 §1.

together and give us an Igbo Catholic Bible. The need for the Catholic Bible in Igbo language was perceived as urgent and overdue. When it came to funding, however, resources were scarce.

The bishops who commissioned the translation depended mainly on European funding agencies to fund the project. The translation committee ran into financial constraints at several stages in the translation process. Translators were not adequately paid. Halfway through the project, the Igbo language experts recruited from department of Igbo studies in various institutions of higher learning in Nigeria had to withdraw their services because they could not be paid. The committee resorted to the use of interested seminarians who would camp together in one of the national seminaries for six weeks in a year in *lieu* of their long vacation pastoral experience. They were paid little or nothing. Similarly, the priests on the committee were inadequately paid. They were promised that when the Bible comes out and begins to sell, they would be compensated.

Today, many of the Igbo-speaking bishops have come to realise that parts of the *Baibul Nsọ, Nhazi Katọlik*[2] that was produced by the committee were poorly translated. That should not come as a surprise. A Bible translation done by amateurs cannot but be amateurish. To have a professional translation you need professional translators. The problem of funding in a translation project often decides the question of whether the translation is done by professional or amateurs, and this definitely affects the eventual quality of the translation.

Non-availability of adequate funding affected the *Baibul Nsọ, Nhazi Katọlik* in more ways than one. After the committee had completed translating, proof-reading, typesetting and desktop printing of camera-ready pages of the entire Bible, the next problem was that there was no money for the publishing. To get around the problem, the archbishop of Onitsha, who was the episcopal coordinator of the project, suggested to a religious congregation to publish, market, and take all the financial profit from the Bible sales, so long as they give us the Igbo Catholic Bible. Igbo Catholics were getting increasingly impatient at the non-availability of the Igbo Catholic Bible that was promised them many years before. When the religious congregation could not accept the offer, the project came to a standstill. The project was in this state of limbo for a number of years when the bishops, as a last resort, turned to a commercial publisher, Africana-FEP Publishers, and offered them the Bible manuscript to publish and market, so long as they give us the Bible. In a situation comparable to that of Esau who sold his birthright to Jacob in order to satisfy a biting hunger (Gen 25:29–34), we gave away the copyright of the Igbo Catholic Bible to Africana-FEP Publishers.

Today, the *Baibul Nsọ, Nhazi Katọlik* is in the market. However the supply, pricing and packaging of the Bible are the exclusive rights of Africana-FEP. On the copyright page of the Bible is the legal warning that "No part of this book may be reproduced, stored in a retrieval system, or transmitted, in any form or by any

---

2. *Baibul Nsọ, Nhazi Katọlik* (Onitsha, Nigeria: Africana-FEP, 2000).

means, electronic, mechanical, photocopying, recording, or otherwise, without the prior written permission of African-FEP Publishers Limited." The Igbo Catholic bishops now find themselves short-changed. Their hands are tied as to what they can or cannot do with the very Bible that they had commissioned and sponsored. Now, they cannot take excerpts from the Bible to compile an Igbo missal, an Igbo lectionary, or an Igbo breviary. They cannot produce audio recordings of the Bible for the Igbo Catholic faithful, many of whom are illiterate or semi-literate and would benefit immensely from the use of an audio Igbo Bible. Neither can they produce multimedia electronic versions of the Bible on CD or online for the teaming Igbo youths who are fascinated with the novel information and communication technology. They cannot even produce a new and revised edition of the Bible. To do any of these legally, they would have to obtain the permission and meet the conditions given by African-FEP Publishers, the legal copyright owners of the Bible.

Believing that the Igbo speaking bishops would retain the copyright to the Igbo Catholic Bible, the translation committee had suggested the setting up of a standing Igbo Catholic Bible office to receive feedback from the reading public as they make their way through the Bible. In devotional personal reading, in parish Bible studies, in liturgical reading and preaching, and in classroom academic studies, the Igbo Catholic Bible is being read. Readers may discover typographical errors, as well as unhappy expressions and downright errors which they would like to report to the editorial committee. The standing office would receive such feedback orally or in writing and document them for a subsequent edition of the translation. No Bible translation is a perfect work, least of all the Igbo Catholic Bible. The bishops did not set up such a Bible office. Maybe they could not even legally set up such an office since the copyright was no longer with them. Be that as it may, the lack of an after sales customer care office for the new Bible proved to be a disservice to all stakeholders in the project, especially to the people of God who had no way to make their voices heard, for better or for worse, on their appraisal of the Igbo Catholic Bible.

Having seen some of the extra-textual challenges to Bible translation in Africa, not least of which is the issue of funding, we shall now proceed to examine textual factors that African Bible translators have to contend with, starting with issues relating to source-text.

SOURCE-TEXTUAL FACTORS

Source Text and Explanatory Notes

Much time was lost in the translation process because the translation team did not resolve beforehand the all-important question of what text they are translating. Translators showed up for work carrying the Hebrew and Greek Bibles as well as five or six English translations, picking and choosing text variants on the go, without any pre-established rules for the choice. If they had decided beforehand that they were going to translate, say, the Vulgate, the Jerusalem Bible, the Revised Standard Version (Catholic edition) or any of the existing versions into Igbo, they would have spared themselves the problem of seeming to re-invent the wheel. Note that a new translation from the original languages had been ruled out from the outset, as this would make the project too time-consuming and too expensive.

Specifying beforehand the source text or exemplar from which the translation was to be made would have facilitated the work of the translation committee in another way. Since Church law demands that Catholic Bibles must have introductory and explanatory notes to go with the Bible text, the translators would then have ready-made notes which they could translate and modify for the new Bible rather than starting entirely from a clean sheet. As a result of this oversight, the first drafts of the translation had no explanatory notes at all. The explanatory notes were added much later and in a hurry, after it was pointed out that church authorities would not approve the Bible for publication unless it had explanatory notes. The same observation goes for the few illustrations that were incorporated into the text. They were chosen in a haphazard and random manner compared, for example, to the Good News Bible, with its consistent and systematic illustrations that make it more reader-friendly.

Translating Gender

Fortunately, most of the issues of the politics of translating gender raised in modern European translations of the Bible do not arise in Igbo and many other African languages. Compared to European languages, most African indigenous languages are gender-neutral. I prefer the terminology of gender-neutrality to gender-inclusiveness in reference to African languages. Whereas gender inclusiveness pays attention to both genders, gender neutrality simply does not pay attention to gender at all. Igbo and most African languages belong to the latter category. Let me illustrate with two simple sentences in two European languages and one African language exhibiting varying levels of gender interestedness.

	Italian	English	Igbo
1	Mia amica è venuta.	My friend came.	Enyi m bịara.
2	È venuta presto.	She came early.	Ọ bịara n'oge.

Take the simple sentence, "My friend came." This construction, which uses the nominal form "friend," is gender neutral in the English language. There is no way of saying this in Italian, Spanish, or any of the romance languages without betraying the gender of the friend in question. In Igbo and most African languages, there is no betrayal of the gender of the friend. When we get to the second sentence, "*She* came early," that uses the pronominal form, English betrays the gender of the friend. The friend is either a *he* or a *she*. Similarly, the romance languages give away the gender of the person referred to through the feminine verb form. In the Igbo language, neither the pronoun nor the verb gives away the gender of the friend in question. The pronoun "o" or "ọ" in Igbo language means equally "he," "she" or "it." The grammatical situation is the same in most indigenous African languages. The implication of this is that gender inclusiveness, which is an important question in the politics of Bible translation in European languages, is often a non-issue in Bible translation in Africa. Let us illustrate.

The Gender of God

The reference to God as "he" in traditional Bible translations in European languages is today seen as politically incorrect among feminists and others who are sympathetic to the feminist agenda of gender inclusiveness. While traditionalists argue that the masculine designation of God is found in the original texts of the Bible in Hebrew and Greek, feminists argue that the gender of God in the biblical texts is grammatical rather than natural, whereas in the English language gender is today used naturally rather than grammatically. In these ancient languages, every object, animate or inanimate, is assigned a masculine or feminine (or neuter) gender depending mainly on the word ending. Thus "stone" is feminine in Hebrew and masculine in Greek, even though it is clear that there is no natural gender attached to a stone. In the English language today, masculine and feminine genders are generally reserved for animate objects that are naturally so. An inanimate object that has no natural gender is usually referred to with the pronoun, "it." This complicated question does not arise with the same urgency for Bible translators in Africa, since in most African languages, as in Igbo, the third person singular is gender neutral and could mean "he," "she" or "it."

"Man" as Masculine versus "Man" as Human

In most European languages, the same word (*man* in English, *homme* in French, *uomo* in Italian, for example) is used to designate an adult male as well as the human person in general. This thorny problem in modern European languages is not shared in most African languages. In African languages, as in the biblical languages of Hebrew, Aramaic and Greek, there is a clear distinction between these two usages. *Adam* (Hebrew) or *anthropos* (Greek) is exactly equivalent to *mmadụ* in Igbo, designating the generic human being, and *ish* (Hebrew) or *aner* (Greek) is equivalent to *nwoke* in Igbo, designating a male person.

The implication of this observation for the politics of Bible translation in Africa would be merely academic if African language translations are done directly from the original languages. Unfortunately, this is not the case. Most African language Bible translations are done using European language Bibles as primary, if not exclusive, source texts. The Igbo Catholic Bible is a case in point. The seminarians who translated them did not have sufficient knowledge of Hebrew and Greek to work from the original biblical languages. They translated from English Bibles, with the unfortunate result that sometimes generic man, *mmadụ*, is rendered in Igbo as *nwoke*, a masculine person. The result would be funny if it did not have such tragic hermeneutical consequences. Fortunately, the editors of the Igbo Catholic Bible picked up the wrong translation of "man" as *nwoke* in Gen 2:18 and corrected it to read *mmadụ*.

Take the example of Genesis 2:18 "It is not good that *the man* [human] should be alone . . ." (NRSV), which is popularly translated into Igbo as "It is not good that *a man* [male] should be alone . . ." This is popularly understood to mean that it is all right for women to be alone in the house while the man goes gallivanting. God made men social animals, but women are different. If the passage was rightly translated as *adam*, a human person, *mmadụ*, then it would be easy to see that social life and relatedness is a human need, applicable equally to men and women. This would help overcome the problem of unfair gender discrimination in Africa.

The absence of gender specific third person singular pronoun in Igbo and most African languages is a plus when translating the use of the third person singular masculine pronoun in general statements, even when translating from European languages. Take a text like,

> Who shall sojourn in thy tent? Who shall dwell on thy holy hill?
> He who walks blamelessly, and does what is right, and speaks truth from his
>   heart. (Ps 15:1 RSV)

Since the third person singular pronoun in Igbo is gender neutral, this passage reads better in the Igbo language as applying equally to men as to women. As a result, there is no need for such biforked expressions as have become necessary in English, such as "he or she." Another hendiadys that is unnecessary In Igbo language is the common expression, "brothers and sisters." In Igbo, as in many African languages, there is only one gender neutral word for a sibling, (*nwanne* in Igbo) which means equally "brother" or "sister," thus rendering the double expression unnecessary.

Translating Number

Many African languages are in many ways closer to the biblical languages of Hebrew and Koine Greek than most European languages. This creates a problem in the translation of the Bible when it is done with Bible translation in European languages as the source text. The English language, for example, has lost the distinction between the second person singular and the second person plural pronoun. In today's English language, the word "you" is used interchangeable to address a single person as well as a group of people. In the biblical languages of Hebrew and Greek, as in African languages, there is a clear distinction between the singular and the plural of the second person. When translations are made from the English by amateur translators with no knowledge of the original languages, there may be some difficulty in distinguishing when "you" is used as singular and when it is used as plural.

Take, for example, the dominical saying in Luke 17:21, "the kingdom of God is within you" (KJV). There is a tendency in certain schools of spirituality to under-stand this as addressed to the individual Christian, taking "you" here as singular. It is psychologically comforting and morally reassuring to imagine the kingdom of God as an inner reality deep within the soul of the individual believer. Be that as it may, the fact of the matter is that "you" in Luke 17:21 is in the plural. Jesus is addressing his followers as a group and reassuring them that the reign of God is present among them in their assembly or as a community. Reading it literally in the plural, as it should, the statement is seen to be an endorsement of community, whereas reading it out of context in the singular, it becomes an endorsement of its opposite, the cult of individualism. If the kingdom of God is within you and me as individuals in isolation, who, then, needs the community of believers, the church? Failure to distinguish between the singular and the plural "you" in Luke 17:21 and similar passages has created a serious problem in African Christian spirituality, especially among the so-called Bible-believing Christians, the problem of "righ-teous individualism."

Translating Race

Translators work with certain racial biases and assumptions, conscious as well as unconscious. This is inevitable, neither is it necessarily a disadvantage. African translators are no exceptions. Among the most determinant of these assump-tions for the work of Bible translation is how a translator images the world of the Bible, its dominant culture and its people. Until recently, most Eurocentric translators come to the task of Bible translation with the assumption that the world and people of the Bible were culturally and racially akin to those of their experi-ence in Europe. On the other hand, *personae non grata* in the Bible, such as Judas Iscariot, were painted in dark colors. There is, for example, a popular image titled "Jacob sees Joseph again in Egypt"[3] in which a White Joseph flanked by Black Egyptians is receiving his White father, who is escorted by some of his White sons. The anachronism in the painting is clear. If Joseph were a Whiteman living among Black Egyptians, why then did his visiting brothers mistake him for an Egyptian, even when he was meeting and speaking with them face to face (Gen 42:7–8). The great artists of Europe, at least from the time of the Renaissance, painted the major characters of biblical history as Europeans. Jesus was often painted complete with blonde hair and blue eyes.

How does this influence Bible translation? A translator with a Eurocentric re-construction of the biblical world and its people will invariably transfer this black-denying attitude to the text of his or her translation. Here is a classical example. Virtually all English Bible translations before the 1990s had a problem translating the autobiographical statement of the Shulammite, the most celebrated beautiful

---

3. Available online: http://pdbb.files.wordpress.com/2009/06/jacob-sees-joseph-again-in-egypt.jpg.

woman in the Bible, Solomon's bride in the Song of Songs. The Shulammite says of herself, "*Shehorah ani wenawah*" (Song of Songs 1:5). They usually translated it with an adversative conjunction, "I am black, *but* beautiful," as if being black and being beautiful were mutually exclusive realities.[4] It took the concerted effort of Afrocentric Bible scholars to draw attention to the fact that the conjunction here translated adversatively has, in fact, a basic and usually progressive, copulative meaning. The translators of the New Revised Standard Version were the first to muster the courage to correct this politically incorrect translation and restore its original, literal and contextual meaning: "I am black and beautiful."

Bible translations made in Africa from European language Bibles end up importing their embedded cultural assumptions and biases into African translations, thus reinforcing and perpetuating a negative stereotype. I feel ashamed to report that the Igbo Catholic Bible actually uses the adversative conjunction "but" in Song 1:5, which goes to prove the point. It is a challenge to African translators to avoid replicating Eurocentric biases against blackness in Bible translations meant to be good news for Africans.

RECEPTOR-TEXTUAL FACTORS

Standard Vernacular versus Dialects

The Igbo language, like most languages spoken by a large number of people, has dialects and dialectal variants. There is, for example, the case of the Southern or Owerri Igbo usage of *ha* ("they") where the Northern or Onitsha Igbo would use *fa*. The same word sometimes comes out as *va* in some variants of Onitsha Igbo, and as *wa* in Delta Igbo. In making a Bible translation for the collective use of all Igbo speaking populations, which of these variants is the translator to use? This scenario is repeated over many more terminologies and phraseologies where the southern Igbo differs noticeable from northern Igbo. Should the translator use *rie* or *lie* (eat), *gaa* or *jee* (go), *laa* or *naa* (return), *ahụ* or *arụ*(body), *kwewe* or *kwebe* (keep singing). The list goes on.

Authors and broadcasters, who have the general Igbo population as their intended audience, usually settle for what is called central or standard Igbo. Central Igbo had its beginnings from the Igbo language as spoken in large urban centres, such as Owerri, Onitsha, Enugu and Umuahia, that serve as melting points for all Igbos of all localities and dialects. In practice, however, the resultant Igbo that is spoken in these urban centres still enjoys the flavour of the local dialect. There is no agreement of the *locus classicus* of central Igbo. The *locus classicus* of standard Italian has been traced to Dante Alighieri who popularised

---

4. The same adversative "but" in found in most other European language translations, such as the 1988 French *Traduction Oecuménique de la Bible*: "Je suis noire, moi, *mais* jolie," the 1952 German *Schlachter* Version: "Schwarz bin ich, *aber* lieblich," and the 1991 Italian *La Nuova Diodati*: "Io sono nera *ma* bella."

the Florentine dialect. Standard German is believed to have its *locus classicus* in the *September Bible*, Martin Luther's 1522 publication of the Bible in the high German dialect.

The Igbo language has no such literary giants who wrote in Igbo and whose writings have galvanised the national imagination. The early Anglican and Catholic missionaries settled in Onitsha and translated their Bibles and catechisms into the Onitsha dialect. Onitsha was then the *locus classicus* for central Igbo. After the missionary era, the *locus classicus* shifted from Onitsha moving towards Owerri, the city that hosts the annual national Odenigbo lecture, the only conference of such magnitude held entirely in Igbo language. Nevertheless, the question has not been finally settled. Translators of the Bible into Igbo must, therefore, contend with the fact that they are making a major contribution in the evolution of standard or central Igbo. Translators of the Bible in other indigenous African languages find themselves in similar situations.

To Indigenise or Not to Indigenise

For reasons best known to them, the pioneer translators of Catholic church documents into Igbo used many loan words from the English language and indigenised or Igbonised them, as we like to say. Such words include: virgin, apostle, bishop, Bible, altar, and person. Translators today argue that the use of these loan words has contributed to a shallow understanding of these concepts and the teaching that are expressed with them, and are resolved to find functional Igbo equivalents for them. Yet the Igbo Catholic population, the intended readers of the translation, are already conversant with these loan words and often find their functional equivalents prosaic, especially when an Igbo phrase is employed to translate a loan word, such as *nwanyị na-amaghị nwoke* for virgin, *ebe nchụ aja* for altar and *nnukwu ụkọchukwu* for bishop. Should translators Igbonise or not Igbonise? Should they maintain the loan words and perpetuate the shallow understandings that go with them, or should they insist on using functional equivalents in the vernacular and risk being rejected by the intended readers? This is one of the important questions that Bible translators in Africa must have to deal with. In the case of the Igbo Catholic Bible, there was no policy on Igbonization. Different translators did different things with the different books they were assigned to translate.

Latinisms or Anglicisms

There are two major languages of Christian religious discourse in the Igbo experience of Christianity. These are the Roman Catholic and the Anglican languages of religious discourse. The Catholic is distinguished by its use of Latinisms and the Anglican by its use of Anglicisms. This is evident in the way they Igbonise English Bible names. Whereas the Anglicans would take the English form of the word as a point of departure, the Catholics would take the Latin form of the name. The following table illustrates the phenomenon.

English	Anglicized Igbo	Latin	Latinized Igbo
Jesus	Jisọs	Iesus	Jesu
Mary	Meri	Maria	Maria
Titus	Taitọs	Titus	Taitus

Here again, the African Bible translator must decide how to transcribe these proper names into the receiving language. Functional equivalence does not function when it comes to proper names. The translators of the Igbo Catholic Bible, as a policy, decided to use the Latinized forms of proper names. Their reasoning is that their intended readers, the Igbo Catholic population, are more familiar with them. Besides, in the case of Jesus and Mary, the Latin forms of the names are closer to the Greek than their Anglicized versions.

Harmonization of Many Translation Hands

Translation projects are often handled by a team of translators. In such a case provision has to be made for a general editor who will go through and harmonize all the different translations to read smoothly. As far as the average reader of the Bible is concerned, the entire Bible is regarded as a homogeneous book. The harmonization process is necessary if the translated work is to be any good for literary and word studies. You cannot study the frequency of occurrence of a particular term in a particular book or set of books unless that term is consistently translated with a corresponding term. This may sound like formal equivalence. That's right, formal equivalence does have its place.

The need to harmonize the work of many hands is perhaps nowhere more evident than in the translation of the divine name, the tetragram YHWH. Different English Bibles translate the divine name in different ways, as Yahweh, Jehovah or Lord, yet they translate it with consistency. No less a standard is to be expected from translators working with African languages.

The translators of the Igbo Catholic Bible did not make sufficient provision for a thorough editorial work of harmonization. Though the translators avoided translating the Tetragrammaton as *Yawe* of *Jihova*, preferring the traditional Igbo Catholic usage of *Dinwenu* or *Osebrụwa*, little effort was made to harmonize the translations and ensure that these terms are used consistently.

The decision as to which name to use is a political decision in that what is at stake is not the understanding of the text but the best way to render it in the receiving language such that when readers of the translation hear that name, it arouses in them sentiments comparable to those aroused in the Hebrews of the Bible when they heard the divine name YHWH.

In examining the politics of Bible translation in Africa, we have tried, in general, to highlight the practical challenges facing translators who work with African indigenous languages and for the African church. In particular, we tried to illustrate these challenges with reference to the Igbo Catholic Bible in which translation I played a major role.

First, under extra-textual factors, we looked at the crucial importance of administrative interests. The authorities that commission a Bible translation decide on the type of translation they want. How much time and funding are available for the work depends also on them. The decision to use professional or amateur translators often depends on the resources available for the work. Hurry and lack of financial wherewithal could impair the task of translation. Quality translation, using the critical texts in the original languages, demands a generous investment of time, expertise and money.

Next we considered the source-textual factors that influence the work of translation. We highlighted the problems associated with using the English Bible or a translation in another European language as the primary, if not the exclusive, source-text. When a hurried and *pro tem* translation is all that is required, as in the case of the Igbo Catholic Bible, the next best thing to do would be to select an existing English translation, such as the Jerusalem Bible, the American Bible, or the Revised Standard Version, and translate that, together with the text as already established and incorporating the introductory and explanatory notes. This is better and faster than doing an eclectic translation, picking and choosing passages from various English translations with no concern for stylistic consistency or literary homogeneity.

Then we turned to the vexed question in Western scholarship of translating gender. We saw that, thanks to the gender neutrality of nouns, pronouns and verbs in Igbo and other indigenous African languages, much of the concern for gender inclusiveness in Western scholarship does not arise in the African context. The pronoun used for God or for the generic human being does not suggest masculinity any more than femininity. A greater concern, in the African linguistic context is the increasing individualistic and individualising understanding and translation of the second person plural as singular, a danger that pertains to those who translate from English Bibles rather than from original biblical languages. Similarly, we warned that overdependence on European language translations could result in the transference of a biased Eurocentric view of Africa and Africans into a biblical text that originally glorified them. This would vitiate the Bible's message for the people of God in Africa, changing good news into bad.

The last part of the work focussed on receptor-textual choices that translators in African languages must make. These include the issue of whether and to what extent the particular African language has been standardised and, if not, the dialect to use in the translation. Then there is the question of whether and to what extent technical terms in the source language are to be imported as loan words into the receiving language or given a loose translation. The translation of proper names raises the question of whether to use the Latinised or the Anglicised forms of the names as model. Finally we pointed out that since a Bible translation is usually undertaken by a team of translators from different dialectal backgrounds and with different literary tastes, there is need for a general editing of the translations to harmonise them for consistency of expression.

Bible translation is not something that one does every day. The aim of this essay has been to document the experience and tease out the lessons learnt in the process of translating and publishing the Igbo Catholic Bible. It is my hope that subsequent translations of the Bible into African languages will build on the strengths and learn from the weaknesses of the Igbo Catholic Bible translation committee in order to do a better job.

WORKS CITED

Baibul Nso, Nhazi Katolik. Onitsha, Nigeria: Africana-FEP, 2000.

Bea, Augustin, and Marc Boegner. *Traduction Oecuménique de la Bible: Comprenant l'Ancien et le Nouveau Testament Traduits sur les Textes Originaux Hébreu et Grec*. Paris: United Bible Societies, Société biblique française, 1988.

La Nuova Diodati. Italian Revised Diodati Translation: Geneva, 1607, rev. 1991. http://www.davepohl.com/winonlinebible.html.

Peters, Edward N. *The 1917 or Pio-Benedictine Code of Canon Law: In English Translation With Extensive Scholarly Apparatus*. New York: Ingatius, 1983.

Schlachter Bible. German translation, 1952. http://pdbb.files.wordpress.com/2009/06/jacob-sees-joseph-again-in-egypt.jpg.

The Shona Bible and the Politics of Bible Translation

Lovemore Togarasei

Although the translation of the Bible into African languages aimed to avail the Bible in Africans' mother languages, it was not a completely objective process. As has already been observed by many scholars, no translation is free from interpretation.[1] Thus translation studies examine "the literary and cultural history of translation practices with an emphasis on the role of the ideology of the translator in the praxis of translation."[2] Translation does not take place in a vacuum. Each translator is guided by a certain ideology(ies). This essay discusses the politics of Bible translation, focusing on the Shona Bible. Specifically it looks at the translation of the word *banquetings* into *mabira* in the *Union Shona Bible*, the first complete translation of the Shona Bible.

The Shona language is spoken by over ten million[3] people in Zimbabwe and some parts of Mozambique, Botswana, and Zambia. This chapter discusses the history of the translation of the Bible from the time the missionaries arrived among the Shona in the 1890s to the time when the first complete Bible was translated into the Shona language in the late 1940s. It discusses the political and cultural factors that influenced the way the Bible was translated. How did missionaries' (the first Bible translators) understanding of the Shona worldview influence the translation? How did the translators address the dialectical differences in the Shona language considering that Shona has five dialects? How did Shona cosmology and spirituality influence translation? To answer these and other questions concerning the politics of biblical translation, specific biblical texts (the translation of banquetings into *mabira* in 1 Pet 4:3) are analyzed. The essay also briefly looks at subsequent "improvements" to the Shona Bible to see how translators have responded

---

Originally published in *SWC* 15, no. 1 (2007): 51–64. Published here with permission.

1. André Lefevere, "Introduction," in *Translation/History/Culture: A Source Book* (London and New York: Routledge, 1992), and Jiri Levy, "Translation as a Decision Process," in *The Translation Studies Reader,* ed. Lawrence Venuti (London and New York: Routledge, 2000).

2. W. Randolph Tate, *Interpreting the Bible* (Peabody, MA: Hendrickson , 2006), 381.

3. This is an estimate I arrive at on the basis that about 80 percent of Zimbabwe's around twelve million people, according to the 2005 census, are Shona-speaking.

to cultural and linguistic changes over the years of the use of the Bible among the Shona.

A BRIEF HISTORY OF THE TRANSLATION OF THE SHONA BIBLE

Christianity in Zimbabwe, like in most African countries, is closely associated with colonialism. Although several attempts to Christianize the country were made from as early as the mid–sixteenth century, all those attempts did not bear any lasting fruits.[4] It was with the colonization of the country in 1890 that the doors to effectively evangelize the nation were opened. Various missionary bodies quickly moved in and with Cecil Rhodes's promotion of Christianity for civilization, the missionary bodies were not only given freedom to evangelize but were also granted large tracts of land for their missionary activities.[5] These missionaries were very quick to realize that if their message was to be accepted, there was need for them to translate their foreign message into the language of the people. Then began the process to translate the various books of the Bible into the Shona language.

To understand the history of the translation of the Shona Bible, it is important for one to first get a picture of how the missionaries operated soon after the colonization of the country. The entry of the Pioneer Column of Cecil John Rhodes in Zimbabwe in 1890 marked the colonization of the country. As soon as the missionaries who accompanied the Pioneer Column arrived in Harare, they divided the area around Harare amongst themselves.[6] This was probably meant to avoid missionary conflicts as later when Pentecostal preachers like L. Kruger and E. Gwanzura, started preaching freely without observing these boundaries, some missionary boards complained to the state and the official status that the Apostolic Faith Mission had previously been given was withdrawn.[7] The Salvation Army went to the north around Mazowe valley, the Catholic Church went northeast to Chishawasha, the Methodist Church went southeast to Epworth and the Anglican Church went southwards to Seke.

The same was happening throughout the country. The Anglican Church and the United Methodist Church concentrated their work in the eastern region of the country, the Evangelical Lutheran Church concentrated in the south-western part of the country, the Dutch Reformed Church were in the southern part. It is important to note that different Shona dialects are spoken in these different regions of

---

4. J. Weller, and J. Linden, *Mainstream Christianity to 1980 in Malawi, Zambia, and Zimbabwe* (Gweru, Zimbabwe: Mambo, 1984), 1.

5. Paul H. Gundani, "The Land Crisis in Zimbabwe and the Role of the Churches towards Its Resolution," *SHE* 28 no. 2 (2002): 122–69.

6. Carl F. Hallencruetz, *Religion and Politics in Harare, 1890–1990* (Uppsala, Sweden: Swedish Institute of Missionary Research, 1998), 24.

7. D. Maxwell, "Historicizing Christian Independency: The Southern African Pentecostal Movement ca. 1908–1960," *JAH* 39, no. 2 (1999): 243–64.

the country. In the southern region where the Evangelical Lutheran Church and the Dutch Reformed Church operated, Karanga is the dominant Shona dialect. In the east, Ndau and Manyika are the common dialects. The Zezuru dialect is dominant in the central region of the country, while Korekore is spoken in northern Zimbabwe.[8] What this means then is that when the missionaries translated the books of the Bible, they used the dialect used in the region they were operating in. Not only were the missionaries to translate the Bible, they also had to come up with an orthography of the language since the Shona themselves were then a nonliterate society.

The translation of the Bible into Shona happened in various stages. Initially the different mission bodies translated different biblical texts and other worship materials. For example, as early as 1891, Andrew Louw of the Dutch Reformed Church in southern Zimbabwe wrote in his diary, "Today I found time to review the translation of Psalm 23, John 3:16 and 'Our Father.'"[9] Thus bit by bit the missionaries translated different texts of the Bible. By 1897 Louw had completed translating the Gospel of Mark into ChiKaranga (the Shona dialect for the southern Shona). He was also the first to complete a Shona translation of the full New Testament in 1900. Other mission bodies were also doing the same in other regions of the country. John White of the Methodist Church in Epworth as early as 1898 published his *Ivangeri ya Marako* (the Gospel of Mark) with the British and Foreign Bible Society. He used the Shona dialect of Zezuru. He followed this with a translation of the Gospel of John in 1903 and by 1907 he had translated and published the whole New Testament. As for the Manyika dialect, translation of the Bible into Shona began as early as 1905 when E. H. Etheridge translated the Gospels and Acts followed by the translation of the whole New Testament in 1908. Another Shona New Testament was also published in the Ndau dialect at Mount Selinda mission before 1910. In fact by 1910 there were four versions of the New Testament in Shona in Karanga, Manyika, Zezuru and Ndau.[10]

Obviously because of the different dialects and the different theological backgrounds of the translators, the four versions differed not only in the choice of Shona words but in theology as well. For example whereas the Catholic translations would translate prophets as *masvikiro aMwari* (God's spirit mediums) accommodating the Shona cosmology to some extent, the Dutch Reformed Church translations rather decided not to translate the word prophets, thus transliterating it *vaprofita* (prophets).

The missionaries soon realized that the parallel translation of the Shona Bible in different dialects did not make sense both financially and missiologically. Thus from the beginning of the translation of the Bible, the need for a common version

---

8. George Fortune, "75 Years of Writing in Shona," *Zambezia* 1, no. 1 (1969): 55–67.

9. W. J. van der Merwe, *The Day Star Arises in Mashonaland* (Morgenster, South Africa: Morgenster Press, 1953), 24.

10. Fortune, "75 Years," 55–67.

of the Shona Bible was raised. But for this to be achieved there was need for a common orthography. This process was spearheaded by the Southern Rhodesian Missionary Conference beginning in 1903.[11] It was, however, a mammoth task which took very long to see the light of the day. Several committees were put up by the Conference between 1915 and 1928 with the objective of developing this orthography.

It was only after the government decided to teach the vernacular language in schools that the process of developing a common Shona orthography was accelerated. This saw the engagement of Professor C. M. Doke of the University of the Witwatersrand in 1929 to lead a Language Committee tasked with the development of a common Shona orthography. But although the government, through the Language Committee, was responsible for the production of the final orthography, missionary influence to this final orthography was strong. For example, Fortune notes that the missionaries' earlier suggestion that Shona orthography be standardized on the basis of two dialects, Karanga and Zezuru, is the one that Doke adopted.[12] Also in the process of standardization, notes on Karanga and Manyika forms of the Shona language were contributed by missionaries, Rev. A. A. Louw of the Dutch Reformed Church and Father Barnes of the Roman Catholic church respectively.[13]

The government approved the Doke orthography in 1931. Although some missionaries had reservations on the orthography, generally they welcomed it. The Missionary Conference then started the work of producing a Shona Bible on the basis of this common orthography. This Shona, in the common orthography, came to be called "Union Shona" since it tried to present Shona language that unified the five Shona dialects. The Mission Conference left this work (of producing a Shona Bible in Shona arthography) to Rev. Louw of the Dutch Reformed Church. In 1941 his translation of the New Testament in Union Shona was published by the British and Foreign Bible Society. The translation was well received but not without criticism. The problem of dialects resurfaced. The major criticism was that it was essentially a Karanga translation. Father Buck who tested it with Shona speakers from all the different dialects concluded that some 40 alterations would be necessary in the first two pages alone if the translation was to be understood by the greatest number of Shona people in all the regions of the country.[14] Be that as it may, Rev. Louw's translation was the first Union Shona translation. After its publication he continued with the translation of the Old Testament in Union Shona and in 1950 the whole Bible in Union Shona was published.[15] The problem of dialecti-

---

11. Ibid., 60.
12. Ibid., 55–67.
13. Ibid., 62.
14. Ibid., 63.
15. Van der Merwe, *Mashonaland*, 38.

cal differences was only resolved in this translation by having a glossary of words in other dialects (*Mashoko pane dzimwe ndimi*) as an appendix to the Bible.

THE POLITICS OF TRANSLATION: GENERAL

Having briefly traced the history of the translation of the Shona Bible in the last section of this essay, let me now turn to look at the politics involved in this process of translation. However, before I do so in the next section, let me in this section briefly define translation and consider some of the factors that influence the process of translation. Peter Newmark gives a simple definition of translation.[16] He defines it as, "the transfer of the meaning of a text (which may be a word or a book) from one language to another for a new readership." This is a simple definition, one which presents translation as a straightforward, objective, process. But as Newmark himself acknowledges, translation is not a simple and straightforward process. It is a difficult operation especially in the case of the missionaries among the Shona who were not native speakers of the receptor language. As J. C. Kumbirai notes, translation can be horizontal (from one contemporary language into another) or vertical (from an ancient language to a contemporary language).[17]

Because Bible translation involves consulting both contemporary and ancient languages like Hebrew and Greek, it is a blending of both horizontal and vertical translations. The translator needs knowledge not only of the source language and the source world but also of the receptor language and the receptor world. Often and especially in the case of the translators of the first Shona Bible, the translators did not have much knowledge of the source texts and source world. A. A. Louw of the Dutch Reformed Church who was responsible for translating the earliest Shona Bible, had not even completed his basic theological training.[18] Also, as we have seen above, missionaries began translating the Bible into Shona hardly a few months after they settled among the Shona. Obviously they were themselves still learning both the language and the customs of the people. English and other European languages Bible translations were used to produce Shona bibles and this should have limited the translation to the missionaries' Eurocentric worldviews. The Shona Bible, like other African languages Bibles, was therefore a translation of other translations.[19]

Another factor that influences translation is that there are no two languages that are identical, either in the meanings given to corresponding symbols or in

---

16. Peter Newmark, *Textbook of Translation* (London: Prentice Hall, 1996), 5.

17. J. C. Kumbirai, "The Shona Bible Translation: The Work of the Revd. Michael Hannan, S.J.," *Zambezia* 2, no. 1 (1979): 61–74.

18. Van der Merwe, *Mashonaland*, 12.

19. Aloo O. Mojola, "Foreword," in *Bible Translation and African Languages,* ed. Gosnell L. O. R. Yorke and Peter M. Renju (Nairobi: Acton. 2004), i–iv.

the ways in which such symbols are arranged in phrases and sentences.[20] Translation is therefore a decision making process making it the most direct form of commentary.[21] It is thus not an objective process as noted above. The translation of "a drunkard" (Greek *methusos*) (1 Cor 5:11) or "drunkards" (1 Cor 6:10) in the Union Shona is a case in point here. The Shona Bible translates these as *kana anosinwa doro* (singular) and *kana vanosinwa doro* (plural). This means someone or some people who sometimes drink beer. Reading this the Shona, most of whom would not bother to compare the translation with English Bibles concluded then that a Christian should not even test beer. Thus it is not surprising to find some Shona readers of the Bible today who think that being intoxicated by wine is not against the Christian teaching since the Bible (1 Cor 5:11) forbids beer (*doro*) not wine consumption. The translation of a drunkard therefore was a commentary meant, not to avoid alcohol abuse, but any drinking of beer.

Obviously understanding Christianity from Eurocentric perspectives, the missionary translators of the African Bibles sought to present such a Eurocentric form of Christianity in their translations. Although translation requires that one minimizes his or her biases, putting this into practice is often difficult if not impossible. It has been observed that translations are not made in a vacuum.[22] This is because translators function in a given culture and at a given time. They are therefore often influenced in their work by the way they understand themselves and their culture. J. N. Amanze describes how European missionaries to Africa understood themselves and the people they were to minister to. He says,

> Salvation (for the missionaries) was only possible if they (the Africans) renounced their past, that is, their beliefs and practices and show willingness to live according to the Christian principles. This involved a wholesale transformation of African ways of life for Africanness or blackness was, to the Europeans, a symbol of evil.[23]

An analysis of the way they translated some texts into the Shona language, as I shall demonstrate in some detail below, reflects this. This attitude to the receptor culture and religion affected the way they translated the Bible. As Mojola says, considering that African languages and cultures are closer to the cultures of the ancient biblical worlds than are, for example, to European languages and cultures, it could be argued that basing an African translation on a European version was likely to produce more translational difficulties and distortions than would result by working from the original source texts.[24]

---

20. Eugene Nida, "Principles of Correspondence," in *The Translation Studies Reader*, ed. Lawrence Venuti (London and New York: Routledge, 2000), 126.

21. Levy, "Process," 148–59.

22. Lefevere, "Introduction," 14.

23. James N. Amanze, *African Christianity in Botswana* (Gweru, Zimbabwe: Mambo Press. 1998), 52.

24. Mojola, "Forward," i–iii.

Translation to André Lefevere also has to do with authority and legitimacy and ultimately power. It is not a "window opened to another world", but rather, it is, "a channel opened, often not without a certain reluctance, through which foreign influence can penetrate the native culture, challenging it and even contribute to subverting it."[25] This was more often in the translation of the Bible into African languages as translation marked the introduction of African orthographies by the translators. For this reason, Musa Dube is therefore right to think of biblical translation in Africa as the "colonization of local languages."[26] Let me then look at how some of these 'political' factors influenced the translation of the term 'banquetings' (KJV) or 'carousing' (RSV) in 1 Pet 4:3 in the Shona Bible.

POLITICS IN THE TRANSLATION OF THE SHONA BIBLE

Before I proceed to discuss the politics of the translation of the Shona Bible, let me define what I mean by "politics" in this essay. *The Random House Dictionary of the English Language* has seven entries defining the word politics. The first entry defines politics in the general sense in which the word is often used, that is, as the science or art of political government. However, for purposes of this essay, I find the sixth entry as the most appropriate. Here politics is defined as the "use of intrigue or strategy in obtaining any position of power or control."[27] Following this definition, I use the word 'politics' to refer to strategies used by Bible translators to influence the meaning of the texts to the recipients of the translated texts. Therefore in this section I consider the strategies used by the missionaries to influence the meaning of the Bible to the Shona readers by looking at how the word "banquetings" was translated into Shona.

Studies on the politics of the translation of the Shona Bible are scarce. Apart from Dora R. Mbuwayesango's study of how local divine powers were suppressed through a translation of the Christian God into Mwari, I am not aware of any other such studies. Mbuwayesango's study traces the history of the translation of the biblical God into the Shona Bible.[28] She looks at some of the terms that early missionaries used to render the biblical God in Shona; terms such as *Wedenga, Mudzimu, Yave*, etc until there was a general consensus to use Mwari. Her conclusion is that the use of Mwari to translate the biblical God was a 'political' move meant to win the Shona to Christianity. She writes:

The missionary translation of the Bible was aimed at replacing the Shona Mwari

---

25. Lefevere, "Introduction," 2.

26. Musa W. Dube, "Consuming a Colonial Cultural Bomb: Translating Badimo into 'Demons' in the Setswana Bible (Matthew 8:28–34; 15:22, 10:8)," *JSNT* 73 (1999): 33–59.

27. *The Random House Dictionary of the English Language* (unabridged ed.; 1971), 1113.

28. Dora R. Mbuwayesango, "How Local Divine Powers Were Suppressed: A Case of Mwari of the Shona," in *Other Ways of Reading: African Women and the Bible,* ed. Musa W. Dube (Atlanta: Society of Biblical Literature, 2001), 63–77.

with the biblical God in everything else but the name. If the missionaries had come to introduce a new God to the Shonas, they might have met much resistance, as happened in the earlier mission ventures. The adoption of the Shona name Mwari for the biblical God was in reality the religious usurpation of the Shona. The missionaries took the Shona captive by colonizing the Shona Supreme Being.[29]

It is not only in the translation of the name of the biblical God that the missionaries sought to win the Shona from their religious and cultural practices. The translation of "banquetings" into *mabira* in Shona was another attempt to win the Shona. In 1 Pet 4:3, the author gives a list of vices his readers had turned away from. These are given in the King James Version (KJV) of the Bible as ". . . lasciviousness, lusts, excess of wine, revellings, banquetings, and abominable idolatries." I am interested in the translation of "banquetings" into the *Union Shona Bible*, the oldest Shona Bible. Banquetings is rendered as '*mabira*'. If the adoption of Mwari as a name for the biblical God was a usurpation of the Shona, translating banquetings into *mabira* (thus presenting *mabira* as vice) was a total blow to the Shona religion and cosmology. This is because of the place that *mabira* played among the Shona.

The Place of "Mabira" among the Shona

Mabira is the plural form of *bira*. In traditional Shona society *bira* was a very important ritual. The ritual expressed the full Shona world view.[30] The Shona believe that the universe is a spiritual world where they, as human beings are ontologically linked to nature, fellow human beings, the ancestors and God.[31] The ancestors occupy a very important place in Shona religion and cosmology. The ancestors (*vadzimu*-plural and *mudzimu*-singular) are spirits of one's patrilineal and matrilineal relatives who died as adults. For one to be a *mudzimu* he/she was supposed to have lived an exemplary life; being morally upright and having left children. He/She was also supposed to have received a proper burial with all rituals and ceremonies properly observed; otherwise his/her spirit would haunt rather than protect the living family.[32] *Vadzimu* are responsible for the well being of their living family members. They are the mediators between the living and the Supreme Being. This is because the Shona believe that *kukwira gomo hupoterera* meaning that God is

---

29. Ibid., 67.

30. *Mabira* can generally be used to refer to all Shona rituals to appease ancestors. Taona T. H. Chabudapasi, "Three Ceremonies for the Dead," in *Shona Customs: Essays by Shona Writers*, ed. Clive Kileff and Peggy Kileff (Gweru, Zimbabwe: Mambo Press, 1970), 65–66, for example, also uses the word *bira* to refer to *kurova guva* (ritual to bring home the spirit of a dead relative).

31. S. Banana Canaan, *Come and Share: An Introduction to Christian Theology* (Gweru, Zimbabwe: Mambo Press 1991), 23.

32. Y. Turaki, "The Role of Ancestors," in *The African Bible Commentary*, Tokunboh Adeyemo, gen. ed. (Grand Rapids: Zondervan; Nairobi: WordAlive, 2006), 480.

so great that approaching him directly is perceived as being disrespectful to him. He therefore should be approached indirectly through the ancestors. Among the Shona, like in most traditional African societies, ancestors are the symbols of family, tribal and ethnic unity, community cohesiveness and custodians of kinship, religion, morality, ethics and customs.[33] Thus although the Shona were monotheistic,[34] their religion was complicated to outsiders who often took their belief in ancestors as some form of polytheism. The ritual of *bira* should be understood in the context of this Shona world view.

Although we can talk of *bira* (singular), there were in fact many types of *mabira* among the Shona. *Bira* was a ritual feast meant to give offerings to the ancestors. It could be for appeasement, for thanking or for honouring the ancestors for the protection of the family. *Mabira* were therefore meant for specific purposes: asking for rainfall (*mukwerekwere*), giving a name (*kugadza zita*), bringing home the spirit of the dead (*kurova guva*) and many other ceremonies. Generally a *bira* took place as follows:

> The head of the family organizes the brewing of beer, possibly collecting contributions of grain from close family members. The women brew the beer. When it is ready, the whole extended family gathers, with other relatives, in-laws and neighbours. Offerings of beer (and some times snuff) are made to the spirits and the remainder distributed to those present. The ceremony often involves traditional music with singing and dancing.[35]

I need to emphasise that there were indeed many *mabira* and sometimes following slightly different procedures from the one described above, depending on each Shona tribe. However, all in all, *mabira* were meant to venerate the ancestors. They were associated with beer drinking, meat eating and general feasting. It was the occasion when members of the extended family and indeed the whole tribe came together. Therefore participation in the *mabira* gave one a sense of belonging and indeed identity. Thus Charles Nyamiti, referring to ancestor veneration in general, says, the cult (of ancestral veneration) was characterized by solidarity (relationality,

---

33. Ibid.

34. I am aware of the debate concerning traditional African religions and monotheism. Contrary to the position I take in this essay, there are scholars who think that the view that African traditional religions were originally monotheistic is a result of Christian and Muslim influences (Kwame Bediako, *Christianity in Africa: The Renewal Of Non-Western Religion* [Edinburgh: Edinburgh University Press 1997], 98). The debate is over whether ancestors were "gods" themselves or were intermediaries between the living and the Supreme Being. K. Núrnberger, *The Living Dead and the Living God: Christ and the Ancestors in a Changing World* (Pietermaritzburg: Cluster, 2007), 33, thinks because ancestors, in most cases, did not speak in the name of the Supreme Being then they were authorities themselves. I think otherwise.

35. Michael F. C. Bourdillon, *Where Are the Ancestors? Changing Culture in Zimbabwe* (Harare: University of Zimbabwe, 1997), 71–72.

totality and participation.[36] Often the ancestral spirits took the occasion, through their mediums, to talk to the living advising them on issues of life. Depending on the type of the *bira*, *mabira* involved all members of the family from young to old. What then were the effects of translating banquetings into *mabira*?

The Politics of Translating "Banquetings" into "Mabira"

I mentioned above that the Shona traditional worldview appeared polytheistic to an outsider. There is little doubt that the missionaries who translated the Shona Bible considered *mabira* to be some form of worship and therefore idolatry for the Shona Christians who continued participating in them. Talking about how the Dutch Reformed Church came to the Shona people of southern Zimbabwe as a day star (Morgenster), van der Merwe describes the Great Zimbabwe ruins, where most *mabira* used to take place as, "once the centre of pagan worship."[37] Translating banquetings into *mabira* was therefore not just a translation but an interpretation meant to deal with what the translators thought to be the Shona people's hindrance to fully embrace Christianity. Just as Musa Dube noted in the translation of demons into *badimo* (ancestors) in the Setswana Bible, that such a translation was a structural device used by the missionaries to alienate natives from their cultures, the same can be said on the translation of banquetings into *mabira*.[38]

Except for achieving their objectives of alienating natives from their cultures, I find it difficult to understand how banquetings was specifically translated *mabira*. The word translated *mabira* is the Greek word *potos* which Rogers and Rogers translate to "drinking" or "drinking parties."[39] Now *mabira* were not drinking parties for the Shona. Although drinking by both the living and the dead was part of the ritual, the Shona did not understand this to be a party. It was a ritual, whose significance was communication between the living and the dead. As M. F. C. Bourdillon says, during these rituals, the living asked the ancestors to take care of the family, protecting it from illnesses and other misfortunes.[40] Also if the family (the living) considered the spirits (ancestral) have been failing in their obligations towards them, the formal address of the spirits by the living could involve harangues with shouts of support from the attendants.

To use Musa Dube's language, translating banquetings into *mabira* was therefore "dropping a cultural bomb" that shattered and fragmented the Shona culture.[41] Reading the translation in the context of the whole verse (1 Pet 4:3), the Shona readers of the *Union Shona Bible* were told that the time they had played *mabira* was over and doing so as Christians was as bad as worshipping idols. What comes

---

36. Charles Nyamiti, in http://www.afrikaworld.net/afrel/nyamiti.htm.

37. Van der Merwe, *Mashonaland*, 18.

38. Dube, "Translating," 33–59.

39. Cleon L. Rogers Jr. and Cleon L. Rogers III, *The New Linguistic and Exegetical Key to the Greek New Testament* (Grand Rapids: Zondervan, 1998), 577.

40. Bourdillon, *Ancestors?* 228.

41. Dube, "Translating," 33–59.

out loud and clear from this translation then is the missionaries' attitude to the
Shona culture and religion. They did not respect the Shona religion and culture.
For them the whole Shona way of life was a life of iniquity. Through the translation of banquetings into *mabira*, all traditional Shona ceremonies associated with
mabira were demonized. Participation in them was seen as participation in idol
worship. The result of this has been Shona identity crisis and total colonization of
Shona culture and religion. Writing on the problems of pastoral care among the
urban Shona, Tapiwa N. Mucherera correctly notes that when most Shona urban
Christians go to seek pastoral counseling, often it is on issues of personal and religious identity confusion caused by the demonisation of their traditional religion
by the missionaries.[42]

Translating banquetings into *mabira* has succeeded not only in demonizing the
Shona culture and religion but also in dividing Shona families. As described above
mabira, were occasions for the extended family to come together, know each other
as individuals and commune with the living dead. It was also a time family members learnt to cooperate, forgive each other for whatever evils that had developed
among them and learnt to honour the family structures for the good of all. With its
demonisation, the extended family has been broken up and in some cases rivalries
created. Christians who no longer want to take part in *mabira* are often accused of
witchcraft by their traditional relatives. Since they do not want to participate in the
honour of the departed, family misfortunes are attributed to them. Divided, the
Shona have therefore been conquered by the missionary translation of banquetings into *mabira*.

Not "Mabira" but "Kuraradza": Improvements to the Union Shona Translation

The entrance of native speakers into the business of Bible translation has seen
some improvements made to the Shona Bible. In 2005 the United Bible Society
published *Testamente Itsva MuChishona Chanhasi* (The New Testament in Today's
Shona). This New Testament has "corrected" some of what the translators thought
were wrong translations in the *Union Shona Bible*. For example instead of translating a drunkard *anosinwa doro*, they have translated it *chidhakwa*. This is the right
translation of a drunkard. They have also translated banquetings to *kuraradza*. Indeed in the context of the vices mentioned in 1 Pet 4:3, *kuraradza* is the best meaning for banquetings. It is understandable to say the author of Peter had in mind
drinking parties when he mentioned banquetings than to think that he was referring to ancestor veneration (*mabira*) whose practice is not explicitly mentioned in
the New Testament. There has also been attempts to try as much as possible to use
the contemporary Shona language but without loosing the dignity of the word of
God. Thus translators have avoided using what M. F. C. Bourdillon calls *chitaundi*,

---

42. Tapiwa N. Mucherera, *Pastoral Care from a Third World Perspective: A Pastoral
Theology of Care for the Urban Contemporary Shona in Zimbabwe* (New York: Peter Lang,
2001), 45.

Anglicized Shona language.[43] Unfortunately besides having modern translations, the Shona still believe that the *Union Shona Bible* is *the Bible*. Often modern translations are approached with suspicion, being understood to be more of interpretations than translations. It is therefore not surprising for many to question the sacrality of modern translations.

CONCLUSION

In this essay I have looked at the politics of translating the Bible into the Shona language. I have approached the subject understanding politics as a strategy used by someone to obtain a position of power and /or control. I have looked at the politics of the translation of the Shona Bible by first tracing the history of the translation of the Shona Bible. Here I have highlighted the contribution of different mission bodies and their realization of the need for Union Shona in the light of the five dialects of the Shona language. I then focused on the translation of "banquetings" in 1 Pet 4:3 highlighting the effects of translating that word into *mabira*. Underlining the centrality of *mabira* in Shona religion and culture, I have concluded that such a translation was influenced by a Europeanized Christianity which saw nothing good in the Shona, their culture and their religion. It was a translation meant to evangelize and to conquer, "a cultural bomb" in the words of Musa Dube.[44]

I, however, do want to end by noting that the politicization of the translation of the Bible was not the work of missionaries only as even modern translators also are influenced by the politics of the day: their educational, doctrinal, personal, social and even denominational sensitivities.[45] As Lefevere, whom I cited above, noted, translation does not happen in a vacuum. However, translators must, as much as possible, avoid bias and deliberate interpretation in their translation.

Missionaries should indeed be given credit for the work they did in translating the Bible into the Shona language. It should be emphasized that they did their work under very difficulty conditions: without native orthographies, with limited knowledge of the native languages and world views, with very few educated natives to seek opinion from, and so on. This, however, should not be used to exonerate them from clear politicization of the translation process.

More work therefore needs to be done as work continues to revise African Bibles translated during the missionary era. As Mojola correctly argues, "[I]t is vitally important that biblical exegesis be done in the languages in which the majority of believers interact with the word of God—their mother languages."[46] For this to happen, he goes on to say that, the pioneering translations of the missionaries

---

43. Bourdillon, *Ancestors?* 233.

44. Dube, "Translating," 33–59.

45. Aloo O. Mojola, "Foreword," in *Bible Translation and African Languages,* ed. Gosnell L. O. R. Yorke and Peter M. Renju (Nairobi: Acton, 2004), 77–104.

46. Aloo O. Mojola, "Bible Translation in Africa," in Adeyemo, *Commentary,* 1315.

need to be revised, more translations need to be made for those languages lacking vernacular Bible translations and more culture-, age-, and gender-sensitive study Bibles need to be produced in many African languages. Over and above this more work also needs to done to educate African Christians on the effect of translation on scripture. It is my conviction that an awareness of "the politics of translation" will help modern translators avoid some of the problems caused by the missionary translations of the Bible into African languages.

WORKS CITED

Adeyemo, Tokunboh, gen. ed. *Africa Bible Commenatry*. Grand Rapids: Zondervan; Nairobi: WordAlive, 2006.

Amanze, James, N. *African Christianity in Botswana*. Gweru, Zimbabwe: Mambo, 1998.

Banana, Canaan S. *Come and Share: An Introduction to Christian Theology*. Gweru, Zimbabwe: Mambo, 1991.

Bediako, K. *Christianity in Africa: The Renewal of Non-Western Religion*. Edinburgh: Edinburgh University Press, 1997.

Bourdillon, Michael F.C. *Where Are the Ancestors? Changing Culture in Zimbabwe*. Harare: University of Zimbabwe, 1997.

Chabudapasi, Taona T. H. "Three Ceremonies for the Dead." In *Shona Customs: Essays by Shona Writers*, ed. Clive Kileff and Peggy Kileff. Gweru, Zimbabwe: Mambo, 1970.

Dube, Musa W. "Consuming a Colonial Cultural Bomb: Translating *Badimo* into 'Demons' in the Setswana Bible (Matthew 8:28–34; 15:22, 10:8)," *JSNT* 73 (1999): 33–59.

Dube, Musa W., ed. *Other Ways of Reading: African Women and the Bible*, Atlanta: Society of Biblical Literature, 2001.

Fortune, George. "75 Years of Writing in Shona." *Zambezia* 1, no. 1 (1969): 55–67.

Gundani, Paul, H. "The Land Crisis in Zimbabwe and the Role of the Churches towards Its Resolution." *SHE* 28, no. 2 (2002): 122–69.

Hallencreutz, Carl, F. *Religion and Politics in Harare, 1890–1990*. Uppsala, Sweden: Swedish Institute of Missionary Research, 1998.

Kumbirai, J. C., "The Shona Bible Translation: The Work of the Revd. Michael Hannan, S.J." *Zambezia* 2, no. 1(1979): 61–74.

Lefevere, André, ed. *Translation/History/Culture: A Source Book*. London and New York: Routledge, 1992.

Maxwell, D. "Historicizing Christian Independency: The Southern African Pentecostal Movement *ca.* 1908–1960." *JAH* 39, no. 2 (1999): 243–64.

Mucherera, Tapiwa N. *Pastoral Care from a Third World Perspective: A Pastoral Theology of Care for the Urban Contemporary Shona in Zimbabwe*. New York: Peter Lang, 2001.

Newmark, Peter. *Textbook of Translation*. London: Prentice Hall, 1996.

Núrnberger, K. *The Living Dead and the Living God: Christ and the Ancestors in a Changing World*. Pietermaritzburg: Cluster, 2007.

Nyamiti, Charles. http.www.afrikaworld.net/afrel/nyamiti.htm (accessed 14 November 2007).

Rogers, Cleon L., Jr., and Cleon L. Rogers III. *The New Linguistic and Exegetical Key to the Greek New Testament*. Grand Rapids: Zondervan, 1998.

Stein, Jess, ed. *The Random House Dictionary of the English Language*. New York: Random House, 1971.

Tate, W. Randolph. *Interpreting the Bible*. Peabody, MA.: Hendrickson, 2006.

van der Merwe, W. J. *The Day Star Arises in Mashonaland*. Morgenster, South Africa: Morgenster, 1953.

Venuti, Lawrence, ed. *The Translation Studies Reader*. London and New York: Routledge, 2000.

Weller, J., and J. Linden. *Mainstream Christianity to 1980 in Malawi, Zambia, and Zimbabwe*. Gweru, Zimbabwe: Mambo, 1984.

Yorke, Gosnell L. O. R., and Peter M. Renju, eds. *Bible Translation and African Languages*. Nairobi: Acton, 2004.

Ideology, History, and Translation Theories: A Critical Analysis of the Tshivenda Bible Translation of 1 Kings 21:1–16

Elelwani B. Farisani

Although Christianity came to South Africa in 1652, the expansion of Christianity in South Africa began with different missionary societies working among different tribes. For the spread of Christianity to make meaningful impact in the lives of the indigenous people, there arose the need to translate the Bible into various local languages. This may not render the same meaning to local people in their own vernacular. Perhaps this may have contributed to the quest for new translation of the Bible by various locals in order for more meaningful usage of their own vernacular. This essay, therefore, calls for a critical analysis of the Tshivenda Bible (1936 version) as it relates to translation ideology, history and translation theories with particular reference to the Tshivenda Bible translation of 1 Kgs 21:1–26. This will be done in the following six steps. First, we will discuss translation ideology. Second, we will examine translation history. Third, we will analyse translation theory. Fourth, we will look at the translation of 1 Kgs 21:1–16. Here we will start off by examining the 1936 Tshivenda Bible translation of 1 Kgs 21:1–16. Thereafter we will go on to examine our own translation of the above-mentioned text. Fifth, we will compare our own translation to the 1936 Tshivenda one. And, finally, we will spell out few challenges facing both translation studies and African Biblical Hermeneutics.

Translation Ideology

In as much as ideology vary from, and depend on contexts to live fully their meanings, I would like to explore the ideology behind the biblical translations. In this case I will put translation into contexts to show the variations found in the translation ideology. South African chief translator of the new Tshivenda Bible declared to eager speakers of the language at its publication celebration that the ideology behind this translation is that it "will empower the church of Christ to conquer the

An earlier version of this article was published in *OTE* 23, no. 3 (2010): 597–626. Republished here with permission.

199

country for Christ."[1] In a similar spirit, it could be deduced that Tshivenda Bible translation is geared towards giving the Tshivenda speakers power to conquer the country and the inhabitants for Christ via the instrument of Tshivenda language. It is also designed to make the peoples' belief stronger than ever before owing to a thorough understanding of the bible available in their own language. The idea not being only allowing the locals to be in touch with the scripture in their own language but also to handle the bible as their own and in their own language thereby guard and protect the values contained therein as theirs too.

Furthermore, the ideology of translation also hinges on the sense of freedom and belonging. The life and light that the bible gives in own language, tends to abolish the darkness that the foreign language may throw on the interpretation and understanding of the values that the bible holds for the readers. It is argued that "translation is a complex process because meaning is 'created' by decoding the source text on several levels (for instance, grammatical, structural, literary, and socio-cultural levels."[2] This meaning as Van der Watt and Kruger went further to argue must then "be encoded into the target language by means of linguistic, literary, and cultural conventions of the target language."[3] The different aspect of translation like grammar, structure, and others are combined in an interactive process that results in meaning. So the ideology of translation points to two basics. Firstly, it is, an acknowledgement that there are different languages in which the Bible could be written. Secondly, there is a need for the locals to read the Bible in their own mother tongue, which at the same time will help in the spread of the message of the Bible. However, it does not mean that the translation should be word for word from the original source. This is because "languages do not overlap in their use of words, structures, genres, and social conventions."[4] In this way, the various aspects of distorted communication and message to some peoples due to language difficulty may by means of translation curbed.

Translation varies from one translator to another, thus, it becomes an aspect of translation ideology to expose the variations and make a critical impact on the course of the translation process. This deals with breaking down the original language to avert it from language dominance. Another significant measure of the ideology of translation is to make the Bible message and meaning more focused and direct to the locals for whom the translation is made. For example, citing Lar-

---

1. World Report, 1998. "Venda Bible Said to Give Church Power to Conquer Country for Christ," n.p. (accessed 4 September 2007). http://www.biblesociety.org/wr_336/wr_336 .htm#Venda.

2. Jan van der Watt and Yolanda Kruger, "Some Considerations on Bible Translation as Complex Process," in *Contemporary Translation Studies and Bible Translation: A South African Perspective,* ed. Jakobus Naudé and Christo van der Merwe (ATS 2; Bloemfontein: UFS, 2002), 118.

3. Ibid.

4. Ibid.

son,[5] Van der Watt and Kruger assert that "a translator should discover the meaning in the source language and then reformulate that meaning in the language tools of the target language in a clear and natural way."[6] Decoding and encoding of meaning of a translated Bible is an ideology in translation, which is focused on the influence on the receiver. It is important to know that "the satisfaction and requirements of receivers of the translation should be met rather than rendering the source text closely as possible even if it means laying a different emphasis in the translation or leaving out/adding materials to the translation."[7]

The value of literary translation of the Bible is one of the ideologies found in translation theory. While Biblical support needs to be explicitly demonstrated, it is certainly clear that in the Bible there are many different texts that manifest both "beauty and power in the presentation of their intended message"[8] which are very crucial to the receivers, hence, the ideology. It is on this note that Wendland would want us to believe that "information transmission is what most contemporary Bible communicators including translators see as their primary objective or ideology."[9] In this way, getting the content of the scripture across to the constituencies is an ideology also behind translation. However, the task of translation is "daunting enough." The truth is that local language translated version is beauty and power in the needed information justifies the task. So translation of the Bible enhances the beauty and increases the power of the word to the hearing of the local receivers. It is therefore important to note that the ideology of translation of the Bible could as well involve all the reasons behind the advantages and disadvantages of a dominant language that could not deliver in every environment of the world.

In addition, in interpreting a text, there are some constituent elements involved that points to the ideology of interpretation. Some of the aspects of the constituent elements in interpretation as Van der Watt and Kruger wrote include "the construction and semantics of words (including phonology and lexicography), the construction of sentences (syntax and some stylistic elements such as figurative language, metaphors, idioms, symbolism, sarcasm, irony)."[10] True and deeper knowledge of the bible via language advantage is a factor. In support of this view, Van der Watt and Kruger cited Gutt[11] who holds that:

We should be clear to ourselves that some inadequacies in our linguistic knowl-

---

5. Mildred Larson, *Meaning Based Translation: A Guide to Cross-Language Equivalence* (Lanham, MD: University Press of America, 1984), 4–5.

6. Van der Watt and Kruger, "Some Considerations on Bible Translation," 118.

7. Ibid., 119.

8. Ernst Wendland, *Translating the Literature of Scripture: A Literary-Rhetorical Approach to Bible Translation* (Dallas: SIL International, 2004), 33.

9. Ibid.

10. Van der Watt and Kruger, "Some Considerations on Bible Translation," 120.

11. Ernst-August Gutt, "From Translation to Effective Communication," *NT* 2, no. 1 (1988): 34.

edge of the receptor language (e.g., about some morphological rules of the language) will probably be far less detrimental to our communication efforts than an inadequate knowledge of the religious beliefs, concerns and overt and convert spiritual needs of the receptor language people; misjudgement in this area will almost certainly do considerable damage to our communication effort.[12]

In this way, the ideology behind translation could be to make the meaning of the translated words more effective than it is in the foreign language in the hands of local users. The paradigmatic cohesion of a text is also of importance. Van der Watt and Kruger further argues that "an adequate translation must reflect the internal cohesion on syntactic and thematic levels."[13] However, with the view to the ideology of translation, a due attention is given to details that can boost the message in the local language. In a similar vein, care should be taken not to divide paragraphs, in ways that would predispose meaning by serving sentences that belong together.[14] The import of this, is, that, word for word translations usually have paragraphs divisions. It helps group idea and makes the many, whole in any complicated translation process.

Another important aspect in translation is the methodology. Under this, there are some of the more important literary movements and schools that have influenced biblical studies, hermeneutics in particular. These important literary movements can be classified under the following, "Rhetorical criticism, Formalism or New criticism, Structuralism, Receptionism or Reader-Response Criticism and Deconstruction or Postmodernism."[15] The import of hermeneutics is the determination that local speakers should as well receive the biblical message in their own languages. Methodology, with effect to ideology should aim towards the packaging of the message that belongs to a particular people specifically and uniquely, for them. It is part of the original communication process. Camery-Hoggatt holds that, "an act of reading is valid to the extent that it fills in the gaps of text with the schemas that were operative for culture in which the text was composed."[16] In as much as understanding the ideology behind translation in general and the biblical message in particular is important, it is of special importance to also note that if translation is defined as conveying meaning, all aspects will be taken seriously. It therefore means that "translation implies interpretation which means that the translator aims to 'retell' what the original text offers. This 'retelling' should come as close as possible to the original process of communication."[17]

Clarification of mixture of languages can be sighted as one of the reasons be-

---

12. Van der Watt and Kruger, "Some Considerations on Bible Translation," 122.

13. Ibid, 125.

14. Ibid., 125.

15. Wendland, *Translating*, 21–22.

16. Jerry Camery-Hoggatt, *Speaking of God: Reading and Preaching the Word of God* (Peabody, MA: Hendrickson, 1955), 84.

17. Van der Watt and Kruger, "Some Considerations on Bible Translation," 130.

hind the continuous survival of ideology of translation. It is clear that different languages use different mixtures and different mixtures place different weights on same words. This, possibility can lead to misrepresentation of the original text in the eyes of translated receptors. Taking into account that the manner in which the elements that form part of the process of creating meaning, combine, it differs from one language to another. It is observed that different languages 'mix-meaning' differently. So the ideology behind the clarification of mix meaning is primarily to enable the receptors tackle locally, languages that could have appeared confusing were they found in any language that is foreign. So, translation ideology deals with simplifying the complexities involved in process of decoding and encoding of meanings of languages. The essence is to guarantee the understanding of the message by the receptor. One can sum this argument by saying that "translation can as well be regarded as a creative process in which the translator should endeavour to combine the different elements in such a way that the meaning in the target language comes as close as possible to that of the source language."[18]

Translation History

In this subsection, we will focus on two main issues, namely the translation history of the Tshivenda bible and the translation history in general.

History of the Tshivenda Bible Translation

In South Africa, there are eleven officially recognized languages which Tshivenda is one of them. Venda is a region to the north of South Africa bordering on Zimbabwe. Tshivenda is a language spoken by over 1, 000 000 people in South Africa, mainly living in Limpopo. It is also spoken in Zimbabwe.[19] Translation of the Gospels and Acts into Tshivenda, by Dr. P. E. Schwellnus assisted by Mr. Isaak Mulaudzi and Mr Fineas Mutsila, were published by the BFBS in London in 1920, the New Testament was published in 1925, and the complete Bible in 1936.[20]

The second translation led by Van Rooy was published in 1998. Dr. T. S. Farisani and Rev. Mahamba were initially appointed to work with Van Rooy in translating this second Tshivenda Bible in 1973.[21] In 1974 the three translators were sent to Israel to study Hebrew and the geography of Israel in order to be fully equipped to handle this second bible translation. On completion of the Hebrew studies, both Mahamba and Farisani returned back to South Africa to continue with bible translation. To their utter surprise, Van Rooy demanded that before they could

---

18. Van der Watt and Kruger, "Some Considerations on Bible Translation," 135.

19. Census 2001, "The Languages of South Africa," n.p. (accessed 14 December 2010). http://www.southafrica.info/about/people/language.htm.

20. Eric Hermanson, "A Brief Overview of Bible Translation in South Africa," in Naudé and van der Merwe, Contemporary Translation, 6–18, 16.

21. Personal conversation with Tshenuwani Farisani on 3 January 2011 at Maungani.

continue with further translation, they need to sign a declaration to the effect that they will respect and not undermine the leadership and authority of Van Rooy.[22] The two refused to sign such a document.

Their arguments for refusing to sign such a declaration were as follows. First, such a declaration should not only favour Van Rooy, but should be signed by all three translators, Farisani, Mahamba and Van Rooy stating that respect will be mutual and no one would undermine the other. Second, they asked why such a declaration only came after the return of the three translators from a Hebrew course in Israel, which both Mahamba and Farisani completed successfully and not at the beginning of the translation process. Farisani completed this eighteen months Hebrew course in only five months with a distinction. Both Farisani and Mahamba were dismissed from the translation panel for refusing to sign such a document in February 1975 by the then General Secretary of the Bible Society of South Africa, Van der Merwe. The two dismissed translators were replaced by F. C. Raulinga and A. R. Mbuwe who worked with Van Rooy until this second bible translation was published in 1998.[23]

Translation History in General

The translation history has several branches that make up the history account. It is the opinion of Naudé and Van der Merwe that in about 1980s, there was a cultural turn in translation studies with its focus on the way culture impacts and constrains translation. This they argue that "as a result of this development, the focus of translation studies shifted from the source text to the translation process, the product and /or reception of translation as well as the cultural-social bound character of translation."[24]

In the above account, the methodological impact is a shift from normative linguistic-based theories of translation. For example, the functional equivalents approach. It is in a similar spirit that Naudé and Van der Merwe citing Jacobus Naudé and Alet Kruger offered an overview of current trends in contemporary translation studies that are relevant to Bible translation. After a review of developments away from functional equivalence in translation studies since the cultural turn of the early 1980s, Naudé and Van der Merwe emphasizes "the advantage of the functionalist approach of the Christiane Nord with its focus on the intention/ purpose of translation as it follows from the translation brief."[25] The consequence is that Bible translation at the time is normal translation and opens up all the concerned foreign cultures.

Translation history observes that Bible translation could be created for a specific purpose, and translation strategies must be followed instead of striving to-

---

22. Ibid.
23. Ibid.
24. Naude and van der Merwe, "Introduction," *Contemporary Translation*, 1.
25. Ibid., 2.

wards equivalence. It is based on this claim that Kruger in the history, provides an overview of "corpus-based" translation research, which builds upon the studies of scholars working within the descriptive translation studies (DTS). This involves using computerized corpora to study translated text, not in terms of its equivalence to source texts but as a valid object of translation. The effect is that a new approach was embraced unlike the word to word translation. The new approach was based on linguistic and textual features of different translation and or revision of the same "Bible in respect of consistency of terminology, orthography and register."[26] This was believed that it could shed light inter-alia on the main two factors: linguistic and textual features. Consideration was also given to the effects of dialectical variation; interference of the source language and recurring patterns and typical strategies utilized.

Accounts available, with effect to translation history also suggest that Bible translation is a "full-fledged" interdisciplinary activity. It involves knowledge and insight from the fields of Biblical studies, this is because it is believed that in "translation history, translation studies, as well as linguistics and the literary sciences (i.e. in both source and target text languages)"[27] are several parts of the whole. With a special mention to Bible translation in South Africa, history shows that,

> Bible translation in South Africa, where 70% of its citizens consider themselves Christians has the benefit that it can reap from a rich tradition of study of the Bible. Further more, in a country with 11 official languages, bible translation also benefit from the fact that the study of different languages, the training of translators and academics research in the field of translation studies enjoy a very high profile.[28]

This position unvails that Bible translation faces a number of exciting challenges both in South Africa and other parts of the world. Given the availability of human resources, the challenges could be easily dealt with by scholars who will in turn make an important contribution to Bible translation in South Africa and in the world in general.

Although, Christianity came to South Africa in about 1652 through missionaries, the outreach was only effective in 19 century and from then emerged the need for translation to meet with the needs of the locals. The missionary period is important in translation history because "history of expansion of Christianity in south Africa began with different missionary societies working among different tribes."[29] In this way, early bible translation was undertaken by individual or group of missionaries usually from the same society and are working towards a defined goal.

---

26. Ibid., 3.
27. Ibid., 5.
28. Ibid.
29. Hermanson, "Brief Overview," 7.

UNIVERSITY OF WINCHESTER
LIBRARY

Translations done by the missionaries were made available in the mission press, or commercial press in the missionaries' country of residence or in their home countries. It is on record that the early missionaries studied Hebrew, Greek and Latin. Translation theory was not well developed as such. Thus the missionary period was marked by formal equivalence form of translation and it was widely contested as it failed to portray values of messages in the native languages. For example, "judging a translation against one another in languages rather than against the original is certainly misguided. However, one would question whether one who adhered closely to Greek and Hebrew and sometimes strained Xhosa idiom was indeed ahead of his[her] time in the principle of Bible translation."[30]

The Bible Society of South Africa which has contributed immensely to the publishing of Bibles in different local languages became an autonomous body on 1 November 1965. It was at the time "Dr. E. A. Nida was developing his theory of dynamic-equivalent translation in publications such as *Towards a Science of Translation* (1964*)* and *The Theory and Practice of Translation* (1969)."[31] For the purpose of efficient translation, a pattern was adopted. The pattern has been to select an Editorial Committee, consisting of a co-coordinator who has had theological training including Hebrew, and Greek who has at least a thorough working knowledge of indigenous languages and two mother-tongue speakers, who do not necessarily have any knowledge of the original language as translators. So translation history deals with the phases the missionary went through with the locals with the view to effect communication of bible message. It also emphasizes the impact made by the locals in translating the Bible from a foreign language to the local languages.

It was not without pains of loss of meaning and weights of words, sentences etc, it is because of lack of professionally trained personnel in the business of translation. This was at the early stage of translation which may have contributed to a huge failure in Bible translation. This is because transformation and communication of the text as it functions within the functional-equivalent approach, is aimed not only at making the bible message understandable for the contemporary readers but also, and particularly at making it communicable. Transformation of the text then leads to adapting idiomatic expression and a figurative language which falls outside the realm of the experience and language usage of the contemporary reader to a level upon which it communicates approximately the same message as the original.[32]

Making idiomatic expression understandable in native/receptor language was a factor that troubled translation. It was because the then word to word way of translation, does not make provision for idiomatic expressions. However, the use

---

30. Ibid., 8.

31. Ibid., 9.

32. Gert Jordaan, "Problems in the Theoretical Foundation of the Functional-Equivalent Approach" in Naudé and van der Merwe, *Contemporary Translation*, 25–26.

of idioms in the Bible seems to have same value as it could be depicted in traditionally or culturally inclined sentences that might have run across the different cultures in the respective languages. Translation history accessed the translation process used in bringing Bible message to a heterogeneous audience of non original Bible language speakers.

TRANSLATION THEORY

During 20th century, literary theories were intensely concerned with the meaning of text and textual theories and sophisticated reading strategies were developed. These theories refer to three prominent strands in theoretical thinking namely: intrinsic literary theory, the Kantian view and the Romantic tradition.[33]

It is important to note that "the pioneers of meaning-based Bible translation studies did not say a great deal if anything, about a specifically literary rendition during decades of the sixties and seventies."[34] Their emphasis was apparently focused so much on conveying the basic content of the scriptures in a natural, idiomatic way that not much attention could be devoted to the refinements of this procedure. The aim here is to break translators, who were increasingly mother-tongue practitioners of their typical preference for a literal approach, opening them up to a freer methodology that will direct their energies to producing a translation that can convey in an appropriate style to the target language the sense of the original.[35] However, it is my intent here to give a brief discussion on secular theorists as regards to translation. I will not be broad as it is not my chief aim, but a little overview to enable me look into the TshiVenda translation of 1 Kgs 21:1–16 which is my chief aim.

The secular theorists to translation comprise varieties of different approaches especially on the subject of literary translation. Among these approaches is the literalist approach. According to Wendland, "the practitioner makes a serious attempt to reflect the recognized literary style of the original text in the language of translation, [. . .] that is 'in English dress but with a Hebraic voice.' "[36] This translation theory approach type is guided by the principle that the Hebrew Bible, like much of the literature of antiquity was meant to be read aloud and translated based on the rhythm and sound. In this case, translation tires to mimic the particular rhetoric, preserving such devices as repetition, alliteration etc.[37] This perhaps is intended to lead the reader back to the sound structure and form of the original words and sentences. A greater recognition of the importance and potential

---

33. Heilna Du Plooy, "Listening to the Wind in the Trees: Meaning, Interpretation, and Literary Theory," in Naudé and van der Merwe, *Contemporary Translation*, 268, 269.

34. Wendland, *Translating*, 43.

35. Ibid.

36. Ibid., 47–48.

37. Ibid., 48.

literariness of explicitly recursion in the biblical text is indeed very necessary in literalist approach theory.

Another approach to literary translation is the functionalist approach. It is interesting to observe that fully functional approach to translation according to functionalist writers naturally stress "the purpose (normally referred to only in the singular) that a particular translation is designed to perform for its primary target audience within a given sociocultural setting."[38] In functionalist approach there is a notable difference between the perspective and that of functional equivalence in the practice of Bible translation. The translation goal as de Waard and Nida (1986:36) is cited is to "seek to employ a functionally equivalent set of forms in so far as possible in order to match the meaning (i.e., functions) of the original source language text."[39] In this way, in Bible translation, it is the communication functions of the text which are preeminent and determinative. Functionalist theorists believe that functions may be fulfilled by either a literal or a more idiomatic translation (a documentary or an "instrumental" version in Nord's terms) depending on particular circumstances of communication at hand.[40] The principal intentions of the original are not ignored in the operation, however, in view of impossibility of satisfying them all, translation are evaluated for, in relevance to the light of setting and then prioritized for application in the translation itself.

Further approach is the descriptive approach, a school of thought called "descriptive Translation Studies" which was developed in the early 1970s more or less in opposition to what its originators viewed as the prevailing "prescriptive" approach to translation.[41] This approach according to Hermans[42] "rejected the idea that the study of translation should be geared primarily to formulating rules, norms or guidelines for the practice or evaluation of translation or to developing didactic instrument for translators training."[43] While descriptive approach is important in translation theory, it certainly needs to be included as part of comprehensive methodology of literary translating, we can observe that due to their fear of being prescriptive, DTS theorists tend to produce studies that are not as helpful as they might be to Bible translators.[44]

One more approach under the secular theorists is the textlinguistic approach which is represented by Hatim and Mason[45] whose theoretical studies provide

38. Ibid., 51.
39. Ibid.
40. Ibid., 52.
41. Ibid., 54.
42. Theo Hermans, *Translation in Systems: Descriptive and System-Oriented Approaches Explained* (Manchester, England: St. Jerome, 1999), 7.
43. Wendland, *Translating*, 54.
44. Ibid., 55.
45. Basil Hatim and Ian Mason, *Discourse and the Translator* (London: Longman, 1990). See also Basil Hatim and Ian Mason, *The Translator as Communicator* (London: Longman, 1997).

many examples of how this methodology can assist translators in their text-transformation efforts.[46] In an early application of textlinguistic approach to the translation of poetry, Robert de Beaugrande noted that "a great poetry is in some manner innovative, whether it derives from a native or foreign source. He underscores that texts are translatable into a given language only if the resulting translated text fulfills at least some of the readers expectation in that language concerning the constitution and transmission of discourse."[47] Text-linguistic approach seeks to engage in the explanatory annotation with regards to artistic and rhetorical matters in any translation.

There is also the "relevance approach," which the insight are important to Bible translation as has been pointed out to be central to the fact that human communication crucially creates an expectation of optimal relevance, that is, an expectation on the part of the hearer that the attempt at interpretation will yield adequate contextual effects at minimal processing cost. Wendland citing Pilkington is of the view that relevance theory is also depicted in literariness which is seen in terms of cognitive events triggered in minds/brains by linguistic stimuli. It can be characterized in terms of distinctive kind of mental process involving extensive guided exploration of encyclopedic entries.[48] The extent to which translators are able to take such phenomena into consideration in their work depends on their level of expertise and experience. This shows that the work of translation is an up-hill task.

Apparently, another approach that is important to note is the "interpretive approach." In a concise comparative overview of an interpretive approach to translation, John Delise provides a summary:

> The expressive (emotive) function of language is predominant. Correspondingly, connotation—the power to evoke—plays a major role in the text. That literary form is important in and of itself; it manifests aesthetic qualities that enrich its referential content. With respective to interpretive theory, the text is not limited to a single interpretation. Also, that, interpretive theory, that message features a certain timelessness that needs to find periodic re-expression through translation, in order to preserve its content and give new life to its form, and that works given universal values and contemporary expression to ancient themes.[49]

It is therefore of importance that Bible translators should consider the extent the Holy Scriptures manifest literary qualities as mentioned above before they begin their work. For failure to do this may bring complication in interpretation of trans-

---

46. Wendland, *Translating*, 57.

47. Ibid., 60.

48. Adrian Pilkington, *Poetic Effects: A Relevance Theory Perspective* (Amsterdam and Philadelphia: Benjamins, 2000), 189, 191.

49. Wendland, *Translating*, 66.

lated text. Other approaches that can as well be of helpful assistance in translation are the "comparative approach and professional approach."

The comparative approach theory to literary translation is less systematic in the theoretical terms and correspondingly more adhoc in its practical application than the other approaches that have been described. According to Gaddis-Rose[50], the general aim of a comparative approach is a "stereoscopic reading" that utilizes "both the original language text and one (or more) translations", whether literal or free in style so as to asses the latter from an "interliminal" perspective.[51] In this case therefore, the desired goal of relational process from the secular view point of comparative literature is "to hoe translating and translations make the reading of literary texts richer."[52] On the other hand, the 'professional approach' has a distinct perspective on literary translation. Those who translate, edit, and critique translations of secular literature as their profession, constitute the professional theorists. It is however important to read what they say since they are both author-and audience-centred in their approach.[53]

Having looked at ideology, history and translation theories, it is now time to look at the translation of 1 Kgs 21 from the 1936 Tshivenda Bible translation, give my own translation and further look at the similarities and differences before spelling out the significance of such a comparison for Bible translation and African biblical scholarship.

THE 1936 TSHIVENDA BIBLE TRANSLATION OF 1 KINGS 21:1–16

1. Zwo daho nga murahu ngezwi: Nabothe wa Yeseriele o vha e na tsimu ya mitokola mudini wa Yeseriele, tsimu yo vhandakanaho na nndu ya Ahaba khosi ya Samaria.

2. Ahaba o amba na Nabothe a ri: Mphe tsimu yau ya mitokola ndi i ite tsimu ya miroho, ngauri i tsini na nndu yanga. Nne ndi do u nea inwe tsimu ya mitokola ine ya fhira heino; kana u tshi funa, ndi u nee masetha ndi i renge.

3. Nabothe a fhindula a amba na Ahaba ari: Yehova nga a nthivhele u ita izwo, nda rengisa ifa la vho-khotsi-anga.

4. Ahaba a vhuyelela mutani wawe o sinyuwa, o vhifhelwa nga zwe Nabothe wa Yeseriele a mu fhindula ngazwo a tshi ri: A thi nga U nei ifa la vho-khotsi-anga. A yo lala kha vhulalo hawe, a nala, a hana na ula zwiliwa.

---

50. Marylin Gaddis-Rose, *Translation and Literary Criticism: Translation as Analysis* (Manchester, England: St Jerome, 1997), 88, 90.

51. Wendland, *Translating*, 71.

52. Ibid.

53. Ibid., 76.

5. Ha da Isebele musadzi wawe, a amba nae ari: Naa wo sinyuiswa ngani, U tshi vhuya wa hana na ula zwiḽiwa?

6. Ene ari: Ndo amba na Nabothe wa Yeseriele nda ri: Litsha ndi U rengele tsimu yau ya miṱokola nga mali; kana U tshi funa ndi U nee iṅwe tsimu ya miṱokola. Ene a ri: A thi nga U nei tsimu yanga ya miṱokola.

7. Isebele musadzi wawe a ri: Iwe zwino ita zwo fanelaho khosi ya Isiraele. Takuwa, Uḽe, U takale. Nne ndi do U nea yeneyo tsimu ya Nabothe wa Yeseriele.

8. Isebele a mbo ṅwala luṅwalo nga dzina ḽa khosi, a lu kandisa nga tshi ṅina tsha thovhele, a lu rumela vhahulwane na vhakoma vha uyo mudi we Nabothe a vha a tshi dzula khawo.

9. Kha lwonolwo luṅwalo o vha o ṅwala a ri: Vhuthani vhathu ni ite duvha ḽa u di dzima. Nabothe ni mu dzudze na vhahulwane vha mudi.

10. Ni dzudze vhathu vhavhili vhavhi vha livhane nae; vhenevho vha mu hwelele vha ri: Wo sema Mudzimu na khosi. Ni kone u mu bvisela nnda na mu kanda nga matombo, a fa.

11. Vhathu vha uyo mudi vhahulwane na vhakoma vho dzulaho mudini muthihi na Nabothe vho ita zwe Isebele avha laya nga ulwo luṅwalo lwe a vha rumela.

12. Vho huwelela vhari: Vhathu vha didzime vha dzudza Nabothe na vhahulwane.

13. Ha mbo da avho vhanna vhavhili vhavhi vha dzula vhalivhana nae. Vhenevho vhanna vhavhili vhavhi vha hwelela Nabothe vhathu vha tshi zwi pfa vhari: Nabothe o sema Mudzimu na khosi. Vha mbo mu bvisa nnda vha mukanda nga matombo a fa.

14. Vha ruma vhathu vha vhudza Isebele vhari: Nabothe o kandwa nga matombo ofa.

15. Isebele a tshi pfa uri Nabothe o kandwa nga matombo a fa, a yo amba na Ahaba ari, Takuwa u dzhie tsimu ya Nabothe, ye a hana u tshi i renga nga maseṱha. Nabothe hatsheho ofa.

16. Ahaba atshi pfa uri Nabothe ofa, a vuwa a tsela tsimuni ya Nabothe ya Yeseriele ha vha u i dzhia.

My Translation of 1 Kings 21:1–16

1. Nga Murahu ha aya mafhungo Nabothe Mujeziriele o vha e na tsimu ya ndirivhe ye ya vha i ngei Jeziriele, i tsini ha pfamo ya Ahaba khosi ya Samaria.

2. Ahaba a mbo amba na Nabothe ari: Mphe tsimu ya u ya ndirivhe, uri ndi i ite ngade ya muroho sa izwi i tsini ha pfamo yanga. Vhudzuloni ha yo nne ndi do ufha tsimu ya ndirivhe ya khwine kha iyo.

Kana arali zwi tshi takadza maṱo au (u tshi zwi takalela) ndi ḓo u fha tshelede i eḓanaho mutengo wa yo.

3. Nabothe ambo fhindula Ahaba ari: zwi a ila uri ndi u fhe ifa ḽa vho makhulu-kuku wanga ḽe vha newa nga Yehova.

4. Ahaba a ṱuwa aya pfamoni yawe o vhifhelwa na u sinyuswa nga fhungo ḽe Nabothe Mujeziriele a mu vhudza ḽone a tshiri: ndi nga si kone u ufha ifa ḽa vho makhulukuku. A mbo ganama kha mmbete wawe o vhifhelwa nahone a tshi hana u ḽa vhuswa/u kungulusa malinga.

5. Isabele muṱanuni wawe a vhuya a ya khae a mu vhudzisa ari: ndi ngani muya wavho wo vhaisala? Ndi ngani vha sa ṱoḓi u kungulusa malinga/u ḽa vhuswa?

6. Vhone vha mbo aravha Isabele vha ri: Ngauri ndo amba na Nabo-the Mujeziriele ndari khae: nthengisele tsimu yau kana arali zwi tshi u takadza ndi ḓo ufha iṅwe tsimu vhudzuloni hayo. Fhedzi ene ari: ndi nga si ufhe tsimu yanga.

7. Isabele muṱanuni wawe a amba nae ari: ndi yone nḓila ine vhone muhali vha vhusa ngayo kha ḽa Isiraele? Kha vha takuwe vha kun-guluse malinga (nga vha ḽe vhuswa). Mbilu yavho kha i rule/takale. Nne ndi ḓo vha nea tsimu ya Nabothe Mujedziriele.

8. A mbo ṅwala maṅwalo nga dzina ḽa vho-Ahaba, a a ganḓa/rwa tshiṱemmbe/tshigivho tshavho (vhamusanda). O no ralo-ha a mbo rumela maṅwalo kha vhalisa, vhahulwane vha muḓi na kha vhaka-laha vhe vha vha vha tshi dzula muḓini muthihi na Nabothe.

9. A mbo ṅwala kha ayo maṅwalo ari: Vhidzani thabelo ya u ḓi dzima ni dzudze Nabothe hune vhathu vhoṱhe vha ḓo kona u mu vhona.

10. Ni vhee vhanna vhavhili (vharwa vha Beliala) tsini hawe, vhane vha ḓo ṱanziela (nga hae) vha ri: Wo sema Mudzimu na khosi. Nga murahu ni mu dzhie ni mu bvisele nnḓa ni mukanḓe nga matombo u swikela a tshi lovha.

11. Vhalisa na vhakalaha vha muḓi vha no dzula muḓini muthihi na Nabothe vha tevhedza ndaela ya Isabele i re maṅwaloni e a ḓo vha rumela one.

12. Vha vhidza vhathu uri vha ḓe thabeloni ya u ḓi dzima, vha dzudza Nabothe phanḓa ha vhathu vhoṱhe.

13. Vhanna vhavhili, vharwa vha Beliala, vha sendela vha ḓa vha dzula tsini/u livhana hawe/nae. Vha nea vhuṱanzi nga ha Nabothe phanḓa ha vhathu vhoṱhe vhari: Nabothe o sema Mudzimu na khosi. U bva afho vha mu bvisela nnḓa ha muḓi vha mu kanḓa nga matombo (u swika a tshi lovha), ambo ḓi lovha.

14. Vha mbo isa fhungo kha Isabele vha ri: Nabothe o kanḓwa nga matombo, o lovha.

15. Musi Isabele a tshi to u pfa uri Nabothe o vhulawa nga u to u

kandwa nga matombo, a mbo amba na Ahaba ari: Nga vhatakuwa
vha ye u dzhia tsimu ye Nabothe Mujeziriele a hana u vha rengisela
yone. Ha tsheho, o ri siya.

16. Ha ri musi Ahaba a tshi pfa uri Nabothe ha tsheho, a mbo di
takuwa a livha tsimuni ya Nabothe Mujedziriele, u i dzhia (u ri i
vhe yawe).

COMPARISON BETWEEN MY TRANSLATION
AND THE 1936 TSHIVENDA TRANSLATION

Similarities

I agree with the 1936 TshiVenda bible translation that the word *yir* "city" (vv. 8,
11, etc.) should be translated "mudi", equivalent of "village" as the set up described
in these verses of a chief/king, traditional court etc fits the Venda village setup as
opposed to the use of the direct Hebrew word *yir*, city.

Differences

Below follows a critique of the use of several phrases in the 1936 Tshivenda Bible
translation:

1. The use of the word *"a/o fa"* "he is dead" (vv. 10, 13, 14, 15
   twice,16) referring to Naboth is insensitive in Venda culture, the
   better phrase is *"o lovha/o ri sia"* he is gone or *"ha tsheho"* he is no
   more.

2. The use of Venda royal language would be appropriate to describe
   certain events/acts with reference to both king Ahab and queen
   Jezebel.
   a. The word *"musadzi"* (vv. 5 and 7) in the Tshivenda 1936 bible
      translation refers to any woman. However, the word for the
      queen is *"mutanuni"*.
   b. The words *U la zwiliwa* (vv. 4, 5) "to eat food" have been used
      in reference to the king's refusal to eat food. However, *U la
      zwiliwa* refers to the eating by ordinary citizens, the correct
      phrase for the Venda king is *"u kungulusa malinga"*
   c. The words *"Mutani wawe"*(v. 4) is used in the 1936 translation
      to refer to the king's house. However, the king's house should
      be referred to as *pfamo*, hence the appropriate phrase should
      be *"pfamoni yawe"*.
   d. The use of words such as *"Iwe, Takuwa, Ule, U takale"* in
      verses 7 and 15 in reference to Jezebel's command to Ahab to
      stand up and be happy do not show respect to the king in the
      Tshivenda context. More respectable words such as *"Muhali*

kha vha takuwe, vha kunguluse malinga, vha takale" would be more appropriate in this context.

3. The words *"Zwiliwa"* (vv. 4, 5) "food" should read *"vhuswa"* which is a traditional Venda stable meal.

4. The word *"rengela"* (v. 6) in the 1936 Tshivenda bible translation above may give the impression that Ahab wanted to buy the vineyard for Naboth and not from him. I would rather use the word *"nthengisele"* as opposed to *"rengela."*

5. The 1936 Tshivenda Bible translation has *"ifa la vho khotsi anga"* (v. 3) in reference to "my ancestral land", but literally it reads *"the land of my fathers"*. I would prefer *"ifa la vho-makhulu-kuku"* as this refers to both paternal and maternal ancestors.

6. The 1936 Tshivenda translation uses *"vhavhi" "evil"* in verses 10 and 13 with reference to the two men, sons of Belial. Although the MT text does not clearly say that the two are evil, the Tshivenda translation uses this adjective not only to show the evil intentions of the two men in falsely accusing Naboth of "cursing both God and the King." Importantly, it shows the ideological inclination of the translators of this text. Clearly the translators have taken sides in the trial of Naboth. They are on the side of Naboth, they probably felt that he was a victim of the two men' evil actions orchestrated by both Ahab and Jezebel.

CURRENT CHALLENGES TO BIBLE TRANSLATION IN AFRICA

Although serious progress has been made in translating the Bible into African languages, there are still several challenges facing us. First challenge is that speakers of certain African languages or dialects have no access to the Bible through their own vernacular. Their only access to the Bible is through a second language.[54] The second challenge is the availability of well-qualified and well-trained mother-tongue biblical scholars and translators.[55] The third challenge is the hermeneutic, i.e., responsibly reading and interpreting African-language Scriptures in manner that seriously respects both the languages and cultures of the biblical text and those of the receptor contexts.[56] Accordingly, it is not enough to know Hebrew, Greek and Latin for translation purposes, as shown above in the analysis of the 1936 Tshivenda bible translation. Rather, you also need to understand both the language usage and the cultural thought patterns of the language into which you intend to translate. Fourthly, word for word translation does not accurately con-

---

54. Aloo O. Mojola, "Bible Translation in Africa," in *A History of Bible Translation,* ed. Philip A. Noss (Rome: Edizioni di storia e letteratura, 2007), 160–61.

55. Ibid., 161.

56. Ibid.,162.

vey a clearer translated text. Fifth, as we have attempted to do in our translation of 1 Kgs 21 above, translation should be used to undermine sexist language and patriarchal thought patterns. Sixthly, translation is not an ideologically neutral process.

From the above discussion, we would like to say the following about ideology in biblical texts. There is the overall sexist/partriachal ideology of the author of 1 Kgs 21:1–16 which indirectly blames Jezebel as the chief mastermind behind the death of Naboth. Ahab, in contrast, is portrayed as the king of Israel who understands the ancient Israelite (settlement) view on the role and significance of an *ancestral land* in that when Naboth refused to sell it to him, he "understood" Naboth's *rationale* although he found it difficult to accept it. So according to this ideology, Ahab is innocent of Naboth's death as he had nothing to do with it.

There is a need to subject translated texts to a rigorous sociological analysis in order to understand the ideological power play in the translated texts before us. What, then, is the contribution of a sociological analysis of any biblical text including 1 Kgs 21 in our African context? First, it warns against any uncritical reading of the Biblical text. By uncritical reading, we refer to any reading of the Bible which does not engage in an in-depth manner with the text. Any uncritical reading of the Biblical text tends to further oppress and sideline the poor and marginalised by appropriating the ideologically undifferentiated Biblical text as the "revealed word of God." [57] Instead of empowering the poor and marginalised, an uncritical reading of the text disempowers and weakens them. A straightforward reading of 1 Kgs 21 tends to uncritically support the ideologies in 1 Kgs 21, in portraying Naboth as the "stubborn" Israelite who had no respect for the king by refusing to accept a generous offer from the king. Furthermore, this ideological inclination will tend to blame Jezebel alone and exonerate Ahab in the death of Naboth. A sociological reading shows that such an uncritical reading of 1 Kgs 21 is dangerous, and should not be left unchallenged.[58]

Such a sociological analysis has to be aware of the fact that both the translators of the biblical text into a particular language and the author of the translated text are not ideologically neutral. Rather, they have particular ideologies. Thus, a sociological analysis argues that African biblical scholarship will have to take seriously, in its theological endeavours in Africa, the fact that each and every text in the Bible is the product of both its socio-historical context and of its translators. And that, in order to effectively use any text in Africa, without it further oppressing and silencing the already silenced and marginalised people, both the text's and

---

57. Itumeleng J. Mosala, *Biblical Hermeneutics and Black Theology in South Africa* (Grand Rapids: Eerdmans, 1989).

58. Elelwani Farisani, "The Ideologically Biased Use of Ezra-Nehemiah in a Quest for an African Theology of Reconstruction," *OTE* 15, no. 3 (2002): 628–46; Elelwani Farisani, "The Use of Ezra-Nehemiah in a Quest for an African Theology of Reconstruction," *JT SA* 116 (2003): 27–50.

the translators' ideologies have to be subjected to a rigorous sociological analysis, so as to de-ideologize it.[59]

Second, a sociological reading of the text goes further, to read the 1 Kgs 21 text "against the grain." It tries to retrieve the voices of the marginalised Naboth, and also attempts to read this text from the perspective of the traditional farmers who hold dear the values of the *nahala* in the monarchic system. By so doing, such an analysis hopes that in appropriating the 1 Kgs 21 text, theologians will be sensitive to the voices and needs of all stakeholders in taking up their theological task in Africa.[60]

WORKS CITED

Camery-Hoggatt, Jerry. *Speaking of God: Reading and Preaching the Word of God.* Peabody, MA: Hendrickson, 1955.

Census 2001. "The Languages of South Africa." Accessed 14 December 2010. http://www.southafrica.info/about/people/language.htm.

Farisani, Elelwani B. "The Ideologically Biased Use of Ezra-Nehemiah in a Quest for an African Theology of Reconstruction." *OTE* 15, no. 3 (2002): 628–46.

———. "The Use of Ezra-Nehemiah in a Quest for an African Theology of Reconstruction." *JTSA* 116 (July 2003): 27–50.

Gaddis-Rose, Marylin. *Translation and Literary Criticism: Translation as Analysis.* Manchester, England: St Jerome, 1997.

Gottwald, Norman K. *The Hebrew Bible: A Brief Socio-Literary Introduction.* Minneapolis: Fortress, 2009.

Gutt, Ernst-August. "From Translation to Effective Communication." *NT* 2, no. 1 (1988): 24–39.

Hatim, Basil, and Ian Mason. *Discourse and the Translator.* London: Longman, 1990.

———. *The Translator as Communicator.* London: Longman, 1997.

Hermans, Theo. *Translation in Systems: Descriptive and System-Oriented Approaches Explained.* Manchester, England: St. Jerome, 1999.

Larson, Mildred. *Meaning Based Translation: A Guide to Cross-Language Equivalence.* Lanham, MD: University Press of America, 1984.

Mosala, Itumeleng J. *Biblical Hermeneutics and Black Theology in South Africa.* Grand Rapids: Eerdmans, 1989.

Noss, Philip A., ed., *A History of Bible Translation.* Rome: Edizioni di storia e letteratura, 2007.

Naude, Jacobus, and Christo van der Merwe, eds. *Contemporary Translation Studies and Bible Translation: A South African Perspective.* ATS 2. Bloemfontein: UFS, 2002.

Personal Conversation with Tshenuwani Farisani on 3 January 2011 at Maungani, Limpopo Province, South Africa.

Pilkington, Adrian. *Poetic Effects: A Relevance Theory Perspective.* Amsterdam and Philadelphia: Benjamins, 2000.

---

59. Farisani, "Ideologically Biased Use," 628–46, and "The Use of Ezra-Nehemiah," 27–50.

60. Ibid.

Wendland, R. Ernst: *Translating the Literature of Scripture: A Literary-Rhetorical Approach to Bible Translation.* Dallas: SIL International, 2004.

World Report. "Venda Bible Said to Give Church Power to Conquer Country for Christ." No. 336 (1998), accessed 4 September 2007, http://www.biblesociety.org/wr_336/wr_336.htm#Venda on.

4. SCRAMBLING FOR THE LAND: READING THE BIBLE AND LAND

"The Land Is Mine!"
Biblical and Postcolonial Reflections on Land with Particular Reference to the Land Issue in Zimbabwe

Robert Wafawanaka

Land is a valuable commodity without which human life and existence would be difficult to conceive. From ancient biblical times to the present, land has played a major role in human life. Throughout history, there have always been struggles for land. The modern struggle for land in Africa in general and Zimbabwe in particular is not a unique phenomenon. It is merely a manifestation of an ancient issue and problem. Using postcolonial hermeneutics, this essay argues that at the heart of the struggle for land is the issue of unequal land redistribution.

The Concept of Land in Biblical Times

Leviticus 25:23 states unequivocally, "The land shall not be sold in perpetuity, for the land is mine; for you are strangers and sojourners with me."[1] This text argues that the land belongs to Yahweh and Israel was not to regard it as its own personal property. Human beings have violated this mandate by viewing the land as their own private possession, rather than as a grant from God. We can argue that this has also contributed to some of the ancient and modern ideologies and problems regarding land.

The history of ancient Israel reveals that land was one of the basic requirements for the "survival" of the nation.[2] Israel needed land in order to realize the fulfillment of the promise to the patriarchs.[3] However, the biblical narrative indicates that the Promised Land was not an unoccupied land. It belonged to the Canaanites and other inhabitants. According to Joshua 3:10, the land of Canaan, a land "flow-

---

1. Biblical quotations are from the NRSV.

2. See Jerome C. Ross, *The History of Ancient Israel and Judah: A Compilation* (Pittsburgh: Dorrance, 2003) xi, xv, 117 n. 34, 158 n. 12. Ross argues that "survival" is the key to understanding Israelite history and there are seven elements for survival: land, people/population, common language, administrative structure, ideological standardization, economic independence, and selective appropriation/assimilation.

3. See Gen 12:1–3; Deut 1:8 21; 3:18.

ing with milk and honey" also belonged to the Hittites, the Hivites, the Perizzites, the Girgashites, the Amorites, and the Jebusites.[4] The acquisition of the Promised Land necessarily implies the conquest of others in order to occupy. Although biblical scholars have endlessly debated various models and theories of land occupation, the biblical text is quite clear about the manner of the conquest.[5] The book of Deuteronomy sets the scene by describing Israel's need to be obedient to the Mosaic Torah by putting every living thing in Canaan to the *ban*.[6] The *ban* or the *herem* was the destruction and dedication of all life to Yahweh. Blessings of land occupation were impinged upon obedience to this rule of military engagement. It is with this divine mandate that Israel operates in the land of Canaan. Robert Allen Warrior, a Native American scholar, argues that our reading of the Exodus narrative often ignores "those parts of the story that describe Yahweh's command to mercilessly annihilate the indigenous population."[7]

The books of Joshua and Judges reveal this theological justification for the occupation of the land, however, the land is not easily conquered as battles continue to rage between the Israelites and the Canaanites, despite Joshua's glorified description of the walls of Jericho tumbling down. The book of Judges (cf. Judg 1–2) carries the story of the conquest further because not all the land had been conquered. Why was this land so important?

The land of Israel lay in the Fertile Crescent, which was a highly desirable portion of land in the ancient Near East. Because of its strategic location in a buffer zone between warring ancient superpowers of the time, Israel was further conquered by different empires in succession: Egypt, Assyria, Babylon, Persia, Greece, and Rome. Israel returned from Assyrian and Babylonian exile under Persian rule, but only to be conquered again by the Greeks and the Romans. This brief history offers a preview on the significance of the land in biblical times.

The theological justification of Israel's conquest of the land of Canaan has given impetus to the modern history of imperial expansion and the spread of Christianity around the world. The history of European and western imperial expansion was justified on the biblical premise of land occupation. Imperial masters saw them-

---

4. See also Gen 15:13–14; Exod 3:17; cf. Josh 9:1–2; Ezek 47:21–23.

5. For example, see Iain Provan, V. Philips Long, and Tremper Longman III, *A Biblical History of Israel* (Louisville, London: Westminster John Knox, 2003), 138–47; Hershel Shanks, ed. *Ancient Israel: From Abraham to the Roman Destruction of the Temple* (rev. and expanded ed.; Prentice Hall, NJ: Biblical Archaeology Society, 1999), 55–89; Victor H. Matthews, *A Brief History of Ancient Israel* (Louisville: Westminster John Knox, 2002), 15–34; Norman K. Gottwald, *The Tribes of Yahweh: A Sociology of the Religion of Liberated Israel, 1250–1050 B.C.E.* (Maryknoll, NY: Orbis Books, 1985), 189–233; and idem, *The Hebrew Bible: A Socio-Literary Introduction* (Philadelphia: Fortress Press, 1987), 261–88.

6. See Deut 3:3f.; 7:16; cf. Josh 6:21.

7. Robert Allen Warrior, "A Native American Perspective: Canaanites, Cowboys, and Indians," in *Voices from the Margins: Interpreting the Bible in the Third World,* ed. R. S. Sugirtharajah (new ed.; Maryknoll, NY: Orbis Books; London: SPCK, 2000), 277–85, 279.

selves as fulfilling the biblical mandate by conquering lands that were occupied by native peoples under the guise of the spread of Christianity and bringing light to the darkest continents. The belief in Manifest Destiny certainly encouraged the European appropriation of indigenous lands despite the consequences.

LAND IN MODERN HISTORY

Postcolonial theory has convincingly revealed that the colonizers often identified themselves with the conquering Israelites of the Bible. Imperial masters and missionaries saw themselves as reenacting the Exodus story in which they were the victorious conquerors. The colonized victims were often portrayed and treated as the biblical Canaanites, fit to be degraded, devalued, and destroyed. Postcolonial biblical scholars such as Musa Dube and R. S. Sugirtharajah have amply demonstrated the role and function of the Bible in the precolonial, colonial, and postcolonial contexts of the Two-Thirds World. Dube has convincingly argued that the colonizers traveled to other people's lands to teach, but never to learn from their subjects in the "contact zone."[8] They simply went to dispossess others and possess for themselves.

THE SCRAMBLE FOR AFRICAN LANDS

According to *The Economist* (Sept. 14, 1996), Africa is the world's richest continent in terms of natural resources. It has some of the world's most precious minerals such as gold, copper, chrome, iron ore, and aluminum. Africa has 40 percent of the world's hydro-electric power; most of the world's diamonds and chromium; 50 percent of the world's gold; 70 percent of cocoa; 60 percent of coffee; and 50 percent of palm oil.[9] Yet despite such wealth, Africa is grappling with grinding poverty, misery, political and economic instability. The two greatest ironies of independent Africa are that Africans are worse off today than they were at independence, and that many countries can no longer afford to export food, let alone feed themselves. Something is seriously wrong with this picture.

Colonial Africa, a period spanning five centuries, saw most of the continent colonized by Europeans from the fifteenth century (1492) on. With few excep-

---

8. Musa Dube, *Postcolonial Feminist Interpretation of the Bible* (St. Louis: Chalice Press, 2000). See also Dube's essay "Go Therefore and Make Disciples of All Nations" (Matt 28:19a): A Postcolonial Perspective on Biblical Criticism and Pedagogy," in *Teaching the Bible: The Discourses and Politics of Biblical Pedagogy*, ed. Fernando F. Segovia and Mary Ann Tolbert (Maryknoll, NY: Orbis Books, 1998), 224–46; and R. S. Sugirtharajah, *The Bible and the Third World: Precolonial, Colonial, and Postcolonial Encounters* (Cambridge: Cambridge University Press, 2001).

9. "Hallo China—or Is It Taiwan? China, Taiwan Compete for Recognition in African Countries with Economic, Military Aid," *The Economist*, 14 September 1996, 68.

tions (Liberia and Ethiopia), most of the countries in Africa were colonized at one time or another. During this period commonly known as "the scramble for Africa" or "the gold rush," Europeans plundered Africa at will and partitioned it arbitrarily. At the Berlin Conference of 1884, they met to divide the continent of Africa among themselves without African involvement.[10] These divisions ignored the way Africans were traditionally grouped. The effects of these decisions contributed to the hostilities that arose among the same people who were divided and treated differently, such as the Tutsis and Hutus of Rwanda and Burundi. Independence in Africa promised to rectify some of these historic problems.

The coming of majority rule to Africa meant that Africans needed to reclaim their land rights. It is important that the land issue in Zimbabwe be understood in this larger historical context, rather than as a mere whimsical appropriation of European farms. Other land struggles have also been witnessed in countries such as South Africa, Kenya, Mozambique, and others.

Knowledge of African history is important as we try to understand its problems. In this postcolonial or independent period, some African leaders have emulated the oppressive lessons of colonialism.[11] African leaders have also inherited foreign systems of government and different economic standards for which they were ill equipped to emulate.[12] Yet European culpability is inevitable in the context of global history.

Writing in *Reading from This Place* (vol. 2), Mary Ann Tolbert, a descendant of English and Dutch colonists, paints a grim picture of the connection between Christianity and imperialism in human history. She confesses:

> As a First World biblical scholar at such an international gathering [the Society of Biblical Literature and the American Academy of Religion Annual Meeting], I found it impossible to avoid the realization of the devastation and misery brought to most of the inhabited world by the imperialist expansion of European nations into the lands and cultures of Africa, Asia, and the Americas during the fifteenth to nineteenth centuries. Much of this expansion was justified by and indeed fuelled by calls to 'spread the gospel to the nations.' What this 'godly pilgrimage' left in its wake was the devastation of rich and influential cultures, complete restructurings of traditional land allocations, and the deaths of millions of generally peaceful, cooperative people. Moreover, European hegemony was not attained... through cultural supremacy or exceptional military strategy but most often by the perniciousness of our ancestors' viruses. It has been estimated, for example, that 90 percent of the Native American population was wiped out by contact with European diseases like diphtheria, smallpox, and syphilis, for which they had no natural immunity. Contrary to popular lore, the North American West and much

---

10. Musa W. Dube, "Go Therefore and Make Disciples of All Nations," 227; idem, *Postcolonial Feminist Interpretation of the Bible*, 4.

11. See Paulo Freire, *Pedagogy of the Oppressed,* trans. Myra Bergman Ramos (New York: Continuum, 1987).

12. George B. N. Ayitteh, *Africa in Chaos* (New York: St. Martin's Press, 1998).

of the so-called New World was 'won,' not by the mighty gun, but by the mighty germ. How great the suffering, how great the destruction of God's good creation have been wrought in the name of Christian piety and biblical authority.[13]

Tolbert goes on to add that "since Christianity and colonial occupation arrived together in most parts of the Two-Thirds World, many native Christians find themselves in the uncomfortable position of representing a belief that supported the destruction of their cultures and families."[14]

This admission buttresses the often cited African short story that goes as follows: "When the white man came to Africa, he had the Bible and we had the land. The white man said to us, 'come, let us pray.' We closed our eyes to pray. After the prayer, the white man had the land and we had the Bible."[15] In his classic novel, *Things Fall Apart,* Nigerian author, Chinua Achebe, captures the history of European behavior with these immortal words by Okonkwo's friend, Obierika:

> Does the white man understand our custom about land?' 'How can he when he does not even speak our tongue? But he says that our customs are bad; and our own brothers who have taken up his religion also say that our customs are bad. How do you think we can fight when our own brothers have turned against us? The white man is very clever. He came quietly and peaceably with his religion. We were amused at his foolishness and allowed him to stay. Now he has won our brothers, and our clan can no longer act like one. He has put a knife on the things that held us together and we have fallen apart.'[16]

These descriptions provide the background within which formerly colonized countries have tried to redress some of the historical injustices and imbalances regarding land possession. The case of the struggle for land in Zimbabwe is by no means an isolated event. It may very well be the tip of the iceberg, or a harbinger of things to come.

THE STRUGGLE FOR LAND IN AFRICA

In addition to the biblical description and the struggle for land between Jews and Palestinians today, land struggles have also taken place elsewhere around the world. There have been struggles for land in South Africa due to the apartheid system that discriminated against the majority Blacks. More than seventeen years after independence, 16% of whites in South Africa currently own 87% of all arable

---

13. Fernando F. Segovia and Mary Ann Tolbert, eds., *Reading from this Place: Social Location and Biblical Interpretation in Global Perspective* (Minneapolis: Fortress, 1995), 2:348–49.

14. Ibid., 353.

15. Dube, *Postcolonial Feminist*, 3.

16. Chinua Achebe, *Things Fall Apart* (London: Heinemann, 1958), 124–25.

land.[17] In Kenya, the Mau Mau Uprisings were fomented by Kenyans who sought a fair share of their land from their British colonial masters. In his book, *Decolonising the Mind,* Kenyan writer, Ngũgĩ wa Thiong'o, clarifies the issue:

> The land question is basic to an understanding of Kenya's history and contemporary politics, as indeed it is of twentieth century history wherever people have had their land taken away by conquest, unequal treaties or by the genocide of part of the population. The Mau Mau military organization which spearheaded the armed struggle for Kenya's independence was officially called the Kenya Land and Freedom Army.[18]

The issues of land, freedom, political and economic independence, have defined much of the history of Africa in the postcolonial era. The struggle for land in Zimbabwe is no exception to this history and background of colonialism and imperial expansion.

Despite what some may perceive the land issue to be in Zimbabwe today, it has an extensive and complex history. The problem did not just surface in the last decade or two. It dates back to the close of the 19th century when the British imperialist Cecil John Rhodes ironically "discovered" Zimbabwe in 1890 and appropriately named it after himself as Rhodesia. It would be almost a century (90 years) of British rule before Africans reclaimed their independence and renamed the country Zimbabwe in 1980.[19] A brief analysis of the history of the land in Zimbabwe is appropriate in order to give sufficient background to the current land crisis in Zimbabwe.

The period of independent Africa saw many African governments emerging everywhere, and all of Africa was finally independent by 1994. Independent Africa was characterized by pride at self-rule, as well as the problems of inheriting foreign systems of government, lack of leadership and vocational training, inferior education, and the negative effects of colonialism. While colonialism in Africa spans five centuries (fifteenth–twentieth centuries), Africa has only been independent a mere five decades.[20] Given the ravages done to Africa in those five centuries, it will take much more than five decades to right the wrongs and problems of colonialism.

A History of the Land Issue in Zimbabwe

The question of land has dominated the political, social, and economic history of Zimbabwe. It can be traced back to the period of the Pioneer Column in the late

---

17. Danielle Owen, "The Progress Report: Land Reform Overdue in South Africa." Available at http://www.progress.org/land16.htm.

18. Ngũgĩ Wa Thiong'o, *Decolonising the Mind: The Politics of Language in African Literature* (Nairobi: EAEP, 1981), 44.

19. Mugabe became prime minister of independent Zimbabwe in 1980 and president in 1987.

20. That is, fifty-four years, starting with Ghana's independence in 1957 through 2011.

1800's and the subsequent laws that were designed to provide more land to whites than to Africans.[21]

Prior to the occupation of Zimbabwe in 1890, the Lippert Concession of 1889 allowed would-be settlers to acquire land rights from indigenous people. The British South African Company began expropriating African lands and sending revenues back to Britain while the African owners of the land received nothing.

The Native Reserve Order Council of 1898 created the infamous Native Reserves which were intended for Blacks only. The Native Reserves were designed to keep indigenous Africans in infertile areas of Zimbabwe while the whites retained most of the productive land.[22]

The period from 1890 to 1920 was characterized by the conquest of Africans and the seizure of their land. The British South African Company spearheaded the occupation of the best areas. This occupation was also the beginning of national uprising known as the first *Chimurenga* war in 1893. Its leader, an old woman named Mbuya Nehanda, urged her followers to fight for their land and independence. At this time, a minority 3% of the population controlled 75 percent of productive land while 97 percent of the population was confined to 25 percent of infertile land areas.[23]

In *The Political Economy of Land in Zimbabwe,* historian Henry V. Moyana describes the reasons why the Reserve areas were created in Zimbabwe. He writes,

> The institution of the Reserves was the first major step in the direction toward land segregation which later became a marked feature of the country. . . . The creation of the Reserves was partly inspired by a desire on the part of the settlers to eliminate the African from competition in the economic field.[24]

Several Land Apportionment Acts were passed. Following the recommendations of the Morris Carter Commission of 1925, The Land Apportionment Act of 1930 was intended to legalize the separation of Blacks and whites and their respective lands. The fertile high rainfall areas became large-scale privately owned white farms.

In 1951, the Native Land Husbandry Act was passed. This law enforced private ownership of land and the removal of Blacks from their traditional lands. Blacks owned poorer land and had neither titles nor capital to develop it. The Dutch oc-

---

21. "Pre-Independence Legislation on Land," http://www.raceandhistory.com/Zimbabwe/factsheet.html.

22. Growing up in the Reserve areas myself, I never understood why there were no white people living in them, but only in the cities. It was much later when I grew up that I began to understand the politics of the land of Zimbabwe.

23. "Pre-Independence Legislation," 3.

24. Henry V. Moyana, *The Political Economy of Land in Zimbabwe* (Gweru, Zimbabwe: Mambo Press, 1984), 51.

cupation of Gazaland, a highly desirable area in Eastern Zimbabwe, shows how Africans were displaced to poor areas far removed from markets.[25]

Between 1945 and 1965, the land issue continued to dominate politics. The growing dissatisfaction with the Rhodesian government fuelled nationalist sentiments and the desire for independence among African political leaders. With Rhodesian Prime Minister Ian Smith's defiant Unilateral Declaration of Independence (UDI) in 1965, and his infamous statement that Black majority rule would come to Zimbabwe "not in a thousand years," the armed struggle for independence and land rights began in earnest and flowered in the mid-1970s. When majority rule came to Zimbabwe in less than two decades, Paul L. Moorcraft published his appropriately titled book, A Short Thousand Years, which showed how misguided Smith had been.[26] Majority rule was a major irony of British politics because colonial masters did not train or educate Africans to rule themselves, but rather to serve them.[27]

At the height of colonial rule, many nationalist leaders such as Mugabe and Nkomo in Zimbabwe, Jomo Kenyatta in Kenya, Samora Machel in Mozambique, Patrice Lumumba of Congo, and Nelson Mandela in South Africa were jailed, exiled, or killed. Many others were detained, tortured, or simply "disappeared."[28]

A discussion of the land issue in Zimbabwe would be incomplete without reference to the legendary saga of Chief Rekayi Tangwena of the Inyanga Highlands in Eastern Zimbabwe. From 1966 to independence in 1980, Chief Tangwena's struggle became the symbol of national resistance to British land policies and "a classic model for resistance to oppression."[29] His defiant stances symbolized the costly price Africans were willing to pay for their freedom and land rights. Chief Tangwena and his people were evicted from their traditional homelands numerous times. He fled to the hills but returned to rebuild his huts on his land that a white farmer had claimed. In the 1970s, the government would demolish his huts and take him to court, but he was persistent in returning to rebuild.[30] At the end of

---

25. The Native Land Husbandry Act was massively resisted and scrapped in 1961. At this time minority whites owned more than 70 percent of the best and arable land.

26. See Paul L. Moorcraft, A Short Thousand Years: The End of Rhodesia's Rebellion (rev. ed.; Zimbabwe: Galaxie Press, 1980).

27. It is equally ironic that Ian Smith, who defied the British government and declared UDI, also had a rebellious son, Alec, who published a book soon after independence, on his father's regime and the revolutionary war, with the catchy but reconciliatory title, Now I Call Him Brother (Grosvenor, 1989).

28. Ayittey, Chaos.

29. Moyana, Political Economy, 174.

30. In the mid-1970s, Chief Tangwena joined the now full-fledged struggle for liberation in Zimbabwe and even assisted Mugabe in escaping to Mozambique (Moyana, Political Economy, 173).

the war the chief returned to his ancestral land and was made Senator in the House of Assembly as a result of his heroic achievements.[31]

The current land conflict in Zimbabwe dates in earnest from the three-month Lancaster House Conference which began on September 10, 1979, in the UK. On the eve of independence, Zimbabwean nationalist leaders of the Patriotic Front, Mugabe and Nkomo, and a delegation led by Bishop Muzorewa, Prime Minister of Zimbabwe-Rhodesia, were entrenched in deep negotiations with the British government on the terms and conditions for self-rule. Among nine major issues, the question of the land dominated the negotiations. The British government insisted on the protection of private property with provisions for compensation. The Patriotic Front wanted the government to determine the compensation, but the British government to provide the money. The conference nearly broke down over the land issue. An agreement was finally reached and it basically reaffirmed the African need for land and economic development and the assistance that would come from Britain, the United States of America and other donor countries.[32]

At independence in 1980, 97 percent of Black Zimbabweans owned forty-five million acres of poor land while 3 percent of the whites owned fifty-one million acres of mostly fertile land—more than half of the country. Britain agreed, under the willing seller/willing buyer principle, to fund the resettlement programs to avoid compulsory land acquisition without compensation by the new government. Negotiators agreed that there would be no compulsory land acquisition during the first decade of independence.[33]

The resettlement program, however, did not go as envisioned. Under the willing seller/willing buyer principle, land was not offered in sufficient bulk to the government. Moreover, the land which was offered was located in poor agricultural regions. Because of the "fair market price" clause, the government was constrained because there were no sufficient funds available to buy land.[34]

In 1980 the Zimbabwe Conference on Reconstruction and Development (ZIM-CORD) was held to mobilize financial support by Britain, West Germany, the USA and others. Britain pledged more than 630 million pounds of aid. The aid promised was not coming in sufficient amounts to extinguish land hunger.[35] The Land Act of 1985 was drawn in the spirit of the Lancaster House Conference and it gave the government the right to buy large-scale farms for resettlement of people, however, the problem was the lack of sufficient funds to compensate landowners.

The Land Reform and Resettlement Programme amended the Constitution following the expiration of the Lancaster House requirements. The government was unable to resettle people because landowners were unwilling to sell, or asked for

---

31. Ibid., 155–76.
32. "Pre-Independence Legislation," 3.
33. Ibid.
34. Ibid.
35. By 1987, only forty thousand families out of 162,000 had been resettled (ibid.).

double or triple the price of their land. The government implemented enforced land acquisition policies.[36] In the meantime, people grew frustrated and hungry for land. Some took matters into their own hands and forcibly resettled themselves on bordering commercial farms. Against this background the government decided to acquire land compulsorily but owners had the right to go to court if they did not agree with the price offered.

The Land Acquisition Act of 1992 was intended to speed up reforms by removing the willing buyer/willing seller principle and acquire more land to resettle Blacks in congested and unproductive areas. The government planned to acquire land that was defined as derelict, under-utilized, owned by absentee landlords, owned by farmers with multiple farms, or land adjacent to communal areas. Objectors were encouraged to submit objections in writing within 30 days of notice of compulsory acquisition.[37] Opposition by landowners increased between 1992 and 1997. Due to perceived government mismanagement and corruption charges, Britain and the United states suspended their aid to Zimbabwe during this period. Only about seventy thousand people had been resettled but without the necessary skills and infrastructure needed for commercial success. By the end of the 1990's land redistribution had not succeeded much due to shortage of funds. Although the War Victims Compensation Act had been passed in 1993, war veterans had not been sufficiently compensated until 1997. This explains their forcible demand for land and compensation.[38]

When British Prime Minister Tony Blair took office in 1997, his secretary of state, Clare Short, argued that Britain had no responsibility to meet the cost of land purchase in Zimbabwe. She would only support a poverty eradication program. On 5 November 1997, she wrote a letter to Zimbabwe's Minister of Agriculture, Kumbirai Kangai, and stated, "I should make it clear that we do not accept that Britain has a special responsibility to meet the costs of land purchase in Zimbabwe. We are a new government from diverse backgrounds without links to former colonial interests."[39] In other words, she believed that the Lancaster House agreements applied only to the first decade of independence.

On 10 June 2004, however, a British Embassy spokesperson stated: "The UK has not reneged on commitments [made] at Lancaster House. At Lancaster House the British Government made clear that the long-term requirements of land reform in Zimbabwe were beyond the capacity of any individual donor country."[40]

---

36. Ibid., 4. However, only seventy-one thousand families (out of a targeted 162,000) had been resettled by 1990. By 1999, eleven million hectares of land were owned by 4,500 white commercial farmers.

37. Ibid., 4.

38. In 1997 the government finally paid them over Z$5 billion as payback, plus free health care, free education, and land.

39. Letter to Kumbirai Kangai, 5 November 1997.

40. Nelson Banya, *Financial Gazette*, 6 October 2004. Sophie Honey, the embassy spokesperson, went on to state that since independence Britain had provided 44 million pounds

From 9–11 September 1998, the Donor Conference and the Second Phase of Land Reform and Resettlement Programme was held in Harare, the capital of Zimbabwe. The purpose was to inform the donor community on the resettlement program and mobilize them for support. About forty-eight countries and international organizations were represented. At the conference, the donors unanimously endorsed the need for land reform and resettlement and affirmed the urgency of poverty reduction, economic growth, and stability. Many donors pledged technical and financial support to reduce poverty, ensure peace, and remove imbalances in land ownership.[41]

In 1999 the Commercial Farmers Union offered to sell land to the government for redistribution. A new constitution was drafted and widely discussed. It also had some limitations on presidential powers and terms of office. The government, however, inserted a clause on compulsory acquisition of land without compensation. The new constitution was defeated 55 percent to 45 percent in 2000 thereby empowering the MDC opposition party, but also prompting farm seizures by war veterans and their followers.

There were also Alternative Land Acquisition and Resettlement Approaches designed. In the Communal Participation and Implementation Model, the government acquires land and communities plan their own settlement.[42] In 2000, Fast-Track Land Reform began. The intention was to redress the historic land inequities. The National Land Identification Committee would identify tracts of land for redistribution.[43] Thousands of farms were listed for compulsory acquisition, however, due to perceived injustices, the Commercial Farmers Union filed suit in the Zimbabwe Supreme Court challenging the legality of fast-track methods.[44]

The tragedy of the resettlement program was that much of this land went to government ministers, the rich, or dubious war veterans and youth brigades, instead of the real veterans who had been promised land, due to their sacrifices in the struggle for independence. The other problem was the lack of sufficient training and manpower on the part of new farm owners. The loss of commercial farming contributed to low production of cash crops such as tobacco and maize (corn). This loss of commercial farms resulted in the recent food shortages, unemployment, hyperinflation, and price increases that have characterized Zimbabwe's most recent history. In addition, drought has worsened the problem of food se-

---

for land reform in Zimbabwe and 500 million pounds in bilateral development assistance, but she was critical of the government's fast-track land reform measures.

41. "Pre-Independence Legislation," 5.

42. The government estimated the entire land resettlement program at 1.1 billion US dollars ("Pre-Independence Legislation," 7).

43. *Models of Resettlement* (A1 and A2) were proposed to create village farms and 51,000 commercial farms.

44. By 2002, 11.5 million hectares of white commercial farms had been given to Blacks.

curity in Zimbabwe.[45] Despite the government's good intentions to redistribute much needed land to the population, land problems still persist.

In 2004 the government announced that all land would soon become state property. In 2005 a constitutional amendment was passed and it nationalized farms acquired through the fast-track process and denied original owners the right to legally challenge the government. In 2006 the government announced its intention to compel commercial banks to finance Black peasants awarded formerly white farms, or risk losing their licenses. These measures were taken due to the fact that banks were refusing to lend to Black farmers because historically they owned no land titles, had no commercial farming experience, and had no collateral for their loans. They were simply a bad risk.

Recently, there has been increasing tensions over land between the government, the opposition, war veterans, and commercial farmers, some of whom are fighting court battles with the government. The government may also fear that the opposition will return land to white farmers, many of whom have left Zimbabwe for Britain, surrounding countries, and countries such as Nigeria.

The problem of the land in Zimbabwe has had major economic implications. While historically white commercial farmers were the backbone of the economy and Zimbabwe was once the "breadbasket" of Africa, land reforms have had to contend with historic problems. The resettled black Zimbabweans lacked the necessary commercial farming skills, land titles, cash capital, infrastructure, farm equipment, and farm management skills. The plight of the black farmer was also worsened by the refusal of banks to loan them money due to lack of land titles or collateral of any kind. In the context of political and economic problems, foreign investments and tourism declined leading to lost revenue, food shortages, and extremely high inflation rates. Needless to say this has increased the suffering of the general populace.

CONCLUSION

The problem of land possession is timeless and without national boundaries. It is manifested in the biblical text as well as the modern history of Israel. It persists in the history of the world in general and in the last five centuries of African history in particularly. The biblical stance with regard to the land is unequivocal. The land belongs to Yahweh and human beings are granted it as stewards. However, human beings have sought to acquire the land for themselves as if it were personal property. Part of the problem is the Bible's ideological justification of the possession of land that was not unoccupied. The biblical text identifies the land of Canaan as the land of several native inhabitants but nevertheless gives theological justification of their extermination and dispossession. This perspective was embraced

45. By 2008, about two hundred to three hundred of 4,500 commercial farmers remained in Zimbabwe.

by Europeans who colonized much of the world including Africa in the name of imperial expansion and the spread of Christianity. This history has affected the entire world and resulted in land-grabbing, as well as the mistreatment and suffering of indigenous peoples. This trend is reflected in biblical history as it is in European, American, Asian, South American, Australian, and African history. The aftermath of land appropriation ventures has resulted in the universal struggle for land rights. The dispossessed often attempted to reclaim their lost lands as can be deduced from the many struggles for independence around the world. While most of Africa was once colonized, all of it is now independent but the effects of centuries of colonialism and land dispossession are still evident in the increasing rates of poverty, suffering, failing economies, and political instability. The issue of land in Zimbabwe is to be understood in this larger biblical, global, and historical context of colonial domination and land dispossession.

WORKS CITED

Achebe, Chinua. *Things Fall Apart*. London: Heinemann, 1958.

Ayitteh, George B. N. *Africa in Chaos*. New York: St. Martin's Press, 1998.

Banya, Nelson. *Financial Gazette*. 6 October 2004.

Dube, Musa W. *Postcolonial Feminist Interpretation of the Bible*. St. Louis: Chalice Press, 2000.

Freire, Paulo. *Pedagogy of the Oppressed*. Trans. Myra Bergman Ramos. New York: Continuum, 1987.

Gottwald, Norman K. *The Hebrew Bible: A Socio-Literary Introduction*. Philadelphia: Fortress, 1987.

———. *The Tribes of Yahweh: A Sociology of the Religion of Liberated Israel, 1250–1050 B.C.E.* Maryknoll, NY: Orbis Books, 1985.

"Hallo China—or Is It Taiwan? China, Taiwan Compete for Recognition in African Countries with Economic, Military Aid." *The Economist*, 14 September 1996, 68.

Matthews, Victor H. *A Brief History of Ancient Israel*. Louisville: Westminster John Knox, 2002.

Moorcraft, Paul L. *A Short Thousand Years: The End of Rhodesia's Rebellion*. Rev. ed. Zimbabwe: Galaxie Press, 1980.

Moyana, Henry V. *The Political Economy of Land in Zimbabwe*. Gweru, Zimbabwe: Mambo Press, 1984.

Owen, Danielle. "The Progress Report: Land Reform Overdue in South Africa." http://www.progress.org/land16.htm.

"Pre-Independence Legislation on Land." http://www.raceandhistory.com/Zimbabwe/factsheet.html.

Provan, Iain, V. Philips Long, and Tremper Longman III. *A Biblical History of Israel*. Louisville: Westminster John Knox, 2003.

Ross, Jerome Clayton. *The History of Ancient Israel and Judah: A Compilation*. Pittsburgh: Dorrance, 2003.

Segovia, Fernando F., and Mary Ann Tolbert, eds. *Reading from This Place: Social Location and Biblical Interpretation in Global Perspective*. Vol. 2. Minneapolis: Fortress, 1995.

————. *Teaching the Bible: The Discourses and Politics of Biblical Pedagogy.* Maryknoll, NY: Orbis Books, 1998.

Shanks, Hershel, ed. *Ancient Israel: From Abraham to the Roman Destruction of the Temple.* Revised and expanded ed. Prentice Hall, NJ: BAS, 1999.

Smith, Alec. *Now I Call Him Brother.* Grosvenor, 1989.

Sugirtharajah, R. S. *The Bible and the Third World: Precolonial, Colonial, and Postcolonial Encounters.* Cambridge: Cambridge University Press, 2001.

————, ed. *Voices from the Margin: Interpreting the Bible in the Third World.* London: SPCK; Maryknoll, NY: Orbis, 2000.

Wa Thiong'o, Ngũgĩ . *Decolonising the Mind: The Politics of Language in African Literature.* Nairobi: EAEP, 1981.

Land Concept and Tenure in Israel and African Tradition

Temba L. J. Mafico

The full import of Ps 24 unfolds when viewed in the context of the concept of land tenure among the ancient Israelites and traditional Africans. This study uncovers some underlying facts regarding the creation of the land/earth. The study of Psalm 24 from this perspective provides insight to understanding differently the biblical story of creation.

> The land (*'erets*) is the Lord's and all that is in it, the world (*tebel*), and those who live in it; for he has founded[1] it on the seas, and established it on the rivers. (Ps 24:1–2)

Traditions of land ownership in Africa and ancient Israel have as their foundation the basic idea expressed in Ps 24:1–2: that God, the creator or founder of the earth, all living things and all that is in it, is the primary owner of the land. In Genesis chapter one, God gave the people whom God created in the divine image the land for their use (Gen 1:29) but they were not free to use it in any way that they might wish, but in accordance with the providence of God (Gen 2:15). The traditional African and ancient Israelite people's relationship to their land—and the ways they used and distributed it—was governed by this historic obligation to God and to all generations, past, present and future, who shared the land's largess.

Traditional African and ancient Israelites' creation myths depict primordial events, in which land first appeared and with it God created life. Four themes emerge in these creation stories: (1) Water and earth (matter) were in existence when God created the universe; (2) union between God and earth that would ultimately result in the creation of living things and plants was prevented by another competing power that, apparently, God did not create; (3) God surmounted the obstacle to creation, establishing order out of chaos; and (4) God (male) joined with the land (female) to produce all life.

The creation myth of the Masai people of Kenya states: ". . . when God came to

---

1. Hebrew avoids the word *bara'* when referring to God establishing the land. This suggests that the earth already existed but was submerged under the *tehom*, "watery chaos."

prepare the world, God found three things in the land, a Dorobo,[2] an elephant, and a serpent, all of whom lived together [on the land]."[3] Thus the land was already in existence when God, according to the Masai, visited the earth. This view accords with the Priestly account in Gen 1 where it is evident that both water and land pre-existed God's creation of the universe. As far as the earth and water are concerned, the concept of *creatio ex nihilo*[4] does not apply.

An African myth from the Dogon people of Mali, West Africa, also shows parallels with the account of creation in Genesis, in that, before the earth could be populated with living things, God had to remove major obstacles, darkness and the deep (Gen 1:2). It was following the appearance of light and land that God was able to connect with the earth and began to redesign everything that is in it (Ps 24). In the Dogon myth God's union with Earth, and subsequent creation of progeny, was prevented by the termite hill (clitoris):

> At the beginning of time, Amma (a supreme God who lived in the celestial regions and was the origin of all creation) created the Earth and immediately joined with it. But the Earth's clitoris [termite hill] opposed the male penis. Amma destroyed it, circumcising his wife, and they had a child, Ogo, and the twins, the Nommo.[5]

In Gen 1, God's ru^ach (spirit, wind) could only hover above the watery chaos (*'al-p^{e}ne t^{e}hom*) (Gen 1:2). It is fascinating to realize that just as God cleared the termite hill out of the way in order to have a union with the earth in the Dogon myth, in Gen 1:9 God moved the watery chaos out of the way in order for dry land to appear. It was after the deep (*t^{e}hom*) had been removed that the dry land, and commanded by God, produced all kinds of vegetation, birds of the air, swarming and creeping things, animals and fishes (Gen 1:24). A closer scrutiny of this text seems to present the earth as a woman who gave birth to all living things and vegetation. Hence, God did not create the creatures out of nothing.

In reading the Priestly story of creation in Genesis 1, it is important to note that the Hebrew verb *'asah*, "to make" does not always refer to God manually making or forming something directly. In some texts it refers to God instructing the earth to produce, and in other texts, ordering the thing itself to come into being. Because God initiated the action, God is seen as having made whatever emerged follow-

---

2. A Dorobo was a nomadic person, and, like Enkidu in the Babylonian creation myth, Enuma Elish lived among and with the animals.

3. In this myth, God did not create the land; it was already there when God visited it. But reading the entire myth one realizes that God was in control of everything in the land because he gave instructions to the Dorobo on how to obtain cattle. The Masai overhead the instructions and stole the secret. That is why, as the Masai believe, they are cattle herders.

4. An uncritical reading of the creation story gives the impression that God created everything (such as earth, water, and air) out of nothing.

5. The latter paragraph is quoted in L. V. Thomas, R. Luneau, and J. Doneux, *Les Religions de L'Afrique Noire* (Paris: Fayard-Denoël, 1969).

ing God's word or fiat. Thus, even though God instructed the earth to produce all
sorts of creatures (as recorded in Gen 1:24–25), in verse 25 we read that God created those same creatures. Likewise, the Dogon believed that for anything to be,
it must have been divinely thought prior to its being. As they put it: "The world is
conceived as a whole, this whole having been thought, realized, and organized by
one creator God in a complete system..."[6]

An Egyptian creation myth found at Hermopolis repeats some of the creation
themes found in the Israelite and Dogon myths. In the Egyptian story, the God
Atum, who was self created, sat on a hillock that shot out of the primordial waters.
It was on this hillock surrounded by waters that Atum began to create other gods.
While it is quite clear that Atum did not create the hillock and the masses of water,
which pre-existed, Atum brought order and structure to the chaos that already
existed, and was the source of new beings.[7]

In both the Priestly and Yahwistic accounts of creation, after God had created
everything on the earth, God entrusted the land to human beings to use and enjoy.
In Gen 1:28 God said, "Be fruitful and multiply, and fill the earth and subdue (*ka-
bash*[8]) it; and have dominion over the fish of the sea and over the birds of the air and
over every living thing that moves upon the earth." In Gen 2:16 the Lord God said,
"You may freely eat of every tree of the garden; but of the tree of the knowledge of
good and evil you shall not eat . . ." (Gen 2:16–17). These verses make it clear that
human beings were to take care of the land they had been given, as well as the animals, the fish, and birds of the air. They were not to abuse or exhaust the land.[9]

Thus, in the Book of Joshua, as the people of Israel arrived in the land of Canaan, God appointed Joshua to allot portions of the land to leaders of households
or families. Josh 14:1 states, "These are the inheritances that the Israelites received
in the land of Canaan, which the priest Eleazar, and Joshua son of Nun, and the
heads of the families of the tribes of the Israelites distributed to them." Land was
always given to family or tribe; but it was never given to an individual for personal

---

6. M. Griaule and G. Dieterlen, *The Pale Fox* (Arizona: Continuum Foundation, 1965),
57–58.

7. Urk. V, 6 = BD, 17.

8. I am more persuaded to interpret this word in the sense of squeezing, kneading, or
massaging the body. In line with Gen 2:15, Yahweh place *ha'adam* in the garden to till it and
watch it. No subjection is referred to here.

9. The Hebrew term *radah* does not mean "dominate" in the modern sense. It meant to
administer as a benevolent head the land that God had entrusted to them to guard on behalf
of all the people and creatures. Directed by God, as the people's shepherds, the later kings
of Israel were to rule their kingdoms in a way that honored this sacred trust and preserved
the land that the people shared as a common heritage. The leaders of Israel, by the authority that God had given them, were in charge of allocating land to new generations as they
came along.

use or gain. The concept of individual buying and selling of the land was unthinkable, except in a very few exceptional situations.[10]

In most African ethnic groups, the extended family held rights to the land and it became a *nahalah*, "heredity," in the sense that it was to be handed down in perpetuity. Family leaders, when they died, passed authority over a family to the new leader, who, as the new patriarch of the ancestral land was now responsible for allocating plots of the family land to new members of the ever extending family. Each married member of the family was allocated a piece of the ancestral land to build their own home.

All the generations of the African family lived on the land, including the dead—who were believed to be still living among their descendents—and shared the rich, common legacy of the land.[11] Ancestral graves became permanent markers that perpetually identified and declared the family's claim to a particular piece of land. The practice of burying the umbilical cords of family members on the ancestral lands further solidified the Africans' connection to the land of their birth.

The land defined who a person was among the Africans and the Israelites. The land was one's mother, providing comfort, identity and security. Without the land of one's birth, a person had no stability and history. They had no protection from the other people who might ultimately kill him/her, as shown in a text like Gen

---

10. In both traditional African society and ancient Israel, the only time when a stranger could acquire land belonging to another family was in certain dire situations. For burial of the dead, a stranger could compensate the owner of the small piece of land with money or property exchange. In Gen 23 we read a story of Abraham living as a sojourner in the land of the Hittites. There was no problem in his sharing the land of the Hittites to feed his livestock and his family. The problem arose when his wife, Sarah, died. The dead could not be buried in a strange land where they might be abandoned later on. This explains why Abraham had to go through an elaborate custom of haggling for Ephron's cave in Machpelah. After paying Ephron four hundred shekels, Abraham possessed the cave of Machpelah and the surrounding field for use only as a burial place for his dead. The Hittites had no choice but to grant Abraham's request in order to avoid desecrating their land with the unburied dead. If the dead were not properly buried, it was assumed that their wondering spirits would torment the land.

The purchase of a plot to bury the dead was common practice in the ancient Near East. The inscription on a sarcophagus clearly states that Abba, a stranger in Babylon, buried his dead in the grotto that he acquired:

> I, Abba, son of the priest Eleazar, son of Aharon the Elder, it is I, Abba, the oppressed, the persecuted, who was born in Jerusalem, exiled in Babylonia, and who brought back Mattatia, son of Judah. And I have buried him in the grotto that I acquired by deed.

Inscription 263 in Yael Hestrin and Ruth Israeli, *Inscriptions Reveal: Documents from the Time of the Bible, the Mishna, and the Talmud* (Jerusalem: Israel Museum, 1972), 122.

11. For the African belief in the living dead, read John Mbiti, *African Religions and Philosophy* (New York: Doubleday, 1970), 35–36, 76–82.

4:12b which relates that the Lord God cursed Cain, following the murder of his brother Abel: ". . . you will be a fugitive and a wanderer on the earth/land." That meant that Cain no longer belonged to a particular piece of land. Although God did not kill him, a distraught Cain, having no land, was compelled to beg God for clemency as is written in Gen 4:13–15:

> My punishment is greater than I can bear!
> *Today you have driven me away from the soil,*
> and I shall be hidden from your face;
> I shall be a fugitive and a wanderer on the earth,
> and anyone who meets me may kill me."

To Cain, as is also the case for Africans, to be landless is worse than death itself.[12]

The traditional practices of land ownership in Africa and Israel worked well when populations were small and land abundant; but eventually adjustments had to be made to the old system that had guaranteed every new generation their plot of land. A common outcome of population growth and attendant discords was migration of people to other lands, which were sometimes available for the taking; at other times already populated and could only be taken by force.[13]

In the Bible, the fact that ancestral lands eventually became too small to accommodate an extended family is illustrated in the case of Abraham and Lot, who shared the same land in the Negeb. Abraham as the senior member of the family offered Lot the choice of where he would like to migrate with his own family. As Gen 12:8–10 states:

> Then Abram said to Lot, "Let there be no strife between you and me, and between your herders and my herders; for we are kindred. *Is not the whole land before you?* Separate yourself from me. If you take the left hand, then I will go to the right; or if you take the right hand, then I will go to the left."

But peaceful migration to other lands was not always possible. Contention over land often resulted in conflicting claims over the area resulting in bloodshed, as one group moved into another's territory.

The current black populations of Zimbabwe and Mozambique are a tribal mix that are the result of migrations and territorial wars that started in the second half of the nineteenth century. The Ndau and the Ndebele people of Zimbabwe and Mozambique both originally lived in Zululand, part of South Africa. In the time of Tshaka, the powerful king of the Zulu people, bravery and victory at battle were expected. Defeat was punishable by death of the entire platoon that lost the battle.

---

12. I attribute the African Americans' anguish and anger to the fact that they were uprooted from their motherland and forced to live like wanderers in a strange land in which they have no traditional attachment.

13. The conquest account in the book of Joshua is a good example of tribes fighting to displace the Canaanites in order to establish a homeland, an 'ahhuzah.

Several army captains who lost battles, or who were disenchanted with Tshaka's oppressive power, escaped with their soldiers (*impi*) and headed north to the lands now called Zimbabwe and Mozambique. Sotshangana Manikusa and Muzilikazi escaped during the time of Dingaan who succeeded Tshaka. While one captain, Manikusa, went to the land now known as Gazaland, another, Muzilikazi, went to the land which was later called Matebeland. These two conquerors shed a trail of blood along their escape route. They harshly subjugated the people; seizing their livestock and terrorizing the population.[14] Such atrocities are vividly remembered today and are at the root of distrust and dissension among the tribal people of Zimbabwe, as currently tribes that have lived for centuries in Zimbabwe and Mozambique live alongside those who seized their lands in the 19th century. Both feel the land is their rightful inheritance.

The biblical Pentateuchal narratives record how Abram left his ancestral land because Yahweh called and said, "Go from your land and your kindred and your father's house (i.e., your ancestral residence) to the land that I will show you." (Gen 12:1). Additionally, Yahweh would bless and make him a great name. He eventually made a new homeland in the land of Canaan—which was already settled. Yahweh revealed this land to Abram and gave it to him as a holding, possession, *'ahuzzah*.[15] To establish their new home in this land that God had shown to their patriarchs, the Israelites had to eliminate the Canaanites. Annihilation of the Canaanites by the Israelites under the leadership of Joshua was seen as fulfilling God's commandment to occupy lands that the Canaanites no longer had a right to because of their iniquity.[16] God had previously given the land to the Canaanites, but later changed God's own mind—as was his right as the primary owner of the land.[17]

---

14. I still recall one of the warriors who converted to Christianity and attended the same church as me. In his testimony that he often repeated, he recalled a person he killed kneeling on his knees pleading for mercy. Because no male among the defeated army was to be spared in these battles, he thrust him with his spear. His tearful lament was, "I wish Jesus' teaching of forgiveness had come a bit earlier to Gazaland."

15. Contra several scholars who confuse the terms *nahalah* and *'ahuzzah*, the Hebrew verb *'ahaz*, "possess," "seize," "grasp," "take hold of," infers that the land that Abraham and his progeny would possess would be seized from its original inhabitants. The substantive *nahalah*, on the other hand, refers to land that has been handed down from generation to generation. See Norman Habel, *The Land Is Mine* (Minneapolis: Fortress, 1995).

16. The question regarding the credibility of the conquest in the book of Joshua is raised by the fact that the land of Canaan was not completely conquered until the time of David. See Mafico, "Joshua," *Africana Bible: Reading Israel's Scriptures from Africa and the African Diaspora* (Minneapolis: Fortress, 2010), 115–19.

17. The Genesis account repeatedly states that the land that the Israelites regarded as their own "possession" once belonged to the Canaanites. As is clearly stated in Genesis 12:6b, "At that time the Canaanites were in the land" (see also Gen 13:7b). The same notion is expressed in different ways in Deut 32:49 in which Yahweh says to Moses: *Re'eh 'et-'erets kena'ani 'asher 'ani noten libne yisra'el la'ahuzzah* ". . . view the land of Canaan, which I am giving to the Israelites for a possession."

For both Israelites and most Africans, despite circumstances that created distances between families, a sense of unity and cohesion as a people was able to be maintained. In Israel, family genealogies clarified for individuals their place in a chain of relationships stretching back to Abraham. Often, whole biblical texts were devoted to relating family genealogies, which were not just historical facts.[18] The genealogies grounded a person in a network of kinship that extended beyond his immediate time and place, and ultimately led back to the ancestral homeland.

Most Africans who have dispersed from their homeland often cannot trace themselves back to a common ancestor or piece of land the way the Israelites could trace themselves back to Abraham. But anthropologists and linguists have identified similarities in vocabulary and linguistic patterns that indicate that people from different parts of Africa had common ancestry. Moreover, most African groups have solidified their permanent relationship by sharing the same totem. The totem relational principle is primary in much of Africa and fosters a sense of social cohesion among communities both within and outside of Africa.

Africans with the same totem animal (such as zebra, baboon, monkey, buffalo, etc.) are considered closely related.[19] This traditional relationship holds true for people with the same totem, even if they live in different countries and even have a different word for the totem animal. Embedded in the totem relational principle is the belief that two people with the same totem are descendants of the same original family from the same ancestral land. Their relationship to each other emerges from their primary relationship to the land. They are related to each other as the offspring, *mwana wevhu*, "the child of the soil/land." The totem animal evokes in them a constellation of positive emotions about the place of their origins, in much the same way as a flag or a national animal represents a country and can evoke an accompanying set of patriotic emotions in a westerner.[20]

African and Israelite history (as is all history) in ancient and modern times is full of examples of the land being seized from a traditional group of people by a more powerful group. The traditional ways of living on the land that created deep, enduring identification with ancestral places and the other people who shared these places could not withstand assaults by the greedy and powerful. The biblical story of Naboth's vineyard clearly shows the tension between traditional,

---

18. Gen 5; 10; 11; etc.

19. There are also special relationships between some clans. For example, I, as a member of the Ndau clan, whose totem is the zebra, regard members of the baboon or monkey as nephews and nieces. People having the same totem could not marry, but people from different clans, even clans that have a special relationship, could marry, as these relationships were considered more distant.

20. Even though Africans have Westernized surnames these days, often their identity is still more strongly tied to their totem animal than to that name. It is still the case that if an African does something good to another, the beneficiary of the good deed will ask, "What is your thank-you name?" A person being thanked was addressed by his totem animal and not by the acquired surname.

collective concepts of land ownership, as it was practiced in Israel, and other more individualistic, self-aggrandizing views of land possession that were developing by the ninth century B.C.E. following Solomon's reign, with its disregard of tradition.

Naboth had a vineyard in the Jezreel Valley near King Ahab's palace (1 Kgs 21:1–4). Ahab (876 to 854 B.C.E.) wanted to purchase and develop it into his own vegetable garden.[21] But because it was a family possession, Naboth could not sell it, even to the king of Israel. For that reason, he swore to King Ahab by Yahweh: "The Lord forbid that I should give you my ancestral inheritance." (1 Kgs 21:3) Ahab, who respected Israelite traditional law, grudgingly acquiesced to Naboth's refusal. But Jezebel, his wife, who came from Phoenicia—where peasants did not have the same rights to traditional family lands as they did in Israel—forged letters to the elders and nobles in Naboth's neighborhood, advising them to have Naboth accused of blasphemy. This done, Naboth was subsequently killed and his land seized by Ahab. But because Yahweh[22] owned the land, God sent the Prophet Elijah to convey the divine judgment: ". . . Have you killed, and also taken possession? . . . In the place where dogs licked up the blood of Naboth, dogs will also lick up your blood" (1 Kgs 21:19). Both Ahab and Jezebel died ignominious deaths (2 Kgs 9:30–37).

Naboth's unfortunate experience was not something novel when it occurred in the ninth century B.C.E. In the second half of the tenth century B.C.E., Solomon's secular administration had led to the development of an aristocracy, which, by the time of the Prophet Amos, had become powerful (Amos 8:4–6). Solomon had made a radical departure from the traditional land holding practices, distributing land to the wealthy and redistricting it based on fiscal policies rather than family and tribal tradition. Solomon viewed land as a commodity. He gave away the Galilee area to King Hiram of Phoenicia in exchange for timber for his building enterprises (1 Kgs 9:10–14). He redistributed the land according to the dictates of commerce needs and thus disregarding traditional boundaries (1 Kgs 4:3). In Deut 19:1 it is clearly stated: "You must not move your neighbor's boundary marker, set up by former generations, on the property that will be allotted to you in the land that the LORD your God is giving you to possess."

In southern Africa, especially in Zimbabwe, Namibia, and South Africa, in colonial times, massive land redistribution by white newcomers benefited the powerful and destroyed ancient traditions of land ownership. When the whites colonized Gazaland, Mashonaland, and Matebeleland in the late nineteenth century, they redistricted their territories, reserving most of the good land for the whites;

---

21. Subsequent to the reign of King Solomon, an aristocratic class arose in Israel that did not respect traditional land ownership. Land could be sold and bought. A person's land could be seized regardless of the fact that the poor person has been living on it as an inheritance from past generations.

22. Yahweh and God are synonymous at this time. See Temba L. J. Mafico, *Yahweh's Emergence as "Judge" among the Gods: A Study of the Hebrew Root Špt* (Lewiston, NY: Mellen, 2007), for the coalescence of God and Yahweh into Yahweh Elohim.

tracts of arid land were designated as "Native Reserved Areas." Making it illegal for native Africans to live in what were then termed "European" areas, the white governments forcibly evicted native Africans as squatters and sold their land to the white settlers to develop into commercial farms. The Zimbabwe war of liberation that began in the late 1960s, culminating in Black African majority rule in 1980, was precipitated by the Zimbabweans' desire to reclaim *nyika yemadzibaba edu,* "the land of our progenitors." But, unfortunately, thirty years following independence, the majority of the black Zimbabwean peasants are still landless. Instead of redistributing land, the black aristocratic class who campaigned for independence under the guise of a socialistic society, has grabbed the European farms for themselves. Many black Zimbabweans, as a result, fare as badly, if not worse, in post-independence Zimbabwe as they did in Rhodesia prior to independence. The disparity in land redistribution, or the lack of it, is causing great pain and suffering to the majority of the people of Zimbabwe and elsewhere in Southern Africa.

A tragic situation of displacement and land conflict also exists in the modern Middle East. The Palestinians, forced from their native land in 1948, when the United Nations set into motion a chain of events that resulted in the establishment of the modern state of Israel, still consider Palestine as their legitimate homeland. The Israelis base their claim to the land of Palestine on the Hebrew Bible, which states that God gave the Canaanite (Palestinian) land to the descendants of Abraham (Gen 12:1–3). This land conflict and the ones in Southern Africa seem unending and impossible to resolve. But unless the land issues in these areas are decided fairly and equitably, acknowledging the rights to the land of all the people of the region, the poor as well as the rich, the weak as well as the powerful, men as well as women, there can be no real justice or stability.

This brief examination of the concept of land tenure in ancient Israel and traditional Africa has unveiled some significant facts. The land was like a mother; at God's command she produced creatures and vegetation (Gen 1:11–12). Land was a divine gift from God to families, clans and tribes to live in and enjoy. Belonging to family land provided security to a person (Gen 3:14). This land was to be passed down from generation to generation as a *nahalah,* "an inheritance" in perpetuity (Gen 13:15). It could also be owned as an *'ahuzzah,* "land possession" following its seizure from other people following the divine command. Because land was a divine trust, it could not be sold for gain. In dire circumstances, however, a person could acquire a portion of the family land belonging to others for burial of loved ones. (Gen 23:1–12). This land was called an *'ahuzzah,* "land possession" and not a *nahalah,* "an inheritance." Although the terms *nahalah* and *ahhuzah* appear to be synonyms, they differ in the original way the land was owned.

Solomon's rule initiated the aristocratic class, a privileged class of people who owned land as a commodity that could be sold to make money. This new view of land led to land aggrandizement, forcing the poor peasants to sell their land during a time of exigency. The regulation regarding the redemption of land by the next of kin or the release of land to its traditional owner during the year of Jubilee (Lev

25) was meant to restore the land to its traditional owners. With the aristocratic onslaught on the traditional land, borders were being redrawn increasing land for the rich at the expense of the poor. This is the reason why the Book of Deuteronomy strongly prohibited those who moved boundary markers: "You must not move your neighbor's boundary marker, set up by former generations, on the property that will be allotted to you in the land that the LORD your God is giving you to possess" (Deut 19:4). Cursed be anyone who moves a neighbor's boundary marker. All the people shall say, "Amen!" (Deut 27:17).

In Africa, traditional boundary markers are now history since colonialism not only redrew the land boundaries; but it also introduced the idea that land was a commodity for sale. The spurning of the traditional land tradition to people who, hitherto, are family oriented in their conceptual worldview is causing great pain and suffering in the Middle East and Africa. I conclude with the painful words of a song we used to sing at school:

> *Liza fika nini ilanga elinjabulo?*
> *Lizafika nini ilanga elijabulo?*
> *Abantu abamyama bayahlupheka.*
> *Kudhala, kudhala, kudhala.*

> When will the day of happiness arrive?
> When will the day of joy arrive?
> Black people are suffering,
> It's been long ago, long ago, long ago!

WORKS CITED

Feldman, Susa. *African Myths and Tales.* New York: Dell, 1965.

Frankfort, Henri, et al. *Before Philosophy: The Intellectual Adventure of Ancient Man. An Essay on Speculative Thought in the Ancient Near East.* Chicago: University of Chicago Press, 1946.

Griaule, M., and G. Dieterlen. *The Pale Fox.* Arizona: Continuum Foundation, 1965.

Habel, Norman. *The Line Is Mine.* Minneapolis: Fortress, 1995.

Heidel, Alexander. *The Babylonian Genesis.* Chicago: University of Chicago Press, 1942.

Hestrin, Ruth, and Yael Israeli. *Inscriptions Reveal: Documents from the Time of the Bible, the Mishna, and the Talmud.* Jerusalem: Israel Museum, 1972.

Mafico, Temba L. J. *Yahweh's Emergence as "Judge" among the Gods: A Study of the Hebrew Root Špt.* Lewiston, NY: Mellen, 2007.

Mbiti, John. *African Religions and Philosophy.* New York: Doubleday, 1969.

Page, Hugh, ed. *Africana Bible: Reading Israel's Scriptures from Africa and the African Diaspora.* Minneapolis: Fortress, 2010.

Sankenfeld, D. K., ed. *The New Interpreter's Dictionary of the Bible.* Vol. 4. Nashville: Abingdon, 2009.

Thomas, L. V., R. Luneau, and J. Doneux. *Les Religions de L'Afrique Noire.* Paris: Fayard-Denoël, 1969.

"I Am What You Are Not!"
A Critical Postcolonial Reading of the
Africa Bible Commentary's Abraham–Lot Stories

Robert Wafula

This essay is a critique of Barnabe Assohoto and Samuel Ngewa's reading of Abraham-Lot stories in the *Africa Bible Commentary* (hereafter called the *ABC*).[1] I would like to propose that, although Assohoto and Ngewa read Genesis with a keen eye on African issues, they are oblivious of the developments in biblical studies and they show disinterest in matters that postcolonial biblical critics have lately been raising. I will proceed in two parts. In part 1 I will outline briefly the concerns of postcolonial criticism. In part 2, I will focus on Assohoto and Ngewa's reading of the Abraham-Lot stories with nuances and insights that would have been useful for their reading, had they paid some attention to a postcolonial reading strategy.

PART 1: CONCERNS OF POSTCOLONIALISM

Postcolonialism and Present-Day Biblical Studies

Assohoto and Ngewa write their commentary on Genesis in a decade that has witnessed increasing agitation within the field of biblical studies. It is an agitation that Fernando Segovia calls an eruption of a fourth paradigm shift[2] that has produced a theoretical methodology now called Postcolonialism, which is defined by R. S. Sugirtharajah as follows:

> . . . a textual and praxiological practice . . . undertaken by people who were once part of . . . European and American Empires, but now have some sort of territorial freedom while continuing to live with burdens from the past and enduring

---

1. Tokunboh Adeyemo, general ed., *Africa Bible Commentary* (Nairobi: WordAlive, 2006), 9–84.
2. Fernando Segovia, "Cultural Studies and Contemporary Biblical Criticism: Ideological Criticism as a Mode of Discourse," in *Reading from This Place: Social Location and Biblical Interpretation in Global Perspective,* ed. Fernando Segovia and Mary Ann Tolbert (Minneapolis: Fortress Press, 1995), 2:1–17.

newer forms of economic and cultural neo-colonialism . . . [and people] who are
now current victims of globalization and who have been continually kept away
from and represented by the dominant First World elements.[3]

From this definition one can argue that, in terms of biblical texts, postcolonialism
interrogates Western interpretations that have sustained the meta-narrative superiority over the rest of the world. Through this process the West is seen as having
taken on the Israelite meta-narrative of a history of a nation. Just like Israel, the
West becomes "the subject of history and its identities, experiences, aspirations,
and its destinies [are] asserted as the history of the world."[4] Western biblical scholars have continued narrating the same meta-narrative. For Kim they have followed
suit in tracing Western civilization in the traditions of Deuteronomistic history.[5]
Segovia describes this process in terms of the binary opposites of the imperial
center and the periphery. The imperial center is firmly in control of the economic,
political and cultural processes while the periphery is subordinated to the imperial center, often described in negative terms as uncivilized, primitive, barbarian,
backward, underdeveloped and so forth. The periphery suffers under the shadow
of the empire's power. So for Segovia what postcolonialism does is to interrogate
these differential projections in their sociopolitical environment in order to expose the empire's workings with the hope of working towards liberation of the
marginalized periphery. This liberation, in the postcolonial era, comes in terms
of placing the periphery at the center hence producing multiple voices that de-
centers the center by infusing third world voices and interpretive strategies with
Euro-American voices.[6]

The origin of a postcolonial criticism theory has been attributed to the works of
Edward Said, Gayatri Chakravorty Spivak, and Homi Bhabha.[7] In his posctcolnial
classic, *Orientalism*, Said examines the effects of colonialism on the world and
on cultural texts. He argues that without understanding the enormous influence
cultural texts have on the mind-set of people of the West and the Rest, one could

---

3. R. S. Sugirtharajah, *The Bible and the Third World: Precolonial, Colonial, and Postcolonial Encounters* (Cambridge: Cambridge University Press, 2001), 246–47.

4. Uriah Kim, "Postcolonial Criticism: Who Is the Other in the Book of Judges?" in
Judges and Method: New Approaches in Biblical Studies, ed. Gale A. Yee (Minneapolis: Fortress Press, 1995), 165–82.

5. Uriah Kim, *Decolonizing Josiah: Toward a Postcolonial Reading of the Deuteronomistic
History* (Sheffield: Sheffield Phoenix, 2005), 55–56.

6. Fernando Segovia, *Decolonizing Biblical Studies: A View from the Margin* (Maryknoll,
NY: Orbis Books, 2000), 121–32.

7. See Sugirtharajah, *Bible and the Third World*, 247–48, and idem, *The Postcolonial
Bible: Colonial and Postcolonial Encounters* (Sheffield: Sheffield Academic Press, 1998), 93.
Sugirtharajah in *Postcolonial Criticism and Biblical Interpretation* (Oxford: Oxford Univer-
sity Press, 2002), 14ff., argues that our attention to the three scholars may overlook the
supposed "real" progenitors of postcolonialism such as Frantz Fanon, Albert Memmi, and
Ngũgĩ wa Thiong'o.

not access the damage caused by colonialism. He argues that there is a relationship between the production of knowledge and the colonization of the Rest by the
West. Orientalism was therefore a science of understanding that represented the
non-Western peoples as different from the West—as the Other for the purpose
of constructing and advancing the identity and interest of the West. For Said, the
Orient was seen as a place of "inferior, irrational and weak peoples" as compared
to Western peoples.[8] Orientalism is, therefore for Said, a Western ideology in the
service of Western identity discourse.[9] Postcolonialism as a theory, in this case,
seeks to address this disparity between the West and the rest of the world. It questions knowledge that has been shaped around narrating the "Other" in differential
terms in order to justify Western supremacy.[10]

Bhabha and Spivak focus more on the subjectivity of the colonized rather than
on what had been done to the colonized by the colonizer. Bhabha argues for the
fact that the nation is not a fixed social formation. He states that the relationship
between the colonizer and colonized was often in a constant state of fluidity. People and culture do not simply comply with the script of the nation and a process of
hybridity takes place. Here Bhabha seeks to break away from dualistic tendencies
that are at the heart of Orientalism—the us and them culture that sees community imagined as insiders and outsiders. Hybridity, argues Bhabha, constantly sees
people negotiating the middle spaces destabilizing the nation's effort to write a coherent identity through cultural texts.[11] For Bhabha, "Resistance is not necessarily
an oppositional act of political intention, nor is it the simple negation or exclusion
of the 'content' of another culture, as a difference once perceived. It is [rather] the
effect of an ambivalence produced within the rules of recognition of dominating
discourses as they articulate the signs of cultural difference. . . .[12] Power dynamics
under this format, for the colonial subject, becomes negotiable around the middles
spaces created by resistance and embrace.

Spivak, on the other hand, challenges Western discourses that purport to speak
for the colonized when in actual fact such discourses participate in subjugating
the colonized further.[13] She shares a story where the case of the *Sari* represents the
British example of "White men saving brown women from brown men" when in
actual sense they misunderstood completely the Hindu ceremony in which women
themselves wanted to die in these ceremonies.[14] She also problematizes the notion—prevalent in subaltern studies—that in order to write a national history one

8. Edward Said, *Orientalism* (New York: Vintage Books, 1978), 32–40.

9. Ibid.

10. Kim, "Postcolonial Criticism," 161–82.

11. Ibid.

12. Homi Bhabha, *The Location of Culture* (London: Routledge, 1994), 110–11.

13. Gayatri Chakravorty Spivak, "Can the Subaltern Speak?" in *Marxism and the Interpretation of Culture*, ed. Cary Nelson and Larry Grossberg (Urbana: University of Illinois
Press, 1988), 271–313.

14. Ibid., 295.

simply has to make subalterns the subjects of their own history.[15] She argues that the subalterns cannot speak because they are in a position where they can only be known, represented and spoken of and for by others. Moreover the subalterns are not a unified group. She points out the invincibility of women in subaltern studies. Women belong to the silenced areas in all discourses.[16] In this way Spivak critiques the assumptions that the colonized are "a unified and undifferentiated group [and also that] racial difference is the only primary base . . . of colonialism."[17]

Although the three theorists above imply that Postcolonialism is far from a unified methodology, they all point to the idea that it is about questioning Western meta-narrative of power. It is about contesting how the West has narrated colonial subjects and a quest to give the colonial subject a voice not only to be heard but to challenge Western power and chart a self definition.

The Ethics of Reading

Alongside a postcolonial reading current biblical scholars have also increasingly been asking for an ethical responsibility on the reading practices. For example, Elisabeth Schüssler Fiorenza calls for a "Public-Political Responsibility in our reading practices."[18] She urges us to be conscious of how the ideologies inherent in texts and in our readings affect the lives of people on the periphery. This consciousness calls for a keen reading of texts captured by Jonathan Magonet. Magonet tells the story of some Czech Jewish youth who surprised him with their deep understanding of biblical nuances considering they had never studied the Bible before. When he asked them how they can read the Bible so keenly, they answered:

> You see, in Czechoslovakia, when you read a newspaper, first you read what is written there. Then you say to yourself, "If that is what they have written, what really happened? And if that is really what happened, what are they trying to make us think? And if that is what they are trying to make us think, what should we be thinking instead?" You learn to read between the lines and behind the lines. You learn to read a newspaper as if your life depended upon understanding it—because it does![19]

The story of these young Jewish readers reminds us that there is more than just words in texts—that texts are political instruments of the state used to communicate slanted messages to serve certain political ends. Thus, Schüssler Fiorenza suggests that we must be attentive to questions such as: How is meaning constructed

---

15. See Kim, "Postcolonial Criticism," 164–65.

16. Spivak, "Can the Subaltern Speak?" 295.

17. Tat-siong Benny Liew, "Postcolonial Criticism: Echoes of a Subaltern's Contribution and Exclusion," in *Mark and Method: New Approaches in Biblical Studies,* ed. Janice Capel Anderson and Stephen Moore (Minneapolis: Fortress Press, 2008), 211–31.

18. Elisabeth Schüssler Fiorenza, *Rhetoric and Ethic: The Politics of Biblical Studies* (Minneapolis: Fortress Press, 1999), 17–18.

19. Jonathan Magonet, *A Rabbi Reads the Bible* (London: SCM, 2004), 28–29.

in texts? What values are being advocated? And whose interests are being promoted in the texts and readings of texts before us?[20] Jonathan Culler makes explicit what seems to be implicit in Schüssler Fiorenza's and the young Jewish readers' explanations. He argues that we must go a step further and ask who is writing what we are reading? He alerts us to the fact that it makes a whole world of a difference if the writer is a man and not a woman, for example.[21] So a lot is at stake in what we read. We must be vigilant and alert to what is at stake in our readings. Philosophies inherent in texts and textual readings are behind some of the world's greatest evils such as racism, colonialism, apartheid, the holocaust and so forth so much that Elie Wiesel urges us in these words: "In times of crisis, [and] danger, no one has the right to choose caution, [or] abstention; when the life . . . of a human community [is] at stake, neutrality becomes criminal."[22]

What Is at Stake for an African's Reading of the Bible?

Musa Dube has shown us that the colonization of Africa is inseparably linked with the use of the Bible.[23] She reminds us of the famous African story that when the "white man came to Africa, he asked the African to close his eyes for prayer. When the African opened his eyes, the African had the Bible in his hands and the white man had the African land."[24] The African was then told to obey those in authority, for thus says the Bible. One finds, therefore, that the biblical text was used to dispossess Africans and to urge them to support this dispossession. Authority forced down the African throat did not stop by the end of territorial colonization of African. Instead it has, "Under the façade of multinational corporations, universalism media, and international monetary bodies, military and ideological muscle imperialism has proven its capacity to mutate and persist in ever new and remarkable forms."[25] Woe to an African of the postcolonial era. In colonial times Africans knew who their enemy was. They knew the oppressive powers against them too well since these powers were openly expressed through the power of the gun. But in the postcolonial era, one has to work extra hard to identify who and how Western nations exercise imperial power—the more reason why a careful reading of texts is called for.

---

20. Schüssler Fiorenza, *Rhetoric and Ethic*, 27.

21. Jonathan Culler, *On Deconstruction: Theory and Criticism after Structuralism* (Ithaca, NY: Cornell University Press, 1992), 42.

22. Elie Wiesel, *Messengers of God: Biblical Portraits and Legends* (New York: Summit, 1976), 213.

23. Musa Dube, *Postcolonial Feminist Interpretation of the Bible* (St. Louis: Chalice, 2000), 16.

24. Musa Dube, "Reading for Decolonization (John 4:1–42)," in *Voices from the Margin*, ed. R. S. Sugirtharajah (Maryknoll, NY: Orbis Books, 2006), 297–318.

25. Dube, *Postcolonial Feminist Interpretation*, 48.

Conclusion for Part 1

Following my argument above, I would propose that Africans, like the Czech Jews, must learn to read the Bible between the lines and behind the lines. A Postcolonial reading strategy can enable us do this kind of reading. We will be able to inquire into the philosophy underlying the biblical meta-narrative(s) and the agendas they advance and particularly how biblical meta-narratives have advanced the Western meta-narrative of imperial power with all its evils.

PART 2: READING ABRAHAM-LOT STORIES

Barnabe Assohoto and Samuel Ngewa's Reading of Abraham-Lot Stories in the Africa Bible Commentary

My critique of Assohoto and Ngewa's reading in the *ABC* will take into account how a postcolonial reading strategy may yield different nuances from those that Assohoto and Ngewa elucidate. I will highlight specific passages in the Abraham-Lot story.

Genesis 11:31–12:4

Lot and Abram are first introduced to us in Gen 11:27–32 as uncle and nephew in the midst of a family on its way to Canaan. But as chapter 12 opens, the focus moves from family to one man—Abram. Assohoto and Ngewa praises Abram for being so kind as to take in his orphaned nephew along with him (Haran Lot's father had died in Gen 11:28). They state that Lot together with Sarai, and others provide Abram "with community, culture and family." In other words, they help advance the meta-narrative of the text. The family journey has quickly turned into a one person journey—the journey of Abram—who receives a divine directive. Lee W. Humphreys points out that God does not mention Lot in his directive to Abram.[26] We also note that God does not mention Sarai either. These crucial components of Abram's family from here henceforth become mere accompaniments on the God-Abram plan. They become subplots in the grand meta-narrative of Abram. Even before chapter 12 (Gen 11:30), Sarai had already been demarcated with a problem: She is barren. This sets her apart as an impediment rather than a blessing to Abram. When God states that Abram will be the father of a great nation, he implicitly casts Sarai ominously as one whose status would threaten the Abram-God plan hence differentiates her from her husband. But Sarai's seedlessness also puts Lot in an ambiguous relationship with the family. On the onset we begin thinking that he might be the one that would provide seed to sustain God's promise to Abram. But this is not to be. God dispels this ambiguity in Gen 12:7 when he states that Abram's own seed will inherit the land. This clarity marks Lot

---

26. Lee W. Humphreys, *The Character of God in the Book of Genesis: A Narrative Appraisal* (Louisville: Westminster John Knox, 2001), 84.

in differential terms in relation to Abram's future. Lot at once becomes a none-entity in the grand God-Abram story. Therefore, unlike the serene picture that the *ABC* gives of this text, we begin seeing a text tensely loaded with imperialistic notions of setting one person over and against others. It forms what Christopher Heard calls the first pair of dis/elect characters in Genesis with significant resemblances to the Isaac/Ishmael, Jacob/Esau, and Jacob/Laban relationships.[27]

Genesis 13

Genesis 13 presents us with the story of a quarrel between Abraham's servants and Lot's servants. This quarrel necessitates a separation between uncle and nephew. In 13:9, Abram uses a niphal imperative masculine הפרד (separate) to urge Lot to separate from him. The *ABC* indicates that "the suggestion to separate was an appropriate decision" and that it was better for them to live apart in peace than to live together in constant quarrels. Thus the *ABC* sees Abram as being concerned about maintaining family ties. It states that Abram "shows his generous and unselfish spirit [in his willingness] to waive his right as the older party to choose where to go" ahead of his nephew. In this way the *ABC* casts Lot as selfish and Abram as a generous. In making this statement, the *ABC* falls in line with interpretations that assume that if Abram had taken the first choice he would have chosen the cities in the Plains. And also that if Lot had chosen the land of Canaan, Abram would have gone to Sodom and Gomorrah. Larry argues that this interpretation ignores the larger context of the story.[28] We know that prior to this God had already promised the land of Canaan to Abram's seed (Gen 12:7). Moreover, immediately after Lot had separated from Abram, God reiterates his promise of giving the land of Canaan to Abram (Gen 13:14–17). So, although, in the minute form of the story, we can agree with the *ABC* that "in terms of pastoral economics", it is good for the two men and their folks to separate, but not so in terms of the plot and larger context of the story. In this regard, the two must part "in order that Lot be removed from further consideration" as being the heir apparent to Abram.[29] Therefore, in God's framework of things, Lot's choice was really no choice. His choice was what Calvinists would call predestined choice. Long before Lot verbalized his choice, God had already fore-planned that he would choose the land of the plains.

If separation was God's plan, what is its implication? Heard locates the answer to this question in the narrators' statements that Lot's choice precedes Yahweh's destruction of Sodom and Gomorrah (Gen 13:10) and that the people of Sodom were wicked to the Lord (Gen 13:13). Heard thinks that the function of the separation then, in light of the narrator's statements, is to line up Abram and Yahweh

---

27. Christopher Heard, *Dynamics of Diselection: Ambiguity in Genesis 12–36 and the Ethnic Boundaries in Post-exilic Judah* (Atlanta: Society of Biblical Literature, 2001), 25.

28. Larry Helyer, "The Separation of Abraham and Lot: Its Significance in the Patriarchal Narratives," *JSOT* 26 (1983): 77–88.

29. Lou Silberman, "Listening to the Text," *JBL* 102 (1983): 3–26.

on one side against Lot, alongside moral concerns. By virtue of his choice, Lot's inclinations are merged with those of the "wicked Sodom," and by implication laying responsibility on Lot for the misfortunes he would later suffer among these wicked people.[30] The story in this context, then serves as an introduction to the Sodom-Gomorrah episode. It begins the first round of sealing Lot's fate and electing Abram for God's favor.

Genesis 14

Genesis 14 relates the story of Lot as a captive of war. Abram goes to rescue Lot. With only 317 people he defeats a combined army of five kings, whom another combined army of four kings had been unable to defeat! The *ABC* praises Abram's "wise strategy and a good team" by stating that "a good leader does not need a multitude of people to succeed." By so doing, the *ABC* credits Abram for saving Lot's family. He is cast as a heroic figure who risks his life to save his nephew.[31] But in the larger Abrahamic cycle, this story consolidates Abram's status as a worthy man. It builds his character in contrast to the character of Lot, who is portrayed as defenseless and dependant on Abram for his life. To bolster this image further, the text has Abram refuse taking any war spoils from the king of Sodom (Gen 14:22–23). He is portrayed as a just man who is worthy to relate with kings and kingdoms. After the rescue Abram meets Melchizedek, the king of Salem and offers him a tenth of everything. Melchizedek blesses Abram. This episode takes us back to Gen 12:3 where the Lord blesses Abram and promises to curse anyone who stands in his way. In this mix, Lot's status is completely submerged under Abram's rising star.

Genesis 18:16–33

In this episode, Yahweh goes to destroy Sodom and Gomorrah due to the outcry he has had. The *ABC* states that, "It was not that the Lord was ignorant of the exact situation in Sodom and Gomorrah. Rather, God's justice demanded that proof of sin be demonstrated to the sinner." The *ABC* praises Abram's prayer request for the Lord to spare the city as an "excellent example of intercessory prayer." Abram prays for the city to be spared if there are fifty, forty-five, thirty, and twenty, down to ten. In each case Yahweh assures Abram that he will not destroy the city if he found righteous people there. The *ABC* further states that Abram had made his plea and "now it was the Lord's business to do what was right."

But by raising a couple of questions, this text becomes more complicated than the *ABC* puts it. Whom does Abram have on his mind when he pleads with Yahweh? Is he thinking about Lot and his company or is he thinking about a hypothetical number of righteous people in the city (considering that Gen 19:12–14 seems to imply that there were other people other than Lot's nuclear company that would

---

30. Heard, *Dynamics*, 31.
31. Ibid., 39.

have been saved)? If we take it that Abraham is pleading for un-named number of people in the city, does Abram's plea then not represent a human public opinion that the city should not be destroyed? The *ABC* says that God gave Abram all the time and patiently answered his questions. But did God listen to Abram? Was not his mind made up when he said, "I shall not hide from Abraham what I am about to do" (Gen 18:17)? Finally, did God do what was right?

These questions indicate that the text is fraught with moral and ethical problems. Feminist scholars have alerted us about the text's silence on the fate of children and women. Assuming that the total destruction included these groups, Holly Joan Tuensing decries God's merciless act against women and children, and vegetation too considering that these groups of people and vegetation are not accused for any wrong doing![32] Taking into account what Tuensing states, Danna Fewell's advice is worth our attention. She argues that when we read texts like this we must be aware that we are reading "texts that are not ours, texts that were not written for us, or by others like us."[33] The Rwandan genocide of 1994, the present mass killings in Darfur region of Southern Sudan, The legacy of the evils of Apartheid, and the despotic African leaders who would have their way no matter the public opinion, should warn us about reading superimposing power lightly.

Genesis 19: 29:38

The last that we hear of Lot is the sad story of a sexual relationship between him and his two daughters. The *ABC* accuses Lot of having gone to live in a cave alone with his daughters—implying that his choice to live in a cave with two young women with wayward hormones would have left room for what the daughters did. It condemns him also for his choice to live in Sodom and raise his girls in a morally depraved city. The *ABC* implies that it serves Lot right that the daughters would do such an act with him. It is the fruits of his uncouth raising of his daughters. It blames Lot for twice failing to return to Abram: once when he is rescued from captivity and secondly when Sodom is burned down, as though this was a choice that Lot had.

The *ABC*'s interpretation ignores the function of this story in the larger context of the Abraham-Lot stories. Way back in 1960 Herman Gunkel had argued that this story is a legend about the origin of the Moabites and Ammonites that honor their founding mothers. But Van Zyl had disagreed with him by arguing that the story is a legend that is directed against the ancestors of these mothers. It is a reflection of the Israelite feeling of disdain towards the Moabites. He argues that sexual intercourse between relatives of the first degree was forbidden and regarded

---

32. Holly Joan Tuensing, "Women of Sodom and Gomorrah: Collateral Damage in War against Homosexuality," *JFSR* 21 (2005): 61–74.

33. Dana Fewell, "Reading the Bible Ideologically: Feminist Criticism," in *To Each Its Own Meaning: Biblical Criticism and Its Application,* ed. Steven L. McKenzie and Stephen R. Haynes (Louisville: Westminster John Knox, 1999), 268–82.

as abhorrent among all the nations of the ancient Near East (ANE). The fact that Lot's daughters are not even named lends credence to the notion that the narrative is meant to dishonor them and their ancestors.[34]

More recently, Heard has sought to strike a middle ground between Gunkel and Van Zyl by stating that the narrative does not blame either Lot or his daughters. Lot is simply stated as having drunken sex, of which he is completely unaware. So Heard concludes that the text is ambiguous in relation to Lot's character portrayal.[35] Lee W. Humphreys, has reasserted Van Zyl's thesis, which, as I have argued earlier, represents the direction of events in the story. He argues that the Moabite and Ammonite origins are set in the context of separation between Lot and Abraham—that Moab and Ammon, unlike Isaac/Ishmael, Jacob/Esau pairs, are born without God's presence or reaction.[36] Indeed, a reading of the narrative shows that they are born without a word from Yahweh concerning either their birth or their future.

If this story is about separating Lot from Abraham and later their descendants, then it relies on vilification as the methodology to justify its separation process. In light of this the daughters' act of causing their father to get drank is not unambiguous statement as Christopher Heard would put it. To take sexual advantage of their drunken father is a serious judgment on the daughters. Similarly, Lot is not entirely off the hook either. The idea that sex could be performed on him twice without his slightest idea of it stretches a rational mind to the extremes. It is later in Deut 23:2 when Israel holds dubious parentage against the Moabites as one of the reason why they are to be excluded from the congregation of Israel that we begin to understand that Lot and his daughters are made to take the blame for their actions for political reasons.

Conclusion of Part 2: Uriah Kim and Postcolonialism

In conclusion, I would like to make a reference to Kim's work in *Decolonizing Josiah.* Kim has argued that the Hebrew Bible orients biblical history as the history of the Israelites against all other nations.[37] Israel's identity, experiences, aspirations and destinies are summoned to submerge the identities of all other groups. In our case, Lot and his future descendants are demeaned and devalued in order to extol and exalt Abram and his descendants. This process allows philosophical concepts that would justify dispossession, depopulation, and annihilation of all those who are perceived to be on the wrong side of things with God. It also deadens Israel's consciousness concerning the destruction of entire cities and cultures and renaming these cities with Israelite names.[38]

---

34. A. H. Van Zyl, *The Moabites* (Leiden: Brill, 1960), 20.
35. Heard, *Dynamics*, 47ff.
36. Humphreys, *Character of God*, 124ff.
37. See n. 4 above.
38. Fewell, "Achsah and the (E)razed City of Writing," in Yee, *Judges and Method*, 115–37.

Uriah argues further that the Hebrew Bible's philosophical framework has been fundamental in the development of Western civilization. According to this framework, there are human beings (Whites) that are superior and others (Africans) who are inferior. By categorizing Africans this way colonialism was justified. The postcolonial era has fared no better than the colonial era. Tyranny continues to be justified against African peoples on the same principle that they are of a lesser importance than the Euro-American imperial powers. The *ABC*'s failure to deal with complex moral questions implicitly justifies the Western meta-narrative which the West transplanted from biblical philosophy. By so doing, the *ABC* implicitly participates in putting weapons in the hands of our killers and justifies our subjugation to Euro-American imperial powers. The imperialistic tendencies in the texts should sensitize our reading process. A work of so huge a pool of African scholars as the *ABC* should have provided a perfect arena to begin this discussion.

I would like also to mention one issue that is important to the *ABC* contributors, and which contributes greatly to its weaknesses. The *ABC* editors acknowledge that the work is a product of the Association of Evangelicals in Africa (AEA) and that every one of the scholars who contributed an article had "to sign an AEA statement of faith" (ix). Herein lies the quandary: A doctrinal statement inevitably muzzles what scholars can or cannot write. Assohoto and Ngewa had to write a narrative that would please their masters, which unfortunately ignored recent scholarship in Biblical Studies.

Finally, I would like to suggest that the acronym *ABC* is appropriate for this commentary. Christopher Peppler, who reviews parts of this commentary, is right on target in saying that the *ABC* demonstrates a work that has just begun.[39] It should, however, mean that we still have *D–Z* letters for its work to be completed.

Works Cited

Bhabha, Homi. *The Location of Culture*. London: Routledge, 1994.

Culler, Jonathan. *On Deconstruction: Theory and Criticism after Structuralism*. Ithaca, NY: Cornell University Press, 1992.

Dube, Musa. *Postcolonial Feminist Interpretation of the Bible*. St. Louis: Chalice, 2000.

Fewell, Nolan Danna. "Achsah and the (E)razed City of Writing." Pages 115–37 in *Judges and Method: New Approaches in Biblical Studies*. Ed. Gale A. Yee. Minneapolis: Fortress Press, 2007.

———. "Reading the Bible Ideologically: Feminist Criticism." Pages 268–82 in *To Each Its Own Meaning: Biblical Criticisms and Their Application*. Ed. Steven L. McKenzie and Stephen R. Haynes. Louisville: Westminster John Knox, 1999.

Heard, Christopher. *Dynamics of Diselection: Ambiguity in Genesis 12–36 and Ethnic Boundaries in Post-exilic Judah*. Atlanta: Society of Biblical Literature, 2001.

---

39. Christopher Peppler, "A Review of *Africa Bible Commentary*," n.p. (accessed 14 April 2010). http://www.satsonline.org/sats_drupal6/userfiles/ReviewofAfricaBibleCommentary .pdf.

Helyer, Larry. "The Separation of Abraham and Lot: Its Significance in the Patriarchal Narratives." *JSOT* 26 (1983): 77–88.

Humphreys, Lee W. *The Character of God in the Book of Genesis: A Narrative Appraisal.* Louisville: Westminster John Knox, 2001.

Kim, Uriah. *Decolonizing Josiah: Toward a Postcolonial Reading of the Deuteronomistic History.* Sheffield: Sheffield Phoenix, 2005.

———. "Postcolonial Criticism: Who Is the Other in the Book of Judges?" Pages 161–82 in *Judges and Method: New Approaches in Biblical Studies.* Ed. Gale A. Yee. Minneapolis: Fortress Press, 2007.

Liew, Tat-siong Benny. "Echoes of A Subaltern's Contribution and Exclusion." Pages 211–31 in *Mark and Method: New Approaches in Biblical Studies.* Ed. Janice Capel Anderson and Stephen Moore. Minneapolis: Fortress Press, 2008.

Magonet, Jonathan. *A Rabbi Reads the Bible.* London: SCM, 2004.

Peppler, Christopher, "A Review of Africa Bible Commentary," n.p. (accessed 14 April 2010). http://www.satsonline.org/sats_drupal6/userfiles/ReviewofAfricaBibleCommentary.pdf.

Said, Edward. *Orientalism.* New York: Vintage Books, 1978.

Schüssler Fiorenza, Elisabeth. *Rhetoric and Ethic: The Politics of Biblical Studies.* Minneapolis: Fortress Press, 1999.

Segovia, Fernando. "Cultural Studies and Contemporary Biblical Criticism: Ideological Criticism as a Mode of Discourse." Pages 1–17 in *Reading from This Place,* vol. 2: *Social Location and Biblical Interpretation in Global Perspective.* Ed. Fernando Segovia and Mary Ann Tolbert. Minneapolis: Fortress Press, 1995.

———. *Decolonizing Biblical Studies: A View from the Margin.* Maryknoll, NY: Orbis Books, 2000.

Silberman, Lou. "Listening to the Text," *JBL* 102 (1983): 3–26.

Spivak, Gayatry Chackravorty. "Can the Subaltern Speak?" Pages 271–313 in *Marxism and the Interpretation of Culture.* Ed. Cary Nelson and Larry Grossberg. Urbana: University of Illinois Press, 1988.

Sugirtharajah, R. S. *The Bible and the Third World: Precolonial, Colonial, and Postcolonial Encounters.* Cambridge: Cambridge University Press, 2001.

———. *Postcolonial Criticism and Biblical Interpretation.* Oxford: Oxford University Press, 2002.

———, ed. *The Postcolonial Bible.* Sheffield: Sheffield Academic Press, 1998.

———. *Voices From the Margin.* Maryknoll, NY: Orbis Books, 2006.

Tuensing, Holly Joan. "Women of Sodom and Gomorrah: Collateral Damage in War against Homosexuality." *JFSR* (2005): 61–74.

Van Zyl, A. H. *The Moabites.* Leiden: E. J. Brill, 1960.

Wiesel, Elie. *Messengers of God: Biblical Portraits and Legends.* New York: Summit Books, 1976.

5. Afrocentric Biblical Interpretations: Unthinking Eurocentrism

The African Origin of Jesus: An Afrocentric Reading of Matthew's Infancy Narrative (Matthew 1–2)

Ernest M. Ezeogu

There is a widespread assumption among people of African descent, both in the continent and in the Diaspora, that Christianity is a foreign, White man's religion as opposed to Islam, which they hail as the African religion. Given the African experience of both religions and their varying dispositions towards African peoples and their cultures, there may be some grounds for such assertions. The purpose of this study, however, is to show that the foundational stories of the Christian religion, historically speaking, have more to do with Africa and Africans than most people, Africans and non-Africans alike, realise. Through a historical and intercultural reading of Matthew's infancy narrative (chs. 1–2), I intend to show that Matthew is attempting a Jewish retelling of a story that had so much to do with Africa and Africans that it can, in fact, be called an African story.

My submission is that the tradition available to Matthew was one in which Mary and her son Jesus, were known to be Africans of Egyptian origin. This tradition created difficulties for the Jews of Matthew's time in accepting Jesus as their Messiah, since the Messiah was expected to be a Hebrew (descendant of Abraham) of the line of David.[1] Marshall D. Johnson, in his study on the purpose of biblical genealogies corroborates this assertion. "Never in the OT is the future Messianic deliverance to come from any tribe than that of Judah and within that tribe from the house of David."[2]

In spite of the popularity of this expectation that the Messiah would come from the bloodline of David, when Jesus finally came on the scene, his Davidic descent was not at all evident. On the contrary, some contemporaries of Jesus, who supposedly knew his family background, seemed to have knowledge that Jesus was not of biological Davidic descent, nor was he born in Bethlehem. The expected Messiah, however, was to have both of these qualities. This is at least the picture we get in John's gospel.

---

1. See, for example, 2 Sam 7:11–16; Ps 132:1; Isa 16:5; Jer 33:17–31.

2. Marshall D. Johnson, *The Purpose of the Bible Genealogies: With Special Reference to the Setting of the Genealogies of Jesus* (2nd ed.; Eugene, OR: Wipf and Stock, 2002), 116.

When they heard these words, some in the crowd said, "This is really the prophet." Others said, "This is the Messiah." But some asked, "Surely the Messiah does not come from Galilee, does he? Has not the scripture said that the Messiah is descended from David and comes from Bethlehem, the village where David lived?" So there was a division in the crowd because of him. (John 7:40–43)

The questions and division in the crowd of Jesus' followers are symptomatic of a wider problem. One problem that tormented the Jewish Christian community in the early church was the fact that what they got in Jesus did not measure up to their expectations, at least as far as ethnicity and ancestry were concerned. Like John, Matthew's gospel is also believed to be addressed to a Jewish Christian community. Matthew's community would, therefore, have the same problem of perceived discontinuity between the expected origins of the Messiah who was to come and the reality of the origins of the historical Jesus. This disparity between the Jesus they knew and the Torah they read was a stumbling block in the way of Jewish commitment to the messianic faith in Jesus that characterized the Jesus movement.

No proclamation of the gospel to the Jewish people would be complete or effective without attempting a resolution of this problem. This must be one reason why Matthew's community saw the Gospel of Mark as deficient and went on to produce their own version. How does Matthew handle this problem? He does so by retelling the story of Jesus (redacting the received tradition) in such a way as to portray Jesus as providentially, if not naturally, a son of Abraham of the bloodline of David (Matt 1:1).

Matthew's attempted make-over of the received tradition, however, leaves many gaps that are easily discernible to the attentive reader. What I intend to do, within the limits of this study, is to point out some of these historical and narrative gaps and show how the thesis of the African origin of Mary and Jesus helps to fill them.

In doing this we will utilize the tools of textual and historical criticism. In particular we will employ the new tool of intercultural criticism[3] to shed light on

---

3. James Leslie Houlden, ed., *The Interpretation of the Bible in the Church* (London: SCM Press, 1995), n. 12. *The Interpretation of the Bible in the Church* presented by the Pontifical Biblical Commission to Pope John Paul II on April 23, 1993, describes the intercultural approach to biblical interpretation as follows:

In general, cultural anthropology seeks to define the characteristics of different kinds of human beings in their social context—as, for example the "Mediterranean person"—with all that this involves by way of studying the rural or urban context and with attention paid to the values recognized by the society in question (honor and dishonor, secrecy, keeping faith, tradition, kinds of education and schooling), to the manner in which social control is exercised, to the ideas which people have of family, house, kin, to the situation of women, to institutionalized dualities (patron–client, owner–tenant, benefactor–beneficiary, free person–slave), taking into account also the prevailing conception of the sacred and

the birth of Jesus as a flesh-and-blood, culturally-situated event that happened in Palestine some two thousand years ago. Again, our aim is to show that, at least in its foundational stories, Christianity, even more than Islam, can validly lay claim to being an African religion, and to challenge people of African descent in the continent and in the Diaspora to rise up and reclaim the Christian heritage that belongs to them.

WHAT IS AFROCENTRIC EXEGESIS?

As the subtitle of this study shows, I intend to do a reading of Matthew's Infancy Narrative from Afrocentric perspective? What does that mean? What is the difference between Afrocentrism and the mainstream approach to biblical exegesis?

First, what it is not! Afrocentrism is not a new exegetical methodology. Afrocentric exegesis employs the established tools of standard biblical criticism: textual, historical and literary, in its reading of the biblical text. What sets Afrocentric exegesis apart from other ways of reading are not the technical tools of exegesis but the questions and interests that inform the reading. There is widespread assumption, implied or expressed, in conventional, Eurocentric biblical scholarship that Africa and persons of African descent play but a minor, insignificant role in the history of salvation and of civilization. Against this ideological background that tends to marginalize or erase Africa and Africans from the history of civilization and salvation, Afrocentrism seeks to reread these histories with Africa and Africans in the centre, hence the term Afro-centric.[4]

For centuries the Christian woman or man who is a person of visible African descent, has felt like the prairie eagle. You know the story: a man finds an eagle egg and puts it with prairie chicken eggs. They hatch but the eagle spends all its life thinking that it was a prairie chick. All its life it never gets to fly or experience the glorious freedom of the eagle but trots about eating waste from the garbage heaps like prairie chicken do.

This story can function as a model to understanding the existential desperation and incessant self-interrogation plaguing the lives of Black individuals and communities everywhere. It portrays a tragedy that is playing out in African and African-American communities, but a tragedy which we can help turn around by

---

the profane, taboos, rites of passage from one state to another, magic, the source of wealth, of power, of information, etc. On the basis of these diverse elements, typologies and "models" are constructed, which are claimed to be common to a number of cultures. Clearly this kind of study can be useful for the interpretation of biblical texts.

4. Henry Louis Gates and Kwame Anthony Appiah, eds., *Africana: The Encyclopedia of the African and African-American* (New York: Oxford University Press, 2005), 1:111. Cf. also James Cone, *Black Theology and Black Power* (Maryknoll, NY: Orbis Books, 1997; orig, Harper and Row, 1969); idem, *A Black Theology of Liberation* (Maryknoll, NY: Orbis Books, 1986; orig., J. B. Lippincott, 1970).

telling the lost eagle the true history of its glorious past. Afrocentrism is a commitment to doing just that. Afrocentrism is not a denial of the contributions of
Europeans, Asians or Americans to the history of civilization and salvation. It is a
commitment to rewriting the one-sided conventional history in such a way as to
give honour to whom honour is due.[5]

Here is an example of what Afrocentric biblical scholarship is all about. If you
look up Song of Songs 1:5 in your Bible, chances are that it reads, "I am black *but*
beautiful" or something similar. It took the efforts on Afrocentric biblical scholars
to raise the awareness of the academic community that this translation is ideologically biased. As a result of their work, the latest major translation of the Bible
in English, the New Revised Standard Version, changed its translation of Song
1:5 to "I am black *and* beautiful." The old translation marginalized blackness as
something negative, something that normally should not go together with beauty,
hence the adversative "but." The new translation, on the other hand, celebrates the
beauty of blackness, which is in line with the viewpoint of the author of Song of
Songs. The old translation was bad news for people of African descent, while the
new translation is good news. By identifying and exposing anti-black ideology
embedded in traditional Bible translations and conventional biblical interpretations, Afrocentric biblical scholarship helps people of African descent experience
the word of God as the good news that it is meant to be.

Given the high premium that Afrocentric scholarship places on history, one
would expect Afrocentric exegesis to be interested in the historical-critical method
of biblical exegesis, and it is. This is the branch of biblical scholarship that views
biblical texts primarily as products of history and seeks to reconstruct their historical settings in order to better understand them. The historical settings include
such elements as time, place, circumstances, authors, and primary audiences.

One element that has been neglected in such historical reconstruction is culture,
understood as expected patterns of behaviour. There is a growing awareness today
of the importance of cultural anthropology and the knowledge of the customs of
the time and place in which a text originated as a key element in reconstructing
what actually is going on in the text. As a matter of fact, cultural anthropology has
always been a factor in biblical interpretation. For example, when we are told that
the young girl Mary was betrothed to Joseph, it is cultural anthropology that tells
us that betrothal usually took place at puberty. From there scholars conclude that
Mary must have been about thirteen years of age. In this example we see how the
cultural reality of the day helps us in the task of historical reconstruction. The use
of cultural anthropological data in the reconstruction of the historical settings of
a text is variously referred to as cultural criticism or intercultural exegesis. In the
Afrocentric re-reading of Matthew's infancy narratives, which we intend to do in

---

5. See Cain Hope Felder, "Afrocentrism, the Bible, and the Politics of Difference," *JRT* 50
nos. 1/2 (1993/94): 45–57, on some pitfalls of Afrocentric readings of the Bible.

this study, we shall employ intercultural exegesis as a tool in the reconstruction of the history in the text and behind the text of Matthew's infancy narrative.

TEXT AND STRUCTURE OF MATTHEW'S INFANCY NARRATIVE (MATTHEW 1–2)

A cursory look at the critical apparatus shows that there is hardly a verse in the entire Infancy Narrative of Matthew (Matt 1–2) that has no manuscript variants. Many of these variants, fortunately, are minor and do not affect the narrative in any significant way. One particular set of variants, however, could be very significant for this study. It is the set of variants found in Matthew 1:16.

Raymond Brown has synthesized the many variants of Matthew 1:16 into three major readings, as follows:

(a) Jacob was the father of Joseph, the husband of Mary; of her was be-gotten Jesus, called the Christ.
(b) Jacob was the father of Joseph, to whom the betrothed virgin Mary bore [gave birth to] Jesus, called the Christ.
(c) Jacob was the father of Joseph, and Joseph to whom the virgin Mary was betrothed, was the father of Jesus, called the Christ.[6]

On both external and internal criteria, reading (a) is the preferred reading. Yet, in spite of the poor attestation of readings (b) and especially (c), they remain significant. As Brown explains, "These would attract little attention if scholars had not seen in them a hint, direct or indirect, of a natural conception of Jesus with Joseph as the biological father."[7] He discusses these variant readings extensively and demonstrates convincingly that (a) is the authentic reading.[8]

Matthew 1–2 can be structured in many different ways according to different criteria. Some scholars have structured the narrative based on the five explicit Old Testament citations, and others on geographical motifs.[9] The difficulty of arriving at a universally accepted structure for Matt 1–2 lies in the fact that it is not clear whether the evangelist is composing this narrative himself or simply piecing together material from different sources, oral or written. For the purpose

---

6. Reading (a) is supported by the best Greek codices, including the Vaticanus (B) and the Sinaiticus (‫א‬), which are the two oldest uncial manuscripts that we possess. Reading (b) is found in the codex Koridethi (Θ), the Ferrar family of mss (φ), and some Old Latin versions. Reading (c) is found only in the Sinaitic old Syriac version (sys).

7. Raymond E. Brown, *The Birth of the Messiah: A Commentary on the Infancy Narratives in Matthew and Luke* (New York: Doubleday, 1977), 62.

8. See also W. D. Davies and D. C. Allison, *The Gospel according to Matthew*, vol. 1: *Introduction and Commentary on Matthew I–VII* (International Critical Commentary; London: T & T Clark, 1988), 183–84.

9. For the merits and demerits of these and others ways of structuring Matt 1–2, see Brown, *The Birth of the Messiah*, 50–54.

of this study, we shall use the simple outline found in most bibles and general commentaries.

This outline divides Matthew's infancy narrative into six narrative sections, namely:

(1) the Ancestors (and Ancestresses) of Jesus (Matt 1:1–17)
(2) Joseph Becomes Foster Father to Jesus (Matt 1:18–24)
(3) the Visit of the Magi (Matt 2:1–12)
(4) the Holy Family Takes Refuge in Egypt (Matt 2:13–15)
(5) Herod Kills Innocent Children (Matt 2:16–18)
(6) the Holy Family Returns from Egypt and Settles in Nazareth (Matt 2:19–23)

Using this outline, we shall now proceed with a section by section study. For each section, we shall, first, identify the narrative gaps in it, and then proceed to show how the thesis of the African origin of Jesus helps to fill the gaps. The approach here is similar to the approach used in the study of Paul's letters. In Paul's letters, it often happens that what we are reading is the answer to an undeclared question or an issue that is bothering Paul and the community he was writing to. The reader works backwards to reconstruct what the question or the issue was. In other words, we are not working simply from cause to effect, but from effect to probable cause.

As is the case with all historical reconstructions, the results of our investigation make no claim to absolute certainty. They necessarily remain within the ambit of probability. Our support for the theory of the African origin of Jesus is informed by our conviction that, more than other competing theories, it explains most satisfactorily the well-known incongruities of Matthew's infancy narratives.

THE ANCESTORS (AND ANCESTRESSES) OF JESUS (MATTHEW 1:1–17)

In this session, four incongruities or gaps immediately spring to our attention, namely:

• Why does Matthew give us Jesus' lineage from Joseph when Joseph is not Jesus' real father?
• Why are women included in a genealogy that traces lineage through fathers?
• If women were to be included, why select only these little-known women and leave out the well-known matriarchs of Israel, such as Sarah, Rebecca, Rachel and others?
• Why does Matthew tamper with history and statistics to arrive at the symmetrical figure of 14 x 3 generations between Abraham and the Christ?

First, we start with a general observation. The fact that Matthew needed to prove the Davidic-Abrahamic ancestry of Jesus shows that the Davidic-Abrahamic ancestry of Jesus was not evident to his contemporaries. Either the fact was contestable or else was known to be non-existent. Most likely it was known to be nonexistent as a historical fact since, for Matthew, to call Jesus "son of David" was a statement of faith.[10] This would not be such a laudable statement of faith were it known to be a historical fact.

The synoptic gospels preserve a tradition where Jesus disputes with the Pharisees in a bid to disabuse their minds of the popular expectation that the Messiah was to be a natural son of David (Mark 12:35–37a//Matt 22:41–46//Luke 20:41–44). Matthew was particularly interested in this question and reported it in greater detail than the other evangelists did. Matthew also edits out Mark's concluding observation that the large crowd that Jesus was addressing listened to him with delight (Mark 12:37). For him the questioning of the Davidic descent of the Messiah was a serious problem and no laughing matter at all.

> While Jesus was teaching in the temple, he said, "How can the scribes say that the Messiah is the son of David? David himself, by the Holy Spirit, declared, 'The Lord said to my Lord, "Sit at my right hand, until I put your enemies under your feet." David himself calls him Lord; so how can he be his son?" And the large crowd was listening to him with delight. (Mark 12:35–37)

> Now while the Pharisees were gathered together, Jesus asked them this question: "What do you think of the Messiah? Whose son is he?" They said to him, "The son of David." He said to them, "How is it then that David by the Spirit calls him Lord, saying, 'The Lord said to my Lord, "Sit at my right hand, until I put your enemies under your feet"'? If David thus calls him Lord, how can he be his son?" No one was able to give him an answer, nor from that day did anyone dare to ask him any more questions. (Matt 22:41–46)

In this passage, Jesus questions or distances himself from the popular expectation that the Messiah would come from the bloodline of David. As Christian readers, we tend to gloss over or spiritualize passages such as this. But a passage like this, which is preserved in all the synoptics, is very significant for a historical reconstruction of what Jesus and his contemporaries knew about Jesus' ancestry. On a literary level, the passage makes sense only on the assumption that both Jesus and his contemporary audience knew that Jesus was not literally descended from David.[11]

---

10. The use of the title "son of David" as a statement of faith occurs in the triple tradition only in the story of the healing of the blind man/men in Jericho (Mark 10:46–52 // Matt 20:29–34; Luke 18:35–43). Matthew uses it four more times in this way (Matt 9:27—two blind men; Matt 15:22—the Canaanite woman; Matt 21:9—the crowds at the triumphal entry into Jerusalem; Matt 21:15—the children in the temple).

11. In his correspondence with Gentiles who had no messianic expectations, Paul, who

Matthew presents Jesus' claim to Davidic ancestry as a legal convention. This point is totally missed in the growing genre of "royal blood" literature, which assumes as a cardinal principle that Jesus carried the royal blood of David in his veins. Such books as Michael Baigent and Richard Leigh's *Holy Blood, Holy Grail*, and *The Jesus Papers*, not to talk of Dan Brown's novel *The Da Vinci Code* come immediately to mind.

Why Does Matthew Give Us Jesus' Lineage from Joseph When Joseph Is Not Jesus' Real Father?

Matthew is at pains to impress upon the reader that Joseph was not the biological father of Jesus. He tells the reader that Joseph had no marital relations with Mary until she had given birth to Jesus (Matt 1:25). Yet he traces the genealogy of Jesus not from Jesus' only natural parent, Mary, but from his foster parent, Joseph (Matt 1:16). Why does he do that? The genealogy establishes a legal framework that gives Jesus a claim to Davidic ancestry. This would hardly be necessary if Jesus' Davidic ancestry was an obvious fact. But it wasn't.

Most commentators are of the view that by establishing Jesus' Davidic and Abrahamic ancestry, Matthew wanted thereby to prove Jesus to be the Messiah. But as Paul S. Minear has rightly pointed out, simply proving that Jesus was a son of Abraham and a son of David was not enough to positively identify him as the messiah to an unbelieving Jewish population, since there were a host of other individuals of equal pedigree.[12] It is more plausible to see the purpose of Matthew's genealogy more negatively as an attempt to surmount a perceived impediment to Jesus' messianic title among those who were otherwise positively disposed to accept him as the Messiah.

Matthew and his Jewish Christian community had a problem. Jesus, they knew, was not literally a descendant of David or Abraham. But, according to the Hebrew Scriptures and popular Jewish belief the Messiah would be a descendant of Abraham (Gen 12:3b; 22:18) from the line of David (2 Sam 7:12; Pss 89:3–4; 132:11). How then could Jesus be the Messiah? Matthew's answer is that even though he was not naturally descended from David, the moment that Joseph married Jesus' mother, Mary, Jesus became Joseph's stepson and a bona fide heir to the patrimony of David and Abraham. Naturally, Jesus came from an immigrant community that had a bad reputation among the Jews. Nathaniel in John's Gospel expresses the stereotypical attitude of the mainstream Jewish population to the ethnic minorities

did not know the historical Jesus, took for granted the natural Davidic ancestry of Jesus. "This is the gospel concerning his Son, who was descended from David according to the flesh and was declared to be Son of God with power according to the spirit of holiness by resurrection from the dead, Jesus Christ our Lord" (Rom 1:3–4). In the Pauline tradition, "son of David" is not regarded as a statement of faith; the statement of faith is "son of God."

12. Paul S. Minear, *Matthew: The Teacher's Gospel* (New York: Pilgrim Press, 1982), 29.

of Nazareth to whom Jesus belonged when he said, "Can anything good come out of Nazareth?" (John 1:46).

Excursus

Who Are the Jews and What Is Their Connection with Galilea?

The primary meaning of the word "Jew" (Heb: *yehûdî*; Gk: *Ioudaios*) in New Testament times was a Judean, that is a citizen of Judea, the land centred around Jerusalem, in which the returning exiles of the former southern kingdom of Judah settled after their Babylonian exile. This meaning was subsequently extended to include a believer in the God of the Jews, which worship was centred in the Jerusalem temple. Thus, by the time of Jesus, to be a Jew could be an ethnic as well as a religious phenomenon. If Mary adopted the religion of her husband Joseph, as was usually the custom, and consequently raised her son Jesus in it, we cannot conclude from this that Mary was Jewish in the ethnic sense. The gospels nowhere suggest that Mary was Jewish by ethnicity. As Raymond Brown rightly observes, "Despite later Christian speculation, we really do not know that Mary was a Davidic."[13]

The centre of the Jewish cultural and religious life was the district of Judea, especially Jerusalem and the temple establishment. Galilee in the north was inhabited mainly by foreigners, hence the appellation "Galilee of the Gentiles" (Matt 4:15; 1 Macc 5:15, 21). Judea, in its more glorious past had conquered Galilee and forcibly converted its foreign population to the religion of the Jews. Nevertheless, the Jews of Judea did not regard their co-religionists in Galilee as true Jews. No prophet ever rose from Galilee and none was expected to arise therefrom (John 7:52). Much of what we have tried to say in this short excursus has been succinctly articulated in an *SBL Forum* article by Jodi Magness.

> Being a Jew in the time of Jesus was not, strictly speaking, a religion, as it is today. Instead, Jews in the time of Jesus were Judeans—that is, people from the district of Judea, the area around Jerusalem. Judeans worshiped the national god of Judea (the God of Israel) and lived according to his laws. Other ancient peoples had their own national deities. During the two centuries before Christ, the Hasmonean kings (a Jewish dynasty descended from the Maccabees) had established an independent Jewish kingdom in Judea (this kingdom was eventually taken over by the Romans). The Hasmonean kings conducted a campaign of expansion, conquering neighboring peoples who they forcibly converted to Judaism. Under the Hasmoneans, Galilee (to the north of Judea) and Idumaea (to the south) were

---

13. Brown, *The Birth of the Messiah*, 89. Such Christian "speculation" includes the later Christian belief that Mary's parents, Anna and Joachim, being childless asked God for a baby. The answer to their prayer was the conception and birth of Mary. When Mary was weaned at the age of three, her parents took her to the Temple and dedicated her to God. From then on, Mary lived and grew up in the Temple serving God night and day.

Judaized, which means their non-Jewish populations began to worship the God of Israel and live according to his laws.[14]

Why Are Women Included in a Genealogy That Traces Lineage through Fathers?

Matthew departs from custom by including women in his genealogy. Altogether he mentions five women: Tamar, Rahab, wife of Uriah, Ruth, and Mary. Some scholars discount Mary and speak of the four women of Matthew's genealogy.[15] This is a grave mistake because Matthew's interest is more on Mary, the single parent of Jesus, than on the four women of the Old Testament.

Having disassociated Mary from the company of the women of Matthew's genealogy, scholars who follow this approach see the reason for the inclusion of women either, as autobiographical, ecclesiological or devotional. As autobiographical, Matthew is believed to have included the women as illustrations of the transformative power of God. The former tax collector identified with these women who were sinners held in contempt by the society and later redeemed. As ecclesiological, Matthew, they hold, wanted to underline the universality of the church. By including these women, who were Gentiles, he wanted to indicate that the kingdom of God preached by Jesus was for Jews and Gentiles alike. As devotional, it is opined that Matthew wanted to make the point that divine providence works in strange and unpredictable ways. What is, therefore, required of believers is complete self-abandonment to divine providence.[16]

I submit, however, that Mary must be central in a search for the reason or reasons why Matthew includes women in his genealogy. This is because, for the Jewish Christians of Matthew's community, Mary was the unknown factor in the series of the five women in his genealogy. From the Hebrew Bible and tradition the reader knows the stories of the first four women in the series, but not that of the fifth woman, Mary. Matthew intends that from what is known of the four women, the reader should be able to solve the riddle of the fifth woman.

The *Catechism of the Catholic Church* lists as the "holy women of the Scriptures: Sarah, Rebecca, Rachel, Miriam, Deborah, Anne, Judith and Esther" and associates them with "that most pure Virgin of Nazareth, Mary."[17] Isn't it intriguing that Matthew does not include a single one of these holy women among the four women from Scripture that he chooses to associate with Mary? What is going on here? Let us start by asking the question, "What do the first four women that Mat-

---

14. Jodi Magness, "Has the Tomb of Jesus Been Discovered?" *SBL Forum*, http://www.sbl-site.org/Article.aspx?ArticleId=640. Accessed 5 March 2007.

15. See, for example, Lawrence O. Richards, *New Testament Life and Times* (Colorado Springs, CO: Cook Communications Ministries, 1994, 2002), 14.

16. Ibid. These are the reasons Richards why Matthew includes women in his genealogy.

17. *Catechism of the Catholic Church* (Vatican City: Libreria Editrice Vaticana, 1994), n. 61.

thew includes in Jesus' genealogy have in common?" These women of the Hebrew Scriptures in Matthew's genealogy have five things in common:

(a) They are all foreigners.
(b) They are all involved in questionable sexual conduct, at least in the eyes of the people.
(c) They were all well disposed and committed to the land, people and God of Israel.
(d) They were all married to Jewish men, and
(e) Each of them gave birth to a male child through whom God continued and advanced the fulfillment of his covenant promises to Abraham and David.

What Matthew is probably saying by including these women in his genealogy is this: in the history of God's dealings with Israel, God has brought some foreign women, even when they were of questionable moral integrity, into the covenant community through marriage and, through them and their sons, has gone on to progressively fulfill his covenant with Abraham and the house of David. This is exactly what God is now doing in and through Mary.

Let us take a cursory look at what the reader must have known about each of these women from Scripture.

Tamar (verse 3), a Canaanite woman, disguised herself as a prostitute and seduced her father-in-law, Judah (Gen 38). She became the mother of Perez through whom the covenant promises made to Abraham were continued.

Rahab (verse 5), a woman of Jericho, was a professional prostitute who saved the spies sent by Joshua to Jericho (Josh 2). In return she and her family were saved at the destruction of Jericho and granted citizenship rights in Israel (Josh 6:25). She married Salmon and became the mother of Boaz, the grandfather of King David.

Ruth (verse 5) was a Moabite woman. Even though the Law states explicitly that "No Ammonite or Moabite shall be admitted to the assembly of the LORD" (Deut 23:3; Neh 13:1), she became an exception by her faithful love and devotion to her mother-in-law, Naomi. Urged by Naomi, she seduced Boaz (Ruth 3) and finally married him. She became the mother of Jesse, the father of King David.

The Wife of Uriah. The unnamed wife of Uriah the Hittite was a woman of Sheba. *Bath Sheba* literally means "a daughter or woman of Sheba." Her personal name was not preserved in the Hebrew Scriptures. That explains why Matthew referred to her simply as "the wife of Uriah" (Matt 1:6). She is the woman who was involved in adultery with king David (2 Sam 11). She later married the king and became the mother of the great king Solomon who inherited the throne and the promises God made to the Davidic dynasty.

In the company of these four women Matthew includes *Mary*. So what is Matthew telling us about Mary? Matthew is saying that even though Mary was a foreigner (she lived in Galilee of the Gentiles, an immigrant community) and was involved in mysterious sexual relations (she conceived by the Holy Spirit, but in the eyes of the community Mary was suspected to be an adulteress that deserved to be stoned to death), she got married to a Jewish man, Joseph, son of David (Matt 1:20), and God used her, on account of her faith in the people, land, and God of Israel, to fulfill God's covenant promises to Abraham and David, the promise of the Messiah.

WHY DOES MATTHEW TAMPER WITH STATISTICS TO ARRIVE AT THE SYMMETRICAL FIGURE OF 14 X 3 GENERATIONS BETWEEN ABRAHAM AND THE CHRIST?

Matthew is known to be a very careful writer. Here he gives us a neat schema of 14 x 3 generations between Abraham and Jesus the Christ. Yet, in order to arrive at this neat schema he had to omit some of the pre-exilic kings as we have it in the Hebrew Bible.[18] Moreover, the last group of fourteen actually only adds up to thirteen generations. Why does Matthew make these apparently mathematical and statistical errors?

First, we know that in many ancient forms of writing, such as Hebrew, Greek and Latin, the alphabet also served as numerals. This means that names have numerical values. The name David, for example, has the numerical value of fourteen (D=4 + V= 6 + D=4). Matthew is probably making the point that Jesus is the quintessential son of David, the son of David par excellence. Jesus is superlatively (threefold, *trés*) Davidic, the long awaited Messiah. As we saw above, the over-riding intention of Matthew in the infancy narrative is to show that, in spite of all the empirical evidence to the contrary, Jesus remained a veritable son of David, son of Abraham (Matt 1:1).

Some scholars have pointed out that the 14 x 3 schema could also be taken as 7 x 6. If that is so, and I see no reason why it couldn't, this would be as a secondary intention to Matthew, the primary intention being the explicit 14 x 3 schema. The support for the 7 x 6 interpretative schema comes from the *Apocalypse of Weeks* in 1 Enoch (91–108) which narrates an outline history of the world, from creation to consummation, in ten periods or "weeks." The first three weeks are from Adam to Abraham. From Abraham, where Matthew begins his genealogy to the final end would take seven weeks of generations. A day in the apocalyptic vision is a generation, and a week is an age, an aeon. What the *Apocalypse of Weeks* says about the ninth and tenth weeks are very relevant to what Matthew is doing here.

> After this, in the *ninth week*, shall the *judgment* of righteousness be revealed to the whole world. Every work of the ungodly shall disappear from the whole earth;

18. See 1 Chron 3:11–12 that has three names of kings Ahaziah, Joash, and Amaziah that were omitted by Matthew.

the world shall be marked for *destruction*; and all men shall be on the watch for the path of integrity. (1 Enoch 92:14–15)[19]

It seems that Matthew consciously has six generations in the final set of seven, which coincides with the Ninth Week in 1 Enoch in order to make room for the evangelist's own generation, which was the generation following that of Jesus.

	Abraham to David	David to Deportation	Deportation to Jesus
1	Abraham	Solomon	Shealtiel
2	Isaac	Rehoboam	Zerubbabel
3	Jacob	Abijah	Abiud
4	Judah (+ Tamar)	Asa	Eliakim
5	Perez	Jehoshaphat	Azor
6	Hezron	Joram	Zadok
7	Ram	Uzziah	Achim
8	Amminadab	Jotham	Eliud
9	Nahson	Ahaz	Eleazar
10	Salmon (+ Rahab)	Hezekiah	Matthan
11	Boaz (+ Ruth)	Manasseh	Jacob
12	Obed	Amos	Joseph (+ Mary)
13	Jesse	Josiah	Jesus
14	David (+ Mrs. Uriah)	Jechoniah	Matthew's second-generation Christian community (?)

In this way, Matthew's community would still be living in the seventh day of Enoch's ninth week and still expecting the *parousia* in their own lifetime, as 1 Enoch has prophesied, and as Jesus had promised, "Truly I tell you, there are some standing here who will not taste death before they see the Son of Man coming in his kingdom" (Matt 16:28//Mark 9:1//Luke 9:27). If Matthew had put Jesus' own generation as the seventh day (generation) of the ninth week, that would mean that his community of believers would then be living in the tenth week and still awaiting the phenomena that would mark the end of the ninth week. This would be absurd. Here Matthew is being more careful than the writer of Hebrews who holds that the coming of Christ marked the end of the age (Heb 9:26). How could the coming of Christ mark the end of the age (ninth week), Matthew's Jewish

19. *The Book of Enoch,* trans. Richard Laurence (London, 1883). Retrieved 15 March 2009 from http://www.johnpratt.com/items/docs/enoch.html. Emphasis mine.

Christian readers would ask, when the signs that would accompany the consum-mation of the age were nowhere evident?

In brief, we suggest that Matthew's primary intention in using the fourteen by three generations schema is to show that Jesus is the ultimate fulfilment of the Davidic messianic expectation. It could also function as a *double entendre*, in the seven by six schema, to address the apocalyptic eschatological expectations of Matthew's Jewish-Christian community.

EXCURSUS II

Who Is Mary of Nazareth?

> Picture a teenage girl—perhaps even as young as 12—with dark skin and dark hair, tending her baby in a village on a hillside in the Roman-occupied province of Palestine, 2,000 years ago. . . . a far cry from the pale-faced, exquisite Virgin Mary usually depicted in European art.[20]

The Name Mary

What is the meaning of the name "Mary?" For a long time no one really knew. Hence the famous rhetorical question in the *Sound of Music*, "How do you find a word that means Maria?" How come no one knew the meaning of Mary? Because everyone presumed that Mary was Jewish and was looking for the meaning of the name within the context of the Hebrew language. The search was a failure. All that scholars who limited their searches to the Hebrew context could come up with were inexact approximations, such as "rebellion" or "bitterness." What a disap-pointing name that would be for God's most beautiful creature in a culture where names were believed to portray a person's inner character or destiny! If Mary's name had meant "rebellion" or "bitterness" she would have been given a new name that more exactly reflected her exalted role in the divine plan of salvation.

According to the 1913 *Catholic Encyclopedia*,[21] it is possible and even probable that the name *miryam* is of Egyptian origin. Here are the reasons:

a. Moses, Aaron, and their sister Miriam were born in Egypt and were probably given Egyptian names. Scholars recognize that the names Moses and Aaron are Egyptian in origin. The same could be said for the name Mary.

b. No other woman in the Old Testament excepting the sister of Moses,

---

20. See *ABC News*, 19 December 2001. Accessed 25 December 2001 from http://abcnews .go.com/sections/2020/DailyNews/2020_mary_011219.html.

21. Anthony Maas, "The Name of Mary," *Catholic Encyclopedia,* vol. 15 (New York: Rob-ert Appleton Company, 1912). Accessed 13 September 2007 from http://www.newadvent .org/cathen/15464a.htm.

who also was born in Egypt, bore the name Mary. If Mary were a Hebrew name you would expect it to be borne by more Hebrew women.

The meaning of the name as derived from the Egyptian *Mery* (cherished, beloved), is most suitable for a young girl, especially an only daughter. The approximate Hebrew derivation as a compound of the noun *meri* and the pronominal suffix *am*, meaning "their rebellion" is not a suitable name for a young girl. Less probable still is the assumption that the name derives from two Hebrew words *mar* (bitter) and *yam* (sea), hence "bitter sea."

According to the *Catholic Encyclopedia*:

> These and all similar (Hebrew) derivations of the name Mary are philologically inadmissible, and of little use to the theologian . . . since in Hebrew the adjective follows its substantive . . . and even if the inverse order of words be admitted as possible, we have at best *maryam*, not *miryam*.[22]

The *Catholic Encyclopedia* article poses a question which it does not answer, "Why was the name Mary chosen by the parents of Our Blessed Lady and by a number of others mentioned in the New Testament, if the word was Egyptian?" The simple and logical answer, which the encyclopaedic author did not contemplate, is, "Because Mary, the mother of Jesus, and the other Marys of the Gospels were of Egyptian origin."

The Four Marys of the Gospels

Mary of Magdala and Mary of Bethany. Popular Christian tradition identified Mary of Magdala with Mary of Bethany. This, however, cannot be sustained because: (a) Mary of Magdala was from Galilee while Mary of Bethany was from the suburbs of Jerusalem. (b) Mary Magdalene was one of the "ministering women" who accompanied Jesus in his journey from Galilee to Jerusalem. Mary of Bethany, sister of Martha and Lazarus, seemed to enjoy a more sedentary lifestyle.

Mary the Mother of Jesus and Mary the wife of Clopas. Among the "many women" at the foot of the cross, Matthew mentions three, two of them by name. The names of these two are Mary: "Many women were also there, looking on from a distance; they had followed Jesus from Galilee and had provided for him. Among them were Mary Magdalene, and Mary the mother of James and Joseph, and the mother of the sons of Zebedee" (Matt 27:55–56). John mentions three women, two of them by name; again they are named Mary. The mother of Jesus is not mentioned by name, but we know already that her name is Mary. "Standing near the cross of Jesus were his mother, and his mother's sister, Mary the wife of Clopas, and Mary Magdalene" (John 19:25).

---

22. Anthony Maas, "The Name of Mary," *Catholic Encyclopedia*.

In effect, John mentions three women at the foot of the cross, all of them named Mary. Two points will interest us here. Firstly, Mary the mother of Jesus had a "sister" also named Mary. How could this be? What does "sister" mean here? Secondly, how do you explain the fact that the name Mary was rare among the Jews of Jesus' time but common among Jesus' die-hard women followers who remained with his mother at the crucifixion even when other followers had abandoned him? How does one explain the exceptional Marian density at the foot of the cross?

Here we appeal to Middle Eastern culture then and even now, which is essentially African. When someone who is a public figure is arrested as a fraud, tried before the public eye, found guilty and rejected by the people, and finally executed publicly by the most shameful death imaginable, naked and hanging on the cross, who are the few who would remain behind to claim the body and give it a decent burial? You are right, not his friends but his own blood relations. This cultural particularity enables us to reconstruct the scenario as follows:

> Mary the mother of Jesus is a woman of Egyptian descent living in a neighbour-hood for foreigners in Nazareth (Galilee of the Gentiles). So also were Mary Magdalene and Mary the wife of Clopas. Mary was a popular Egyptian girl name, meaning "beloved." Mary the wife of Clopas is referred to as sister of Mary the mother of Jesus because they were closely related, probably belonging to the same extended family or clan. In a foreign land the bonding between them grows even stronger. This Mary is probably the same Mary that Matthew refers to as "Mary the mother of James and Joseph." If that is so, then this explains why Matthew earlier calls James and Joseph "brothers" of Jesus (Matt 13:55). Their mother and the mother of Jesus were "sisters," so they are Jesus' cousins or close relations on the mother's side.

It remains a common practice in African culture for women of a common land of origin who live abroad in the same foreign locality to bond together into a tight sorority for mutual support. Their support is nowhere more evident than in times of bereavement. Should a member of their sorority lose her husband or breadwinner, as Mary would have lost in the death of her son Jesus, the support the women render to their colleague is unqualified. I submit that all the Marys who came from Galilee were Egyptians women resident in a foreign land who had bound themselves together as a sorority for mutual support.

What about Mary of Bethany? She too, together with her sister Martha, and brother Lazarus, could be Egyptian immigrants. In intercultural perspective, the researcher asks, "Where do people of a certain extraction stay when visiting a city in which they are not resident." The answer, from a Western perspective, would be in an inn or lodging for travellers, as in Luke, the Gentile Gospel. From African, including Middle Eastern, perspective, the answer is that the visitor's privileged place of lodging is with a relation who lives in the city that one is visiting. Thus, when Jesus of Galilee, who is Egyptian in origin, visits Jerusalem, his first port of inquiry for lodging would be with an Egyptian family living in Jerusalem or its suburb Bethany. The text does not tell us that. But cultural anthropology, which has always been employed, albeit sporadically, in exegesis, suggests this conclusion.

Joseph Becomes Foster Father to Jesus (Matthew 1:18–24)

> Is not this *the carpenter, the son of Mary* and brother of James and Joses and Judas and Simon, and are not his sisters here with us? (Mark 6:3)

> Is not this *the carpenter's son*? Is not his mother called Mary? And are not his brothers James and Joseph and Simon and Judas? (Matt 13:55)

Earlier tradition as represented by Mark seems not to know that Jesus had a foster father called Joseph. Mark knows Jesus only as "the carpenter, the son of Mary" (Mark 6:3). Joseph is not mentioned directly or indirectly in Mark's gospel. Similarly, the Pauline corpus, which was written before the Gospels, knew no Joseph. All that Paul knows of the birth of Jesus is that "when the fullness of time had come, God sent his Son, born of a woman" (Gal 4:4). By the time Matthew wrote his gospel, Jesus is no longer "the carpenter, the son of Mary" but "the carpenter's son" (Matt 13:55). Why then does Matthew retell Mark's story, adding a new character, Joseph?

Matthew makes it clear that Joseph is not the real father of Jesus (Matt 1:25). Mary conceived by the power of the Holy Spirit. The character of Joseph serves two purposes in the story: (a) to provide legitimacy to a would-be illegitimate birth, and (b) to adopt Jesus and so give him a legal claim to Davidic ancestry. Jesus is "son of David" and "son of Abraham" only through adoption by Joseph.

Note the many similarities between this Joseph and the Old Testament Joseph who was sold into slavery in Egypt:

a.   They have same first name, Joseph.
b.   They have same father's name, Jacob (not Heli as in Luke 3:23).
c.   They are both paragons of chastity, who could be trusted with women.
d.   They are both master dreamers, who use dreams as a means of communicating with God.
e.   They are both silent sufferers who bear the responsibility and shame, rather than blow the whistle on a woman.
f.   They are instrumental in bringing the covenanted family of God into Egypt, thus saving them from a death threat that would have frustrated the realization of God's covenant promises.

On account of these similarities, some scholars see Joseph in Matthew and subsequent traditions as more of a literary than a flesh-and-blood character.[23]

---

23. See John Shelby Spong, *Liberating the Gospels: Reading the Bible with Jewish Eyes* (San Francisco: Harper, 1996), 201–18, esp. ch. 12: "Joseph: The Shadowy Figure."

The Visit of the Magi (Matthew 2:1–12)

Matthew 2:1—In the time of King Herod, after Jesus was born in Bethlehem of Judea, wise men *from the East* came to Jerusalem asking, "Where is the child who has been born king of the Jews?"

2:2 For we have seen his star in the East, and have come to worship him. (RSV)	2:2 For we observed his star at its rising, and have come to pay him homage. (NRSV)	2:2 We saw his star at its rising and have come to do him homage. (NAB)	2:2 We saw his star as it rose and have come to do him homage. (NJB)

On account of the popular translation of *anatolê* as "the east," many scholars conclude that the magi must have come from eastern lands, such as Persia or the Far East (Asia). But scholars today are beginning to realise that anatolê primarily means "a rising (of the sun or stars)" and then only by inference, "the east (the direction of the sun's rising)." The rising in question here, in Matthew's story, is probably that of the star and not the sun, since no sun is mentioned in the narrative.

Anatolê, therefore, probably tells us nothing about the geographical direction from which the magi came. In other words, the magi do not necessary have to have come from an eastern country, although one could argue that since Jerusalem is east of Bethlehem and the magi came from Jerusalem, they invariably came from the east, from the eastern direction. But as for their country of origin, they could as well have come from the south or even the north, for that matter. They came from the land of the rising star.

The point of this observation is to suggest that the magi might as well have come from Egypt. It is a normal traditional African cultural practice for a woman's family elders to visit her with presents for her and her child when she gives birth to a child, particularly her first child. Such a visit could subsequently acquire theological significance and the story embellished with such theologically rich motifs as the star and the symbolic gifts.

It is important to note that the change from "East" to the "land of the rising star" is effected in recent translations, such as the NRSV, NAB and NJB only in Matt 2:2, 9 but not in Matt 2:1, where the "East" is still retained. This is textually justifiable given that the occurrence of *anatolê* in Matthew 2:2, 9 is in the singular whereas its occurrence in 2:1 is in the plural.[24] Even so, there is evidence that Egypt

---

24. Compare Matt 8:11, where *anatolê* occurs again in the plural and its meaning is obviously the East, the Eastern lands.

was sometimes regarded as "East" in biblical tradition[25] and that it was famous for its wise men or magicians (Gen 41:8; Exod 7:11; Is 19:11–12). So, there is nothing in the text that rules out Egypt as the possible land of origin of Matthew's magi.

THE HOLY FAMILY TAKES REFUGE IN EGYPT (MATTHEW 2:13–15)

Would the magi be truly wise men if, knowing that the child Jesus, the long-expected messiah, was in mortal danger, they would worship him privately and depart secretly without saying a word to Jesus' parents about the severe danger they were in? If they were truly wise men you would expect them not only to intimate Mary and Joseph about the secret plans of Herod but also to offer to help them escape from Herod's domain, probably by fleeing with them to the safety of their country of origin. Given that the flight into Egypt follows immediately after the visit of the magi, it is only natural to believe that they must have played an important role in the escape of the holy family. This plausible scenario would again point to Egypt as the homeland of the magi, because it is to Egypt that the parents of the child Jesus took him for sanctuary.

Some scholars think that the flight into Egypt was a historical event, while others think it is a literary device used by Matthew, to explain what was common knowledge in his community, namely, that Jesus was of Egyptian descent. We looked at the story in both of these ways and found that, either way, the story points to the Egyptian origin of Mary and Jesus.

If it was a historical event and the holy family did indeed escape to Egypt, this raises the questions: Why Egypt? Who was there in Egypt to receive them and provide for them? Or did they just turn into street beggars in Egypt? Did they know the Egyptian language already or did they have to learn a new language there in order to survive? If the flight into Egypt is Matthew's embellishment of the story, why did Matthew have to do it? In either case, the proposal that Mary is of Egyptian provenance seems to provide adequate answers.

If the flight into Egypt was factual, Mary would simply have returned to her maiden home, to her own people in Egypt. They would be the ones to provide for her, and the question of the language of communication is solved. It is a cultural ethos in biblical times, and still is in traditional African societies, that when a person's life is threatened in his or her fatherland, the surest and safest place of sanctuary available to him or her is his or her mother's maiden home. Thus Jacob had to flee to his maternal uncle Laban in the face of death threats from Esau (Gen 27:41–44) and Absalom, after murdering Amnon, had to do likewise to escape his father's anger (2 Sam 13:37–38; 3:3). One's maternal home was regarded as one's

---

25. See, for example, 1 Kings 4:30: ". . . so that Solomon's wisdom surpassed the wisdom of all the people of the east, and all the wisdom of Egypt," where Egypt and East are used in parallelism.

second home and the privileged place of sanctuary when one's life is threatened in one's fatherland.

If, on the other hand, the flight into Egypt did not actually happen, as many scholars now believe, then the question reverts to: why then did Matthew deem it necessary to include it? What purpose does it serve for Matthew and his Jewish Christian community? It is no secret that Jesus of Nazareth, coming from Galilee of the Foreigners, would not easily be acceptable by mainline Jews as the definitive teacher and interpreter of the Torah, much less as the long-expected Jewish Messiah, the promised son of David. But this is precisely what Matthew and Jewish Christians believed him to be. The story of the flight into Egypt, therefore, would be Matthew's way of explaining how this man Jesus, who was known to be of Egyptian descent, came to be said to be the Jewish Messiah. His answer is that Jesus was indeed a Jew of the line of David (at least by adoption) who was taken to Egypt as a child and raised there. This was the way God had ordained it to be, Matthew argues by citing Hosea 11:1: "Out of Egypt I called my son" (Matt 2:15).

A traditional Catholic scripture scholar of the Roman Theological Forum, John F. McCarthy, having examined the facts, has come to accept the likelihood of Mary's Egyptian origin and reassures concerned Catholics that this is a theologically sound position to take. According to him, "As far as some aspects of the theology are concerned, nothing would be lost if Mary's biological father were an Egyptian. That could better explain why the Holy Family fled into Egypt."[26]

HEROD KILLS INNOCENT CHILDREN (MATTHEW 2:16–18)

There is no historical record of Herod killing the children of Bethlehem, although scholars observe that such brutality was consistent with what is known about the character of Herod. Scholars have pointed out that Matthew is probably portraying Jesus as the new Moses, miraculously saved from a massacre of Hebrew children decreed by the king in Egypt only to later become the leader through whom God would save his people from the bonds of slavery. The motif of Jesus as the new Moses runs through Matthew's gospel. Yet the function of the massacre of the innocent children in its immediate literary context is to provide an incentive for the flight into Egypt.

THE HOLY FAMILY RETURNS FROM EGYPT AND SETTLES IN NAZARETH (MATTHEW 2:19–23)

The prophecy Matthew cites in verse 23 ("He shall be called a Nazarene") cannot be found in the Hebrew Bible or the Septuagint. Matthew sometimes quotes the scriptures creatively to agree with his theological understanding of the matter.

---

26. John F. McCarthy, "New Light on the Genealogies of Jesus," *LT* 11 (1987). Accessed 15 March 2009 from http://www.rtforum.org/lt/lt11.html.

In Matthew, as in many other early Christian writings, we find instances of what could be termed theology-to-fact reasoning which, by today's standards of logical argumentation would be termed *petitio principii* or begging the question. It is a circular reasoning which portends to demonstrate a conclusion by means of premises that assume that conclusion. It goes somewhat like this: "The prophets said that the Messiah was to be a son of David. Jesus is the Messiah. Therefore, Jesus is son of David." A good example of Matthew's theology-to-fact reasoning is Matt 21:2–3, 7 where Matthew makes Jesus do the triumphal entry into Jerusalem sitting on two different animals at the same time, in fulfilment of his (Matthew's) literalistic understanding of the Septuagint Greek of Zech 9:9.[27]

According to Luke, Mary and Joseph lived in Nazareth prior to the birth of Jesus and had to travel to Joseph's ancestral home, Bethlehem, the city of David, for a census, and while there in Bethlehem, Jesus was born. For Matthew, Mary and Joseph lived in Bethlehem, where Jesus was born. There is no need for a census to bring them to Bethlehem. From Bethlehem they fled to Egypt and to Bethlehem they made to return but were directed by an angel to make a detour to Nazareth. Isn't it strange that the same angel who told Joseph in a dream (Matt 2:20) to go back home (Bethlehem) because those who sought to kill Jesus were dead, suddenly tells him in another dream to divert and take refuge in Nazareth (Matt 2:22)?

One thing is sure: the man Jesus was known historically to be a resident of Galilee. He was "Jesus of Nazareth," a Galilean city. As we saw above, Galilee was a district populated by non-Jewish settlers, so much so that it was nick-named "Galilee of the Gentiles." One problem that the Jews of Matthew's time had in accepting Jesus as their Messiah was that they could not figure out how this "outsider" could be the Jewish Messiah, the promised son of David. Matthew tried to solve the problem by telling the story of how Jesus, supposedly of Bethlehem (city of David) came accidentally to live and grow up in Galilee and so came to be known as "Jesus of Nazareth."

CONCLUSION: DOES IT MATTER WHETHER JESUS WAS BLACK OR WHITE?

We have attempted to read Matthew's story of the birth of Jesus as the story of an event that evolved on *terra firma*, and not as a fairy tale that took place in "winter wonderland" as it sometimes appears to the historically-minded reader. We have seen how the thesis that Mary and Jesus were people of African descent provides answers to many of the difficulties one would otherwise encounter in a traditional reading of the infancy narrative in Matthew's gospel. To conclude we would like

---

27. A similar relevant instance of theology-to-fact reasoning is found in St. Augustine's argument that Mary had to be of the family of David, because Jesus was born "from the seed of David," and no male seed was involved in Jesus' conception (St. Augustine, "Contra Faustum," in *PL* 42:§471–72).

to take one other question: Does it make a difference whether Jesus was Black or White? Our answer is: No, it makes no difference; and yes, it makes a world of difference.

Insofar as faith is concerned, it makes no difference whether one images Jesus as a Blackman or a Whiteman. What matters is believing in him, trusting in him, and following his teachings in one's daily life. On judgment day, no one will be thrown into hell because they thought Jesus was White, and no one will be admitted into heaven just because they believed Jesus to be Black. This is simply to put the hypothesis in proper perspective.

When it comes, however, to the existential question of how people of African descent see themselves and how others see them, the African origin of Jesus becomes a critical issue. I will share with you three unfortunate incidents or cases where the knowledge that Jesus was a Black African could have saved the situation:

a.   A religious community of Whites and a few Blacks received a replica of an ancient statue of the Madonna and Child. The statue was black in colour. The White members of the community rejected to mount the statue in the chapel for the simple reason that a Black Mary and Jesus was a falsification of history. This generated racial tension in the community. If they had known, as a matter of fact, that Jesus and Mary were indeed African, it might have saved the situation.

b.   A six-year old Black child attending a predominantly White school in Maryland, came back from school one day and announced to his parents that he was dropping from school. The reason? The little White boys in his class were teasing this little Black boy, saying that they looked like God (meaning the picture of Jesus) and he did not. If his little White friends had for once in their lifetime been exposed to a picture of an African Jesus, they would not make school life so miserable for their little Black friend.

c.   Finally, during the apartheid era in South Africa, members of the Dutch Reformed church were demonstrating against the admission of Black South Africans into their church. One of the demonstrators carried a placard which read: "We want only pure white blood like the pure white blood of Jesus." The irony of this tragedy is exposed by the knowledge that the historical Jesus was indeed a Blackman of African descent.

The African origin of Jesus is an idea that would radically transform the negative way that people of visible African descent are generally perceived around the world as people who have made a significant contribution neither to the history of civilization nor to that of salvation. As we saw in the examples above, it would minimise racial tension and lead to greater harmony in today's multicultural societies and globalized world.

Acknowledging the African origin of Jesus and Mary would lead to the logical conclusion that Christianity, at least in its origins, is an African religion. The Christian faith is increasingly under attack in the African continent and Diaspora as the Whiteman's religion, in contrast to Islam, which is deemed to be the Blackman's religion. The realisation that the founding father and mother of the Christian religion were African would lead to Africans confidently and boldly embracing the Christian religion as part of their common heritage and contribution to humanity. Through centuries of European enslavement and colonisation, Africans have been programmed to be their own worst enemies. They have been conditioned, through language and the visual arts, to see whatever is African as inferior, if not altogether negative. The structures of apartheid have been overthrown, but only after the dynamics and principles of apartheid have been erected in the African mentality. Africans now share with their erstwhile colonial masters the conviction that white is good and black is evil. We freely use the racially exclusive and self condemning language of Eurocentric origin, such as, black Tuesday, black market, black magic, black lie, blackmail, blacklist, black book, and even black Mass, with the understanding that black is negative or evil, whereas their white counterparts, white magic, white lie, white list, etc. are regarded as positive. If we realised that God sent his only begotten son into the world, and sent him as a Black man, then we can begin to revisit and reverse this residual prejudice in the awareness that being black is not so bad after all.

The African origin of Jesus is an idea that could liberate Africans to see themselves as active agents in the interpretation and transmission of the Jesus tradition and not just as passive consumers of Europeanised and Americanised versions of Christianity. This is the task of inculturation at its best. From this endeavour, an authentic African expression of Christianity and theology would emerge that could be more faithful to the original teachings of Jesus than we have had in the past two thousand years. Authentic African impact would be felt in the areas not only of worship and the visual arts, but also in the deeper and more faithful understanding and articulation of Christian doctrine and morals as we, as a church, move forward to face the enormous challenges of the third Christian millennium.

Works Cited

ABC News. 19 December 2001. Accessed 25 December 2001. http://abcnews.go.com/sections/2020/DailyNews/2020_mary_011219.html.

The Book of Enoch. Trans. Richard Laurence. London, 1883.

Brown, Raymond E. *The Birth of the Messiah: A Commentary on the Infancy Narratives in Matthew and Luke*. New York: Doubleday, 1977.

Catechism of the Catholic Church. Vatican City: Libreria Editrice Vaticana, 1994.

Cone, James. *Black Theology and Black Power*. 1969; Maryknoll, NY: Orbis Books, 1997.

———. *A Black Theology of Liberation*. 1970; Maryknoll, NY: Orbis Books, 1986.

Davies, W. D., and D. C. Allison. *The Gospel according to Matthew: Introduction and Com-*

mentary on Matthew I–VII. Vol. 1. The International Critical Commentary. London: T & T Clark, 1988.

Felder, Cain Hope. "Afrocentrism, the Bible, and the Politics of Difference," *JRT* 50 nos. 1/2 (1993/94): 45–57.

Gates, Henry Louis, and Kwame Anthony Appiah, eds. *Africana: The Encyclopedia of the African and African-American*. Vol. 1. New York and London: Oxford University Press, 2005.

Johnson, Marshall D. *The Purpose of the Bible Genealogies: With Special Reference to the Setting of the Genealogies of Jesus*. 2nd ed. Eugene, OR: Wipf and Stock, 2002.

Maas, Anthony, "The Name of Mary." *Catholic Encyclopedia*. Vol. 15. New York: Robert Appleton, 1912.

Magness, Jodi, "Has the Tomb of Jesus Been Discovered?" *SBL Forum*. http://www.sbl-site .org/Article.aspx?ArticleId=640. Accessed 5 March 2007.

McCarthy, John F. "New Light on the Genealogies of Jesus." *LT* 11 (May 1987): n.p. http:// www.rtforum.org/lt/lt11.html.

Minear, Paul S. *Matthew: The Teacher's Gospel*. New York: Pilgrim Press, 1982.

Pontifical Biblical Commission. *The Interpretation of the Bible in the Church*. Presented to Pope John Paul II on 23 April 1993.

Richards, Lawrence O. *New Testament Life and Times*. Colorado Springs, CO: Cook Communications Ministries, 1994, 2002.

St. Augustine. "Contra Faustum." *PL* 42:§471–72.

Spong, John Shelby. *Liberating the Gospels: Reading the Bible with Jewish Eyes*. San Francisco: Harper, 1996.

HER APPROPRIATION OF JOB'S LAMENT? HER-LAMENT OF JOB 3, FROM AN AFRICAN STORY-TELLING PERSPECTIVE

Madipoane Masenya (ngwan'a Mphahlele)

He [Mmanape][1] knows that his [her] friends' common sense and their traditions, their rationality and their revelations are inconsistent with his [her] *own* experience. For Job [Mmanape], to hold fast to his [her] integrity means *to insist on the validity and authority of his [her] own experience*, even when it seems to be contradicted by all the [those who belong to the hegemonic cultures of the] world to be true.[2]

BEGINNING HER STORY

After almost two days of labor pains, a baby boy is born to Mmanape. Like most of her contemporaries in African cultures, she has looked forward not only to a heterosexual marriage relationship, but also to fulfilling her marital role as a mother within her husband's family.

> *Midwife:* (Reporting excitedly) A baby boy is born to you! What is his name?
> *New mother:* Tumisho a Sepedi (name meaning "praise").
> *Midwife:* (A rhetorical question) *Le tumiša badimo ba botatagwe*! (So, you are praising his Dad's ancestors!)
> *New mother:* We are praising *Modimo* (God).

Originally published in *Theologia Viatorium* 33, no. 3 (2009): 385–408. Published here with permission.

1. As part of her storytelling approach, the author diverges from the conventional article-writing style and uses a fictitious character named "Mmanape" to designate not only the mourner in the present article, but also the main narrator, who laments her way through Job's lament in Job 3. In a communal African setting, Mmanape's lament is likely to depict some of the concerns that influence modern female readers of the Bible in their struggles with lamentation. More details on the storytelling approach: Musa W. Dube, ed, *Other Ways of Reading: African Women and the Bible* (Atlanta: SBL; Geneva: WCC, 2001), as a way of giving background to the text.

2. Carol A. Newsom and S. H. Ringe, eds., *The Women's Bible Commentary* (Louisville: Westminster John Knox, 1992), 133. Brackets and italics added.

The new mother, that is Mmanape, was at that moment struggling with how to handle her mixed feelings: (1) tiredness after a very long period of labor; (2) severe pains caused by minor surgery, and; (3) the excitement of being a mother at last.

> Elderly village woman: O boile madibeng Moremadi'a bo Sememeru! You have returned from the deep waters. Moremadi wa bo Sememeru!
> Moremadi (New mother's praise name): Ke boile (I have returned).

The underlying implication of the village woman's rhetorical question, simply put, is that Mmanape, as the new mother, has undergone the process culturally referred to as *go ya madibeng*. The literal meaning of this phrase is: "to go to the depths (of the waters)" or "to go to the deep waters." Mmanape the woman and Mmanape the mother can thus resonate with the Psalmist that her own frame, while she herself was still a fetus in her mother's womb, was not hidden from God (Ps 139:15). This new mother, unlike the male psalmist, had not only been intricately woven in the depths of her mother's womb, or the womb of Mother Earth in the metaphorical sense (cf. Ps 137:15b). Mmanape had also just tasted the experience craved by many (African) women, that of having successfully returned from the deep waters / the depths of Mother Earth.

Mmanape, unlike women whose babies were not privileged to see the light of day, but were stillborn (cf. Job's problematic wish in 3:16), was fortunate enough to return from *madiba* with a human being in her hands! A strapping baby boy! What a joy it was for her and her family, both nuclear and extended! Indeed, this was a major achievement in the patriarchal culture. She knew that in some African cultures patriarchy had always dictated that a woman could become authentically human/woman only after the birth of her first child/son.[3] She would now find her place in the patriarchal family household. Not only was Mmanape the bride (*ngwetši*) in her husband's family, but was also the mother of Tumisho, *leitšibulo*[4] *la gagwe,* her first-born son.

Like many mothers, Mmanape also tasted what it meant to nurture Tumisho from the moment of his emergence onto Mother Earth until he reached adulthood. Little did she know, however, that she, like many parents all over the world, would sooner or later experience what most of them dread: the death of a child.

---

3. E. J. Krige, *Social System of the Zulus* (Cape Town: Via Africa, 1956), 62, notes that, among the Zulus, marriage is considered complete only after the birth of a child. The first child, particularly a boy, is very important to this group. The latter point also applies perfectly for the Northern Sotho patrilineal family groups (cf. Madipoane Masenya [ngwana' Mphahlele], *How Worthy Is the Woman of Worth? Rereading Proverbs 31:10–31 in African-South Africa* [New York: Peter Lang, 2004], 129).

4. The word *leitšibulo* or *lethaše*, depending on the particular context, is an African word/noun which refers to the name of the firstborn child. In her culture, both the baby who is the first to open the womb of a woman, as well as the one who closes it (*bofejane*), have specific names!

The latter is, in all probability, not the object of Job's dread in Job 3:25.[5] A few months ago, Mmanape performed what is taboo in the African cultures. She buried her own son.[6] Tumisho died suddenly in a car crash. A part of Mmanape has essentially gone! A few years ago, she held a human being in her hands. Although at the point of his death she could no longer hold him in her arms, Mmanape could hold Tumisho in her heart. As of now, both her hands and her heart are empty. Why? Because the son she brought out of the deep waters twenty six years ago has now made a transition. Mmanape, not alone, but with her nuclear and extended families, as well as the community members, had to take Tumisho's body back to the depths of the earth! If Tumisho were still physically alive, perhaps he would resonate with the words of the prosaic Job as his story of misery begins to unfold: ". . . Naked I came from my mother's womb, and naked shall I return there. . . (Job 1:21)."

MMANAPE'S ENCOUNTER WITH HIS-LAMENT IN JOB 3

Causality through Misery? Contemplating the Connections

As Mmanape desperately searches for answers during her conversation with the Sacred Other, she chances on the book of Job in the Hebrew Bible. She has read the book before, as could be expected, but she reads it differently this time. She has to. She struggles through the book, painfully and with expectation as she, like the poetic Job, vents her anger and frustration on what she perceives to be continued unjust misery in her life. Where is God in these struggles? Where is God's justice? Where was God when the white Afrikaner youngster reportedly collided with her son's car and left him to bleed profusely[7] at the scene of the accident before the paramedics intervened and he eventually died?

The death of Mmanape's son was, in fact, the culmination of other calamities that had plagued her family even before Tumisho's sudden death. The family continues to experience one calamity after the other. In the African context, which sets great store by causality,[8] a human being cannot simply die without a specific

---

5. Truly the thing that I fear comes upon me, and what I dread befalls me (Job 3:25; NRSV)

6. In one practical example, Mmanape was informed that a seminary student, who was a native of Nigeria, passed on while he was studying in Kenya. The parents, inspired by the preceding taboo, refused not only to transport the corpse of their son to Nigeria, but also to attend the funeral!

7. Mmanape experienced a painful moment of witnessing the blood-soaked part of Mother Earth on the accident scene even as she had to wash Tumisho's blood-soaked clothes.

8. A. Kamp, "With or Without a Cause: Images of God and Man in Job 1–3," in *Job's God*, ed. E. van Wolde (London: SCM, 2004), 9–17, holds a different view: "Within the boundaries of a divine worldview, retribution is not necessary and the logic of causality does not

reason.[9] Mmanape, like the biblical Job, who in fact shared the same worldview, cannot but ask the question that typifies the Biblical lament: *lāmâ* (למה), "Why?"

Like Job, the legendary rich non-Israelite, Mmanape is an outsider to Israel and its traditions, even though her calamity might not be as intense as his. In her view, though, both she and Job are troubled by the same basic questions, which are informed by the worldviews underlying their philosophies/theologies: Why do righteous people suffer unjustly? The philosophy underlying the optimistic mentality of Africa inevitably haunts her: Good people will always prosper while the bad will reap accordingly. According to the African worldview, does it make sense that the *Modimo* (God) and *badimo* (the ancestors) can punish those who live harmoniously with their neighbors? Can one's relationship with the Sacred Other be sustained even in the midst of what one perceives to be unjust suffering? Mmanape continues to ask these disturbing questions as she presses on through the Book of Job with the hope of finding answers, even pointers towards her healing.

As Mmanape reads about Job and his struggles, she encounters Job's lament (Job 3). She becomes curious and concerned about how Job the man, in his distress and anger, and prompted by his desire for death (Job 3:1, 16, 20, 21, 23), attacks, with his incantations, both the day of his birth, and, more pointedly so, the night of his conception.[10] This will be considered later.

---

necessarily apply to God's actions. People's worldviews and religious beliefs depend on God, but God does not depend on their views, beliefs and actions."

9. The African proverb *Letlalo la motho ga le bapolelwe fase*—literally, the skin of a human being cannot be skinned on the ground—has the following tenor: a human being cannot die without a "legitimate" cause. May the proverb also have the connotation that a human being, particularly a child, was not supposed to die?

10. As a mother who bore a child/son, she resonates with the lament of the mother of Damu (cf. its Mesopotamian roots from the cult of the dying god Tammuz) over her son who had forcibly been removed from his home only to die in a military campaign: "I am the mother who gave birth!

Woe to that day, that day!
Woe to that night!"
the day that dawned for my provider,
That dawned for the lad,
My Damu!
A day to be wiped out,
That I would I could forget,
You night [. . .] that should [never]
Have let it go forth,
When my gendarmes shamelessly
Made their way
Into my presence [to take away my Damu] (brackets mine)

Mmanape's resonance with the words of the lament of Damu's mother is based on her observation that the latter, wishes into oblivion, not the day on which she bore Damu (cf.

Lamentation, A Gendered Act/Process?

As she starts Job 3, Mmanape cannot avoid asking whether lamentation/an expression of grief due to some kind of loss, particularly that of a child/children (Job 1:18–19) is gendered. Why? The chapter opens with the scene depicting the breaking of silence after the period of seven days and nights.[11] As the communal mourning period ends, Job breaks the silence by vehemently attacking both the day of his birth and the night of his conception:

אִיּוֹב וַיֹּאמַר: יֹאבַד יוֹם אִוָּלֶד בּוֹ

וְהַלַּיְלָה אָמַר הֹרָה גָבֶר: (Job 3:3)

Let there be destruction on the day on which I was born;
[Let there be destruction] on the night that said: a new male is conceived. [12]

Job's incantations, speculates Mmanape, are subtly directed at Job's mother, particularly on her female reproductive anatomy (Job 3:3; 3:7; 3:11–13), and his father (cf. Job 3:3; 3:10). In Mmanape's opinion, contrary to the popular view on the curse of the day of Job's birth the pointed attack is not aimed at Job's birthday.[13] No! It is directed mainly at his mother's womb. As far as Mmanape is concerned, this is on account of its efficiency in (1) receiving the "politically correct?" sperm cell; (2) providing the male seed with a healthy egg cell; (3) nurturing the fetus with success for nine months; and eventually (4) successfully delivering a healthy baby to Mother earth! Contrary to Mmanape's view, Habel, a male commentator, finds no connection between the womb which comes under attack in Job 3 and a human womb. In his view, the mythological language in which the incantations have been coached, makes the identity of the word *rehem* or *beten* (womb) to be ambivalent.

Job's incantation), but the day on which he was taken away from her, to die eventually. In essence, ponders Mmanape, Damu's mother levels incantations against the day of his son's death, not the day on which she ushered him onto Mother Earth (S. Langdon, *Babylonian Penitential Psalms* [Oxford Edition of Cuneiform Texts 6; Paris, 1927], l. 15. K5208 rev. 3'–10'). Cf. Harps, 65, as quoted by Thorkild Jacobsen and Kirsten Nielsen, "Cursing the Day," *SJOT* 6 (1992): 187–204, 188.

11. X. H. T. Pham, *Mourning in the Ancient Near East and the Hebrew Bible* (Sheffield: Sheffield Academic Press, 1999), 24. Such a period of silence formed part of some of the ancient Near Eastern mourning rituals. Pham asserts: "In summary, the mourning rites of the ancient Near East are closely related to the rites of supplication or lamentation. . . . They include loud weeping (usually aided by professional wailing women), the tearing of clothes and donning of sackcloth, sitting or lying on the dirt, gashing the body, strewing dirt on the head, fasting, abstaining from anointing oil. . . . The ritual morning period lasts seven days and seven nights, after which the mourners returns to normal life."

12. My translation.

13. Cf. Newsom and Ringe, *Women's Bible*, 132; Jacobsen and Nielsen, "Cursing," 193–94. Toweldemedhin Habtu, "Job," in *Africa Bible Commentary*, ed. Tokunboh Adeyemo (Grand Rapids: Zondervan; Nairobi: WordAlive, 2006), 571–604.

Argues Habel:

> But whose womb is intended? His mother's? The womb of the night (Michel)?
> Or the womb of Mother earth (as in 1:21)? Given the mythological overtones in
> these incantations, the word may be deliberately ambiguous since his parents are
> clearly excluded from the curse of his origins in the preceding verses.[14]

Mmanape cannot agree with Habel though. Informed about Job's incantations by
the plot of the poem of his lament in Chapter 3, she concludes that the "womb"
that is primarily under attack in that chapter is neither that of the night nor that
of Mother earth. It is the womb of a female human being. She thus agrees with
Klein that:

> Whereas rehm (רחם) refers specifically to the womb (בתן—*btan*) pertains pri-
> marily to the "belly" in the sense of "source of hunger" or "abdomen"; and it
> is also used in Job in this sense (15:2, 20:23, 32:18,19; 40:16). *However, Job
> uses beten more frequently in its secondary sense, to refer to the female organ of
> reproduction.*[15]

The womb that is being attacked is the womb of Job's mother coming under the
scathing attack of her own son! The words of the wise in Africa quickly dawn in
Mmanape's mind: *Ka hlagolela leokana, la re go gola la ntlhaba*: I hoed and pruned
(for) the baby thorny plant, after growing bigger, it prickled me!

Informed by the words of the Psalmist (Ps 139:13–15; cf. also Job 10:8–9) as
well as her understanding that the people of Israel believed that everything, including babies, was birthed by God the Mother, Mmanape is adamant that Job's
incantations are also directed at God (*Eloah*),[16] albeit indirectly:

> 13. For it is was you who formed my inward parts;
>   You knit me together in my mother's womb.
> 14. I praise you, for I am fearfully and wonderfully made
>   Wonderful are your works;
>   That I know very well.
> 15. My frame was not hidden from you,
>   When I was being made in secret,
>   Intricately woven in the depths of the earth (*madiba*).
>   Your eyes beheld my unformed substance. . ..
>   (Ps 139:13–15: NRSV)

Perhaps, speculates Mmanape, at that early stage, Job was not yet bold to speak ill

14. N. C. Habel, *The Book of Job: A Commentary* (London: SCM Press, 1985), 109.

15. L. R. Klein, "Text about Men, Subtext about Women," in *A Feminist Companion to
Wisdom Literature,* ed. A. Brenner (Sheffield: Sheffield Academic Press, 1995), 198.

16. Newsom seems to share the same view when she argues: "*Though he does not exactly
curse God*, he curses the day of his birth" (Newsom and Ringe, *Women's Bible*, 132) (emphasis added).

(badly) to/ about God? Could it be that for Job and his community, it was hard to "curse" God? (cf. the use of the Hebrew *bārâk* [bless/curse] instead of *qālal* [curse] in the first two chapters of the book).[17]

As Mmanape struggles through Job's lament, she continues to hold on to her suspicion that lamentation in Israel/Yehud might have been gendered. What does it mean to lose a child to a mother and a father as well as the deceased's siblings? Did the loss of eight children in the family of Mr. and Mrs. Job (Job 1:19) have the same impact on their mother as it had on their father? What formed the core of Job's misery, *'āmāl* (עמל)? Was Job bothered by the loss of his property, the deaths of his children or the loss of his own health? If the loss of his own health was not the main cause of his misery, why is Job heard as being so pious after the traumatic reports of the loss of his property and his children?

> 20 Then Job arose, tore his robe, shaved his head, and fell on the ground and worshipped:
> 21 He said, "Naked I came from my mother's womb, and naked I shall return there; the LORD gave, and the LORD has taken away; blessed be the name of the LORD." (Job 1:20–21)

Mmanape had noticed that the change of Job's tone from politeness to sharpness (cf. Job 3:1ff.) occurs only after his body had been inflicted by sores. She thus continues to raise questions in her quest for the gendered nature of lamentation. Do fathers and boy children grieve the same way as mothers and girl children? Is the pain of grief, particularly on account of the loss of a child or children, the same across the people of different cultures? She suddenly remembers the African wisdom saying, *monna ke nku, o llela teng*, literally translated, a man is a sheep, he cries from within.

Although the sighing of Job, the man (male human being), does not seem to resonate with Mmanape's African reality (cf. the preceding Sepedi proverb), she thinks that many men, not only African men, but all adult male human beings globally, can learn a great deal from Job's *human* encounter with the pain caused by the misery of grief or suffering in general: the courage and capacity to weep.

> 24 For my sighing comes like bread,
>   And my groanings are poured out like water
>   (Job 3:24 NRSV)

As an aggrieved parent, overwhelmed by the pain of loss, Mmanape could attempt to investigate some of these questions. On account of the nature of the present topic of her storytelling, her focus is more on the gendered nature of lament as

---

17. See the use of the play on these words by Sarojini Nadar, "Barak God and Die! Women, HIV, and a Theology of Suffering," in *Grant Me Justice: HIV/AIDS and Gender Readings of the Bible*, ed. Musa W. Dube and Musimbi R. A. Kanyoro (New York: Orbis Books, 2004), 60–79.

it continues to unfold through her re-reading and re-hearing of the story of Job's lamentation.

As already narrated, Mmanape's main concern is what she perceives to be an attack on female reproductive anatomy, something, which does not augur well for her African context. In the latter context, one's mother's private parts are usually cited in a context of fight in order to let the offender feel *really* hurt! It follows that in her culture, one does not swear by another's mother's genitals because then one would be inviting war. A situation which, in Mmanape's view, shows not only the close bond between mothers and their children, but also, the value placed on the communities to women as mothers.

The story of her concerns will be heard at a later stage. For now, we revisit her earlier observation that what is more pointed in Job's incantations (cf. 3:3–9), is not the "curse" on his day (of birth) and night as many commentators have argued (Murphy1999:19 (*day* and *night*), Newsom and Ringe, (*day*); Jacobsen, (*day*) van Wolde (*day* and *night*), Habtu, 574 (*day*), Habel, 103 (*day* and *night*).[18] In her reading of Job's story, she is convinced that Job's incantations are leveled more at the night on which Job was conceived than on his birthday. The following proverb quickly comes to her mind: *Bošego ga bo rone nta*

BOŠEGO GA BO RONE NTA/ THE NIGHT IS RISKY

3   **Let the day perish in which I was born,**
       and the night that said,
       "A man-child is conceived"
4   **Let that day be darkness!**
       May God above not seek it,
       Or light shine on it;
5   **Let gloom and darkness claim it**
       Let clouds settle upon it
       Let the blackness of the day terrify it.
6   **That night—let thickness seize it!**
       Let it not rejoice among the days of the year;
       Let it not come into the number of the months,
7   **Yes, let that night be barren;**
       Let no joyful cry be heard in it.
8   **Let those curse it who curse the Sea**
       Those who are killed to rouse up Leviathan

---

18. Newsom and Ringe, *Women's Bible Commentary*, 132; Jacobsen, "Cursing," 193–94; van Wolde, *Job's God*, 36; Habtu, "Job," 574; Habel, *Job*, 103. Mmanape finds it interesting that many English translations deviate from the MT's rendering of the opening line in Job 3. The line is basically translated as follows: "After this Job opened his mouth and cursed (קלל) the day *of his birth*" (Job 3:1 NRSV). What makes Mmanape marvel is why the translators freely add "birth" to what in the MT can simply be translated as "his day" *yômô* (יומֹ).

9   **Let the stars of its dawn be dark;**
     let it hope for light, but have none;
     may it not see the eyelids of the morning—
10   because it did not shut the doors
     of my mother's womb,
     and hide trouble from my eyes. (Job 3:3–10 NRSV)

So, ponders Mmanape, Job, like the wise of Africa should have believed that *bošego ga bo rone nta*. (A) night cannot remove lice from (the seams of clothes). The underlying meaning of the proverb is that it is difficult to work efficiently in the night even as dangerous experiences are usually linked with the night. The night can thus not be safe, it cannot be trusted!

Perhaps it is no wonder that acts of witchcraft in the African cultures, were and are still usually linked with the night. In Mmanape's view, Job is not only scared of the night, its darkness and all the images which were conjured by the ancients when they thought about the night. Job seems to have had a great distaste for the night and all that goes with it. He seems to Mmanape to have believed that nothing good could come from the night, that *bošego ga bo rone nta*! Why?

First, in the incantations Job leveled against the day on which he was born (cf. Job 3:4–5), he calls on what he perceives to be negative, which is night, *bja go se rone nta*, that is, that which cannot remove lice (from the seams of clothes), to come upon the day and mess it up: (1) darkness (Job 3:4a); (2) no shining of light (Job 3:4c); (3) and blackness (Job 3:4d). All of the preceding images in Job's "narrow" view of God are also a distaste for God: "May God above not seek it" (Job 3:4b). As the day becomes darkened, deprived of light and thus blackened, Job's God will not seek it! Has his view of creation suddenly changed? Mmanape wonders. Was the night and its darkness not created by the same God if the ancients believed that God was responsible for all of creation?

Second, as for the night of his conception, just like the day of his birth, Job wishes that it comes into oblivion (Job 3:3b). In fact, the word "curse" (ארר and קבב and קלל) *arr* and *qbb* and *qll* as coming from Job himself, not the narrator as in Job 3:1 *only* comes into the picture in the more and elaborate incantations leveled against the night of his conception (cf. particularly verse 8):

8   Let those **curse** it [the night] who **curse** the Sea
     Those who are skilled to rouse up Leviathan (Job 3:8 NRSV; brackets mine)

The mention of Leviathan the sea monster in the second stanza, makes Mmanape resonates with the rendering of the word *yām* (ים) as "sea" rather than as yōm (יום), for "day." The preceding incantation falls within the *nine* incantations (Job 3:6–9) which are leveled against the night of Job's conception. What Mmanape finds interesting though, is that even though Job vehemently attacks the night of his conception, the "curse" can apparently not come from his mouth. It is to be said though, by the skilled cursers who can even rouse the Sea monster by their curses.

In fact, what Mmanape finds interesting is that what is conventionally known as a chapter on the curse of Job's day of birth is devoid of any word for "curse" (*qll, arr,* and *qbb*) as coming from Job's mouth. Also, as noted previously, the focus of the present pericope, or the emphasis of the lament as a whole, is placed more on the night of Job's conception than on the eventual day of his delivery on Mother earth. That the two are intricately bound together cannot be disputed. The foregrounding of the night of his conception as well as the subsequent important period of the nurturing of life in the mother's womb is, in Mmanape's view, very crucial. Why? It shows the importance of women's bodies, not only in providing a suitable home/security (*menûhâ*; cf. Ruth 1:9) for human life at its beginning, but also in nurturing life through the very early stages of its formation, influencing it even before its arrival on Mother earth. In essence, Mmanape, unlike Job and the wise of Africa, regards the night of Job's conception as one with the capacity to remove lice from the seams of clothes. That night in her view can thus not be regarded as unsafe and dangerous: *bošego bjola bo ronne nta!* That night, which not only reported Job's conception but also provided space for it to happen, removed the lice from the clothes' seams!

Third, Mmanape notes that the incantations leveled against the night of conception are not only three times more than those leveled against the day of Job's birth; they are also more elaborate. Indeed, in Job's view, *bošego ga bo rone nta*: The images emerging from the incantations on the night understandably comes from the night itself, with more intensity: (1) intense darkness (as it is said in the Pedi African jargon with regard to "the heaviness of darkness": "it is so dense that one can touch it!"); (2) sadness; (3) no fertility/barrenness;[19] (4) light-less/dark stars; (5) permanent darkness (no morning eyelids). What interests Mmanape is Job's/the ancients' belief that conceptions happened in the night. In that sense, it follows that the night could have the capacity to remove lice from clothes! Could this be linked with the fertility cults in which the fertility god operated in the night?[20] Could it be linked with the fact that the pleasure of men "knowing" (*yadah*) their wives usually was experienced in the night (cf. Gen 4:1, 28; Ruth 4:13)? Couldn't conceptions occur during the day? These are questions coming from a modern mother, questions which may not have bothered the male narrator(s)/author(s) of the book of Job.

In Job's view, that night must not only be darkened, it should never have been fertile! The night's provision of suitable space for the fruitful sexual relationship between Job's parents is viewed with distaste by their offspring. In Mmanape's

---

19. Mmanape finds it curious that in the Hebrew Bible, depending on the situation of a particular male at a certain point in time, female wombs can be expected to nurture and eventually deliver more babies (cf. the early chapters of the book of Exodus) or be barren! For more details on the former aspect, cf. Masenya(ngwan'a Mphahlele)'s article: " '. . . But You Shall Let Every Girl Live': Reading Exodus 1:1–2:10 the Bosadi (Womanhood) Way," *OTE* 15, no. 1 (2002): 99–112.

20. Cf. Habel, *Job,* and Jacobsen and Nielsen, "Cursing," in this regard.

view, Job particularly shuns the fact that his mother's womb became fertile ground for the beginning of his existence in that night! Hence, Job's negative images about that night because in his view, *bošego ga bo rone nta*! The night can and should not be trusted!

Verse 6:	*Thick* darkness (6a)
	No joy (sadness: 6b)
	Not to be counted/Perish- [cf. the opening incantation in Job 3:3b (6c)]
Verse 7:	Barrenness (no fertility: 7a)
	No joyful cry (sadness: 7b)
Verse 8:	Cursed by the cursers
Verse 9:	Darkened stars (: 9a)
	No light (darkness: 9b)
	No morning eyelids (darkness: 9c)

Contrary to Job and the wise of Africa, Mmanape thinks though, that in fact *bošego bo rona nta*! The night, particularly the one which comes under attack in Job 3, had the capacity to remove lice from the seams. Why?

First, it is that night which has fore grounded the significant role which women as mothers play in the co-creation business. Second, had it not been for that night, where would modern Bible readers have gotten the story of a devout man whose relationship to God could apparently not be tampered with by what he perceived to be God's unjust dealings with him? Third, Job's character affords readers with a rare model of a male human being who faces the pain caused by grief with both frankness and humanness. Fourth, through Job's lament, the reader is also provided with a positive view of death and the place of the dead.

Mmanape, coming from the Two Thirds world, is naturally empowered by Job's observation that in and through death, the ground is level: both great and small, royalty and those with no royal blood (*balata*), the rich and the poor, those designated wicked and those designated righteous. All these will be and are united in death. Yes, affirms Mmanape, that night which gave birth to the beginning of Job's life *e rona nta*! It can thus be trusted.

Before she ends her story, Mmanape must still ascertain that her earlier concerns reach the listeners' ears. She has noted that verse 10 is the key verse upon which the preceding incantations are based. The night which enabled the conception of Job must perish ". . . because it did not shut the doors of my mother's womb, and hide trouble from my eyes" (Job 3:10). Mmanape realises that the attack which is leveled against the female reproductive anatomy, an attack which becomes even more visible in the opening verses of the immediate section of Job's lament (Job 3:11), was basically inspired by Job's misery. In the face of untold suffering, Job focuses on Job, and on himself only—at all costs. Mmanape is concerned!

EXPOSING MISOGYNY IN HIS-LAMENT: AN AFRICAN MOTHER'S GAZE

Mmanape's first concern is the assault of Job on his mother's reproductive organs (cf. the incantations leveled on the day of his birth/ the attack his mother's womb (Job 3:3–5); the night of his conception/ the attack on the cervix of his mother's womb (Job 3:7–9). As though that were not enough, Job, the frustrated and angry man attacks his mother's thighs and breasts! Although Mmanape also reels with pain because of several losses in her life, including that of her son, Job's attack (swear?) of her mother's reproductive organs does not resonate with her socio-cultural reality. As already noted, in the African cultures, one who wants his/her rivalry to feel the real pinch, will swear at them by swearing at their mother's private parts.

The misery upon which the body of an elitist, self-righteous (?) male patriarch is thrown, urges him to make incantations on the patriarchal subjects of his day: some items from nature (night and day) as well as aspects of female anatomy. Mmanape cannot but be disturbed. In her view, Job's misogyny, is revealed not only in his distaste for women (women's anatomy), but also, and pointedly ironically, in his lack of respect for women as human beings in their own right. An irony indeed, if one considers that his frustrations and anger might have been inspired by those of his children's mother in the preceding chapter: "...Do you still persist in your integrity? Curse –(ברך-bārak [curse/bless?]) God and die!" (Job 2:9).

Job, surmises Tumisho's mother, does not have any appreciation for the importance of the human womb: a symbol of life for both, women and men, the great and the small, etc.; Job 3:11–19). As life was precarious then, as well as the lack of modern sophisticated technology in ancient Israel/the post-exilic era,[21] it follows that there were more risks entailed in the pregnancies and the birthing processes. How could Job trivialize such crucial processes? Mmanape is concerned. The African ancestors were right that *seso se baba mongwai wa sona*, a sore itches to its owner. A patriarch, who probably played a lesser or no role in communal mothering and never tasted what it means to carry a human being in the womb, has the "luxury" to speak about the female body as Job does in this text. In his anger,

---

21. Elusive as the dating of the book of Job is, a general dating postulated by scholars for the book of Job is the early postexilic era (cf. Newsom 1992:130; Ceresko 1999:68). In our view though, Murphy is right when he argues about the timelessness of matters pertaining to suffering and personal responsibility (1999:6). Similarly, Habel argues convincingly that "consistent with the orientation of traditional wisdom thinking, the author of Job has created an artistic work with universal dimensions *rather than a text directed at a particular historical situation or theological issue alive in Israel at a specific time. . . .* Thus, while cumulative evidence may tend to suggest a postexilic era, the book's literary integrity, paradoxical themes, heroic setting, and uncomfortable challenge are pertinent for students of wisdom and life in any era and far more important than the precise date of this ancient literary work" (1985:42, italics mine).

against God (?), his parents (more specifically his mother?) and nature (forces/gods[22] controlling nature?), Job (3:11) can simply say:

"Why did I not die at birth,
    come forth from the womb
    and expire?

Mmanape continues to be disturbed by the lack of empathy from an outsider (to female anatomy) for someone who had treasured a human being and nurtured life in her womb for nine months, only to have it "expire." What a pain would accompany such a loss? Such outsiders to female anatomy can in their moments of distress, wish that their mothers' wombs were their graves! Similarly, Mmanape remembers Jeremiah's lament:

Jer 20:17   because he[God] did not kill me in the womb;
             So my mother would have been my grave,
             And her womb for ever great (brackets: mine).

The sense of Jeremiah's frustration in the preceding text is detected by Mmanape in Job's lament:

Job 3:16   Or why was I not buried like a stillborn child,
            Like an infant that never sees the light?

What about the life of a woman in such circumstances? Distressed men, like Job whose misery has also inspired him to long for the tomb, apparently do not want to die alone. No! Their mothers, these women who should have possessed "failed" wombs, were then expected to serve as their son's graves. In essence, these mothers have a responsibility to accompany their sons to their own tombs!

As Mmago Tumi (Tumisho's mother) continues to interrogate the lens through which Job reads female anatomy, she wonders whether Job's assault on this anatomy could be an indication of the control which men as property-owners (then and today), both in ancient Israel/ Yehud, Africa and globally, continue to have on the bodies of those who are power-less. In the latter category, within the present textual context, one finds: the body of Job's mother; the body of his children's mother; and the body of Mother earth! Outside of the text under discussion, the following images quickly come to Mmanape's mind: married women, sex slaves, strangers, widows, prostitutes, virgins (in their father's households), girl children and women from the Two Thirds World who are usually used for sex trafficking by the rich.

Mmanape's reading of Job's lament on his assault of female anatomy seems to endorse the preceding argument:

---

22. For more details on a reading of Job 3 that views the "day" and the "night" which comes under attack in this text as personifications of some of the ancient Near Eastern gods, cf. Jacobsen, "Cursing," 87–204.

Job 3:12   Why were there knees to receive me,
                or breasts for me to suck (NRSV)

Elsewhere Job, who was the *ba'al* (בעל—"master") of his wife's body, in his attempt
to prove his (self)-righteousness ironically reveals the control which he has on his
wife's body:

Job 3:9   "If my heart has been enticed by a woman [who is not
                    my wife]
                And I have lain in wait at my neighbor's [fellow property-owned
                    male/husband] door;
Job 3:10   then let my wife grind for another,
                And let other men kneel over her." (Brackets mine)

In Mmanape's view, although the preceding text reveals Job's sense and assur-
ance of fidelity in a monogamous marriage context, an action which needs to be
lauded as it hardly typifies the majority of men then and now, it reveals the power
which Job has over the sexuality of his property, that is, the body of his wife.

ENDING THE STORY

As the story of Mmanape's struggle to approapriate "his-lament" through her-la-
ment comes to an end, she painfully observes that "his-lament" may not be helpful
for (African) women who struggle with various losses, in particular, the loss of
their children. In her view, such women are likely to end his-lament more pained
than they were before they begun to read it. Says the African proverb: *Tswala ga
e gane ka teng fela, le ka gare e a gana!* (Translated: "Birth [it] does not only fail
inwardly, even on the outside it does fail.") Mmanape cannot but remember the
preceding proverb which is usually cited by parents who had raised deviant children, children who dared among others, to swear at their mothers. If Job had an
African mother, not only would she have cited the preceding proverb, speculates
Mmanape, Job's African mother, would out of frustration have leveled the following incantation at him:

bakgekolo nke ba go dule godimo!
(Translated: "For all that you [Job] have said against female
anatomy, would that the old mid-wives would have sat on you,
immediately after your delivery onto Mother earth!")

WORKS CITED

Adeyemo, Tokunboh, ed., *Africa Bible Commentary*. Grand Rapids: Zondervan; Nairobi:
    WordAlive, 2006.
Brenner, A., ed. *A Feminist Companion to Wisdom Literature*. Sheffield: Sheffield Academic
    Press, 1995.

Ceresko, A. R. *Introduction to the Old Testament Wisdom: A Spirituality for Liberation.* Maryknoll: Orbis Books, 1999.

Dube Musa W., and Musimbi R. A. Kanyoro, eds. *Grant Me Justice: HIV/AIDS and Gender Readings of the Bible.* New York: Orbis Books, 2004.

Habel, N. C. *The Book of Job: A Commentary.* London: SCM Press, 1985.

Holladay, W. L. *A Concise Hebrew and Aramaic Lexicon of the Old Testament.* Leiden: Brill, 1971.

תרה נביאים וכתובים *The Holy Scriptures.* New York: Hebrew Publishing Company, 1939.

Jacobsen, Thorkild, and Kirsten Nielsen. "Cursing the Day," *SJOT* 6, no. 2 (1992): 187–204.

Kittel, R., W. Rudolph, and H. Ruger, eds. *Biblia Hebraica Stuttgartensia.* Stuttgart: Deutsche Bibelstiftung, 2002.

Krige, E. J. *Social System of the Zulus.* Cape Town: Via Africa, 1956.

Langton, S. *Babylonia Penitential Psalms.* Oxford Edition of Cuneiform Texts 6. Paris, 1927.

Masenya (ngwana' Mphahlele), M., " '. . . But You Shall Let Every Girl Live': Reading Exodus 1:1–2:10 the Bosadi (Womanhood) Way." *OTE* 15, no. 1 (2002): 99–112.

———. *How Worthy Is the Woman of Worth? Rereading Proverbs 31:10–31 in African-South Africa.* New York: Peter Lang, 2004.

Murphy, R. E. *The Book of Job: A Short Reading.* New York: Paulist Press, 1999.

Newsom, C. A., and S. H. Ringe, eds. *The Women's Bible Commentary.* Louisville: Westminster John Knox, 1992.

O'Connor, K. M. *The Wisdom Literature.* Collegeville, MN: Liturgical Press, 1988.

Pham, X. H. T. *Mourning in the Ancient Near East and the Hebrew Bible.* Sheffield: Sheffield Academic Press, 1999.

Van Wolde, E. *Job's God.* London: SCM, 1997.

Decolonizing the Psalter in Africa

David Tuesday Adamo

The book of Psalms is one of the most widely read books of the Bible. The reason, perhaps, is because the Christian church finds this book the easiest to approach personally and directly in every situation in life (joy, sorrow, pain, and confusion). One of the eminent Old Testament scholars, Arthur Weiser, calls it "the favourite book of the saints."[1]

Among Western scholars, this book has received considerable attention, perhaps more than any other books of the "Christian" Bible. These scholars have paid much attention to what might be the best approaches to the understanding of the book. Some of these approaches include determining the author, the date, literary types and forms, the basic theological thoughts amongst many others. In the majority of cases, these Eurocentric approaches to the Psalter are considered universal and imposed on the scholars of the so-called "Third World" as the main, if not the only, criteria by which the study of the Psalter can be judged authentic and scholarly.

The old paradigm of historical critical exegesis in the "First World" is becoming obsolete. To a certain extent, it has become an obstacle to our critical thinking in the light of African culture. Western exegesis has subjected the Bible to abstract, individualized and neutralized reading, "characterized by positivism, empiricism or radical detachment" in the name of objectivity. This method has undermined other methods such as African cultural approaches. This is the "academic sin" of most Western biblical scholars that are clearly offensive, and have called for unapologetic hermeneutical response.[2] Our Bible and our interpretation must be indispensable for the academy, the church, and society at large, not only for the West.[3]

Originally published in *Black Theology* 5, no. 1 (2007): 20–38. Republished here with permission. © Equinox Publishing Ltd 2007.

1. Aurthur Weiser, *The Psalms: A Commentary*, trans. Herbert Hartwell (OTL; Philadelphia: Westminster, 1962), 19.

2. Krister Stendahl, "Dethroning Biblical Imperialism in Theology," in Heiki Raisamen et al., *Reading the Bible in the Global Village* (Atlanta: SBL, 2000), 62.

3. Ibid., 61.

The main purpose of this article is to present the fact that there are other legitimate, authentic and scholarly ways of understanding the Psalms. In other words, I want to bring to your attention the various ways of decolonizing the study of the book of Psalms in Africa. These approaches can be termed "African Cultural Hermeneutics." In addition, I want to lay emphasis on the Bible as "Power approach" to the study of the book of Psalms that has been championed by African Indigenous churches in African.

COLONIZATION OF THE BIBLICAL STUDIES

Whenever one thinks of colonization, what immediately come to my mind are the partition of Africa and the eventual physical conquest of that continent. Modern imperialism has to do with market inequality among the "Third World" and the Western people, foreign aid as weapon for colonization, debt domination, political repression and state terror, globalization and others.[4] Thus colonialism is not limited to the partition of Africa and the eventual domination of that entire continent by the European nations. It includes the colonization of our thought and the entirety of our way of life.

The concern here, however, is how African biblical studies, especially of the Psalter, have also been colonized in various ways.[5] Colonization of biblical studies began with the establishment of Bible colleges, seminaries and universities in Africa by the missionaries and the colonial masters. These Bible colleges and Seminaries became places where priests, pastors and evangelists were trained. During the early period the teachers in these colleges were missionaries from the Western

---

4. Michael Perenti, *Against Empire* (San Francisco: City Lights, 1995), 18–35.

5. R. S. Sugirtharajah, *The Bible and the Third World* (Cambridge: University Press, 2001), 61–73. Sugirtharajah lists and discusses the various marks of colonial biblical interpretation, as follows:

1. Inculcation, that is, "the use of the Bible as a vehicle for inculcating European manners."
2. Encroachment, that is, "the introduction to the 'other' of alien values, under the guise of biblicization," in order to repudiate the local culture which is considered incapable of transmitting Christian truths.
3. Displacement, that is, the displacement of local culture.
4. Analogies and implication, that is, the juxtaposition of biblical and secular history as a weapon against those who resisted colonial intervention. The Bible stories were read to justify the cruelty and suffering caused by violent invasion of the Europeans.
5. The textualization of the Word of God, that is, the idea that no religious teaching was of any value except in written form. This is in order to discredit the oral tradition of the local people.
6. The historicization of faith, that is, the affirmation of biblical religion as a historical faith.

world. Their methods of teaching were Western. In their enthusiasm to teach students how to communicate the gospel, they also taught Western cultures and ways of life. All students must learn how to interpret the Christian scripture the way it is interpreted in the West. To the missionaries, African cultures and religions were not important, and therefore, were not taught to the students.

In many parts of Africa, and right from the earliest times, the interpretation of the Bible took place in the "religious room." In the contemporary era, the Bible is read and interpreted within the institutionalized realms of synagogues, churches, and mostly interpreted in a way that is directly or indirectly related to the agenda of a particular church denomination. Such church denomination is still being controlled by their mother church in the Western world.[6] In our universities, especially the Departments of Religious Studies in Africa, our curriculum betrays us as still being slaves to the tradition of Western biblical scholarship. In other words, in our interpretative mode, we are still colonized. In 1960, there were only six universities and very few seminaries in the whole continent of Africa.[7] Edward G. Newing conducted a survey of how Old Testament research was conducted at this period, throughout Africa, and found that most institutions employed the method of higher critical approaches developed in the Western tradition.[8] The universities and theological institutions at that time were parallel to those of the West.

Although by the 1980s and 1990s the establishment of universities and theological institutions increased (more than one hundred universities and one thousand seminaries by the end of the 1990s), most of these universities and seminaries do not have postgraduate programmes in biblical studies, which is why much of the training has continued to take place in Europe and America.[9] Still, it is interesting to note that the overseas training of African biblical intellectuals followed ecclesiastical and denominational traditions (i.e., Catholic students go to Rome, Evangelicals to USA and Britain), and along with their colonial masters (Great Britain, France, Belgium, and the USA who are former colonial and neo-colonial masters).[10]

In fact, it is unfortunate that up till now there has not been any outstanding center for biblical studies to boast of in Black Africa. The bitter truth is that the training of African scholar in a context that is both culturally and scholarly non-African is gradually becoming a problem. Knut Holter points out these problems:

6. Mary Etui, Knut Holter, and Victor Zinkuratire, "The Current State of Old Testament Scholarship in Africa: Where Are We at the Turn of the Century?" in *Interpreting the Old Testament in Africa,* ed. Mary Getui, Knut Holter, and Victor Zinkuratire (New York: Peter Lang, 2001), 32. See also Knut Holter, *Yahweh in Africa: Essays on Africa and the Old Testament* (New York: Peter Lang, 2000).

7. Holter, *Yahweh in Africa*, 10–11.

8. E. G. Newing, "A Study of Old Testament Curricula in Eastern and Central Africa," *ATJ* 3 (1970): 80–98.

9. Holter, *Yahweh in Africa*, 15.

10. Ibid., 15–16.

... it is increasingly being experienced as a problem that the training is given in
a context that both culturally and scholarly is non-African. One result of this is
that questions emerging from cultural and social concerns in Africa only to some
extent are allowed into the interpretation of the OT. As a consequence, there is a
gap between the needs of ordinary African Christians for modes of reading the
OT, and the modes provided by scholars trained in the western tradition of biblical scholarship. Another result of the location of the training outside Africa is a
feeling, at least in some cases, of inferiority vis-à-vis the massive western tradition. This might eventually lead some scholars to neglect their African context,
and instead see '(. . .) themselves as ambassadors of Cambridge, Oxford, (the)
Tubingen school, etc.'[11]

The majority of eminent African biblical scholars that we have today are trained
in the Western institutions where their training was a Eurocentric approach to
biblical studies

Although one appreciates the opportunity to study in many of these great Western institutions, one thing is certain: the overseas training in biblical studies and
theology is one of the ways by which African biblical scholars have been colonized.
By the time many of us graduated we became expert Eurocentric interpreters of
the Bible. When we came back to our institutions at home, we spread the good
news of Eurocentric biblical interpretation. We teach pastors, priests, and other
leaders in the church, the Eurocentric method and these pastors, priests and leaders have passed them on to their congregations. All the pastors, priests, their congregations, other leaders and biblical teachers became colonized with Eurocentric
methods of biblical interpretation. (The reader should note that I am one of the
beneficiaries of the colonization.)

Consciously and unconsciously, the establishment of churches became another means of colonizing Africans. As discussed previously, the African biblical
scholars who are immersed in Eurocentric approach to biblical interpretation and,
therefore colonized, passed on the process of colonization to pastors and priests
and other leaders. They, in turn, have passed it on to their congregations. To think
and interpret in Afrocentic ways has become a problem, because we have been
thoroughly schooled in Eurocentric frameworks.

Another way in which the colonization of African biblical studies has taken
place is the domination of the field of biblical studies by Eurocentric scholars. Eurocentric scholars, who write through Eurocentric lenses, write most of the commentaries, Bible Introductions, Bible Atlases, History of Ancient Israel, and the
major Bible Translations that we use in universities and seminaries all over the
world. Not only are they Eurocentric in their approach to biblical scholarship, they
feverishly attempt to de-Africanize the Bible. Yet, these are what we read and con-

---

11. Holter, *Yahweh in Africa*, 16; see J. S. Ukpong, "Rereading the Bible with African
Eyes," *JTSA* 91 (1995): 3–14; see also S. O. Abogunrin, "Biblical Research in Africa," *AJBS* 1
no. 1 (1986): 13.

sume in many of our universities and seminaries in Africa.[12] These authors write with scholastic prejudice and hold tenaciously to the conception that the Eurocentric methods of biblical interpretation are "the interpretation." These approaches are, therefore, superior and universal. Such a view also has led to using Eurocentric criteria as a yardstick for judging all Afrocentric scholarship. As a result, the major publishers in religion in the Western world reject most of our manuscripts for publication. They also reject most of our manuscripts with the pretence that there will be no market for them when published.[13]

COLONIZATION OF THE PSALTER

The Psalter being one of the most read books of the Bible cannot and has not escaped colonization in its history of interpretation. It is important to mention in outline how Psalms interpretation has been colonized. Traditionally, the book of Psalms was considered to be the book of individual persons who composed it as prayers and songs for either private devotional use or in response to a particular historical event in life. As such, Psalms interpretation took the shape of finding the authors of Psalms, and the discernment of that very historical circumstance of the authors' composition. They attempted at dating each Psalm as specifically as possible. The tendency is to date most Psalms very late, usually to the third and second century BCE.[14] The Psalms were therefore viewed as an individualized spirituality superior to the corporate worship of early ancient Israel. [15] David and his musicians became the decisive clue to the authorship of the book of Psalms. It was largely read as the expression of the piety of David. The superscriptions in the book of Psalms became the means by which the authorship of the book of Psalms was defined. This largely controlled the interpretation of the book of Psalms in the early period of this literature. The early interpreters did not actually consider David as a historical figure; rather, he was seen as the paradigm and prototype in the canonical context.[16] He exemplified prayers, praise and piety for Israel. Psalms are considered his prayer, praise and piety, which are useful for instruction and prophecy.

During the early to middle part of the nineteenth century, the authors of the

---

12. Cain Hope Felder, ed., *Stony the Road We Trod: African American Biblical Interpretation* (Minneapolis: Augsburg Fortress, 1991), is a notable exception.

13. For example, in 1989, I sent an article on African presence in the Bible to a reputable journal, and, in return, I was accused of trying to "smuggle Africa and Africans into the Bible."

14. J. Clinton McCann Jr., *A Theological Introduction to the Book of Psalms* (Nashville: Abingdon, 1993), 16.

15. Ibid.

16. James Luther Mays, "Past, Present, and Future Prospects in Psalm Study," in James Luther Mays, David L. Petersen, and Kent Harold Richards, *The Old Testament Interpretation, Past, Present, and Future* (Nashville: Abingdon, 1995), 147–57.

historical critical method called the Davidic authorship of Psalms into question. This was based on some incongruities between the many accounts in the book of Psalms attributed to David and the account of David's career in Samuel and the connection between some of the Psalms and the biblical literature of the late period after David's life.

The historical critics examined the individual and the corporate experiences and hymns in the light of the historical rather than the spiritual and theological perspectives.[17] The historical critics considered Psalms as the voice of some historical persons or occasions which do not match the person and the experiences of the person of David. They, therefore, searched through the biblical literature for other plausible people and times for the context with which to interpret the Psalms. The tendency with the historical critical scholars was to locate Psalms later rather than early in Israelite history. The result of this research was largely inconclusive because of the absence of the details that could link the Psalms with the particular historical context.[18]

In the early years of the nineteenth century a German scholar, Hermann Gunkel, was convinced that the work and method of the historical critics was inadequate. After his recognition of the presence of liturgical materials such as singing, dancing, shouting, sacrifices, prayers, temple, house of the Lord, courts, and others, he concluded that the Psalms were related to the worship in ancient Israel and not the meditation of pious individuals. He then started the classification of the book into different forms and types or genres (*gattung*) and tried to determine the life setting in ancient Israel. Although he was not satisfied with the historical critical method, he did not completely break from it.

For example, he still maintained that the Psalms were of a later time period. He believed, further, that the composers based their poetic creation on the "prototypes" that originated in the worship life of an earlier period.[19] According to Gunkel, (1) "Hymns," (2) "Laments of the People," (3) "Laments of the Individual," (4) "Songs of Thanksgiving of the Individual," (5) "Spiritual Poems" are the real treasure of the Psalter. Certainly, Gunkel's form critical approach to the Psalms was the most widely utilized approach in the twentieth-century research.[20]

Sigmund Mowinkel took the next step in Psalm interpretation. According to him, the Psalms represent the actual songs and prayers produced for and used in the public worship of ancient Israel before the destruction of the temple in 587/586 BCE. This is the main goal of this approach, referred to as the "cult functional approach," is to, first of all, classify the Psalm literature and then determine the setting of where that particular Psalm functioned in the life of the ancient Isra-

17. Ibid., 148.
18. Ibid.
19. McCann, *Introduction*, 17.
20. John H. Hayes, *Introduction to Old Testament Study* (Nashville: Abingdon, 1979), 291.

elite.[21] The form criticism and the functional approach to Psalms are inseparable, and also became very dominant approaches in the interpretation of Psalms. Both methods continue to be hugely influential in contemporary scholarship, although they are being refined and extended, to include many different settings.

Other scholars, having recognized the limitation of the approach of form-critical and functional approaches to the study of the book of Psalms, have called for a totally new direction in which scholarship should travel. James Muhlenberg, one of the dominant scholars, called for the need to supplement form-critical approaches with what he called rhetorical criticism. According to him, scholars should take very seriously the rhetorical and literary features of each Psalm in order to recognize "the actuality of the particular text." Today, rhetorical criticism has joined the form-critical approach to become one of the major forces in biblical interpretation.

Brevard Childs has called for the need to go beyond the form-critical and functional method of the Psalter.[22] He emphasized that more attention should be given to the final form of the Psalter. This is referred to as "canonical criticism." According to him, the canonical approach will help scholars to determine how the meaning of the individual Psalter may be affected by their titles and their placement in that particular place in the canon. Gerald H. Wilson has also paid serious attention to the canonical shape of the Psalter for many years and concluded that the Psalter is not a random collection of songs and prayers.[23] According to Childs, Wilson and others, the Psalter is not a mere collection of the liturgical materials, but has the purpose of being read and heard—"a source of *torah*." That is, as a source of instruction. As such, they are songs and prayers that originated from the response of the faithful persons to God.[24] It is, therefore, regarded as the words of God. James Luther Mays' acceptance of this canonical approach was reflected in his article entitled "The Place of the Torah-Psalms in the Psalter,"[25] where he argued that torah Psalms are present throughout the Psalter for the purpose of orienting the faithful to hear the Psalms as instructions of God. Eventually, form-critical and cult-functional approaches became subordinated to the question of content and theology.

The above methods of approach to Psalm study became dominant in America, Europe and Africa. These approaches were imposed on African biblical scholars who passed them on, often forgetting the fact that his or her religion and culture

21. McCann, *Introduction*, 17.

22. B. Childs, "Reflections in the Modern Studies of the Psalms," in *Magnalia Dei, the Mighty Acts of God: Essays in Memory of G. Ernest Wright*, ed. F. M. Cross, W. E. Lemke, and P. D. Miller Jr. (Garden City, NY: Doubleday, 1976), 378.

23. Gerald H. Wilson, *The Editing of the Hebrew Psalter* (SBLDS 76; Chico, CA: Scholars, 1985).

24. Ibid., 204–7; Brevard Childs, *Introduction to Old Testament as Scriptures* (Philadelphia: Fortress, 1979), 513–14.

25. James Luther Mays, "The Place of Torah-Psalms in the Psalter," *JBL* 106, no. 1 (1987): 3–35.

could also form an interpretative tradition. Though such methods of the study of the Psalter that we have discussed, thus far, do not have real value and meaning in African context, scholars continue to impose them on students, lecturers and scholars in Africa, as if there are no other methods relevant to our context.

DECOLONIZATION OF THE PSALTER

Having discussed how biblical studies, especially the Psalter, have been colonized in Africa, we need to discuss how such studies can be decolonized. Decolonization of the Psalter can only be possible by employing African cultural hermeneutics or inculturation hermeneutics. African cultural hermeneutics entail the use of African comparative, evaluative, Africa-and-African-in-the-Bible, the Bible as power, African bibliographical, and reading with the ordinary people approaches.[26] The following section presents a brief description of each these approaches

African Comparative Approach

African comparative approach in biblical studies is the comparison of the Old and New Testament with African cultures and religions. The field of Eurocentric comparative biblical studies has been dominated by the comparison of biblical materials with the cultures and religions of the ancient Near East and not Africa. Although African comparative studies do not exclude the materials from the ancient Near East, our emphasis and concentration is on African cultures and religions, such as African literature, archaeology, and the entirety of African tradition. In the case of the Psalter, there is a comparison of the African potent words (the so-called incantation) and the biblical Psalm. Some similarities and differences have been highlighted. This African comparative approach includes some elements of critical evaluation of both African cultures and the Old Testament. After comparing African cultures and Christianity or the Old and New Testaments, the relevance of African cultures to the study of the Bible and the relevance of the Bible to African cultures is clear.

African Bibliographical Studies

African bibliographical study is the study of the collection of published and unpublished articles, books and monographs, and dissertations that deal with African contextual studies. Prof. Samuel Abogunrin of the Department of Religious Studies, University of Ibadan, Ibadan, Nigeria, lamented, "As late as 1987, there was no center of Biblical Studies in Africa South of the Sahara," and of course, if we look at the contemporary scene, there is still no center for African Biblical Studies. There is an urgent need for a center of African biblical studies where African cultural and religious documents will be gathered and stored for academic use. More

---

26. David T. Adamo, "The Historical Development of Old Testament Interpretation in Africa," *OTE* 16, no. 1 (2003): 9–33.

than any other biblical book, the Psalter is used in the light of African cultures, especially by African indigenous churches and non-Christians in Africa.[27]

African Evaluative Approach

African evaluative approach refers to essays on books produced by Africans or non-African biblical scholars for the purpose of criticizing the work of African Old Testament scholars. This criticism may be constructive, negative, or both. Somebody said that if one does not want to be critiqued; such a person should not publish. For progress, correction and readjustment in African biblical scholarship, there is need for evaluation of our work. Some scholars stand out in their evaluation and criticism of the work of African Old Testament scholars. Knut Holter and his student Marta Holland seem to be at the forefront of such work.[28]

These criticisms are valuable in that they call our attention to the opinions of other scholars. These criticisms not only help us to know the areas for further research, they also assist us to know how other Western Old Testament scholars, who are concerned with African Old Testament scholarship, understand us.[29]

---

27. David T. Adamo, *Reading and Interpreting the Bible in African Indigenous Churches* (Eugene, OR: Wipf and Stock, 2001); Knut Holter and Grant LeMarguand did most of the few bibliographical studies in the area of biblical studies respectively. As far as I know, Holter was the first scholar to publish extensive studies on African bibliographical studies. He published *Tropical African and the Old Testament: A Selected and Annotated Bibliography* (Oslo: University of Oslo, 1990) and *Old Testament Research for Africa* (New York: Peter Lang, 2002). Grant LeMarguand also published an outstanding bibliographical work (containing 167 pages) in Gerald West and Musa Dube, eds, *The Bible in Africa: Transactions, Trajectories, and Trends* (Leiden: Brill, 2000), 633–800.

28. Knut Holter, "Should Old Testament Cush Be Rendered 'Africa'?" in *Yahweh in Africa*, 107–14. Despite his criticism, I certainly believe that his interest in African Old Testament scholarship and his publication have done an important service to African Old Testament, especially as he spends his energy in bringing African Old Testament scholarship to the attention of the Old Testament scholars in the Western world. See Getui, Holter, and Zinkuratire, *Interpreting the Old Testament in Africa*, 43–54; Knut Holter, "The Institutional Context of Old Testament Scholarship in Africa," *OTE* 11 (1998): 50–58; Marta Hoyland Lavik, "The 'African' Texts of the Old Testament and their African Interpretations," in Getui, Holter, and Zinkuratire, *Interpreting the Old Testament in Africa*, 50.

29. After summarizing and presenting the work of "four contrasting scholars"— E. Mveng, G. A. Mikre-Selassie, S. Sempore, and David Adamo—and accrediting me with the honor of "probably being the African scholar who has made the simple most important contribution to the field" of African presence in the Old Testament, she saw the possible "danger in" my interpreting some biblical texts existentially since it "may potentially divorce us from the original historical setting of the text." She thinks that there should be more emphasis on the negative roles of Africa and Africans in the Old Testament.

"Reading with the Ordinary Readers" Approach

This is one of the latest approaches to African Biblical Studies championed by two African biblical scholars: Professors Gerald West, a South African, and Justin Ukpong, a Nigerian. They advocate doing biblical studies with ordinary people. By ordinary people, they mean the poor, the oppressed, the under-privileged, and the untrained in the art of biblical interpretation. Professor Ukpong calls this reading "inculturation hermeneutics."[30] Gerald West calls this a "contextual Bible reading."[31] This form of hermeneutics is contextual in nature, and it "seeks to make any community of ordinary people and their socio-cultural context the *subject* of interpretation of the Bible."[32] What this means is that trained biblical scholars sit down with untrained biblical scholars and study the Bible without directing the reading. It means that the reading agenda becomes that of the community. The trained biblical scholars do not control the reading process;[33] instead, they read as part of the community. They only facilitate the reading process. The hermeneutical tools include African socio-religious and cultural institutions, thought systems and practices, the African oral narrative genre, and African arts and symbols. The interpretation, therefore, reflects their concerns, values and interests. One of the advantages of this reading is that it does not only create critical reading masses but also builds "the community of faith that reads the Bible critically."[34]

In the case of the Palms, the Psalter becomes the community document, which addresses the concern of the community and not just the private individual. The Psalter is read and interpreted as a sacred document which addresses how the community can be protected from enemies, as a document for healing and success, which the main concern of many African people.

This approach is a form of hermeneutics from which Western readers can learn from their African counterparts. This is the case because many ordinary people read the Bible more than scholars. If Western academic readers refuse to learn this African method, the Bible could eventually become meaningless for the ordinary people, as it now seems to be in many parts of Europe, where the Bible is mainly interpreted abstractly solely for the sake of scholarship.[35]

---

30. J. S. Ukpong, "Inculturation Hermeneutics: An African Approach to Biblical Interpretation," in *The Bible in the World Context: An Experiment in Contextual Hermeneutics,* ed. Walter Dietrich and Ulrich Luz (Grand Rapids: Eerdmans, 2002), 17–32.

31. Gerald West, *The Contextual Bible Study* (Pietermaritzburg: Cluster, 1993).

32. Ukpong, "Inculturation Hermeneutics," 18 (emphasis in original).

33. Ibid., 21.

34. Ibid., 22.

35. Dietrich and Luz, *World Context,* ix.

Africa and Africans in the Bible Approach[36]

Throughout my eight years at the ECWA (Evangelical Church of West Africa) Bible College and Seminary (1968–1977) in Nigeria, my dedicated evangelical lecturers never made any mention of the presence of Africa and Africans in the Bible. Eminent Professors in the four universities in the United States where I received my education did not give me any hint of the possibility of an African presence in the Bible. Most of the textbooks that I used were authored by Eurocentric scholars and they tended to de-Africanize the Bible.

I discovered later that Africa and Africans were mentioned more than any other foreign nations and peoples in the Bible. They were mentioned in every strand of biblical literature. They made economic, religious, military, social and political contributions in ancient Israel. In Fact, Africa and Africans were mentioned in the pages of the Old and New Testament about 867 times. (I mean that no other nations, except Israel, were mentioned so frequently in the Bible.) But, unfortunately, this aspect of biblical studies is neglected even in Africa.

The biblical, archaeological, scientific evidence shows that if the Garden of Eden (Gen 2–3) ever existed at all, it was probably located in Africa as the cradle of human race. The presence of the African wife of Moses (Num 12:1), Ebed-melech (Jer 38:7–13), and African military men who defended King David (1 Sam 18) from his son, and Ancient Israel from the powerful Assyrian (2 Kgs 19:9), demonstrate the importance of Africa and Africans and their participation in the drama of redemption. Africa as a place of refuge for Jesus, the conversion of Ethiopian Eunuch, and the assistance of Simon of Cyrene to carry the cross also demonstrate the importance of Africa and Africans in the Bible.

To decolonize the Psalter, such methodology (Africa and Africans in the Bible) should be employed in the study of the Psalter. Passages that mention the acknowledgment of God's gifts by Africans (Ps 68:31) and Africans gaining the universal knowledge of Yahweh (Ps 87:4) should be studied critically, and not with the Eurocentric purpose of de-Africanizing the passages, by saying that those passages are latter additions, or interpolations and therefore not authentic passages.

The-Bible-as-Power Approach

One of the most important ways of decolonizing African biblical studies is the use of the Bible as power approach in our reading and interpretation of the Bible. This way of reading is an important development in African cultural hermeneutics and "existential" and "reflective" approaches to the interpretation of the Bible. Unlike the Eurocentric conservative biblical scholars who are preoccupied with the subject of inerrancy and infallibility of the Bible, African Christian scholars believe and respect the Bible without any attempt to defend it or apologize for it.

---

36. An example of this methodology is discussed fully in my book, D. T. Adamo, *Africa and Africans in the Old Testament* (Benin City, Nigeria: Justice Jeco Press, 2005; orig., San Francisco: Christian University Press, 1998).

The Bible, to African Christians, is the "Word of God" and is powerful. Such is its claims in Heb 4:12.

> For the word of God is quick, and powerful, and sharper than any two-edged sword, piercing even to the dividing asunder of soul and spirit, and of joins and marrow, and is a discerner of the thoughts and intents of the hearts.

The Bible is not only powerful; its power is relevant to the everyday life of Africans.[37] The Bible is used as a means of protection, healing and success. This method is mostly prevalent among the African Indigenous Churches in Africa and the Diaspora. They recognize that many of Eurocentric biblical interpretations and theologies, nourished in the Western biblical intellectual context have no root in the life of Africans. These methods make the Bible relevant to the African communities by employing African cultures in their interpretation of the Bible. It is important to demonstrate how the Psalms are used as protection, healing and success.

Protective Use of Psalms

The existence of evil ones is real in Nigerian indigenous tradition. Witches, sorcerers, wizards, evil spirits and all ill wishers are considered enemies. The consciousness of the existence of these enemies is a significant source of fear and anxiety in the Nigerian indigenous society. Among the Yoruba people of Nigeria, there is a belief that every person has an enemy, known or unknown. The activities of such enemies can be deadly.

The belief in enemies as the main sources of all evil and bad occurrences is so strong that nothing happens naturally without a spiritual force behind it. The Nigerian way of dealing with such enemies is to learn some "potent words" (the so-called incantation) and/or medicine to deal with such enemies. There is a strong belief in the power of words if spoken correctly, in the correct place, and at the correct time. Such words in Yoruba tradition are called *ogede*. The "potent words" are "performative words" that can be repeated two, three or more times without any addition. They attain the desired effect.

As Nigerian Christians examine the Bible to find potent words for protection against perennial problem of witches and all forces of evil, they discover some words in the book of Psalms that resemble the ones used in their traditions against one's enemies. As such the so-called "imprecatory Psalms" (Pss 5, 6, 28, 35, 37, 54, 55, 83 and 109) and are classified as protective Psalms by West African Indigenous Churches. The words in these Psalms are not only divine; they are also potent and

37. Zablum Nthaburi and Douglas Waruta, "Biblical Hermeneutics in African Instituted Churches," in *The Bible in African Christianity*, ed. Hanna Kinoti and John Waliggo; Nairobi: Acton Press, 1997), 40–57. See also D. T. Adamo, "The Use of Psalms in African Indigenous Churches," in West and Dube, *The Bible in Africa*; idem, *Reading and Interpreting the Bible*; idem, "The Distinctive Use of Psalms in Africa," *MJT* 9, no. 2 (1993): 94–111.

performative words that can be used for protection against enemies, if recited with faith in God and the power of words. Examples of these words are:

> Make them bear their guilt O God;
> Let them fall by their own counsels,
> Because of their many transgressions
> . . . All my enemies shall be shamed
> And sorely troubled; they shall turn
> Back and be put to shame in a moment. (5:10 RSV)

Sometimes the psalmist invoked death on their enemies as in Ps 55:15, 23.

> Let death come upon them;
> Let them go down to sheol alive;
> Let them go away in terror into their grave. . .
> [They] shall not live out half their days. (RSV).

They regarded these Psalms as psalms for protection against enemies since the recitation makes them "die by their own evil deeds."[38] This Psalm can be read everyday with Yahweh's holy name. In the Nigerian context, Psalm 35 is used to drive away evil plans of enemies and especially witches and evil men.

Therapeutic Use of Psalms

Before the advent of Christianity and Western medicine, West Africans had developed certain effective ways of rescuing themselves from various types of diseases. These ways include the use of herbs, powerful, mysterious or potent words, animals parts, living and non-living things, water, fasting, praying and laying on of hands, and other rituals for restoration of harmony among the people and the wider environment.

When Western missionaries came to West Africa, they concluded that indigenous therapeutic methods were barbaric and even abominable for converts, but they did not provide any substitute. With the total devotion of missionaries who left their beautiful countries to the so-called African jungle, and with the emphasis on the importance of the Christian book, the converts believed that there must be something equally potent that could be used for healing in the Bible. Psalms 1, 2, 3, 20 and 40 are identified as Therapeutic Psalms.[39] They are said to be good for stomach pain.

The Use of Psalms for Success

The examination of the classification of some Psalms into success psalms will be more readily understood and intelligible within the context of the discussion on

---

38. Chief J. O. Ogunfuye, *The Secrets of the Uses of Psalms* (Ibadan, Nigeria: Ogunfuye Publications, n.d.) 37.

39. Adamo, *Interpreting*.

the use of medicine and potent words to enhance success in all walks of life in West African indigenous traditions. Success in all walks of life is an important aspect of African society. Lack of success is viewed with all seriousness. Medicine or potent words are employed for success in academic life (especially passing exams), in business, embarking on a journey, and in securing love from a person. Such medicine for success in academic work and business, among the Yoruba people of Nigeria, is called *isoye* and *awure* respectively. *Isoye* in Yoruba practically means "quickening the memory or intelligence."[40] *Awure* means the thing that activates success or what uncovers success.

Whenever an important venture is being embarked upon in West African indigenous traditions, a strong awareness exists that their enemies (human or spirits, seen and unseen) are struggling to bring bad luck to particular groups of people. This thought is indisputable in a typical West African traditional society. Hence, when an important venture is undertaken such as business, building houses, marriage, hunting for a new job, or attending an interview, a medicine-man/woman is often consulted to narrow down the chances of failure and increase success. Unfortunately, the missionaries did not provide a substitute for securing success when they condemned the West African indigenous traditions.

Identification of Success Psalms

West African Christians, however, identified some Psalms as success psalms. These are Psalms believed by the West African Indigenous Christians to have the power to bring success if used with faith, rituals, prayer, fasting, and rehearsal of some specific symbols (such as the sign of the cross or standing at the crossroad at midnight), and a combination of other animate or inanimate materials. Christians in West Africa, who were no longer comfortable with using pure indigenous ways of obtaining success, mostly because of the condemnation by Western orthodox Christians and missionaries, had no choice but to find an alternative method of achieving success. They turned to the Christian Bible, and found, in the book of Psalms, the equivalent powers, which they had discarded.

For success in examination or studies, Pss 4, 8:1–9, 9, 23, 24, 27, 46, 51, 119:9–16, 134 are identified. For success in securing the love of a woman or man Ps 133 is recommended.[41] For success or good luck in winning court cases, Pss 13, 35, 46, 51, 77, 83, 87, 91, 110, 121, 148, with specific instructions, are recommended. Psalms 4, 108 and 114 are special psalms for success in any venture that one embarks upon such as laying the foundation of a house, promotion in government work, and embarking on a business trip.

---

40. S. Ademiluka, "The Use of Psalms" (M.A. thesis, University of Ilorin, Nigeria, 1990), 88; David T. Adamo, "African Cultural Hermeneutics," in *Vernacular Hermeneutics*, ed. R. S. Sugirtharajah (Sheffield: Sheffield Academic Press, 1990).

41. Ogunfuye, *Secrets*, 88–89.

CONCLUSION

I may be accused of trying to dethrone the dominant, universally acceptable, and authoritative Eurocentric method of interpretation, but my aim, which I think should be the aim of all African biblical scholars, is rather to seek to dethrone the biblical imperialism of the Western world, which Western biblical scholars have imposed on their African peers. I know that for an African biblical scholar to try to do this is like trying to read and interpret "against the grain," or to read and interpret against the overwhelming scholarly view. I may be accused of bias and lack of objectivity. The fact is that I have no choice but to oppose biblical imperialism and to apply the "hermeneutic of suspicion" to the entire dominant and biblical Western interpretation. There is the need to promote Afrocentic biblical scholarship.

A closer look at the "Africa-and-Africans-in-the-Bible approach" shows that it is time for African biblical scholars to begin to ask the question "Who am I? What did the Holy Scripture say about me, my people, and my ancestors?" The contextual/reading with ordinary people and the "Bible as power" approaches demonstrate that our reading and interpretation must be indispensable for the academy, the church and the society at large.

The use of the "Bible-as-power" approach may seem fetishistic and magical (this is the opinion of many Eurocentric biblical scholars), but biblical scholars, especially of the Psalter, should ask the questions, "What was the intention of the original authors of the Psalter when they composed the Psalm orally? Were these passages recited repetitively? Was there any expectation, by faith, that when those words were recited they would achieve the desired effect? Were those words spoken and recited for fun, for aesthetic or scholarly purpose in ancient Israel?"

As an Old Testament scholar, my understanding of the culture of the ancient Near East makes me believe that the words of the Psalter were memorized and recited not for fun or aesthetic or scholarly purposes, but there was a faith behind the recitation or singing of the Psalms, with the expectation that they would achieve a desired effect. In ancient Israel, those words were potent and performative words that sought to invoke a particular result. Like the ancient Israelites, who were the original authors of the Psalter, many African biblical scholars see the Psalter as divine, potent and performative words that can be used to protect one from enemies, to heal diseases and to bring about success. A few eminent biblical scholars (E. Jacob, W. Eichrodt, O. Prockesh, G. Von Rad, G. A. F. Knight, and R. Bultmann) agree with African biblical scholars that the spoken word in ancient Israel was "never an empty sound but an operative reality whose action cannot be hindered once it has been pronounced."[42]

---

42. E. Jacob, *Theology of the Old Testament*, trans. Arthur W. Heathcote and Philip J. Allcock (New York: Harper & Row, 1958), 127; W. Eichrodt, *Theology of the Old Testament* (London: SCM Press, 1967), 2:69; G. Kittel, *Theological Dictionary of the New Testament* (Grand Rapids, MI: Eerdmans, 1967), 4:93; G. von Rad, *Old Testament Theology* (Edin-

African and Africanist biblical scholars must genuinely face the task of formulating further Afrocentric hermeneutics for the purpose of decolonizing, not only the Psalter but the Bible as a whole.

WORKS CITED

Abogunrin, O. *Africa and Africans in the Old Testament.* Benin City, Nigeria: Justice Jeco, 2005; orig. San Francisco: Christian University Press, 1998.

———. "Biblical Research in Africa," *AJBS* 1, no. 1 (1986): 7–24.

———. "The Distinctive Use of Psalms in Africa," *MJT* 9, no. 2 (1993): 94–111.

———. "The Historical Development of Old Testament Interpretation in Africa." *OTE* 16, no. 1 (2003): 9–33.

———. *Reading and Interpreting the Bible in African Indigenous Churches.* Eugene, OR: Wipf and Stock, 2001.

Childs, B. *Introduction to the Old Testament as Scripture.* Philadelphia: Fortress, 1979.

Cross, F. M., W. E. Lemke, and P. D. Miller Jr., eds. *Magnalia Dei, the Mighty Acts of God: Essays in Memory of G. Ernest Wright.* Garden City, NY: Doubleday, 1976.

Dietrich, W., and U. Luz. *The Bible in the World Context: An Experiment in Contextual Hermeneutics.* Grand Rapids: Eerdmans, 2002.

Eichrodt, W. *Theology of the Old Testament.* Vol. 2. London: SCM, 1967.

Felder, C.H. *Stony the Road We Trod: African American Biblical Interpretation.* Minneapolis: Fortress, 1991.

Getui, M., K. Holter, and V. Zinkuratire, eds. *Interpreting the Old Testament in Africa.* New York: Peter Lang, 2001.

Hayes, J. H. *Introduction to Old Testament Study.* Nashville: Abingdon, 1979.

Holter, K. "The Institutional Context of Old Testament Scholarship in Africa." *OTE* 11 (1998): 50–58.

———. *Old Testament Research for Africa.* New York: Pert Lang, 2002.

———. *Tropical Africa and the Old Testament: A Selected and Annotated Bibliography.* Oslo: University of Oslo, 1990.

———. *Yahweh in Africa: Essays on Africa and the Old Testament.* New York: Peter Lang, 2000.

Jacob, E. *Theology of the Old Testament.* Trans. A. W. Heathcote and P. J. Allcock. New York: Harper & Row, 1958.

Kinoti, Hanna, and John Waliggo. *The Bible in African Christianity.* Nairobi: Acton, 1997.

Kittel, G. *Theology of the Old Testament.* Vol 4. Grand Rapids: Eerdmans, 1967.

Knight, G. A. F. *A Biblical Approach to the Doctrine of the Trinity.* Edinburgh: T&T Clark, 1953.

Mays, J. L. "The Place of Torah-Psalms in the Psalter." *JBL* 106, no. 1 (1987): 3–35.

Mays, James Luther, David L. Petersen, and Kent Harold Richards, eds. *The Old Testament Interpretation, Past, Present, and* Future. Nashville: Abingdon, 1995.

McCann, J. C. Jr. *A Theological Introduction to the Book of Psalms.* Nashville: Abingdon, 1993.

---

burgh: T&T Clark, 1965), 2:85; G. A. F. Knight, *A Biblical Approach to the Doctrine of the Trinity* (Edinburgh: T&T Clark, 1953), 14–16.

Newing, E. G. "A Study of Old Testament Curricula in Eastern and Central Africa." *ATJ* 3 (1970): 80–98.

Ogunfuye, J. O. *The Secrets of the Uses of Psalms.* Ibadan, Nigeria: Ogunfuye Publication, n.d.

Parenti, P. *Against Empire.* San Francisco: City Lights Books, 1995.

Raisamen, Heiki, and Elisabeth Schüssler Fiorenza. *Reading the Bible in the Global Village.* Atlanta: SBL, 2000.

Sugirtharajah, R. S. *Vernacular Hermeneutics.* Sheffield: Sheffield Academic Press, 1990.

———. ed. *The Bible and the Third World.* Cambridge: Cambridge University Press, 2001.

Ukpong, J. S., "Rereading the Bible with African Eyes." *JTSA* 91 (1995): 3–14.

von Rad, G. *Old Testament Theology.* Vol 2. Edinburgh: T&T Clark, 1965.

Weiser, A. *The Psalms: A Commentary.* Trans. Herbert Hartwell; Philadelphia: Westminster, 1962.

West, G., and M. Dube, eds. *The Bible in Africa: Transactions, Trajectories, and Trends.* Leiden: Brill, 2000.

West, W. *The Contextual Bible Study.* Pietermaritzburg: Cluster Publication, 1993.

Wilson, G. H. *The Editing of the Hebrew Psalter.* SBLDS 76. Chico, CA: Scholars, 1985.

Interpreting τὸν ἄρτον ἡμῶν τὸν ἐπιούσιον in the Context of Ghanaian Mother-Tongue Hermeneutics

John D. K. Ekem

"The Lord's Prayer," considered by many as Jesus' most significant teaching on prayer, is recorded specifically in Matt 6:9–13 and in Luke 11:2–4, with some variations. If one were to ask about the extent to which these Gospel accounts have been able to recapture the original prayer spoken by Jesus, presumably in the Aramaic language, the answer would not be conclusive enough. Common to both Matthew and Luke is the phrase τὸν ἄρτον ἡμῶν τὸν ἐπιούσιον (Matt 6:11 and Luke 11:3) whose interpretation has posed a big challenge to New Testament exegetes.

This essay examines some European and Ghanaian translations of the phrase. It argues that from a Ghanaian hermeneutical perspective, the question of "economic survival" and the need to strive for moral and economic excellence should play a crucial role in the interpretation of the text. In attempting to understand the text from a diachronic perspective, cognizance should also be taken of the precarious living conditions of first century Palestinian workers. The hermeneutical relevance of this essay for Theological Education in the Ghanaian/African context lies precisely in the challenge it throws to communities to use the text as an important springboard to rise above their poor economic circumstances and to strive for moral as well as economic excellence. This carries profound implications for the preparation of context-sensitive study Bibles and commentaries.

A Brief Comment on Mother-Tongue Biblical Hermeneutics

In the process of translating and interpreting the Judeo-Christian scriptures, scholars have, since ancient times, been faced with the Herculean task of making these scriptures relevant to their target audiences through the dynamic process of "vernacularization." In such a process, the "original texts" are expected to be communicated in a way that will meet the needs of receptor audiences whose worldviews are quite different from those of the original recipients. It involves, so to speak, the re-packaging of thoughts embedded in an "original revelation/message" for speakers of other languages taking cognizance of relevant theological, linguistic, and cultural factors.[1] Sugirtharajah sums up this point as follows:

> Vernacular interpretation seeks to overcome the remoteness and strangeness of these biblical texts by trying to make links across the cultural divides, by employing the reader's own cultural resources and social experiences to illuminate the biblical narratives.[2]

If the vernacular may refer to the common language used by a particular community, region or nation, the mother tongue is a person's own indigenous language into which he or she is born and with which he or she grows up.[3] It is clear from such a distinction, however, that a mother tongue can eventually become a people's vernacular, depending on how widely it is spoken across geographical boundaries. Biblical Interpretation in Africa has a lot to offer through the use of various mother tongues. Herein lies the crucial importance of Bible translations in local Ghanaian/African languages as viable material for interpretation, study Bibles and commentaries.

SOME PRELIMINARY EXEGETICAL REMARKS ON THE TWO VERSIONS OF "THE LORD'S PRAYER"

An examination of the two Gospel accounts shows that there are significant similarities and differences between them. Scholars have pointed to the fact that this popular prayer begins in a manner similar to the *Kaddish*, a Jewish prayer that magnifies and sanctifies the name of God. Whereas Matthew's version is located within the textual unit usually referred to as the "Sermon on the Mount," Luke's version is captured within the larger text bloc dealing with Jesus' journey to Jerusalem (Luke 9:51–19:27). This follows the Galilean ministry account recorded in 4:14–9:50. The account in Luke is a response to the disciples' request to be taught how to pray. A doxology, most probably emerging from the liturgical needs of some early Christian communities, is sometimes appended especially to the Matthean account. But it is neither part of the "actual text" nor supported by evidence from the best and most reliable ancient Greek manuscripts.[4] Its popular version[5] runs as follows:

---

1. For a discussion of this delicate subject with reference to the translation of "The Lord's Prayer" by an eighteenth-century theologian of the Gold Coast (now Ghana), see J. D. K. Ekem, "Jacobus Capitein's Translation of 'The Lord's Prayer' into Mfantse: An Example of Creative Mother Tongue Hermeneutics," *GBOT* 2 (July 2007): 66–79.

2. R. S. Suirtharajah, *The Bible and the Third World: Precolonial, Colonial, and Postcolonial Encounters* (Oregon: Wipf & Stock, 1998), 14.

3. For a good discussion, see B. Y. Quarshie, "Biblical Studies in the African Context-The Challenge of Mother-Tongue Scriptures," *JACT* 5, no. 1 (2002): 7.

4. For a good discussion, see B. M. Metzger, *A Textual Commentary on the Greek New Testament* (London: UBS, 1971), 16–17.

5. Ibid., 16, for some other renditions.

ὅτι σοῦ ἐστιν ἡ βασιλεία, καὶ ἡ δύναμις, καὶ ἡ δόξα, εἰς τοὺς
αἰῶνας ἀμήν.

That liturgical adaptation continued even after the gospels had been written down
is shown by the inclusion of this doxology in the *Didache* version of "The Lord's
Prayer" (*Didache* 8:2), which comes quite close to the text of Matthew, with some
minor variations. It has quite rightly been observed that

> Variations in the form of the LP [Lord's Prayer] did not cease with the writing
> of the Gospels and the *Didache*. Such variations are in no way surprising in the
> transmission of a text which was soon, and perhaps from the start, central in
> Christian liturgy and instruction. The operation of both liturgical and instruc-
> tional use can be discerned. Thus, over a long period various mss have alterations,
> whether the addition of the liturgical doxology to Matthew or the harmonizing
> expansion of Luke's shorter version with Matthew's fuller and soon more widely
> used version. Both the gospel settings and that of the Didache reflect instruc-
> tional needs, and the provision of a guide for Christian prayer.[6]

Some scholars are inclined to consider the Matthean and Lucan versions as being
from the same source (possibly Q) from which the Gospel writers embarked on
their creative editorial work. According to this viewpoint, the prayer was a well-
known liturgical material and each of the Gospel writers adapted it to the needs of
his audience.[7] Hence it is quite understandable when Matthew opts for the phrase:
Πάτερ ἡμῶν ὁ ἐν τοῖς οὐρανοῖς (Matt 6:9b) rather than simply Πάτερ, as in Luke
11:2b.[8] Luke also omits Matthew's γενηθήτω τὸ θέλημά σου, ὡς ἐν οὐρανῷ, καὶ ἐπὶ
τῆς γῆς Matt 6:10b) as well as Matthew's reference to deliverance from evil/the evil
one (Matt 6:13b). Again, whereas the Matthean account expresses the petition for
the supply of needs just a day at a time (δὸς ἡμῖν σήμερον), Luke's version conveys

---

6. J. L. Houlden, "Lord's Prayer," in *The Anchor Bible Dictionary* (New York: Doubleday,
1992), 4:357.

7. W. G. Kümmel, *Einleitung in das Neue Testament* (Heidelberg: Quelle & Meyer, 1983),
84, argues strongly for an adaptation of the Matthean version to a Jewish liturgical setting.
An interesting discussion of the Gospel's relation to Judaism is offered by A. J. Saldarini,
"Reading Matthew without Anti-Semitism," in *The Gospel of Matthew in Current Study*, ed.
D. E. Aune (Grand Rapids: Eerdmans, 2001), 166–84.

8. B. M. Newman and P. C. Stine, *A Handbook on the Gospel of Matthew* (New York:
UBS, 1988), 165, observe that "questions regarding the original form, whether to be found
in Matthew or Luke, remain unresolved. Scholars have often argued in favor of the original-
ity of the Lucan form, since it reflects less of a liturgical structure." For an exegetical comment on the shorter Lucan version, see J. Reiling and J. L. Swellengrebel, *A Handbook on
the Gospel of Luke* (New York: UBS, 1971), 428–30; M. Goodacre, "A Monopoly on Marcan
Priority? Fallacies at the Heart of Q," *SBLASP* (2000): 538–622, argues that Luke has rewritten the Matthean version in line with another version more familiar to him from frequent
use in his own community.

the impression that these needs are to be supplied continually on a daily basis (δίδου ἡμῖν τὸ καθ᾽ ἡμέραν).

Of particular importance for the exegesis of the text is the understanding of the difficult phrase τὸν ἄρτον ἡμῶν τὸν ἐπιούσιον. This phrase has been variously interpreted as:

1. "Bread for the current day/for today"
2. "Bread for the following day"
3. "Bread necessary for our existence"
4. "Bread for the future."[9]

Before we take a closer look at this text and attempt locating it in a Ghanaian hermeneutical setting, it would be useful to remark that considering the similarities between the Matthean and Lucan texts, it is doubtful whether the two versions were derived from separate sources, namely, M and L, thereby reflecting independent translations from an Aramaic original. Or did Luke depend on Matthew, having reduced the latter's text to certain essential theological components relevant to his community? Such a theory would square up with the Griesbach hypothesis whereby Matthew is purported to have been the earliest among the Gospels. It would also agree with ancient Church tradition represented by Clement of Alexandria, Eusebius and Augustine. But there is also the possibility that Luke's version is closer to the original text which was later expanded by Matthew for liturgical purposes. If this prayer did indeed exist originally in Aramaic, then it could be argued that Luke's use of the simple form Πάτερ suggests a close leaning on the Aramaic *Abba* = "Father" which had in fact been employed by his contemporary Paul the Apostle (Rom 8:15–16; Gal 4:6–7). Hence Luke's predominantly non-Jewish audience might have influenced his choice of the Greek form. Matthew, on the other hand, might have introduced some creative additions to this prayer in order to meet the specific needs of his community.

THE COMPLEXITIES UNDERLYING THE TRANSLATION AND INTERPRETATION OF ἐπιούσιον

If Matthew's use of the aorist imperative δὸς in relation to σήμερον seems to focus on the supply of needs for the "present day" and Luke's use of the present imperative δίδου, in conjunction with τὸ καθ᾽ ἡμέραν, envisages the continual supply of needs "on a daily basis," there has been no unanimous scholarly conclusion regarding how the accusative form of the adjectival word ἐπιούσιον should be translated

---

9. For a useful summary of these interpretations, see W. F. Arndt and F. W. Gingrich, *A Greek-English Lexicon of the New Testament and other Early Christian Literature* (Chicago: University of Chicago Press, 1965), 296–97; Newman and Stine, *Handbook on Matthew*, 169–70. For the possible Aramaic background of the text, see the discussion of P. Grelot, "La Quatrieme Demande Du 'Pater' et son Arrière-Plan Sémitique," *NTS* 25 (1978): 299–314.

and interpreted. This rare word can only be clearly attested in the Matthean and Lucan versions of "The Lord's Prayer." Grave doubts have been cast on its extra-biblical occurrences and many wonder whether it should not be treated as a biblical *hapax*.[10] The following observation of Davies and Allison is apposite in this regard:

> One of the great unresolved puzzles of NT lexicography is the derivation and meaning of ἐπιούσιον upon which hinges the interpretation of the present verse. The word has not, despite assertions to the contrary, been found outside the gospels, save in literature influenced by them . . .[11]

The various linguistic derivations of ἐπιούσιον can be summarized as follows:

1. The word can be derived from ἐπι and οὐσια denoting that which is "necessary for our being/existence" or "that upon which our existence depends," an interpretation favored by Origen, Chrysostom and Jerome. Betz is therefore on track when he remarks with reference to ἄρτος that "bread is a *synecdoche* (collective term) of the type *species pro genere* (the particular representing the whole) in which bread represents all the necessities for sustaining life."[12]

2. The word is a substantivized form of the phrase ἐπι τὸν οὐσαν, denoting that which is applicable "for the current day" or "for today." Going by this derivation, the translation "bread that we need today"/ "bread that is necessary for us today" would be quite legitimate.

3. The word can be derived from the feminine participial phrase ἡ ἐπιοῦσα denoting "that which follows immediately" and thus "for the following day" suggesting also "the day that is about to dawn." In this case, the translation "bread that we need for the day that is immediately going to dawn" assumes validity. It is significant to note that in the ancient Near East to which the world of Matthew and Luke belonged, the day also began in the evening. The request in "The Lord's Prayer" could therefore be a morning or evening prayer anticipating the provision of subsequent needs in the day into which the supplicant is about to be ushered.

4. The word can be derived from ἐπιεναι "be coming" on the analogy of τὸν ἐπιον = "the future" and hence a possible reference to "bread for the future." But this interpretation is somewhat remote from the Matthean and Lucan contexts which also envisage the precari-

---

10. See B. M. Metzger, "How Many Times Does ἐπιούσιον Occur outside the Lord's Prayer?" *ExpTim* 69 (1957–58): 52–54.

11. W. D. Davies and D. C. Allison, *A Critical and Exegetical Commentary on the Gospel According to Saint Matthew* (Edinburgh: T&T Clark, 1988), 607.

12. Hans-Dieter Betz, *The Sermon on the Mount* (Minneapolis: Fortress, 1995), 377.

ous living condition of day labourers and daily wage earners of first century Palestine. Although an eschatological interpretation cannot be ruled out, given the eschatological tone of the previous petitions in both Matthew and Luke, and "the circumstance that in Jesus' ministry table fellowship was an anticipation of the eschatological banquet,"[13] the reality of material provision for the day cannot be overlooked.

5. In the wake of this eschatological interpretation, some early exegetes even thought it inappropriate to view ἄρτον as a reference to physical food, having been influenced by Jerome's Latin translation of ἐπιούσιον as *supersubstantialem*. Hence, the rendering: "Give us . . .our 'Supersubstantial bread'" would have pointed to "The Lord's Supper" or even to the "Word of God" rather than the supply of material needs.[14] But this is again an artificial rendition that hardly addresses the immediate concerns of the Matthean and Lucan target audiences.

A Look at Selected Translations in Some Major European and Ghanaian Languages

Revised Standard Version (1952)

Matt 6:11 Give us this day our daily bread (footnote: or our bread for the morrow)

Luke 11:3 Give us each day our daily bread (footnote: or our bread for the morrow)

New International Version (1984)

Matt 6:11 Give us today our daily bread
Luke 11:3 Give us each day our daily bread

Today's English Version (1992)

Matt 6:11 Give us today the food we need (footnote: or for today/for tomorrow)

Luke 11:3 Give us day by day the food we need (footnote: or food for the next day)

Biblia Sacra Vulgata (1983 Edition)

Matt 6:11 *panem nostrum supersubstantialem* (footnote: *cotidianum*) *da nobis hodie*

---

13. Davies and Allison, *Critical and Exegetical Commentary,* 609.

14. For a discussion, see D. A. Carson, *The Expositor's Bible Commentary: Matthew* (Grand Rapids: Zondervan, 1984), 8:171–72.

Luke 11:3 *panem nostrum cotidianum da nobis cotidie*

Nouvelle Version Segond Révisée (1978)

Matt 6:11 Donne-nous aujourd'hui notre pain quotidian
Luke 11:3 Donne-nous chaque jour notre pain quotidian

Traduction Oecuménique de la Bible (1988)

Matt 6:11 Donne-nous aujourd'hui le pain dont nous avons besoin
Luke 11:3 Donne-nous le pain dons nous avons besoin pour chaque jour

La Bible en Français Courant (1997)

Matt 6:11 Donne-nous aujourd'hui le pain nécessaire (footnote: autres traductions: de ce jour/ du jour qui vient)
Luke 11:3 Donne-nous chaque jour le pain nécessaire (footnote: autre traduction: pour le lendemain)

Die Luther Bibel (1984)

Matt 6: 11 Unser tägliches Brot gib uns heute
Luke 11: 3 Unser tägliches Brot gib uns Tag für Tag

Die Gute Nachricht (1997)

Matt 6:11 Gib uns, was wir heute zum Leben brauchen
Luke 11:3 Gib uns jeden Tag, was wir zum leben brauchen

Translations into Key Akan Dialects of Ghana

Yen Wura ne Agyenkwa Iesu Kristo Apam-Foforo wo Tyi kasa mu: Unified Twi NT (1864)

Matt 6:11 Ma yen yen dā aduan ne ["Give us today our daily food"]
Luke 11:3 Ma yen yen dā aduan dā ["Give us each day our daily food"]

Anyamesem anase Kyerew Kronkron Apām-Dedaw ne Apām-Foforo nsem wo Twi kasa mu: The Holy Scriptures (Old and New Testaments) in the Twi language (1871)

Same as above.

1878 revised NT edition

Same as above

Nwoma Krønkrøn: Fante Bible (1948)

Matt 6:11 Ma hän hän daa daa edziban ndä [same translation as in the previously listed Twi dialect]

Luke 11:3 Ma hän hän daa daa edziban daa [-do-]

Kyeräw Kronkron: Akuapem-Twi Bible (1964)

Matt 6:11 Ma yän yän daa aduan nnä [-do-]
Luke 11:3 Ma yän yän daa aduan daa [-do-]

Apam Foforo: Akuapem-Twi NT (1974)

Same renditions as above.

Twerä Kronkron: Asante-Twi Bible (1964)

Matt 6:11 Ma yän yän daa aduane nnä [-do-]
Luke 11:3 Ma yän yän daa aduane daa [-do-]

Ewe Translations of Ghana and Togo

Nya Nyui h'akpale ene le wegbe me: The Four Gospels in the Ewe language (1861)

Matt 6:11 Na mi miaŵe nududu ši asu mia nu egbe ["Give our today food that will suffice us"]
Luke 11:3 Na mi gbawo dšio gbe miahe nududu ["Give us each day food that is sufficient"]

Nubabla yeye we agbalewo kata. Le Ewe gbe me: All the books of the New Testament in the Ewe language (1877)

Matt 6:11 Na mi miaŵe nududu ši asu mia nu egbe [same as the 1861 translation]
Luke 11:3 Na mi miaŵe nududu ši asu mia nu gbawo-dšogbe ["Give us our food that will suffice us daily"]

Biblia alo Ñøñlø Køkøe la le Eœegbe me: The Bible or The Holy Scriptures in the Ewe Language (1913)

Matt 6:11 Na míafe nududu si asu mía nu egbe la mi [same translation as in previous versions except for a slight change in orthography]
Luke 11: 3 Na míafe abolo si asu mía nu gbesiagbe la mí ["Give our bread that will suffice us daily to us"]
These translations were subsequently reproduced in the 1931 revision and re-prints of 1957, 1981 and 1983.

Nubabla yeye la: The New Testament (1990)

Matt 6:11 Nà nududu si hiã mî egbe la mi ["Give food that we need today to us"]
Luke 11:3 Na míafe gbesiagbe nududu mi ["Give our daily food to us"]

Gã Translations of Ghana

Wo Nyontso ke Yiwilaherelo Jesu Kristo Kpãnmo He le, ye Gã wiemo le mli: The New Testament of our Lord and Saviour Jesus Christ in the Gã language (1859)

Matt 6:11 Hãwo nmene wodã nmã ["Give us today our daily food"]
Luke 11:3 Hãwo dane wodã nmã ["Give us each day our daily food"]

Biblia alo Nmale Kronkron le, Kpãnmo Momo ke Ehe, ye Gã wiemo le mli : The Bible or The Holy Scriptures, Old and New Testaments, in the Gã language (1866)

The same translation was reproduced in this Premier Bible Version to be followed by revisions/reprints in 1872, 1889, 1907, 1955, 1966, 1974, 1983 and 1984.

Kpañmø Hee Lä Käha Yinø Bii: The New Testament for the Present Generation (1977)

Matt 6:11 Ha wø ñmänä wødaa ñmaa [same translation as in previous versions except for a revised orthography]
Luke 11:3 Ha wø wødaa ñmaa daa gbi ["Give us our daily *food* every day"].

It is clear from these European and Ghanaian translations that they have attempted to make use of the options available for the interpretation of ἐπιούσιον. It is noticeable from the various Ghanaian renditions that no alternatives have been offered and that translators have made their choices based on exegetical conclusions they arrived at. But the Ewe translations are particularly intriguing because they (except for the Lucan renditions of 1913 onwards) not only translate ἄρτον in the generic sense of food provision, but also go beyond the notion of "daily bread/food," popular in some translations of ἐπιούσιον by drawing attention to the aspect of "food that will be sufficient for us" and hence "necessary for our existence."

This point should not be overlooked in the preparation of study Bibles and commentaries for Ghanaian audiences. Popular and legitimate though the interpretation of ἐπιούσιον as "daily bread/food" might be and expressing, as it does, the thought of trust in God for the constant supply of our needs, it also carries the subtle danger of promoting a "living from hand to mouth syndrome" reminiscent of the precarious living conditions of first century Palestinian daily wage earners in Jesus' time. What Ghanaians and Africans need is not merely survival based on a subsistence economy, but a leap from mediocrity to economic and moral excellence. This in turn needs to be buttressed by the optimal use of our resources and trust in God for wisdom to develop modest but dignified life-styles that will not make us perpetually dependent on other people's benevolence.

Precisely, a mother-tongue hermeneutics that is relevant to our people will need to apply the biblical text intelligently to correct imbalances in society. That which disturbs the equilibrium of society, including the wasteful use of resources and opportunities, must be thoroughly dealt with. In hermeneutical terms, it is essential for African biblical interpreters to ensure a careful balance between the diachronic and synchronic dimensions of texts they examine and expound for their audi-ences. All the available interpretational options must be carefully evaluated and the choice made adequately substantiated in mother-tongue commentaries and study Bibles. To use the Mfantse example with which I am most familiar, a legiti-mate translation of the Matthean and Lucan texts containing ἐπιούσιον would be:

> Matt 6:11 Ndä so ma hän dza øbødøø hän so ["Today too, give us
>   that which will be sufficient for us"]
> Luke 11:3 Na daa so ma hän dza øbødøø hän so ["And each day
>   too, give us that which will be sufficient for us"].

CONCLUDING REMARKS

Our study has shown that translating and interpreting biblical texts in the con-text of Ghanaian mother-tongue hermeneutics have profound implications for the preparation of context-sensitive study Bibles and commentaries. This has been il-lustrated using ἐπιούσιον from the Matthean and Lucan contexts as a case study. It is hoped that more attention will be devoted to this important discipline which will also help shape the future of Biblical Studies in Africa.

WORKS CITED

Arndt, W. F., and F. W. Gingrich. *A Greek-English Lexicon of the New Testament and Other Early Christian Literature*. Chicago: University of Chicago Press, 1965.

Aune, D. E., ed. *The Gospel of Matthew in Current Study*. Grand Rapids: Eerdmans, 2001.

Betz, Hans-Dieter. *The Sermon on the Mount*. Minneapolis: Fortress, 1995.

Carson, D. A. *The Expositor's Bible Commentary: Matthew*. Vol. 8. Grand Rapids: Zonder-van, 1984.

Davies, W. D., and D. C. Allison. *A Critical and Exegetical Commentary on the Gospel Ac-cording to Saint Matthew*. Edinburgh: T & T Clark, 1988.

Ekem, J. D. K. "Jacobus Capitein's Translation of 'The Lord's Prayer' into Mfantse: An Ex-ample of Creative Mother Tongue Hermeneutics." *GBOT* 2 (2007): 66–79.

Freedman, D. Noel. *The Anchor Bible Dictionary*. Vol. 4. New York: Doubleday, 1992.

Goodcare, M. "A Monopoly on Marcan Priority? Fallacies at the Heart of Q." *SBLASP* (2000): 538–622.

Grelot, P. "La Quatrieme Demande Du 'Pater' et son Arrière-Plan Sémitique." *NTS* 25 (1978): 299–314.

Kümmel, W. G. *Einleitung in das Neue Testament*. Heidelberg: Quelle and Meyer, 1983.

Metzger, B. M. "How Many Times Does ἐπιούσιος Occur outside the Lord's Prayer?" *ExpTim* 69 (1957–58): 52–54.

———. *A Textual Commentary on the Greek New Testament*. London and New York: UBS, 1971.

Newman, B. M., and P. C. Stine. *A Handbook on the Gospel of Matthew*. New York: UBS, 1988.

Quarshie, B. Y., "Biblical Studies in the African Context—The Challenge of Mother-Tongue Scriptures," *JACT* 5, no. 1 (2002): 4–14.

Reiling, J., and J. L. Swellengrebel. *A Handbook on the Gospel of Luke*. New York: UBS, 1971.

Suirtharajah, R. S. *The Bible and the Third World: Precolonial, Colonial, and Postcolonial Encounters*. Oregon: Wipf & Stock, 1998.

6. Biblical Interpretations for Reconstruction

The Ideologically Biased Use of Ezra-Nehemiah in a Quest for an African Theology of Reconstruction

Elelwani B. Farisani

While this essay does discuss theologies of reconstruction in general terms, its specific focus is to examine how Ezra-Nehemiah has been used by certain theologians in a quest for a theology of reconstruction and, furthermore, how these theologians' use of Ezra-Nehemiah could be strengthened in a quest for a theology of renewal, transformation and reconstruction.

In their quest for a renewal theology, scholars have suggested different biblical paradigms. The most popular one is Ezra-Nehemiah.[1] This popularity is certainly because the Ezra-Nehemiah text may contribute considerably to the current ongoing and crucial debate on the theology of renewal, reconstruction, transformation and reconciliation in Africa. Certain scholars[2] have used Ezra-Nehemiah in a quest for a theology of reconstruction. However, their use of Ezra-Nehemiah "lacks clear and direct biblical pointers for useful and contextual discussion on reconciliation, reform, reconstruction, redress and transformation, because it is not based on solid exegesis"[3] of the text of Ezra-Nehemiah. Furthermore the text "does not serve the community as a whole."[4]

This essay reviews the research done on the use of Ezra-Nehemiah in the African continent with focus on how Ezra-Nehemiah has been used by three scholars

---

An earlier version of this article was published in *OTE* 15, no. 3 (2002): 628–46. Republished here with permission.

1. Elelwani Farisani, "The Use of Ezra-Nehemiah in a Quest for a Theology of Renewal, Transformation, and Reconstruction" (Ph.D. thesis, University of Natal, 2002).

2. Jesse Mugambi, *From Liberation to Reconstruction* (Nairobi: EAEP, 1995); Charles Villa-Vicencio, *A Theology of Reconstruction* (Cape Town: David Phillip, 1992a); André Karamaga, "A Theology of Reconstruction," in *Democracy and Development in Africa: The Role of the Churches,* ed. Jesse Mugambi (Nairobi: AACC, 1997), 190–91.

3. E. A. Turner, "Reconciliation amidst a Socio-Economic Crisis: A Rhetorical Critical Reading of Nehemiah against the Background of the Socio-Economic Situation in Judah during the Reign of the Achaemenids" (Ph.D. thesis, University of Stellenbosch, 1998).

4. John De Gruchy, "African Theology: South Africa," in *The Modern Theologians,* ed. D. F. Ford (2 vols.; Oxford: Blackwell, 1997), 450–51; Turner, "Reconciliation," 9.

to bolster the quest for a theology of reconstruction in the African context. The three scholars are: Charles Villa-Vicencio, Jesse Mugambi and André Karamaga.

C. Villa-Vicencio—1992: A Theology of Reconstruction

Villa-Vicencio was prompted by the changing situation in South Africa (before the democratic elections of 1994) and Eastern Europe to investigate the implications of transforming liberation theology into a theology of reconstruction and nation-building.[5] Explaining the changes that were taking place in Eastern Europe, the Soviet Union and South Africa, he declared that "the old is dying even though the new is not yet born, and there is no clear indication what form the new society might take."[6] He believes, then, that the new "is likely to be manifest in situations of genuine crisis, where the context demands creativity and change as the only reasonable basis for just and peaceful coexistence. Renewal occurs, not where empires endure and power reigns, but where ideologies crumble and failure is acknowledged."[7] Thus, as part of the "old" giving way to the "new," he argues that liberation theology has to be transformed into reconstruction theology.

Reconstruction Theology

Villa-Vicencio believes that the challenge now facing the church in South Africa is different from the challenge before 2 February 1990. Before 2 February 1990,[8] Villa-Vicencio argues, theology had to respond in a resistant manner. Today, after 2 February 1990, in a different context, he argues that theology "is obliged to begin the difficult task of saying 'Yes' to the unfolding process of what could culminate in a democratic, just and kinder social order."[9] Thus, he proposes reconstruction theology as a new theology which will better address the challenges of post—2 February 1990.

While acknowledging that the task of liberation theologians has essentially been to say "No" to all forms of oppression, he maintains that the prophetic—'No' must continue to be part of a reconstruction theology's role.[10] Hence it should continue to say no to all forms of exploitation and injustice wherever and whenever it

---

5. Villa-Vicencio, *Reconstruction*, i.

6. Ibid., 2.

7. Ibid.

8. On 2 February 1990, the last white president to rule South Africa, F. W. de Klerk, delivered a speech in Parliament in which he unbanned the previously banned liberation movements (namely the ANC, PAC, AZAPO, SACP, COSATU, MDM, etc.) and their leaders. Furthermore, de Klerk also announced the possible release of Nelson Mandela from twenty-seven years' imprisonment. De Klerk's speech was seen by many South Africans as the beginning of the new era in South African politics.

9. Villa-Vicencio, *Reconstruction*, 8.

10. Ibid., 1.

occurs.[11] However, reconstruction theology, according to Villa-Vicencio, will have to do more than saying "no," it will have to be more than a theology of resistance.[12] So Villa-Vicencio believes that in the new context, the task of reconstruction theology must include "thoughtful and creative 'yes' "[13] to meaningful political socio-economic and cultural changes such as one person one vote, economic justice, ecological renewal, gender sensitivity and so on.[14]

Villa-Vicencio's concern though, is that theology has perhaps never got the relationship between saying "no" and saying "yes" correctly. He argues that it tends either to be part of the resistance process (saying "no") or to provide religious legitimation of the status quo (saying "yes"). His suggestion is that by combining both the "no" and the "yes," reconstruction theology will be demonstrating its "critical solidarity with a democratically elected government of the people."[15]

And, he says that a theology of reconstruction is about facilitating, promoting and supporting actions which make and sustain human life. Thus, he calls it "a positive and constructive theology, concerned with social, economic and political structures."[16] Moreover, a theology of reconstruction involves the task of breaking-down prejudices of race, class and sexism, and also the task of creating an all-inclusive (non-racial and democratic) society, built on the values denied the majority of people under apartheid (7–8).

Postexilic Metaphor

Villa-Vicencio argues that reconstruction theology must be based on a postexilic metaphor, as opposed to liberation theology's Exodus metaphor. He, however, seems to be aware that "not all in the Bible and Christian tradition is 'of God' in the sense of being liberatory and redemptive. A clear distinction needs to be made between the residue of oppression within the Christian tradition and that part which points to, and symbolizes, the true message of liberation" (26).

Moreover, he points out that not all within the exilic and postexilic period and literature immediately offers itself for appropriation in a theology of reconstruction. The homecoming for the Jews was largely a restrictive and oppressive event, resulting in isolation from other nations. And yet, "metaphor" is "pure and adventure" (27). The "post-exilic metaphor" is used as a tentative, open-ended "symbol" which draws on the liberative spirit of hope located alongside all else within the exilic period and the return of the exiles (27). Furthermore, he believes that a postexilic biblical theology has not been fully developed by biblical scholars. He charges that,

---

11. Ibid.; Villa-Vicencio, "Beyond Liberation Theology: A New Theology for South Africa," *CM* (1993): 24.

12. Villa-Vicencio, *Reconstruction*, 274.

13. Ibid., 1.

14. Ibid.; Villa-Vicencio, "Beyond Liberation," 24.

15. Ibid., 25.

16. Villa-Vicencio, *Reconstruction*, 274. In-text references that follow are to this book.

> The dichotomy suggested by some scholars between doom, judgment and law in the pre-exilic period over against hope, salvation and grace in the post-exilic period is an oversimplification of the more complex biblical shift in emphasis at the time of the return from exile. (27)

As a way of explaining this shift, he goes on to explain that prior to the pre-exilic time in the history of Israel the prophets and poets looked back to the former times and old traditions:

> Then come the exilic poets, no longer appealing to the continuing power of the old tradition, but enunciating new actions of God that are discontinuous with the old traditions. The promise of the old tends to give way to the new. It is this shifting emphasis that is employed in what follows in the "metaphorical" use of post-exilic theology as a theology of reconstruction and nation-building. (29)

Thus, in summing up, Villa-Vicencio states that "there are resources within the biblical literature which give credence to the use of the post-exilic metaphor as a basis for a theology of prophetic reconstruction and political stability rather than revolution" (28). He identifies Ezra-Nehemiah together with several other texts that could be used as a basis for a reconstruction theology.

Other Texts

Villa-Vicencio argues that the prophetic and priestly themes tended towards "a closer synthesis, with the prophets Haggai and Zechariah calling for the rebuilding of the temple, while in the third Isaiah, especially chapter 56, there is a blend of cultic and ethical concerns." His argument here is that there is renewed emphasis on worship and social justice (27–28).

He explains his use of this postexilic metaphor when he states,

> The post-exilic metaphor as used here is built on the emphasis of Gerhard von Rad who identifies the poetry of Jeremiah, Ezekiel and Deutero-Isaiah as an important turning point in the traditions of the Old Testament. It is this that causes him to make Isaiah 43:18–19 the hinge between the two volumes of his Old Testament Theology: "Do not remember former things. Behold, I am doing a new thing." (28–29)

He then goes on to state that inherent to the metaphor of a postexilic theology is the expectation of the emergence of something new. He thus states,

> Biblically the renewing poems of Jeremiah, Ezekiel and Deutero-Isaiah constitute a reorientation of prophetic literature within which God's promise is not found by looking back, but by anticipating the future. The exilic prophets also knew, however, that the new age is born in present struggle. It was in obedience to God and in solidarity with one another that the new society would be born. The kind of society that will prevail in different parts of the world tomorrow is being forged on the anvil of struggle today. The church of tomorrow is also in the process of being born today. (48)

Ezra-Nehemiah

According to Villa-Vicencio, liberation was built largely around the biblical symbol of "Exodus." A theology of reconstruction, then, will have to look for additional symbols within the postexilic period. In other words, a paradigm shift from liberation theology to reconstruction theology means a shift of emphasis from the Exodus (pre-exilic) to Ezra-Nehemiah and other texts (postexilic).[17]

He, however, does not use Ezra-Nehemiah alone, as a basis for a theology of prophetic reconstruction and political stability.[18] Rather, he sees it as part of these other texts mentioned above:

> Post-exilic theology at the same time incorporates the contradictions and conflicts inherent to most theologies. It includes the moralisms of Deuteronomy, the passionate rebellion of Job against these impositions, the prophetic judgement and suffering of Jeremiah, Ezekiel's theology of renewal and the hope and anticipated home-coming of Deutero-Isaiah. After the return these contradictions continued in the ideological conflicts inherent to Nehemiah, Ezra and other reconstructionists, counter-balanced against the apocalyptic dreams of Zechariah and Joel.[19]

It is worth noting here, that though Villa-Vicencio does talk of "ideological conflicts" in Ezra-Nehemiah, his use of this text neither indicates that he identifies nor analyses such ideological conflicts.

A Critique of Villa-Vicencio's Reconstruction Theology and His Use of Ezra-Nehemiah

The main critique is that Villa-Vicencio's use of Ezra-Nehemiah does not examine critically the ideology behind the conflict between the returned exiles and the *am haaretz*. A careful reading of the text of Ezra-Nehemiah demonstrates that there is a contestation between at least two groups, namely the returned exiles and the *am haaretz*. Elsewhere I have shown that the Ezra-Nehemiah text has a particularly bias or ideology which tends to promote the view of the returned exiles rather than of the *am haaretz*.[20]

It follows, therefore, that if Ezra-Nehemiah is to be used in a theology of reconstruction, it should not be read as representing the voice of only one group, that is, that of the returned exiles. The suppressed voices of the *am haaretz* have to be heard as well. Unfortunately, Villa-Vicencio's use of Ezra-Nehemiah suppresses the voice of the *am haaretz*, in that he neither identifies nor analyses critically the ideology within the text, an ideology which is biased against the *am haaretz*.

Though he does mention that there is an ideological conflict inherent in Ezra-

17. Villa-Vicencio, "Beyond Liberation," 25.
18. Villa-Vicencio, *Reconstruction*, 27.
19. Ibid., 28.
20. Farisani, "Renewal,"

Nehemiah, his use of Ezra-Nehemiah does not seriously take into consideration the fact that the Ezra-Nehemiah text is not neutral, when setting forth a theology of reconstruction based on Ezra-Nehemiah and other reconstructionists. In fact, he does not read the text carefully. He has spoken of reconstruction theology as being based on, among other texts, Ezra-Nehemiah. By using the reconstruction theme in Ezra-Nehemiah without isolating the ideological agenda of the text and identifying the group which is dominant in the text, he has inadvertently identified reconstruction as that which is driven by the returned exiles at the exclusion of the *am haaretz*. Such a reading of the text is insensitive to the plight of the *am haaretz*. Our study of the text of Ezra-Nehemiah, elsewhere, takes seriously the fact that this text is not neutral, it is embedded within an ideological world of its author, which suppresses and oppresses the voice of the marginalized group, namely the *am haaretz*.[21]

If African biblical hermeneutics is to have an impact on our continent, it cannot only relate the text as is to the African context, without de-*ideologizing* that particular text in the first place. For such a reading may be counter-productive, in that instead of supporting and advancing the cause of the poor and marginalized, such a reading may further marginalize the poor by continuing to enslave them with the "revealed word of God."[22]

Moreover, though Villa-Vicencio argues for a postexilic metaphor as a basis for his reconstruction theology, he hardly develops or unpacks what and how these metaphors could be used effectively. He includes in his postexilic metaphors different texts from different socio-political contexts without doing a sociological analysis of any of them.

Conclusion

Villa-Vicencio's reconstruction theology correctly points out that we are in a different context in South Africa today than we were before the unbanning of the liberation movements in 1990 with the subsequent election of the democratic government in 1994. This new or different context requires, for him, a theology which in the first instance acknowledges that the context has changed, and then goes on to analyze the new context with a view to proposing creative solutions to the socio-economic conditions of this new context. This theology he calls "reconstruction theology." Accordingly, reconstruction theology should be based not on the old liberation theology's Exodus metaphor, rather it will have to use postexilic metaphors, ranging from Deuteronomy, Ezekiel, Isaiah, to Ezra-Nehemiah.

My main concern with Villa-Vicencio is not with the concept of reconstruction, which is relevant not only to South Africa but to the rest of our continent as well. Rather, it is with the manner in which he uses Ezra-Nehemiah in his recon-

---

21. Ibid.

22. Itumeleng Mosala, *Biblical Hermeneutics and Black Theology in South Africa* (Grand Rapids: Eerdmans, 1989), 6.

struction theology. He lists Ezra-Nehemiah together with other postexilic texts as having the same reconstructive theme. But he does not go on to read the text carefully in order to isolate certain ideological agendas which are prevalent in the text. By not doing so, he tends to succumb to the ideology of the author, which tends to be biased against the *am haaretz*, the very poor and marginalized that his reconstruction theology is designed to support.

J. N. K. MUGAMBI, 1995: FROM LIBERATION TO RECONSTRUCTION

Introduction

As indicated earlier, Mugambi's reflection on the reconstruction theme precedes Villa-Vicencio's, though his published work is later. Jesse Mugambi introduces reconstruction as a new paradigm for African Christian theology in Africa. He explores the role of Christian theology in the social reconstruction of Africa. He argues that the reconstruction theme is evoked partly by the changes that have taken place during the 1960s, 1970s and 1980s, and partly by the emergence of the "New World Order," after the end of colonialism, apartheid and the cold war.[23]

Mugambi sees the 1990s as a very difficult decade for peoples in all nations of the world. The Old Secular Order has passed away suddenly, he argues, and the New World Order is hardly here with us. Mugambi views the arrival of the New World Order as posing a challenge for us to be very creative and innovative. Thus he argues, "Theologically, Christians are challenged to look at the Gospel anew all the time, and re-discover the freshness of its message for every generation in every culture" (18).

Mugambi, like Villa-Vicencio before him, argues for a shift of paradigms from liberation to reconstruction theology. His concern is that in the recent past, liberation and inculturation have been taken as the "most basic concepts for innovative African Christian theology" (2).

Reconstruction Theology

Mugambi suggests that as we end the twentieth century and enter the twenty-first, a time has come for African Christians to discern themes other than "liberation and the Exodus." Thus he explains, "The themes of reconstruction and restoration are also powerful and relevant as concepts for motivating the Hebrews to transform their own society and culture at different times in their history. There are also the themes of renewal and survival" (24). It was in March 1990 that the process to address the above question was begun, when the Executive Committee of the All Africa Conference of Churches met in Nairobi. Mugambi was invited to reflect on the "Future of the Church and the Church of the Future in Africa." Thus he elaborates,

---

23. Mugambi, *From Liberation*, x. Subsequent in-text references are to this book.

> The theme of reconstruction appeared most appropriate in the New World Order. My presentation proposed that we need to shift paradigms from the Post-Exodus to Post-Exilic imagery, with reconstruction as the resultant theological axiom. It turns out that the 1990s are a decade of reconstruction in many ways, with calls for national conventions, constitutional reforms and economic revitalization. The 21st century should be a century for reconstruction in Africa, building on old foundations which, though strong, may have to be renovated. (5)

Here he introduces reconstruction as a new paradigm for African Christian theology in the "New World Order." Mugambi believes that reconstruction should be of interest to African theologians of all doctrinal persuasions, "considering that the task of social reconstruction after the Cold War cannot be restricted to any religious or denominational confines." Like Villa-Vicencio, he thinks reconstruction theology has to be interdisciplinary. Thus, he maintains that,

> At the same time, reconstruction is a concept within the social sciences, which should be of interest to sociologists, economists and political scientists. The multi-disciplinary appeal of reconstruction makes the concept functionally useful as a new thematic focus for reflection in Africa during the coming decades. (2)

Mugambi argues that the shift from liberation to social transformation and reconstruction begins in the 1990s. He points out that,

> This shift involves discerning alternative social structures, symbols, rituals, myths and interpretations of Africa's social reality by Africans themselves, irrespective of what others have to say about the continent and its peoples. The resources for this re-interpretation are multi-disciplinary analyses involving social scientists, philosophers, creative writers and artists, biological and physical scientists. (40)

Using engineering and construction terminology, he explains that, an engineer constructs a complex according to specifications in the available designs. Some modifications are made to the designs, in order to ensure that the complex will perform the function for which it is intended. Reconstruction is done when an existing complex becomes dysfunctional, for whatever reason, and the user still requires it. New specifications may be made in the new designs, while some aspects of the old complex are retained in the new (12). He then goes on to elaborate that social reconstruction belongs to the social sciences, and involves reorganization of some aspects of a society in order to make it more responsive to changed circumstances (13).

> This theology should be reconstructive rather than destructive; inclusive rather than exclusive; proactive rather than reactive; complementary rather than competitive; integrative rather than disintegrative; programme-driven rather than project-driven; people-centred rather than institution-centred; deed-oriented rather than word-oriented; participatory rather than autocratic; regenerative rather than degenerative; future-sensitive rather than past-sensitive; co-operative rather than confrontational; consultative rather than impositional. (xv)

In this sense, he says, Africa has been undergoing processes of social reconstruction during the past five hundred years (xv). Ultimately, he suggests several biblical metaphors that are discussed below.

Biblical Metaphors

Mugambi believes that after the abolition of apartheid, the "metaphor" of the Exodus has become "inapplicable and irrelevant." He then asks the question: What other metaphors are possible (165)? Mugambi argues that the Bible is replete with illustrations of social reconstruction over a long span of time. He identifies them as follows. Mugambi takes his first example of the reconstruction metaphor from Deuteronomy:

> Theologically, we need to appreciate that entry into the land of Canaan from Egypt is only the beginning of a long process of human fulfillment. The Exodus is only a prelude to that process. Moses did not enter the promised land, but he provided the bridge for the people to cross the Red Sea, the wilderness and the River Jordan. He established the foundation upon which the new nation was to be built, but later generations would have to build that new society. The Book of Deuteronomy, written perhaps more than six centuries later, recaptures that significant role of Moses, but highlights the necessity of later generations to revise the plans to match new circumstances and resources. (166)

Explaining the reconstruction theme in Deut 1:19–20, he argues that,

> It is important to note that the book of Deuteronomy was written in the 7th century B.C., long after the settlement in Canaan. The book represents an effort, under the long reign of King Josiah, to formulate a theology of reconstruction based on Mosaic law and highlighting those aspects of society which required further explanation. Thus, Deuteronomy is based on the exodus, but offers an updated version of Mosaic law. How can this text be applied in a relevant manner so as to discern a new ideological emphasis to propel African churches into the future? Quite obviously, Africa today needs a theology of reconstruction, just as King Josiah needed such a theology in 622 B.C. (65)

The second text Mugambi identifies is from the New Testament, namely, Matt 5–7. Explaining the context of this text, he states that the critics of Jesus accused him of trying to destroy Judaism and its institutions. In response, Jesus replied that his mission was reconstructive rather than destructive. Thus, Mugambi contends that the Sermon on the Mount (Matt 5–7) can be considered as most basic of all reconstructive theological texts in the synoptic gospels (13).

Ezra-Nehemiah

Mugambi states that the challenge, as we enter the twenty-first century, is to discern other biblical motifs that would be relevant for a theology of transformation and reconstruction. He maintains that such texts might, for example, be the Exilic motif (Jeremiah), the Deuteronomic motif (Josiah), the restorative motif (Isa

61:4), the reconstructive motif (Haggai and Nehemiah), and so on (39). Having identified these several motifs, he goes on to focus, though superficially, on Ezra, Haggai and Nehemiah. He argues that if we were to opt for the Exilic motif, "the logical follow-up would still be social transformation and reconstruction identified with Ezra, Haggai, and Nehemiah" (40).

He focuses specifically on the text of Nehemiah, as a possible postexilic text appropriate for reconstruction theology. For him, the book of Nehemiah explains the process of reconstruction in Jerusalem and Judah after the exile. And so he predicts that the central biblical text for African Christian theology in the twenty-first century will, perhaps, be the Book of Nehemiah, rather than the Book of Exodus. Of course, the book should be read critically, taking into consideration all the hermeneutical, exegetical, theological and ethical limitations associated with the reconstruction project of Nehemiah (166). It is worth noting here, that though Mugambi advocates a critical reading of the book of Nehemiah, he does not do it. He does not seem to read the text carefully at all!

Even though, like Villa-Vicencio, Mugambi mentions the book of Ezra-Nehemiah as part of an array of biblical texts that deal with the theme of reconstruction, he seems to put greater emphasis on the Ezra-Nehemiah text. Using Ezra-Nehemiah as a model for a reconstruction theology, he declares that,

> After the Babylonian exile, a new nation was reconstructed under the direction of Ezra and Nehemiah. The role of Nehemiah as the director of the reconstruction project is lucidly explained in the book bearing his name. Nehemiah becomes the central text of the new theological paradigm in African Christian theology, as a logical development from the Exodus motif. (13)

Mugambi sees the figure of Nehemiah not only as an exemplary character, but also as a leader who represents the aspirations and contradictions of Africa's social reconstruction at this time in history.[24]

We have so far attempted to outline both Mugambi's theology of reconstruction and how he uses Ezra-Nehemiah in his theology. It is important to note that Mugambi does not say anything more than we have outlined above on the role of Ezra-Nehemiah's text in the reconstruction process.

A Critique of Mugambi's Reconstruction Theology and His Use of Ezra-Nehemiah

Let us make some preliminary observations about Mugambi's use of Ezra-Nehemiah for a theology of reconstruction. First, Mugambi, like Villa-Vicencio, does not seem to have read the text of Ezra-Nehemiah carefully. Like Villa-Vicencio, he does not seem to identify or examine critically the ideology behind the conflict between the returned exiles and the *am haaretz*. Second, like Villa-Vicencio's use of Ezra-Nehemiah, he also suppresses the voice of the *am haaretz*, in that he

---

24. J. N. K. Mugambi, "Foreword," in *Theology of Reconstruction,* ed. Mary Getui and Emmanuel A. Obeng (Nairobi: Acton, 1999), i–iv.

neither identifies nor analyses critically the ideology within the text, an ideology which is biased against the *am haaretz*. Third, like Villa-Vicencio, by using the reconstruction theme in Ezra-Nehemiah without isolating the ideological agenda of the text and identifying the group which is dominant in the text, he has inadvertently identified reconstruction as that which is driven by the returned exiles at the exclusion of the *am haaretz*. Such a reading of the text is insensitive to the plight of the *am haaretz*. Finally, like Villa-Vicencio, he argues for a postexilic metaphor as a basis for his reconstruction theology, he hardly develops or unpacks what and how these metaphors could be used effectively. Rather, he includes in his postexilic "metaphors different texts from different socio-political contexts without doing a sociological analysis of any of them."

Having critiqued Mugambi's use of Ezra-Nehemiah, we briefly critique his reconstruction theology. First, unlike Villa-Vicencio, while calling for a paradigm shift from liberation to reconstruction theology, he does discuss in a detailed way what liberation theology is all about, and goes on to advance reasons why a shift of paradigms is necessary. Second, unlike Villa-Vicencio, his reconstruction theology's immediate context seems to be Africa.

However, there seems to be a contradiction with the place of inculturation within Mugambi's reconstruction theology. To start with, he advocates for a paradigm shift from inculturation to reconstruction theology, but as one of his components of a theology of reconstruction he lists cultural reconstruction alongside personal, social and ecclesiastical reconstruction. Does he see cultural reconstruction as something totally different from inculturation?

Furthermore, we also need to acknowledge the following about Mugambi. In the first place, like Villa-Vicencio, he is quite tentative at times about his identification of reconstruction as a new metaphor, for he uses the word "perhaps" when suggesting reconstruction theology as a new theological paradigm. In addition we need to note that he admits that the reconstruction theme needs "further development as a paradigm of Christian theological reflection in Africa."[25] Second, both Mugambi and Villa-Vicencio see reconstruction theology as positive and constructive in its nature. Third, unlike Villa-Vicencio and Karamaga (to be discussed later), Mugambi is the only one who identifies metaphors or symbols from both the Old and New Testaments.

Summary

Mugambi, like Villa-Vicencio, observes that we are no longer living in the previous decade of colonialism and apartheid, but that we have attained political liberation. This presupposes that we are in a different context today than we were before. It is this new context which justifies his proposal for shifting theological paradigms from liberation and inculturation to reconstruction. His reconstruction theology addresses challenges facing the African continent on the following levels: socio-

---

25. Mugambi, *From Liberation*, 15.

UNIVERSITY OF WASHINGTON
LIBRARY

economic, personal, ecclesiastical, and cultural. He uses Ezra-Nehemiah as a possible reconstruction metaphor, together with other biblical metaphors from both the Old and the New Testaments. Like Villa-Vicencio, he does not do a sociological analysis of the texts he mentions as possible basis for a reconstruction theology. All he does is just to mention them. By so doing he fails to get behind the ideological issues embedded in these texts.

The need for the two theologies to join hands together has been succinctly expressed by Pityana when he states,

> Theological discourse will continue to predominate in the shaping and construction of a new South Africa. Theology, therefore, must proceed from the social and religious pluralism of South Africa. Social critical tools will be necessary to analyse social dynamics. Culture is a critical element in that understanding of society. A critical and dynamic understanding of culture thus becomes essential for a meaningful theological discourse.[26]

Mugambi's suggestion of shifting paradigms from inculturation to reconstruction, while he still includes cultural reconstruction as part of his reconstruction theology, may underlie the fact that the two theologies should complement each other rather than exclude each other.

ANDRÉ KARAMAGA, 1997: THEOLOGY OF RECONSTRUCTION

Reconstruction theology

Unlike Villa-Vicencio and Mugambi, André Karamaga did not write a book on reconstruction theology, rather his is just an article. Nevertheless, in his article he demonstrates how Ezra-Nehemiah (or rather Nehemiah) could be a model for reconstruction theology. Therefore, we have decided to give him the same attention as the other two scholars discussed earlier.

Karamaga argues that the theology of reconstruction is necessary today in order to face vital challenges.[27] However, he does not mention any of those vital challenges. According to him, we need to reconstruct both the church and the nation: "Some countries in Africa are completely destroyed, pillaged, cultures disorganised. One finds countries where the church is sterilized and characterised by a multitude of divisions." In these circumstances, he sees human beings as co-creators with God and who need to be active role players in the reconstruction of both the church and the nation (190).

---

26. Barney Pityana, "Beyond Transition: The Evolution of Theological Method in South Africa: A Cultural Approach" (unpublished Ph.D. thesis, University of Cape Town, 1995), 288.

27. André Karamaga, "A Theology of Reconstruction," in *Democracy and Development in Africa: The Role of the Churches,* ed. Jesse Mugambi (Nairobi: AACC, 1997), 190–201. Subsequent in-text references are to this article.

Like Villa-Vicencio and Mugambi, he argues for a shift of paradigms from liberation to reconstruction theology, saying: "The liberation theology had become reactionary and we changed to a proactive one of reconstruction" (190). Though Villa-Vicencio calls liberation theology "resistance" theology, Karamaga sees it as "reactionary." Like Villa-Vicencio and Mugambi, he sees liberation theology as no longer relevant today and instead he suggests that we shift paradigms to reconstruction, which will be able to address the socio-economic crises or challenges that Africa is faced with.

Karamanga's Use of Nehemiah

What is Karamaga's biblical basis for his reconstruction theology? His use of Nehemiah is based on Neh 2:1ff. But does he say anything about this text or any other text of Nehemiah other than just mentioning Neh 2:1ff.? Not at all! Rather he seems just to mention this text and then goes on to talk about the reconstructive measures undertaken by Nehemiah. He argues that the process of reconstruction "has a theme of liberation" (190). Although he calls liberation theology a reactionary theology, his above-mentioned statement of a link between liberation and reconstruction theologies may be undermining his aim of separating the two theologies. Perhaps he should be suggesting a complementary interaction between the two theologies rather than a total independence from each other.

Like the other two, Karamaga sees Nehemiah as a proper role model for reconstruction theology, for "Nehemiah was able to mobilise masses to do the reconstruction. The Jews did the work with a morale that was unparalleled. Nehemiah was action oriented and his example inspired the reconstruction of the temple, city and nation." Clearly he sings a praise song to Nehemiah. He takes the text at face value, that is, literally, and he does not bother to note that most of Nehemiah's actions were done at the exclusion of the people of the land. While portraying Nehemiah as the role model on reconstruction, Karamaga, unlike Villa-Vicencio and Mugambi, acknowledges certain weaknesses in Nehemiah's reconstructive role: "He was a human being with faults for we learn that he excluded mixed marriages." Nonetheless Karamaga maintains that "on the basis of this (Nehemiah's) biblical experience, we should look at our function in reconstruction" (190). So his reconstruction theology takes Nehemiah as our role model for our reconstruction purposes today in our African context.

A Critique of Karamaga's Reconstruction Theology and Use of Ezra-Nehemiah

We make the following observations about his reconstruction theology. First, Karamaga does not clearly explain what he means by a theology of reconstruction. Unlike Villa-Vicencio and Mugambi, his definition and methodology of his reconstruction theology has not been clearly spelled out. We also need to observe that, though Karamaga feels that Nehemiah has to be a role model, he is the only one of the three discussed, who actually acknowledges what he calls Nehemiah's "weaknesses" in dealing with the intermarriage matter. Furthermore, he is the only

scholar of the three who focuses only on Nehemiah's reconstruction process, excluding Ezra. The question that needs to be raised is whether this is a deliberate
move, and if so, why? Does it suggest a lesser role for Ezra in reconstruction? His
approach may be narrow as he only concentrates on Nehemiah without taking
into consideration the role played by Ezra.

Second, unlike Villa-Vicencio and Mugambi, he uses only one exilic motif (Nehemiah) for his reconstruction theology, whereas both Villa-Vicencio and Mugambi uses Ezra-Nehemiah together with other biblical metaphors.

Third, though his point of departure seems to be Neh 2:1ff, in his discussion of
reconstruction theology, he does not seem to refer anywhere to this or any Nehemiah text. Like Villa-Vicencio and Mugambi, Karamaga appropriates the reconstruction metaphor without actually dealing with ideological issues raised in the
text of Ezra-Nehemiah.

Summary

Karamaga's definition of reconstruction is not clearly formulated. He seems to take
it for granted that we all know what is meant by reconstruction theology. He argues that we need to shift paradigms from liberation to reconstruction. But he
does not give any justification for such a move. He argues that reconstruction is
the most relevant theology for today as it will address both the religious and the
socio-economic challenges facing our continent today. What we have said about
Villa-Vicencio and Mugambi about the lack of isolating the ideological issues
within the text equally applies to Karamaga. He does not read the text carefully to
make it a strong basis for his reconstruction theology.

Toward an African-Oriented Sociological Exegesis of Ezra-Nehemiah

The Ezra-Nehemiah text has been used by Mugambi, Villa-Vicencio and Karamaga in a quest for a theology of renewal and reconstruction. While the quest
for this theology should be supported by all who are serious about the challenges
facing Africa today, the way the three African scholars have used Ezra-Nehemiah
undermines their basic call for a theology which aims at addressing the needs and
plight of the poor and the marginalized in Africa. This is precisely because they
appropriate the Ezra-Nehemiah text without engaging with the text in any exegetical depth. By not so doing, the three scholars have failed to identify an ideology
prevalent in the Ezra-Nehemiah text, an ideology which is biased in favor of the
returned exiles, and against the *am haaretz*.[28]

An important resource for identifying the ideology of Ezra-Nehemiah (and any
other biblical text) is a sociological reading. The purpose of a sociological reading of Ezra-Nehemiah is threefold. First, to demonstrate that the Ezra-Nehemiah
text has a particular exclusivist ideology which tends to be biased against the *am*

---

28. Farisani, "Renewal."

haaretz, while favouring of the returned exiles.[29] It argues that when one reads Ezra-Nehemiah, one immediately detects a contestation between the returned exiles and the *am haaretz*. Furthermore, a sociological reading argues that if Ezra-Nehemiah were to be used in a theology of reconstruction, it has to be read taking into consideration the voice of the *am haaretz*, as well, rather than only address the voice of the returned exiles.

Second, a sociological analysis also demonstrates that the Ezra-Nehemiah text is a product of several authors and was compiled in different layers and years. Thus, it argues that the final editor, who may have been an unknown Jew, has compiled the whole text round about 300 B.C.E., using both the Ezra "Memoirs" and the Nehemiah "Memoirs" which were probably written by both Ezra and Nehemiah round about 440 B.C.E. and 432 B.C.E. respectively.

Third, a sociological analysis goes on to analyze the ideology in Ezra-Nehemiah. In this case purpose of sociological analysis is to provide a socio-historical analysis of the conflict between the *am haaretz* and the returned exiles. Such a sociological analysis covers the period from the fall of the Southern kingdom up to the period after the return to Judah of the Babylonian exiles.

Accordingly, such a sociological analysis identifies the ideology of each of the layers of the text of Ezra-Nehemiah with respect to the *am haaretz*. The first return of the Babylonian exiles to Jerusalem, recorded in Ezra 1–6, represents the ideology of the final redactor of Ezra-Nehemiah. Ezra 1–6 tells us that on returning from Babylon, the returned exiles embarked on the rebuilding of the temple, at the exclusion of the *am haaretz*. So, the ideology of the final redactor of Ezra-Nehemiah, while favoring the returned exiles is biased against the *am haaretz*. The second return of the exiles to Jerusalem is recorded in Ezra 7–10. We have argued elsewhere that Ezra is the author of Ezra 7–10. So the second return is Ezra's ideology.

A sociological analysis has shown that immediately after his return, Ezra embarked on a program of redefining the returned exiles in ethnic terms. He encouraged them to separate themselves from the *am haaretz*. Thus, he excluded the *am haaretz* from assembly participation and also urged the returned exiles to divorce their *am haaretz* wives. The third return, under the leadership of Nehemiah, is recorded in Neh 1–5. This text represents the ideology of Nehemiah himself. Nehemiah 5 records a debate by the returnees about the shortage of food, taxation, debt, slavery etcetera. This debate excludes the *am haaretz*. It is important, however, to note that though Nehemiah has failed to reconcile the returned exiles with the *am haaretz*, he succeeded, in chapter 5, to reconcile the debtors and the creditors within the returnee community.

---

29. By the returned exiles here we are referring to all the Jews who were taken into exile by the Babylonian king, Nebuchadnezzar, in 586 BCE and returned back home with the assistance of the Persian king Cyrus in 539 BCE. The *am haaretz* are those Jews who did not go into Babylonian exile but stayed in Palestine.

The above summary of the ideologies of the authors of each of the layers of Ezra-Nehemiah tell us that the entire Ezra-Nehemiah text is colored with an ex-clusivist ideology which is biased in favor of the returned exiles, while being bi-ased against the *am haaretz*. Such a sociological analysis of the exclusivist ideology of the text of Ezra-Nehemiah is an important step in our quest for a theology of renewal, transformation and reconstruction. The purpose of such an analysis is to enable us to de-ideologise effectively the exclusivist ideology in the text and read the text against the grain, that is, from the perspective of the excluded and mar-ginalized *am haaretz*.

What, then, is the contribution of a sociological analysis of the text of Ezra-Nehemiah to a theology of renewal? While not questioning the concept of re-construction as propagated by Mugambi, Villa-Vicencio, and Karamaga, a soci-ological reading of Ezra-Nehemiah's contribution to the project of renewal and transformation in Africa is on the theological level. First, it warns against any un-critical reading of the biblical text, like the ones by Mugambi, Villa-Vicencio, and Karamaga. By uncritical reading, we refer to any reading of the Bible which does not engage in an in-depth manner with the text. Any uncritical reading of the biblical text tends to further oppress and sideline the poor and marginalized by appropriating the ideologically undifferentiated biblical text as the "revealed word of God."[30] Instead of empowering the poor and marginalized, an uncritical reading of the text disempowers and weakens them.

A straightforward reading of Ezra-Nehemiah tends to uncritically support the ideologies in Ezra-Nehemiah, in portraying the returned exiles as the legitimate Israelites who should lead the reconstruction and renewal process in postexilic Palestine at the exclusion of the *am haaretz*, who are portrayed as "enemies" and "foreigners". A sociological reading shows that such an uncritical reading of Ezra-Nehemiah perpetuates the ideology of sidelining, excluding and marginalizing the *am haaretz* from any meaningful participation in the renewal and reconstruction process in postexilic Palestine. Such an uncritical reading is dangerous, and should not be left unchallenged.[31]

Such a sociological analysis has shown, contra Mugambi, Villa-Vicencio, and Karamaga, that, for a theology of renewal, transformation, reconciliation and re-construction to be effective, it will have to be conscious of the fact that the Ezra-Ne-hemiah text is not neutral. Rather, it has a particular ideology, an ideology which is biased against the *am haaretz*. Thus, a sociological analysis argues that reconstruc-tion theology will have to take seriously, in its theological backing of the process of renewal and transformation in Africa, the fact that each and every text in the Bible is the product of its socio-historical context. And that, in order to use any text ef-fectively in the reconstruction process in Africa, without it further oppressing and

---

30. Mosala, *Hermeneutics*.
31. Farisani, "Renewal."

silencing the already silenced and marginalized poor, the text's ideology has to be subjected to a rigorous sociological analysis, so as to de-ideologize it.

Second, a sociological reading of the text goes further, to read the Ezra-Nehemiah text "against the grain." It tries to retrieve the voices of the marginalized *am haaretz*, and also attempts to read the Ezra-Nehemiah text from the perspective of the *am haaretz*. By so doing, such an analysis hopes that in appropriating the Ezra-Nehemiah text in the renewal and transformation of Africa, theologians will be sensitive to the voices and needs of all stakeholders in taking up this theological task in Africa.

Works Cited

Farisani, Elelwani B. "The Use of Ezra-Nehemiah in a Quest for a Theology of Renewal, Transformation, and Reconstruction." Ph.D. thesis, University of Natal, 2002.

Ford, D. F., ed. *The Modern Theologians*. Cambridge, MA.: Blackwell, 1997.

Getui, Mary, and Emmanuel A. Obeng. *Theology of Reconstruction*. Nairobi: Acton, 1999.

Mosala, Itumeleng J. *Biblical Hermeneutics and Black Theology in South Africa*. Grand Rapids: Eerdmans, 1989.

Mugambi, J. N. K. *Democracy and Development in Africa: The Role of the Churches*. Nairobi: AACC, 1997.

———. *From Liberation to Reconstruction*. Nairobi: EAEP, 1995.

Pityana, N. Barney. "Beyond Transition: The Evolution of Theological Method in South Africa. A Cultural Approach." Ph.D. thesis, University of Cape Town, 1995.

Turner, E. A. "Beyond Liberation Theology: A New Theology for South Africa." *CM* (1993): 24–25.

———. "Reconciliation amidst a Socio-Economic Crisis: A Rhetorical Critical Reading of Nehemiah 5 against the Background of the Socio-Economic Situation in Judah during the Reign of the Achaemenids." Ph.D. thesis, University of Stellenbosch, 1998.

Villa-Vicencio, Charles. *A Theology of Reconstruction*. Cape Town: David Phillip, 1992.

In Quest of Survival: The Implications of the Reconstruction Theology of Ezra-Nehemiah

Robert Wafawanaka

This essay attempts to take a critical look at the reconstruction program of Ezra and Nehemiah and its implications for African biblical hermeneutics of reconstruction. I seek to defend the thesis that Ezra and Nehemiah's activities may be understood in the context of their history; however, this rationale is not sufficient in our modern context. To this end, I contend that the issue of "survival" influences the nature of their theology and reconstruction program. However, a reading of Ezra-Nehemiah in contemporary culture sends a message of intolerance, othering, and separatism, thereby challenging the whole question of religious ideals and identity. What then are the implications of Ezra-Nehemiah's reconstruction program? I will discuss Ezra and Nehemiah in the context of Old Testament history and theology. My conclusion will be a critical analysis of the implications of Ezra and Nehemiah's reconstruction theology for an African biblical hermeneutics of reconstruction.

Ezra-Nehemiah in Old Testament History and Theology

The books of Ezra and Nehemiah are regarded as one book in the Hebrew Bible although Christian Bibles separate them into two individual books. While there is some debate among scholars, the consensus is that Ezra-Nehemiah may be attributed to the Chronicler historian. These books are generally thought to have been written in the postexilic period between 400 and 300 B.C.E.[1]

A close reading of the Hebrew Bible demonstrates that the books of Chronicles, Ezra, and Nehemiah recount the history of Israel and Judah although it largely

---

1. See the following references: Joseph Blenkinsopp, *Ezra-Nehemiah: A Commentary* (Philadelphia: Westminster, 1988), 35–72; F. Charles Fensham, *The Books of Ezra and Nehemiah* (Grand Rapids: Eerdmans, 1982), 1–37; Mark A. Throntveit, *Ezra-Nehemiah: Interpretation* (Louisville: Westminster John Knox, 1992, 1–11; H. G. M. Williamson, *Ezra and Nehemiah* (Sheffield: JSOT, 1987), 14–47; and Ralph W. Klein, "The Books of Ezra and Nehemiah," in *The New Interpreter's Bible: Kings–Judith* (Nashville: Abingdon, 1999), 3:661–851.

departs from, or redacts the Deuteronomistic History upon which it is based. We first read about the history of Israel in the Priestly and the Deuteronomistic History. Chronicles, Ezra, and Nehemiah belong to the third type of History we find in the Hebrew Bible, the Chronicler's History. When we compare and contrast these histories, we can clearly see that the Chronicler's History is a heavily edited work. Scholars are not always in agreement about the reasons for the drastic editing of the history of Israel and Judah in the Chronicler's History. As part of the Chronicler's History, Ezra and Nehemiah extend Israel's history into the post-exilic period. These books conclude with the return of the Jews from exile. This is the period of renewal, restoration, and reconstruction.

The history of Israel as reported in the Priestly and Deuteronomistic History is a history punctuated by covenantal relationship between Israel and Yahweh. Yahweh makes a covenant with Abraham the father of the nation and promises him land and progeny (Gen 12:1–8; 15:1–21; 17:1–27). In the legal and historical narratives, Israel emerges as a nation of former slaves which is given the land of promise. Israel is liberated by Yahweh and Moses leads the Israelites to freedom. Through their wilderness wanderings, Yahweh makes a covenant with Moses as he had with Abraham (Exod 24:1–18; 34:1–35; Deut 5:1–33). The book of Deuteronomy illustrates the importance of Israel's obedience to the covenant as a guarantee of success in the Promised Land. Blessings are given for obedience and covenant fidelity while curses are threatened for disobedience and covenantal infractions (Deut 27–28). Hence the book of Deuteronomy may be viewed as Moses' extended sermon on the importance of obedience. Consequently, a Deuteronomistic perspective which equates success with obedience and sin with disobedience informs the theology of this important book.

After Israel has settled in the land of Canaan, the Deuteronomistic Historian narrates the nature of Israel's history. While kingship is established (1 Sam 8–12), in general, it is a history of failure due to disobedience and covenantal infidelity. Israel forsakes Yahweh and worships other gods. The nation is judged on the basis of the king's rule. In theological perspective, the nation of Israel succumbs to Assyrian domination and ends up in exile (722 B.C.E.). Although the southern nation of Judah survives for a little while longer (135 years), it too succumbs to Babylonian domination (587 B.C.E.). Judah ends up in exile in Babylon and the theological premise is that the nation had sinned by forsaking the covenant with Abraham, Moses, and David (1 and 2 Kings).

Through the tragic experience of the exile, Israel had lost much of its former heritage and glory. Gone were the temple, kingship, and the priesthood. Even classical prophecy ceased at this time. These losses were significant in terms of giving an identity to Israel. Even the Psalmist laments by the rivers of Babylon, "How can we sing the Lord's song in a strange land?" (Ps 137:4).[2] The exile lasted but a half century (587–538 B.C.E.). At the end of the exile, Israel was determined to

---

2. Biblical quotations are from the NRSV.

reconstitute itself as a nation once again. The exile itself had indeed been a bitter pill to swallow.

The Chronicler Historian opens a new window in Israel's history by extending this history into the post-exilic period. The books of Ezra and Nehemiah give us an account of the nature of Israel's return to its homeland. The new Persian king, Cyrus, issues a decree that the Jews could return to their homeland to rebuild the temple of the Lord in Jerusalem and restore their community (2 Chron 36:22–23; Ezra 1:1–4). Ezra the priest, scribe, and expert in Mosaic Law, and Nehemiah the governor take turns and lead delegations of the returnees. Among other things, Ezra is in charge of the rebuilding of the temple (Ezra 3–6) while Nehemiah oversees the rebuilding of the wall of Jerusalem (Neh 3–6). They both attempt to rebuild the shattered lives of the people. Their reform and reconstruction efforts appear harsh, separatist, and extreme to modern sensibilities. However, we can understand the nature of these measures in light of Ezra and Nehemiah's historical context. I contend that these measures have as much to do with history as they have with the issue of survival.

SURVIVAL

The history and theology I briefly outlined is central to our understanding of the question of survival. Given the fact that Israel was a blessed nation that lost its land, legacy, and identity primarily due to disobedience and covenantal infidelity, it was incumbent upon the returnees not to repeat the mistakes of the past. The very survival of the nation of Israel was at stake because of the displacement of the exile. Consequently, the return period was to be characterized by an obedient nation struggling for its very survival and identity as a people of God.

The concept of survival suggests a people threatened who will do everything in their power to avert this threat. According to Jerome Ross, survival means "the perpetuation and preservation of a people" as a community.[3] Ross identifies seven elements that are needed to fulfill the requirements for survival. These are: administrative structure, economic independence, ideological standardization, common language, cultural assimilation, people, and land.[4] Each of these requirements is a factor in Ezra and Nehemiah's reconstruction theology. Ezra and Nehemiah provide the administrative arms of the community while they strive for economic independence and living as a pure nation among the people. The problems of language, repopulation, and control of the land become critical issues upon return. By assuring that all these elements were in place, the survival of the nation was guaranteed. Conversely, the lack of these elements would be a threat to the very existence and survival of the emerging and reformed nation.

---

3. Jerome Clayton Ross, *The History of Ancient Israel and Judah: A Compilation* (Pittsburgh: Dorrance, 2003), xi.
4. Ibid., xi–xii, 158.

Ezra-Nehemiah's Reconstruction Program

The reconstruction program of Ezra and Nehemiah begins with King Cyrus' liberation edict that freed the Jews to return to their homeland (2 Chron 36:22–23; Ezra 1:1–4). Scholars are divided about the nature of the return in terms of the delegations and their chronology. However, the central elements of the restoration program are clear. With the backing and funding of the Persian government, Sheshbazzar is entrusted with the return of the temple vessels which had been plundered by Nebuchadnezzar, while Joshua and Zerubbabel begin laying the foundation of the temple. The prophets Haggai and Zechariah also encouraged their rebuilding efforts.

This rebuilding program is interrupted by the enemies of Judah who want the process to stop. The completion and dedication of the temple is achieved during King Darius' reign. Passover is celebrated to mark this milestone (Ezra 6:1–22). Ezra returns with the Law of Moses, reads it publicly, and addresses some of the social problems such as mixed marriages. Foreign wives and their children are to be send away. Nehemiah returns to rebuild the wall of Jerusalem and completes it in fifty-two days under strong opposition and threat to his life. He also addresses socio-economic problems, mixed marriages, and how to repopulate Jerusalem. In light of previous history, Ezra and Nehemiah ensure that the community makes a pledge to keep the law of God (Neh 9:38–10:39; 13:10–31).

The completed wall is also dedicated, the feast of Booths is celebrated and the Sabbath is observed. When Nehemiah goes away to Babylon and returns to find a backsliding people, he takes even more drastic measures by advocating separation from foreigners, preventing intermarriage with foreigners, and breaking up marriages. The traditional enemies of Israel, the Ammonites, the Moabites, and the Ashdodites are singled out as those causing religious impurity. The issues of language and cultural assimilation clearly stand out in Nehemiah's diatribe. He complains:

> In those days also I saw Jews who had married women of Ashdod, Ammon, and Moab; and half of their children spoke the language of Ashdod, and they could not speak the language of Judah, but spoke the language of various peoples. And I contended with them and cursed them and beat some of them and pulled out their hair; and I made them take an oath in the name of God, saying, "You shall not give your daughters to their sons, or take their daughters for your sons or for yourselves. Did not King Solomon of Israel sin on account of such women?" Among the many nations there was no king like him, and he was beloved by his God, and God made him king over all Israel; nevertheless, foreign women made even him to sin (Neh 13: 23–26).

It is clear from this passage that cultural mixing was viewed negatively because it was deemed as leading to syncretism. Therefore, it was necessary to circumscribe the circle of those viewed as holy, religious, pure, and true Jews. It was a question of Jewish identity and survival. However, it was not a question without problems and serious implications.

Implications of the Reconstruction Program of Ezra-Nehemiah

The text of Ezra-Nehemiah demonstrates the need for us to reflect critically upon our theologies of reconstruction. Given the history of Israel and the context of Ezra-Nehemiah, the biblical text also reminds us that nations may go through periods of despair, destruction, and hopelessness. Due to this dire experience, nations are urged to plan carefully how they may reconstruct their shattered lives. The idea of reconstruction is certainly one that any nations that may have experienced what the ancient Israelites experienced must seriously wrestle with. How do we rebuild our devastated communities in the face of hopelessness and so much devastation? What is the best approach to take? Do we dare repeat some of the mistakes of the past? How do we reconstruct our communities in a world characterized by diversity and differences?

These questions force us to consider some challenging situations and solutions. One response is that of Ezra and Nehemiah. After witnessing the destruction of the nation of Israel, Ezra and Nehemiah return and embark upon a serious program of reform and reconstruction. They rebuild the temple, reinstitute traditional festivals, reorganize the people, begin economic initiatives, and rededicate themselves to the demands of the Torah. These initiatives are commendable in the sense that they signal attempts to reconstruct a nation that has been severely devastated. We can understand how they do not want to repeat the mistakes of the past, the very mistakes that contributed to the destruction of the nation in the first place. As a result, they take the opposite extreme position. They seek to construct a pure and holy Jewish nation and an identity that is exclusive of foreign elements. Essentially, they attempt to return to their traditional values. The problem I see in these measures is that Ezra and Nehemiah do not consider the implications and effects of their reform measures on other people who lived among them. Rather than working on how to construct a new inclusive and diverse society, they embark upon a program whose very intention is to prevent any inclusiveness and diversity. The effects of this drastic program are such that the very same people are divided and turned against each other. These divisions persisted through the centuries such that by the time of Jesus in the first century, New Testament writers believed that "Jews have no dealings with Samaritans" (John 4:9). One may well argue that the history of conflict between Israel and Palestinian Arabs may well have its antecedents in these centuries of division and separate identities.

Biblical scholars have much to say about the implications of Ezra-Nehemiah's reconstruction program. Ralph Klein finds no redeeming theological value in texts that promote separation through divorce and argues, "While divorce was permitted . . . there are strong voices critical of divorce in the Bible."[5] Malachi 2:16 categorically states that God hates divorce. Jesus put some limitations to this problem as well (Matt 19:1–12; Mark 10:1–12). As for marrying foreigners, there are

---

5. Klein, 746.

many supportive texts but the text of Ruth is a classic example of this opposing view. We also know that King David and King Solomon married many foreign women although primarily for political and diplomatic reasons. Therefore, mixed marriages were not a new phenomenon at the time of the return from exile. Klein concludes that "the biblical ambivalence toward outsiders and the excesses re-counted in Ezra 10 call us to serious reflection on these questions today. Ignoring interfaith questions is irresponsible."[6] He also asks a very relevant question, "How do we maintain the integrity of the faith without excluding others?"[7] Despite fears of apostasy and cultural contamination, Klein concludes that "Nehemiah's anxiet-ies come perilously close to what we would see as racial prejudice or the hatred that goes with ethnic cleansing."[8] Other scholars attempt to sanitize the extremism of Ezra and Nehemiah. For example, Throntveit argues that the redefinition of Israel demanded purification of the people on religious grounds, rather than racial terms.[9] It was a separation from all that was viewed as unclean. Others feel that "disobedience to the law threatened the very existence of the Jewish identity,"[10] or that intermarriage corrupts the home and "strikes at the very basis of marriage."[11] Williamson also agrees that marriages with indigenous populations were forbid-den for fear of sanctioning religious apostasy.[12] Despite these reservations, mixed marriages continued to be a part of ancient Israel's life.

While many biblical scholars fully understand the implications of Ezra and Nehemiah's reconstruction efforts, I do not think that they sufficiently critique this problem. It is true that we can make sense of Nehemiah's strict measures and almost berserk reaction in light of his context and the situation of the nation of Is-rael. However, reading such texts in a postmodern and postcolonial context reveals the many disturbing layers of the text. For example, a postmodern interpretation grapples with the question of identity or presence. It demonstrates that by creating identity, we often embrace ideologies of exclusion of others. In our search for dif-ference and distinction, we also embrace universals which negate any particulari-ties. As a result, we privilege some things while at the same time negating others. Deconstructing the problem of identity demonstrates the problematic nature of the reconstruction program of Ezra-Nehemiah. By creating such a strong identity of who belongs to the inner circle, the outsiders are automatically excluded. They are viewed as the opposite of the insiders or basically those who are to be removed

6. Ibid., 747.

7. Ibid.

8. Ibid., 850.

9. Throntveit, 57.

10. John White, *Excellence in Leadership: Reaching Goals with Prayer, Courage, and De-termination* (Downers Grove, IL: InterVarsity Press, 1986), 129. See also Cyril J. Barber, *Ne-hemiah and the Dynamics of Effective Leadership* (Neptune, NJ: Loizeaux Brothers, 1976).

11. Barber, 174.

12. Williamson, 95.

from among the insiders. Such an attitude naturally results in the demonization and degradation of the other.

I also find the measures of Ezra and Nehemiah troubling because the majority of ordinary and faithful Bible readers who live in the developing world read the Bible hoping to find in what way it addresses their needs. Historical, cultural, and contextual questions are of secondary concern if at all raised. Reading Ezra and Nehemiah from this perspective would be troubling for readers who might feel excluded, discriminated against, or unwanted as believers in God. Indeed, texts like these can be interpreted as sanctioning hate, hostilities, intolerance, and even genocide. In our modern world, we have indeed witnessed wars and genocides premised on religious differences and intolerance of the other. It is my contention that the text of Ezra-Nehemiah has some serious implications for African biblical hermeneutics of reconstruction. This text provides a timely warning for us who live in an unpredictable and often volatile world where differences seem to imply disparagement of the other rather than tolerance or celebration of diversity as a human race.

IMPLICATIONS OF THE RECONSTRUCTION PROGRAM OF EZRA-NEHEMIAH FOR AFRICAN BIBLICAL HERMENEUTICS OF RECONSTRUCTION

The reconstruction measures of Ezra and Nehemiah provide some important lessons for reforms and reconstruction programs in Africa as well as African biblical hermeneutics of reconstruction. Like the history of the Israelites, I agree that Africa has indeed been decimated as a continent and is in need of a viable reconstruction program. Like Ezra and Nehemiah, we need to return to our traditional values as we embark on this program. Our traditional values of community, unity, hospitality, respect, and togetherness have served us well. However, colonial domination, oppression and poverty have created more problems for Africa. As we reconstruct our societies, we need to be careful to avoid divisions and pitfalls such as those promoted in Ezra-Nehemiah.

The text of Ezra-Nehemiah provides a timely warning for African biblical scholars. As Africans, we are all familiar with the history of conflicts, wars, genocides, tribalism, and religious differences. We know too well how the construction of identity may create problems among the same people. We know how differences and distinctions may pull us apart and even lead us to serious conflict.

The construction of identities and distinctions may be seen in the recent conflicts in Rwanda and Burundi. Historically, these are the same people who were divided and treated differently by their colonial masters at a time when "divide and conquer" was their *modus operandi*. The results of this tactic are familiar and too painful to relate. Ever since the European arbitrary partition of Africa, we have existed as the same people but with divisions, differences, and barriers among us. Throughout Africa we know the many conflicts that have occurred are due to perceived differences among people. We are also familiar with the problems that tribalism, nepotism, and corruption can create. In our postcolonial context, perhaps we can learn something from Ezra and Nehemiah that may bring us together rather than apart. It is the major irony of our independence and postcolonial era that we are faced with so many crises in Africa today.

Many African thinkers and theologians have wrestled with this problem and how best to aid Africa in its reconstruction efforts in the postcolonial period. It is ironic that independent Africa should be defined by a host of problems rather than unity and peace. Mugambi and others rightly argue that independent Africa no longer needs a theology of liberation but a theology of reconstruction.[13] They state, "Africa today needs a theology of reconstruction, just as King Josiah needed such a theology in 622 B.C.E. We need to shift our theological gear from *liberation* to *reconstruction*."[14] Mugambi believes that such a theology is based on the hope for a better future and it should be similar to the reconstruction theology in the book of Deuteronomy. C. K. Omari believes it is the responsibility of the African Church to address social evils and offer hope rather than keep silent.[15] Kä Mana observes that salvation for Africa lies in the construction of a new African society using a hermeneutics of resourcefulness. This is a creative venture where all Africans work together toward the creation of a better society.[16]

Perhaps some of the most stimulating and beneficial work on reconstruction in Africa has been done by Samuel Kobia through his work with the World Council of Churches. The report of the General Secretary of the World Council of Churches on his visit to Kenya and Rwanda in 2004 is chronicled in the book, *For a New Africa with Hope and Dignity.*[17] Essentially, Kobia argues that Africa needs a new vision in which poverty, injustice, tyranny, war, and genocide will never again reign.[18] In words reminiscent of W. E. B. DuBois's "problem of the twentieth century," Kobia argues, "the 21st century will be dominated by the politics of identity."[19] He adds, "Given the fact that religion is a powerful source of

---

13. See Jose B. Chipenda et al., *The Church of Africa: Towards a Theology of Reconstruction* (Nairobi: All Africa Conference of Churches, 1990); J. N. K. Mugambi and Laurenti Magesa, eds, *The Church in African Christianity: Innovative Essays in Ecclesiology* (Nairobi: Initiatives Ltd., 1990); J. N. K. Mugambi, *African Christian Theology: An Introduction* (Nairobi: East African Educational Publishers, 1992); J. N. K. Mugambi, *Critiques of Christianity in African Literature* (Nairobi: East African Educational Publishers, 1992); Samuel Kobia, *The Courage to Hope: The Roots for a New Vision and the Calling of the Church in Africa* (Geneva: WCC, 2003); WCC, *For a New Africa with Hope and Dignity* (Geneva: WCC, 2004); and Kä Mana, *Christians and Churches of Africa: Salvation in Christ and Building a New African Society* (Maryknoll, NY: Orbis Books, 2004).

14. Mugambi et al., *The Church of Africa*, 35 (emphasis in original).

15. Omari, *Church of Africa*, 57–62.

16. Kä Mana, *African Society*, 90–106.

17. WCC report of Sam Kobia's visit, 2004.

18. WCC, *New Africa*, 27.

19. Ibid., 33. See also W. E. B. Dubois, *The Souls of Black Folk* (New York: Knopf, 1993).

identity, human conflicts and projects of conquest are likely to gain ontological justification. . . .The question of identity as a social construction in naming the other is often based on power relations."[20] Furthermore, Kobia argues that Africa, as cradle of humanity, needs to create a new world in which all live together as good neighbors. He chronicles the horrors caused by the "politics of division" and colonialism in Rwanda. His conclusions support the substance of my argument. He observes, "If religion is used as an instrument to gain political power and emphasize the exclusiveness and primacy of one's own group at the expense of others, it will be a most destructive contribution. The political idea of "the otherness" fuels conflicts."[21] I agree with this assessment since it sheds light on the problem of the reconstruction theology of Ezra-Nehemiah. Applying these comments to the text of Ezra-Nehemiah, the problem of identity and distinctions suddenly makes sense. One can argue that identity creates the very problem it seeks to avoid.

Kobia believes a new Africa needs hope and dignity that can be provided by stressing ethics and humanity, giving voice to the voiceless, focusing on inclusiveness and hope, cultural mixing, and by being ecumenical.[22] In prophetic fashion, he declares, "the 21st century will be dominated by the politics of naming otherness, hence the need to comprehend ethnic/tribal identities as resources of diversity rather than differences to be condemned."[23] As a means of providing hope and creating a new African society, Kobia argues that we need to engage in reconstruction and renaissance. Among other issues, some of the central features of this reconstruction program for Africa are embracing life-giving values, democracy, a theology of development, people's participation in the political process, social transformation, and above all, the courage to hope.[24] In this age of globalization, it is also important to ensure that African people participate in decision making processes and that they are the ultimate beneficiaries of economic programs.

Conclusion

This paper has sought to defend the thesis that the drastic measures taken by Ezra and Nehemiah in their reconstruction efforts are understandable in their historical context. However, within that context, there are dissenting voices already, and consequently, an ambivalent attitude toward cultural mixing and assimilation especially as expressed in the problem of mixed marriages. I have also attempted to demonstrate that an uncritical appropriation of Ezra and Nehemiah's reconstruction theology can lead to divisiveness and conflict in the African context as it has also done in other contexts. Therefore, I have attempted to read the narratives

---

20. Ibid.
21. Ibid., 64.
22. Ibid.
23. WCC, *New Africa*, 77.
24. Kobia, *Hope*, ch. 7, 118–48.

of Ezra-Nehemiah as cautionary reminders in our often volatile world and modern communities of faith. Rather than stressing identity and distinction, Africa has a better chance of achieving lasting unity, peace, stability, success, and hope by stressing our common humanity and taking seriously the warning signs that are evident in a critical reading of the reconstruction program and theology of Ezra-Nehemiah.

WORKS CITED

Barber, Cyril J. *Nehemiah and the Dynamics of Effective Leadership.* Neptune, NJ: Loizeaux Brothers, 1976.

Blenkinsopp, Joseph. *Ezra-Nehemiah: A Commentary.* OTL. Philadelphia: Westminster, 1988.

Chipenda, Jose B., et al. *The Church of Africa: Towards a Theology of Reconstruction.* Nairobi: AACC, 1990.

DuBois, W. E. B. *The Souls of Black Folk.* New York: Knopf, 1993.

Fensham, F. Charles. *The Books of Ezra and Nehemiah.* NICOT. Grand Rapids: Eerdmans, 1982.

Keck, Leander E. *The New Interpreter's Bible: Kings–Judith.* Vol. 3. Nashville: Abingdon, 1999.

Kobia, Samuel. *The Courage to Hope: The Roots for a New Vision and the Calling of the Church in Africa.* Geneva: WCC, 2003.

Mana, Kä. *Christians and Churches of Africa: Salvation in Christ and Building a New African Society.* Maryknoll, NY: Orbis Books, 2004.

Mugambi, J. N. K., *African Christian Theology: An Introduction.* Nairobi: EAEP, 1992.

———. *Critiques of Christianity in African Literature.* Nairobi: EAEP, 1992.

Mugambi, J. N. K., and Laurenti Magesa, eds. *The Church in African Christianity: Innovative Essays in Ecclesiology.* Nairobi: Initiatives, 1990.

Ross, Jerome Clayton. *The History of Ancient Israel and Judah: A Compilation.* Pittsburgh: Dorrance, 2003.

Throntveit, Mark A. *Ezra-Nehemiah.* Interpretation. Louisville: Westminster John Knox, 1992.

White, John. *Excellence in Leadership: Reaching Goals with Prayer, Courage, and Determination.* Downers Grove, IL: InterVarsity Press, 1986.

Williamson, H. G. M. *Ezra and Nehemiah.* Sheffield: JSOT, 1987.

World Council of Churches. *For a New Africa with Hope and Dignity.* Geneva: WCC, 2004.

Collective Memory and Coloniality of Being, and Power as a Hermeneutical Framework: A Partialised Reading of Ezra-Nehemiah

Gerrie Snyman

Introduction: Disgraced

In an interview with BBC News in April 2006, Archbishop Desmond Tutu is reported to have said that the white community does not seem to have shown an appreciation for the incredible magnanimity of those who were the major victims of a system that benefited white people so much.[1] In August, a former apartheid cabinet-minister, Adriaan Vlok, asked the forgiveness of Rev. Frank Chikane, the director-general in the President's Office. In October 2006, another former apartheid cabinet minister, Dr. Stoffel van der Merwe, and currently chairperson of the board of the directors of the *Afrikanerbond*, formerly the *Broederbond*, claimed that the "Afrikaner" is tired of trudging, tired of apologizing, tired of being blamed.[2]

Antjie Krog asks whether the South African community have lost the ability to deal with the disgraced.[3] Nothing human is seen past the "distorted faces, punned names and mangled expressions" of perpetrators, whether black or white. Krog argues that there has been no room in civil society in which people are allowed to create a vocabulary of admitting to wrongdoing without being trashed. She misses a language of care: "[W]e will destroy everything we have achieved over the past sixteen years if we assume that we do not need a vocabulary of care—also and especially for the disgraced."

However, to develop a vocabulary of care for the disgraced (which I take to imply a perpetrator culture in which apartheid could thrive), the disgraced needs to develop an eye for the victim. In the congregation of which I am a member, I have never seen so much activity going on regarding taking care of the poor, in the

---

Originally published in *OTE* 20, no. 1 (2007): 53–83. Published here with permission.

1. Cf. Peter Biles, "Transcript: Desmond Tutu Interview," accessed October 2006. http://news.bbc.co.uk/2/hi/africa/4961144.stm.

2. Pieter du Toit, "Onder Vier oë: Broeders en Bog," *Beeld* (21 October 2006): 8.

3. Antjie Krog, "A Space for the Disgraced," *Mail & Guardian*, 15–21 September 2006, 31.

squatter camps of Olievenhoutbosch and the needy of Danville. Yet I have to hear a sermon in the Reformed Churches of South Africa (*Gereformeerde Kerke in Suid-Afrika*) about our complicity in maintaining apartheid. Four individual members risked appearing before the Truth and Reconciliation Commission to apologise, but the Synod failed miserably to send a deputation, despite the fact that many members were active in apartheid politics and large numbers of church members kept apartheid in place through their votes.

My Old Testament lecturer at seminary, Jaap Helberg, referring to war as a reality in Ps 137:9, made the following salient remark (my translation): "These words [Ps 137] should be seriously thought about: Those who are prepared to make war, should be prepared to follow it through into the fullest consequences of reality, and accept responsibility for it." [4]

To read the Bible in a literal way implies to translate the Israelite situation directly to the context of a congregation. Thus, if Israel was asked to discriminate against others because that is what obedience to God implies, that kind of obedience is transferred to a community 2000 years later. I have not seen that we have taken responsibility of the consequences of this kind of reading.

For this reason, I suggest that memory of apartheid should make us apprehensive of transferring ancient values of 2000 years ago as if they are divine revelation and universally applicable. To be more precise, memory of apartheid should indicate the untenability of the divine nature we have attributed to some of these values. What I am pleading for is to let the memory of apartheid be part of the hermeneutical framework in reading the Bible.

To argue my case, allow me to illustrate the dilemma with a problematic reading and sermon within the RCSA of the strange or foreign women in Ezra 9–10. To address my concerns and support my appeal, I intend looking at the following: the role of memory, coloniality of being and power and whiteness within a perpetrator culture, a theology of reconstruction and another understanding of the strange women in Ezra 9–10.

EZRA 9–10: BENEVOLENCE AND ATROCITY

This sermon[5] represents something of what Kä Mana in his book on the theology of reconstruction, refers to as *l'imaginaire*: it is the entire constellation of a group's beliefs, patterns of thought and the inner drive that motivates behaviour in particular circumstances.[6]

---

4. Jaap L. Helberg, *Verklaring en Prediking van die Ou Testament* (Potchefstroom, South Africa: PTP, 1983), 123.

5. See http://www.gkcenturion.org.za/prediking17b.html. The sermon was written by Rev. Martin van Helden of the *Gereformeerde Kerk*, Centurion.

6. Kä Mana, *L'afrique va-t-elle Mourir?* (Paris: Editions du Cerf, 1991), 6, borrows the term from Albert Camus's *La Peste*. In his book he analyses the *imaginaire social* of contemporary black Africa in her collection of myths, utopias, and expectations. Cf. also Valentin

The message of the sermon is summarised by its topic or heading: *Obedience to Yahweh (God) costs a lot sometimes.* In the story, Ezra learns from his leaders that the people did not set themselves apart from what is said to be the alien population. He was shocked and grieved over the people's unfaithfulness and neglect of God's commands. After having prayed and confessed, it was decided that the only way to make amends is to take strong action. The people were assembled and asked to repent by cutting themselves off from the people of the land and from the foreign wives. However, the assembly was hesitant and requested a commission to investigate the matter and to list the culprits. But the story is not clear on whether the people thus named did in fact dismiss their foreign wives and children. Ezra 10:44 simply states that they all had married foreign women and amongst them there were women with children.

Referring to these foreign women as heathens, the sermon formulates the problem in terms of the probability of these women leading the men astray by practicing idolatry, a path away from the true religion revealed by God. The covenant, a concept that plays a major role in the sermon, needs to be maintained and kept holy. Intermarriage will jeopardise this project. Moreover, these intermarriages are sacrilegious and the men need to submit themselves to a process of purification.

The sermon acknowledges the human catastrophe that is about to take place, but the atrocity is brushed aside in favour of the argument that faithlessness of the people towards God cannot be tolerated. God demands obedience, even when it concerns drastic measures that would end in a heartless deed. The counter-arguments based on the infringement of human rights and the accusation of ethnic cleansing are discarded, because nothing dare stand in the Lord's way. Yielding to these arguments amounts to yielding to sin.

The audience of the sermon is a white middle class faith community whose cohesion is seriously weakened by secular society's erosion of its boundaries.[7] Not only do they perceive that Christianity is under threat, but also that their interpretation of the Bible in terms of norms and values are no longer absolute. The relativising of their norms and values is regarded with suspicion and interpreted as an attack on the authority of the Bible.

From this story, the sermon deduces a rule regarding marriage. A believer or confessing Christian cannot marry someone from outside his or her faith. The faithful and the unfaithful cannot share the same bed. What is more, children

---

Dedji, "The Ethical Redemption of African *Imaginaire*: Kä Mana's Theology of Reconstruction," *JRA* 31, no. 3 (2001): 254–72.

7. David Janzen, *Witch Hunts, Purity, and Social Boundaries: The Expulsion of the Foreign Women in Ezra 9–10* (Sheffield: Sheffield Academic Press, 2002) 54, states that societies with strong external boundaries and weakening internal cohesion will out of necessity institute acts of purification when a particular disquiet sets in about the society's increasing inability to continue to comply with values and norms that used to have been held high by communities.

should be taught that their choices of friends are important. Even differences within church may pose a problem.

The message of the sermon is one of conversion: Israel has been liberated from exile and their reaction to the gracious act should have been repentance. Repentance implies obedience to God's word. One should be more obedient to God than to other human beings. Moreover, the separation between faith and unbelief must be drawn sharper. Therefore, the congregation is called to be obedient to God no matter the cost in contrast to the world that remains disobedient. As a deterrent the preacher installs fear in the congregation by invoking judgement in the last days.

I was struck by the ease with which perpetrators were turned into martyrs for doing the will of God. In the safe space of the disgraced, to use Krog's term, this community within the Calvinist tradition, was led to deliberate about their relationship with God with the help of a text that brings forth in me a memory of the past, namely apartheid's *Prohibition of Mixed Marriages Act no. 55 of 1949* and the *Immorality Amendment Act no. 21 of 1950*. The sermon does not legitimate apartheid, but it employs the same argument that has been used in the legitimating of apartheid: If God proclaims it, it is right and the believer must follow suit.

In my quest[8] to understand how it was possible for pious and honest people to justify apartheid from the biblical text, the sermon's use of the biblical text unexpectedly gave me an inkling: *Uncritical acceptance as benevolent everything the text says*. Relating an argument to God is the ultimate argument against which no one can bring anything.

Reading the biblical text as a benevolent text blinds the reader for the possibility that the text itself may be oppressive. What I miss from the sermon is subjectivity, a problem Africa has in general with what she calls the Western perspective that reduces the human to an object.[9] The sermon rejects subjectivity outright. God's demands are dictatorial and there simply are no excuses. Without any sensitivity or care for the victim, it expresses a theology of the powerful, in which the perpetrators would become victims of God's wrath if they do not comply.

How would one interpret this story taking into account racism, the power of whiteness and middle class values, in effect the entire history of colonialism? I cannot escape the fact that my own existence is the product of sexual relations in the second half of the seventeenth century between a Christian (presumably Protestant) Dutch soldier and a "heathen" Asian woman, a union drowned by sinful lust and oppressive patriarchy.[10] Nor can I escape the function this text with its

8. Cf. Gerrie Snyman, "Social Identity and South African Biblical Hermeneutics: A Struggle against Prejudice?" *JTSA* 121 (2005): 34–55; idem, "The Rhetoric of Shame in Religious and Political Discourses: Constructing the Perpetrator in South African Academic Discourse," *OTE* 19, no. 1(2006): 183–204.

9. Kä Mana, *Mourir?* 62.

10. Gerrie Snyman, "Playing the Role of Perpetrator in the World of Academia in South Africa," *BOTSA* 12 (2002): 8–20.

concomitant parts in Deuteronomy once played in the theological justification of apartheid.

My origins make it rather difficult to read the story of the strange women in Ezra as a benevolent revelation of God. I cannot imagine him sending away children and mothers from the fathers for the simple fact that they are from a different culture and religion. The vividness of that separation makes it extremely difficult to accept the theological sense attributed to the story by the sermon. In fact, not only did the story underscore my problematic origins, but it also highlighted in my thinking the coloniality of power, my whiteness, my share in the perpetration of apartheid.

Between Tutu's remark about lack of appreciation and Krog's reference to a life of disgrace, there appears to be a need to develop a hermeneutic that will enable those who are associated with a perpetrator disgraced culture to reconstruct themselves. A hermeneutic that fails to take seriously the effects of reading would be powerless to address the concerns of those dealing with the bad memories of the past and the construction of a new identity.

MEMORY

The history of colonialism left us with what seems to be an incommensurable difference between indigenous Africans and settled[11] Africans. For example, there is a marked difference between the indigenous African's way of being in the land and the settled African's claim of possession.[12] As will be seen when I discuss the coloniality of power, apartheid left us with two separate communal identities with two separate memories trying to live in one space.[13]

---

11. In postcolonial studies the usual reference is between indigenous and settler. But the slogan "one settler, one bullet" of the apartheid struggle implies that settlers are invaders and not committed to the continent. The phrase "settled African," I hope, would indicate those of colonial origins who have settled permanently in Africa. However, the claim of incommensurability may undermine the notion of a settled African, as the Western way of thinking within which the settled African was educated may differ from an indigenous African's way of thinking about the self and identity. Cf. Jane Haggis, "Beyond Race and Whiteness? Reflections on the New Abolitionists and an Australian Critical Whiteness Studies," *Borderlands e-journal* 3, no. 2 (2004): §22. Accessed 21 September 2006. http://www .borderlandsejournal.adelaide.edu.au/vol3no2_2004/haggis_beyond.htm.

12. Haggis, "Beyond Race?" §20.

13. For example, memories of happy family holidays in Durban occur with the memory of being deprived and marginalised by being unable to (legally prohibited) go to the beach. The process of colonisation in South Africa is largely regarded by the colonisers as benign, comparatively peaceful, and filled with good intentions. It is perhaps not that gentle, passive, and non-confrontational, but the end result is regarded as being of tremendous value: strong economy, infrastructures, etc. To the colonised, the process was far from being benign. It evokes a memory of oppression and limitation to freedom. Cf. Jan Larbalestier, "White over Black: Discourses of Whiteness in Australian Culture," *Borderlands e-journal* 3, no. 2

POSTCOLONIAL PERSPECTIVES

These two identities are not of equal strength. The one with the political power would be able to enforce his or her memory on society. Brian Havel refers to *official public memory* that is a deliberate attempt by ruling elites to influence public recollection of the past.[14] In what appears to be very similar to James Scott's "public transcript,"[15] official public memory is the construction of a claim that seeks to supersede actual memory to displace or assimilate competing memories. It treats the past as a construct that serves ideological purposes while, at the same time, constructing a canonical past.[16]

Havel regards the official public memory as an imposture from its inception, a "product of drastic selectivity."[17] In constructing a claim about a past occurrence, it culls, organises and reformulates supporting data, giving official public memory its constructivist nature. It is less concerned with historical fidelity than with re-working and extrapolating data in order to simplify a complex past that would fit a canonical master narrative. It absorbs any counter-narrative that may challenge its hegemony.[18] As an instrument of the state, official public memory serves the purpose of social control of the citizens in order to achieve social stability and order. Memory is not only based on a struggle, but it can become a site of struggle if the memory is one of a conflicted past. It is a struggle over power and who gets to decide the future.[19] The ruling elite's use of power to inscribe a particular memory is pervasive.

Remembered events are more political than objective facts. As social constructs they cannot be understood as natural objects with an existence outside language. They are 'plastic' and open to construction and reconstruction to serve other ideological needs.[20]

Havel appeals to the omnipresent contestation of official public memory. Mindful recollection and conscious observation cannot bring about authentic recapture. Official public memory cannot mask the emotional and affective resonance that an individual retains of the past. For this reason, Havel introduces the concept of affectivity into memory, that is, the memory of how an individual felt in the past,

---

(2004). Accessed on 21 September 2006. http://www.borderlands ejournal.adelaide.edu .au/ vol3no2_2004/larbales tier_white.htm, §24–5.

14. Brian Havel, "In Search of a Theory of Public Memory: The State, the Individual, and Marcel Proust," *ILJ* 80 (2005): 608.

15. James A. Scott, *Domination and the Arts of Resistance: Hidden Transcripts* (New Haven: Yale, 1991), 4. A public transcript suggests a discourse in public by which the ruling elite maintain power and the subordinates their position of subservience. A public transcript refers to the self-portrait of those in power as they see themselves. It also constitutes the ideology that they want the subordinates to accept.

16. Havel, "Public Memory," 616, 668, 670.

17. Ibid., 680.

18. Ibid., 632–635.

19. Ibid., 653.

20. Ibid., 698.

the capacity to experience emotional resonance with the past. It is an autonomous condition of lived experience, which defines and limits the reach of official public memory.[21]

The basis of affective memory is Marcel Proust's monumental work *À la recherche du temps perdu*. In the first book, *Du côté de chez Swann*, Proust ruminates on his sensations when taking a sip of tea and a crumb of a Petite Madeleine between his lips:

> Et bientôt, machinalement, accablé par la morne journeé et la perspective d'un triste lendemain, je portai à mes lèvres une cuillerée du thé où j'avais laissé s'amollir un morceau de madeleine. Mais à l'instant même où la gorgée mêlée de miettes de gâteau toucha mon palais, je tressaillis, attentive à ce qui se passait d'extraordinaire en moi.[22]

When one hears a noise, smells a scent, savors a taste or see something from the past, the past sensation surges forward and pushes against present reality, forcing itself into consciousness. In personal memory, says Havel, there is a core of heightened affectivity that has no analogy in the structural memory work of official public memory.[23] What are experienced are fragments of existence that have escaped from time. The affectivity of personal memory cannot be imitated by official public memory. This ability to transcend makes official memory dull and unspecific. Proust illustrates how affective memory can overcome the distance that separates the recall of an event from the lived experience of those events.[24]

Paul Ricoeur refers to the duty of memory.[25] It is a duty to do justice to another than the self. He refers to the indebtedness to those who have gone before us for part of what we are. The duty of memory is not a mere preservation of material traces (documents, films, videos, letters) of past events, but encompasses the feeling of being obligated with respect to these others of whom will be said later not that they are no more, but that they were. In the act of remembering the moral priority goes to the victim that is other than ourselves.

To Marc Augé the duty to remember is of special concern to those who have not been direct witnesses or victims of events that is preserved in memory. Those who have endured apartheid need not be reminded of their duty to remember. But those who have not been victims, who therefore would be unable to conjure up affectivity towards these experiences, will find it difficult to imagine. The duty of memory is intended for the descendants of victimised and perpetrator com-

---

21. Ibid., 714–20.

22. Proust, *Swann*, 58–59: "And soon, mechanically, overwhelmed by the overcast day and the perspective of a dismal next day, I took to my lips a spoonful of tea in which I have left to soften a piece of madeleine. But the moment the mouthful mixture of crumbs of cake touched my palette, I got a thrill, carefully noting the extraordinary that took place in me."

23. Havel, "Public Memory," 715–16.

24. Ibid., 719. See also 610.

25. Paul Ricoeur, *Memory, History, Forgetting* (Chicago: University of Chicago Press, 2004), 89.

munities and people not directly related to the events of suffering themselves. The duty to remember brings about vigilance, imagining in the present what might resemble the past, remembering the past as present, returning to the present to find the hideous shape of the unspeakable again, says Augé.[26]

Trauma survivors have an impaired ability to forget central features of disturbing events.[27] However, the brain has a metabolic feature that proves to be indispensable for one's sanity: the function of memory is to flush and void. Failure to flush the memory leads to an incapacity for thought, as was the case for the main character in Jorge Luis Borges's story "Funes the Memorious." Having fallen from a horse at age eighteen, Funes found it impossible to forget anything and he dies eventually of too much detail that has been preserved in his memory![28]

But preserving memories can overwhelm our capacity to remember. On the one hand, to forget is a human way to cope with information overload. On the other hand, intentional forgetting becomes wilful exclusion as certain events are simply ignored. Bjorn Krondorfer opts for the term "oblivion" that is less emotionally charged and asks whether one can grant a perpetrator and his or her descendants the privilege of oblivion.[29] From his experience perpetrators usually resist acknowledgement of individual wrongdoing in collective evil and fail to recognise the full weight of their moral failure as human beings. Subsequently, perpetrators blend out the perspective of the victim. When evil is committed within a collective identity, the individual does not see the cruelty of the deeds in the moment of the atrocity. For this reason, argues Krondorfer, perpetrators remember correctly when they fail to recollect the victim or fail to ascribe agency to themselves. After all, the victim has always been absent from their sight. To block out the victim, is an act of oblivion: "Oblivion as the refusal of a memory that requires the acknowledgement of one's own moral failure is ultimately a resistance to the spillage of shame."[30] Ironically, such a refusal gives the perpetrator back his or her humanity. Krondorfer argues: "If we want perpetrators to be morally accountable, we must grant them the right to be human, the right to oblivion, and yet also allow for the possibility that they are able to acknowledge and repent the evilness of their deeds."[31]

To return to the sermon: One has to grant the minister who constructed the sermon his right to oblivion. But within a faith community that has been up to now unable to acknowledge their complicity as church members in the moral failure of the apartheid system, oblivion looks more like wilful exclusion. Add to this

---

26. Marc Augé, *Oblivion* (Minneapolis: University of Minnesota Press, 2004), 87–88.

27. Havel, "Public Memory," 698.

28. Jorge Luis Borges, "Funes, the Memorious," in *Imagining Language: An Anthology*, ed. Jed Rasula and Steve McCaffery (Cambridge: MIT Press, 1998), 320–24.

29. Bjorn Krondorfer, "Is Forgetting Reprehensible? Holocaust Remembrance and the Task of Oblivion," *JRE* 36, no. 2 (2008): 233–67.

30. Ibid., 264.

31. Ibid., 265.

the blending out of a victim perspective by claiming obedience to God. The exclusion of subjectivity forces the reader to keep the victim absent from view.[32] Failure to keep the victim in view is part of the West's mythopraxis, the *imaginaire* that was instrumental in colonialism, namely the coloniality of power.

COLONIALITY OF BEING AND POWER

South African President Thabo Mbeki's reference at the Fourth Annual Nelson Mandela lecture[33] at the University of the Witwatersrand to the individual acquisition of material wealth as a defining social value in the organisation of white society that negatively influenced indigenous African societies in South Africa brought into play the coloniality of being and the geopolitics of knowledge.[34]

Coloniality of being and power suggests patterns of power that are the result of colonialism and which defines relationships of power long after the demise of colonial structures. Coloniality outlives colonialism. A coloniality of power suggests some form of power or domination by the former colonial masters and coloniality of being suggests a "conversion (to the ideals of Christianity, to civilization and progress, to modernization and development, to Western democracy and the market) or by adaptation and assimilation (the willingness of the native elites in the colonies to embrace imperial designs and values leading to colonial subject formation). That is, it means accepting dwelling in the coloniality of being by narcotizing the colonial wound, ignoring it with all sorts of painkillers."[35]

For example, a coloniality of power was established when the name "America" was imposed on that continent by European Christians at a time when Europe was the central and privileged continent with the power of naming. Since then particular imperial epistemic privileges remained in place: the universal idea of human being as well as the universal idea of a planet validated by a Christian idea

---

32. The absence of women is conspicuous at the synods of the RCSA. The past decisions about women in the ministry are in tandem with their exclusion from representation.

33. Thabo Mbeki, "Fourth Annual Nelson Mandela Lecture by President Thabo Mbeki, University of the Witwatersrand 2006." Accessed 26 September 2006. http://www.info.gov .za/speeches/2006 /06073111151005.htm. He argued that "the new order born of the victory in 1994 inherited a *well-entrenched value system* that placed individual acquisition of wealth at the very centre of the value system of our society as a whole."

34. The annual lecture left me a bit bewildered, since a few years ago President Mbeki, as adjunct-president under former President Nelson Mandela, declared in Parliament that a subject like biblical studies is no longer worthy to pursue in a technocratic society. But here he becomes a man of ethical principle locating him in the moral universe while condemning greed and the deification of personal wealth on the basis of, inter alia, a few biblical texts. See also Charles Villa-Vicencio, "SA Needs to Dig Deeper for its Soul," *Sunday Independent*, 27 August 2006, 8.

35. Walter D. Mignolo, *The Idea of Latin America* (Blackwell Manifestos; Malden, MA: Blackwell, 2005), 77.

of continental division. [36]A coloniality of power is evident in the 9th century so-called "Christian T-in-O" map. It shows a tripartite division of Asia, Europe and Africa, but Asia takes the top half and Europe and Africa each shares a quarter of the other half. This division is only found in Western Christianity and each part is assigned to one of the sons of Noah.[37]

Coloniality is the darker side of modernity.[38] Its geo- and body politics remain hidden:

> The overall classification and ranking of the world do not just reveal a reality out there, in the world, that they reflect, like in a mirror. They also hide the fact that such classification and ranking are valid only from a "given perspective" or locus of enunciation—the geo-historical and bio-graphical experience of the knowing subject of the philosophical principles of theology, the historical experiences of Western Christians, and the way of looking at the world as a male. [39]

The epistemological privilege of the West implies that its reality is assumed to be the reality that matters. It is their experiences that become universal and that ultimately define reality, not only for themselves but also for others. Their definition becomes authoritative. Racism then emerges when the authority to define gives one ethnic group the privilege to classify people in terms of the concepts of that particular group.

For example, Heidegger regarded Europe to have been in a crisis due to nihilism and rootlessness. As an antidote for Germany, he prescribed the Athenian myth in which the city's greatness resided in its citizens and the soil.[40] His geopolitics is a politics of epistemic racism and imperialism, which is regarded as an intrinsic part of the Western *imaginaire*. He thought the people could not do without Europe's achievements; he thought the French could no longer get by without Germany; he regarded the USA as a land without history; the Jews were thought to be rootless and urban. Even Levinas, who challenged his thoughts, remained within the limits he set in looking for the relevance of Judaism within the *Western* world (Europe). However, Heidegger and Levinas forgot Fanon's wretched of the earth, those found in the wastelands of empires, countries or cities.[41] Says Maldonado-Torres (2001:36): "The forgetfulness of the damned is part of the veritable sickness of the

---

36. Ibid., 151–52. The name "Africa" is apparently rooted in an ancient Egyptian word meaning good or beautiful.

37. Ibid., 24–26. With the realisation that there is indeed a fourth continent, the T-in-O map was invisibly imposed upon Ortelius's *Orbis Universalis Terrarum*. The Americas were conceived of as a continent separated from Asia, Africa, and Europe.

38. Nelson Maldonado-Torres, "The Topology of Being and the Geopolitics of Knowledge: Modernity, Empire, Coloniality," *City* 8, no. 1 (2001): 39.

39. Mignolo, *Latin America*, 15.

40. Maldonado-Torres, "Topology," 31.

41. Frantz Fanon, *The Wretched of the Earth* (New York: Grove Press, 1991).

West, a sickness that could be likened to a state of amnesia that leads to murder, destruction and epistemic will to power—with good conscience."[42]

Is it is a forgetfulness similar to the sermon's forgetfulness of the damned in Ezra 9–10, the foreign women and their children, the consequence of the West's *imaginaire* in which a particular geopolitics and spatiality subconsciously receive a privileged epistemic position?

The sermon's distinction between belief and unbelief is in line with the typical Western construction of binary oppositions.[43] The context of the sermon is white middle class men and women in a religious community in whose broader context there is a dispute about women in the ministry.[44] With the colour line largely broken, the significant ill against which the congregation needs to be vaccinated is that which would take them away from their true Christian self. The foreign women become the pagan or heathen and the idolater, two concepts the believers would claim from their memory of what they have been taught in the church. The construction in the sermon is understandable in the light of Wynter's explanation of the Western *imaginaire*. The effect, though, is that the foreign women are reduced to non-being.

The discourse of coloniality ascribes to whiteness, as a continuous part of the colonising force, a particular privilege. However, Nobel Prize–winner for literature J. M. Coetzee (a former South African citizen) rejects the power and privilege colonialism bestowed upon him.[45] In an interview he queried the possibility to

---

42. Maldonado-Torres, "Topology," 36.

43. Sylvia Wynter, "Unsettling the Coloniality of Being/Power/Truth/Freedom towards the Human, after Man, It's Overrepresentation—An Argument," *TNCR* 3, no. 3 (2003).

44. Gerrie Snyman, "Telling Women to Be Like Men? Some Theoretical Aspects Regarding the Interpretation of the Bible on Gender Issues," *Koers* 67, no. 1 (2002): 1–26.

45. Fiona Probyn, "J. M. Coetzee: Writing with/out Authority," *Jouvert* 7, no. 1 (2002), accessed 21 September 2006 (http://english.chass.ncsu.edu/jouvert/v7is1/probyn .htm), and idem, "Playing Chicken at the Intersection: The White Critic of Whiteness," *Borderlands e-journal* 3, no. 2 (2004). Accessed 21 September 2006. http://www.borderlands ejournal.adelaide.edu.au/vol3no2_2004/probyn–playing.htm. Coetzee argued that he is a white male without authority in South Africa in contrast to the images of power and privilege associated with white men in the country (§15). He later emigrated to Australia where the agency of white Australians appears to be central to its imagined nation: a society with a mix of cultures brought together by the goodwill of whites, a showcase of benign whiteness (cf. Rachel Standfield, "'A Remarkably Tolerant Nation'? Constructions of Benign Whiteness in Australian Political Discourse," *Borderlands e-journal* 3, no. 2 (2004). Accessed 21 September 2006. http://www.borderlandsejournal.adelaide.edu.au/vol3no2_2004/stand-field_tolerantnation.htm §30). Australia is a white-majority society where the racialised nature of power and privilege remain masked or hidden (Haggis, "Beyond Race?" §4). The position of weakness lies with the Aborigines, and power and privilege are indeed associated with white men.

question power from the position of power. He wanted to do it from a position of weakness.[46]

A position of weakness is indicated by the construction of whiteness along the lines of disempowerment. In other words, other entanglements of power complicate whiteness, so that it appears less privileged and more palatable. In the process, whiteness is never owned directly. It is mitigated by other circumstances, for example I am white *and* middle class, or white *and* male, or white *and* privileged.[47] As a social category, whiteness encompasses numerous interests and intersects with other categories. Whiteness constitutes diverse groupings. However, over against that which is not white, whiteness presents itself in a homogeneity in which other categories with which it intersects, are suppressed or overridden.[48]

In the film *Forrest Gump*, whiteness receives a social injury and Forrest Gump is rendered discursively black through the analogy between his mental and physical disability and black social disenfranchisement. Segregation is rewritten "as a discourse of injury no longer specific to black bodies, which installs whiteness as injury; and they define that injury as private, motivated not by a social system but by prejudices and moral lacks of individuals who seem simply not to know better."[49] Gump's injury is a negation of privilege.

It is a question in what way whiteness in South Africa still operates as an ordering principle that organises the social discourses of race privileging those classified as white. In terms of political power in a liberal democracy with black majority rule whiteness lost its political privilege. However, there is still a coloniality of power in the economical sphere, with the largest companies still in white (male) hands.[50] What about smaller fields such as parochial religious groupings? In these instances, social reproduction of dominance and privilege takes place without any intention of domination and oppression in the minds of the white social actors. They are simply unaware of the broader meanings and implications of their dispositions, practices and habits, that is, their coloniality of power.[51]

Whiteness within black discourse is constructed in ways fairly diverse from its construction in white discourse. In the former whiteness is constructed as dominance and exclusion. In the latter the discourse does not always testify to

---

46. Probyn, "Playing Chicken," §2.

47. In a reverse way white feminists come under scrutiny by black feminists for being white. In this instance, you are not only a feminist, but also a white (or black) feminist. Subsequently, gender oppression becomes hierarchical.

48. Simeon Moran, "White Lives in Focus: Connecting Social Praxis, Subjectivity, and Privilege," *Borderlands e-journal* 3, no. 2 (2004). Accessed 21 September 2006. http://www .borderlandsejournal.adelaide .edu.au/vol3no2_2004/moran_lives.htm §16.

49. Robyn Wiegman, "Whiteness Studies and the Paradox of Particularity," *Boundary 2* 26, no. 3 (1999): 124, 127.

50. Ann Crotty and Renée Bonorchis, "Where Is the New (Corporate) South Africa?" *Sunday Independent,* 29 October 2006, 9.

51. Moran, "White Lives," §5.

any awareness regarding the structural location of privilege.[52] The reproduction of racialised systems of knowledge, power and privilege is rooted in ignorance with the result that the knowledge systems appear to be natural and part of the common sense ordering of reality, a phenomenon remarkably similar to religious fundamentalism in Western Protestant Christianity. Moreover, this blissful ignorance feeds the collective fantasies of being good and of being a just society:

> The epistemic, symbolic and physical violences which sustain the racial hierarchy, in both the past and the present, are repressed to maintain both personal and collective fantasies of being good selves and a just and equitable society. Thus repression and denial are psychic mechanisms that function to manage the incompatibility between manifest aggression and the fantasised good self.[53]

I am aware that to think beyond race in a country that is still racially divided is tantamount to build castles in the air. Racism is not undone once we have seen through it.[54] In addition, racism is not merely located in the epidermal reality of a white or black skin, but in a myriad of complex, contradictory and competing discourses and discursive practices that are always contested.[55] If racism is a system of a relationship of power, hierarchy and privilege that remains invisible, then perhaps the task is not to deny one's location in these practices of oppression but to develop ways of exploring one's complicity. Nevertheless, it remains an extremely discomforting process.[56]

To own whiteness is to liberate a white into being a perpetrator. But this is not a very satisfying role as no one bothers to inquire into what happens in the space of the disgraced, as Krog argued.[57] Yet, the "revelation" of whiteness must go somewhere. I am left with two options: Either convert others to own their whiteness, or, faced with the horrors of the role of being an oppressor, think through the ambiguity and ambivalence of the position of perpetratorhood and trace its paradoxical nature in one's own praxis.

Perpetrators

The sermon's interpretation of the foreign women in Ezra 9–10 called my attention to our understanding of racism. Racism does not merely declare that if you are black, you are inferior. It says that if you are not like me, you are inferior. Racism goes beyond the physical characteristics pertaining to blood and colour to include

---

52. Ibid., §18.

53. Ibid., §37.

54. Sara Ahmed, "Declarations of Whiteness: The Non-Performativity of Anti-Racism," *Borderlands e-journal* 3, no. 2 (2004). Accessed 21 September 2006. http://www.borderlands ejournal.adelaide.edu.au/vol3no2_2004/ahmed_declarations. html §48.

55. Karen Anijar, "Into the Heart of Whiteness," *AJB* 3, no. 2 (2003): 29.

56. Haggis, "Beyond Race?" §24.

57. Snyman, "Role of Perpetrator," 8–20.

the interpersonal realm of human activities, like language, religion, knowledge, nationality and countries and continents.[58] What is problematic in the sermon's interpretation of the story is the divine sanction attributed to the racism found in the text. The ability to read in a benevolent way a biblical story that links God to cruelty, has been fundamental to the perpetuation of apartheid by church-going pious men and women, people like me, my parents, my grandparents and great-grandparents. The biblical text was read to justify a coloniality of power. I am not sure that we have moved away significantly from this kind of hermeneutic or have developed a critical sensibility towards apartheid so that it can become an irrita-tion for our belief in a just God.[59] The community in which I live and in which I practice my faith has not yet developed an eye for a coloniality of being.

Just after World War II, German theologians were unable to express any consciousness of the significance of the Holocaust for Christianity. For example, Theodor Wurm, who was influenced by the German monarchy and expressed a strong nationalist perspective, put Germany in the same salvational framework as Israel: the same God elected both and both suffered the same fate.

> Wenn die nachkriegsdeutsche Kirche dem deutschen Volk in seinem Schiksal helfen will, dann predigt sie ihm das gleiche, was Jesaja dem Volk Israel verkün-det hat, den verborgenen Gott des Alten Testaments, der plötzlich hervorbrechen und Neues schaffen kan für seine deutschen Knechte auserwählt im Ofen des Elends.[60]

But the furnaces of misery in Auschwitz were filled with Jews, Poles, Gypsies and Soviet nationals, all subordinated to the Nazi ruling elite.

According to Krondorfer, Wurm's statement expresses a mixture of the mis-siological consciousness of the monarchic period, a national victim mentality and

---

58. Mignolo, *Latin America*, 17.

59. Norbert Reck, "Der Blick Auf Die Täter—Zur Einführung," in *Mit Blick Auf Die Täter. Fragen an Die Deutsche Theologie Nach 1945,* ed. Bjorn Krondorfer and Katharina von Kellenbach (Gütersloh: Gütersloher Verlaghaus, 2006), 12, argues that in the last years of the Nazi-regime the churches and theologians did not experience the reports about the death camps as an irritation for their belief in a just God. And sixty years later, the ques-tion remains: How was it possible that the murderers in the Holocaust could have been Christians? Reck (13) says: "Anstelle der nervösen *Abkehr* von der, Vergangenheit kommt der traditionelle Weg der *Umkehr* wieder in den Blick: die reuevolle Betrachtung des Ge-schehens, das Eingestehen eigenen Versagens und die Arbeit an der Überwindung irriger Vorstellungen."

60. Bjorn Krondorfer, "Nationalsozialismus Und Holocaust in Autobiographien Prot-estantischer Theologen," in Krondorfer and Kellenbach, *Mit Blick Auf Die Täter*, 70: "If the post-war German church wants to help the German people with their fate, she must preach to them the same message Isaiah once proclaimed to Israel, the hidden God of the Old Tes-tament who suddenly breaks through and creates something new for his German servants selected in the furnace of misery."

a traditional anti-Jewish historical theology.[61] Wurm returns to a biblical and his-torical-theological model that allows him to draw fatal comparisons between the German people and the people of Israel. Krondorfer calls it an unholy historical-theological pulp (*unseligen, geschichtstheologischen Brei*) in which an awareness of guilt disappears in favour of a vulnerability vis-á-vis the allied victors, making them (the Germans) the real victims of Auschwitz.[62]

Norbert Reck sees more or less the same in Karl Rahner. Rahner saw the prob-lem as unbelief, a process that originated in the European emancipation history and whose aim was to set free humanity, to discover the autonomous personality of unassailable worth. Reck argues that Rahner remains unable to link German guilt as failure to acknowledge God to specific concrete perpetrations. All he can ask is a return to God. The guilt remains vague and creates an insufferable burden from which one can only pray (without real hope) to be relieved.[63]

Joseph Ratzinger, the current pope (Benedict XVI) also sees National-Social-ism as unbelief and Hitler's victory was a victory for an anti-Christian apocalypti-cal period.[64] He operates from a natural contrast between Nazis and Christians. The question of guilt concerns belief in God or unbelief, and not the atrocities committed to Jews. The Nazi-period is judged, but not exposed.

Another theologian, Helmut Thielicke, recognises guilt towards the victims of the Holocaust. He was prohibited by the Gestapo to publish books and to deliver public speeches. His teaching permit was also withdrawn. However, on closer scrutiny, thus Krondorfer, his rhetoric is filled with self-pity and cast as a national Passion narrative.[65] The real victim is the ill-treated German, and the perpetrator the Allied justice. His autobiography is regarded as total absorption with the own suffering to the exclusion of the suffering of other. Thielicke rejected the denazifi-cation process, and renounced it as "Seelenmord" and "Glaubensmord", an anti-Christian course of action with a murderous goal![66]

Krondorfer deplores Thielicke's unwillingness to question himself.[67] He consid-ers Thielicke's theology to be a deceiving illusion of guiltlessness. Thielicke's depic-tion of his own discrimination by the Gestapo, and the suffering of the Germans in general, presents Krondorfer with a harmless picture of National Socialism, a political thinking that has shortly blinded people and caused them only to err briefly. However, it was more systemic than Thielicke thought.

---

61. Ibid., 71.

62. Ibid., 72.

63. Norbert Reck, " '. . . Er vervolgt die Schuld der Väter an den Söhnen und Enkeln, an der Dritten und Vierten Generation' (Ex 34,7): Nationalsozialismus, Holocaust und Schuld in den Augen Treier Katholischer Generationen," in Krondorfer and Kellenbach, *Mit Blick Auf Die Täter*, 180–82.

64. Ibid., 200.

65. Krondorfer, "Holocaust," 85.

66. Ibid., 105, 109.

67. Ibid., 101, 110.

One will look in vain for a theological and narrative presence of the victim in the autobiographies of most German theologians just after the war. They focussed on a new beginning, a reconstruction of the land and society, a program of re-Christinianising of the German people.[68] For this reason a lot of energy went into the counselling of perpetrators in the internment camps and prisons. The victims of national socialist persecution did not get any attention, or at least, not those who survived. Factually, very few Jews were left in Germany.

Besides the physical absence of Jews in Germany after the war, there is a theological reason why there was a lack of focus on the victim. Katharina von Kellenbach refers to the distinction between the Jewish and Christian traditions towards reconciliation.[69] In the Jewish tradition, reconciliation with God is only possible once reconciliation between human beings has been achieved. The damage must be repaired or compensated and the victim must be asked for forgiveness. The request for forgiveness and the compensation restores the worthiness of the victim. The restoration of the dignity of the victim has not been taken over by the Christian tradition's doctrine of redemption. The perpetrator can be released without being confronted with his or her victim who is compelled to give up any claim to restitution or reparation. Reconciliation with God is more important, but according to Von Kellenbach, it means that the victim is disparaged and condemned to silence.

Von Kellenbach's idea of reconciliation is based on Claudia Card's atrocity paradigm.[70] The atrocity paradigm does not focus on the innocence of the victim. Innocence is neither necessary nor sufficient for suffering to count as evil.[71] The presumption is simply that no one should have to suffer atrocities, regardless of individual character.

The atrocity paradigm assumes a relationship of dependence between the perpetrator and victim. The perpetrator stands in debt to the victim and is unable to freely liberate him or herself from this position. It stands the victim free to liberate the perpetrator or to request reparation or restitution. Perpetrator dependency on the victim cannot be solved by a substitutionary reconciliation of the traditional Christian doctrine of redemption and reconciliation in Christ.[72] Moreover, argues Von Kellenbach, such a one-sided reconciliation act renders the integrity of the Christian doctrine of redemption questionable.

Emphasis on God's power and omnipotence within the reconciliation process leaves the perpetrators' responsibility towards the victims of no consequence. It is

---

68. Ibid., 115.

69. Katharina von Kellenbach, "Schuld Und Vergebung. Zur Deutschen Praxis Christlicher Versöhnung," in Krondorfer and Kellenbach, *Mit Blick Auf Die Täter*, 266–67.

70. Claudia Card, *The Atrocity Paradigm: A Theory of Evil* (Oxford: OUP, 2002).

71. Ibid., 13.

72. Von Kellenbach, "Schuld," 271–73.

only in the confrontation with the consequences of cruelty within the life of a victim that a perpetrator is able to recognise the destructive force of his or her acts.[73]

THEOLOGY OF RECONSTRUCTION

After World War II, Germany embarked on a radical reconstruction initiative with the help of the Allied forces that occupied them. After all, the country was physically in ruins. However, with very few Jews left, the victims of the Holocaust did not really come in sight.

After the demise of the apartheid system in 1994, the newly born nation embarked on a Reconstruction and Development programme that changed gear to become GEAR (growth, employment and redistribution strategy), only to change gear into a developmental state with Pres. Mbeki's Nelson Mandela lecture. A new world order required a new understanding of the blossoming South African state.

Similarly, in his book, Jesse N. K. Mugambi referred to a new world order that requires a new understanding of the church and a new corresponding theology.[74] He suggests a theology of reconstruction that would correct the distortions imposed on the world by imperialism.[75] The missionary has an obligation to listen to the newly formed Christian community and become a partner instead of an overlord, whereas Africans must carry their own cross in the context of their own cultural limitations and opportunities.[76]

Mugambi finds the Bible abounding with examples of social reconstruction. After the exile, Ezra and Nehemiah, the characters in the books as well as the books themselves, became the matrix for his theology of reconstruction.[77] However, Elewani Farisani finds this concept of reconstruction theology incapable of examining the ideologies embedded in the biblical text. He says that by using the reconstruction theme in Ezra-Nehemiah without isolating the ideological agenda

---

73. Ibid.

74. Jesse N. K. Mugambi, *From Liberation to Reconstruction: African Christian Theology after the Cold War* (Nairobi: East African Educational Publishers, 1995), xv. He based his reconstruction on the metaphor provided by the Peters Projection, a geographical map of the world that reflects each country in an equitable way. See Gerrie Snyman, "Eurocentrism and Africantrism: What Is Western/African Research?" in *Research, Identity, and Rationalism: Thinking about Theological Research in Africa,* ed. Cornel W. Du Toit (Pretoria: RITR, 2002), 5–9.

75. Mugambi. *Reconstruction*, 12.

76. Ibid., xvi. In contrast, Tinyiko S. Maluleke, "The Proposal for Theology of Reconstruction: A Critical Appraisal," *Missionalia* 22, no. 3 (1994): 245–58, does not provide much space for these "missionaries" as he suspects them of a liberal agenda trivialising liberation theology.

77. Ibid., 13.

of the text, reconstruction is identified as that which is driven by the returned exiles at the exclusion of the *am ha'aretz*.[78]

In fact, Mosala once argued for an approach to reading the Bible that will be able to recognise the texts as products of definite historical and social material conditions.[79] These texts are the sites of struggles that caused their production: "[T]hey radically and indelibly bear the marks of their origins and history."[80] One not only finds in the biblical texts records of historical, cultural, gender and social struggles, but these texts become themselves a *site* of struggle as well as a *weapon* of struggle.[81] To him, not everything in the Bible is on the side of human rights or of the oppressed and marginalised people. Moreover, oppressive texts cannot be totally tamed or subverted into liberating texts. Failing to recognise that, would mean that oppressors and exploiters in the text become comrades in arms.[82]

Mugambi fails to do sociological analyses that will enable him to get behind the ideological issues embedded in these texts.[83] He appears to read the text and accept the code in which the message has been inscribed. Thus, the biblical text remains an innocent and transparent container of messages in which possible signified practices of oppression go largely unrecognised.

In response to criticisms of his first book, Mugambi wrote a second one, invoking the call of the builders of the wall of Jerusalem in Neh 2:18.[84] He compares Nehemiah to Moses' spiritual emancipation at the burning bush. Nehemiah leaves the luxurious life in the palace to lead a project of reconstruction, which is regarded as "essentially a spiritual project, inspired by the inner commitment to do the will of God."[85] Nehemiah becomes a larger figure than Moses in epitomising endeavours to rebuild Africa out of the ruins of the wars against racism, colonial domination and ideological branding.

Nehemiah's leadership in terms of managerial knowledge and experience is evoked. His ability to mobilise skills and resources to accomplish the building, is what attracts Mugambi.[86] He views Nehemiah and his power in a benevolent

---

78. Elelwani Farisani, "The Ideologically Biased Use of Ezra-Nehemiah in a Quest for an African Theology of Reconstruction," *OTE* 15, no. 3 (2002): 633.

79. Itumeleng Mosala, *Biblical Hermeneutics and Black Theology in South Africa* (Grand Rapids: Eerdmans, 1989), 7: "This approach should also recognize that these texts are *productions*, or 'signifying practices,' that reconstitute in very specific ways the realities of the material conditions of which they are the products."

80. Ibid., 20.

81. Ibid., 11.

82. Ibid., 30–31.

83. Elelwani Farisani, "The use of Ezra-Nehemiah in a Quest for an African Theology of Reconstruction," *JTSA* 116 (2003): 27–50.

84. Jesse N. K. Mugambi, *Christian Theology and Social Reconstruction* (Nairobi: Acton, 2003).

85. Ibid., 68.

86. Ibid., 58–59.

way. However, not everybody's skills are welcome. There is a limit. As with Ezra and Nehemiah, the foreign women are not welcome. Those who married them are shunned (Neh 13:28).

It is an exclusion I experienced in Mugambi's brief reply to a debate in the *Bulletin for Old Testament Studies in Africa,* where he distinguishes between African and Africanist scholarship according to which a white academic is Africanist and not African.[87] Mugambi does not refer to the colonial remnant in his geographical context of Kenya. They are, according to Chris McGreal's perception in the *Guardian* newspaper in the UK a "30,000-strong white community, which, through more than 40 years of black rule, has clung to its privileged lifestyle—and in the case of 12 or so old settler families, great swathes of land—largely by keeping its collective head down."[88] In avoiding politics and public life, they did not become integrated socially, and would thus be, in Mugambi's experience, Africanists.

Where would Ezra's, and Nehemiah's, handling of the situation of the foreign women leave the reconstruction theologian regarding the colonial remnant in an African country? Portraying the white academic as Africanist and not African pushes the colonial remnant to the margins. Add to this the current debate on the ills of Western culture, does the colonial remnant not become a polluting agency, a site of impurity?

For Kä Mana's reconstruction theology, the West's polluting agency is pathological[89] in the African *imaginaire* and Africa needs psychic reform to change the implantation of the West into African minds. The imaginary of Africa has been broken in the sense that people are dehumanised and conditioned to see themselves without any human possibilities. Africa thinks she is already predetermined by the fatality of certain political and social contingencies so that she cut herself off from innovation and creativity.

In response to Western domination, Africa developed a mythic cultural identity in French speaking Africa with the concept *Négritude* with its precursor in African-American circles' search for their African roots.[90] It is within this context that young Africans in Paris in 1930 started to think about their roots, giving birth to the Négritude movement of *inter alia* Aimé Césaire and Leopold Senghor. Nonetheless, Kä Mana is of the opinion that the concept of Négritude gave Africa a false consciousness of grandeur, a fictive glory disconnected from the African reality.[91] Under Négritude, argues Kä Mana, African identity turned out to be without a soul. It was a magic word that would open the door of the cavern. Only, according to Kä Mana, the cavern never existed. It was a chimera. Moreover, under the cloak

---

87. Mugambi, "African and Africanist Scholarship," *BOTSA* 14 (2003): 9–12.

88. "A Lost World," *Mail & Guardian,* 27 October–2 November 2006, 34.

89. Kä Mana, *Mourir?* 58, 66. Africa is entranced by the world that dominates it politically, economically, and culturally, despite being the symbol of her misery.

90. Ibid., 68.

91. Ibid., 71.

of Négritude, several political and economic movements promoting the African personality have reduced African culture to an amusing folklore that drowned any creative energy in a sea of submission to a single language of power, glorifying new leaders by dance and poetry and turning the people to the simple function of *griot*, a mixture of poets, musicians and sorcerers. Cultural identity became a worthless weapon (*un arme de pacotille*) against the more powerful. Incapable of addressing the more powerful (the colonisers, the West, men), cultural identity transformed into a power of new black masters over their black brothers.[92]

EZRA 9–10: THE STRANGE WOMEN

What good is there in a text like Ezra 9–10 for a theology of reconstruction? It depends where one sides oneself along the axis of power. If one has power, this text will exclude groups of people of a particular identity. From a subordinated position, the employment of the text to define a particular identity may be experienced, yet again, as discrimination. If the text invites us to inquire from an exilic consciousness, from the perspective of their worries and experiences, does it mean one can follow the imperative at all costs?[93]

After the building of the temple and Passover (Ezra 6:16–22), Ezra was sent to Jerusalem to establish the temple service. A few families accompanied him (Ezra 7). On arrival in Jerusalem, Ezra assumed his leadership position (Ezra 8), and the leaders visited him to bemoan the fact that the people, the priests and the Levites did not separate themselves from the peoples of the land (Ezra 9). One finds a similar need for separation from the people of the land or local inhabitants and foreign peoples of Ammon and Moab in Neh 10 and 13.[94]

The expulsion of defenceless women and children and their abandonment to an unknown fate can be understood within the framework of purity and impurity laws. The feminine is associated with the unclean, signifying an "irreparable trauma at the core of Jewish identity."[95] The narrative attests to a situation in which women

92. Ibid., 77. He (14) suggests a transformation, which is not a question of transforming the relationship with the West, but a process of reconditioning the conscience, the heart, the imagination, and the spirit.

93. Daniel L. Smith, "The Politics of Ezra: Sociological Indicators of Postexilic Judean Society," in *Second Temple Studies. 1, Persian Period,* ed. Philip R Davies (Sheffield: Sheffield Academic Press, 1991), 97.

94. Daniel L. Smith-Christopher, "The Mixed Marriage Crisis in Ezra 9–10 and Nehemiah 13: A Study of the Sociology of the Post-exilic Judean Community," in *Second Temple Studies 2, Temple Community in the Persian Period,* ed. Tamara C. Eskenazi and Kent H. Richards (Sheffield: Sheffield Academic Press, 1994), 259, the problem of mixed marriages in Nehemiah is a political problem that involved the Jewish aristocracy, that is, marriage of convenience.

95. Harold C. Washington, "Israel's Holy Seed and the Foreign Women of Ezra-Nehemiah: A Kristevan Reading," *BibInt* 11 nos. 3–4 (2003): 428.

bore the brunt of a larger social conflict.[96] This conflict resulted in a confrontation between the different population groups that inhabited Jerusalem and environments when Ezra returned. The story has us believe that the land was empty, *terra nullius*, with everyone being deported to Babylonia. However, only the cream of the population, the ruling elite, was deported. Most of the population remained in Judea, and they were still there when Ezra returned. But they are not recognised by Ezra and Nehemiah. They are simply grouped together with the people of the land, whom the story accuses of idolatry.

Eskenazi ascribes to the presence of the foreign women an economic and political basis. Her evidence is the Elephantine texts' picture of women in the Jewish community who can divorce husbands, hold property, buy, sell and inherit. The ability to inherit could present a problem in the community of Yehud. If this was indeed the case, land could be lost to these women when their husbands die.[97]

Philip Esler regards the Books of Ezra and Nehemiah as narratives that reconstruct or re-invent their ethnic identities.[98] He argues that the exile and the subsequent return entailed major adjustments for the people concerned. They had to deal with major challenges. For example, survival in exile, as captives in a foreign land without access to an ancestral cultic centre, requires other ways of maintaining an identity and establishing boundaries that separated them from outsiders. On return, they had to establish yet again their identity and set up new boundaries to secure their survival in fresh circumstances. From their point of view, a return to those measures that defined their identity before the exile in order to restore what they have lost in terms of the temple and the cult, was a possibility. But given the time span between the exile and the return, it would have been difficult to install a precise copy of what has been before the exile. They were rather forced to engage in cultural imagining and engineering *de novo*. The people they encountered in Jerusalem at their return were not particularly receiving them with open arms. To succeed, they had to reinvent themselves.

For this reason, Ezra drew up a list (Ezra 2) to indicate who will constitute the people and who will play powerful roles.[99] Only those listed would constitute the new Israel. But this list contains names of men who cannot prove whether they once belonged to Israel. Nevertheless, they could become part of the new rein-

96. See Gerrie Snyman, "Carnival in Jerusalem: Power and Subversiveness in the Early Second Temple Period," *OTE* 9, no. 1 (1996): 88–110. Tamara Eskenazi's ("Out From the Shadows: Biblical Women in the Postexilic Era," *JSOT* 54 [1992]: 36) remark is noteworthy: "In reflecting on the subject of foreign wives, it is important to remember that an opposition to foreign women, so easy to criticize from a distance, is at the same time an affirmation of women who belong to the group."

97. Eskenazi, "Shadows," 31, 33.

98. Philip Esler, "Ezra-Nehemiah as a Narrative of (Re-invented) Israelite Identity," *BibInt* 11, nos. 3–4 (2003): 417.

99. Ibid., 419.

vented identity of Israel, if and when they separate themselves from the pollution of the nations (Ezra 6:21).

On the basis that the list is not cast in iron, Harold Washington (2003:431) asks why was it impossible for the foreign women to join.[100] A possible answer could be Esler's assumption that with intermarriage the maintenance of a particular ethnic identity turns out to be hazardous in facilitating the adoption of the culture and the concomitant religious cult of the foreign spouse.[101] But the narrative never states that those who married had indeed abandoned their worship of Yahweh. It is as if the narrative cannot follow through its own injunction. The problem appears to be a blurring of boundaries that constitute a breach of the divine commandment in Deuteronomy 7:3–4. Ezra's concern, according to Esler is that the symbolic boundary that has been breached needs to be reinstated, no matter if the means is draconian in nature resulting in the divorce of wives who do not fit the criteria and the abandonment of children.[102]

The leaders tell Ezra with which nations the people of Israel appeared to have mixed. Ezra tore his clothes (Ezra 9:1–5) and prayed (Ezra 9:6–15), whereupon the Israelite community in Jerusalem decided to separate from these foreign women (Ezra 10:1–11). But that project seemed a bit too overwhelming, and a commission was constituted to look into the matter (Ezra 12–17). The commission indeed found quite a few perpetrators and their names were published (Ezra 18–44). The story simply concludes with the following: "All these had married foreign women, and some of them had children by these wives."[103]

The reference to the holy seed in verse 2 and the defilement of the land in verse 11 are of considerable interest. Washington observes a particular gendered construction at work in the story in terms of the holy seed (*zara' haqadosh*, Ezra 9:2)[104] that indicates the community's holiness. Over against the community's holiness the narrator posits a threatening contaminant, the impurity (*niddah*, Ezra 9:11). This impurity is usually associated with female menstrual activities. The *holy seed* is a male symbol of purity and *niddah* is linked to female pollution. Says Washington: "This language therefore unavoidably positions women as signifiers of the stranger within. The female body represents … the abject, that which must be expelled."[105]

---

100. Washington, "Holy Seed," 431.

101. Esler, "Ezra-Nehemiah ," 421.

102. Ibid.

103. The Masoretic text is said to be corrupt here and some translations follow 1 Esdras 9:36. However, the LXX (2 Esdras 10:44) follows the Masoretic text.

104. Washington, "Holy Seed," 431. Smith-Christopher ("Mixed Marriage," 256) states that the term "holy seed" indicates group xenophobia. Smith ("The Politics," 97) interprets Ezra's use of exclusive terms as the preoccupation of a self-conscious community to preserve itself in a religious and in a material sense. They formulated a theology of innocence and purity against the defilement of those who remained behind.

105. Ibid., 431.

In other words, the body reflects what is going on in society. Washington argues that purity as a signifier of holiness implies the integrity of a society:

> The language of purity and impurity takes the individual body as a symbol for—a microcosm of—the larger social body. Concern about things entering and exiting the body, foods, excretions and secretions, signify anxiety about the boundaries of a society. Bodily orifices represent those boundaries themselves.[106]

In Ezra 9:11 these orifices represent insecure boundaries: "They have filled it with their impure ways from end to end" (*mapeh el peh*), which literally means from mouth to mouth.[107] Cultic impurity is graphically placed as a defilement in the mouth, "stirring in the reader an irresistible urge to expel, a nauseous desire to vomit . . . the abject." The land defiled with a pollution (*erets niddah*) signifies a similar expulsion and relates to the discharge of menstrual blood. The stigma of people defiling the land is presented in feminine terms, turning the foreign women into objects of abjection and exclusion.[108]

CONCLUSION

It is quite ironical that Ricoeur's original book, *La Mémoire, L'histoire, L'oubli*, was published when a debate in France about the role of the French in Algeria in the colonial period was raging.[109] The only problem was that Ricoeur failed to address French colonial memory. It was as if the memory of colonialism in France was repressed, distorted and forced in a book that discussed repressed, forced and manipulated memory. Says Abdelmajid Hannoum: "Yet the publication of a book on memory void of any discussion of the memory of colonialism, in the midst of an intense debate about the Algerian war, is an interesting coincidence."[110] France has elected to eradicate three centuries of colonialism from its memory, choosing as the founding event of its identity the bourgeois revolution.

In this essay, the issue of memory and forgetting put Western thinking in the spotlight. To many the Holocaust and its memory serve as a test case for the humanistic and universalistic claims of Western civilisation. Perhaps the same is true for the memory of apartheid. Bible reading that fails to bring into play the experience of apartheid in terms of white complicity (coloniality of power) might refer to a fundamental inability to accept difference and otherness and a failure to

---

106. Ibid., 432. See also Hennie Viviers, "The Politics of Bodily Disability," *Scriptura* 90, no. 3 (2005): 799.

107. Ibid., 433.

108. Ibid., 435.

109. Paul Ricoeur, *La Mémoire, L'histoire, L'oubli* (Paris: Seuil, 2000).

110. Abdelmajid Hannoum, "Paul Ricoeur on Memory," *TCS* 22, no. 6 (2005): 134.

draw the consequences from the insidious relationship between modernity and apartheid.[111]

The official public memory of apartheid left white identity with a scar. In Ezra 9–10, women are scarred for their impurity in being female. Apartheid was not simply a brief aberration, but was systemic and a logical consequence of the Western *imaginaire*. Denial or suppression of subjectivity disables the reader to take the victim in his or her view. When the Bible is read for others, denial of subjectivity (a hallmark of coloniality of power) has the possibility to reduce those who will bear the marks of reading to non-being (a hallmark of coloniality of being).

My main problem with the sermon is that coloniality of power in the reading process translates into a failure to take the victims' situation in the text seriously. This failure, in turn, enables the reader to commit cruel acts in the name of God, thereby continuing coloniality of power. A hermeneutic that remains insensitive to oppressive biblical texts, disempowers the reader to construct a new way of being after apartheid. It is a forgetfulness similar to Ezra 9–10's forgetfulness of the damned, the foreign women and their children. It is a forgetfulness set off by the West's *imaginaire* that favours a particular geopolitics and spatiality. The latter makes for an affective memory that is disparate from the affective memories of discrimination and humiliation of a coloniality of being. Because of an incommensurable difference between a coloniality of power and a coloniality of being the official public memory will always be open for contestation.

The affective memory of coloniality of power is one of benevolence, but it will always be in tension with the memory of discrimination and humiliation which mark coloniality of being. Everyone likes to be good, but those structures that make us feel good need to be challenged. One such challenge is the practice of reading the Bible as a benevolent text. The assumed benevolence masks those texts that are oppressive and its cruelty hides behind the will of God. And doing the will of God is what about every Christian intends to do. It makes one feel good and not evil.

I believe apartheid shattered the belief in a benevolent biblical text and those still in the sphere of a coloniality of power need a critical sensibility to recognise oppressiveness in biblical texts. Ezra and Nehemiah's handling of the foreign women render their reconstruction projects questionable. Reading the story of the strange women in Ezra 9–10 in terms of the patriarchal world view of holy seed and impurity might explain the thinking behind the construction of the story in the postexilic period. But one should realise, without recognition of coloniality the concept of foreign women may become an ideal metaphor to legitimate the Western *imaginaire*'s binarity of salvation/selectedness versus significant ill/dysselectedness. After apartheid, I am left with some serious questions about the story's moral vision, even when God is drawn into the argument.

111. Andreas Huyssen, "Monument and Memory in a Postmodern Age," in *The Art of Memory: Holocaust Memorials in History,* ed. James E. Young (New York: Prestel Verlag, 1994), 10.

Works Cited

Ahmed, Sara, "Declarations of Whiteness: The Non-Performativity of Anti-racism," *Border-lands e-journal* 3, no. 2 (2004). Accessed 21 September 2006. http://www.borderlands ejournal.adelaide.edu.au/vol3no2_2004/ahmed_declarations.html.

Anijar, Karen. "Into the Heart of Whiteness," *AJB* 3, no. 2 (2003): 29–31.

Augé, Marc. *Oblivion*. Minneapolis: University of Minnesota Press, 2004.

Biles, Peter, "Transcript: Desmond Tutu Interview." Accessed October 2006. http://news .bbc.co.uk/2/hi/africa/4961144.stm.

Card, Claudia. *The Atrocity Paradigm. A Theory of Evil*. Oxford: Oxford University Press, 2002.

Crotty, Ann, and Renée Bonorchis. "Where Is the New (Corporate) South Africa?" *Sunday Independent*, 29 October 2006, 9.

Davies, Philip R. *Second Temple Studies: 1 Persian Period*. Sheffield: Sheffield Academic Press, 1991.

Dedji, Valentin, "The Ethical Redemption of African *Imaginaire*: Kä Mana's Theology of Reconstruction." *JRA* 31, no. 3 (2001): 254–74.

Du Toit, Cornel W. *Research, Identity, and Rationalism: Thinking about Theological Research in Africa*. Pretoria: Research Institute for Theology and Religion, Unisa, 2002.

Du Toit, Pieter. "Onder Vier Oë: Broeders en Bog." *Beeld*, 21 October 2006, 8.

Eskenazi, Tamara C., "Out from the Shadows: Biblical Women in the Postexilic Era." *JSOT* 54 (1992): 25–43.

Eskenazi, Tamara C., and Kent H. Richards, eds. *Second Temple Studies. 2 Temple Community in the Persian Period*. Sheffield: Sheffield Academic Press, 1994.

Esler, Philip. "Ezra-Nehemiah as a Narrative of (Re-invented) Israelite Identity," *BibInt* 11, nos. 3–4 (2003): 413–26.

Farisani, Elelwani, "The Ideologically Biased Use of Ezra-Nehemiah in a Quest for an African Theology of Reconstruction." *OTE* 15, no. 3 (2002): 628–46.

———. "The Use of Ezra-Nehemiah in a Quest for an African Theology of Reconstruction." *JTSA* 116 (2003): 27–50.

Haggis, Jane, "Beyond Race and Rhiteness? Reflections on the New Abolitionists and an Australian Critical Whiteness Studies." *Borderlands e-journal* 3, no. 2 (2004). Accessed 21 September 2006. http://www.borderlandsjournal.adelaide.edu.au/vol3no2_2004/ haggis_beyond.htm, Accessed 2006/09/21.

Hannoum, Abdelmajid. "Paul Ricoeur on Memory," *TCC* 22, no. 6 (2005): 123–37.

Havel, Brian. "In Search of a Theory of Public Memory: The State, the Individual, and Marcel Proust," *ILJ* 80 (2005): 605–726.

Helberg, Jaap L. *Verklaring en Prediking van die Ou Testament*. Potchefstroom, South Africa: Potchefstroomse Teologiese Publikasies, 1983.

Janzen, David. *Witch Hunts, Purity, and Social Boundaries: The Expulsion of the Foreign Women in Ezra 9–10*. JSOTSup 350. Sheffield: Sheffield Academic Press, 2002.

Krog, Antjie. "A Space for the Disgraced." *Mail & Guardian*, 15–21 September 2006, 31.

Krondorfer, Bjorn, and Katharina von Kellenbach. *Mit Blick Auf Die Täter: Fragen an Die Deutsche Theologie Nach 1945*. Gütersloh: Gütersloher Verlaghaus, 2006.

Krondorfer, Bjorn. "Is Forgetting Reprehensible? Holocaust Remembrance and the Task of Oblivion." *JRE* 36, no. 2 (2008): 233–67.

Larbalestier, Jan, "White Over Black: Discourses of Whiteness in Australian Culture." *Bor-*

derlands e-journal 3, no. 2 (2004). Accessed 21 September 2006. http://www.borderlands ejournal.adelaide.edu.au/vol3no2_2004/larbalestier_ white.htm.

Maldonado-Torres, Nelson. "The Topology of Being and the Geopolitics of Knowledge: Modernity, Empire, Coloniality." *City* 8, no. 1 (2001): 29–56.

Maluleke, Tinyiko S. "The Proposal for Theology of Reconstruction: A Critical Appraisal." *Missionalia* 22, no. 3 (1994): 245–58.

Mana, Kä. *L'afrique Va-t-elle Mourir?* Paris: Editions du Cerf, 1991.

Mbeki, Thabo. "Fourth Annual Nelson Mandela Lecture by President Thabo Mbeki," University of the Witwatersrand, 2006. Accessed 26 September 2006. http://www.info.gov.za/speeches/2006 /06073111151005.htm.

McGreal, Chris, "A Lost World." *Mail & Guardian*, 27 October–2 November 2006, 34.

Mignolo, Walter D. *The Idea of Latin America*. Blackwell Manifestos. Malden, MA: Blackwell, 2005.

Moran, Simeon. "White Lives in Focus: Connecting Social Praxis, Subjectivity, and Privilege." *Borderlands e-journal* 3, no. 2 (2004). Accessed 21 September 2006. http://www .borderlandsejournal.adelaide.edu.au/vol3no2_2004/moran_lives.htm.

Mosala, Itumeleng J. *Biblical Hermeneutics and Black Theology in South Africa*. Grand Rapids: Eerdmans, 1989.

Mugambi, Jesse N. K. "African and Africanist Scholarship." *BOTSA* 14 (2003): 9–12.

———. *Christian Theology and Social Reconstruction*. Nairobi: Acton, 2003.

———. *From Liberation to Reconstruction: African Christian Theology after the Cold War*. Nairobi: East African Educational Publishers, 1995.

Probyn, Fiona. "J. M. Coetzee: Writing with/out Authority." *Jouvert* 7, no. 1 (2002). Accessed 21 September 2006. http://english.chass.ncsu.edu/jouvert/v7is1/probyn.htm.

———. "Playing Chicken at the Intersection: The White Critic of Whiteness." *Borderlands e-journal* 3, no. 2 (2004). Accessed 21 September 2006. http://www.borderlandsejournal .adelaide.edu.au/vol3no2_2004/probyn–playing.htm.

Proust, Marcel. *À la Recherche du Temps perdu: Du Coté de Chez Swann*. Paris: Gallimard, 1954.

Rasula, Jed, and Steve McCaffery. *Imagining Language: An Anthology*. Cambridge, MA: MIT Press, 1998.

Ricoeur, Paul. *La Mémoire, L'histoire, L'oubli*. Paris: Seuil, 2000.

———. *Memory, History, Forgetting*. Chicago: University of Chicago Press, 2004.

Scott, James. *Domination and the Arts of Resistance: Hidden Transcripts*. New Haven: Yale University Press, 1990.

Snyman, Gerrie F. "Carnival in Jerusalem: Power and Subversiveness in the Early Second Temple Period." *OTE* 9, no. 1 (1996): 88–110.

———. "Playing the Role of Perpetrator in the World of Academia in South Africa." *BOTSA* 12 (2002): 8–20.

———. "The Rhetoric of Shame in Religious and Political Discourses: Constructing the Perpetrator in South African Academic Discourse." *OTE* 19, no. 1 (2006): 183–204.

———. "Social Identity and South African Biblical Hermeneutics: A Struggle against Prejudice?" *JTSA* 121 (2005): 34–55.

———. "Telling Women to Be Like Men? Some Theoretical Aspects Regarding the Interpretation of the Bible on Gender Issues." *Koers* 67, no. 1 (2002): 1–26.

Standfield, Rachel. " 'A Remarkably Tolerant Nation'? Constructions of Benign Whiteness in Australian Political Discourse." *Borderlands e-journal* 3, no. 2 (2004). Accessed 21 September 2006. http://www.borderlandsejournal.adelaide.edu.au/vol3no2_2004/standfield _tolerantnation.htm.

Villa-Vicencio, Charles. "SA Needs to Dig Deeper for Its Soul." *Sunday Independent*, 27 August 2006, 8.

Viviers, Hennie. "The Politics of Bodily Disability." *Scriptura* 90, no. 3 (2005): 799–808.

Washington, Harold C. "Israel's Holy Seed and the Foreign Women of Ezra-Nehemiah: A Kristevan Reading." *BibInt* 11, nos. 3–4 (2003): 427–37.

Westcott, R. "Witnessing Whiteness: Articulating Race and the 'Politics of Style.'" *Borderlands e-journal* 3, no. 2. Accessed 21 September 2006. http://www.borderlandsejournal .adelaide.edu.au/vol3no2_2004/westcott_ witnessing.htm.

Wiegman, Robyn. "Whiteness Studies and the Paradox of Particularity." *Boundary* 2 26, no. 3 (1999): 115–50.

Wynter, Sylvia. "Unsettling the Coloniality of Being/Power/Truth/Freedom towards the Human, after Man, Its Overrepresentation—An Argument." *NCR* 3, no. 3 (2003): 257–337.

Young, James E. *The Art of Memory: Holocaust Memorials in History.* New York: Prestel Verlag, 1994.

7. SOCIAL ENGAGEMENT AND BIBLICAL INTERPRETATIONS

"Hermeneutics of Transformation?"
A Critical Exploration of the Model of Social Engagement between Biblical Scholars and Faith Communities

Sarojini Nadar

As a biblical scholar, and graduate student of Gerald West, I feel greatly honoured to critically reflect on my esteemed supervisor's model of social engagement. My dissertation centred on social engagement and the biblical scholar.[1] What follows is a dialogue between his work and that of my own. This chapter will seek to explore the ideological, academic and socio-political implications of the model of social engagement as advocated and developed by Gerald West, during the past two decades. It will do so through an examination of three focus areas, namely, *motivation*, *method* and *representation*.

Motivation

The question raised here concerns the motivation and rationale behind social engagement. At the 1983 Azanian People's Organisation (azapo) Congress, held in Lenasia, South Africa, in a paper entitled "Black Theology Revisited," Itumeleng Jerry Mosala made the following observation:

> Theologians and Christian activists must first be rooted in a community before they can begin to evoke a theology meaningful and challenging for and with a community. As painfully "slow" as the process may seem at times, anything less than this would still be elitist or paternalistic.[2]

Originally published in *Scriptura* 93 (2006): 339–51. Published here with permission.

1. Sarojini Nadar, "Power, Ideology, and Interpretation/s: Womanist and Literary Perspectives on the Book of Esther as Resources for Gender-Social Transformation" (Ph.D. diss., University of Natal, 2003).

2. I am grateful to Gary Leonard for allowing me to use this quote from his unpublished paper, "Revelation in the Information Society: Escaping our Cultural Boxes," presented at the ICCJ Youth Conference, Madrid, July 2000. See Itumeleng Jerry Mosala, "Black Theology Revisited," paper presented at Azapo Congress (Lenasia, 1983).

Some theological scholars in South Africa have attempted to rise to Mosala's challenge. As Kwame Bediako remarked during a presentation given recently at the University of KwaZulu-Natal, the uniqueness of African theological scholarship is that it works with what he termed, "living data." This claim of Mosala and Bediako seems more difficult for biblical scholars than theological scholars, for how can a biblical scholar work with "living data" when the primary source is actually a *written* text, in this case the Bible, or as what Emily Dickinson characteristically described as "an antique volume written by faded men."[3]

Yet, biblical scholars in Southern Africa and in Africa have attempted to do precisely this—to engage, challenge and work with "living data." The 1996 *Semeia* volume *"Reading With": African Overtures* is testimony of this. Here scholars argued persuasively for an engagement between biblical scholars and faith communities, not just as a way to produce "meaningful" biblical scholarship, but as a way to *transform* society. As John Pobee can cogently argue:

> The scholarly study of Scripture is not an island unto itself; it is answerable to the hopes and fears of the society in which it is done. . .I do affirm the accountability of scholarship to the community of faith. . .In short, the Bible proves central in and for human transformation in Africa and elsewhere.[4]

If we take what Mosala, Bediako and Pobee are saying seriously, the motivation for a hermeneutical model of social engagement can be three-fold:

1. Scholarship must be firmly rooted in the community if it is to be meaningful;
2. Scholarship that fails to engage "living data" can be considered elitist and paternalistic;
3. Scholarship must be responsible to the community, if it is to have the potential to transform.

In this article, I will argue that of these three underlying principles of social engagement the third is the most important, leading to what I would call a *hermeneutic of transformation*. As I have argued elsewhere, "a hermeneutic of transformation cannot be applied to the text. A hermeneutic of transformation can only be applied and tested within a community of real readers."[5] This leads to the all-important issue of method. Simply put, the question revolves around two related core issues.

---

3. Emily Dickinson, *The Complete Poems of Emily Dickinson, with an Introduction by Her Niece Martha Dickinson Bianchi* (Boston: Little, Brown, 1924).

4. John S. Pobee, "Bible Study in Africa: A Passover of Language," *Semeia* 73 (1996): 161–80, 162.

5. Nadar, *Power*, 175.

What Does This Method of Social Engagement Imply, and Who Does It Involve?

Method

Gerald West can be credited with pioneering a methodology that engages with real readers outside of the academy. Leaning heavily upon literary modes of reading the biblical text, West has developed what has become known as the "Contextual Bible Study" (*hereafter,* CBS) method.[6] This methodology, although proving a good tool for social engagement, contains certain epistemological problems. To explicate these, I suggest three crucial questions that need to be answered:

(a) What is the aim of the CBS?
(b) Who are the participants in the CBS?
(c) Who is the facilitator and what is the facilitator's role in the CBS?

What Is the Aim of Contextual Bible Study?

If social transformation is to be taken seriously, the aim of the CBS method should be to enable, or at least initiate discussion around social transformation. In order for this to be meaningful, I submit that such method has to be interventionist, while still respecting the community of faith. This however is not the primary aim of the CBS method as described by West and practiced by the Institute for the Study of the Bible (*hereafter,* ISB) now known as the Ujamaa Centre. Commenting on issues of process West makes the following comment:

> The socially engaged biblical scholar is called to read the Bible with them, but not because they need to be conscientised and given interpretations relevant to their context. No, socially engaged biblical scholars are called to collaborate with them because they bring with them additional interpretative resources which may be of use to the community group.[7]

West is here clearly making a case for a non-interventionist strategy on the part of the scholar. Although he provides cogent arguments for this, I submit that the reason he argues against an interventionist model has more to do with his own social identity and location[8] than with his need to respect a community's own interpretative resources, although I doubt that this forms part of his original equation.

6. Gerald West, "Contextual Bible Study in South Africa: A Resource for Reclaiming and Regaining Land, Dignity, and Identity," in *Towards an Agenda for Contextual Theology: Essays in Honour of Albert Nolan,* ed. T. McGlory, T. Speckman, and Larry T. Kaufmann (Pietermaritzburg: Cluster, 2001), 169–84.

7. Gerald West. "Contextual Bible Study in South Africa: A Resource for Reclaiming and Regaining Land, Dignity, and Identity," in *The Bible in Africa: Transactions, Trajectories, and Trends,* ed. Gerald West and Musa W. Dube (Leiden: Brill, 2000), 601.

8. Given that most of the participants in West's CBS's are black, female, and poor as opposed to his social position as a privileged white male.

As a socially engaged, South African Indian Christian woman scholar, I strongly make the case for a conscientisation motive, or interventionist method. An apt way to explain this conscientisation motive is through the wisdom gleaned from a famous Chinese fortune cookie—"Knowing and not doing are equal to not knowing at all."[9] In other words, sharing the liberating knowledge gained from my academic work, and helping to transform the ways in which my community understands the roles of women in church and society, is what makes my knowledge valuable. Socially un-applied knowledge gained in the academy becomes therefore equivalent to "not knowing at all."

Arguing against this view, West calls for a shift of focus of the socially engaged biblical scholar. Utilising the analysis of James Scott, of the way in which the dominated react to their domination, West argues that while the oppressed possess creative ways of dealing with their oppression, they often do not exhibit them because revolution is a dangerous process. Instead, the dominated exhibit a public transcript of subservience until the situation is no longer threatening, after which they activate their hidden transcript of resistance. According to West, the role of the biblical scholar is to activate the hidden transcript of the oppressed, although he freely admits that he is not sure that biblical scholars ever have access to the hidden transcript.[10] I find agreement with West on this point, that the dominated do possess creative ways of dealing with their domination. Scott quotes an engaging Ethiopian proverb to illustrate this point—"When the peasant Lord walks past, the peasant bows very low and silently farts."[11] On this point, West and Scott agree, that the power of the resistance of the dominated lies in the power of their silent fart! Although an interesting simile, I would argue that the silent resistance of the dominated, although admirable, does not result in their much-needed social transformation.

For Latin American liberation scholars, the dominated are in need of conscientisation. I find agreement with this assertion, my contention being that it is only during a period of conscientisation that the hidden transcript (if one exists at all) can be activated. This point has been ably demonstrated in the various community Bible studies I have conducted. Although space does not permit me to give much detail, it is significant to note that the aim of the CBS method, as espoused by West is not centrally motivated by conscientisation, although it is conceded that conscientisation can be a by-product of the CBS process.

---

9. Quoted in E. Messer-Davidow, *Disciplining Feminism: From Social Activism to Academic Discourse* (Durham, NC: Duke University Press, 2002), 1.

10. James C. Scott, *Domination and the Arts of Resistance: Hidden Transcripts* (New Haven and London: Yale University Press, 1990); Gerald West, *The Academy of the Poor: Towards a Dialogical Reading of the Bible* (Sheffield: Sheffield Academic Press, 1999), 39–52.

11. The full and correct quote reads as follows: "when the great lord passes the wise peasant bows deeply and silently farts" (see Scott, *Domination*, epigraph, v).

Who are the Participants in the Bible Study?

The term "ordinary reader" has come to represent those in the faith community with whom scholars engage.[12] West and Dube define the term "ordinary" in the following way:

> The term 'ordinary' is used in a general and a specific sense. The general usage includes all readers who read the Bible pre-critically. But we also use the term 'ordinary' to designate a particular sector of pre-critical readers, those readers who are poor and marginalised.[13]

The ideological underpinnings of the use of the word "ordinary" to describe the people (of faith) who participate in the CBS have been strongly challenged. Although most African scholars agree that social engagement is important, not all agree on how this goal should be achieved. In this debate, Tinyiko Maluleke has been the most rigorous, contending that West's use of the term "ordinary reader" is intentionally ambiguous in terms of race, gender and economic location. Central among his carefully argued suspicions, is his line of argument that states:

> While "ordinary" and "trained" are power-relation categories, the tentative, evasive and "innocuous" nature of the terms tend to obscure, trivialise or palliate the economic, race and gender (especially as it relates to Black women) basis of the power discrepancy concerned.[14]

Another notoriously slippery term that is used interchangeably with "ordinary" is that of "other." As with Maluleke's argument concerning the use of "ordinary" this expression is also patently unhelpful in terms of its generality. Daniel Patte has argued that anyone can be "ordinary" depending on where they are positioned at any given time.[15] In similar vein, I would argue that anyone can be "other" depending on where they are positioned at any given time. In other words, everyone, including my spouse and my children, can be "other" to me. My spouse is "male"

---

12. Although it is commonly asserted that the term was made famous by West, other scholars have used the term regularly within their work. See for example Gerald West, *Biblical Hermeneutics of Liberation—Modes of Reading the Bible in the South African Context* (Pietermaritzburg: Cluster, 1991); Daniel Patte, *Ethics of Biblical Interpretation—A Re-evaluation* (Louisville: Westminster John Knox, 1995); and Musa W. Dube, "Readings of Semoya—Batswana Women's Interpretations of Matt. 15:21–28," *Semeia* 73 (1996): 111–29.

13. Gerald West and Musa W. Dube, "An Introduction: How We Have Come to 'Read With,'" *Semeia* 73 (1996): 7–20, 7.

14. Tinyiko S. Maluleke, "The Bible among African Christians: A Missiological Perspective," in *To Cast Fire upon the Earth: Bible and Mission Collaborating in Today's Multicultural Global Context*, ed. Teresa Okure (Pietermaritzburg: Cluster, 2000), 87–112, 93.

15. See Daniel Patte, "Biblical Scholars at the Interface between Critical and Ordinary Readings—A Response," *Semeia* 73 (1996): 263–76, esp. 266. Patte notes that "the same person can be at any given moment an 'expert-critical reader' or an 'ordinary reader' of the Bible. It is a matter of attitude and not of person."

and I am "female" therefore he is "other" to me. My children are "younger" and I am "older" therefore they are "other" to me. I readily admit that these may seem extremely frivolous examples, and hence, I do not mean to trivialize the issue. However, I think that a critical review of the original use of the term "other" might help us see that it has to become more nuanced in our discourses; otherwise it might not be as useful as we might think, particularly in the ways in which we appropriate it.

The term was made popular by Edward Said in his book *Orientalism*, where he depicts how Western Europe envisaged the Other, thereby enabling the colonial authorities a means of dealing with the "otherness" of Eastern culture, customs and beliefs.[16] Since then, the term has been appropriated by the colonised in rhetorical, sarcastic, and even derisive ways. Equally, the term has become commonplace in its use within the academy. For the immediate purpose of describing particular participants in a community Bible study session, I think that the term has to be thoroughly interrogated; being careful not to make the assumption that it has been "ordained from above," to use Maluleke's telling words.

It seems that the way in which we (scholars) describe those with whom we are socially engaged depends on our own located-ness as scholars undertaking research. For example, James Cochrane entitles a chapter of his book, *Circles of Dignity*, "Voices of the Other."[17] In it he gives a series of personal reflections of the processes involved in the conducting of a group Bible study in Amawoti, a Black township, north of Durban. Throughout the whole chapter, Cochrane attempts to grapple with the question of representivity.[18] For Cochrane, the notion that the participants were "other" to him (and perhaps also his research assistants, although he does not indicate this), is taken for granted. This fact is assumed from the preliminary questions that were asked by the group committee, namely, "What does it mean for us and who are you? (Why should we trust you?)." In other words, Cochrane contends that inherent in their questions was an indication that they did not trust that as research subjects they would be fully recognised and respected within his research. As Cochrane asserts, "The claim for recognition posits both a self, and in relation to the one spoken to, an otherness."[19] This implies that the participants posited themselves in relation to the researcher as "other."

The question I want to raise is not *whether* the sense of "otherness" was recognised by both subjects as being valid, but *why* either subject felt such a sense of "otherness." In other words, it is not enough to assume the position of "otherness" without first investigating the factors that underlay such "otherness." Hence the

16. Edward W. Said, *Orientalism* (Harmondsworth, England: Penguin, 1985).

17. James R. Cochrane, *Circles of Dignity: Community Wisdom and Theological Reflection* (Minneapolis: Fortress, 1999), 95–117.

18. For the concept of representativity, see Gayatri C. Spivak, "Can the Subaltern Speak?" in *Marxism and the Interpretation of Culture*, ed. G. Nelson and L. Grossberg (London: Macmillan, 1988), 271–315.

19. Cochrane, *Dignity*, 95.

questions that Maluleke asks about the "ordinary" have to be asked in relation to the "other" as well.[20] In other words, we should not take for granted that subjects are "other," but we should be asking *how*, *which* and *why* people are "othered?" I contend that if we socially engaged biblical scholars follow this process before naming our research subjects as "other" it would reveal that there is what I would call "degrees of otherness" and that the "degrees of otherness" determine the amount of trust the "other" is willing to invest in us. The consequence of this is that the amount of trust that the "other" endows to us will determine not only the validity of scholars' representation of them, but also the validity of their responses to the scholar as "other." This brings us to the role of the scholar in this relationship.

Who Is the Facilitator, and What Is the Facilitator's Role in the Bible Study?

One of the most significant factors in the CBS process is the person who facilitates the Bible study. It is important to establish the aims and the role of the facilitator. In West's description of the CBS process it is clear that in his understanding the biblical scholar who writes the academic paper on the bible study is not necessarily the facilitator.[21] This of course raises the issue of a "double representivity," since neither the facilitator nor the biblical scholar are neutral participants in the Bible study. There are numerous problems attached to this approach. In what follows, instead of interrogating the problems inherent in that approach, I choose rather to highlight my own approach, by examining my own role in the Bible studies I have conducted as both facilitator and biblical scholar.

Who is, or who should be the facilitator? is an important question. I would suggest that there are three fundamental characteristics of a facilitator:

1. The facilitator should be trained in the tools of critical scholarship (this needs to be unmasked, particularly given the dominance of Global-north training methods in Africa);
2. S/he should be committed to liberation in the community (not simply as a by-product of the process, but as a conscious effort on the part of the facilitator);
3. S/he should be an organic member of the community.

Each of these characteristics is not mutually exclusive, but complementary; hence, I will endeavour to discuss them collectively.

Firstly, *What does it mean to be trained in critical scholarship?* As a critical reader I have been trained to read the Bible critically. Hence, to quote Dube and West, "I have access to the structured and systematic sets of resources that constitute the craft of biblical scholars," but because of my commitments to the community and to liberation, I choose to read the Bible for the purposes of liberation.[22] This

---

20. Maluleke, "African Christians," 93.
21. West, "Contextual Bible."
22. West and Dube, "Introduction," 7.

approach does not always imply rejecting the methods I have been trained with. It simply implies a critical engagement with those methods. In other words, it negates Audre Lorde's terse, yet cautionary statement, "The master's tools will never dismantle the master's house."[23]

In making the admission that I may not read the Bible in the same way as other critical readers in the academy already decreases the space in the measurement of the "degrees of otherness" between myself and the community of women with whom I read; indeed most would be daunted by the use of academic jargon and intellectual methodologies. The need to unmask the identity of the scholar is therefore crucial to this process. Hence, of first importance is the necessity to declare my social location as a South African Indian Christian woman. The groups of women with whom I engaged in my own Bible studies were not as suspicious of me, or of my intentions, as the participants in the Amawoti Bible study group were of Cochrane and his researchers. In fact their enthusiasm for the Bible study was at times overwhelming. This may have something to do with the sense of pride which they felt, having someone from their own community who having advanced to the "centre" has now come back with that knowledge to empower those at the "periphery." Mogomme Masoga argues strongly for the organic presence of the biblical scholar when reading the Bible with African faith communities.[24]

By locating organic academics at the centre, and the community at the periphery, he argues, "Organic readers are produced by the periphery and advanced to the centre to learn the ropes in the centre, and their sole responsibility is the periphery."[25] Given this assumption, the women from my own community did not need to ask who I was, because most of them already knew me from the community. Some had even watched me as a child grow up, and others had known me from participating in previous Bible studies on violence against women, conducted in collaboration with the ISB. To say this, however, is not to downplay the question of trust, nor to sound arrogant or completely self-assured in my role. To the contrary, I think that the question of trust is and remains an important concern, even for scholars.

I do not think that it is possible that they trusted me completely, but I think being part of the community, and having established a relationship with them through other Bible studies, and by laying bare my intentions and motivations, they were able to trust me possibly more than they would have, had I been a complete outsider. This makes a difference to the way in which they responded to me. To use the term "other" to describe them or myself seems to indicate space or

23. Quoted in Elisabeth Schüssler Fiorenza, *Wisdom Ways: Introducing Feminist Biblical Interpretation* (Maryknoll, NY: Orbis Books, 2001), 4–5.

24. Magomme A. Masoga, "Re-defining Power—Reading the Bible in Africa from the Peripheral and Central Positions," in *Towards an Agenda for Contextual Theology: Essays in Honour of Albert Nolan,* ed. T. McGlory, T. Speckman, and Larry T. Kaufmann (Pietermaritzburg: Cluster, 2001), 133–47, 146.

25. Ibid.

distance, which is not fully compatible with my experience in the community. I did not see the people with whom I interacted as completely "other." To be honest, my university education, and even my class status to some degree, did make me different from them, but not to the extent that I can claim with full confidence that those with whom I worked were "other" than I.

The way in which the facilitator conceptualises her/his role in the Bible study process is also related to the way in which s/he conceives of their relationship with the community, with regard to the act of reading the biblical text. West uses the term "reading with" or "speaking with" as opposed to "speaking for" or "speaking to," to describe the ways in which the biblical scholar and those within the community interact.[26] He argues that the term "speaking with" or "reading with" takes seriously the subjectivities of both partners in the dialogue, that is, both the scholar and the poor and marginalised reader. Notwithstanding that it is indeed admirable that a scholar takes the agency of the oppressed seriously, I would argue that this might be an idealistic notion, even though West plainly argues that it is not.[27] One of the central reasons for my argument lies in the fact that West sees the readers in the community as "other" to himself.

I submit that "speaking with" or "reading with" does not ensure a "genuinely dialectical interaction between two vigilantly fore-grounded subject positions."[28] In fact, I suggest that the preposition "with" camouflages the respective power categories associated with identity that is associated in each subject position. It implies that the scholar comes alongside the community reader and hence reads "with" them. West counters this by arguing that "reading with" accepts real difference.[29] If this is true, there seems little space for conscientisation, as the method itself accepts that real differences exist between the ways in which scholars and those in the community read, but does not move much beyond simple recognition.

I would argue for an alternative perspective. I would suggest that "reading with" the community should only be a preliminary step to the Bible study, for "reading with" implies that the scholar understands (even if the scholar does not agree with) the position from which the community is reading. By first "reading with" the community, the scholar already grasps the processes involved in the ways in which the community reads, before the actual Bible study formally begins. In most cases, this phase is almost automatic for organic scholars. In other words, there is a shared or common understanding of the way in which the community approaches the biblical text. In the process of the actual Bible study it would perhaps be misleading to suggest that the scholar "reads with" the community. In other words, "reading with" is a notion that only works as an initial phase in order that

---

26. Gerald West, "Reading the Bible Differently: Giving Shape to the Discourse of the Dominated," *Semeia* 73 (1996): 21–42, 26.

27. West, *Academy of Poor*, 52–53.

28. West, "Reading Differently," 25.

29. Ibid., 26.

the scholar does not simply "observe" but goes on to genuinely comprehend the community's motivations and principles behind their reading practices.

For example, in reading the book of Esther "with" my community, I understand why the character of Vashti is perceived by the Bible study group as a bad woman. I understand, both as scholar and as a member of the community, the cultural and the theological codes which embed and aid such an interpretation. It is in this sense that I "read with" my community. In the process of the Bible study however, it is not always possible for scholars and the community to speak together, especially when the scholar sees her/his role as that of conscientisation, as for example in challenging the notion that Vashti is a bad wife. This necessitates a certain distance which in turn requires that the scholar transfer from the "reading with" paradigm to a "reading to" paradigm.

It is in this instance that I prefer Spivak's use of the term "speaking to."[30] Inherent in this paradigm is an acknowledgement that even though we as scholars may gain valuable insights from community wisdom, what is intrinsic to our work is the assumption that we can transform our society. This is not always possible if we stop at the point of "reading with" the community. In this sense, I concur with Cochrane when he asserts:

> Gerald West prefers to substitute the term *speaking with* for the term *speaking to* in contexts where the encounter between trained and untrained readers of the Bible take place. Where the trained person is organically one of the local community, this seems to make sense. But where this is not so (as is most commonly the case of clergy in many churches, for example), the preposition *with* seems too strong an indication of common identity.[31]

REPRESENTATION

To engage the issue of representation, I would like to use the postcolonial feminist critic, Gayatri Spivak's evocative question "Can the subaltern speak?"[32] To facilitate the discussion I wish to bring Gerald West, Beverley Haddad and Gayatri Spivak into dialogue. Both Haddad and West argue that the subaltern does speak. In terms of how the subaltern speaks during his engagement with them, West's arguments are based on an understanding of James Scott's theories of the hidden and public transcript.[33] West argues that intellectuals have assumed that "ordinary readers" do not speak because intellectuals only have access to their public transcript of "apparent submission" to the dominant discourse. He asserts, "the subaltern does

---

30. Spivak, "Subaltern Speak?" 275.
31. Cochrane, *Dignity*, 189.
32. Spivak, "Subaltern Speak?"
33. Scott, *Domination*.

speak, but in forms of discourse we cannot hear if we only listen."[34] West suggests that in order to "hear" what the subaltern is saying we have to move beyond a "listening to" or "speaking for" to a "speaking with" mode of understanding.

Haddad concurs with West, but goes further to suggest that poor and marginalised women "articulate and own their own interpretations of faith" when the intellectual is able to build "alliances of solidarity" through collaboration with the community.[35] Although acknowledging her relationship (as a non-organic activist-intellectual) with the community of Black Zulu-speaking women as being fraught with racial, class and language politics,[36] Haddad nevertheless argues that their "common experience as women was sufficient, even before we had secured common ground to risk collaboration."[37] As with West, Haddad recognises her role as a socially engaged intellectual, but unlike West, conceptualises herself as being closer to the community than West by virtue of her gender. Haddad thus argues that her solidarity with the community and the safe space that is thereby created is what enables the community to speak.

Both West and Haddad seem to indicate that the community does and will speak if they are sure of the intellectual's commitment to creating "alliances of solidarity" with them, and hence a safe site is created whereby they can speak and articulate their subjugated expressions of faith.

I concur with West and Haddad concerning the ability of the subaltern to speak and that in most cases they speak most freely when provided with a safe space to do so. Where I differ, is in their use of the term "reading with" to reinforce their argument that the subaltern does speak in the subsequent representation of them in their scholarship. The reason that both West and Haddad are so intent on foregrounding the notion of "reading with" or "speaking with" is captured well by Haddad when she comments that West's argument:

> Is crucial if, as activist-intellectuals working with women from different backgrounds, we are to avoid constructing what Mohanty terms *colonising discourse* which merely masks unequal relations of power and falsely suggests a *solidarity* with those less privileged.[38]

---

34. Gerald West, "Being Partially Constituted by Work with Others," *JTSA* 104 (1999): 44–54, 52.

35. Beverley Haddad, "Practices of Solidarity, Degrees of Separation: Doing Theology as Women in South Africa," *JCT* 6, no. 2 (2000): 39–54, 49.

36. See Beverley Haddad, "African Women's Theologies of Survival: Intersecting Faith, Feminisms, and Development" (Ph.D. diss., University of Natal, 2000), 25, where she foregrounds her identity as a South African woman of Lebanese descent who was "given" white status in the apartheid era but chooses to align herself with African women; she sees herself as a South African–African woman who is "not quite-white" and who has chosen to be shaped by her "blackness" rather than by "whiteness" as she lives and works in post-apartheid South Africa.

37. Ibid., 296.

38. Ibid., 47.

Haddad's observation points to a crucial position in the debate, that the "reading with" notion is principally and especially (and perhaps only) significant for the activist-intellectual working with women from *different backgrounds*. Hence, their position is clear. In such cases, the foregrounding of the "reading with" method is vital. West acknowledges this, when he says that the "listening to" or "speaking to" method "Fails to take sufficient account of contestation taking place between the public and the hidden transcript, particularly when we are present—particularly when 'we' are people like me who are not *organic* intellectuals.[39]

In other words, West and Haddad argue that the "speaking to" model is not possible for those who are not organic intellectuals. But, you may ask, *What if those intellectuals who are working in the community are organic intellectuals?* In other words, *What happens when the "other" is the "scholar?"* The starting point of their dialogue is then different to that of West's and Haddad's (and consequently their representation of the community would also be different). In other words, organic intellectuals might not want to make as strong a claim for the "reading with" paradigm as seemingly West and Haddad are wont to do.[40] This is because the organic intellectual, (and I refer to myself in this role) might see their role as moving beyond "reading with" (as this might be an automatic process anyway) to actual "conscientisation." On the other hand, Haddad and West do not see their roles as initiating a process of conscientisation. Haddad explicitly states this:

> I now recognise that my role is not to conscientise but to enter into mutual dialogue and collaborative work with those I work with. In so doing, I recognise the need to be re-shaped and re-made. It opens me up to transformation and re-constitution. I am less bold or hasty than I used to be about what action I think should be taken against the many gendered injustices I see around me. I listen more, speak less and do not rush into any prescribed solutions to these evils. . .At times in discussions with women of Sweetwaters and Nxamalala, I have not been able to be quiet and found myself speaking out my perspective on their oppression. Instead of having the desired effect of moving them into unanimous agreement, it has more often than not elicited silence.[41]

Haddad's statement clearly reveals her paralysis in influencing these women in their journey towards transformation. Her speaking out against their oppression elicited only silence. In other words, the women were not able to "speak back" to her when she "spoke to" them. Given that they were not able to "speak back" to her, her argument suggests that the women have other ways of speaking about their oppression, and that her role is not as an interventionist, but simply that of forg-

---

39. West, "Partially Constituted," 49.

40. This argument does not preclude my own already made earlier that the "reading with" paradigm is only a first step in the process of collaboration. Here I simply want to point out that it is not the most crucial part of the process.

41. Haddad, "Solidarity," 49.

ing "alliances of solidarity," which in turn provides a safe space for the women to articulate their "survival theologies." West sees his role in the same way.

So where does Spivak enter this debate? Spivak illustrates her point by referring to the Indian practice of sati, where a wife burns herself on her late husband's funeral pyre. The practice of sati was abolished by the British in the early nineteenth century. In post-colonialist discourse the abolition might be viewed, Spivak argues, as a classic case of "white men saving brown women from brown men." On the other hand Spivak holds that the Indian nativist argument that "the women actually wanted to die," would certainly be problematic from the feminist side. So, she concludes that the subaltern is muted in both discourses.

To relate this to the position of West and Haddad, I would suggest that in arguing for survival theologies and hidden transcripts in representative discourse, they substantively agree with what Spivak calls "the Indian nativist argument" that "the women actually wanted to die," forms the public transcript which contains encoded forms of resistance, and that it is the role of the intellectual by "speaking with" the subaltern to uncover the actual "hidden transcript" which we assume, may affirm that the women did not want to die.[42] Spivak would argue that this in itself is not a bad assumption. Spivak's problem however would be that with West (or any other scholar from a differing background to that of the Indian widow) making such a conjecture as this, it may replicate the common argument made of the British that this was "a case of white men saving brown women from brown men."[43]

Both the arguments that "the women actually wanted to die," and, "white men are saving brown women from brown men" are equally unhelpful in foregrounding the voice of the subaltern. Spivak's conclusion is therefore, that the subaltern cannot speak in representative discourse. She does however concede that the intellectual is able to offer a critique of the subaltern's position if the intellectual is willing to admit s/he is "speaking to" the subaltern, by virtue of the intellectual's status. Hence Spivak can assert:

> In seeking to learn to speak to (rather than listen to or speak for) the historically muted subject of the subaltern women, the postcolonial intellectual *systematically* "unlearns" female privilege. This systematic unlearning involves learning to critique postcolonial discourse with the best tools it can provide and not simply substituting the lost figure of the colonised.[44]

It seems clear that West and Haddad in recognising the need to hear the "ordinary" and "poor and marginalised women" articulate their struggles in their own voices, and with their own covert strategies, they are "simply substituting the lost figure

---

42. Spivak, "Subaltern Speak?" 297.

43. Ibid. Here, Spivak notes that even "white women—from nineteenth century British Missionary Registers to Mary Daly—have not produced an alternative understanding."

44. Ibid., 295.

of the colonised"[45] (poor and marginalised) without critiquing the postcolonial discourse (in this case patriarchal discourse) which under-girds the reason that the subaltern remains colonised (oppressed by patriarchal forces). Their lack of critique is due to their predilection to close down the conversation as soon as they attempt any form of critique as their identities prevent them from entering a meaningful dialogue.

In other words, in taking Spivak's arguments seriously, Haddad and West, gallantly and admirably attempt to avoid the notion of "white men (and women) saving brown women from brown men," by claiming that the community are in possession of hidden transcripts, without feeling *able* (as inorganic intellectuals) to speak out about why they need such hidden transcripts, or to critique the structures that keep them oppressed, as the reaction they might get (as inorganic intellectuals) would be that of silence, as Haddad's statement above confirms. My point here is not that inorganic intellectuals fail to point out what the structures and constraints of oppression are, because as West's and Haddad's work demonstrate, they do. What is clearly in view however is that, although they acknowledge the oppressions, they feel unable to critique these structures because of their own social locations.

In other words, I am not arguing that the theory of a hidden transcript is invalid. It has validity in that a hidden transcript can be a tool used by the oppressed, most times for the purposes of survival. However, the theory cannot be used in isolation of the inherent questioning and revealing of the structures that necessitate the hidden transcript, through for example, making the subaltern conscious of why it is they need a hidden transcript, and if they do not have a hidden transcript, to expose the ways in which the consciousness of the subaltern has internalised these oppressive structures.

To summarise this tri-partite dialogue on representation, I turn again briefly

---

45. R. S. Sugirtharajah, *The Bible and the Third World: Precolonial, Colonial, and Postcolonial Encounters* (Cambridge: University Press, 2001), 280, can argue in similar vein: "The validity of an interpretation does not depend on positing an alternative reading or supporting it with new data. Simply replacing an alternative reading with a subaltern one does not make the latter more legitimate than the one it tries to dislodge. Combating one set of data with a counter set is not enough to unsettle hegemonic readings. Instead the discursive modes through which narratives and facts are produced must also be called into question." Cochrane (*Circles of Dignity*, 4), although noting the value of what he calls "community wisdom" or "local wisdom," also concedes with regard to the critique from Black theologians of the African Independent Churches (hereafter, AICs) that "Black theologians have a point in their negative analysis of the political significance of the AICs. It would be romantic idealism to imagine that the faith and reflection of local Christian communities, because they may be black, poor, or oppressed, is free of distortion, of entrapment in increasingly dysfunctional paradigms, or of contradictions not yet experientially significant. Ordinary believers may well hamper the emancipatory goals for which Black theology strives, and even act as counterrevolutionary agents against freedom."

to my representations with the women of my own community. I am not simply reporting on the ways in which they interpret biblical texts when given a safe space to interpret through their own lenses, because in these cases I would concur with West and Haddad that the women do speak. But, what I also intend reflecting upon is my own role in bringing to consciousness, by helping the women of my own community become more ideological about their own oppression.[46] This crucial process seems to be lacking in West and Haddad's work because as inorganic intellectuals, they do not recognise it as part of their work.

CONCLUSION

This chapter has shown that to be a socially engaged biblical scholar, comes with certain challenges and responsibilities. In examining the focus areas of the motivation of social engagement, the method of social engagement and the subsequent representation of social engagement, I have tried to show the importance of a hermeneutic of transformation. As a socially engaged biblical scholar, the most important function that a hermeneutic of transformation can provide in the academy is that it can highlight my role as an activist. At the heart of such a scholar's reasoning should be the transformation of the community.

The feminist scholar, Lilian Robinson once posed this challenge to feminist academics: "The most important question we can ask ourselves as feminists is 'so what?'"[47] This challenge can equally be made towards socially engaged biblical scholars as well! In other words, Robinson was reminding feminist academics that the point of our work is not only to change the academy but to change our societies. Gerald West and others like him, who share similar social commitments, have

---

46. Most of the essays in the 1996 *Semeia* volume on the "Reading With" methodology seem to focus on the agency of "ordinary" African readers. Without doubting the seriousness of the agency of "ordinary" Africans, I do think that the intellectual at the same time has to critically examine and expose those areas in our cultural communal mind-sets, which oppress (see, for example, Mercy A. Oduyoye, "Women and Ritual in Africa," in *The Will to Arise: Women, Tradition, and the Church in Africa*, ed. Mercy A. Oduyoye and Musimbi R. A. Kanyoro [Maryknoll, NY: Orbis Books, 1992], 9–24). As Cochrane (*Circles of Dignity*, 4), has observed: "It would be romantic idealism to imagine that the faith and reflection of local Christian communities, because they may be black, poor, or oppressed, is free of distortion, of entrapment in increasingly dysfunctional paradigms, or of contradictions not yet experientially significant. Ordinary believers may well hamper the emancipatory goals for which Black theology strives, and even act as counterrevolutionary agents against freedom." Given Cochrane's point above, it seems that critique and conscientisation is necessary, but the levels of critique and conscientisation offered by the intellectual will depend largely on whether the intellectual is an organic part of the community or not.

47. Quoted in "Introduction—Toward a Materialist-Feminist Criticism," in J. Newton and D. Rosenfelt, *Feminist Criticism and Social Change—Sex, Class, and Race in Literature and Culture* (New York and London: Methuen, 1985), xv.

taken up this challenge, albeit in varying degrees. The challenge which remains is to ensure that our work involves not only patronage, charity or an uncritical acceptance of the hidden transcripts of resistance, but a genuine engagement with the community for social transformation.

Works Cited

Cochrane, R. James. *Circles of Dignity: Community Wisdom and Theological Reflection.* Minneapolis: Fortress, 1999.

Dickinson, Emily. *The Complete Poems of Emily Dickinson, with an Introduction by Her Niece Martha Dickinson Bianchi.* Boston: Little, Brown, 1924.

Dube, W. Musa. "Readings of Semoya—Batswana Women's Interpretations of Matt. 15:21–28," *Semeia* 73 (1996): 111–29.

Haddad, Beverley. "African Women's Theologies of Survival: Intersecting Faith, Feminisms, and Development." Ph.D. diss, University of Natal, 2000.

———. "Practices of Solidarity, Degrees of Separation: Doing Theology as Women in South Africa." *JCT* 6, no. 2 (2000): 39–54.

Messer-Davidow, E. *Disciplining Feminism: From Social Activism to Academic Discourse.* Durham, NC: Duke University Press, 2002.

Mosala, Itumeleng Jerry. "Black Theology Revisited." Paper presented at Azapo Congress, Lenasia, 1983.

Nadar, Sarojini. "Power, Ideology, and Interpretation/s: Womanist and Literary Perspectives on the Book of Esther as Resources for Gender-Social Transformation. Ph.D. diss., University of Natal, 2003.

Nelson, G., and L. Grossberg, eds. *Marxism and the Interpretation of Culture.* London: Macmillan, 1988.

Newton, J., and D. Rosenfelt. *Feminist Criticism and Social Change—Sex, Class, and Race in Literature and Culture.* New York and London: Methuen, 1985.

Oduyoye, Mercy A., and Musimbi R. A. Kanyoro, eds. *The Will to Arise: Women, Tradition, and the Church in Africa.* Maryknoll, NY: Orbis Books, 1992.

Okure, Teresa, ed. *To Cast Fire upon the Earth: Bible and Mission Collaborating in Today's Multicultural Global Context.* Pietermaritzburg: Cluster, 2000.

Patte, Daniel, "Biblical Scholars at the Interface between Critical and Ordinary Readings—A Response." *Semeia* 73 (1996): 263–76.

———. *Ethics of Biblical Interpretation—A Re-evaluation.* Louisville: Westminster John Knox, 1995.

Pobee, John S. "Bible Study in Africa: A Passover of Language," *Semeia* 73 (1996): 161–80.

Schüssler Fiorenza, Elisabeth. *Wisdom Ways: Introducing Feminist Biblical Interpretation.* Maryknoll, NY: Orbis Books, 2001.

Said, W. Edward. *Orientalism.* Harmondsworth, England: Penguin, 1985.

Scott, James C. *Domination and the Arts of Resistance: Hidden Transcripts.* New Haven and London: Yale University Press, 1990.

Speckman, McGlory T., and Larry T. Kaufmann, eds. *Towards an Agenda for Contextual Theology: Essays in Honour of Albert Nolan.* Pietermaritzburg: Cluster, 2001.

Sugirtharajah, R. S., *The Bible and the Third World: Precolonial, Colonial, and Postcolonial Encounters.* Cambridge: University Press, 2001.

West, Gerald, "Being Partially Constituted by Work with Others." *JTSA* 104 (1999): 44–54.

―――. *Biblical Hermeneutics of Liberation—Modes of Reading the Bible in the South African Context*. Pietermaritzburg: Cluster, 1991.

―――. "Reading the Bible Differently: Giving Shape to the Discourse of the Dominated." *Semeia* 73 (1996): 21–42.

―――. *The Academy of the Poor: Towards a Dialogical Reading of the Bible*. Sheffield: Sheffield Academic Press, 1999.

West, Gerald, and Musa W. Dube, "An Introduction: How We Have Come to 'Read With.'" *Semeia* 73 (1996): 7–20.

―――. *The Bible in Africa: Transactions, Trajectories, and Trends*. Leiden: E. J. Brill, 2000.

Embodied and Embodying Hermeneutics of Life in the Academy: Musa W. Dube's HIV/AIDS Work

Emmanuel Katongole

Because HIV/AIDS has interrupted our world and our lives in such radical ways, we must allow it to interrupt our scholarship radically as well. Doing so not only leads us to question our existing paradigms, it calls for the adoption of new methodologies and approaches. Even more importantly, it calls us back to the discipline of dreaming new visions in relation to our bodies, sexuality, family life, the church, and the world. But this is where the tension lies. For with HIV/AIDS, we live under the paradigm of shattered dreams. The challenge therefore is how not to allow this deadly body- and dream-shattering virus to shatter the very ability to dream of God's new creation. To put it more positively, the challenge is how to embrace HIV/AIDS not only as a threat, but to see it as a *kairos*, that is, as a moment of truth and a unique opportunity that forces us to dream and inhabit dreams of God's new creation.

I locate Musa Dube's work, especially her *HIV and AIDS Bible* (Scranton: University of Scranton Press, 2006), within this broad challenge. The overall effect of her work has been to force us to see that with HIV/AIDS we live under the paradigm of shattered dreams. What one finds still missing in her work, and what one hopes to see more explicitly developed in her future work, are the theological visions and dreams "from beyond" that can sustain life in a dream-shattered world. I suggest that Dube might be in a better position to provide these big dreams if she pays attention to the notion and practice of lament within the biblical tradition. The issue I am raising goes beyond Dube's work and beyond the specific case of HIV/AIDS. It involves a wider claim about the coherence and integrity of socially engaged African scholarship and how such scholarship must be shaped around the discipline and practice of lament. Before I explore this general claim, a note about Dube's work and the positive challenge it presents in terms of embodied and embodying hermeneutics of life within the academy.

Originally published in *SBL Forum* (March 2006). http://sbl-ite.org/Article.aspx?Article ID=510. Published here with permission.

Musa Dube: Embodied and Embodying Hermeneutics Of Life

I focus on the work of Musa Dube for a number of reasons. First, she is a first rate scholar, one of the most prolific on the African scene. A New Testament professor in the Religious Studies Department at the University of Botswana, Musa Dube has published numerous academic books and essays, and she has edited several monographs.[1] Her research and writing focus on postcolonial feminist ways of reading the Bible. Another reason why Dube's work is significant is that, unlike many "post-colonialists" (for whom postcolonial critique has become the primary goal), Dube's post-colonialism is not a detached academic pursuit. Rather, her postcolonial scholarship is grounded in, and seeks to connect with, the actual struggles of African women in their search for justice and liberation. In this connection, Dube is a key voice in the Circle of Concerned African Women Theologians, where she has served as the chair of biblical research and publication.[2] A third and more immediate reason for focusing on the work of Musa Dube is that she has been involved actively in issues related to HIV/AIDS. In 2002–2003, she worked with the World Council of Churches (WCC) as the HIV/AIDS and Theological Consultant for churches and theological institutions in Africa, training theological lecturers and church leaders to incorporate HIV/AIDS in their programs.

What drives Musa Dube's scholarly activism is a keen awareness that with HIV/AIDS we live in world of shattered dreams. Given this fact, she has consistently noted, our scholarship as well as our church life cannot go on "as usual." Instead, both the academy and the church must become sites of struggle and critical engagement in the fight for liberation and healing in the era HIV/AIDS. Her HIV/AIDS related work and scholarship, therefore, provide a good model for African scholars as we seek to embody the embodying hermeneutics of life in the academy.

I do not know many scholars who would self-consciously describe themselves in such a hyphenated fashion as Musa Dube does: "An African post-colonial-feminist-biblical-scholar." And yet, there is something in Dube's heavily hyphenated self-description that rings true of all African scholars. To be an African is to find oneself richly hyphenated; that is to say, located within a multiplicity of marginalizing and marginalized narratives; thus, if you are a scholar, at the intersection of many disciplines in the academy. What makes Dube's work unique, fresh, and provocative is not only the verve and relentless passion with which she

---

1. See, for example, *Post-colonial Feminist Interpretation of the Bible* (Atlanta: Chalice, 2000); *Other Ways of Reading: African Women and the Bible* (Atlanta: SBL, 2001); *Grant Me Justice: HIV/AIDS and Gender Readings of the Bible* (Maryknoll, NY: Orbis Books, 2005); *John and Postcolonialism: Travel, Space, and Power,* edited with Jeffrey Staley (Sheffield: Sheffield Academic Press, 2002); and *The Bible in Africa: Translations, Trajectories, and Trends,* edited with Gerald West (Leiden: Brill, 1999).

2. In this role, she has edited such volumes as *Other Ways of Reading: African Women and the Bible* (Atlanta: SBL, 2001) and contributed to numerous other publications by the Circle.

inhabits such a world of postcolonial hybridity, but also the commitment to engage and interrogate its limits and possibilities. In other words, for Musa Dube to be an "African post-colonial-feminist-biblical-scholar" does not constitute a combination of "scholarly interests"—for these hyphens are less of "interests" and more of destinies.

Moreover, in Dube's work it is clear that what is at stake is not simply the destiny of this one uniquely gifted, brilliant, and exceptionally capable scholar, but the lives of millions of others who, like her, find themselves within the postcolonial space, but who, unlike her, have neither the skills to fully grasp the machinations of a postcolonial world nor a voice to make their cries heard. Musa Dube thus speaks with, and on behalf of, a corporate identity: She writes, reads, sings, and speaks of, and on behalf of, Mamma Africa. That is why her work provides a positive model of what African scholarship should be about, namely, trying to make sense of these complex narratives that constitute our multiple social locations in a postcolonial Africa. We do not bring "scholarly interests" into the academy, we bring the hyphenated biographies of Africa. In order to preserve its inner integrity and relevance, African scholarship cannot but be deeply socially engaged.

On Being Interrupted

No doubt becoming a deeply and socially engaged scholar may, at least on the surface, appear to be a distraction and even an unwelcome interruption of one's scholarly ambitions. And yet, the type of interruption that HIV/AIDS presents is not one that allows us freedom to decide to respond or not respond. In this connection, the story of how HIV/AIDS "invaded" Dube's work is telling, as it represents the shattering of her dreams to be an "academic" scholar. In the opening essay of *The HIV and AIDS Bible*, she recounts how it was, during her graduate days in the United States, that she became aware of HIV/AIDS and the deadly devastation it was dealing on the African continent. Even as she wrote poems and songs, which were later turned into albums that would raise funds for orphaned children, her vision was fixed on a career in the academy, with fellow scholars as her primary audience. However, on returning to her home country, her teaching soon went through a crisis when she realized that more than half of her students could be HIV positive. This realization began to interrogate her teaching:

> As I went about with the business as usual, teaching the synoptic Gospels from a feminist, narrative, historical or redactional criticism and the like, there came a point that this academic approach began to become artificial and strange even on my tongue.[3]

Her position on the HIV/AIDS front lines impelled her to undertake a different rereading of the miracles of Jesus and to begin to ask, What is the meaning of the

---

3. *HIV and AIDS Bible*, 15.

miracles of healing in the Synoptic Gospels? Are they still relevant? How does one propound a theology of healing where there is no healing?[4]

The HIV/AIDS context was not only beginning to change the way she taught but where she taught. By now, she was sending her students into the community with AIDS-related questionnaires (thus taking her teaching outside the academy). And she was also challenging her colleagues at the university to attend to the issue of HIV/AIDS through scholarly writing and integrating AIDS into their syllabi.

As one thing led to another, with various speaking invitations in and outside of Africa, she was asked by the WCC to serve as the African consultant on HIV/AIDS, and as theological consultant. Thus, in September 2002, she took a leave of absence from her university to take on the WCC position. A key task in her position was to mobilize, equip, and challenge theological educators and church leaders in Africa to take on HIV/AIDS and to respond to it effectively. In this respect, her task involved, among other things, researching, writing, and publishing theological materials that could be used by both theological institutions and churches.[5]

HIV/AIDS had not only forced Musa Dube to read the Bible with new questions, it had also forced her to embrace a new type of scholarship, a socially engaged scholarship, or what she calls "prophetically healing scholarship."[6] As is clear from the essays in *The HIV and AIDS Bible*, Dube's prophetically healing scholarship, among other things, is grounded in the realization that AIDS has shattered dreams of our basic social plots and has "debunked many known truths and exposed the limitations of many scientific, economic and cultural truths/knowledge."[7] She thus challenges the academy and scholars to face this fact and therefore to "think and design frameworks that nurture a scholarship that is socially engaged and accountable to addressing the most burning issues of our day, time, world and contexts."[8] She also "seeks to unsettle the Christian churches to move beyond the comfortable limits of their ministry by showing that HIV/AIDS is not an event that happens outside the normal, usual pattern of the church, and to come to the realization that the "Church is HIV positive."

Musa reads the Bible creatively with the marginalized, with the People Living with AIDS (PLWA), in order to allow the biblical text to breathe new life. Her reading of such texts as Mark 5:21–43 (*Talitha Cum*) and Luke 4:16–22: ("The Spirit of the Lord is upon me") provide fresh insights into the liberating promises of the gospel. Moreover, hers is not a detached "reading," but one committed to the healing and liberation as a comprehensive struggle that involves, among others, prevention; breaking stigma and silence; provision of quality care; and addressing

4. Ibid., 15.

5. Out of this work grew two key books: *HIV/AIDS and the Curriculum: Methods of Integrating HIV/AIDS in Theological Programs* (Geneva: WCC, 2003), and *Africa Praying: A Handbook of HIV/AIDS Sensitive Sermons and Liturgy* (Geneva: WCC, 2003).

6. *HIV and AIDS Bible*, 5.

7. Ibid., 21.

8. Ibid., 5.

HIV/AIDS as an epidemic within other social epidemics, a factor that makes the marginalized groups of the world more vulnerable.[9]

Given such rich themes, it is obvious that Musa Dube has not just squarely and creatively responded to the interruption of HIV/AIDS, but, in doing so, has also provided a good example of what a socially engaged scholarship for liberation and healing in the wake of AIDS might look like.

THE LIMITS OF AN ACTIVIST PARADIGM

Nevertheless, if Musa Dube's work depicts the urgency and possible direction of socially engaged scholarship in relation to HIV/AIDS, it also reveals the limits of any activist paradigm. Simply put, I find Dube's work too activist. What I mean by this is that while it is strong on strategies and skills for how to respond to HIV/AIDS, it is short on visions and dreams of transformation in the wake of HIV/AIDS. While it helps to display the Bible as a "formidable weapon" in the struggle for liberation and healing, it does not make sufficiently explicit its central characteristic as a journey. At the heart of this journey is God's invitation to God's people to live in the present that has been shaped, indeed transformed, by the visions of the beyond.

There is of course no doubt that the crisis of AIDS is so urgent that it calls for immediate response, which includes advocacy. Nevertheless, grounding a theology of AIDS within an activist paradigm deprives such a theology of the most radical contribution of the biblical tradition; namely, inspiring and drawing its adherents into dreams and radical visions of the beyond. The reason is that an activist paradigm is by its nature always committed to a sense of pragmatic urgency, to what is relevant to the needs and challenges at hand. In other words, even were such a paradigm to succeed (and thus be able to procure liberation and healing), there is a sense in which it would still leave us within the limits of the world as is—a world in which current models of economics, politics, and international relations have been somehow modified but not radically challenged.

To put it differently, an activist theology of advocacy can never be ambitious enough, as such a theology very easily misses *the kairos* that HIV/AIDS is.[10] As *kairos*, HIV/AIDS reveals the limits of our conceptions of the body, sexuality, and gender relations, as well as the social, political, and economic imbalances of our world. If HIV/AIDS exposes these limits of our established canons, then responding to the HIV/AIDS *kairos* calls for nothing short of dreaming radically new visions of

9. Ibid., 6.

10. Here I use the term *kairos* in the sense that the South African theologians used it in their famous Kairos Document of 1986. Referring to apartheid as a Kairos, the theologians noted, "For many Christians in South Africa, this is the Kairos, the moment of grace and opportunity, the favourable time in which God issues a challenge to decisive action" (cited by Maluleke in "The Challenge of HIV/AIDS for Theological Education," *Missionalia* 29 no. 2 [2001]: 129).

human flourishing. Such a call finds ready resonance in Scripture, for dreaming of a radically new creation is what is at stake in the Bible. But this is what might easily be missed by an activist paradigm that tends to view the Bible as simply another formidable weapon in the struggle against AIDS that can be mined for usable insights and strategies in the struggle towards liberation and healing. No doubt the Bible contains many such insights, but these are secondary to the basic plot of Scripture, which is the story of a dream: God's dream for the world.

What the work of Dube (and other scholars like Itumelang Mosala and Gerald West) have helped us to see is that, as a written text, the Bible can easily legitimize or underwrite gender, imperialistic, and colonizing inequalities (thus the need for different hermeneutical skills, including postcolonial hermeneutics). Nonetheless, as a Christian, what I find most fascinating and refreshing are the ways in which the Bible's stories and narratives constantly thrust the reader back to the origins—Genesis—in order to reorient us toward a future to which everything is headed—Revelation. This future comes as a dream in which John, facing persecution and imprisoned on the island of Patmos, is nevertheless still able to see "a new heaven and a new earth coming down from heaven" (Rev 21:1).

With HIV/AIDS we face a similar situation of tribulation and "persecution." The challenge is whether, like the seer John, we are still able to dream of, and see signs of, "a new heaven and a new earth" in the wake of the dream-shattering reality of HIV/AIDS. To put it more succinctly, the biblical and theological challenge, even as it involves advocacy, has to do more with the recovery of dreams and visions. That is why a biblically inspired social engagement in the era of HIV/AIDS, rather than being grounded in an activist paradigm, needs to grow out of, and be deeply connected to, a biblically inspired discipline of lament. The reason for this has to do not only with the fact that the stubbornness to dream of God's new creation in the wake of AIDS involves the discipline of sustained memory, but also with the realization that dreaming is deeply engaged commitment that requires community. Recovering the biblical tradition of lament not only helps to maintain the balance between memory, community, and the search for a transformed future, it also provides a more promising starting point for Christian social engagement in the wake of AIDS.

LAMENT, MEMORY, AND COMMUNITY

Modern psychology has increasingly highlighted the need for grieving as a necessary step towards healing. Such accounts might lead us to think of lament as a process of grieving that an individual or family goes through in the journey towards recovery. In the biblical tradition, however, lament is not simply a process or a stage towards recovery. It is a posture, grounded in the memory of God's promises, that makes possible the dreaming of a new future. In this context, no biblical text comes more readily to my mind than Joel 2:28: "Then, I will pour out my spirit on all the people; your sons and daughters will prophesy; your old men will dream dreams, and your young men will see visions." It is helpful to realize that the context and setting for this promise is not very different from ours. The prophet is responding to a similar catastrophe and destruction. In the sections preceding this particular passage, Joel uses different images to convey the plight: a nation has invaded my land (Joel 1:16); the fires have devoured the pastures of the wilderness, and flames have burned all the trees (Joel 1:19); the fields are devastated (Joel 1:9) by locust and plague (Joel 1:4)

What is particularly significant is the manner in which Joel responds to the national tragedy and devastation, namely, by calling for a period of lament: "wake up you drunkards and weep" (1:4); "be dismayed your farmers, wail your vinedressers" (Joel 1:11); "put on sackcloth and lament you priests, wail you ministers of the altar" (Joel 1:13); "return to me with all your heart, with fasting, with weeping, and with mourning" (Joel 2:12).

We should also notice that in contrast to our modern, individual-centered notions of grieving, for Joel lament is not an individual cry of dereliction. It is first and foremost a communal practice. The context and setting for the practice of lament is within a particular assembly. Thus, twice Joel invites the priests to "sanctify a fast, call a solemn assembly" (Joel 1:14) and "to gather the people, sanctify the congregation; assemble the aged, gather the children, even the infants at the breast" (Joel 2:16). In other words, the invitation to lament is at the same time a calling into existence of a distinctive community, an assembly—the *kahal Yahweh*.

Another striking difference with the modern understanding, where we tend to associate lament simply with the grieving process, is that for Joel lament is not so much an action, even less a process of grieving towards recovery. It is more a way of facing the present crisis—a posture of attentiveness, of recalling or remembering what Yahweh has done in the past on behalf of God's people. It is a practice of communal memory. Thus for Joel to call "a solemn assembly" is to invite the community to hear again the story—not only of their origin and their unfaithfulness, but also of God's constant love and constant promise of salvation, healing, and deliverance. In other words, it is an invitation to remember hope. Thus, calling the community to remember at this critical time of crisis is not to distract it away from the crisis and what needs to be done to avert the crisis, but to help it locate the crisis at hand within the wider story of God's relationship with God's people. Thus, in inviting the people to lament, Joel seeks to relocate the people's lives into the imaginative landscape of both God's dream of the old creation and the promise of a new creation.

It is the relocation into the imaginative landscape of God's story that then allows Joel to dream of—indeed, see—a hopeful future at the intersection of a remembered past and a painful present.

HIV/AIDS, Lament, Hope, and Visions from Beyond

One can draw a number of conclusions from this brief discussion of the book of Joel. One obvious conclusion is that the devastation of HIV/AIDS calls for a recovery of a substantive notion and discipline of lament. In this connection, what the book of Joel helps us to highlight is the fact that lament is not a cry of despair, but an affirmation of hope. To engage a discipline of lament is to face the present with hope, a hope grounded in memory. Clifton Black is right when he notes: "The spine of lament is hope; not that vacuous optimism that 'things will get better,' which in the short run is usually a lie, but the deep and irrepressible conviction, in the teeth of present evidence, that God has not severed the umbilical cord that has always bound us to the Lord."[11]

What Joel also helps us to recover is the discipline of lament not as a socially detached attitude, but as a deep form of social engagement, indeed, a powerful political practice. As such, it calls into existence and shapes a new reality of church as a wounded community, which in its woundedness lives out visions of the beyond. A theology of AIDS has to draw attention to a new reality of church, a fresh imagination of ecclesia—ecclesial communities that are at once capable of lament and that are made possible through lament. In the struggle against HIV/AIDS the church is not simply another NGO; the Bible is not simply another tool in the quest for healing. What the bible constantly does is to draw us back to a memory of "in the beginning" in order to reorient us to a future beyond—all the while calling into existence new assemblies (communities, congregations) that already live in the present transformed by those visions of the beyond.

If, through the devastation wrought by HIV/AIDS, we are able to become such a community, then we would have begun to face the moment that AIDS is. This is where one might begin to see HIV/AIDS as a *kairos*, even as a gift (a strange gift to be sure)—through which God is shattering our social, political, economic, and individual dreams and forcing us to live out or, rather, reassembling us into, new and fresh ecclesial imaginations that are beyond East or West, African or Western, black or white, infected or not infected.

In *The HIV and AIDS Bible*, Musa Dube has already pointed out to us the urgent need for new theological and biblical paradigms to confront the reality of HIV/AIDS. In doing so, she has not only provided a model of African scholarship that is both intellectually lucid and socially engaged, she has also brought us to the threshold of radically fresh engagement with HIV/AIDS. The challenge now is how to move beyond the threshold into the nitty-gritty of dreams and visions able to sustain Christian life in the wake of HIV/AIDS. Our exploration here has shown that getting there requires us to recover the practice and discipline of la-

---

11. See C. Black, "The Persistence of Wounds," in *Lament: Reclaiming Practices in Pulpit, Pew, and Public Square*, ed. Sally A. Brown and Patrick D. Miller (Louisville: Westminster John Knox, 2005), 54.

ment. What still needs to be done is to display how and what a biblically inspired practice of lament might look like in our time. What is, nonetheless, sufficiently clear is that the recovery of such practice is not only urgent, but allows for more explicit glimpses of the dreams and visions from beyond that are able to sustain Christian life and hope in the era of shattered dreams. At any rate, it is clear to me that any Christian social engagement that is at once biblically grounded, historically relevant, intellectually compelling, and existentially hopeful—more so in the wake of HIV/AIDS—must be shaped around the notion of lament.

WORKS CITED

Brown, Sally A., and Patrick D. Miller, eds. *Lament: Reclaiming Practices in Pulpit, Pew, and Public Square*. Louisville: Westminster John Knox, 2005.

Dube, Musa Wenkosi. *Africa Praying: A Handbook of HIV/AIDS Sensitive Sermons and Liturgy*. Geneva: World Council of Churches, 2003.

———. *Grant Me Justice: HIV/AIDS and Gender Readings of the Bible*. Maryknoll, NY: Orbis Books, 2005.

———. *HIV/AIDS and the Curriculum: Methods of Integrating HIV/AIDS in Theological Programs*. Geneva: World Council of Churches, 2003.

———. *The HIV and AIDS Bible: Selected Essays*. Scranton, PA: University of Scranton, 2006.

———. *Other Ways of Reading: African Women and the Bible*. Atlanta: SBL, 2001.

———. *Post-colonial Feminist Interpretation of the Bible*. Atlanta: Chalice, 2000.

Dube, Musa, and Gerald West, eds. *The Bible in Africa: Translations, Trajectories, and Trends*. Leiden: Brill, 1999.

Dube, Musa, and Jeffrey Staley. *John and Postcolonialism: Travel, Space, and Power*. Sheffield: Sheffield Academic Press, 2002.

Maluleke, Tinyiko Sam. "The Challenge of HIV/AIDS for Theological Education." *Missionalia* 29, no. 2 (2001): 125–43.

The Liberative Power of Silent Agency: A Postcolonial Afro-Feminist-Womanist Reading of Luke 10:38–42

Alice Y. Yafeh-Deigh

Luke 10:38–42, a small five-verse story about Jesus' visit with Martha and Mary, is among the most popular stories in the Lucan narrative for many female readers.[1] Albeit its popularity, the interpretation of the story remains a significant bone of contention among interpreters. The multivalent nature of key terms in the story, its built-in gaps and ambiguities have been read and interpreted in diverse ways. The variety of differing interpretations is not only a reflection of semantic ambiguities of key terms in the story; it is also a manifestation of the many different sociopolitical, ideological, theological, and ecclesial situations and commitments of interpreters. This paper seeks to offer *one* of the many potential readings of the story within the context of a postcolonial Afro-feminist-womanist biblical hermeneutics.[2] A postcolonial Afro-feminist-womanist approach takes the concerns of disadvantaged, marginalized grassroots women as the starting point of analysis. The approach will discern ways in which this story that is not written with contemporary Cameroonian women's experience in mind can be critically recontextualized and hermeneutically reappropriated within the context of their own lived experi-

---

1. Its popularity for female readers probably stems from the fact that it is one of the very few narratives in the New Testament that has women as the main characters, where they are actually the protagonists. Thus, the story has a particular relevance to women.

2. My choice of the tripartite phrase "Afro-feminist-womanist" is informed particularly by my desire to move away from oppositional rhetoric that characterizes much of the conversation about women's experiences and realities. To be sure, oppositional rhetoric can provide a critical step forward, but the ultimate goal is to move beyond oppositional arguments in the search for a space where women can constructively address our common concerns. The concept "Afro-feminist-womanist" carries the weight of the collective and multilateral experiences of women. It assumes and recognizes shared aspects as well as unique ones, thereby holding up the tension between real differences and commonality which the binary definitions of womanism/feminism do not properly capture. Until a more inclusive term is coined, in an effort to adopt a holistic, tri-polar approach to speaking about women's experiences and realities, I situate my work in the context of an Afro-feminist-womanist hermeneutics. My hope is that the Afro-feminist-womanist paradigm will add parameters for dialogue and also construct bridges for "a way forward" for women.

ences.[3] The working hypothesis of this paper is that in Luke 10:38–42, Mary creates and enables a unique kind of agency—silent resistance to patriarchal gender relations. I show that Jesus' consent to and affirmation of Mary's subversive decision forces the reader to reassess the meaning of agency, especially in the contemporary context where, influenced by Eurocentric cultural ideals, silence is generally deplored as a symbol of passivity and disempowerment. Mary's silent agency, I argue, could not only be construed as an emancipatory strategy for contemporary women in marginalized communities in rural Cameroon,[4] it could also be a tool for liberation that effectively challenged established gender roles and forge sustainable change. Ultimately, I maintain, the space that Mary silently intrudes and creates is a space that is truly pregnant with possibilities for Cameroonian rural women's struggle for liberation and empowerment.[5]

My analysis will proceed as follows. First, to support my contention that wherever one enters the story inevitably dictates how one reads and interprets the story, I briefly present examples of interpretations that result from two very different starting points. One strand of interpretation is based on the premise that the story in Luke 10:38–42 is a description of an event from the life of the historical Jesus. The second strand is based on the assumption that the story is a pure creation of Luke or the Lucan community, not an event in the life of the historical Jesus. Second, I evaluate how the ancient Mediterranean social structures of honor and shame affected gender relationships in the world of Luke's Gospel. Third, I use the lens of postcolonial Afro-feminist-womanist hermeneutics to reevaluate gender relationships in rural communities in Cameroon within its own contemporary

---

3. Notwithstanding the historical and cultural distance between the lived experiences of women in the first century Mediterranean world of the Lucan community and the lived experiences of contemporary Cameroonian rural women's, one can still presuppose a great amount of cultural overlap due to multiple parallels and similarities between the biblical world and the traditional African communities. The parallels and similarities allow one to make analogical connections between the two worlds while, at the same, being cognizant of and taking seriously the historical particularity of the story.

4. Women in urban settings have more political and economic power than those live in rural areas. Because of access to information, greater employment potentials, and income-earning capacity that an urban setting provides, urban women have more decision-making power compared to rural women, and can consequently break out of the system easily. Since two-thirds of the population of women live in rural areas, rural women comprise the majority of women who are affected by patriarchally structured relationships. This essay, therefore, intentionally privileges the plight of rural women who, though victims of harmful patriarchal values, cannot easily break out of the patriarchal system. For some of these women, Mary's silent yet subversive agency may offer positive model in their struggles for survival.

5. To be sure, there are plural postcolonial African women interpretations. They share, however, a common goal of empowering women through interpretive strategies that decolonize the biblical text and its ideologies.

cultural systems of honor and shame and make suggestions about the implications of Luke 10: 38–42 for contemporary women in Cameroonian rural communities.

LUKE 10:38–42: AN EVENT FROM THE LIFE OF THE HISTORICAL JESUS

Notwithstanding the different strands in interpretation, there is a general consensus among interpreters that gender issues are central to the narrative of Luke 10:38–42. Every interpreter agrees that the narrative has implications for women in leadership and women in all areas of ministry. Regardless of what epistemological framework is used as an interpretive lens to the narrative, the variety of analyses of the story center on (1) what the story conveys through the portrayal of Martha and Mary's characters, (2) Jesus' statements regarding the actions of the two sisters, and (3) what the text implies about women's leadership roles in the church. These central questions have been assessed and addressed in multiple ways in the aforementioned approaches.

In this section, I present a variety of interpretations that read Luke 10:38–42 as a narrative that is based on an event in the life of the historical Jesus. Interpreters, especially feminist apologists, who read Luke 10:38–42 as a story that describes an event of in the life of the historical Jesus generally read the story through the lens of a hermeneutic of trust; that is, they read with the text rather than against it.[6] Based on this hermeneutical starting point, a majority of interpreters strongly emphasize the emancipatory potential of the story for women.[7] In terms of conven-

---

6. Although applying different methods to the pericope, they share a common approach in that they all locate the occurrence of this story in the life and ministry of Jesus. It should be noted that this is not an uncritical approach to the text. Those who approach the text via a hermeneutic of trust or who read with the text rather than against it do not simply accept uncritically what the story says about gender relations. The distinctiveness of this approach lies in its treatment of Mary and Martha as historical characters, and its pivotal assumption that the broader countercultural ministry of the historical Jesus is a necessary starting point for understanding gender dynamics in the story in Luke 10:38–42.

7. Cheryl Townsend Gilkes, "'Go and Tell Mary and Martha': The Spirituals, Biblical Options for Women, and Cultural Tensions in the African American Religious Experience," *SC* 43 (1996): 563–81; Ben Witherington, *Women and the Genesis of Christianity* (Cambridge: Cambridge University Press, 1990), 100–101; Mary Cartledge-Hayes, *To Love Delilah: Claiming the Women of the Bible* (San Diego: Lura Media, 1990), 72; Loveday Alexander, "Sisters in Adversity: Retelling Martha's Story," in *Women in the Biblical Tradition*, ed. George J. Brooke (Lewiston, ME: Edwin Mellen, 1992), 167–86; Adele Reinhartz, "From Narrative to History: The Resurrection of Mary and Martha," in *Women Like This: New Perspectives on Jewish Women in the Greco-Roman World*, ed. Amy-Jill Levine (Atlanta: Scholars, 1991), 161–84; Kathleen E. Corley, *Private Women Public Meals: Social Conflict in the Synoptic Tradition* (Peabody, MA: Hendrickson, 1993), 137; Dorothée Soelle, "Mary and Martha," in *The Window of Vulnerability: A Political Spirituality*, trans. Linda M. Maloney (Minneapolis: Fortress, 1990), 93–96; Marjorie Kimbrough L, *She Is Worthy: Encounters with Biblical Women* (Nashville: Abingdon, 1994); Rose Sallberg Kam, *Their Stories, Our*

tional patriarchal ethos or customs of Luke's world, the story is viewed as radically countercultural. For this reason, many interpreters considered it the "Magna Carta" for women's liberation.[8] Generally, scholars who have assessed the story in terms of its emancipatory potential for women almost invariably focus on the statement that Mary," sat at the Lord's feet and listened to what he was saying" (Lk 10:39). In its ancient Mediterranean patriarchal and androcentric context, the posture of Mary at the feet of Jesus evokes the posture of a male disciple/student vis-à-vis his master.

Mary's posture at the feet of Jesus has been the subject of a wide variety of interpretations. It is generally viewed by interpreters in this category as uncharacteristically subversive of culturally assigned positions. Accordingly, the countercultural thrust of Luke 10:38–42 is thus assessed through the lens of Mary's positioning in the narrative and Jesus' affirmation of her positioning even though Mary is clearly "violating the household codes and social norms."[9] The idiomatic expression "sitting at the feet" is traditionally interpreted as a rabbinic idiom for learning from a rabbi. So Mary sits at Jesus' feet, demonstrating an appropriate posture of a disciple.[10] Leonard Swidler argues that Jesus' endorsement of Mary's unusual behavior indicates that he "explicitly rejected the housekeeping role as the female role."[11] For Ben Witherington, "Luke is intimating that Mary is a disciple, and as such her behavior is to be emulated."[12]

While Swidler and Witherington assessment above might indicate that Jesus' appraisal of Mary's attitude provides a strong difference to traditional perspectives, some puzzling questions still come to the reader's mind. Why did Jesus rebuke Martha for complaining that Mary has left her alone "to serve" (diakonein, 10:40)? What is Martha being anxious and troubled about? What is the "one thing,"

Stories: Women of the Bible (New York: Continuum, 1995); Satoko Yamaguchi, Mary and Martha: Women in the World of Jesus (Maryknoll, NY: Orbis, 2002); Joel Green, The Gospel of Luke (NICNT; Grand Rapids: Eerdmans, 1997), 433–34; Paul Borgman, The Way according to Luke: Hearing the Whole Story of Luke-Acts (Grand Rapids: Eerdmans, 2006); Mitzi J. Smith, "A Tale of Two Sisters: Am I My Sister's Keeper?" JRT 2 (1996): 69–75; Robert C. Tannehill, Luke (ANTC; Nashville: Abingdon, 1996), 185; Luke T. Johnson, Luke (Sacra Pagina; Collegeville, MN: Liturgical, 1991), 175; Sharon H. Ringe, Luke (WBC; Louisville: Westminster John Knox, 1995), 161–62; Gordon Fee, "One Thing is Needful? Luke 10:42," in New Testament Textual Criticism: Essays in Honour of Bruce M. Metzger, ed. E. J. Epp and G. D. Fee (Oxford: Clarendon, 1981), 61–75.

8. L. Swidler, Biblical Affirmations of Women (Philadelphia: Westminster, 1979), 272–73.

9. Smith, "Two Sisters," 72.

10. Cf. B. Witherington, Women in the Ministry of Jesus (SNTSMS 51; Cambridge: Cambridge University Press, 1984), 101. For other occurrences of the idiomatic phrase "sitting at the feet," see Luke 8:35 and Acts 22:3.

11. Swidler, Biblical Affirmations of Women, 272

12. Witherington, Women in the Ministry of Jesus, 100; cf. Renita J. Weems, Just a Sister Away: A Womanist Vision of Women's Relationships in the Bible (San Diego: LuraMedia, 1988), 39–50. It should be noted, though, that although it is unusual for women to be described in the role of a disciple, it is not unknown in the ancient world.

the "good portion," chosen by Mary? How did Martha respond to Jesus' response? Did she stay annoyed with Mary? These basic yet very important questions remain unrequited just like many other unanswered questions in the story, thereby leaving the plot open-ended. As a result, a wide range of possible interpretations exist. In regard to Jesus' rebuke of Martha, the most popular proposal is that Jesus' displeasure with Martha results from her distraction or preoccupation with "many things" as opposed to the "one thing" required (Lk 10:41).

For example, Green argues that "the manner of Martha's hospitality is ill adapted to the sort of hospitality for which Jesus seeks."[13] To Howard Marshall, "Martha, as the hostess, was distracted from listening by her preparations for a meal."[14] Joel Green thinks it is because "Martha's speech is centered in 'me-talk.'"[15] Thus, her service of hospitality is "marked by distractions and worry that conflict with the growth and expression of authentic faith."[16] In contrast to Martha, Mary, "sitting at Jesus' feet in childlike trust and openness to learning, exemplifies love of God."[17] This evaluation of the problem sets up a false dualism between Mary and Martha. Following this line of reasoning, early Christian patristic writings, beginning with Origen,[18] reduced the two sisters to theological principles of the embodiment of justification by faith and by works, while still another view is used to reject the traditional housewife role of Martha and opt for Mary's nonconventional role. [19]

Basically, most traditional allegorical readings of the narrative often served to perpetuate dichotomies between the characters of the two sisters. The often androcentric focus of traditional interpretations establish an irreconcilable "good woman/bad woman" polarization of Mary and Martha.[20] Schüssler Fiorenza and other feminist apologists have rightly criticized interpretations that view the two women as polarities, forcing the reader to choose between the two sisters and pit one against the other.[21] Concurring with Schüssler Fiorenza, Mitzi Smith main-

---

13. Green, *Gospel of Luke*, 434.

14. I. Howard Marshall, *The Gospel of Luke: A Commentary on the Greek Text* (NIGTC; Grand Rapids: Eerdmans, 1978), 451.

15. Green, *Gospel of Luke*, 437.

16. Ibid., 436.

17. Borgman, *The Way*, 103.

18. See Origen, "Homilies on Luke," trans. Joseph T. Lienhard, in *The Fathers of the Church* (Washington, DC: Catholic University of America, 1996), 94:192–93. cf. Mary Elizabeth Mason, *Active Life and Contemplative Life: A Study of the Concepts from Plato to the Present* (Milwaukee: Marquette University Press, 1961).

19. Schüssler Fiorenza, "Interpretation for Liberation," 26.

20. Ibid., 27.

21. Barbara Reid, Schüssler Fiorenza, and others also caution against anti-Jewish readings of the story. Jesus' boundary-breaking practices took place within Judaism. Therefore, it is important that Christian women's role not be construed over and against that of Jewish women's because Jesus advocated liberative possibilities within Judaism. Cf. Schüssler Fiorenza, "A Feminist Critical Interpretation for Liberation," and Reid, *Choosing* .

UNIVERSITY OF WINCHESTER
LIBRARY

tains, "it was not Jesus' intention to juxtapose or compare housework and education."[22] Loveday Alexander notes that elsewhere in Luke Jesus often declines involvement in sibling rivalries (cf. Lk 6:41–42; 12:13–15; 15:25–32).[23] In Alexander's
contention, "Jesus' rebuke of Martha is the result of his general attempt to shock
his audience. Not only should Mary, the spiritual disciple, serve as a role model for
women, but Martha too is important as sister, as hostess, as servant of Christ, as
disciple."[24] Ultimately, Alexander notes, "the Lucan Jesus is more concerned with
the reversal of existing value-systems than with the setting-up of new ones; and
paradox plays an important part in this process."[25]

In Witherington's argument, "Luke's intention is once again to convey a certain
male-female parallelism in order to stress the equality of man and woman in God's
plan of salvation, and their equal importance to the new community."[26] Thus, Jesus'
words "are neither an attempt to devalue Martha's attempts at hospitality, nor an
attempt to attack a woman's traditional role; rather Jesus defends Mary's right to
learn from him and says this is the crucial thing for those who wish to serve him."[27]
Cartledge-Hayes agrees. He states: "Jesus was making a radical statement for his
time, not setting up women for conflicts between home and career."[28]

In Joseph Fitzmyer's opinion, "to read this episode as a commendation of contemplative life over against active life is to allegorize it beyond recognition and to
introduce a distinction that was born only of later preoccupations."[29]

Ultimately, even though there is plurality of interpretation among interpreters
who discuss the story in relation to the historical Jesus, the interpretations invariably highlight the story's stress on the need for disciples to listen to the word of the
Lord.[30] Hearon cogently concludes, "If we hear this story within the context of the
community of faith, we hear echoes of the struggle to be faithful to the demands
of ministry, and, in that ministry to be faithful to Jesus. It is not a matter of one

---

22. Smith, "Two Sisters," 73.

23. Loveday, "Sisters in Adversity," 181–82.

24. Alexander, "Sisters in Adversity," 213. In like manner, Smith contends, "sisters
must stop searching for reasons to undermine, downplay, and ignore another sister's ac-
complishments, goals, dreams, and calls. Instead, we must actively empower each other"
("Two Sisters," 69).

25. Alexander, "Sisters in Adversity," 179.

26. Witherington, *Women and Genesis*, 215.

27. Ibid., 101.

28. Cartledge-Hayes, *Delilah*, 72.

29. Joseph A. Fitzmyer, *The Gospel according to Luke X–XXIV* (New York: Doubleday,
1985), 892–93.

30. Cf. John N. Collins, "Did Luke Intend a Disservice to Women in the Martha and
Mary Story?" *BTB* 28 (1998): 104–11. Cf. idem, *Diakonia: Reinterpreting the Ancient Sources*
(New York: Oxford University Press, 1990).

or the other. It is learning to hold both Martha and her sister Mary in dynamic tension."[31]

LUKE 10:38–42: A PRODUCT OF THE LUCAN COMMUNITY

Interpretations whose interpretive starting point is the assumption that the story about Martha and Mary is a product of the Lucan Community have typically been suspicious of Luke's account and have rightly been skeptical and critical of traditional interpretations of the narrative. Schüssler Fiorenza argues that the story "is generated by and addressed to a situation in the life of the early church."[32] The story is thus read as transparent of gender issues faced by the Lucan community. Interpreters in this category, therefore, reject Luke's assumptions and prejudices against women. Jane Schaberg, for instance, maintains that Luke's narrative as a whole is "extremely dangerous" because it deftly portrays women "as models of subordinate service, excluded from the power centre of the movement and from significant responsibilities. Claiming the authority of Jesus, this portrayal is an attempt to legitimate male dominance in the Christianity of the author's time."[33]

In regards to the narrative in Luke 10:38–42, the hermeneutical stance here is that, at its core, the story of Martha and Mary is inherently misogynistic and oppressive. To interpreters in this category, the story is influenced and/or shaped by androcentric point of view. The critical reader should therefore employ the hermeneutical lens of suspicion to examine the oppressive function of the story by identifying its androcentric-patriarchal character and dynamics.[34] For interpreters in this category, what is problematic about Luke 10:38–42 is the way Martha is depicted? Her characterization in the story betrays a conflict surrounding the ministerial service performed by Christian women in the early church. Though Mary is elevated at Martha's expense and depicted as an ideal disciple, she is a passive and

---

31. Holly Hearon, "Between Text and Sermon: Luke 10:38–42," *Int* 58 (2004): 95.

32. Schüssler Fiorenza, "Interpretation for Liberation," 29.

33. Jane Schaberg, "Luke," in *The Women's Bible Commentary*, ed. S. Ringe and C. Newsom (Philadelphia: Westminster John Knox, 1992), 275.

34. Elizabeth Schüssler Fiorenza, "Theological Criteria and Historical Reconstruction: Martha and Mary, Luke 10 28–42," *Colloquy* 53 (Berkeley, CA: CHSHMC, 1986), 1–12; cf. idem, "A Feminist Critical Interpretation for Liberation: Martha and Mary, Lk. 10:38–42," *RIL* 3 (1986): 29; idem, *But She Said: Feminist Practices of Biblical Interpretation* (Boston: Beacon, 1992), 52–76; Barbara E. Reid, "Choosing the Better Part," *BR* 42 (1997): 23–31; Mary Rose D'Angelo, "Women in Luke-Acts A Redactional View," *JBL* 109 (1990): 441–61; Hal Taussig, "The Sexual Politics of Luke's Mary and Martha Account: An Evaluation of the Historicity of Luke 10:38–42," *FFNT* 7 (1991): 317–19; Warren Carter, "Getting Martha Out of the Kitchen: Luke 10:38–42," *CBQ* 58 (1996): 272, 275–76; Ranjini Rebera, "Polarity or Partnership?" *Semeia* 78 (1997): 93–108; Turid Seim, *Double Message of Luke-Acts: Patterns of Gender in Luke-Acts* (Edinburgh: T&T Clark; Nashville: Abingdon, 1994).

silent disciple. Martha, on the other hand, though the active and vocal character, is seen as a traditional woman in her kitchen duties.[35]

Answering the question regarding the object of Martha' distraction, readings in this category maintain that Martha "is preoccupied with *diakonia and diakonein,* terms that in Luke's time had already become technical terms for ecclesial leadership."[36] Carter concurs. He argues, "By the end of Acts, Luke's audience has encountered the noun διακονία eight times in contexts that concern not kitchen activity but participation with others in leadership and ministry on behalf of the Christian community."[37] So, what is the point Luke or the Lucan community is making about gender relations? For Schüssler Fiorenza, Luke wants to "silence women leaders of house churches who like Martha might have protested and at the same time to extol the silent and subordinate behavior of Mary."[38] Luke does this by stressing "that the *diakonein* of Martha is not the 'one thing needful' and must be subordinated to the 'listening to the word.'"[39] Thus, Schüssler Fiorenza notes, "Martha, the independent and outspoken woman, is rejected in favor of the dependent Mary who chooses the posture of a subordinate student."[40]

This, to Schüssler Fiorenza, is indicative of Luke's concerted strategy of subordinating women. While early Christian women struggled "against patriarchal restrictions of women's leadership and ministry at the turn of the first century,"[41] Luke "appeals to a revelatory word of the resurrected Lord in order to restrict women's ministry and authority."[42] As already noted, Warren Carter contends that Martha's "much ministry" consists rather of leadership or ministry in the Christian community and on its behalf."[43] For him, the context of Martha's complaint and request concern partnership in ministry and leadership. Martha "is distracted by her responsibilities of leadership and ministry on behalf of the church."[44] She is "one of several women in roles of ministry and leadership, in partnership with the church's wider ministry."[45]

To be sure, the conclusion reached by Schüssler Fiorenza, Carter, and others is predicated on a specific interpretation of the polysemous verb διάκονέω in

---

35. Cf. Christopher Hutson, "Martha's Choice: A Pastorally Sensitive Reading of Luke 10: 38–42," *RQ* 45 (2003): 139–50. It should be noted that the pericope has traditionally been interpreted as a story about proper hospitality; hence, it is often placed within the context of a meal and other domestic duties.

36. Schüssler Fiorenza, "Interpretation for Liberation," 30.

37. Carter, "Kitchen," 272.

38. Schüssler Fiorenza, "Interpretation for Liberation," 31

39. Ibid.

40. Ibid., 29

41. Ibid., 33

42. Ibid., 31

43. Carter, "Kitchen," 272.

44. Ibid., 273

45. Ibid., 274.

terms of participation in leadership and ministry rather than "waiting on tables" or "serving guests." Through Luke's use of the words διακονία and διάκονέω elsewhere in Luke-Acts, Carter argues that Martha "is not distracted by her kitchen duties. Consistently with the actions of the male leaders of Acts denoted elsewhere by διακονία, her 'much ministry' consists rather of leadership or ministry in the Christian community and on its behalf. By analogy with these uses of διακονία, her [Martha's] responsibilities include care for believers, teaching, and preaching, perhaps as a leader of a house church."[46]

Contra Carter and feminist interpreters, Tannehill's reads διακονία in its restricted/literal sense of serving food and argues that "in Luke διακονία and διάκονέω always refer to the work of preparing and serving food, work normally performed by those regarded as social inferiors, such as women and servants."[47] John Collins offers linguistic evidence that precludes the possibility of reading Martha's *diakonia* in terms of her leadership or ministry in the Christian community.[48] Essentially, for feminist critical interpreters like Schüssler Fiorenza and Carter, by the time Luke is writing, the terms διακονία and διάκονέω had achieved the technical meanings and used in the context of ministerial service.[49]

At the end of her analysis, Schüssler Fiorenza concludes, "feminist interpretation that is interested in defending the story as positive for women perpetuates the androcentric dualism and patriarchal prejudice inherent in the original story."[50] Barbara Reid agrees. She states: "contemporary readers of Luke choose the better part when they read against the grain of Luke's rendition of this story."[51] Thus, from a rhetorical and a pragmatic standpoint, Luke 10: 38–42 does actually re-inscribe the cultural status quo.

Unavoidably, to analyze the pericope in a gender-critical perspective implies the analysis of issues of power relations, gender oppression, and many other forms of oppressive power relationships. If a key premise to understanding these issues is the assumption that the Lucan narrative offers the readers "direct information about the theology of the early church and not about the teaching of the historical Jesus,"[52] then Schüssler Fiorenza's claim that the narrative in Luke 10: 38–42 contributes to the continued marginalization of women and to the further reinforcement of a patriarchal relations is a logical, even plausible conclusion.

An equally gender-sensitive approach that treats Mary and Martha as historical characters, that takes as starting point the assumption that Luke 10:38–42 narrates an event that took place in the life of the historical Jesus, and that locates the story

46. Ibid.
47. Tannehill, *Narrative Unity*, 2:22.
48. See John N. Collins, "Did Luke Intend a Disservice to Women in the Martha and Mary Story?" *BTB* 28 (1998): 109–10.
49. Cf. Schüssler Fiorenza, *But She Said*, 64.
50. Schüssler Fiorenza, "Interpretation for Liberation," 33
51. Reid, *Choosing*, 31
52. Norman Perrin, *What Is Redaction Criticism?* (Philadelphia: Fortress, 1969), 69.

within Jesus' boundary breaking ministry and call for the liberation will certainly underline the countercultural impulses within the story. This is what most interpreters of the first category did. Certainly, the approach does acknowledge and critiques androcentric and patriarchal assumptions in story. Yet, it sees a radical subversion of those assumptions in the countercultural, boundary breaking praxis of Jesus. Both of the approaches, therefore, have an advocacy position in the reading and interpretation of the story.

In sum, the various interpretations that result from these approaches confirm that by dealing with specific aspects and functions of a narrative, interpreters inevitably elicit results in conjunction with their questions, methods, theories, and hypotheses, and values. As a result, certain interpretations are brought to the foreground while others, wittingly or unwittingly, are overlooked.

As a result of this presupposition, I disagree with Schüssler Fiorenza's conclusion that "feminist interpretation that is interested in defending the story as positive for women perpetuates the androcentric dualism and patriarchal prejudice inherent in the original story."[53] Interpreters situated in different contexts access the meaning potential of the story differently. My reading will show that in some specific situations or contexts, especially in contexts where there is a strong culture of gender inequality, and where women who publicly challenge the status quo experience harassment and violence, women can act to challenge established gender hierarchies and to effect change through silent agency. For these women, the Mary and Martha narrative in Luke 10:38–42, particularly Mary's subversive attitude in the narrative, could be appropriated and used as the basis for transformative praxis. Thus, the silence of women cannot be universally deplored as a symbol of passivity and powerlessness. Ultimate, I will contend that Jesus' consent and affirmation of Mary's silent agency authorizes resistance to relations and structures of domination.

The aim of this brief review was to provide an overview of two major hermeneutic frameworks underlying the various interpretations of the Mary and Martha narrative in Luke 10:38–42. My analysis has revealed that some interpreters read Luke 10:38–42 as an event in the life of the historical Jesus while others read it as a creation of the Lucan community. Both of these hermeneutical starting points have given rise to a plurality of interpretations. The plurality of interpretations could be largely attributed to Luke's use of language that has an "indeterminate surplus of meaningful possibilities," and the various interpretations are "a production of meaning from the surplus."[54] Diversity in interpretation is also a result of

53. Schüssler Fiorenza, "Interpretation for Liberation," 33

54. T. K. Beal, "Ideology and Intertextuality: Surplus of Meaning and Controlling Means of Production," in *Reading between Texts: Intertextuality and the Hebrew Bible* (Louisville: Westminster John Knox, 1992), 30–31, quoted in Steve Moyise, "Intertextuality and the Study of Old Testament in the New," in *The Old Testament in the New Essays in Honour of J. L. North* (JSNTSup 189; Sheffield: Sheffield Academic Press, 2000), 33.

the social and cultural location of the interpreter; it is a dynamic between text and interpretive context. As Brian Blount rightly notes, "each interpretation is a single piece of a larger picture of potential meaning, and therefore represent an acquisition of only a segment of that potential."[55] In other words, "the reader accesses as 'meaning' that part of the potentiality that is most applicable to his or her social and linguistic context."[56] This means that no one interpretation can claim a position of interpretive authority.

Following this very brief review of examples of interpretations reached using the two aforementioned hermeneutical lenses, I move in the next section to reread and reinterpret the story using ideological framework of ancient Mediterranean concepts of honor and shame. It is my conviction that the ancient categories of honor and shame provide analogies and models to help reevaluate gender relationships in rural communities in Cameroon within the Cameroonian cultural systems of honor and shame.

Luke 10:38–42 and the Ancient Mediterranean Social Structures of Honor And Shame

In this section, I have elected to reread the story through the hermeneutical lens of the ancient categories of honor and shame because (1) the story is couched in language that evokes those categories and (2) those categories resonates well with the conceptual framework of women in rural communities in Cameroon. My approach is also postcolonial in that I am primarily interested in reading the story from the perspective of oppressed and marginalized rural women in Cameroon struggling for emancipation.

In recent decades, there has been a proliferation of works in social anthropology that have focused attention on the ancient Mediterranean social and cultural values of honor and shame.[57] These studies have shown that the concepts of honor and shame was a code of behavior that was very prevalent in the Mediterranean world, and that was consciously or unconsciously acquired or internalized by those

---

55. Brian K. Blount, *Cultural Interpretation: Reorienting New Testament Criticism* (Minneapolis: Fortress, 1995), 90.

56. Blount, "If You Get MY Meaning: Introducing Cultural Exegesis," in *Exegese und Theoriediskussion,* ed. Stefan Alkier and Ralph Brucker (Tübingen and Basel: Francke-Verlag, 1998); cf. "Righteousness from the Inside: The Transformative Spirituality of the Sermon on the Mount," in *The Theological Interpretation of Scripture: Classic and Contemporary Readings,* ed. Stephen E. Fowl (Cambridge, MA: Blackwell, 1997), 268–84, 263.

57. H. Moxnes, "Patron-Client Relations and the New Community in Luke-Acts," in *The Social World of Luke-Acts: Models for Interpretation,* ed. J. H. Neyrey (Peabody, MA: Hendrickson, 1991), 241–68; Bruce J. Malina, *The New Testament World: Insights from Cultural Anthropology* (1981; Louisville: Westminster John Knox, 2001), 25; Jerome H. Neyrey, "Despising the Shame of the Cross: Honor and Shame in the Johannine Passion Narrative," *Semeia* 69 (1996): 113–37.

living in that world. Based on cultural evaluation, "honor is a claim to positive worth along with the social acknowledgment of that worth by others."[58] People establish their honor, hence their identity on the basis of how they are seen through the eyes of others.[59] Shame thus "refers to a person's sensitivity about what others think, say, or do with regard to his or her honor."[60] People gained honor either through ascription or through achievement. Ascribed honor is gained by birth, adoption into a family and appointment to an office. Achieved or acquired honor is honor "actively sought and garnered most often at the expense of one's equals in the social contest of challenge and response."[61]

The narrative Luke 10: 38–42 is particularly framed in language that evokes the two categories of honor and shame.[62] Crucial to my reevaluation of the narrative through the lens of the ancient categories of honor and shame are two hermeneutical premises. First, my approach to the story assumes an interconnection of a hermeneutic of suspicion and a hermeneutic of trust that basically recognizes that "the Bible is a resource for liberation, but it is also a source of oppression and domination."[63] Thus, even though I approach the narrative with a critical, even suspicious, mind, recognizing that the narrative has sometimes functioned as a powerful tool of oppression, I also acknowledge that the story contains potentially emancipatory meanings to women who occupy various spaces and lifestyles.[64] Second, I assume that a "both/and" approach is capable of achieving an emancipatory alternative when gender relations are interpreted against the backdrop of the boundary-breaking ministry of Jesus.[65]

A core theme in the story of Jesus' visit with Martha and Mary is the theme of hospitality. As the narrative opens, Martha assumes the role of a male host by

---

58. Bruce Malina and Jerome Neyrey, "Honor and Shame in Luke-Acts: Pivotal Values of the Mediterranean World," in Neyrey, *Social World*, 26.

59. Cf. Vernon Robbins, *Exploring the Texture of Texts: A Guide to Socio-Rhetorical Interpretation* (Valley Forge, PA: Trinity Press International, 1996), 76.

60. Ibid.

61. Ibid.

62. Although the words "honor" and "shame" do not actually appear in the narrative, codes of honor and shame govern the key themes of hospitality and service.

63. Gerald West, "Biblical Hermeneutics in Africa," n.p. (accessed 26 June 2011). http://www.chora-strangers.org/files/chora/west2008_Parratt.pdf.

64. One must particularly read against the grain of traditional readings that are disempowering, that elevate Mary at Martha's expense, thereby setting sister against sister. Only by highlighting the effects of patriarchal expressions in the story can one effectively reclaim the story for the struggles of the oppressed and the marginalized.

65. I am assuming here a more inclusive "both/and" (rather than an "either/or") framework that analyzes the Mary and Martha narrative from a hermeneutic of trust and from a hermeneutic of suspicion. The approach reads the story as a depiction of an event in the life of the historical Jesus as well as a reflection of a situation in the Lucan community.

receiving Jesus into her house.[66] She welcomes Jesus into her house (*hypodecho-mai*, "Martha welcomed him into her home" [Lk 10:38]). The term *hypodecho-mai* denotes hospitality, a crucial value everywhere in the ancient world. In the Greco-Roman world, hospitality was generally perceived as a symbol of honor. Thus, Martha's reception of Jesus in her house brought public praise and honor to the family as a whole given that family honor usually subsumed personal honor. The Ancient Mediterranean world was not individualistic. It was a collectivist cultures. In a collectivist or group oriented culture, individuals are expected to seek the benefit of their family instead of pursuing selfish objectives. Martha, therefore, faithfully carries out the social role of hospitality in conjunction with the Mediterranean societal cultural expectations.[67]

Surprisingly, in contrast to Martha who responds to Jesus' word with acts of hospitality, the reader is told that Mary "sat herself down" (*parakathezomai*) at the feet of Jesus. Construed within the broader context of the social values of honor and shame, Mary bold self-determined decision to sit herself down at the Lord's feet instead of helping Martha could be interpreted as a potential source of shame to the family. In a culture where the quest of honor was essentially the driving force of life, where family honor is on the line in every public or private interaction,[68] Mary behaves inappropriately in that she does not respect social and cultural expectations and assumptions about gender behavior. Her attitude indicates that she is unconcerned about the opinion of others.[69] Martha's concern or complain is thus legitimate. She is concerned about the potential loss of family honor; she perceives Mary's behavior as potentially detrimental to the family's honor, particularly because Jesus, the Lord, is capable of ascribing honor to the family or stripping the family of honor. Thus, family honor is on the line in for Martha, especially

---

66. Note here that Jesus' traveling entourage has suddenly disappeared from the scene. Martha receives "him" (*auton*) into her house. The focus of the narrative is shifted to Jesus and the two women.

67. Jerome H. Neyrey, "Loss of Wealth, Loss of Family, and Loss of Honor: A Cultural Interpretation of the Original Four Makarisms," in *Modeling Early Christianity: Social-Scientific Studies of the New Testament in Its Context,* ed. Philip F. Esler (London: Routledge, 1995), 139–58; Halvor Moxnes, "Honor and Shame," *BTB* 23 (1993): 167–76; cf. *The New Testament World: Insights from Cultural Anthropology* (Atlanta: John Knox, 1993); "Honor and Shame," in *The Social Sciences and New Testament Interpretation,* ed. R. L. Rohrbaugh (Peabody, MA: Hendrickson, 1996), 20–40; Malina and Neyrey, "Pivotal Values," 25–65; cf. Jerome H Neyrey and Eric C. Stewart, eds, *The Social World of the New Testament: Insights and Models* (Peabody, MA: Hendrickson, 2008).

68. Cf. Moxnes, "Honor and Shame," 19.

69. Particularly since, as Joseph Hellerman notes, "in the collectivist culture of antiquity, one's honor was almost exclusively dependent upon the affirmation of the claim to honor by the larger social group to which the individual belonged" ("Challenging the Authority of Jesus: Mark 11:27–33 and Mediterranean Notions of Honor and Shame," *JETS* 43 [2000]: 214).

so because the defense of the family's honor was of paramount importance in the ancient world and women were looked upon as potential threat to it.

Given that within the cultural context of the Lucan narrative, Martha and Mary's self-worth and social status were achieved and maintained through family honor, Mary's move away from her culturally allocated position and her posture at the feet of Jesus subverts a central cultural requirement that is used for legitimation of public honor. She essentially does not embody those actions and qualities that the group values as honorable. By consenting to and by affirming Mary's decision, Jesus recognizes that the patriarchal code of honor and shame generates and obligates gender oppression. His affirmation of Mary's choice thus subverts the cultural notion of what constitutes an honorable behavior; he gives Mary divine legitimation, thereby indicating that "God's perspective on what kind of behavior merits honor differs exceedingly from the perspective of human beings."[70] In so doing, Jesus challenges the debilitating cultural codes of conduct or standards of behavior that constrain women's agency. Therefore, the climatic pronouncement that "Mary has chosen the better part, which will not be taken away from her," is hugely countercultural in that it gives Mary the power of self-determination; it underlines that Mary is sufficiently autonomous to make her own decisions even at expense of personal and family honor. As such, the salient point in Jesus response to Martha is that Mary has the right and ability to make her own choices and decisions about the right course of behavior.

In view of the above analysis, I argue against the grain of much scholarly opinion that Jesus climatic and categorical assertion in Luke 10:41–42 ("there is need of only one thing. Mary has chosen the better part, which will not be taken away from her" [10:41–42) does not target nor devalue Martha's own choice of service, but Martha's choice of service for Mary. In my reading, it is not Martha's *diakonia* with which Jesus has issues. At issue is what Mary chooses as opposed to what Martha wants Mary to choose. So, even though Jesus' choice of language "better portion" is contrastive in nature, in my reading, it is not contrasting Mary's better to Martha's good, but Mary's better to Martha's good for Mary. In this reading Mary's choice is at the heart of the problem. The entire narrative revolves around her behavior albeit she does not speak. As Jesus' response to Martha reveals, Mary's silence does not imply the absence of agency or the absence of voice. In the narrative, Mary's silence is a tool of resistance and empowerment.

Read from the point of view of Jesus' affirmation of Mary's action, the Mary and Martha narrative can provide resources for liberatory practices for contemporary women in rural communities in Cameroon. Mary's silent resistance can be used to mobilize women in their struggle against patriarchal relationships that re-inscribe social structures which spawn disempowerment and victimhood. It is very significant that Jesus affirms Mary's self-determined decision in a context where choices

---

70. David deSilva, *Honor, Patronage, Kinship, and Purity: Unlocking New Testament Culture* (Downers Grove, IL: InterVarsity Press, 2000), 51.

were very often, if not always, made for women.[71] Also, it is noteworthy that Jesus emphasize very clearly and unambiguously that Mary's choice will not be taken away from her. In my contention, this theological affirmation should be retrieved for emancipatory practices, and should serve as a principle for social critic and not as principle for maintaining the status quo. By authorizing a new social relationship that allows women to make their own choices, the Lucan Jesus confers honor to Mary and Martha's family. Therefore, Martha does not need to worry about her sister's choice. Mary has chosen the better part with regards to what is good for her. Ultimately, Jesus' affirmation of Mary's behavior ascribes honor not only to Mary, but also to Martha.

A Postcolonial Afro-feminist-womanist Re-evaluation and Re-contextualization

Reading Luke 10:38–42 from the ideological framework of the ancient Mediterranean concepts of honor and shame has enabled us to underline some of the cultural scripts inherent in narrative of Luke 10:38–42. Attention to the cultural script of shame and honor allows us to draw analogies between the experiences of the two sisters and those of contemporary women in rural communities in Cameroon. Analogies can be particularly drawn in terms of the portrayal of women.

In a collectivist society like Cameroon, honor and shame are dominant cultural values. The concepts are inexorably linked to the institutionalized patriarchal system of Cameroon. They are important aspects of the Cameroonian social life. The centrality of group honor, especially in rural tribal communities, results in individuals being tightly linked to their in-groups. In the collectivist model of family, gender relations are characterized with a strict hierarchy. The relationship between men and women is described in honor and shame categories. Within the shame and honor paradigm, women are socialized to conform to their prescribed roles within the household. They are expected to be subordinate to men and any attempt at gaining autonomy is considered a threat to the family. The only way women can acquire honor s by being good wives. The androcentric culture of Cameroon defines the ideal wife in terms of her prescribed roles within the community and household. She brings honor to her family and tribal community by being unwaveringly devoted to her husband. She is expected to sacrifice her own good for the greater good of the family and community. In terms of traditional family values, Martha is an embodiment of the ideal woman/wife.

When analogies are drawn, it becomes evident that the narrative of Luke 10:38–

---

71. Jesus' consent to Mary's decision is significant in ancient Mediterranean agrarian society, which, like most contemporary sub-Saharan African societies, involves a "hierarchically ordered, mostly male dominated, stratified social order" that subordinates women (Stuart L. Love, *Jesus and Marginal Women: The Gospel of Matthew in Social-Scientific Perspective* [Cambridge: Clark, 2009], 31).

42 addresses gender issues that are highly relevant to the modern day gender concerns in the rural communities in Cameroon. In these communities women have internalized their oppressed condition. They have particularly internalized and valued the idea that they are responsible for the honor of their husbands and their tribal groups. Mary's daring courage to resist stereotypical gender roles can inspire these women to equally take actions that resist oppressive systems that denigrate them.

IMPLICATIONS OF LUKE 10: 38–42 FOR CONTEMPORARY WOMEN IN CAMEROONIAN RURAL COMMUNITIES

The Bible has had a tremendous impact in the Cameroonian culture and society. Unlike some Western countries, in Cameroon, religious practices have an especially pragmatic social dimension. Many people use the Bible as a towering theological resource in search of meaning for their lives. Because of this, one fundamental challenge facing churches in Cameroon in this century is to wrestle theologically with the issue of women's empowerment in constructive ways, so that churches can effectively empower Cameroonian women who are sincerely committed to finding Scripture's relevance for daily life. Almost all Christian churches in Cameroon are embroiled in the contemporary controversy over women in leadership and women in all areas ministry. Each church, however, approaches the discussion differently. The controversy over women in leadership is emblematic of a much larger systemic problem. The controversy exposes some of the dangers of patriarchally structured relationships that are, by definition, discriminatory against women.

A reevaluation of gender relationships in rural communities in Cameroon from the perspective of an Afro-feminist-womanist hermeneutics requires us to bring a hermeneutic of decolonization to bear on our reading of the Lucan story. This is because, from the outset, missionary institutional discourses were oriented toward supporting the dominant interests of European colonialists. As West asserts, "African social and cultural concerns were not reflected in missionary and Western academic forms of biblical interpretation."[72] The missionary-colonial interpretations, therefore, promoted Christian principles that were grounded in European ideologies. By implication, biblical interpretation in colonial and post-colonial Cameroon, in particular, and in Sub-Saharan Africa, in general, is inextricably tied up in and shaped by political agendas and strategies. It is not surprising, then, that Colonial missionary readings and interpretations of the Bible were legitimating the political and economic subordination of women.

In the Cameroonian male dominated society, interpretation of the Bible is still largely still done through the lens of the colonial paradigm. The Bible remains an important ideological tool used to advance patriarchal agenda. Readings of the Bible are therefore powerfully shaped by the complex and subtle pressures

---

72. West, "Biblical Hermeneutics."

of imperial legacies. As such readings and interpretations even now reflect the presuppositions and prejudices of colonial mission churches. Rather than promote social justice for all, the Bible was/is use as a weapon that legitimated the oppression of women. In a nutshell, many of the assumptions which underlie the logic of colonial missionary ways of interpreting the Bible are still active forces in contemporary ecclesial communities in Cameroon. This means that most women, especially located in rural communities are still psychologically and mentally colonized. Reading for decolonization and for liberation implies then a reading "in opposition to the forms of biblical interpretation imposed by and inherited from missionary Christianity and Western academic biblical studies."[73]

From the aforementioned, it become clear that reading the narrative of Martha and Mary for decolonization and for liberation within the context of Cameroon should systematically take as starting point the lived experiences and the contextual particularities of oppressed and marginalized women. It should be "consciously informed by the worldview of, and the life experience within [their] culture."[74] Such a reading must be sensitive to and challenge inherent assumptions about gender in the narrative; it must always be "resolutely situated over against missionary colonial imperialism."[75] Thus, it takes an oppositional stance towards the legacies of missionary colonial interpretations of the Bible, which, most often, were influenced by the racial, gender, and imperial ideologies of the West.

With respect to the particular narrative of Luke 10:38–42, a postcolonial Afro-feminist-womanist reading acknowledges with Perrin that "Luke the historian becomes a self-conscious theologian, and the details of his composition can be shown convincingly to have been theologically motivated."[76] This means that Luke's theological imprint is unavoidably stamped upon the narrative. However, to admit that the Gospel writers shaped and modified traditions to fit their distinctive theological agendas does not necessarily mean that their narrative is unhistorical. It

---

73. West,"Biblical Hermeneutics." Cf. Musa Dube, *Postcolonial Feminist Interpretation of the Bible* (St. Louis: Chalice, 2000), 16, 21. In Musa Dube's contention, African postcolonial hermeneutics must read the Bible for decolonization. For her, reading for decolonization is reading against the sanctioning of unequal power relations in biblical texts. She particularly focuses her critique on the suppression of the female presence in the Bible. I totally share Dube's attitude of suspicion toward biblical texts. However, in my perspective, reading Luke 10:38–42 for decolonization and empowerment means reading with and for marginalized and oppressed women, especially paying attention to the questions that arise from their lived experiences. For those women who feel unsafe to speak out against oppressive structures, silent agency is a possibility worth considering. I therefore propose the space that Mary intrudes and creates as a space of resistance that subverts the status quo. It is an emancipatory space pregnant with possibilities. Women can inhabit it in their diverse struggles to re/claim their right to self-determination.

74. Ukpong, "Rereading," 5.

75. West, "Biblical Hermeneutics."

76. Perrin, *Redaction Criticism?* 29.

fundamentally necessitates sensitivity to gender roles and power dynamics inherent in the story. In the context of these power dynamics, I have located my reading of the story within the broader counter-cultural, boundary-breaking thrust of
Jesus' ministry. An important implication of locating the Lucan story within Jesus'
boundary breaking call for the liberation is that, at the end of the story, Mary is
not presented as a passive, submissive, and subservient woman. Jesus' affirmation
of Mary's agency is a subtle critique of patriarchy from within. At the end of the
story, it becomes clear that Mary creates and enables a different kind of agency—
silent resistance. We have come to associate silence with lack of agency, but Jesus'
evaluation of Mary's decision goes contrary to the patriarchal model of the passive
submissive woman. Mary's subversive attitude in the story challenges the reader
to reconsider the conventional definition of agency. The reader is compelled to
reassess the common assumption that agency is a synonym for activity and the
capacity to speak out. Personally, I do not think that women's silence can be attributed mainly to the absence of agency. To be sure, in some contexts and situations,
silence may function to maintain the status quo and perpetrate oppression and
subjugation. In such situations, women need to demonstrate agency through vocal
challenge against patriarchal hegemony and for the transformation of gender relations in an egalitarian direction. Still, in some specific situations like that of the
Lucan narrative, rather than being a symbol of passivity and powerlessness, silence
is ultimately construed as a form of agency and empowerment for Mary. Through
silent agency she was able to act and to effect change. Thus, Mary exemplifies a different kind of agency, a subtle form of agency that is affirmed and applauded by the
Lucan Jesus as an empowering choice, a better choice that will not be taken away
from her. Thus her silent agency is not only empowering strategy, it is a tool for the
liberation that effectively challenged established gender hierarchies.

Through silent agency, Mary undermines patriarchal hegemony without openly
challenging it. The space that Mary silently intrudes and creates is a space that is
truly pregnant with possibilities for Cameroonian rural women's empowerment.
It is a potentially liberatory space that allows women to autonomously make their
own choices unencumbered by patriarchal constraints. If the choice made moves
"against the prevailing winds of patriarchy,"[77] then why should anyone complain
that it is the wrong choice? At the end of the day, some women will choose silent
agency that might very wrongly be construed as submission to patriarchal cultural
practices. However, silence does not necessarily imply conformity. It might simply
mean that the women do not yet have the resources to deal with the consequences
of active confrontation of patriarchal cultural expectations. As Reid cogently puts
it, some women "will swim securely in the liberating waters; others will need to
cling to the debris of the sinking ship until they gain footing on *terra firma*."[78]
Those of us who are swimming "securely in the liberating waters" should be there

77. Reid, *Choosing*, 31
78. Ibid.

to affirm our sister and consent to her choice as situationally, or contextually a "better part" that will not be taken away from her.

Ultimately, the story in Luke 10:38–42 is a story about Mary's liberating choice. Although she is silent in the story, she is the central figure around whom all the actions of the story revolve. Jesus' advocacy on behalf of Mary's right to make her own decisions, when read in the context of Cameroonian rural women struggles for agency, becomes radically countercultural and emancipatory. With Mary, Jesus invites all women who are oppressed by patriarchal gender relations that deny them the dignity of making informed choices about their lives to enter the space that Mary creates and make it a space in which diverse subversive praxis are created and nurtured.

WORKS CITED

Achtmeier, Paul J., ed. *Harper's Bible Dictionary*. San Francisco: Harper and Row, 1985.

Alkier, Stefan, and Ralph Brucker. *Exegese und Theoriediskussion*. Tübingen and Basel: Francke-Verlag, 1998.

Bailey, Randall C., and J. Grant, eds. *The Recovery of Black Presence: An Interdisciplinary Exploration*. Nashville: Abingdon Press, 1995.

Birkett, Margaret. "The Inculturation of the Gospel Message from the Context of African Women Theologians." *FT* 5 (1994): 92–105.

Blount, Brian K. *Can I Get a Witness? Reading Revelation through African American Culture*. Louisville: Westminster John Knox, 2005.

———. *Cultural Interpretation: Reorienting New Testament Criticism*. Minneapolis: Fortress, 1995.

———. *Then the Whisper Put on Flesh New Testament Ethics in an African American Context*. Nashville: Abingdon, 2001.

Blount, Brian K., et al., eds. *True to Our Native Land: An African American New Testament Commentary*. Minneapolis: Fortress, 2007.

Carr, Anne, and Elisabeth Schüssler Fiorenza, eds. *Motherhood: Experience, Institution, Theology*. Concilium 206. Edinburgh: T&T Clark, 1989.

Carter, Warren. "Getting Martha Out of the Kitchen: Luke 10:38–42." *CBQ* 52 (1996): 264–80.

Cartledge-Hayes, Mary. *To Love Delilah: Claiming the Women of the Bible*. San Diego: Lura Media, 1990.

D'Angelo, Mary Rose. "Women in Luke-Acts. A Redactional View." *JBL* 109 (1990): 441–61.

———. "Women Partners in the New Testament," *JFSR* 6 (1990): 65–86.

Deen, Edith. *All of the Women of the Bible*. San Francisco: Harper and Row, 1955.

De La Torre, Miguel. *Reading the Bible from the Margins*. Maryknoll, NY: Orbis, 2002.

deSilva, David A. *Honor, Patronage, Kinship and Purity: Unlocking New Testament Culture*. IVP, 2000.

Detrick, R. Blaine. *Favorite Women of the Bible: Ten Sermons on the Lives of Familiar Scriptural Personalities*. Lima, Ohio: C.S.S., 1988.

Draper, Jonathan A., "Reading the Bible as Conversation: A Theory and Methodology for Contextual Interpretation of the Bible in Africa." *GT* 19 (2002): 1224.

Dube, Musa W. *Postcolonial Feminist Interpretation of the Bible*. St. Louis: Chalice, 2000.

———. "Reading of Semoya: Batwana Women's Interpretations of Matthew 15:21–28." *Semeia* 73 (1996): 111–29.

———. "Toward a Postcolonial Feminist Interpretation of the Bible." *Semeia* 78 (1997): 11–26.

———, ed. *Other Ways of Reading: African Women and the Bible*. Atlanta: SBL and WCC, 2001.

Emswiller, Sharon Neufer. *The Ongoing Journey: Women and the Bible*. Cincinnati: United Methodist Church, 1977.

Fitzmyer, Joseph. *The Gospel according to Luke*. AB28A, 28B. Garden City, NY: Doubleday, 1981, 1985.

Funk, Robert W., Roy W. Hoover, and the Jesus Seminar. *The Five Gospels: The Search for the Authentic Words of Jesus*. New York: Polebridge Press, 1993.

Greinacher, N., and N. Mette. *Diakonia: Church for the Others*. Concilium 198. Edinburgh: T&T Clark, 1988.

Hearon, Holly E. "Luke 10:38–42." *Interpretation* 58 (2004): 393–95.

Hellerman, Joseph H. "Challenging the Authority of Jesus: Mark 11:27–33 and Mediterranean Notions of Honor and Shame." *JETS* 43 (2000): 213–28.

Hutson, Christopher Roy. "Martha's Choice: A Pastorally Sensitive Reading of Luke 10:38–42. *RQ* 45 (2003): 139–50.

Johnson, Luke Timothy. *Luke*. SacPag 3. Collegeville, MN: Liturgical Press, 1991.

Kercheval, Mary L. "Women Balancing Work and Family." *Horizons* 8 (1995): 14–15.

Kilgallen, John J. "A Consideration of Some of the Women in the Gospel of Luke." *SM* 40 (1991): 27–55.

———. "Martha and Mary: Why at Luke 10:38–42?" *Bib* 84 (2003): 554–61.

———. "A Suggestion Regarding *gar* in Luke 10:42." *Bib* 73 (1992): 255–58.

Kimbrough, Marjorie L. *She Is Worthy: Encounters with Biblical Women*. Nashville: Abingdon, 1994.

Kraemer, Ross Shephard, and Mary Rose D'Angelo. *Women and Christian Origins*. New York: Oxford University Press, 1999.

Levine, Amy-Jill, and Marianne Blickenstaff, eds. *A Feminist Companion to Luke*. FCNT 3. London: Sheffield University Press, 2002.

Luter, Boyd, and Kathy McReynolds. *Women as Christ's Disciples*. Grand Rapids: Baker Books, 1997.

MacHaffie, Barbara. *Her Story: Women in Christian Tradition*. Philadelphia: Fortress Press, 1986.

Malina, Bruce J. *The New Testament World: Insights from Cultural Anthropology*. Louisville: Westminster John Knox, 1981, 2001.

Marshall, I. Howard. *Commentary on Luke*. NIGTC. Grand Rapids: Eerdmans, 1978.

Meeks, Wayne. *The First Urban Christians: The Social World of the Apostle Paul*. New Haven: Yale University Press, 1983.

Moloney, Francis J., "The Faith of Martha and Mary: A Narrative Approach to John 11:17–40." *Bib* 75 (1994): 471–93.

Moltmann-Wendel, Elizabeth. *The Women around Jesus*. New York: Crossroad, 1992.

Newsom, Carol A., and Sharon H. Ringe, eds. *The Women's Bible Commentary*. Louisville: Westminster John Knox, 1992.

Neyrey, Jerome H. *Honor and Shame in the Gospel of Matthew.* Louisville: Westminster John Knox, 1998.

Neyrey, Jerome H., and Eric C. Stewart, eds. *The Social World of the New Testament: Insights and Models.* Peabody, MA: Hendrickson, 2008.

Nunnally-Cox, Janice. *Foremothers: Women of the Bible.* New York: Seabury, 1981.

Powell, Mark Allan, ed. *The New Testament Today.* Louisville: Westminster John Knox, 1999.

Rebera, Ranjini, "Polarity or Partnership? Retelling the Story of Martha and Mary from Asian Women's Perspective." *Semeia* 78 (1997): 93–107.

Reid, Barbara E. *Choosing the Better Part? Women in the Gospel of Luke.* Collegeville, MN: Liturgical, 1996.

Ringe, Sharon H. *Luke.* Louisville: Westminster John Knox, 1995.

Schaberg, Jane, Alice Bach, and Esther Fuchs. *On the Cutting Edge: The Study of Women in Biblical Worlds. Essays in Honor of Elisabeth Schüssler Fiorenza.* New York: Continuum, 2004.

Schottroff, Luise. *Let the Oppressed Go Free: Feminist Perspectives on the New Testament, Gender, and the Biblical Tradition.* Louisville: Westminster John Knox, 1993.

———. *Lydia's Impatient Sisters: A Feminist Social History of Christianity.* Louisville: Westminster John Knox, 1995.

Schüssler Fiorenza, Elisabeth. *But She Said: Feminist Practices of Biblical Interpretation.* Boston: Beacon, 1992.

———. "A Feminist Critical Interpretation for Liberation: Martha and Mary, Lk. 10:38–42." *RIL* 3 (1986): 21–36.

———. *In Memory of Her: A Feminist Theological Reconstruction of Christian Origins.* New York: Crossroad, 1994.

———. *Jesus: Miriam's Child, Sophia's Prophet.* New York: Continuum, 1994.

———. *Wisdom Ways: Introducing Feminist Biblical Interpretation.* Maryknoll, NY: Orbis, 2001.

Segovia, Fernando, and Stephen Moore. *Postcolonial Biblical Criticism: Interdisciplinary Intersections.* T&T Clark, 2005.

Segovia, Fernando, and M. A. Tolbert. *Reading from this Place: Social Location and Biblical Interpretation in Global Perspective.* Minneapolis: Fortress, 1995.

Seim, Turid. *Double Message of Luke-Acts: Patterns of Gender in Luke-Acts.* Edinburgh: T&T Clark; Nashville: Abingdon, 1994.

Sugirtharajah, R. S. *The Bible and the Third World: Precolonial, Colonial, and Postcolonial Encounters.* Cambridge: Cambridge University Press, 2001.

———. *The Postcolonial Bible.* Sheffield: Sheffield Academic Press, 1998.

———. *Postcolonial Criticism and Biblical Interpretation.* New York: Oxford University Press, 2002.

———, ed. *The Postcolonial Biblical Reader.* Malden, MA: Blackwell, 2006.

Swidler, Leonard. *Biblical Affirmations of Women.* Philadelphia: Westminster, 1979.

Thurston, Bonnie Bowman. *The Widows: A Women's Ministry in the Early Church.* Minneapolis: Fortress, 1989.

———. *Women in the New Testament. Questions and Commentary.* Companions to the New Testament. New York: Crossroad, 1998.

Torjeson, Karen Jo. *When Women Were Priests: Women Leaders in the Early Church and the Scandal of Their Subordination in the Rise of Christianity.* San Francisco: Harper San Francisco, 1993.

Ukpong, Justin S. "Developments in Biblical Interpretation in Africa: Historical and Hermeneutical Directions." In *The Bible in Africa: Transactions, Trajectories, and Trends*, ed. G. O. West and M. Dube. Leiden: E. J. Brill, 2000.

———. "The Parable of the Shrewd Manager (Lk 16:1–13): An Essay in the Inculturation of Biblical Hermeneutics." *Semeia* 73 (1996): 189–210.

———. "Rereading the Bible with African Eyes." *JTSA* 91 (1995): 3–14.

Verheyden, J., ed. *The Unity of Luke-Acts*. Louvain: Louvain University Press, 1999.

Wall, Robert W. "Martha and Mary (Luke 10:38–42) in the Context of a Christian Deuteronomy." *JSNT* 35 (1989): 19–35.

Weems, Renita J. "Biblical Hermeneutics in Africa." Accessed 26 June 2011. http://www.chora-trangers.org/files/chora/west2008_Parratt.pdf

———. "Finding a Place among the Posts for Postcolonial Criticism in Biblical Studies in South Africa." *OTS* 10 (1997): 322–42.

———. "Indigenous Exegesis: Exploring the Interface between Missionary Methods and the Rhetorical Rhythms of Africa. Locating Local Reading Resources in the Academy." *Neot* 36 (2002): 147–62.

———. *Just a Sister Away: A Womanist Vision of Women's Relationships in the Bible*. San Diego: LuraMedia, 1988.

———. "Shifting Perspectives on the Comparative Paradigm in (South) African Biblical Scholarship." *RT* 12 (2005): 48–72.

———. "Taming Texts of Terror: Reading (against) the Gender Grain of 1 Timothy." *Scriptura* 86 (2004): 160–73.

West, Gerald O., ed. *Biblical Hermeneutics of Liberation: Modes of Reading the Bible in the South African Context*. 2nd ed. Maryknoll, NY: Orbis; Pietermaritzburg: Cluster, 1995.

West, G. O., and M. Dube. *The Bible in Africa: Transactions, Trajectories, and Trends*. Leiden: E. J. Brill, 2000.

Witherington, Ben. *Women and the Genesis of Christianity*. Cambridge: Cambridge University Press, 1990.

———. *Women in the Earliest Churches*. Cambridge: Cambridge University Press, 1984 .

Wold, Margaret. *Women of Faith and Spirit: Profiles of Fifteen Biblical Witnesses*. Minneapolis: Augsburg, 1987.

Yamaguchi, Satoko. *Mary and Martha: Women in the World of Jesus*. Maryknoll, NY: Orbis, 2002.

8. EMBODIMENT AND BIBLICAL INTERPRETATION IN THE HIV/AIDS CONTEXT

A Postcolonial Feminist Reading of Mark 14–16

Malebogo Kgalemang

A colonial missionary hymn, composed in Lesotho and widely sung in some Southern African churches, recalls vividly the crucifixion of Jesus. The hymn goes thus: *Sefapanong ke a boha* (At the Cross I behold thee); *Wena Mmoloki waka* (where my saviour is hanging); *Madi a tswa maqebeng, le metsi lehlakore* (the blood gushing from his wound, and the water from his side); *Kaona ke re ntlhatswe* (With the blood, I request the Saviour to cleanse me). The colonial missionary hymn notably seeks not to denounce the "atrocious agony felt by our sensitive savior as the nails were driven through his hands and feet."[1] Rather the song celebrates and elevates suffering to salvific status. Furthermore, the hymn with its allusion to the context of Roman imperial violence glorifies the "central figure of Christianity as the figure of a tortured man."[2] It is clear that the hymn draws its influence from the narrative of the gospel believed to be the earliest, Mark. The passion narrative as a series of individual frames is strongly undercut by a profound motif of difference as each sandwiched narrative works in comparison and contrast. The politics of difference is manifested in the portrayal of the characters and how each reflects the socio-religio-political representation of Mark's interests, rhetoric, and ideology. The passion narrative lends itself to many varied descriptions. It dramatizes the final and epic conflict of the entire Markan narrative of Jesus Christ, the son of God and his opponents.

In this essay, I will focus on the passion narrative of Mark 14–16 and will provide an analytic reading of the passion narrative from a postcolonial feminist methodology. A postcolonial feminist interpretation of the passion narrative takes into full cognizance the patriarchal nature, the imperial context that produced the crucifixion, the role of local politics, its collusion with empire, and the role of women in the passion narrative. I will first look at the scope of postcolonial feminist criticism of the Bible. The second part of the article will be apply the methodology of postcolonial feminist biblical interpretation. This interpretation

---

1. Stephen D. Moore, *Post Structuralism and the New Testament: Derrida and Foucault at the Foot of the Cross* (Minneapolis: Fortress, 1994), 75.

2. Ibid., 76.

of Mark 14–16 from postcolonial and ideological perspectives will be followed by a conclusion.

Postcolonial Feminist Biblical Interpretations

Postcolonial feminist analysis of the Bible "reads" and "writes" women at the collusion and intersection of patriarchy, imperialism, neocolonialism, gender, nation, and religion in the Bible. It is rooted in postcolonial feminist theory, in postcolonial biblical interpretation, and in feminist interpretation of the Bible.[3] It scrutinizes the gendered blind spots of the historical critical methodologies, by pointing out a crucial lack of attention to the colonial and imperial history of the Bible. However, its relationship to feminist interpretation of the Bible is a tense one. On the one hand, it draws from feminist interpretation of the Bible; on the other hand, postcolonial feminist interpretation of the Bible challenges the representation of women in feminist readings of the Bible. Postcolonial feminism interpretation of the Bible has asserted that the feminist biblical critic has ignored the history of imperialism and colonialism which were heavily part of the rise of Christendom[4]. Not only is it a critique of feminist biblical criticism, postcolonial feminist biblical criticism has developed a position from which to speak and a set of issues to be addressed.

The Bible, a book born in the diverse worlds of the Mediterranean, Palestine, Mesopotamia, and Northern Africa, took a journey to the Western culture where it historically became the emblem of Western culture. In the opening of *The Postmodern Bible: The Bible and Collective Culture*, its writers acknowledge the influence of the Bible. They confess, "We begin with a truism: the Bible has exerted more cultural influence in the West than any other single document."[5] This cultural influence enabled a transportation of the Bible to other parts of the world through colonial missionaries. In her book *Discovering the Bible in a Non-biblical World*, Kwok Pui Lan raises the relevance of the Bible in a pluralistic culture of Asia.[6] Her questions surround the interpretation of the Bible in a culture that is both plural-

---

3. See Rosemary Marangoly George, "Feminists Theorize Colonial/Postcolonial," in *The Cambridge Companion to Feminist Literary Theory,* ed. Ellen Rooney (Cambridge: Cambridge University Press, 2006), 211–31. Sara Mills, "Post-Feminist Theory," in *Contemporary Feminist Theories,* ed. Stevi Jackson and Jackie Jones (New York: New York University Press, 1998), 98–112.

4. Musa W. Dube, *Postcolonial Biblical Interpretation of the Bible* (St. Louis: Chalice, 2000); Catherine Keller, "The Love of Post Colonialism: Theology in the Interstices of Empire," in *Postcolonial Theologies: Divinity and Empire,* ed. Catherine Keller et al. (St. Louis: Chalice, 2004), 221–42.

5. George Aichele et al., *The Postmodern Bible: The Bible and Collective Culture* (New Haven: Yale University Press, 1995), 1.

6. Kwok Pui Lan, *Discovering the Bible in a Non-biblical World* (Maryknoll, NY: Orbis Books, 1995), 1–5.

istic and non-biblical, and poses the question, "how do we interpret the Bible in a world that has not been historically shaped by the biblical vision?"[7] Kwok provides an alternative proposal to the reading of the Bible, namely a dialogical model of interpretation. A dialogical model of interpretation imagines the Bible as a "talking book" that engenders "conversations and (creates) a polyphonic theological discourse."[8] Its purpose is to open the Bible, and to bring Asian oral and textual culture into dialogue with the Bible. The model looks also at the role of oral transmission in Asian culture and the potential for biblical interpretation that may lie in focusing on both the written text and the role of oral discussion. The model shifts the Bible from a single religious narrative to possible multiple narratives.[9] It takes the social location of the reader into consideration and applies a "multi-axial framework of analysis, especially in issues like class, race and gender."[10]

However, in her later book, *Postcolonial Imagination and Feminist Theology*, Kwok revisits her initial discussion and assumptions of dialogical model of interpretation and provides some correctives to the model.[11] Kwok credits her formulation of dialogical imagination to a Western liberal influence, in which the subject was a product of the Western liberal subject. Kwok asserts that she initially failed to pay attention to the analysis of the "fragmented subject or the multiple fractures of the colonized subject mind and psyche in the imaginative process.[12] In reconstructing the dialogical model of interpretation, Kwok adds to the dialogical model two models, historical and diasporic, as the three tasks of postcolonial feminist imagination. The three are not linear but work in interrelated and intricate ways. The three "resignify gender, moving from a liberal humanist position and a poststructuralist emphasis on difference to a transnational approach that foregrounds relation of the female subjects in globalization."[13] Furthermore, the three tasks "requeer sexuality, through tracing the genealogy of sexual discourses in the wider nexus of race, class, and religious difference in the colonial process."[14]

Furthermore, Kwok recounts her lack of problematizing the idea of the "Asian story." The "Asian" in *Discovering the Bible* was both essentialized and not thoroughly discussed. Kwok highlights the potential dangers of essentialism, especially her use of the homogenous Asian identity at the expense of the diversity and the complexity of the Asian narrative. Yet, Kwok does not discard her use of Asian identity nevertheless argues that the use of a generalized Asian identity is a dis-

---

7. Ibid., 35.
8. Ibid., 36.
9. Ibid, 38.
10. Ibid.
11. Kwok, *Postcolonial Imagination and Feminist Theology* (Louisville: Westminster John Knox, 2005), 29–51.
12. Ibid, 23.
13. Ibid., 23–24.
14. Ibid., 24

cursive and political construct, arising out of a particular historical moment of the recovery of political and cultural autonomy in the 1960s."[15]

Postcolonial feminist criticism of the Bible pays particular attention to the biblical women and the women of the colonized space in the contact zone. The "contact zone," a concept developed by Mary Louise Pratt in her book, *Imperial Eyes: Travel Writing and Transculturation*, refers to the social spaces where cultures "meet, clash, and grapple with each other, often in context of highly asymmetrical relations of power, such as colonialism, or slavery."[16] It is in essence a place of multiple tensions defined by inequalities. Furthermore, the subjects who meet at the contact zone are separated by geographical and historical disjuncture. Explicating the contact zone through the works of Donaldson and Dube, Kwok observes that the contact zone reflects the theoretical challenges wrought forth by the contacts between women from different geographical and historical locations.[17] She further notes that "reconstructive readings" in the works of Donaldson and Dube are "delineated as counter-narrative."[18] But how does this counter-narrative deploy itself?

Laura Donaldson's article "Native Women's Double Cross: Christology from the Contact Zone" is an example of the contact zone between American Indian women and Euro-American Christian missionaries.[19] Donaldson explores the inculturation of the figure of Jesus in the lives of American Indian women, particularly in the case of one Mrs. Edna Chekelelee, a Cherokee woman. Donaldson observes that Mrs. Chekelelee enunciates a uniquely and a subversive Christology in very different dialects and location than those inhabited by Euro-Americans missionaries. Mrs. Chekelelee's Christology is one, "in which the figure of Christ is defined through the sacred orienting of a Cherokee village."[20] The figure of Jesus is given native worldviews along with a naturalization of the cross, over against the individualized saving cross of the Euro-American Jesus. Moreover, the cross is relocated and repositioned in geographical and spatial ideas. Donaldson contends that the idea of Jesus saving the world is rebalanced and "salvation exists as a daily practice of world renewal instead of a single, atoning act."[21]

And Dube's *Postcolonial Feminist Interpretation of the Bible* explores the disturbing relation of the Western canon, the Bible to colonialism, imperialism, gender, God and how each intersects with patriarchy.[22] Dube insists that imperialism

15. Ibid., 40.

16. Mary Louise Pratt, *Imperial Eyes: Travel Writing and Transculturation* (London: Routledge, 1992), 5.

17. Kwok, *Postcolonial Imagination*, 82.

18. Ibid., 83.

19. Laura Donaldson, "Native Women's Double Cross: Christology from the Contact Zone," *FT* 10 (2002): 96–117.

20. Ibid., 101.

21. Ibid., 102.

22. Dube, *Postcolonial Feminist*.

and patriarchy need to be closely examined in Biblical readings, given that the Bible was instrumental in the colonization of Africa and other two thirds world countries. Second, Dube focuses on what she terms "colonizing feminism"; while appreciating the ground-breaking work of biblical feminists, she argues that they had not sufficiently factored imperial oppression and its ideological manifestations in the reading of the Bible.[23] In an analysis of Elisabeth Schüssler Fiorenza's Western feminist reading of the Bible, Dube holds that Schüssler Fiorenza reproduces imperial strategies of subjugation particularly in her reconstructive and restoration efforts of Western women to the history of early Christianity. Dube asserts that Schüssler Fiorenza's reconstructive efforts conceal "imperial influence and constructions of the biblical texts; hence, they have maintained the violence of imperial oppression against non-Western and non-Christian biblical feminists."[24] Furthermore, Dube says that Schüssler Fiorenza's restoration goal downplays the "imperial setting of the early Christian origins . . . demonstrating no effort to expose its ideology and its impact."[25]

Fourth, the editors of the book *Postcolonial Feminism and Religious Discourse*, Kwok Pui-Lan and Laura Donaldson plot a postcolonial feminist discursive framework that adds religion to patriarchy and colonialism as a category of analysis.[26] They contend that when feminist scholarship in religion fails to take colonial representation seriously, it risks "replicating the colonial gaze in the name of a single feminist agenda."[27] They continue to assert that when postcolonial biblical and theological scholarship fails to pay attention to either gender or religion, it will be severely distorted. Therefore, religion, gender and colonialism should be brought together in a triad connection.[28] The edition through different essays demonstrates that religion shapes both the colonial experiences and anti-colonial resistance. A more nuanced analysis of the triad is articulated by Dube's "Postcoloniality, Feminist Spaces, and Religion."[29] Dube's essay is a critical examination of patriarchy, Christianity, and gender in pre-colonial and colonial Botswana. Her critique is that Christian missionary efforts to colonize and further partriachalize traditional religion in Botswana colluded with traditional patriarchy. Therefore, Dube's per-

23. See Dube's critique of Western feminism in *Postcolonial Feminist*, 157–96. Also Gayatri Spivak has argued that Western feminism is implicated in what she calls the axioms of imperialism ("Three Women's Texts and a Critique of Imperialism," *CI* 12, no. 1 [1985]: 243–61). Further, Laura Donaldson, *Decolonizing Feminisms: Race, Gender, and Empire-Building* (Chapel Hill: University of North Carolina Press, 1992).

24. Ibid., 27.

25. Ibid., 28.

26. Kwok Pui-Lan and Laura Donaldson, *Postcolonial Feminism and Religious Discourse* (New York: Routledge, 2002).

27. Ibid., 3.

28. Ibid., 1.

29. Dube, "Postcoloniality, Feminist Spaces, and Religion," in Kwok and Donaldson, *Discourse*, 100–120.

suasive analysis is her resistance to a glorified and a romanticized pre-colonial Botswana. Dube considers gender as a challenge and a problem in both colonial and
indigenous culture. But how does Dube's analysis relate to pre-colonial Batswana
women? Dube's analysis paints the colonized Motswana woman as one who defies simple identifications. The colonized woman is complex, caught between the
intricacies of a patriarchal culture, imperial Christian religion, and women's narrative and histories.

Postcolonial feminist interpretation of the Bible pays close attention to the politics and poetics of location.[30] The politics and poetics of location are defined as
the "complexity of one's social background, or the socio-context that shape and
affect a woman's life such as gender, race and sexual orientation, as well as institutional context, including one's national and institutional context."[31] In addition,
the economic and educational status determines who speaks and who is likely to
listen. Kwok, citing Mary Ann Tolbert, contends that, "any interpretation of a text
especially a text as traditionally powerful as the Bible, must be assessed not only
on whatever its literary or historical merits may be but also on its theological and
ethical impact on the integrity and dignity of God's creation."[32]

POSTCOLONIAL FEMINIST READING OF THE PASSION NARRATIVE

In the passion narrative, we see the powerful hand of gender and empire dominating narrative, including the practice of profound religious differences. When
Mark writes about gender and empire, it is through the Manichean worldview
that produced two groups of people in an imperial situation. However, considering the Roman empire, Stephen Moore observes that the Roman empire is mostly
invisible until Mark 15, in which the Roman empire comes into explicit focus,[33]
whereas Liew contends that Mark's narrative plot is an apology for the empire of
God realized through the *Parousia*.[34] Even though the empire is explicitly the focus
of Mark 15, the plot of the gospel's passion narrative is dominated implicitly by the
imperial force that structures the narrative, considering that the gospel was written at the height of the Roman domination and Jewish revolts.

Mark, is therefore, written from a male and imperialized peripheral point of
view, consequently marking Mark with gender as a fundamental and a strong
component of the passion narrative. The patriarchal and imperial setting of the
passion narrative is divided into a two-tier setting that focuses on male protagonist and its supporting cast. The first setting (Mark 14:1–72) is grounded in the

---

30. Kwok, *Postcolonial Imagination*, 84.
31. Ibid., 85.
32. Ibid., 84.
33. Moore, *Post Structuralism*, 130.
34. Tat-siong Benny Liew, "Tyranny, Boundary, and Might: Colonial Mimicry in Mark's
Gospel," *JSNT* 73 (1999): 7–31.

colonized periphery world. It is dominated by Jesus, his disciples; Peter, John and Judas Iscariot and Jewish religious leaders made of the chief priests and scribes. The second tier is set in the imperial world of the Roman empire. It includes the Roman prefect Pilate, and the Roman soldiers, the crowds, Sanhedrin council and Jesus, the named women observing at the crucifixion, and empty tomb. Jesus and the Sanhedrin council dominate both settings.

A postcolonial feminist reading of the passion narrative rhetorically reads how Mark narrates and critiques the empire. My reading goal is to show how Mark, the colonized male writer navigates the intricacies of imperial and religious politics, between the Jesus circle, the religious leaders and Pilate. I will draw from Dube's questions to help explicate the imperialized and imperial conflicts. Dube's questions provide a framework that reads Mark from a postcolonial feminist analysis. Because the world of Mark was a dominated world, Dube asserts that we posit questions that reveal the text's stance toward the political and imperial contexts of its time. Dube's second question hinges on markers of difference: "How does an imperial text constructs difference?" She asserts that a text should be scrutinized for its construction of difference. Further, she asks, "Is there dialogue and mutual interdependence, or condemnation and replacements of all that is foreign?"[35] She adds the gender question to the analysis of texts written in the belly of empire as gender is a crucial component of empire. Dube's question is thus, "Does it employ a gender and divine representations to construct relationship of subordination and domination?"[36]

In addition to the critical reading questions offered by Dube, I will draw from the work of Homi Bhabha, "Signs Taken for Wonders."[37] His theory of ambivalence provides insights on the character of Peter and Pilate. Bhabha has shown that a colonized discourse is structured by ambivalence that contradicts, subverts, and undermines the empire. Drawn from psychoanalysis, ambivalence in its simplest form is a "continual fluctuation between wanting one thing and wanting its opposite."[38] It emphasizes a simultaneous attraction toward and repulsion to an object, person or action. Its appropriation in colonial discourse reveals ambivalent as a characteristic feature of the relationship between colonizer and the colonized. However, I am rather still ambivalent toward the Bhabhian concept of ambivalence. On the one hand, it provides insights to the character of Peter, but the loss of agency with Bhabha's formulation leaves little room for any form of resistance. Since colonial and imperial contexts are masculine inscribed, how does Mark orient and narrate itself?

---

35. Dube, *Postcolonial Feminist*, 97.

36. Ibid.

37. Homi Bhabha, "Signs Taken for Wonders: Questions of Ambivalence and Authority under a Tree outside Delhi, May 1817," *CI* 12, no. 1 (1985): 144–65.

38. Bill Ashcroft et al., *Key Concepts in Post-colonial Studies* (London: Routledge, 1995), 12–13.

Scene 1: The Prologue (Mark 14:1–2)

The prologue opens in the colonized world of the chief priests, the scribes, and the Jewish festivals; "Two days before the Passover and the festival of unleavened Bread," the chief priests and the scribes were seeking *(zetein)* for a way to arrest Jesus but they decide against it by declaring "not during the festival" (Mark 14:1–2). The chief priests, and scribes are a power group of colonized priestly aristocracy, and they straddle both the colonized periphery and the Roman centers of powers. The chief priests have their foot on both side of the aisle, they are the Jerusalem leaders of the Jewish religion, yet they have a stake in the imperialist and hegemonic rule of Rome. The opening "plunges the reader into the deepest heart of a Jewish symbolic life."[39] Not only are we thrust into a Jewish religious life, but we are drawn into a defined and complicated world of the colonized periphery, away from the eyes of the Roman imperial power. Furthermore, the decision to not capture Jesus at the beginning of the preparation of the festival does not betray the significance of the decision which reflects the politics of patriarchal and religious privilege and power.

Scene 2: The Anointing at Bethany: Jesus and the Woman (Mark 14:3–11)

With the brief introduction of the chief priests and scribes' plan, we are immediately transferred to an entirely different setting; the opening of which is marked with precision, attention to details and vivid description. We move from Jerusalem to Bethany, a place outside Jerusalem. Jesus is in the house of Simon, the leper and he sits at the table (Mark 14:1). The gender markers inscribe a male dominated space. Bordered and intercalated between the preparation and beginning of the Passover and Judas' conspiracy, the anointing of Jesus functions within its own border space. This border configures a contrast to the hostility of the chief priests and the betrayal of one of the twelve, Judas.

A nameless woman enters the house of Simon. Her namelessness erases her subjectivity despite some scholars remarking that her namelessness is not unusual in a narrative that places emphasis on the words of Jesus and her action. In a colonial context, she is triply colonized; she is colonized by the Roman imperial power, imperial patriarchy, and local patriarchal ideologies.[40] The nameless woman carries with her an expensive bottle of perfume, shatters it, and pours the perfume on Jesus' head (Mark 14:34).

Not only is she the nameless one, but those *(tines)* accompanying Jesus are nameless, except the significant one, the host, Simon, the leper, and Jesus, the protagonist. Her entry indirectly disrupts the colonized patriarchal space dominating

39. Ched Myers, *Binding the Strong Man: A Political Reading of Mark's Story of Jesus* (Maryknoll, NY: Orbis Books, 1988), 343.

40. Oyeronke Oyewumi, "Colonizing Bodies and Minds: Gender and Colonialism," in *Postcolonialism: An Anthology of Cultural Theory and Criticism,* ed. Gaurar Desai and Supriya Nair (New Brunswick, NJ: Rutgers University Press, 2005), 339–69.

Simon's house, yet the nameless men flout her expensive gift. The polyphony of the nameless men's voices receives and appreciates not her deed. There is indignation, utter mutterings and berating, "why is there a total loss of this ointment?" (Mark 14:45). But what do we make of her silence? Gayatri Spivak in her classical essay, "Can the Subaltern Speak?" questions whether it is possible for the oppressed and downtrodden, the subaltern, to speak.[41] The subaltern, in this case, is the woman who anoints Jesus. Is it possible for the anointing woman to represent, speak and act for herself? She succeeds in anointing Jesus, but there are obstacles, Jesus' friends disprove her action. Spivak's compelling analysis is that speech can be substituted for action. Therefore, rephrasing Spivak's question, 'Can the woman who anoints Jesus speak?' Is it possible to read her silence apart from a colonized male defined context? But answering this question can result in reading her action negatively as this is reflected within the trajectory of feminist tradition in which women's silence is a product of the androcentric narrative's bias. Or rather can the woman's silence and lack of consistent speech be redeemed from the usual negativity of a male defined context of absence, lack, and fear as feminine territories? If we read silence in a negative way, we face the danger of inscribing femininity as absence, as a lack and a blank and, we thus reject the importance of the act of renunciation[42].

Despite trying to read some positivity in her character, the woman who anoints Jesus is a character of ambiguities. Further, her character and representation defies easy or simple categorization. Jesus claims the anointing is to prepare him for his death. Yet the anointing touch evokes elements of sexual tension. For instance, her anointing of Jesus, despite the lack of a name, and the bitter murmurings from Jesus' friends demonstrates resistance and subversion to local patriarchal ideology. Her resistance is doubly deployed. When she anoints Jesus, she resists the Rome imperial cult and Roman imperial forms of masculinity. Her resistance contests and disrupts the patriarchal meeting. She ruptures the colonized male space that Jesus, Simon, the host and his friends have created in the house of Simon the leper. But her rupturing of the space is not without consequences, for she is still contained by the narrator, in that she is left nameless.

Scene 3: Prophecy, Prediction, Failures, and the Passover Meal (Mark 14:12–42)

This section is dominated by a sandwich structure; the preparation for the meal (Mark 14:12–16), the initial phase of the prediction of the Judas betrayal (Mark 14:17–21) and the celebration and institution of the Lord's supper (Mark 14:22–

41. Gayatri Chakravorty Spivak, "Can the Subaltern Speak?" in *Colonial Discourse and Post-Colonial Theory*, ed. P. Williams and L. Chrisman (New York: Columbia University Press, 1992), 66–111.

42. Trinh T. Minh-ha, "Not You/Like You: Postcolonial Women and the Interlocking Questions of Identity and Difference," in *Dangerous Liaisons: Gender, Nation, and Postcolonial Perspectives,* ed. Anne McClintock, Aamir Mufti, and Ella Shohat (SCP; London and Minneapolis: University of Minnesota Press, 1997), 415–19.

25). The plot narrative plays on aspects of resistance politics or praxis that are easily part of a resistance movement in an imperialized context, the tensions (betrayal and failure of both Peter, Judas and the three disciples) within the Jesus movement. Second, the manifestation of the divine through a prophetic instruction plays crucial resistance politics to the idea of the Roman imperial cult. The mention of the chief priests solves the problem of verses 14:1–2. The setting of the narrative takes us to Jerusalem, the center of Jewish religious nationalism, then Bethany, but now Mark takes us back to Jerusalem, and the plot continues the introduction of Mark 14:1–2.

"Then on the first day of the feast of Unleavened Bread when they were sacrificing the Passover lambs . . ." (Mark 14:12) is again another one of Markan attention to time. This last meal takes place outside the public space, far away from the imperial centre and the prying eyes of the Sanhedrin council. Jesus instructs (with details) his disciples to obtain goods that will make possible the festival. Mark uses the last supper as a backdrop to Jesus' farewell to the disciples. They are not to request but instruct as Jesus has instructed them, they are to follow as they have been following. The Passover festival emphasizes the maleness of Jesus and his disciples among other things. This meal to commemorate a Jewish religious festival reveals many layers. Second, it projects the violence of the empire as the last supper is metaphorically tied to the imperial violence of the cross. Jesus will celebrate and predict who will betray and give him up to die a violent death. The collusion of the myths of the divine and the mundane in this celebration reveals the tension that Mark stresses between Jesus and his followers.

The observance and celebration of the Passover meal signifies the last supper as a process of re-appropriating a predominantly Jewish festival as a critique and a deconstruction of the Roman Empire's form of imperialism, which was hostile to difference. The resistance in the Passover celebration is that, it is not a redeployment or appropriation of an imperial culture. It is a privilege of a nativist religious praxis, and a nativist representation of identity, one that is part of a collective memory. By nativism, I do not refer to the return of the native, or return to a pre-imperial world.[43] Rather, it is a tool that plays a role in strategies of opposition and decolonization, as its praxis and celebration is a claim of power. To practice the Passover meal is to render the possibilities of a mutual understanding between empire and its subject. Furthermore, this religious praxis of natives means that the Passover celebration is part of the subjugated to "write" their own resistance politics by evoking a religious praxis long held in the psyche and consciousness of a subjugated religious group.

The failure of the three disciples is further revealed in the intimate details of

---

43. Benita Parry, "Resistance Theory/Theorizing Tesistance or Two Cheers for Nativism," in *Postcolonial Studies: A Materialist Critique* (London: Routledge, 2005), 37–54. Also Kwame Anthony Appiah, *In My Father's House: Africa in the Philosophy of Culture* (New York: Oxford University Press, 1992).

Jesus agonizing prayer in Mark 14:32–42. The prayer in Gethsemane reveals the vulnerabilities of the colonized Jesus. If possible, Jesus desperately desires that the hour might pass him. "Abba, Father," Jesus calling out to his father shows the patriarchal and hierarchical relationship of father and son, at a moment of crisis in which the state of the empire of God is thrown into chaos. The difference that has marked Jesus, the colonized male through Mark's story of Jesus collapses. Eric Thurman recognizes a pronounced ambivalence in Jesus' prayer in Gethsemane.[44] The requirement of suffering for the empire is what Jesus prays to resist yet he prays also that the Abba's will be done. There is a deep-seated personal refusal to the "cup of suffering" yet Jesus still leaves room for any possibility. When he prays "let this cup of suffering pass me by . . . everything is possible for you," Jesus negotiates with his Abba. He negotiates the power to resist yet he recognizes the Abba's power to make the cup of suffering pass him or not.

The action moves from Jesus' last supper with his disciples to Gethsemane, where Jesus' passion wanes and a moment of utter desperation engulfs him. Judas, the colonized male, through a kiss identifies Jesus to the high priests as the "Rabbi" and kisses Jesus to identify him to the crowd with swords and clubs from the chief priests and the scribes and the elders (Mark 14:43–44).

Scene 5: Jesus and Peter. An Accusation and a Denial (Mark 14:53–72)

I have titled this section "Jesus and Peter: An Accusation and a Denial" because of the juxtaposition of the trial of Jesus and the denial of Peter. The pericopes are simultaneously narrated. Furthermore, the placing of each pericope side by side reflects Dube's question in which she suggests we critically inquire how a text creates difference. The powerful religious leaders of the Jerusalem all "apprehended (*aphegagon*) and led Jesus away" (Mark 14:53). As Jesus is led away, Peter is "following (*apomakrothen*)" from a distance.

Postcolonial feminist analysis of the Bible seeks to understand how the dynamics of power relations, particularly gendered political power are exercised. Jesus' trial before the Sanhedrin council is about the dynamics of power relations. The decision to capture Jesus, the colonized son of God, reveals the power struggles between the Jesus circle and the chief priests. It brings to epic the conflict and power struggle that has defined Jesus' relationship with the high priests; a relationship defined by struggles to dominate the religious space and competing masculinities. The power groups are gender-specific as, in this case, chief priests, an all-male elite religious group, interrogate Jesus, a male Mark has constructed as the *son of God*.

Dube in her reading of the gospel of Matthew's passion narrative, which is equally applicable to my reading here, notes that the tension between "various interest groups" of the colonized is one in which they "try to gain power to define

44. Eric Thurman, "Novel Men: Masculinity and Empire in Mark's Gospel and Xenophon's *An Ephesian Tale*," in *Mapping Gender in Ancient Religious Discourses,* ed. Todd Penner and Caroline Vander Stichele (BIS 84; Leiden: Brill, 2007), 185–229.

the national (religious) cultural identity of the colonized as well as to compete for the attention of their collective oppressor."[45]

Jesus' appearance before the chief priests, is a conflict initiated by the council to retain and maintain their power, influence and definition of religious and cultural identity, one in which they view Jesus as a threat. Therefore, it is notable that when the high, chief priests and scribes seek (*zetein*) testimony against Jesus, the (false) testimony provided by the witnesses is founded on religious discourse. The search for testimony against Jesus reveals also the gender dynamics which were, from the outset, fundamental to the securing and maintenance of the imperial enterprise and religious power. The witnesses claim to have heard Jesus declare, "I will destroy this temple made by hands. . .not made by hands," (Mark 14:55–59) yet the testimonies are contradictory. From the (false) testimonies, the High priest provokes Jesus by a double question, "Are you not going to respond? What these have testified *(katamartyrein)*[46] against you?" (Mark 14:60).[47] Jesus' chooses to remain silent. This is effectively emphasized by a double negation, (*ouk. . .ouden*)."[48] From a silent response to a specific question by the high priest, the high priest's question is an incriminating one: "Are you the Christ, the Son of the Blessed One?" Jesus promptly responds, "I am," (*ego eimi*)[49] which leads to a charge of blasphemy and of condemnation deserving death" (verse 64).

Moreover, by staging their own trial, they disrupt the colonial power. In a colonized culture of the Roman imperial power, they know the structures and how to maneuver them. But in a context where power is a contested terrain, continuous struggles and illegal trials are part of the challenges. The illegality of the trial is in subtle ways a mockery of the final trial, as both cases will have similar structures in their mode of questioning and responses. Ultimately, when they take him to Pilate, they seek for Pilate to rubber-stamp their desires. The masculine entity and authority of the Sanhedrin council is founded on the Jerusalem temple; in fact, Second Temple Judaism was established and maintained by the priests' close association with the imperial power or imperial patriarchy.

---

45. Dube, *Postcolonial Feminist*, 127.

46. John Donahue and Daniel Harrington, *The Gospel of Mark* (Collegeville, MN: Liturgical, 2002), assert that the "prefix *kata* (against) in the verb *katamartyrein* (witnessing against) is part of the motif of hostility 'against' Jesus in the trial narrative. It is used also in verse 55 (seeking testimony against Jesus), and Mk 14:64 (all condemned)."

47. Myers, *Binding*, 372, reads verse 60 as a "hearing climax." He reads back to the "climatic synagogue confrontation at the end of the Capernaum campaign. Jesus had called a crippled man 'into the centre' and his opponents had been 'silent' (*esiopon*) before his challenge (Mk 3:3–5)."

48. Donahue and Harrington, *Mark*, 422.

49. Myers, *Binding*, 376, says a more appropriate translation is "Am I?"

Scene 6: Peter's Unofficial Trial (Mark 14:66–72)

Markan markers of difference are consistently constructed on class, gender, and colonized space. As noted above, a process of differentiation is already at work in constituting the binary opposition in the Peter and Jesus' relationship. If the trial of Jesus is inherently and consistently dominated by the hegemonic religious male elites, Peter's trial is dominated by a servant girl, and her lower class companions. Mark compares Jesus and Peter, and subordinates Peter to Jesus. Peter is said to be "following from a distance" (Mark 14:54) but follows up to the point where he is not allowed inside. With detailed and vivid descriptive action, Peter's pseudo-trial is described as "down in the courtyard" (Mark 14:66)[50] where he "sits with the attendants at the blazing fire" and is "warming himself" (Mark 14:67). This pseudo-trial fulfils Jesus' prophecy regarding Peter's denial. However, Peter's separation reveals the heterogeneity of a gendered colonized space while the socio-religious politics are the chief motif. In addition, the separation of Peter and Jesus reflects the potential fragmentations of colonized lives under the hegemonic power of empire.

Mark strategically places and compares Peter's "mimic trial" with Jesus' trial. Because imperialism is not only constructed around a single entity of colonized and colonizer, both the trial of Jesus and Peter's pseudo-trial are constructed around the social, and political categories of class, religion, and location within a colonized space. Two men who have walked, and dined together, are now constituted and separated by issues of gender, class, and religious negotiation. Where Jesus responds briefly and at times with absolute silence, Peter stubbornly and passionately responds to the interrogation (like Herod in Mark 6). Where Jesus is predominantly in a colonized male-religious space and interrogated by powerful men, Peter is in a space occupied by both colonized and gendered male and female, a process that both undermines Peter's gender and reflects the tension that plagues the colonized periphery. Stuart Hall's assertion regarding colonized spaces is relevant. Hall asserts that "boundaries of difference are continually repositioned in relation to different points of reference."[51] Jesus and Peter have resided in the same circle but the trial reflects the profound difference between them. Furthermore, Jesus' difference is signified from a different point, in this case, a religious and blasphemous one, in which his otherness stands in different relation to Peter's.

While Peter "sits at the blazing fire" a "servant girl" *(paidiske)* who, on seeing *(idousa . . . emblepsasa)*[52] Peter, declares simply, "You too were with the Nazarene Jesus" (Mark 14:67). To identify her as *paidiske* is to render her through an adjec-

---

50. Donahue and Harrington, *Mark*, 425, observe that this statement suggests that Jesus' trial took place in the second floor of the high priest's house.

51. Stuart Hall, "The Emergence of Cultural Studies and the Crisis of the Humanities," *October* 53 (1990): 11–23.

52. Donahue and Harrington, *Mark*, 425, note that the verb suggests "a first sighting and then a closer look leading to recognition of Peter."

tival description rather than a proper name. The term emphasizes her social insignificance, marks her class and social particularities. The *Paidiske* (Mark 14:66) declares simply, "You too were with the Nazarene Jesus" (Mark 14:67). Had she seen Peter with Jesus? Her direct statement does not tell us. The stark vividness that articulates the young girl is emphasized by "you too" (Mark 14:67) and the verbs of participle of "seeing." Despite her class particularities, the *paidiske* signifies Peter's relation to Jesus through an ethnic epithet that plays to stereotypes. Consequently, her question is one that seeks an affirmation from Peter who denies *(arneisthai)* thus, "I neither know nor understand what you are saying" (Mark 14:68). And a "cock crowed" (Mark 14:68).

She continues her second tirade, yet this time appeals to the bystanders, and points him out to the group; "this man is one of them" (Mark 14:69) a statement that takes a different angle. This is no longer a question but a declarative statement. Again Peter denies it (Mark 14:70).[53] And the bystanders emphasize, "You certainly are one of them, for you are a Galilean" (Mark 14:70). When both the *paidiske* and the bystanders use ethnic markers to refer to both Peter and Jesus, they participate in a process of "othering." Postcolonial theory defines "othering" as an ideological process through which isolated groups are seen as different from the norm. On the other hand, her reference to Jesus reflects the cultural identity of the colonized groups, in which imperial and patriarchal history has shaped the colonized.

A seemingly bewildered and confounded Peter began *(erxato)* to curse *(anathematizein)* and swear *(omnynai)* (Mark 14:71).[54] "I do not know *(ouk oide)* this man you are talking about.[55]" Peter certainly feels besieged. And he remembered *it,* that is, the prophecy of Jesus as the cock crowed for the third and last time.

The scene of Peter's denial yields to many varied potential readings. Despite the fact that Peter is a victim of a prophetic saying, if we ignore the prophetic anecdote; how would we read Peter? Firstly, it is clear that Mark undermines Peter especially by using the maid servant to question his relationship status with Jesus. If we locate Peter's denial within the psychology of a postcolonial feminist analysis, one that evokes the Bhabhaian concept, Peter is vulnerable. Peter's questioning pushes him further into the periphery, and marginalizes him. Peter's presence at the courtyard reflects his desire to be with Jesus; yet he seeks not to publicly identify with him. He is ambivalent, to use the lucid word that describes those who are in such a state. The denials are a mocking circus marked and constantly emphasized by Peter's ambivalent stance. By following and remaining in the courtyard, he

53. Mark uses *erneito,* which signifies repeated denials by Peter. See Donahue and Harrington, *Mark,* 425.

54. Donahue and Harrington, *Mark,* 426, note that this very familiar Markan construction, *erxato* (he began), introduces very strong infinitives: *anathematizein* (curse) and *omnymai* (swear).

55. Myers, *Binding,* 377, observes that Peter's language of his third denial is very strong. Peter commands an anathema and an oath.

seeks to remain loyal to Jesus, yet his denial is a disloyalty to Jesus. Peter's ambivalence will grant Peter neither an identity nor a public affirmation that he was one of Jesus, the Nazarene. His ambivalence serves as an act of resistance. It is never a pure resistance, never a simple one, but is a necessary aspect of what Peter seeks to achieve, that is a constant surveillance on the action of Jesus' trial.

Scene 7: Jesus Before Pilate (Mk 15:1–20)

Jesus' trial before Pilate is a demonstration of the colluding and collision of imperial patriarchy, the colonized masculinity, native religion and politics. This scene opens with what has become a feature of a Markan narration; that is, the specifics and attention to time as a marker of a new plot and action. R. T. France observes that the attention to time comes to define the account of the crucifixion, since Mark sets this scene in an explicit and detailed time of three hour intervals:[56] "Early in the morning, the chief priests convened a meeting (*sunaboulion poiesantes*)."[57]

The time reflects the break from the trial of Jesus, the denial of Peter, and the cockcrows to a new action, the trial before Pilate. They "bound Jesus, brought him and handed him (*paradidonai*) over to Pilate" (Mark 15:1–2). The decision to hand Jesus over to Pilate moves the setting from the colonized periphery world to the Roman imperial power and from the margins to the center of imperial Rome. Overall, the decision to hand Jesus over to Pilate is fulfillment of Mark 10:33, in which the chief priest are said to "hand over to the Gentiles." This stark decision is the political drama and climax of the passion narration. Furthermore, this crossing over is marked by masculine gender as it reflects empire as the ultimate exercise and practice of imperial and imperialized masculine enterprise.

The decision by the chief priests, and the scribes "to hand" Jesus "over" to Pilate, reveals the limited power of the Sanhedrin in the Roman hegemonic world. On the other hand, handing Jesus over to Pilate is an inscription of the centre/periphery separation that serves the institutional function of securing the dominant narrative, namely, that the power of the imperial rule is a manly prerogative. Despite the Sanhedrin council occupying locations in both worlds, the colonized and the colonizers, the power they yielded in the colonized world is now shifted to the Roman imperial centre.

Handing Jesus "over" to Pilate abruptly introduces a meeting between Pilate and Jesus which, to the surprise of the reader, begins with a direct and imposing question. However, Helen Bond in her study of Pontius Pilate observes that the

---

56. R. T. France, *The Gospel of Mark: A Commentary on the Greek Text* (Grand Rapids: Eerdmans, 2002), 627.

57. Some scholars offer a different translation of *symboulion poiesantes*. See Raymond Brown, who makes a compelling note that it means the Sanhedrin Council had "made their consultation which was initially decided in Mark 14:55–65." (*The Death of the Messiah: From Gethsemane to the Grave* [New York: Doubleday, 1994], 721).

lack of a description of Pilate's non-official trial means that Pilate's character may have been well known to Mark's audience.[58]

> And Pilate questioned him: *"Are you the king of the Jews?"* *(Su ho Basileus ton Ioudaion?)* (Mark 5:2).

> Jesus' response is non-committal: *"You say so."* *(Su legeis),* (Mark 15:2b).

And Warren Carter remarks that the verse that introduces the scene with Pilate accentuates "crucial political dynamics and imperial perspectives that shape the whole scene."[59] Carter further asserts that Jesus and Pilate reflect the disparate and intertwining social locations which make "difference in determining who make claims and who do not" (64).[60] Not only are we introduced to political dynamics but the question is heavily marked by gender, ethnic, class and religious overtones which construct difference. Pilate, a Roman imperial male representative of a masculine imperial interrogates Jesus, a colonized male Jew, proclaimed according to Mark 1:1, "the son of God" and of lower class. His power emphasizes the hegemonic masculinity that defines imperial men, and partly secures and maintains imperial enterprise. Pilate represents Augustus, "son of a God." Detailing the nature of Roman imperial theology, John Dominic Crossan traces the historical narrative of the Roman civilization and imperial power as founded on imperial theology centered on the divinity of the emperor. He alludes to the ubiquitous nature of the imperial power which is "better understood not as propaganda from imperial top to colonial bottom but as an extraordinary campaign supported by self-consciously Roman political elites across the entire empire."[61]

Their social, religious and political locations are also symbolical, as they represent gendered kingdoms which underscore hierarchical powers of the Roman empire that sustained it. The difference that Mark marks is one that has undercut the entire narrative of the gospel. Pilate's question begins a dialogue that will lead to a judgment of insurrection. "Are you the King of the Judeans?" threatens the Roman imperial power. Carter notes that the question is a dangerous one for both Pilate and Jesus. Bond contends that the Pilate question is one that "therefore focuses on the political implications of the Jewish charge, in an attempt to gauge how far he might present a threat to Roman stability in the province."[62] Bond further notes that the trial with Pilate makes allusions to another kingdom, which is "important

---

58. Helen Bond, *Pontius Pilate in History and Interpretation* (Cambridge and New York: Cambridge University Press, 1998), 99.

59. Warren Carter, *Pontius Pilate: Portraits of a Roman Governor*, Interfaces (Collegeville, MN: Liturgical, 2003), 59–65.

60. Ibid., 64.

61. John Dominic Crossan, *God and Empire: Jesus against Rome, Then and Now* (New York: HarperSanFrancisco, 2007), 59.

62. Bond, *Pilate*, 106.

in the passion narrative as a whole but comes into special prominence during the Roman trial."[63]

When Pilate asks, "Are you the king of the Jews?" he is questioning the possibilities of a new kingdom, or nation, apart from the Roman imperial one and if Jesus is its king. Under an absolute rule of hegemonic empire, Rome is the sole power and Caesar is its ultimate leader. The question marks the beginning of the dominance of Jesus' kingship discourse in the trial and the crucifixion. It is repeated over and over again. In fact, from then on, Jesus as king of the Jews will be repeated six times. Mark's narrative technique according to Bond is that the title of king of the Jews is never elsewhere used of Jesus except in the trial thus making Jesus' kingship a discursive practice despite Jesus' controlled response.[64]

Yet, despite assumptions and arguments made by postcolonial theorists, that the colonized tend to mimic the colonizers, Pilate's trial is a replica and mimic of the Sanhedrin council's trial of Jesus (Mark 14:43–50). Its political charge builds on the findings of the Jewish court, especially "the central questions of Jesus' messiahship and status."

Pilate declares that he finds no crime in Jesus, yet the priests incite the crowd to push Pilate to serve their own interests as they accuse Jesus of causing strife, contentions and trouble among the people from Galilee to Jerusalem. Because Jesus chooses to not respond to claims of kingship and nation, in the process undermining Pilate's powers, the Markan writer introduces us to another character, Barnabas (Mark 15:6–7). Mark does not inform the reader of any judgment taken by Pilate, but rather, are we to assume that the Sanhedrin council has influenced Pilate's next act? In the exchange between Pilate, the chief priests, and the crowd, Jesus is a "bargain" for the Sanhedrin council and the crowd. The power exchanges at play here do not clearly give leverage to either party, but each party (the crowd at the influence of the Sanhedrin council) will play Pilate to serve their own interests, just as Pilate will play them to serve his own interests. Pilate uses Barnabas to secure imperial Rome by appealing to the colonized male. He is not as dramatic as the Johannine Pilate neither is the Markan Pilate's dance with the crowd and the religious leaders as intense as the dance between the Johannine Pilate and the crowd.[65] Furthermore, by using Barnabas to serve a Jewish tradition of releasing a prisoner during Passover festival, his imperial vision is to tame the crowd, chief priests, and scribes.

Pilate ironically quips, "Do you want me to release to you the king of the Jews?" (Mark 15:9). The chief priests yield their power to have Barnabas released instead because Barnabas seems to not pose a threat to difference that has marked Jesus,

---

63. Ibid., 107.

64. Ibid.

65. See Stephen D. Moore, *Empire and Apocalypse: Postcolonialism and the New Testament* (Sheffield: Sheffield Phoenix, 2006), particularly the essay " 'The Romans Will Come and Destroy Our Holy Place and Our Nation': Representing Empire in John," 45–76.

the chief priests and Pilate's empire neither to patriarchy. The tug of war that ensues between Pilate and the crowd is evident of their own perspectives to Jesus. Second, it reveals the tension that undercuts the relationship of interests groups within an empire. The counter-discourse is between Pilate, the Sanhedrin and, the crowd and Jesus, a pawn in their game.

Scene 8: The King of the Jews on the Cross (Mark 15:16–32)

After an encounter with Jesus, in which he is found guilty and a brief debate with the crowd, Pilate hands Jesus over to the Roman soldiers. Finding Jesus guilty and handing him over is laid out by Dube when she contends that "the trial, the accusation, and the verdict attest to powers of imperial domination that vigilantly guarded against any rebellious individuals in order to maintain its political sovereignty in a foreign land."[66]

"But the soldiers brought him inside the courtyard *(aulē)* and they summon the whole cohort" (Mark 15:16). Mark thus sets the stage for what transpires between the Roman soldiers and Mark describes (through the use of the historical present) in striking vividness what is to be a showdown between imperial Rome represented by the soldiers and Jesus, the divine and colonized whose rejection by the crowd and Sanhedrin council to a pivotal moment. Harrington and Donahue assert that Mark's use of the historical present is to make the narrative more vivid.[67] With Pilate's instruction, Roman imperial forms of violence take precedence, and Jesus is flogged and crucified.

In the detailed narration, Jesus is clothed in royal regal of purple and crowned with thorns (Mark 15:16) and the soldiers begin to salute him, "Hail, King of the Jews?" (Mark 15:17–18). What emerge in the Roman coronation of Jesus are elements of mockery, mimicry and a mode of civil authority and order. The mockery by the soldiers continues the masculine endeavors of empire and reflects an extreme form of Roman masculine practice and performance. Furthermore, the mimicry of the Roman soldiers emerges as dramatic irony for the Markan community who are aware of Jesus' identity. It is the joke upon us, as brilliantly read by Brian Blount. He observes that when the crucifying soldiers kneel before and hail Jesus as "king of the Jews," the reader "nods knowingly with Mark because she comprehends the royal regal and salutation is the 'salute of royalty Jesus deserves.'"[68]

When they mime Jesus' kingdom and lordship, the mockery is produced within the imperial master context yet privileges the colonized subject. Again, when the Roman soldiers endow and serenade Jesus as king, they ironically unsettle the

---

66. Dube, *Postcolonial Feminist*, 130

67. Harrington and Donahue, *Mark*, 435.

68. Brian K. Blount, "Is the Joke on Us? Mark's Irony, Mark's God, and Mark's Ending," in *The Ending of Mark and the Ends of God: Essays in Memory of Donald Harrisville Juel*, ed. Beverly Roberts Giventa and Patrick D. Miller (Louisville: Westminster John Knox, 2005), 15.

Roman notions of Augustus Caesar. The mockery and salutation of Jesus; "Hail, King of the Jews" (Mark 15:17–18) may sound to the Roman readers as a parody of the *Ave Caesar*, the official salutation to the emperor. When the Roman soldiers garb Jesus with royal regal, the mockery is subversive in that it recognizes Jesus as king of the Judeans but polarizes differences in the interstices of mockery and the real. In addition, it blurs and contaminates the real and unreal, the mockery and the non-mockery. It is equally privileges and foregrounds the hierarchy of patriarchy of both kingdoms on par.

Further, a mockery of Jesus destabilizes the Roman privilege of Caesar or Pilate. The destabilization does not reverse power. The destabilization is between systems, between the mockery and mimicry of Jesus. It provides the colonized and divine Jesus the ultimate coronation and inscription: "The King of the Jews." Crucifixion, as historians of Roman imperial power note, was designed "to inflict maximum pain and agony on its victims, by hanging them from a pole or a crossbeam" and to dishonor the "King of the Judeans," yet the lifting up may ironically mean the Markan narrative's opening is fulfilled.[69]

What of resistance in the Markan construction of the mockery of Jesus? However, resistance is between the mockery and mimicry performed by the soldiers, as it gives the colonized and the divine Jesus, the ultimate coronation, and inscription, "King of the Jews." Stephen Slemon contends that "Resistance can never easily be located in the sites of anti-colonial resistance. . ." as resistance is at times an "effect of the contradictory representation of colonial authority."[70] This resistance works through preparatory episodes in the passion narrative. For instance, Abraham Smith opines that "Mark provides a narrative frame of resistance that significantly shapes the way in which Pilate would be read, namely, in the parallels Mark makes between this episode and a previous episode about tyranny in Mark 6:14–29"(2009:202).

Scene 9: The Crucifixion, Burial and the Women (Mark 15:21–16:8)

By crucifying Jesus at Golgotha, the Roman imperial power exercises its ultimate domination and brings to epic its violence against its subjects. Jesus is crucified by the Romans on their colonial cross. Crucifixion, a Roman form of execution was both violent and brutal. Horsley notes it as a form of the imperial and ultimate destruction on its insurgents. Through the colonial cross, the empire leaves "its marks on Jesus of Nazareth, most obviously on his body"[71] and was used to dishonor, demean, and dehumanize its victims and destroy dissident males. Extending from

---

69. Richard A. Horsley, "Jesus and Empire," in *In the Shadow of Empire: Reclaiming the Bible as a History of Faithful Resistance* (Louisville: Westminster John Knox, 2008), 75.

70. Stephen Slemon, "Unsettling the Empire: Resistance Theory for the Second World," in *The Post-colonial Studies Reader,* ed. Bill Ashcroft, Gareth Griffiths, and Helen Tiffin (London: Routledge, 1995), 102, 103.

71. Moore, *Empire and Apocalypse,* 60–61.

Mark 15:20, Jesus is handed over by Pilate, to the soldiers who "lead him out in order that they might crucify him" (Mark 15:21–22). On the way to Golgotha, they encounter Simon, who is described in basic details, ". . .of Cyrene. . .the father of Alexander and Rufus" (Mark 15:22–23), as if the information is necessary for carrying the colonial cross.

In a simple but highly profound present-tense construction, Mark writes, "And they crucify him" (Mark 15:24). "They" describes the soldiers who will divide Jesus' clothes among "themselves" (Mark 15:24b) which leans on the Roman law that awarded garments of those condemned to death to be shared. With the written charge, "King of the Jews" (Mark 15:26), the Jewish nationalist ideology and theology is publicly inscribed on the imperial and colonial cross. Mark's complicity to the colonial cross, in an unsettling way bespeaks the ambivalence that undercuts his resistance politics and locates the summary and declaration of the Mark's theology in the colonial cross. On the other hand, the crucifixion of Jesus offers the ultimate triumph of Roman imperial power over Jesus. The colonial cross objectifies Jesus and his body. In addition, Jesus' crucifixion absolutises the hegemonic empire, as it renders the maleness of Jesus besieged and subdued.

The crucifixion scene is inundated with those who gaze at and vilify Jesus; "you who are destroying the sanctuary and building it in three days. . . save yourself by coming down from the cross" (Mark 15:29–30). And the chief priests uttered, "He saved others, himself he cannot save" (Mark 15:31). In addition, Jesus is an object of the dominant imperial, male gaze of the Roman soldiers, the religious leaders, and the crowd. As they continually gaze at Jesus, their gaze and hostility marks their collaboration with the Roman empire. The gaze and the shouting signify the power of the gaze and its transcription. It is an active instrument of ridicule and, a commanding view of scorn and insults.

Furthermore, their hostility draws us into the Markan time frame and specifics, "And when the sixth hour came, there was darkness over the whole land until the ninth hour" (Mark 15:39). As the hour progresses to the ninth one, it collides with Jesus' cry of desperation, and abandonment and captured thus; "Jesus screamed a loud voice, '*Eloi, Eloi, lama sabachthani,*'" (Mark 15:39). By inserting transcendental and supernatural powers, Mark affirms the role of patriarchal power, and God, in this case, the *Abba* who has allowed the "cup of suffering" in his all-powerfulness. Thereafter, the centurion presumably convinced by the cosmic events of darkness and Jesus' utter cry, proclaims "Truly this man was Son of God," (*hyios theou*) (Mark 15:39) equalizing Jesus with Caesar the emperor. The Greek rendering is "*a son of God*"; the absence of the article is very notable. The centurion's confession is a spontaneous recognition of the divinity of Jesus (1952:597). The lack of an article may not mean much for Mark.

The centurion's proclamation joins the inscription of the colonial cross: two titles at the crucifixion, one inscribed and one confessed but both performed by gentiles, or roman imperial agents. The two titles, "King of the Jews" and "A Son of God" enter the messiness of Roman imperial violence, the colonial cross, and its signification of Roman imperial victory over its dissidents. Moreover, they unsettle and destabilize Roman imperial enunciation. The two titles, both Markan theological constructions are a "writing back" to a Roman imperial theology centered on the divinity of the emperor. Mark demonstrates what Bhabha observes as the constitution of resistance. Bhabha notes that resistance is very complex. It is an "oppositional act of political intention."[72] But it reveals a Markan ambivalence constructed "within the rules of recognition of dominating discourses as they articulate the sign of cultural difference and implicate them within the deferential relations of colonial power."[73]

But the Roman centurions, the religious leaders and the crowd are not the only gazers. Out in the periphery, is a group of women observing and gazing from a distance. From the Roman centurion's gaze and proclamation, Mark moves away from the centre of the Roman imperial cross to the non-Romans characters standing on the margins of the cross. They are observing and gazing at the figure on the Roman imperial cross; "And there were also women looking on from a distance" (Mark 15:40). And among them Mark specifies three; Mary Magdalene, and Mary the mother of James the younger and Joses, and Salome. They are described as having followed Jesus while in Galilee; "they were following *(akolouthen)* him and ministering to him while he was in Galilee" (Mark 15:41). Two of them we will meet at the empty tomb. Women in imperial context are always on the receiving end of their male narrators. For instance, we learn that they were disciples of Jesus, who had followed him from a distance. Mark plays upon gender and imperial context, infused with patriarchal ideology that has undercut the passion narrative to its core, to introduce the named women. Despite Mark signifying the women as having followed Jesus, he places them in the periphery. The women are products of a Markan patriarchal and imperialist ideology. Like the woman who anoints Jesus, the women stand outside the colonial cross yet they are products of the patriarchal Mark's writing.

Further, their gazing from a distance locates them as excess, as fragments, as those who do not qualify to be in the same space with the centurion. To have women at the end, in the periphery, looking from a distance produces patriarchal and colonial intensions. Patriarchy in colonial structures acts as double-colonizing for women. As both a colonial power structure and an ideology that privileges men, and through the discourse of what colonialism or Roman imperialism has produced, it becomes foundational to resistance than privilege the female characters. It seems in Mark that inequalities and empire are essential to the structure of patriarchy, colonial and imperial authority. Although the women are disciples, their discipleship and their following are performed from a distance.

That Mark represents them as those who followed Jesus from his days in Galilee does not provide any hope. Rather, it is as if the patriarchal Mark fractures

---

72. Bhabha, "Wonders," 158.
73. Ibid.

any possible positive analysis of the women. Mary Magdalene and her cohorts occupy contradictory roles. They are visible yet invisible as they observe Jesus from a distance. This distance is at least the interstitial space that blurs their visibility as Mark has relegated them to the periphery. Compared to the centurion, who is standing right at the centre of the colonial cross, and the privilege of Roman imperialism, they do not have that luxury, but remain in the periphery, the doubly colonized periphery.

CONCLUSION

The Markan key issues are the intersection of gender, Roman imperialism, and a Markan theology of the Jesus narrative with the failing disciples which are all brought to bear in the passion narrative. A Markan resistance does not make sense outside the imperial context and outside the politics of gender. Mark is a colonized patriarchal writer, one who is constituted by the very same ideological principles he calls into critical questioning. Mark is shaped by imperial Rome and, in turn, shaped the imperial ideologies of his own context. But the aspects of colonialism or Roman imperialism are experienced and played differently and uniquely by the Markan passion narrative. Mark is enacted in ambivalent spaces. For instance, Mark does not lay the blame for Jesus' death on the Jewish religious leaders but views it as collaboration between the two or more parties, despite that Jesus' death was birthed in the world of the colonized periphery by the Jewish religious leaders.

The Markan passion narrative is a narrative in the excursions of resistance that produces an ambivalent stance towards the empire. Markan strategies of resistance emerge out of the collision of the Markan margins. Mark does not have affinity towards the empire but he realizes the importance of working within the borders and confines of imperial Rome. Mark embodies a resistance that is not a clear cut but one that is complicated. Neither does Mark seek to replace Rome but within the collision of Rome and the colonized, we locate resistance. On the question of gender, it is still peripheral to Mark, out of the specifics of the passion narrative characters; women are presented in very peculiar instances. They are definitely in the periphery as they do not form part of the dominant plot. However it is obvious that Mark works the entanglements of imperial ideology but at the expense of gender politics.

WORKS CITED

Aichele, George, et al. *The Postmodern Bible: Bible and Culture Collective*. New Haven: Yale University Press, 1995.

Appiah, Kwame Anthony. *In My Father's House: Africa in the Philosophy of Culture*. New York: Oxford University Press, 1992.

Ashcroft, Bill, Gareth Griffiths, and Helen Tiffin, eds. *Key Concepts in Post-colonial Studies*. London: Routledge, 1995.

————. *The Post-colonial Studies Reader*. London: Routledge, 1995.

Bhabha, Homi. "Signs Taken for Wonders: Questions of Ambivalence and Authority under a Tree outside Delhi, May 1817." *CI* 12, no. 1 (1985): 144–65.

Bond, Helen. *Pontius Pilate in History and Interpretation*. Cambridge: Cambridge University Press, 1998.

Brown, Raymond. *The Death of the Messiah: From Gethsemane to the Grave*. New York: Doubleday, 1994.

Carter, Warren. *Pontius Pilate: Portraits of a Roman Governor*. Interfaces. Collegeville, MN: Liturgical Press, 2003.

Crossan, John Dominic. *God and Empire: Jesus against Rome, Then and Now*. New York: HarperSanFrancisco, 2007.

Desai, Gaurar, and Supriya Nair, eds. *Postcolonialism: An Anthology of Cultural Theory and Criticism*. New Brunswick, NJ: Rutgers University Press, 2005.

Donahue, John, and Daniel Harrington. *The Gospel of Mark*. Collegeville, MN: Liturgical, 2002.

Donaldson, Laura. *Decolonizing Feminisms: Race, Gender, and Empire-Building*. Chapel Hill: University of North Carolina Press, 1992.

————. "Native Women's Double Cross: Christology from the Contact Zone." *FT* 10 (2002): 96–117.

Dube, Musa W. *Postcolonial Biblical Interpretation of the Bible*. St. Louis: Chalice, 2000.

France, R. T. *The Gospel of Mark: A Commentary on the Greek Text*. Grand Rapids: Eerdmans, 2002.

Gaventa, Beverly Roberts, and Patrick D. Miller, eds. *The Ending of Mark and the Ends of God: Essays in Memory of Donald Harrisville Juel*. Louisville: Westminster John Knox, 2005.

Hall, Stuart. "The Emergence of Cultural Studies and the Crisis of the Humanities." *October* 53 (summer 1990): 11–23.

Horsley, Richard A., ed. *In the Shadow of Empire: Reclaiming the Bible as a History of Faithful Resistance*. Louisville: Westminster John Knox, 2008.

Jackson, Stevi, and Jackie Jones, eds. *Contemporary Feminist Theories*. New York: New York University Press, 1998.

Keller, Catherine, et al. *Postcolonial Theologies: Divinity and Empire*. St. Louis: Chalice, 2004.

Kwok Pui Lan. *Discovering the Bible in a Non-biblical World*. Maryknoll, NY: Orbis Books, 1995.

————. *Postcolonial Imagination and Feminist Theology*. Louisville: Westminster John Knox, 2005.

Kwok Pui Lan and Laura Donaldson, eds. *Postcolonial Feminism and Religious Discourse*. New York: Routledge, 2002.

Liew, Tat-siong Benny, "Tyranny, Boundary, and Might: Colonial Mimicry in Mark's Gospel." *JSNT* 73 (1999): 7–31.

McClintock, Anne, Aamir Mufti, and Ella Shohat, eds. *Dangerous Liaisons: Gender, Nation, and Postcolonial Perspectives*. Studies in Classical Philology. London and Minneapolis: University of Minnesota Press, 1997.

Moore, Stephen D. *Empire and Apocalypse: Postcolonialism and the New Testament*. Sheffield: Sheffield Phoenix, 2006.

————. *Post Structuralism and the New Testament: Derrida and Foucault at the Foot of the Cross*. Minneapolis: Fortress, 1994.

Myers, Ched. *Binding the Strong Man: A Political Reading of Mark's Story of Jesus.* Maryknoll, NY: Orbis Books, 2001.

Parry, Benita, "Resistance Theory/theorizing Resistance or Two Cheers for Nativism." In *Postcolonial Studies: A Materialist Critique.* London: Routledge, 2005.

Penner, Todd, and Caroline Vander Stichele, eds. *Mapping Gender in Ancient Religious Discourses.* BIS 84. Leiden: Brill, 2007.

Pratt, Mary Louise. *Imperial Eyes: Travel Writing and Transculturation.* London: Routledge, 1992.

Rooney, Ellen, ed. *The Cambridge Companion to Feminist Literary* Theory. Cambridge: University Press, 2006.

Spivak, Gayatri C. "Three Women's Texts and a Critique of Imperialism." *CI* 12, no. 1 (1985): 243–61.

Williams, P., and L. Chrisman, eds. *Colonial Discourse and Post-colonial Theory.* New York: Columbia University Press, 1992.

Pauline Bodies and South African Bodies:
Body, Power, and Biblical Hermeneutics

Jeremy Punt

Considering the relationship between body, Bible and the South African context, my primary interest is not Paul's theology of the body.[1] Going about Paul and the body the other way round, and wanting to consider how his perceptions of body contributed to his theology and morality, my point of departure is rather Paul's *body theology*, and its envisaged significance for contemporary South Africa. An earlier paper of mine[2] focused on the construction of the body in the (authentic) Pauline letters as generally either a physical, metaphorical, or bad (sinful) notion, but—somewhat ironically—also that the notion of the body of Christ often occupied a central place in these documents. Important issues related to body in Paul were the body's intersections with power and control, with sex, and, with transformation in the form of both resurrection and glory. Whereas the importance of Pauline body theology was then explored for his morality or moral theology, the question here is related to the power exerted by invoking body theology, and even broader, asking about possible implications for the (Southern) African context today.

When the focus shifts from designing Paul's "theology of the body," contemplating the impact of his theological considerations for bodies, to considering his body theology approach, at least three changes in perspective and resulting spinoffs can be registered. Firstly, body theology allows for the rehabilitation of an important (and, at times, even positive!) concept in Pauline thought. Secondly, a new epistemology of body is signalled in which the contextual nature of the body is taken seriously, *and* the body is understood as a site of revelation, both of which imply a

---

Originally published in *JTSA* 136 (2010): 76–91. Published here with permission.

1. A more common theology-of-the-body approach would attempt to understand how notions (and sometimes concerns) about the body fit into a theological framework or worldview construed for a particular NT author or corpus of writings; in short, a theology of the body is about theological reflection on the body and corporeality. On Paul's "theology of body," see, e.g., Leander E. Keck, *Paul and His Letters* (Proclamation Commentaries; Philadelphia: Fortress, 1979), 99.

2. J. Punt, "Morality and Body Theology in Paul," *Neot* 39, no. 2 (2005): 359–88.

non-essentialist understanding of the body; in other words, body is acknowledged as social construct complete with accompanying power-related issues.[3] In the third place, body theology creates room for a more integrated understanding of human existence and theological reflection, acknowledging a cross-directional hermeneutical flow.[4] The investigation of Paul's body theology is therefore not about an attempt to provide a template for human life, to "read off" (as it were) from the texts a blueprint for a constructive, life-affirming, gender-equal, and so on, community and/or society; it is, rather, about the construction of a discursive space for understanding Paul amidst first- and twenty-first century notions, attitudes and actions from a perspective informed by bodily existence.

SOUTH AFRICAN BODIES, RACISM, XENOPHOBIA AND POLITICAL TURMOIL

A number of recent events in South Africa have driven the materiality of human existence and the nature of our bodily life to some of its furthest limits since the end of Apartheid in April 1994. Our contemporary South African context is, not unlike many other African and Two-Thirds World countries, marked by deep-set problems of hunger and poverty and disease, homelessness and marginalisation, violent crimes and rape, widespread corruption and political instability—to name a few. These conditions are, however, also matched by the indestructible buoyancy of the African spirit, so often misunderstood or diminished by people elsewhere. Nevertheless, within this context South Africans (and the world at large) were shocked by some overtly racist events in the first part of 2008,[5] soon followed by some vicious xenophobic attacks of which the consequences are still lingering. In all of these events, often very different in nature, human beings in their very bodily existence have been and still are in focus. From quite a different direction, body

---

3. These power-related issues include answers to the questions such as: Who constructs bodies? What is the body that is constructed? Where and how does the construction activity take place? Why or for what purpose is it done, in the way it is done? What are the results of these processes?

4. Three distinct influences on body theology can be detected in process thought, liberation theology, and feminist theory. Process thought emphasises the evolutionary principle and undermines dualistic thinking, seeing the world in the broadest and most narrow way as ever becoming. The cosmic drive of evolution and individual drives towards certain goals are brought about by emotional intensity, making the body central to the unfolding of life and the world. In Liberation Theology a central notion is the concern with justice as *the* direction of God who is unfolding through the bodies of individuals, and in the lives of the oppressed in particular. And it is in Feminist Theology where human, individual experience is identified as the centre and touchstone of theology, with the body being the site of experience (L. Isherwood and E. Stuart, *Introducing Body Theology* [FTS; Cleveland: Pilgrim, 1988], 33–41).

5. See J. Punt, "Post-Apartheid Racism in South Africa: The Bible, Social Identity and Stereotyping," *RT* 16, nos. 3–4 (2009): 246–72.

awareness is also stimulated endlessly (even, incessantly) through the popular media at home and abroad, with its focus on manufactured bodies in the interest of health and fitness for example—or maybe more cynically, for commercial interests. In short, corporeality (or, bodiliness) is clearly not some abstract concept in (South) Africa; moreover, it forms an important backdrop for considering Pauline body theology.

The very awareness and effects of the focus on bodily or corporal existence in (South) Africa is often in direct contrast to some trends in the area of religion and spirituality, and to the growth of Pentecostalism on the sub-continent in particular. What is argued for another, context, the Western, about the issue of slavery, that in the history of Western philosophical and theological thought matters of flesh have generally been subordinated to matters of spirit,[6] has over many centuries become largely true in South Africa as well.[7] While the Pentecostal religious experience often does not (simplistically) exclude concern for people in their existential need as evidenced by the movements' social programmes, the contribution of Pentecostalism to an other-worldly focus can also not be denied. To avoid the charge of unfounded claims regarding specific religious experiences—and since Pentecostalism is certainly not the only religious formation invoking concerns regarding its (ambiguous if not negative) stance on the materiality of human, bodily existence—further discussion of religious formations and affiliations, or their societal impact, will be avoided. Suffice it to register the concern with other-worldly focused religious practices in the midst of a deepening crisis for people at existential, and in particular, at corporal level, locally in Southern Africa and globally.

However, and this is the framework for my argument, given the body-aversion theology of (some) Christian formations, the Pauline writings, which are at times considered central to such theological patterns,[8] deserve further and renewed attention for the apostle's body theology, even for his (not always uncomplicated) bodily-infused theology, and especially in South Africa where corporeal concerns are prominent. But Paul's body theology should, of course, be approached from its first-century C.E. context, which therefore will be our starting point.

---

6. J. A. Glancy, *Slavery in Early Christianity* (Minneapolis: Fortress, 2006), 30.

7. Glancy takes issue with the minimising of the effect, conditions, and consequences of enslavement in the first century C.E., when its physical dimensions are ignored with a resulting concentration on spiritual slavery—its disastrous effects were not restricted to colonial slave trade in African bodies, but its legacy endures on the African continent where human life is often denigrated, is often cheap.

8. The role of Bible translations in this regard also needs attention, since curious decisions are often made to avoid corporeal and thus sexual references (e.g., Rom 12:1 *ta somatōn humōn* is in Nuwe Afrikaanse Vertaling 1983 translated as "julle" [you] instead of "julle liggame" [your bodies]).

THINKING ABOUT PAULINE BODIES WITHIN THE FIRST-CENTURY C.E. CONTEXT

The general assumption that Paul's thinking about the human body is dichotomous, taking a division between the flesh (body) and soul within the one human body for granted, requires further explanation. First-century thinking about the human body was more complex than a simple separation between different elements such as body and soul, or ranking them in a hierarchy of values. There was a difference between the Jewish and Greek understandings of body: the view found in the He-brew scriptures presented the body and soul (*nepheš*) as a unity, indissoluble to the point of ceasing to exist at death, which contrasted with the prevailing view in the Greco-Roman world that the mortal body could be understood apart from the immortal soul (*psychē*). The body in fact was often understood by those in the Greco-Roman world to have imprisoned the soul, and that the soul is freed from its trapped existence at death at which point it then ascends to heaven[9] or journey to the underworld. However, understanding the first century C.E. body amounts to more than such rather unsophisticated oversimplifications framed in modernist thinking informed by the biological sciences,[10] and it requires more than simply distinguishing between Semitic and Greco-Roman views, particularly since Paul was after all a Jew living in an, at the time, increasingly Hellenised world.

If, as scholars often argue, Pauline ethics in areas such as sexual morality can be traced back directly to the Jewish tradition,[11] the same was largely true for his perceptions about the human body—however, and again, the thoroughgoing influ-ence of the Hellenistic context should likewise not be neglected. Moreover, from a social-scientific perspective, among second-temple Jews, "the physical body was regulated with the same systematic concern for order as the Temple and the body politic.[12] This meant concern for precise classification, about both the exact role and status of a person, as well as the regulation of who's 'in' or 'out'. Whenever role and status become blurred or ambiguous, the orderly system is threatened; what-ever enters and leaves, is the object of great scrutiny, for such things belong to the realm of the unclean."[13]

9. J. M. Bassler, *Navigating Paul: An Introduction to Key Theological Concepts* (Louisville and London: Westminster John Knox, 2007), 87.

10. Cf. D. B. Martin, *The Corinthian Body* (New Haven and London: Yale University Press, 1995), 3–37.

11. Cf. R. B. Hays, *The Moral Vision of the New Testament: A Contemporary Introduction to New Testament Ethics* (San Francisco: HarperSanFrancisco, 1996), 41.

12. But systematic regulation should be understood within the context of the time. For example, the ancient rabbis understood Gen 1:27–28 to refer to Adam being created inter-sexed, not just male or female but both. This is the image of God in which humankind was created, and God divided Adam into male and female only at a later stage (S. Gross, "Male and Female God Created Them," *Challenge* 59 [2000]: 12–13).

13. J. H. Neyrey, "Nudity," in *Biblical Social Values and Their Meaning: A Handbook*, ed. J. J. Pilch and B. J. Malina (Peabody, MA: Hendrickson, 1993), 119–25.

However, invoking these cultural, Jew versus Greek, or social-scientific paradigms for understanding the first-century body runs the risk of getting stuck in
schematic frameworks, in which perceptions of the body are overshadowed by
other, often theological and mostly essentialist, considerations.[14] Therefore, to
complement but also go beyond such understandings, another useful approach to
the human body in the first century is to look at the exposed or vulnerable body,
the body at the margins of society. Two instances of marginalised corporeality
were particularly pronounced.

First Century C.E. Bodies in a Context of Slavery

If it is true that the body has been neglected in the history of Christian theological
scholarship generally, it is particularly the case regarding the bodily dimensions of
slavery throughout most of the history of interpretation—a neglect exacerbated
through the particular "corporal vulnerability" of the enslaved body, always at risk
in terms of sexual availability *and* in danger of corporal abuse. While first-century
slavery had many faces, slaves were, among others, considered safe and benign
sexual outlets throughout antiquity: the sexual use of male and female slaves[15]
for their owners' pleasure constituted fair and just practice in the Greco-Roman
society.[16]

It has been argued that the ethos of the body[17] in the first centuries of Christian-

---

14. P. R. L. Brown, *The Body and Society: Men, Women, and Sexual Renunciation in Early
Christianity* (New York: CUP, 1988), makes valuable contributions, and certainly not of an
essentialist kind. See also, for example, W. R. LaFleur, "Body," in *Critical Terms for Religious
Studies,* ed. M. C. Taylor (Chicago: University of Chicago Press, 1998), 36–54; G. Loughlin,
"Biblical Bodies," *TSe* 12, no. 1 (2005): 9–27. In similar vein, Mary Douglas's notion of the
body as social map was an important influence on various biblical scholars making use of
social-scientific and social-anthropological methods (see M. Douglas, *Purity and Danger:
An Analysis of Concepts of Pollution and Taboo* [London: Routledge & Kegan Paul, 1996]).

15. Glancy, *Slavery,* 21: "Although some matrons exploited their male slaves sexually,
constraints on the sexuality of freeborn women rendered this practice less acceptable than
the sexual exploitation of male or female slaves by male slaveholders" mainly because of
different outcomes when children were born from such liaisons: children born from slave
women increased the owner's stock, whereas a child born from a male slave to a free women
would wreak havoc in the household, and possibly lead to divorce; the child would be illegitimate although freeborn.

16. Ibid., 21–24, 154, 144.

17. Ibid., 154–55. With increasing interest in asceticism in early Christianity as a form of
disciplining the body and guarding its integrity through rejection of sexual activity, foods,
refinements, sleep, pleasure, and the like, slaves were not, however, in the picture. Partly
because some of these slaves had to endure through no choice of their own (and would
slaves have recognised these activities as such [asceticism] in any case?), and partly because
slaves had the opposite predicament: not being able to refuse the sexual attention of their
slaveholders, and also being reliant on food and rest in order to cope with their workload
and so as to avoid punishment.

UNIVERSITY OF WINCHESTER
LIBRARY

ity requires investigation, given the possible effect that the slave-holding culture would have had on the church that developed within this context.[18] However, prevailing perceptions about the body were part of what made the continuing maintenance of slavery possible, in other words, what made it reasonable and socially acceptable at the time—also within the early Christian church. For example, slaves served as sexual doubles in households, where female slaves in particular on the one hand had to fulfil the sexual favours a married woman could effectively deny, and on the other hand generally were sexual stand-ins for their matrons when the latter for whatever reason opted out of sexual relations with their husbands.[19] Perceptions about slave bodies were indicative of how bodies in general were understood. "In a world where householders treated their slaves as recalcitrant bodies to be restrained by corporal corrections, ascetic Christians emphasized the discipline and the control of their own bodies. Just as householders regarded the control of unruly slave bodies to be a standard part of household management, ascetic Christians regarded the control of their own unruly bodies as a necessary dimension in the management of their spiritual houses,"[20] This does not mean that all Christians aspired to ascetic lives, nor that Christian slaveholders did not also indulge in various excesses; the point is, rather, that as much as slaves were perceived and treated as bodies, in the early church the body was to be treated as a slave (cf. 1 Cor. 9:27).

The impact of slavery on the character of Greco-Roman people was vast and deep, and left its mark in ways that will not ordinarily be associated with practices of slavery. One aspect is especially important for our purposes here (and a matter to which we will return in a moment): a slave-holding culture resulted in a society where characters and habits were moulded by lifetimes of command and obedience, where young and old had become habituated to power, all of which impacted on emerging structures and perspectives of the early churches—and on perceptions of bodiliness in particular.

Theologising First Century C.E. Bodies: Martyrdom Traditions

Sticking to the notion of finding the body more exposed in situations of its own vulnerability, the martyrdom traditions[21] that soon developed in the early Chris-

---

18. Ibid., 154.

19. Ibid., 21–24.

20. Ibid., 155.

21. It is interesting to note that Clark also includes asceticism with her argument about martyrdom, referring to asceticism as the "'long martyrdom' of renunciation" (G. Clark, "Bodies and Blood: Late Antique Debate on Martyrdom, Virginity, and Resurrection," in *Changing Bodies, Changing Meanings: Studies on the Human Body in Antiquity,* ed. D. Montserrat [London and New York: Routledge, 1998], 99–115). She concludes her study with the following remark: "The bodies of the martyrs and the bodies of the ascetics demonstrated the power of God in flesh and blood; and bodily resurrection will be the ultimate transition" (112).

tian church illustrated the ambivalent positions ascribed to the body.[22] Martyr acts and their (sometimes much later) narrative descriptions came from a context where suspected criminals were often publicly tortured, the practice of which endured unchanged among the followers of Christ notwithstanding their beliefs about a loving God.[23] With the martyred, tortured body on public display, the violent exposé was furthered in the remembering and retelling of these deaths of men and women.[24] In the end, the early Christian church triumphed theologically over martyrdom as the very practice which intended to effect the permanent and degrading transformation of the body. This victory (over martyrdom) was accomplished by having the faithful spirit triumph over the vulnerable body, as much as the body triumphed over torment and death. Such perspectives about martyrdom and bodies were grounded in a particular understanding of Jesus' death, accompanied by assumptions about the body of Jesus and its consequences.

The incarnation of God in Christ evidently played an important role in the New Testament documents, and despite the often-remarked upon absence of biographical depictions of Jesus in his letters, the notion of the embodied Jesus Christ was a central concern for Paul. Paul's concern for *and* ambiguity regarding the body became apparent in his attention to the resurrection of Christ as the first fruits of those who "sleep," holding the resurrection of Christ as both the model and the reason for the resurrection of all human beings. In his distinction in 1 Cor. 15 between the physical and spiritual body, explained through the analogy of the grain of wheat, his belief that the resurrected body will not be the same as the original body soon became clear—as much as the stalk of wheat is recognised to be from the grain, but is at the same time also distinct from it. Paul's ambiguous position on the human body, that is, its relative unimportance given what lies beyond the body as well as its undeniable and non-negotiable importance in light of Christ's incarnation and resurrection, and the notion of a general resurrection, soon became—and have to this day remained—hotly debated theological issues.[25]

Amidst first-century C.E. notions of the body, and then also the vulnerable body in particular, Paul's notions about the body, and the bodiliness of human

---

22. Ibid., 99–115.

23. Ibid., 104.

24. Ibid., 106. Such retellings included the martyrdom of women, which probably provoked a different response from an audience. Although accustomed to male control over female bodies, and a discourse of invasive and violent sexuality, audiences would have recoiled from presenting the sexual assault of women martyrs notwithstanding overtly eroticised descriptions of their deaths. Rape, however, was unlike other forms of violence directed at the martyrs—never the "object of loving description and retelling."

25. Ibid., 111–12. In the fourth century Paul's views already led to much discussion, with Gregory reasoning that the resurrected body will be the same as the pre-Fall into sin body. Augustine's position changed form a Platonist view of the soul fallen into a body as a consequence of the Fall, to a position about the "conjugal union" of body and soul that will be maintained in the resurrection.

existence (at least, Paul's construction of it) can briefly be considered, not only for how it impacted upon but also how it actually informed his thinking and theological position.

PAULINE BODY THEOLOGY: TOWARDS A NEW EPISTEMOLOGY

As pointed out above, in a Pauline body theology, a new epistemology of body is signalled in the sense that the contextual nature of the body is taken seriously, but also that the body is understood as a site of revelation. Such considerations involve a non-essentialist understanding of the body, and imply, therefore, reckoning with the body as social construct—and, to be sure, together with all the power-related issues that accompany it. Three important aspects of Pauline body discourse, namely the metaphorical body, the engendered body and Christ's body, can be probed briefly.

Paul and the Body as Metaphor[26]

The body metaphor was not original to Paul, but it is difficult to trace its provenance. No exact parallel exists in Jewish literature, since although the "corporate personality" idea may be present in the Hebrew Bible,[27] it is the Septuagint that introduced "body" into Jewish thought for the first time (e.g., Lev 14:9 and Prov 11:17). While neither the Jewish tradition of the time nor the Intertestamental Literature made use of the body as metaphor, it was in the air in the contemporary and later Greek traditions. The Gnostics, for example, made much of the saved community as body of the heavenly redeemer, although this applies really to post-New Testament writings. Among the Stoics, the cosmos including humanity was taken as the body of the divine world-soul, and society as the body in which each member had a different part to play. With Paul, however, the body was a more restricted metaphor, referring to a more personal community than the Stoic *polis* in which the wider society did not receive priority over the Christian community. Paul's use of the body metaphor was further different from contemporary use in

---

26. See J. D. Crossan and J. L. Reed, *In Search of Paul: How Jesus's Apostle Opposed Rome's Empire with God's Kingdom. A New Vision of Paul's Words and World* (New York: HarperSanFrancisco, 2004), 281–84, on Paul being a mystic himself, intending more with the body-imagery than just metaphor. Unlike the use of slavery as metaphor for a certain identity and ethos but which amounted to a rhetoric of evasion, where the brutality of slavery is hidden in a discourse of other relations, deemphasising its coercive character (see S. Briggs, "Paul on Bondage and Freedom in Imperial Roman Society," in *Paul and Politics: Ekklesia, Israel, Imperium, Interpretation: Essays in Honor of Krister Stendahl,* ed. R. A. Horsley [Harrisburg, PA: Trinity, 2000], 110–23), Paul's use of the body as metaphor puts it squarely into focus, along with the accompanying issues of coercive and constructive power.

27. Against "corporate personality" as an outdated concept, see B. J. Malina, "Understanding New Testament Persons," in *The Social Sciences and New Testament Interpretation,* ed. R. Rohrbaugh (Peabody, MA: Hendrickson, 1996), 41–61.

identifying a community *within* the larger society, and using it to describe *personal* responsibilities for those belonging to the community rather than civic duties.[28]

Against this background, Paul portrayed the community of Jesus' followers in the latter half of 1 Corinthians as a metaphorical body, first to stress unity rather than a focus on diverse gifts (1 Cor 10:17), but then also to stress unity amidst diversity and even multiplicity (1 Cor 11:29). The human body thus came to function as allegory for the Christian community, while a focus on the local community as body of Christ (1 Cor. 12:27) served the important purpose of allocating (different) responsibilities to each other. Not intent on establishing some "universalist" notion of "*the* church", each member of the community was granted ministry to others, which not only maintained diversity but was also required for proper functioning, at least according to Paul's consideration of divine intention. The community as body was seen to have a common nerve, where people shared all experiences without compulsion, in close relation between the community and Jesus Christ. In fact, initially the community was identified with Christ (1 Cor 12:12), although at a later stage, the community was portrayed as the body of Christ.[29] In Paul's later letter to the Romans there is also a focus on body (Rom 12–15), stressing again unity amidst diversity against both the over-evaluation of some gifts at expense of others but also against the overestimation of the gift possessed. The primary application of the body metaphor, therefore, was that through the variety of contributions and proportionate strength, the unity of the community becomes manifest: not just the body *of* Christ but the one body *in* Christ (Rom 12:5a).[30]

On the one hand, the use of body as metaphor shows the importance of bodiliness in Pauline thought, and for the importance of body theology. On the other, it can however be asked to what extent Paul's metaphorical use of the body[31] carried within itself the seeds of the neglect and disavowal of the real-life body in later Christian tradition? And what was the effect of exerting power on bodies through metaphorising the very same body or bodies? But other difficulties also

---

28. R. Banks, *Paul's Idea of Community* (rev. ed; Peabody, MA: Hendrickson, 1994), 66; cf. Martin, *Corinthian Body*, 92–96. In the deutero-Pauline letters the body metaphor is further developed as an aspect of the new religious ideas supplementing faith in Jesus Christ, and it is especially in Colossians and Ephesians where Jesus is portrayed as the head of the church as body and head of his own body, respectively. For further discussion of the development, limits, and applications of the body metaphor in the deutero-Pauline letters, see Banks, *Community*, 61–66.

29. Ibid., 58–61.

30. Ibid., 61.

31. Other aspects related to Paul's invocation of the body as metaphor cannot be addressed here; for example, Banks, *Community*, 67–76, also shows how Paul's use of the body metaphor focused on growth and maturity; even faith was connected to the body and its maturity as in the milk-metaphor (1 Cor 3:1; cf. Heb 5:13 versus 1 Pet 2:22). Knowledge stood central for Paul in as far as the body was concerned, and he uses different terminology to express it.

arise in Paul's body theology, particularly in terms of gendered bodies in Pauline communities.

Men and Women: Pauline Gender Discourse

Christianity was shaped in a world characterised by patriarchy, whether particular Jewish or Greco-Roman sentiments dominated in a certain context. Such patriarchal notions were religiously defined and justified, which meant that natural order and natural laws[32] "were originally seen as such because they supposedly reflect God's design for the universe."[33] The male body was constituted in opposition to that of the woman, the child or the slave[34] and thus defined by mastery, in the first place of the self but also in exercising authority and control over others.[35] Freeborn men were therefore trained to resist servility, and to further their own power. In public, men were most often noted oratorically which made persuasive speech so decidedly important.[36] This was part of the context in which Pauline body theology developed, the results of which have been variously described, both lauded and decried—at any rate, some of these ambiguities[37] deserve attention here.

In Gal 3:28 Paul not only claimed that there are no longer male and female,

---

32. An inkling of Paul's thinking on the natural order of the world, life, and human bodies is reflected in Rom 1.

33. Isherwood and Stuart, *Introducing*, 20.

34. The bodies of slave and child were often conflated, as hinted in the Greek word *pais,* which could refer to both; and also in terminology that referred to (male) slaves as boys; and since male slaves' paternity was not legally recognised. The perception of slaves and servants as immature and effectively being like children, and referred to as "boys" and "girls," was found in among others the racially segregated United States and apartheid South Africa!

35. The patriarchal cornerstone at the time was the family, with the legal authority vested in the *paterfamilias*, extending his power over wife, children, slaves, animals, and land. The power and authority vested in the *paterfamilias* was reflected and expanded in the social and political, military and religious, and others forms of public power wielded by the ruling elite, while excluding women from higher education, elite professions, and military and political leadership. Cultic roles occupied by women in the Graeco-Roman world were restricted to the female sphere, while Second Temple Judaism excluded women from priesthood and the inner sanctuary of the temple through purity laws. However, the relative openness to forms of women leadership in early Christianity is probably indicative of some flux in gender roles in first-century Judaism.

36. Glancy, *Slavery*, 24–26. The importance of public speaking and language in general is underwritten by the way in which a child's paternity was established; unlike our day and age, which relies upon genetic or spermatic evidence as borne out by scientific methods such as DNA testing, paternity in the first century was by decree. A freeborn man could acknowledge or deny a child as his own, with accompanying different consequences.

37. Others are best left to be discussed elsewhere; see, e.g., B. R. Gaventa, "The Maternity of Paul: An Exegetical Study of Galatians 4:19," in *The Conversation Continues: Studies in John and Paul. In Honor of J. Louis Martyn,* ed. R. T. Fortna and B. R. Gaventa (Nashville: Abingdon Press, 1990), 189–201, and idem, *Our Mother Saint Paul* (Louisville and London:

but also that men and women are one in Christ, raising the question of what this would have meant for women converts to become members of the community of Jesus followers but also to have their female bodies become one in the male Christ? Sexuality, to use a modern word, was understood in the Greco-Roman world as a continuum of possibilities rather than a stark contrast between male and female. Unlike the modern notion of a horizontal continuum for gender and sexuality, a hierarchy with a clear top and bottom positioned the male end of the spectrum as exercising a natural dominance over the female end. Masculinity was associated with strength, rationality, self-control, activity, and perfection, and contrasted with weakness, sexuality and procreation, passion, passivity, and imperfection which were associated with the feminine.[38] A body necessarily consisted of male and female aspects, and the location of a particular person at a specific point on the male-female axis depended on the relative strength of these aspects. In fact, male or female aspects could be adjusted or amplified through the impact of a number of internal or external forces, which would affect the position that a person is accorded on the spectrum; in short, "either slipping downward to greater femininity or rising to a greater degree of masculinity."[39]

And therefore Gal 3:28 should probably be read to understand that women in their mystical union with Christ became empowered as males, growing toward the male end of the spectrum. Being fully female in Christ,[40] would have meant being or becoming as male as possible.

Volf's assertion that, "What has been erased in Christ is not the sexed body, but some important culturally coded norms attached to sexed bodies, (such as the obligation to marry and procreate and the prohibition of women from performing certain functions in the church),"[41] therefore, cannot stand.[42] Bodiliness

---

Westminster John Knox, 2007), on Paul's use of maternal language, an interesting aspect of which was his higher reference to the maternity than the paternity of God.

38. For the inherent tendency to violence in ancient gender relations, see P. J. J. Botha, "Submission and Violence: Exploring Gender Relations in the First-Century World," *Neot* 34, no. 1 (2000): 1–38.

39. Bassler, *Navigating*, 45.

40. Ibid., 46. Bassler speculates whether the emphasis on being "in Christ" was not intricately involved with a possible trend among women to an altered sense of self in a masculine direction.

41. M. Volf, *Exclusion and Embrace: A Theological Exploration of Identity, Otherness, and Reconciliation* (Nashville: Abingdon, 1996), 184; cf. D. Boyarin, *A Radical Jew: Paul and the Politics of Identity* (CSJLCS 1; Berkeley: University of California Press, 1994).

42. Other scholars argue for some relaxation of the strict gender codes on the time, through Christianity's forceful introduction of eschatological expectation and divine incarnation influenced by apocalyptic and sapiential Judaisms, fused two horizons: an eschatological future and restored creation. This contributed to the conviction that current social divisions expressed in gender, social, political status, and the like have been invalidated if they have not indeed disintegrated (see R. R. Ruether, "Gender Equity and Christianity: Premodern Roots, Modern, and Postmodern Perspectives" [Lecture Given in Conjunction

and certainly gender are not essences that can be understood outside of cultural codes; function defined form even more in first century C.E. than with us today.[43] Secondly, where would a culturally decoded body have fitted in, and how would it have functioned? And thirdly, in whose interests would such culturally decoded bodies have been, especially since the first century C.E. church gave no indication of even attempting to be culturally neutral or aloof (as, e.g., the household codes, and the focus on order in the Corinthian correspondence, etc, attested)?

In fact, the trend towards emulating a greater masculinity was underwritten by Paul's preference for celibacy and virginity (1 Cor 7), a trend which lasted well into the second century C.E. when women were urged to reject culturally prescribed roles (cf. 1 Tim 5:3–16).[44] The ambiguous situation which Paul was party to, in which women took up a greater sense of masculinity led to some sense of invulnerability to hostile spiritual forces (1 Cor 11:2–16) and even to engaging in public roles reserved for men (1 Cor 14:34–35), invoking the apostle to counter such notions. The "masculinisation" of the congregation in Corinth emerges from the community's claims to authority (1 Cor 4:6), wisdom, strength and honour (1 Cor 4:10); freedom (1 Cor 9:1); and, to knowledge (1 Cor 8:1).[45]

In subsequent developments, in the history of interpretation and Christian-

---

with the Installation of Rosemary S. Keller as Academic Dean of Union Theological Seminary, 12 November 1996], *USQR* 50, nos. 1–4 [1996]: 47–61).

43. See J. Butler, *Gender Trouble: Feminism and the Subversion of Identity* (Thinking Gender 2; New York: Routledge, 1990), 139–40, on gender and performativity.

44. In her investigation of what motivated women to conversion to early Christianity, C. Osiek, "Motivation for the Conversion of Women in Early Christianity: The Case of Pentacostalism," in *In Other Words: Essays on Social Science Methods and the New Testament in Honor of Jerome H Neyrey*, ed. A. C. Hagedorn, Z. A. Crook, and E. Stewart (Sheffield: Sheffield Phoenix, 2007), 186–201, reckons that in the early Christian churches the participation of women was probably more widespread than what the New Testament texts tended to indicate. Osiek finds in contemporary Pentecostal churches hints as to how some conundrums such as Gal 3:28 and women leadership in Rom 16 and Phil 4:2 are to be reconciled with texts such as 1 Cor 11:2–16; 14:34–35. "While in the Pentecostal tradition God is resolutely male, traditional *machismo* is mitigated by presenting God with tender affection, one who never forces the human heart but waits for a response of affection, and opening of the heart to God's love. Jesus is the suffering victim who endured shame that the Mediterranean male would not countenance, yet he is to be worshiped as one who also desires a loving response from the faithful. . . . Thus, the churchgoer is presented with a masculine God and Jesus who nevertheless exhibit certain 'feminine' attributes. While patriarchal language and structures are reinforced, 'feminine' qualities are encouraged through divine modelling" (195). The question, though, remains whether the net effect of the mitigation of structures and systems is not all too often the reimposition of such structures and systems?

45. Bassler, *Navigating*, 46. While no direct criticism of patriarchal culture emerged from Paul, his urging to avoid sexual exploitative behaviour (*porneia*) and for men to control their bodies (or, manage their "tools," 1 Thess 4:3–4), did imply some reining in of

ity as a whole, distrust about the body gradually settled in, often evidenced most clearly in perceptions about the gendered body. So, for example, in the early church fathers, the orthodox or patristic, "the figure of the heretical female" was created "as a negative expression of their own orthodox male self-identity."[46] The heretical was now expressed in terms of gender, and the ground was prepared for engendering heresy and sin.[47]

Paul and the Body of Christ

As suggested earlier, in Paul's letters it was the body rather than the life of Jesus that was in focus, incarnation rather than biography, and it was used to extrapolate meaning and significance for the bodies of believers. The intricate relationship that Paul saw between Christ and believers was often expressed by the Pauline phrase, "in Christ." While much energy has been disbursed in the past in an effort to explain (and also to claim a privileged explanation) of this phrase,[48] and its re-enactment in the baptism and the Eucharist, the ongoing participation in the body of Christ, at once crucified and alive (Rom 6:3–4; 1 Cor 11:26), was according to his letters evidently and eagerly anticipated by Pauline initiated communities.

Rather than focussing on the mystical aspects involved—but certainly without denying them—the emphasis on being in Christ can in Paul's case also be understood to refer to the new identity of Jesus-followers as communities of solidarity with the crucified. Not in a monolithic way, though: "[A] multiplicity of com-

---

the phallus (see N. Elliott, *Liberating Paul: The Justice of God and the Politics of the Apostle* [Maryknoll, NY: Orbis Books, 1994], 203).

46. V. Burrus, "The Heretical Woman as a Symbol in Alexander, Athanasius, Epiphanius, and Jerome," *HTR* 84, no. 1 (1991): 229–48. The background to this was the struggle over the character of the *ekklesia*. Some scholars are of the opinion that the *ekklesia* was radically democratic at first, but as the need to control the influx of newly, and often partly, converted people into the imperial church increased, the pressure to conform to the kyriarchal order of the Roman imperial state increased (E. Schüssler Fiorenza, "Introduction: Transgressing Canonical Boundaries," in *Searching the Scriptures, Volume Two: A Feminist Commentary*, ed. E. Schüssler Fiorenza [London: SCM, 1991], 1–14).

47. The negative perception of women bodies abounded, with Tertullian referring to the woman as "the devil's gateway" and Augustine insisting that only the male body had the full image of God; still later, Thomas Aquinas thought of the woman as a defective human being, the result of an accident to the male sperm. With patriarchal culture firmly established in the church, women were not ordained to the diaconate or the priesthood. See L. Magessa, "From Privatized to Popular Biblical Hermeneutics in Africa," in *The Bible in African Christianity: Essays in Biblical Theology*, ed. J. N. K. Mugambi and C. Houle (Nairobi: Acton, 1997), 25–39, on Augustine's views on women not being the image of God unless connected to a man/husband—unlike man himself—which were views based on Genesis and Pauline letters.

48. See the recent brief summary in Bassler, *Navigating*, 35–47, who concludes that "in Christ" could best be understood as referring to a mystical union between Christ and believers.

munity and personal life patterns is explicitly warranted by Paul's celebration of the diversity that constitutes the Body of Christ."[49] Given Paul's style and content, particularly when interpreted within a context imbued with interests and concerns of the twenty-first century, the radical vulnerability which the apostle posed as crucially important for the *ekklesia's* formation is sometimes neglected. Not only did the apostle identify with Christ as victim, but he also claimed to have suffered bodily, bearing the scars as proof (2 Cor 8:9; Phil 2:5–11). The regular rites of baptism and Eucharist through which the church as community associated itself with the body of the Christ as victim, constituted both the initiation and confirmation of this new identity[50]—in material and bodily ways.

In this context the body of Christ became a compact metaphor, and also a symbol of power for going against and beyond the power of Roman imperialism, which may have been for Paul and others the culmination of the long experience of Israel's oppression by foreign powers. The central position of the Christ-body symbolism disallowed the mystifying of oppression, mystical escape though rapture or acceptance of oppression by the rulers of the age. Although Paul neither offered nor contemplated a programme of social action for those whose humanity was impinged upon—at least as far as twentieth-first century readers are concerned—he advocated community values of mutuality and solidarity with the weak and vulnerable amidst the exigencies of the time.[51] This has led some to argue that Paul should be seen as an early exponent of the "preferential option for the poor," seeing that he so clearly used the logic of the crucified in (among others) 1 Cor 1:27–28. Paul sided with the "weak," with the poor as the primary representatives of people of God, and against the Roman Empire that championed the political and economic interests of wealthy. In the end, Paul's ethos of discernment, resistance and solidarity with the vulnerable understandably met with the most resistance from those congregations which stand to lose most, those in Corinth and in Rome.[52]

---

49. D. J. Good, "Wrestling Biblically with the Changing Shape of the Family," accessed 17 May 2007. Available from http://www.ekklesia.co.uk/node/4844/print.

50. Without denying the tensions between the ideal of community and the normal structures of larger society, it is also a question whether baptism, given Gal 3:28, could be understood as a doing away with distinctions of role and status, and establishing a new status in a continuing social order which plunged community members permanently into new "threshold" state (Elliott, *Liberating*, 181–230). On the other hand, it is difficult to deny that community members' traditional roles and status were reconstructed in the new humanity Paul constructed through Christ, evidence of which was probably seen in the Lord's Supper (1 Cor 11).

51. Paul's awareness that he was operating in an elaborate grid of patron-client relationships is probably evidenced in his refusal to accept obligations implied by aid from the elite of Corinth and their animosity (2 Corinthians).

52. Elliott, *Liberating*, 181–230.

Conclusion: Pauline Body Theology and Human Existence

In all three aspects of Pauline body theology discussed above, the issue of power in the congregations was strongly in focus: formatting and using the body metaphor for structuring community relations; constructing and regulating gendered bodies; and, creating a certain understanding of the body of Christ to exercise and regulate power in the communities addressed by Paul. Rather than discussing the detail of each of these three aspects, the point is that body theology and terminology was evidently not incidental to Paul's thinking, but central in and for his theology, vital for his perspectives on Christ and community, and important for making sense of Pauline thinking. The human body was for Paul not a topic best avoided, and certainly not of peripheral concern, as much as knowledge was not only about thinking and speaking, but also about a way of life: people did not *have* bodies, they did not live *in* bodies, but they existed as bodies, in a *bodily* way.

While the place and role of the body occupied constituted an important element in Paul's thought and life, bodiliness in Pauline thinking was not uncomplicated or uncontested; and, although it cannot be discussed here, it served also an important function in Paul's claims on power and to authority. It achieved a certain centrality in Pauline thinking through the incarnational focus on Jesus,[53] and was an oft-used metaphor for expressing how Paul understood the nature and structure of the communities of Jesus-followers. On the one hand, disregarding the importance of the body and related concepts in the Pauline letters will result in the inability to account for how it informed and steered his theological thinking. On the other hand, Paul's body theology is at best ambiguous and at times properly confusing.[54] Nevertheless, a re-appreciation of the constitutive centrality of the body in and for Pauline thinking, that is, for his body theology, could go a long way towards a re-thinking of theology, of ecclesial structures, of human life—of bodies—in communities and society. As stressed earlier, no easy, ready-made solutions to our South African problems can simplistically be gleaned from a Pauline blueprint. However, the importance of Pauline body theology in the apostle's letters requires a serious reappraisal of theological thinking and hermeneutics—that not only puts the body in focus but that acknowledges the body as its point of departure—on the sub-continent.

Works Cited

Banks, R. *Paul's Idea of Community*. Rev. ed. Peabody, MA: Hendrickson, 1994.

53. Even if not uncontested as the Johannine letters for example show, the bodily presence of Jesus prevails throughout these documents. The governing images of early Christianity such as virgin birth, incarnation, resurrection, and Eucharist relied on the power of body symbolism; see A. Cameron, *Christianity and the Rhetoric of Empire: The Development of Christian Discourse* (Berkeley: University of California Press, 1991), 68; Isherwood and Stuart, *Introducing*, 11.

54. See Martin, *Corinthian Body*, 250–51.

Bassler, J. M. *Navigating Paul: An Introduction to Key Theological Concepts*. Louisville and London: Westminster John Knox, 2007.

Brown, P. R. L. *The Body and Society: Men, Women, and Sexual Renunciation in Early Christianity*. New York: Columbia University Press, 1988.

Botha, P. J. J. "Submission and Violence: Exploring Gender Relations in the First-Century World." *Neot* 34, no. 1 (2000): 1–38.

Boyarin, D. *A Radical Jew: Paul and the Politics of Identity*. Critical Studies in Jewish Literature, Culture, and Society 1; Berkeley: University of California Press, 1994.

Burrus, V. "The Heretical Woman as a Symbol in Alexander, Athanasius, Epiphanius, and Jerome." *HTR* 84, no. 1 (1991): 229–48.

Butler, J. *Gender Trouble: Feminism and the Subversion of Identity*. Thinking Gender 2. New York: Routledge, 1990.

Cameron, A. *Christianity and the Rhetoric of Empire: The Development of Christian Discourse*. Berkeley: University of California Press, 1991.

Crossan, J. D., and J. L. Reed. *In Search of Paul: How Jesus's Apostle Opposed Rome's Empire with God's Kingdom: A New Vision of Paul's Words and World*. New York: HarperSanFrancisco, 2004.

Douglas, M. *Purity and Danger: An Analysis of Concepts of Pollution and Taboo*. London: Routledge and Kegan Paul, 1996.

Elliott, N. *Liberating Paul: The Justice of God and the Politics of the Apostle*. The Bible and Liberation 6; Maryknoll, NY: Orbis Books, 1994.

Fortna, R. T., and B. R. Gaventa, eds. *The Conversation Continues: Studies in John and Paul. In Honor of J. Louis Martyn*. Nashville: Abingdon, 1990.

Glancy, J. A. *Slavery in Early Christianity*. Minneapolis: Fortress, 2006.

Good, D. J., "Wrestling Biblically with the Changing Shape of the Family." http://www.ekklesia.co.uk/node/4844/print. Accessed 17 May 2007.

Gross, S. "Male *and* Female God Created Them." *Challenge* 59 (2000): 12–13.

Hagedorn, A. C., Z. A. Crook, and E. Stewart. *In Other Words: Essays on Social Science Methods and the New Testament in Honor of Jerome H. Neyrey*. The Social World of Biblical Antiquity, 2nd ser., vol. 1. Sheffield: Sheffield Phoenix, 2007.

Hays, R. B. *The Moral Vision of the New Testament: A Contemporary Introduction to New Testament Ethics*. San Francisco: HarperSanFrancisco, 1996.

Horsley, R. A, ed. *Paul and Politics: Ekklesia, Israel, Imperium, Interpretation. Essays in Honor of Krister Stendahl*. Harrisburg, PA: Trinity Press International, 2000.

Isherwood, L., and E. Stuart. *Introducing Body Theology*. Introductions in Feminist Theology. Cleveland: Pilgrim, 1988.

Keck, L. E. *Paul and His Letters*. Proclamation Commentaries. Philadelphia: Fortress, 1979.

Loughlin, G., "Biblical Bodies." *TSe* 12, no. 1 (2005): 9–27.

Martin, D. B. *The Corinthian Body*. New Haven and London: Yale University Press, 1995.

Montserrat, D., ed. *Changing Bodies, Changing Meanings. Studies on the Human Body in Antiquity*. London and New York: Routledge, 1998.

Mugambi, J. N. K., and C. Houle, eds. *The Bible in African Christianity: Essays in Biblical Theology*. African Christianity Series. Nairobi: Acton, 1997.

Pilch, J. J., and B. J. Malina, eds. *Biblical Social Values and Their Meaning: A Handbook*. Peabody, MA: Hendrickson, 1993.

Punt, J. "Morality and Body Theology in Paul." *Neot* 39, no. 2 (2005): 359–88.

———. "Post-Apartheid Racism in South Africa: The Bible, Social Identity, and Stereotyping." *RT* 16, nos. 3–4 (2009): 246–72.

Rohrbaugh, R., ed. *The Social Sciences and New Testament Interpretation*. Peabody, MA: Hendrickson, 1996.

Ruether, R. R. "Gender Equity and Christianity: Premodern Roots, Modern and Postmodern Perspectives (Lecture Given in Conjunction with the Installation of Rosemary S. Keller as Academic Dean of Union Theological Seminary, November 12, 1996)." *USQR* 50, nos. 1–4 (1996): 47–61.

Schüssler Fiorenza, E., ed. *Searching The Scriptures, Volume Two: A Feminist Commentary*. London: SCM, 1991.

Taylor M. C., ed. *Critical Terms for Religious Studies*. Chicago: University of Chicago Press, 1998.

Volf, M. *Exclusion and Embrace: A Theological Exploration of Identity, Otherness, and Reconciliation*. Nashville: Abingdon, 1996.

GO TLA SIAMA, O TLA FOLA:
DOING BIBLICAL STUDIES IN AN HIV AND AIDS CONTEXT

Musa W. Dube

Due to its impact on all aspects of our lives; due to its spread through prevailing social injustice, HIV/AIDS is no longer just a health issue or an issue of individual morality. Rather HIV/AIDS' impact calls for a multisectoral approach. That is all of us, wherever we are and whatever disciplines and departments and institutions we serve, need to use our space to contribute toward the struggle against HIV/AIDS, its stigma, its impact and for the provision of quality care to the infected. This strategy has been adopted to fight HIV/AIDS as a disease of social injustice.[1]

The HIV/AIDS pandemic means that we need to read the Bible in new ways as we begin to think ourselves as a community in new ways.[2]

GO TLA SIAMA. O TLA FOLA

In an article I wrote at by the end of the 1990s, entitled, "Healing Where There is No Healing: Reading the Miracles of Healing in an AIDS Context," I describe the experience of living and teaching biblical studies in the HIV and AIDS context.[3] By that time the infection rate in Botswana was among the highest in the world and anti-retroviral drugs were unaffordable. Death and burial occupied a significant amount of our lives and hopelessness reigned. One of the issues that I discussed in the article was that if one did not see a friend over a long time, one did not ask;

Originally published in *BT* 8, no. 2 (2010): 212–41. Published here with permission.

1. M. W. Dube, "Rahab is Hanging Out a Red Ribbon: One African Woman's Perspective on the Future of Feminist New Testament Scholarship," in *Feminist New Testament Studies: Global and Future Perspectives,* ed. K. Wicker et al. (New York: Palgrave, 2005), 196.

2. Cheryl B. Anderson, "Lessons of Healing from Naaman (2 Kings 5:1–27): An African-American Perspective," in *African Women, HIV/AIDS, and Faith Communities,* ed. Isapel Phiri et al. (Pietermaritzburg: Cluster, 2003), 39.

3. M. W. Dube, "Healing Where There Is No Healing: Reading the Miracles of Healing in an AIDS Context," in *Reading Communities Reading Scripture: Essays in Honor of Daniel Patte,* ed. G. A. Phillips and N. Duran (Harrisburg, PA: Trinity Press International, 2002), 121–33.

for possibly asking would confirm the obvious: namely, that they were dead.[4] I also pointed out how the HIV and AIDS storm had rendered our lives meaningless to the extent that even our greeting expressions sounded hollow and, sometimes, as an outright mockery. That is, in a situation where we all knew that one's health could only get worse, it made no sense to say "how are you," to someone whose body bore the wounds of an incurable and stigmatized illness.[5]

Today we have come a long way, living in the HIV and AIDS storm, to a point where we are not only trying to stop the storm, but to live in it. One such innovation is evident in the creation of a language of self-awareness and hope. For example, expressions such as *Modimo ore file sebakanyana se; go tla siama, o tla fola* have come to characterize our time. *Sebakanyana se* means "this little time," or "this very small opportunity." Songs and expressions of gratefulness to God who has given us *se bakanyana se le motsutsunyana o*—are quite popular. The popularity of the expression of *sebakanyana se* depicts the obvious: namely, a context where we have become intensely aware of our passing. In the HIV and AIDS context, there are no long-guaranteed futures; nonetheless, these very short moments of our lives can still be celebrated with gratefulness. And so we say, *Modimo o re file sebakanyana se le motsutsunyana o.* That is, "God has given us this little time and this very short moment of our existence, of which we are very grateful."

Accompanying this intense awareness of our brief existence, there is, however, a language of hope; a hope for a healed time. This is best characterized by another new popular expression, *Go tla siama. O tla fola.* The expression means, "It will be fine. You will be healed." In the past five years, this expression has become quite popular and part of the lexicon of speaking to one another in Botswana. Whenever one is talking to people or sharing, perhaps about ill-health, some disappointment, failure or some misfortune, one will constantly hear people assuring the other, saying, *Go tla siama. O tla fola.* It is an expression that resists hopelessness, by calling one to look beyond the current situation to another realm of being; to a healed time, a healed future, a good time. It is notable that such expressions rose within a context of dire hopelessness and lack of healing. Be that as it may, I must underline that such expressions do not indicate that we have figured out the art of finding healing where there is no healing. At best, the expressions are indicators of an *a luta continua* search for health and healing.

It is in this very context that I wish to discuss doing biblical studies in the HIV and AIDS era. Some of the questions I seek to explore are: What are the biblical interpretations that have emerged in relation to the search for health and healing in the HIV and AIDS context? How and why do we read the Bible in the HIV and AIDS context? To discuss these questions, I will first describe some aspects of the HIV and AIDS context and the various frameworks it has assumed. Second, I will give a rough sketch of some emerging biblical interpretations in the African context. In

---

4. Ibid., 124.
5. Ibid., 122–24.

conclusion, I will highlight some of the methodological frameworks of reading the Bible in the HIV and AIDS era.

THE HIV AND AIDS CON(TEXTS), RELIGION, HEALTH, AND HEALING

In the three decade history of HIV and AIDS, the epidemic has proven its complexity by affecting all the disciplines and departments of life and impacting on several social frameworks of understanding.[6] The various frameworks that I discuss here are the medical, moral-religious, human rights, psychological and social justice perspectives.[7] These frameworks of understanding HIV and AIDS are intertwined on various levels and they inform the kind of response different individuals and institutions assume. In this paper some of them will be discussed more extensively than others.

The earliest HIV and AIDS framework was, of course, medical. HIV was medically discovered and named in 1981. Its mode of spread was recognized as through exchange of infected body fluids. Its long-term impact was medically named as AIDS—a condition whereby the HIV virus has depleted the body of its immune system, leaving it open to endless opportunistic infections, which finally lead to death. Consequently, HIV and AIDS had been medically named as incurable, infectious and deadly. Accordingly this stage was characterized by scientifically, recommended methods of prevention, such as screening blood products for infection, using disposable needles and adopting safer sexual practices. An information and education campaign was launched. For some, the HIV and AIDS epidemic has remained locked within this paradigm, namely, as a medical issue that calls for purely medical solutions.

Although the history of HIV and AIDS emerged from the medical frame-work, closely tied to this origin was the rise of a moral-religious perspective.[8] The latter perspective gave its explanation of the origin and purpose of the disease, holding that HIV and AIDS is God's punishment and judgment on immoral persons or sin-

---

6. See Barbara Schmid, "AIDS Discourse in the Church: What We Say and What We Do?" *JTSA* 125 (2006): 103, for the development of legal, ethical, and activist discourses of AIDS.

7. One framework that is hinted in this essay, but not discussed, is the conspiracy framework. The perspective holds that HIV was deliberately invented and injected among people of color and homosexuals by racists. Kihumbu Thairu, *The African and the AIDS Holocaust: A Historical and Medical Perspective* (Nairobi: Phoenix Books, 2003), subscribes to a certain angle of this perspective, although covertly. He critiques the strategy of confidentiality as a strategy that served to allow HIV to entrench itself by disabling the powers of doctors from previous practice of addressing STIs, or sexual transmitted infections, by treating people with their partners. He also suspiciously analyses the patterns of the types of HIV and AIDS as inconsistent with a natural spread of disease.

8. See Schmid, "AIDS Discourse in the Church," 96–97.

ners.[9] The perspective was partially fueled by the concentration of HIV and AIDS cases among gay communities in the earliest history of the epidemic. It was further maintained by the association of HIV and AIDS with drug addicts and sex-workers. It was also, ironically, fueled by the popularized ABC HIV prevention campaign strategy. The latter held that HIV prevention was as easy as "abstaining, being faithful to one's partner/ spouse or condomizing." Implied in this message was a hierarchy of sexual morality and the implication was that those who are infected suffer from sexual laxity, for they have failed to abstain; or they have failed to be faithful to their partners and they have somehow failed to "condomise."[10] Similarly, the strategy of confidentiality of one's status, especially in cultures where health was always a shared experience in the family and community,[11] did not only breed unspoken fear and suspicion, it also seemed to suggest that the infected should hold themselves responsible for sexual-moral failure and thereby hide themselves in shame. This religious morality framework marked the earliest interpretation of biblical texts in the light of HIV and AIDS. Unfortunately, it was a reading that was heavily dependent on the theory of retribution. Many texts from the Hebrew Bible supported these perspectives, especially from the Deutronomistic historical tradition.[12] Under this reading, HIV and AIDS would be seen "as punishment from God," for sexual immorality.

The religious moral framework with its politics of sexuality had thus gained prominence from an unfavorable/unhelpful standpoint. Believing that sexual immorality is the key problem, many faith-based organizations would then throw their weight behind the promotion of abstinence from premarital sex and faithfulness in marriage or co-habiting partners.

This interpretation of HIV and AIDS as a consequence of sexual immorality con-

---

9. Ibid. See also L. Togarasei, "Teaching Old Testament Studies in Zimbabwe's Theological Institutions in the HIV/AIDS Era," *HRRC* 14, no. 3 (2002): 254–71; J. Stiebert, "Women's Sexuality and Stigma in Genesis and the Prophets," in *Grant Me Justice! HIV/AIDS and Gender Readings of the Bible*, ed. M. W. Dube and M. R. Kanyoro (Maryknoll, NY: Orbis, 2004), 80–96, and S. Nadar, *Module 4: Reading the Hebrew Bible in the HIV and AIDS Context* (Geneva: WCC, 2007).

10. This is a specific term adopted by the author from the literature pertaining to HIV and AIDS.

11. M. W. Dube, "On Becoming Healer-Teachers of African Indigenous Religion in HIV and AIDS Prevention," *JCT* 10, no. 2 (2004): 131–57.

12. Togarasei, "Teaching Old Testament Studies," 264. See also Anderson, "Lessons of Healing," 28, 32. See also P. Mageto, "Beyond 'Victim Theology': Reconstructing Theological Education in an Era of HIV/AIDS in Africa," in *Theological Education in Contemporary Africa*, ed. G. LeMarquand and J. D. Galgalo (Eldoret, Kenya: Zapf Chancery, 2004), 147–66; P. Djomhoue, "Gender and Ethics in the Fight against HIV/AIDS: A Case Study of Mark 5: 25–34 in an African Context," in *Into the Sunshine: Integrating HIV/AIDS into Ethics Curriculum*, ed. Charles Klagba and C. B. Peter (Eldoret, Kenya: Zapf Chancery, 2005), 131–43.

tributed to the unfortunate rise and intensification of a bigger problem; namely, HIV and AIDS stigma and discrimination. With the addition of the latter, HIV and AIDS was not only an incurable, infectious, deadly disease, it was also a stigmatized condition. HIV and AIDS stigma and discrimination immediately highlighted HIV and AIDS as a human rights issue that raised deep theological questions: Does one cease to be human once infected by HIV? Does God care and love people living with HIV and AIDS (henceforth PLWHA)? How do we become loving and healing families, communities and world in the HIV and AIDS era?[13] HIV and AIDS hermeneutics of healing seek to address individual and community rights and to promote social justice (confronting all inequalities—gender, class/poverty, race, age and sexuality). A crucial part of HIV and AIDS hermeneutics thus involves the quest of building human dignity affirming communities. The latter, focuses on expounding frameworks that encourage the building compassionate communities. As Cheryl Anderson aptly asserts, "The HIV/AIDS pandemic means that we need to read the Bible in new ways as we begin to think ourselves as a community in new ways."[14]

The incurability of AIDS, stigmatization, the mode of controlling the disease and massive amounts of deaths, ushered in the psychological side of the epidemic. The latter became evident in the violent masculinities that erupted. Rape and femicide-suicide[15] sky-rocketed,[16] directly contradicting the educational and information campaign that encouraged high sexual morality. Incest became common and mothers no longer felt safe to leave children in the care of their fathers.[17] These are indicators of how HIV and AIDS became a psycho-logical issue as well. While individuals, families and communities were traumatized, the male-psyche took the worst blow, as indicated by the aforementioned crimes. What happened? The incurability bred helplessness and hopelessness, which is the perceived opposite of patriarchal masculinities that construct men as those in control.

In the HIV and AIDS context men were out of control and the identity of manhood was seriously challenged. The methods of prevention (abstinence, faith-

---

13. Mageto, "Beyond 'Victim Theology,'" 163. See also Musa Dube, "*Talitha Cum!* A Postcolonial Feminist and HIV/AIDS Reading of Mark 5:21–43," in Dube and Kanyoro, *Grant Me Justice!* 140–56.

14. See also Anderson, "Lessons of Healing," 239.

15. In Botswana in the past five years we have experienced another epidemic of violence in what became known as "passion killings," which involves boys in their early twenties killing their girlfriends brutally, and then killing themselves. According to the 2009 Botswana Police report, between 2003 and 2008, 7,577 cases have occurred which claimed women's lives. Even as I was writing this paper one such case occurred in the University of Botswana in the week of 23–29 March 2008, involving first-year students.

16. Botswana Government Statistics (1999), i–viii.

17. P. Lenkabula, "From the Womb into a Hostile World: Christian Ethics and Sexual Abuse against Children in South Africa," *JTSA* 114 (2002): 55–68. See also T. Maluleke and S. Nadar, "Breaking the Covenant of Violence against Women," *JTSA* 114 (2002): 5–18.

fulness and condomising) largely debunked patriarchal rights of manhood over women's bodies, by insisting that they have to stick to one partner and they have to condomise—that is, they have no right to deposit their semen into women's bodies. Resistance took a form of rape, which was a way of insisting on owning women's bodies. Incest served the same purpose. It allowed men to feel in control over a situation in which they were largely out of control. Finally, confidentiality and stigmatization led people to isolation, anger, desperation, silent fear of sharing or exposing their status, and the unspoken fear of impending inevitable exposure and suffering with the arrival of AIDS.

Confidentiality arrested the traditional nature of community by denying its rights to be communitarian through sharing in the health of its members and stigmatization. This itself became indicative of the failure of community to be community.[18] In comparative terms, femininity allows women to express fears and admit weakness, hence they have more avenues of sharing difficult issues within their circles of social support, but male construction does not encourage sharing, especially relating to fear. As they say: *monna o swa senku*, a man must not cry.

By the mid-1990s HIV and AIDS had quickly spilled over the medical and moral-religious frameworks to assume a social-justice perspective. At this stage HIV and AIDS had quickly shifted to the Two-Thirds World populations: infecting more women, more young people, more poor people, displaced persons, immigrants, children and those who live in violent zones. It had shifted from its early history and was now infecting more heterosexual people than gay communities; more Black people than White people.

It was now increasingly located in Two-Thirds World continents and populations. With this larger worldwide picture of the infection, its patterns were much more evident than in the early years. It was becoming evident that HIV and AIDS is an epidemic within other social epidemics; namely, that it attacks the most vulnerable members of our world. It attacked those who are already dwelling in the margins of society, who were either oppressed due to class, age, race, gender, sexual identity, national corruption and international economic injustice. The virus found its fertile soil in social injustice.

The earliest response to HIV and AIDS had embarked on massive information and educational campaigns, believing that knowledge is power. However, monitoring and evaluation indicated that knowledge does not always get translated into practice or behavioral change, given the prevailing social inequalities. New infec-

---

18. This is a much more complex issue than I can address here, but which I have addressed in my article "Adinkra! Four Hearts Joined Together," in *African Women, Religion, and Health: Essays in Honor of Mercy Amba Ewudziwa Oduyoye*, ed. I. Phiri and S. Nadar (Maryknoll, NY: Orbis, 2006), 131–56. Basically, the strategy of confidentiality came as a Western package of controlling HIV and AIDS, but it clashed with the indigenous way of understanding the individual's health as shared within family and community.

tions continued to rise even in places where there was a 90 per cent rate for the most informed education on the facts pertaining to HIV and AIDS.

Worldwide HIV and AIDS research and documentation were increasingly indicating that abstinence from premarital sex among young girls and women is defeated by poverty and gender-based violence. Faithfulness among married couples did not protect women, especially those in patriarchal cultures that often tolerated unfaithfulness from the male spouses, but denied women from having power over their bodies. Faithfulness and good family values were defeated by political upheavals and economic structures that perpetuate poverty and force the scattering and separation of families in search for survival across various borders. Similarly, the correct and consistent use of condoms was hindered by poverty, illiteracy and gender constructions that denied women control over their bodies and constructed boys and men as fearless risk takers. Children were born with HIV, married women were getting infected, and abstaining girls were not immune. Boys and men were not immune despite the massive information and educational campaign. The list goes on. *The story of HIV and AIDS was thus increasingly emerging as a social injustice story.* The moral-religious perspective could not hold ground in the light of these findings. But this does not mean that the moral-religious perspective ceased to proclaim itself both covertly and overtly. In short, HIV and AIDS was a growing discourse that was being interpreted within various competing frameworks, that continued to co-exist, often complementing, contradicting and frustrating each other.

The social justice framework was a critical moment in the history of HIV and AIDS and a crucial lesson for us all in the understanding of health and healing and the role of religion in this context. The framework highlights that health and healing lodges and operates within power relations. It had been shown that healing is as physical as it is spiritual, social, psychological, structural and historical. One big irony in HIV and AIDS tendency to attack Two-Thirds World populations is that it has re-inscribed the colonial and patriarchal sexual stereotypes about the colonized,[19] hence making it a postcolonial issue as well. This epidemiological map seemed to confirm colonial stereotypes about the colonized,[20] thus resulting in much suspicions and silence among the infected and affected communities. In my view, HIV and AIDS have shown us that sexual morality or purity is in fact a discourse of those in power that largely gets sustained through occupying a certain class, race, gender, sexual identity and a particular world class.

Generally the three decades of HIV and AIDS history has highlighted that our health is interconnected; it is related with how we relate with one another and the institutions that we create and inhabit at all levels of our lives; and through various

---

19. See Anthony Balcomb, "Sex, Sorcery, and Stigma—Probing Some No-Go Areas of the Denial Syndrome in the AIDS Debate," *JTSA* 125, no. 1 (2006): 104–15, for an elaboration of this point. See also Mageto, "Beyond 'Victim Theology,'" 156.

20. See Thairu, *African Holocaust*, which maps the link between disease and colonialism.

histories. Consequently in the 1990s it had become undeniable that HIV and AIDS was a medical issue as it was a social justice issue. It became evident that it is about individual morality as it is about the structural morality of our institutions, our relationships, our histories; indeed our whole world. It was as physical as it was psychological. The 1990s context of HIV and AIDS had shown that the search for healing is about the healing of our physical bodies as it is the healing of our social bodies, our histories and our international economic structures. This all-embracing impact of HIV and AIDS highlighted that the search for health and healing should involve all social institutions and disciplines. Biblical studies, like all other disciplines, is not exempt from the search for healing.

O TLA FOLA: TOWARDS A BIBLICAL HERMENEUTICS OF HEALING IN THE HIV AND AIDS CONTEXT

The above contextual description highlights two issues: First, the HIV and AIDS story is a complex social text in itself that needs serious exegesis. Indeed I have to admit that the above description is an inadequate description of a complex issue. Second, that it is a story that raises questions for everyone, including biblical scholars. Perhaps HIV and AIDS hermeneutics can be summarized as relating to a world that is infected and affected by an infectious, incurable, deadly and stigmatized disease that functions through social injustice. The search for healing—the healing of our bodies and social relations—is the key to such a context. Healing, here, should be understood in the wider perspective as described above. The question in such a context for biblical scholars is: Does the Bible say anything about infectious, incurable and deadly diseases that are sustained by social injustice and which evoke stigma and discrimination from the wider public? How do we build healing communities and relationships? As used here, social injustice refers to a whole range of structural oppressions (e.g. poverty, gender oppression, homophobia, racism, age-based discrimination, exploitative capitalist neo-liberal economic structures, etc.) covering various marginalized groups such PLWHA, Blacks, women, widows, children, gay people, sex workers and drug addicts.

As the above discussion indicates, the question of reading the Bible in the HIV and AIDS context was asked early in the history of HIV and AIDS and was answered within an unconstructive moral-religious framework. Basically the question was answered affirmatively by referring to biblical texts that explicitly associate ill-health with sin and punishment (Gen 30; Exod 1–12; Lev 13–15; Num 12, 14; 21:4-9. Texts that explicitly associated obedience with blessings and disobedience with disaster (Deut 7:12-16, 28) were used. This early biblical reading, of course, became part of a larger context of HIV and AIDS, by raising further questions such as: Are there other perspectives in the biblical literature on infectious, incurable and deadly diseases that are propelled by social injustice and accompanied by stigma and discrimination? Do biblical texts provide models for compassionate and supportive communities instead of stigmatizing and discriminating perspectives towards the infected and affected? How can biblical texts be read to promote social justice to all as the promotion of health to all the members of the earth's community? New readings of the Bible were needed to address the complex challenges of HIV and AIDS.

Evidently, academic biblical scholars' reading of the Bible in the light of HIV and AIDS came much later, trailing behind the popular interpretations of communities of faith, which themselves were the result of explicit governmental encouragement.[21] Governments and development agencies underlined that HIV and AIDS is no longer just a health issue; rather, that each and every sector, department and discipline should use their particular social space of existence and influence to interrogate how they are part of the problem. Namely, how might they be aiding the spread of the virus; being complicit in the lack of quality care and how they may be promoting stigma, discrimination and social inequalities? Such a self-situated analysis was a condition for exploring possible ways for being part of the solution in the struggle against HIV and AIDS. The latter was a call to investigate and find innovative ways of being part of promoting effective prevention, quality care, mitigating impact, and promoting social justice to all. In short, just as HIV and AIDS had challenged the medical guild to undertake a great deal of researching and rethinking of their medical practice, products and services, this was applicable to a great number of other disciplines as well.

For biblical studies (and religious studies as a whole) in the African context, the response at this stage can be grouped under three forums: The World Council of Churches' Health and Healing initiative; the Circle of Concerned African Women Theologians' research agenda; and individual scholarly efforts within their particular academic departments. The Health and Healing Department of the World Council of Churches had made an early response to HIV and AIDS by enacting a global commission into the epidemic. They produced one of the earlier texts: *Facing AIDS: The Challenge, the Churches and the Response* in 1997. Towards the end of the 1990s when the HIV and AIDS epidemic was becoming even more critical, the Health and Healing Department conducted a series of continental situation and needs analyses on the response of the church. The process culminated in the production of the Plan of Action, which listed 13 key issues.[22] Theology and ethics were at the top, since it was established that without a constructive framework of thinking, effective and useful practical response could not be expected from faith perspectives.[23]

Part of the agenda included challenging and training academic institutions of

21. *MTP II 1997–2002: Botswana HIV and AIDS Second Medium Term Plan* (Gaborone: Ministry of Health, 1997).

22. World Council of Churches, *Plan of Action: The Ecumenical Response to HIV/AIDS in Africa* (Geneva: WCC, 2001), 7–12.

23. Ibid., 7.

religion to journey with the communities, through curriculum transformation.[24] It was held that faith-based academic training institutions and departments, be they located in University departments, seminaries, Bible colleges and schools, were responsible for training faith leaders. In this context, it was important that faith-based academic institutions should equip communities of faith to be effective in their response to HIV and AIDS through curriculum transformation. The aim was to ensure that all learners would graduate equipped to serve in the HIV and AIDS context and to retrain faith leaders who were already in the field, through work-shops and other informal learning frameworks. I was asked to facilitate this process continent-wide through training of trainer workshops that targeted academic lecturers on the issue of curriculum transformation in the light of HIV and AIDS.[25] The second aim was curriculum transformation in the worship space through the constructive and mainstreaming of HIV and AIDS in liturgy and sermons.[26] Faith leaders were the target of this second type of work-shop. For this task I had to leave my job with the University of Botswana for approximately two years in order to facilitate training and discussions about being effective scholars of religion and faith leaders in the HIV and AIDS context.

This training also entailed production of relevant materials for and with scholars as well as religious leaders. A number of books, articles, and educational materials were produced under this program, some of which focused on reading the Bible in the HIV and AIDS context. Notable edited books and modules here include: *HIV/AIDS and the Curriculum: Methods of Integrating HIV/AIDS in Theological Programmes*; *Africa Praying: A Handbook on HIV and AIDS Sermon Guidelines and Liturgy*; *Studying the Hebrew Bible in the HIV and AIDS Context* and *Reading the New Testament in the HIV and AIDS Contexts*.[27] All these resources are available from the World Council of Churches' publishers and website.

The Circle of Concerned African Women Theologians was the second forum where African scholars grappled with reading the Bible in the HIV and AIDS context. The Circle is a continent-wide academic association that promotes research, writing and publishing on religion, culture and gender. Given that worldwide HIV and AIDS research and documentation was indicating that women are at the centre of the HIV and AIDS storm, at its 2002 Pan-African meeting, held in Addis Abba, the Circle decided to adopt HIV and AIDS as its research focus area for five years. Seven edited books have been produced since that time.[28] The collection includes several articles on reading the Bible in the HIV and AIDS context. *Grant Me Justice:*

---

24. See also Musa Dube, ed., *HIV/AIDS and the Curriculum: Methods of Integrating HIV/ AIDS in Theological Programmes* (Geneva: WCC, 2003), vi–xiii.

25. Ibid.

26. Musa Dube, ed., *Africa Praying: A Handbook of HIV/AIDS Sensitive Sermon Guidelines and Liturgy* (Geneva: WCC, 2003), v–x.

27. See bibliography for full publishing details of these texts.

28. Some of these include Isapel Phiri et al., *African Women, HIV/AIDS, and Faith Communities* (Pietermaritzburg: Cluster, 2003), and Isapel Phiri and Sarojini Nadar, eds, *African*

HIV and AIDS and Gender Readings of the Bible is one of the seven books, which focuses on reading the Bible in the HIV and AIDS context.

The third forum for reading the Bible in the HIV and AIDS context occurred as independent initiatives of individuals or academic departments within their own workplace. Thus book chapters, journal articles, journal volumes,[29] conferences, and research programs have also been run by independent scholars in their various academic settings. A bibliographic publication is needed here to highlight what has been produced so far. Fortunately, CHART (Centre for HIV and AIDS, Religion and Theology) in the University of Kwazulu-Natal has began the process compiling an annotated bibliography. In addition, one notable research program on religion and HIV and AIDS is the African Religious Health Asserts Programme (ARHAP), headed by James Cochrane. The research program is sponsored by the World Health Organization and it covers a number of countries in Southern Africa. Its question is: "what is the contribution of religion and religious entities to the struggle for health and well being in Southern Africa in a time of HIV and AIDS?"[30]

Similarly, the Department of Theology and Religious Studies in the University of Botswana carried out a national study entitled *An Assessment of the Faith-Based Organizations for HIV Prevention in Botswana*, and embarked on Church and HIV and AIDS Prevention among Adolescents. This study will run for the next five years, under the sponsorship of NIH (the National Institutes of Health in the United States) and in collaboration with the scholars from University of Pennsylvania.

Independent academic initiatives have also been characterized by the organization of conferences[31] or establishing interdisciplinary HIV and AIDS centres of research and other related events. For example, upon my return to the University of Botswana in 2005, I headed a team of four, whose mission was to establish an HIV and AIDS Research Centre in the University of Botswana. The Centre was established in 2006. It seeks to facilitate and highlight various HIV and AIDS-related research and pedagogical projects across the academic disciplines. Similarly, the Department of Religion in the University of Kwazulu-Natal has established an HIV and AIDS research and study centre in October 2008.

This is the wider academic setting upon which reading the Bible in the context

---

Women, Religion, and Health: Essays in Honor of Mercy Amba Ewudziwa Oduyoye (Maryknoll, NY: Orbis, 2006).

29. A number of special issues focusing on HIV and AIDS, such as *Missionalia* 29 (2002); *JTSA* 125 (2006); and *JTSA* 126 (2006), have been produced. The articles are written from various disciplines of theology and religious studies, including biblical studies.

30. Steve de Gruchy, ed., "Editorial: Doing Theology in a Time of AIDS," *JTSA* 125, no. 1 (2006): 3.

31. From 3–12 July 2006, the University of Botswana hosted an AASR (African Association of the Study of Religion) on the theme of religion, health, and healing. There were fifty-seven papers presented, and two-thirds of those were on HIV and AIDS. Two sessions on Bible, HIV and AIDS, and pedagogy were held.

of HIV and AIDS occurs among African scholars. This context insists on a form of engaged scholarship that is answerable to the most burning issues of the community. In such a context, the scholarship is challenged to locate itself within the HIV and AIDS infected and affected world and people and to make an option for PLWHA,[32] by fighting stigma and discrimination and being actively involved in reading for hope, compassion and healing. Finally, given HIV and AIDS' tendency to function through various forms of social injustice, means that it attaches itself to most, if not all, disciplines and departments; this, therefore, calls for an interconnection and interdisciplinary approach. This HIV and AIDS context calls for scholars to engage in a form of scholarship that informs and enhances the capacity of communities and their institutions in their social-justice service delivery. Further, an interdisciplinary approach became crucial and social-science methods of research became quite critical, as attested to by some of the aforementioned research programs. It also challenges us to network and collaborate at local and international levels, for solidarity is central to transformation.

READING FOR HEALING:
BIBLICAL HERMENEUTICS IN THE HIV AND AIDS CONTEXT

What then are some of the strategies adopted by biblical scholars? What interpretations are being advanced to deal with the HIV and AIDS context? What are the methods used? I will not attempt to give an exhaustive analysis here, but rather, I intend to give some broad strokes of the emerging colors of biblical interpretations in the HIV and AIDS context. I will highlight the emerging HIV and AIDS biblical hermeneutics under the following categories: Liberative and combative biblical hermeneutics; Biblical texts as constructive theoretical frameworks; Conclusion: Issues of methods in the reading of the Bible in the HIV and AIDS context.

Liberative and Combative Biblical Hermeneutics: Justice-Seeking Biblical Readings

It is evident that the major complications of HIV/AIDS are its incurability, massive death rates, linked with social injustice, plus its generation of stigma and discrimination, hopelessness and helplessness. Liberative HIV and AIDS hermeneutics of the Bible seek to combat the oppressive conditions, structures and perspectives that aid the spread of HIV and AIDS and deny quality care to PLWHA. They are war instruments for the establishment and search for justice to and for all.[33] The initial stigmatizing biblical interpretations capitalized on biblical texts that tend to

---

32. J. Cochrane, "Of Bodies, Barriers, Boundaries, and Bridges: Ecclesial Practice in the Face of HIV and AIDS," *JTSA* 126, no. 2 (2006): 1. See also Gerald O. West and B. Zengele, "The Medicine of God's Word," *JTSA* 125 (2006): 51–63.

33. Dube, "*Talitha Cum!*" 115–40. See also Gerald O. West, "Liberation Hermeneutics after Liberation in South Africa," in *The Bible and the Hermeneutics of Liberation*, ed. A. F. Botha and P. R. Andinarch (Atlanta: SBL, 2009), 36–37.

equate illness with disobedience, impurity and God's punishment. Consequently, interpretations that assist us to understand the historical meaning and context of these biblical texts, and those that explore other constructive perspectives, became central to the HIV and AIDS hermeneutics of healing. Some examples that have taken this path include chapters by Johanna Stiebert, Sarojini Nadar, Cheryl Anderson and Malebogo Kgalemang. They sought to address issues pertaining to stigma. In her article "Does the Hebrew Bible Have Anything to Tell Us about HIV/AIDS?" Stiebert investigates "how disease and illness are depicted in the Hebrew Bible."[34] She explores the various passages relating to illness, diseases, plagues and purity and concludes that in the Hebrew Bible diseases and illness are not invariably a matter of simple causality: of constituting a punishment for disobedience or moral shortcoming. There is no logic or pattern to their distribution: The good are afflicted along with the wicked. Sometimes the reason is to make a theological point, sometimes there appears to be no discernible reason at all; consequently, it is not possible on the basis of the Hebrew Bible to regard illness such as HIV/AIDS as a divine punishment for wrongdoing. Instead it must be acknowledged that the situation is considerably more complex and perplexing. Casting aspersions about the moral character of any person infected with HIV/AIDS is therefore unjust and unfair.[35]

Given that HIV and AIDS stigma is related to the fact that its mode of infection is linked to sexuality, in her follow-up chapter, "Women's Sexuality and Stigma in Genesis and the Prophets," Stiebert explores the depiction of women's sexuality in the Hebrew Bible and its possible contribution to the stigmatization of HIV-positive women. Her exploration of Genesis concludes that the overall picture "is that female sexuality is not necessarily condemned and associated with stigma."[36] Stiebert's exploration of the prophetic literature, however, finds women's sexuality depicted negatively in a way that can sanction their stigmatization and discrimination in the HIV and AIDS context. Stiebert also problematizes the depiction of God in the prophetic literature, holding that "the abusive and distinctively masculine depiction of God alongside the image of the brutalized woman also holds another very dangerous implication in the HIV and AIDS era," given that "there is a documented correlation between male violence against women and women's vulnerability to HIV infection."[37]

The reading of the book of Job has been central to resisting HIV and AIDS related stigma and discrimination and seeking an alternative framework for understanding infectious and incurable diseases that involve social justice, stigmatiza-

34. J. Stiebert, "Does the Hebrew Bible Have Anything to Tell Us about HIV/AIDS?" in Dube, *HIV/AIDS and the Curriculum*, 24–34.

35. Ibid., 31.

36. Stiebert, "Women's Sexuality and Stigma," 85.

37. Ibid., 90.

tion and discrimination. A number of articles have been produced on Job,[38] since "the book most obviously questions the traditional tenets of the wisdom that good deeds are rewarded and evil deeds are punished."[39] In her article " 'Barak God and Die!' Women, HIV and AIDS and a Theology of Suffering," Nadar investigates if the book of Job can be read from the perspective of women and the poor and what it says concerning the link between illness and God's punishment.[40] Nadar argues that it is Job's wife who opens this debate, which occurs between Job and his friends. She further argues that Job who was once a rich patriarch can speak from the position of the poor since he had lost everything. Her conclusion is that the book of Job does not provide us with a conclusive answer (how can God be just when God allows poor people to suffer) but she says it does show us ways of "how not to talk about God!" That is, we should not think the sick have sinned and they are punished by God. Both the good and the bad suffer and we are yet to understand, or may be just a simple dilemma of our lives; namely, that God talks and comes to us in the storm!

In her article, "Lessons on Healing from Naaman (2 Kings 5:1–27): An African-American Perspective," Cheryl Anderson seeks to deconstruct historical stigmas both in the reading communities and in the biblical text. Anderson shows how the response of African-Americans to HIV and AIDS has been characterized by suspicions given such historical cases as the Tuskegee Syphilis Study. Consequently, she points out that, "in a 1990 New York Times survey. . . nearly one-third of black New Yorkers believed that it was true or might be true that the 'virus which causes AIDS was deliberately created in a laboratory in order to infect black people.'"[41] An important part of her reading is to problematize African-Americans' attitudes towards homosexuality and drug addicts and how it impacts their response to HIV and AIDS.[42]

Turning to the biblical passage, Anderson points out that the passage is "a classic Deuteronomistic blessings and curses formula" for "the contrast between Naaman and Gehazi indicates that there is a relationship between suffering and disobedience, a perspective that does not contribute constructively to the struggle for healing and wholeness."[43] Be that as it may, Anderson holds that the story "is countered in the books of Job and Ecclesiastes"[44] for:

---

38. Madipoane Masenya, "Between Unjust Suffering and the Silent God: Job and the HIV/AIDS Sufferers in South Africa," *Missionalia* 29, no. 2 (2001): 186–99. See also Togarasei, "Teaching Old Testament Studies," 265, and West and Zengele, "The Medicine of God's Word," 51–63.

39. Sarojini Nadar, " '*Barak* God and Die!' Women, HIV, and AIDS and a Theology of Suffering," in Dube and Kanyoro, *Grant Me Justice!* 64.

40. Ibid.

41. Anderson, "Lessons of Healing," 23–43.

42. Ibid., 28.

43. Ibid., 36–37.

44. Ibid., 36.

... in Job the concept that God rewards the faithful and punishes the unfaithful is challenged by God's anger at Job's friends who had offered that formula as the explanation for Job's suffering (Job 42:7-9). Similarly, in Ecclesiastes any simplistic notion of rewards and punishments is rejected because "all is vanity" (Ecclesiastes 1:2). Without a doubt the blessings and curses formula exists in the Biblical canon. That formula, however, is not the only human suffering the Bible offers. Any interpretation of a biblical passage, then, must not be considered in isolation but should be evaluated in the full canonical witness of the Old and New Testament.[45]

From the New Testament several texts have been handy. The whole healing ministry of Jesus and his general attitude toward the poor and despised groups (Matt. 9:10-13) is seen as a powerful statement against all forms of stigmatization, against any denial to the right to medicine and against all forms of social injustice.[46] For example, the interrogation of stigma and discrimination has been explored from the healing of people with leprosy (Mark 1:40-42)[47] and Jesus' attitudes towards other marginalized groups (Matt 25:31-46). A good example is Jesus' healing of the man with leprosy in Mark 1:40–42, where Jesus reached and touched the man.[48] This is often seen as a powerful model against stigma and discrimination. Jesus also sent him to the priests for official recognition, which underlines the role of institutions in de-stigmatizing the stigmatized.

The story of the bleeding woman (and the dying twelve-year-old daughter) has been popular in the HIV and AIDS context,[49] for she is seen as embodying both the incurable and an impoverishing, stigmatized illness.[50] She is also credited for her determined search for health and willingness to break the stigma.[51] Some interpretations of Mark 5:25-34 equate salvation with regaining health.[52] They argue that salvation is a relational process, as attested by the bleeding woman's newly established relationship with Jesus, which was established through her trust in him.[53]

---

45. Ibid., 36.

46. See E. Chitando, *Living with Hope: African Churches and HIV/AIDS 1* (Geneva: WCC Publications, 2007), 24.

47. See K. R. Overberg, S.J., "Jesus, the Leper, and HIV and AIDS," in *Vulnerability, Churches, and HIV,* ed. G. Gunner (Eugene, OR: Pickwick, 2009), 33–51.

48. See O. M. Kenia et al., "Embracing, Not Excluding, Mark 1:40–45," in *God Breaks the Silence: Preaching in the Time of AIDS,* ed. U. Hendrich et al. (Basel: United Evangelical Mission, 2005), 87–90. See also Musa Dube, *Module 7: A Theology of Compassion in the HIV and AIDS Context* (Geneva: WCC, 2007), 31–33.

49. Dube, *Africa Praying,* 151–57; Djomhoue, "Gender and Ethics," 132–37.

50. Dube, *HIV/AIDS and the Curriculum,* 83–89. See also West and Zengele, "The Medicine of God's Word," 59.

51. Dube, "On Becoming Healer-Teachers," 134–38.

52. P. Germond and S. Molapo, "In Search of Bophelo in Time of AIDS: Seeking a Coherence of Economies of Health and Economic of Salvation," *JTSA* 126, no. 2 (2006): 42–43.

53. Ibid., 44–45.

In the HIV and AIDS context, stigma and discrimination, incurability and massive death-rates breed intense silence,[54] such that part of carrying out a successful educational campaign and building compassionate communities includes breaking the silence. The bleeding woman is credited for breaking the silence against the imposed exclusion by making it a point to break the rules of impurity in order to attain her health by pushing through the crowds and touching Jesus and coming forward to talk to him.[55] Hendje Toya argues that

> Speaking is breaking the silence. Breaking the silence is not only an act in relation with one's external world or with one's addressee. Breaking the silence is first of all a matter of victory over oneself: By interacting with Jesus, that woman takes something from her intimate and private life (her blood) to expose it in the public place. She gives her own life to Christ. It is an unprecedented act of courage and determination to speak about one's intimate and sensitive life to another person, especially when this person is somebody one is meeting for the first time. . .she does it in a way that liberates her. She is the symbol of evangelical subversion, a subversion that is saving.[56]

Similarly, the story of John 8:1–11, featuring the accused adulterous woman, has been found instructive against tendencies of singling some people or groups of people as the sinful or the most sinful, hence deserving to die or to be infected by HIV and AIDS.[57] The story of John 8:1–11 cautions against "holier than thou" attitudes; as it highlights that sin is not only sexual, woman-centred or located with certain individuals, but we are all sinners, who should desist from judgmental attitudes.[58] As Chitando underlines, we need to assume a position that "refuses to throw stones."[59] Likewise, the reading of Matt 25:31–46 has provided one of the most instructive imperatives for compassionate communities that identify with the sick and marginalized instead of isolating and stigmatizing.[60]

In the HIV and AIDS context, John 9 is to the New Testament what Job is to the

---

54. T. S. M. Maluleke, "Towards an HIV/AIDS-Sensitive Curriculum," in Dube, *HIV/ AIDS and the Curriculum*, 65–66, says, "[T]o the extent that it [silence] is an admission of failure and a sign of a loss of words and plans . . . [t]he first step in the construction of AIDS might be a recognition and exploration of silence, not only in Africa but also in the whole world."

55. S. Hendje Toya, "Touching the Untouchable (Mark 5:25–34)," in Hendrich, *God Breaks the Silence*, 119–20.

56. Ibid., 119.

57. Dube, *Africa Praying*, 128–29. See also J. B. R. Gaie, "Ethics of Breaking the Stigma: African, Biblical, and Theological Perspectives," in Klagba and Peter, *Into the Sunshine*, 106–7. See also West and Zengele, "The Medicine of God's Word," 51–63; and Djomhoue, "Gender and Ethics," 131–43.

58. M. Kgalemang, "John 9: Deconstructing the HIV and AIDS Stigma," in Dube and Kanyoro, *Grant Me Justice!* 141–68, 165.

59. Chitando, *Living with Hope*, 3.

60. Dube, *Module 7*, 42–50.

Hebrew Bible, receiving much attention.[61] In John 9, we perceive that the tendency to associate ill-health and disability with sin persisted, but Jesus disputes this perspective. In her article "John 9: Deconstructing the HIV and AIDS Stigma," Malebogo Kgalemang invests much effort in interrogating stigma, its purposes and impact. She argues that stigma is a social creation of the dominant, and is meant to suppress, control and oppress some people or groups of people through devaluation of their humanity. Kgalemang, who holds that stigma "connotes a power relationship," insists that stigma is a "construction, a creation of society, a reflection of culture and not a property of individuals."[62]

Kgalemang thus argues that "the view that HIV/AIDS is a punishment from God is often done with judgments and preconceived ideas and such religious or moral beliefs lead some people to conclude that having HIV/AIDS is the result of a moral fault, such as promiscuous or deviant sex that deserves punishment."[63] With this understanding of stigma, Kgalemang concludes that "John 9 is a deconstructive text that directly asserts that there is no relationship between (individual) sin and suffering/disease."[64]

Listening to the biblical interpretations of the affected communities and PLWHA is an important part of breaking the stigma and discrimination and building compassionate communities. Thus my earliest quest for HIV and AIDS biblical hermeneutics, represented in the article "Healing Where There Is No Healing: Reading the Miracles of Healing in an HIV and AIDS Context," involved reading with non-academic readers. My aim was to measure the theologies that were arising from affected communities as well as to assess if stigmatizing biblical reading was still prevalent.[65] In his article "(Ac)Claiming the (Extra)Ordinary African Reader of the Bible," Gerald West has also sought for popular biblical interpretation in the light of HIV and AIDS by studying arts and crafts.[66] West gives a close interpretation of artist Trevor Makgoba's artwork, stating that "it [HIV and AIDS] gives sufficient time for repentance: God wants his people."[67] He finds that "like Job of the poetry Makhoba too struggles. . .with how to speak of God in the context of HIV/AIDS."[68] West concludes that Makhoba's piece

> . . . fits the prophetic pattern well. The horror of the punishment that awaits those who refuse God's call is vividly portrayed. But the prophet's voice/text is equally

61. See also Dube, *Africa Praying*, 128–30, and Hendrich, *God Breaks the Silence*, 128–34.

62. Kgalemang, "John 9," 4.

63. Ibid., 150.

64. Ibid., 163.

65. Dube, "Healing Where There Is No Healing, 121–33.

66. G. O. West, "(Ac)Claiming the (Extra)Ordinary African Reader of the Bible," in *Reading Other-Wise: Socially Engaged Biblical Scholars Reading with Their Local Communities*, ed. Gerald West (Atlanta: SBL, 2007), 29–47.

67. Ibid., 45.

68. Ibid.

clear: God wants his people, and there is sufficient time to repent. This work of Makhoba also fits the disciplinary parameters of the Deuterono-mistic theology of retribution. . .but when they cry out to God and/or the ancestors (as Makhoba's pictures do), God hears, raises up a prophet leader and restores the people.[69]

Gerald West and Bongi Zengele's article "The Medicine of God's Word: What People Living With HIV and AIDS Want (and Get) From the Bible" represents the determined effort to read with PLWHA.[70] Given that many communities of faith are still perceived as unsafe spaces, such a reading occurs in other spaces than the church space. Indeed great credit goes to African scholars for taking an option for PLWHA in their HIV and AIDS biblical hermeneutics, since the focus on breaking the stigma and discrimination and building compassionate communities is, ultimately, an option for PLWHA.

Given the epidemic's dependency on social injustice, biblical readings in the light of HIV and AIDS have also focused on prophetic literature. The volume, *HIV/AIDS and the Curriculum: Methods of Integrating HIV/AIDS in Theological Programmes*, carries two articles on prophets and HIV and AIDS by M. Masenya[71] and M. W. Dube.[72] These chapters sought to make a case for biblical readings and responses to HIV and AIDS that are critical to structural oppression. Indeed, one of the issues that became evident in the biblical readings of faith communities in their response to HIV and AIDS has been the failure to fully grasp the role of social injustice in the spread of HIV and AIDS. Consequently, faith leaders' approach to HIV and AIDS capitalized on individual morality such as practicing sexual abstinence and faithfulness to one's partner as the solution to HIV and AIDS prevention.

The structural sins of poverty, gender inequality, violence against women and international economic structures of injustices, which are central to the spread of HIV and AIDS, remained invisible to (or hardly addressed by) most faith leaders. Worse still, focus on individual morality always carries a potential for stigmatization, since the infected can then be seen as people whose sexually standards are questionable. Other readings of prophetic literature in the light of HIV and AIDS include the chapter by Dorothy Akoto,[73] who focuses on Ezek 37:1–12, and Sarojini Nadar's chapters on Hosea and Ezekiel.[74] A volume dedicated to readings from

---

69. Ibid., 44.

70. West and Zengele, "The Medicine of God's Word," 51–63.

71. M. Masenya, "Prophecy as a Method of Speaking about the HIV/AIDS Epidemic in Southern Africa," in Dube, *HIV/AIDS and the Curriculum*, 35–42.

72. M. W. Dube, "The Prophetic Method in the New Testament," in *HIV/AIDS and the Curriculum*, 43–58.

73. Dorothy E. Akoto, "Can These Bones Live? Re-reading Ezekiel 37:1–14 in the HIV and AIDS Context," in Dube and Kanyoro, *Grant Me Justice!* 97–111.

74. Nadar, *Module 4*, 137–66.

HIV and AIDS perspectives and gender-justice also seeks to address issues of social justice.[75]

HIV and AIDS biblical hermeneutics of healing include focusing on masculinities. Given the psychological impact of HIV and AIDS and the crisis of manhood that it ushered in, studying masculinities[76] and investigating life-affirmation have become more central in recent times.[77] Two forums have undertaken this study: the University of Kwazulu-Natal Department of Religion has made it a central part of their study and dedicated a special issue on the *Journal of Constructive Theology* to this issue. Second, the Circle of Concerned African Women have decided to collaborate with African male theologians to interrogate African masculinities, HIV and AIDS and religion. The first such panel occurred in the Pan African Circle of Concerned African Women Theologians meeting held in Yaoundé, Cameroon, 1–6 September 2007. Collaborations along this theme are expected in the next five years of the Circle's focus on HIV and AIDS research.

A biblical reading focusing on HIV and AIDS and masculinities is reflected on in Tinyiko Maluleke's paper "Men, Religion and HIV-AIDS Africa: Complex and Paradoxical Relationship," which asserts that "in the age of HIV and AIDS, masculinity and manhood roles, tendencies and attitudes have become matters of life and death."[78] Maluleke interrogates various forms of masculinities, including his own. In search of life-affirming masculinities that assist us in the struggle against HIV and AIDS he investigates the model of Joseph, the father of Jesus, as one form of masculinity that chooses to protect a woman and a child, even if it means that Joseph was seemingly subjugated.

HIV and AIDS biblical hermeneutics of healing also seek to address the gap between knowledge and practice by embarking on liturgical hermeneutics. The latter refers to the fact that knowledge about HIV and AIDS prevention (condomising, being faithful and abstaining) does not necessarily get translated into practice, even by those who have the power to do so. Similarly, fear-based stigmatization and discrimination continues, even among those who have knowledge about how HIV is transmitted and how it cannot be transmitted. The HIV and AIDS information and education campaign had assumed that "knowledge is power," and that once people are informed on HIV and AIDS facts they would necessarily take pre-

---

75. M. W. Dube, "Twenty-two Years of Bleeding and Still the Princess Sings!" in Dube and Kanyoro, *Grant Me Justice!* 186–200.

76. See *JCT* 12, no. 1 (July 2006), which focuses on masculinities.

77. In his new book, *Acting in Hope: African Churches and HIV/AIDS 2* (Geneva: WCC, 2007), Ezra Chitando dedicated a whole chapter, "Nurturing Faithful Men" (40–54), to the issue, arguing that "the pulpit should also be appropriated in the struggle to transform masculinities. Sermons that challenge men to embrace gender justice must be preached with clarity and compassion" (47).

78. This unpublished paper was presented at the AASR (African Association for the Study of Religion) held at the University of Botswana, 3–12 July 2006.

caution to practice "safer sex," to desist from stigmatizing and to care for PLWHA, but it has proven to be much more complicated than this.

The contribution of biblical studies is not only to develop intellectual instruments on the struggles against HIV and AIDS, but also create resources that speak to the heart in the presence of the community and the Divine. This contribution is in the form of liturgy that is accompanied by HIV and AIDS sensitive biblical interpretation. This work is best represented by *Africa Praying: A Handbook of HIV and AIDS Sensitive Sermon Guidelines and Liturgy*.[79] The latter is a collection of about 80 sermon guidelines, with participatory prayers, songs, rituals and, in some cases, complete service orders for various church occasions, themes, groups and social issues. The method used is liberational in the sense that each sermon guideline begins by describing the context and a particular HIV and AIDS issue, then reading the text in the light of the described context. The exposition of the biblical text is followed by application on the congregation, the society at large and, finally, a call to action. In my view, what we have in *Africa Praying* comes closely to an HIV and AIDS Bible Commentary, but it seeks to speak to the head and the heart in the HIV and AIDS struggle.

The above reviewed chapters, articles, collections and special journal issues on HIV and AIDS biblical readings, scattered in various sources, have largely appeared within the current decade. The five largest and most consistent readings of the Bible in the light of HIV and AIDS include the volume described above, *Africa Praying*, and *Grant Me Justice!*[80] More recent resources include Sarojini Nadar's distance learning module on *Studying the Hebrew Bible in the HIV and AIDS Contexts*,[81] and Musa W. Dube's distance-learning module on *Reading the New Testament in the HIV and AIDS Contexts*,[82] plus my more recent volume *The HIV and AIDS Bible: Selected Essays*.[83] While the above evaluations of various works have largely focused on scholars' attempts to read for destigmatization, these five volumes make a wider attempt to deal with all the critical issues of HIV and AIDS, such as prevention, plus the impact, care, and social issues as they impact on PLWHA.

SEEKING CONSTRUCTIVE LANGUAGE
AND FRAMEWORKS FROM BIBLICAL CONCEPTS

One of the significant contributions of biblical literature and texts is in providing constructive frameworks of thinking and responding to HIV and AIDS. In this area

79. See also Paul L. Leshota and N. M. Hadebe, *Preaching and Liturgy in the HIV and AIDS Context* (Geneva: WCC, 2007).

80. See bibliography for full publishing details pertaining to these texts.

81. See Nadar, *Module 4*.

82. See M. W. Dube, *Module 5: Reading the New Testament in the HIV and AIDS Context* (Geneva: WCC, 2007).

83. M. W. Dube, *The HIV&AIDS Bible: Selected Essays* (Scranton, PA: University of Scranton Press, 2008).

the reading of biblical texts does not necessarily constitute close exegetical reading of books or particular passages. Rather, certain concepts in the biblical texts are used to propound constructive ways of thinking and responding to HIV and AIDS. As used here, constructive refers to ways of thinking that counteract the devastating impact of HIV and AIDS, by promoting healing, hope, valuing of life, compassion and justice. I want to highlight just three of these.

From the Hebrew Bible, the creation story of Gen 1 is quite central. First, it underlines the belief that all life was created by God, and was created good.[84] It also presents the concept of "being made in God's image."[85] The creation story thus offers a powerful framework of thinking and acting about HIV and AIDS that revalues all life and all people as sacred hence deserving of prevention and quality care.[86]

It also underlines that stigma and discrimination are unacceptable since the value of each person is inherently guaranteed by the creator, who bestowed God's own likeness upon all regardless of such person's health status and sexual identity. The creation story framework is also powerful in the sense that it promotes social justice for all, since both male and female were created in God's image, both were blessed and given access to the resources of the earth—a perspective that supports counteracting poverty and all forms of social discrimination and oppression. The creation story framework disavows social discrimination of all forms and disempowerment, especially poverty and gender-based discrimination that fuel the HIV and AIDS epidemic. The ministry of Jesus and his attitude towards the marginalized was also an important frame-work for HIV and AIDS response, by providing a liberation paradigm. This is particularly important because HIV and AIDS works through prevailing social injustice. Sometimes this framework is drawn from such passages as Matt. 25:31-46 but also from the general attestation of Jesus' attitudes towards the marginalized and oppressed.[87] As Ezra Chitando points out,

> Just as Jesus interacted with the marginalized groups of his day—women, children, lepers, tax collectors, sex workers, the Samaritans and other, so does the church of today need to engage in mission at the edges of society. The church in Africa needs to interact with men who have sex with men, sex workers, and other marginalized groups. It needs to increase levels of HIV and AIDS awareness among these groups, while demonstrating love and acceptance.[88]

Turning to the Christian Testament, one of the most powerful texts that pro-

---

84. Dube, *Africa Praying*, 84–91.

85. Mageto, "Beyond 'Victim Theology,'" 164. See also Elias K. Bongma, *Facing a Pandemic: The African Church and the Crisis of AIDS* (Waco, TX: Baylor University Press, 2007).

86. UNAIDS, "Outcome from the Workshop—HIV and AIDS Related Stigma: A Framework for Theological Reflection," in *A Report of a Theological Workshop Focusing on HIV-and AIDS-Related Stigma* (Geneva: UNAIDS, 2005), 11–18.

87. Dube, *HIV&AIDS Bible*, 123–70.

88. Chitando, *Living with Hope*, 24.

vides constructive frameworks for responding to HIV and AIDS is 1 Cor 12:26, which depicts the believers as the body of Christ that cannot separate itself from the joys and pains of all its members. This concept counteracts stigma and discrimination and provides a powerful motivation and metaphor for compassionate communities that identify with the infected and affected people as a whole.[89] This particular passage has served very well in challenging churches to accept its identity as an HIV and AIDS positive church—a church that identifies and supports PLWHA, rather than distancing itself.

Given the assault of HIV and AIDS on life—its massive killing of people in millions and the resultant hopelessness, the concept of resurrection has also been a central framework of thinking and acting about HIV and AIDS.[90] According to Daniel J. Louw, "resurrection implies a recreation of Creation. It reveals the transforming power of God as an expression of the faithfulness of God despite death and suffering."[91] Kenneth R. Overberg holds that "the emphasis on creation-for-incarnation in the resurrection, gives us great hope as we confront the overwhelming suffering of HIV and AIDS."[92] For Letty Russell we need to re-imagine resurrection in the HIV and AIDS context, so that "resurrection is not an escape, but rather God's 'No' to evil suffering and death."[93] In the HIV and AIDS context, Letty Russell insists that what "we find in these texts and in our own lives, is that resurrection is not only something that happens at death. *Resurrection is a daily matter*. It happens over and over in the midst of our struggles."[94]

CONCLUSION: METHODS AND CURRICULUM TRANSFORMATION IN THE HIV AND AIDS CONTEXT

In conclusion what are the methods of reading the Bible in the HIV and AIDS context? From the above descriptions it is obvious that methods of biblical reading are contextual, liberational and theological. HIV and AIDS hermeneutics is a liberational practice, since it is about the healing of people and com-munities by countering oppression and participation in the transformation of our relationships at all levels. Given the tendency of HIV and AIDS to attack the most vulnerable members of the society, HIV and AIDS hermeneutics of healing inevitably have to deal with all forms of inequalities along the lines of class/poverty, gender, race, age, health, disability and sexual orientation. But since HIV and AIDS strategy is both a

---

89. Dube, *Module 7*, 67–76.

90. L. Russell, "Re-imagining the Bible in a Pandemic of HIV & AIDS," in Dube and Kanyoro, *Grant Me Justice!* 205–9. See also D. Louw, "The HIV Pandemic from the Perspective of a Theologia Resurrectionis: Resurrection Hope as a Pastoral Critique on the Punishment and Stigma Paradigm," *JTSA* 126, no. 2 (2006): 100–15.

91. Louw, "The HIV Pandemic," 109.

92. Overberg, "Jesus, the Leper, and HIV and AIDS," 50.

93. Russell, "Re-imagining the Bible in a Pandemic of HIV & AIDS," 207.

94. Ibid., 208 (author's emphasis).

multi-sectoral and multi-dimensional activity, it involves using all available methods as well as inventing new ones. In my article "Methods of Integrating HIV/AIDS in Biblical Studies," I outline how prevailing methods of biblical studies can contribute towards reading the Bible in the HIV and AIDS context.[95] In addition, I suggest thematic and book-orientated approach methods that involve designing new courses along themes that have become critical in the HIV and AIDS context, such as life, compassion, hope and sexuality. Such themes could be studied across books, testaments, cultures and religions or by focusing on particular books.

Needless to say, HIV and AIDS biblical hermeneutics are still on a journey in search of health and healing. HIV and AIDS has only had three decades of history, although it has been a devastating one. Biblical interpretation occurred early, but academic biblical interpretations have largely occurred in the current decade (2001–2011). One of the things that has become glaringly obvious in this journey is the need for a curriculum transformation. Generally, academic biblical studies tends to be too much of a text-centred discipline, despite the fact that it is not only an ancient text, but a text that is read by millions of people everyday, around the world.

Undoubtedly, academic biblical readers are a comparable minority against the massed numbers of ordinary biblical readers and interpreters across the world. Ironically, academic biblical studies largely focuses on the text to the exclusion of studying the millions of its readers and their interpretations in the myriad communities of faith. Of course, readers and readings have been studied and theorized, but this largely involves theorizing textual and academic readers, such as the implied reader, the original reader, first-time reader, the real reader, the trained reader and flesh and blood reader.[96] With few exceptions,[97] the majority of flesh and blood readers and their interpretations in biblical studies have largely remained an unopened "Pandora's box" (to use Stephen Moore's metaphor).[98] Yet I suspect that there might be a class angle to this, for in the past decade, I have seen much excitement and interest in reading and studying the flesh and blood biblical

---

95. Dube, "Methods of Integrating HIV/AIDS in Biblical Studies," in *HIV/AIDS and the Curriculum*, 10–23.

96. See Stephen Moore's chapter, "Stories of Reading," in *The Literary Theoretical Criticism Challenge and the Gospels* (New Haven: Yale University Press, 1989), 71–107. Moore argues that "reader-response criticism of the Gospels, because it is an enterprise that tends to feel accountable to conventional scholarship, has worked with reader constructs that are sensitively attuned to what may pass as permissible critical reading" (107). This means that "the reader-oriented exegete is a *homo institutionis*, just as the more conventional exegete is" (106).

97. G. O. West and M. W. Dube, eds, *Reading with African Overtures* (Semeia 73; Atlanta: SBL, 1996). See also V. Wimbush, *African Americans and the Bible: Sacred Text and the Social Texture* (New York: Continuum, 2000).

98. Moore, *Theoretical Criticism*, 107.

interpretations of Hollywood movies than the willingness to study interpretations of biblical communities of faith.[99]

It seems to me that text-centred biblical studies constitute some form of nativity and purity seeking. Through the text-centred academic approach, academic biblical scholars hold conversations within and between themselves; a very small club indeed. We close off and play "a members only" card, which ignores the majority of biblical readings that occur outside the academic boundaries. Of course, what we do in the academic club of biblical scholars is extremely important and has made significant scientific contributions. However, it is not an exaggeration to say it represents a largely unopened Pandora's box, for, as Stephen Moore intimates, "opened more fully it might release some unsettling, but possibly timely, ways of re-conceiving biblical interpretation."[100]

In the HIV and AIDS context, where about sixty million members of the world have been infected, with a third of these dead and 15 million children orphaned, where the social justice and human rights link are so central, the classy, text-centred academic biblical approach is challenged to expand its boundaries. It becomes evident that it is an approach that is vulnerable to silence and indifference to the social concerns of its world and communities. It becomes evident that, many times, academic biblical studies largely become research for the sake of research, whose findings hardly ever seek to inform social practice and social transformation. They are largely what Gerald West has called "interesting, but not interested" scholars.[101]

With the HIV and AIDS era, however, it has become increasingly evident that biblical studies should also become a social science research that uses field-work-based methods to study contemporary biblical readers and interpretations outside the academic halls. For example, in the HIV and AIDS context one increasingly wished to have fieldwork-based research and documentation that analyse biblical interpretations in communities of faith, to measure, among other things, the stagnancy or transformation from stigmatizing biblical interpretations to the affirming, compassionate and accompanying interpretations of the Bible. Such knowledge calls for social-science fieldwork-based research methods, which are rarely used in text-centred academic biblical studies.

HIV and AIDS history, however, does seem to challenge the guild to break the mould of self-isolation and the exclusive text-centred approach to include the clumsy field of contemporary communities of faith readers of the Bible and their interpretations.[102] This involvement should be a significant contribution in the search for a healed and healing world. Such will be an academic guild that partici-

---

99. See Alice Bach, ed., *Biblical Glamour and Hollywood Glitz* (Semeia 74; Atlanta: Scholars, 1996).

100. Moore, *Theoretical Criticism*, 107.

101. Gerald O. West, *Biblical Hermeneutics of Liberation: Modes of Reading the Bible in South Africa* (Maryknoll, NY: Orbis Books, 1995).

102. Dube, "Rahab Is Hanging Out a Red Ribbon," 186–87.

pates in the pronouncement, *Go tla siama. O tla fola*, and actively seeks to groom and serve justice to all its earth members, for it is in such activities that we participate in healing.

WORKS CITED

Bach, Alice, ed. *Semeia* 74. Atlanta: Scholars, 1996. The theme of the issue is "Biblical Glamour and Hollywood Glitz."

Balcomb, A. "Sex, Sorcery, and Stigma: Probing Some No-Go Areas of the Denial Syndrome in the AIDS Debate." *JTSA* 125, no. 1 (2006): 104–15.

Bongma, Elias K. *Facing a Pandemic: The African Church and the Crisis of AIDS.* Waco, TX: Baylor University Press, 2007.

Botha, A. F., and P. R. Andinarch. *The Bible and the Hermeneutics of Liberation.* Atlanta: SBL, 2009.

Chitando, E. *Acting in Hope: African Churches and HIV/AIDS 2.* Geneva: WCC, 2007.

———. *Living with Hope: African Churches and HIV/AIDS 1.* Geneva: WCC, 2007.

Cochrane, J., "Of Bodies, Barriers, Boundaries, and Bridges: Ecclesial Practice in the Face of HIV and AIDS." *JTSA* 126, no. 2 (2006): 7–26.

De Gruchy, S. "Editorial: Doing Theology in a Time of AIDS." *JTSA* 125, no. 1 (2006): 2–6.

Dube, Musa W. *Africa Praying: A Handbook of HIV/AIDS Sensitive Sermon Guidelines and Liturgy.* Geneva: WCC, 2003.

———. *The HIV&AIDS Bible: Selected Essays.* Scranton, PA: University of Scranton, 2001.

———. *Module 5: Reading the New Testament in the HIV and AIDS Contexts.* Geneva: WCC, 2007.

———. *Module 7: A Theology of Compassion in the HIV and AIDS Context.* Geneva: WCC, 2007.

———. "On Becoming Healer-Teachers of African Indigenous Religion in HIV and AIDS Prevention." *JCT* 10, no. 2 (2004): 131–57.

———, ed. *HIV/AIDS and the Curriculum: Methods of Integrating HIV/AIDS in Theological Programmes.* Geneva: WCC, 2003.

Dube, Musa W., and M. R. Kanyoro, eds. *Grant Me Justice! HIV/AIDS and Gender Readings of the Bible.* Maryknoll, NY: Orbis Books, 2004.

Germond, P., and S. Molapo. "In Search of Bophelo in Time of AIDS: Seeking a Coherence of Economies of Health and Economic of Salvation." *JTSA* 126, no. 2 (2006): 27–48.

Hendrich, U., and Benedict Schubert. *God Breaks the Silence: Preaching in Times of AIDS.* Basel: United Evangelical Mission, 2005.

Klagba, C., and C. B. Peter, eds. *Into the Sunshine: Integrating HIV/AIDS into the Curriculum.* Eldoret, Kenya: Zapf Chancery, 2005.

Lenkabula, P. "From the Womb into a Hostile World: Christian Ethics and Sexual Abuse against Children in South Africa." *JTSA* 114 (2002): 55–68.

Leshota, P. L., and N. M. Hadebe. *Preaching and Liturgy in the HIV and AIDS Context.* Geneva: WCC, 2007.

Louw, D. "The HIV Pandemic from the Perspective of a Theologia Resurrectionis: Resurrection Hope as a Pastoral Critique on the Punishment and Stigma Paradigm." *JTSA* 126, no. 2 (2006): 100–115.

LeMarquand, G., and J. D. Galgalo. *Theological Education in Contemporary Africa.* Eldoret, Kenya: Zapf Chancery, 2004.

Maluleke, T., and S. Nadar. "Breaking the Covenant of Violence against Women." *JTSA* 114 (2002): 5–18.

Masenya, M. "Between Unjust Suffering and the Silent God: Job and the HIV/AIDS Sufferers in South Africa." *Missionalia* 29, no. 2 (2001): 186–99.

Moore, S. *The Literary Theoretical Criticism Challenge and the Gospels.* New Haven: Yale University Press, 1989.

MTP II 1997–2002: Botswana HIV and AIDS Second Medium Term Plan. Gaborone: Ministry of Health, 1997.

Nadar, Sarojini. *Module 4: Studying the Hebrew Bible in the HIV and AIDS Contexts.* Geneva: WCC, 2007.

Phillips, G. A., and N. Duran, eds. *Reading Communities Reading Scripture: Essays in Honor of Daniel Patte.* Harrisburg, PA: Trinity Press International, 2002.

Phiri, Isapel, B. Haddad, and M. Masenya, eds. *African Women, HIV/AIDS, and Faith Communities.* Pietermaritzburg: Cluster, 2003.

Phiri, Isabel, and S. Nadar, eds. *African Women, Religion, and Health: Essays in Honor of Mercy Amba Ewudziwa Oduyoye.* Maryknoll, NY: Orbis, 2006.

Schmid, B. "AIDS Discourse in the Church: What We Say and What We Do?" *JTSA* 125 (2006): 91–103.

Thairu, K. *The African and the AIDS Holocaust: A Historical and Medical Perspective.* Nairobi: Phoenix Books, 2003.

Togarasei, L. "Teaching Old Testament Studies in Zimbabwe's Theological Institutions in the HIV/AIDS Era." *HRRC* 14, no. 3 (2002): 254–71.

UNAIDS. *A Report of a Theological Workshop Focusing on HIV- and AIDS-Related Stigma.* Geneva: UNAIDS, 2005.

West, Gerald. *Biblical Hermeneutics of Liberation: Modes of Reading the Bible in South Africa.* Maryknoll, NY: Orbis, 1995.

———, ed. *Reading Other-Wise: Socially Engaged Biblical Scholars Reading with Their Local Communities.* Atlanta: SBL, 2007.

West, G. O., and M. W. Dube, eds. *Semeia* 73. Atlanta: SBL, 1996. The theme of the issue is "Reading with African Overtures."

West G. O., and B. Zengele, "The Medicine of God's Word." *JTSA* 125 (2006): 51–63.

Wicker, Kathleen O'Brien, Althea Spencer Miller, and Musa W. Dube. *Feminist New Testament Studies: Global and Future Perspectives.* New York: Palgrave, 2005.

Wimbush, V. *African Americans and the Bible: Sacred Text and the Social Texture.* New York: Continuum, 2000.

World Council of Churches. *HIV/AIDS Curriculum for Theological Institutions in Africa.* Geneva: WCC, 2001.

———. *Plan of Action: The Ecumenical Response to HIV/AIDS in Africa.* Geneva: WCC, 2001.

CONTRIBUTORS

David Tuesday Adamo (Ph.D.) is Professor of Biblical and Religious Studies, Department of Philosophy and Religious Studies, Kogi State University, Nigeria, and a Research Fellow in the Department of Old Testament and Ancient Near Eastern Studies, University of South Africa, and Department of Old Testament Studies, University of Pretoria, South Africa. His numerous publications include seminal biblical works entitled *Africa and Africans in the Old Testament* (ISP, 1998) and *Africa and Africans in the New Testament* (UPA, 2006).

Lynne S. Darden (Ph.D.), Adjunct Professor at Rutgers University, New Jersey. An African American biblical scholar interested in examining the New Testament and early Christian origins with an interdisciplinary approach, her research interests include investigating the role of scripture in the formation of identity, African American biblical hermeneutics, postcolonial biblical criticism, and collective cultural memory. Her dissertation analyzed the book of Revelation through an African American biblical interpretative lens supplemented by postcolonial theory.

H. J. M. (Hans) van Deventer (Th.D.), Professor, Biblical Studies at North-West University, Vaal Triangle Campus, South Africa. An ot scholar with a primary research interest in the book of Daniel on which he has published articles in academic journals and essays in collected works. Other research interests include paradigms in biblical studies, literary studies of the Hebrew Bible, feminist interpretation, and the interpretation of the Bible in African contexts.

Musa W. Dube (Ph.D.) is Professor of the New Testament in the University of Botswana. Her numerous publications include *Postcolonial Feminist Interpretation of the Bible* (2000) and *The HIV & AIDS Bible: Selected Essays* (2008).

John D. K. Ekem (Ph.D.), Academic Dean and Associate Professor of Mother-Tongue Biblical Hermeneutics and New Testament Studies at Trinity Theological Seminary, Legon, Accra, Ghana. A Ghanaian biblical scholar, he is a member of Studiorum Novi Testamenti Societas and a former translation consultant for The Bible Society of Ghana/United Bible Societies. With special research interest in mother-tongue biblical interpretation, New Testament, African life and thought, he has authored numerous volumes including most recently *Essentials of Biblical Greek Morphology—with an Introductory Syntax* (Accra: SonLife Press, 2010) and

509

Early Scriptures of the Gold Coast (Ghana): The Historical, Linguistic, and Theological Settings of the Gã, Twi, Mfantse, and Ewe Bibles (Rome: Edizioni di Storia e Letteratura; Manchester, England: St. Jerome, 2011). He is currently working on one major book project—*A Comprehensive Introduction to the New Testament: An African Perspective.*

Elelwani B. Farisani (Ph.D.), Associate Professor, Biblical Studies, Hermeneutics and Biblical Hebrew, University of South Africa. A South African biblical scholar, with a special focus on Old Testament, his other research interests are in biblical hermeneutics, use of African languages in teaching and learning of biblical Hebrew, identity notions in the Persian period, and Bible translation. He is currently working on a book project on Ezra-Nehemiah.

Sylvester Johnson (Ph.D.), Associate Professor of African American Studies and Religious Studies at Northwestern University. His *Myth of Ham in Nineteenth Century American Christianity: Race, Heathens, and the People of God* (Palgrave, 2004) won the American Academy of Religion's Best First Book Award. He teaches religion in the Americas, and his research examines African American religions, race and sexuality, and American empire. He is currently writing *African American Religions, 1500–2000: Colonialism, Democracy, and Freedom.*

Emmanuel Katongole (Ph.D.), Associate Professor, Theology and World Christianity at Duke University. The cofounder and Senior Strategist of the Center for Reconciliation at Duke Divinity School, Katongole's research interests cover a wide range of issues related to theology and violence, especially in Africa, the role of stories in the formation of political identity, dynamics of social memory, and nature and role of Christian imagination. Published works include *Beyond Universal Reason: The Relation between Religion and Ethics in the Work of Stanley Hauerwas* (UONDP, 2000), *A Future for Africa* (Scranton, 2005), and *The Sacrifice of Africa: A Political Theology for Africa* (Eerdmans, 2010).

Malebogo Kgalemang is a scholar of the New Testament in the Department of Theology and Religious Studies, University of Botswana. Her research and interest areas include the Gospels, hermeneutics, the Bible in literature, postcolonial, gender, and masculinity studies. Her published articles include "The Contest for Sacred Power between Kgama the Great and the London Missionary Society: Things Fall Apart, the Centre Cannot Hold," in *Aspects of the History of the Church in Botswana,* ed. F. Nkomazana and L. Lanner (2007), and "John 9: Deconstructing HIV/AIDS Stigma," in *Grant Me Justice: HIV/AIDS and Gender Readings of the Bible,* ed. M. W. Dube and M. Kanyoro (2004).

Temba L. J. Mafico (Ph.D.), Vice President for Academic Affairs/Provost and Professor of Hebrew Bible and Languages at Interdenominational Theological Center,

Atlanta. A Zimbabwean-born biblical scholar, Mafico has a special research interest in the Bible and its ancient Near Eastern setting and in comparison between the Hebrew Bible socio-religious ideas and African traditio-religious thought. Author of *The Emergence of Yahweh as "Judge" among the Gods: A Study of the Hebrew Root Špt* (Mellen, 2007), he has contributed to the *Anchor Bible Dictionary, New International Bible Dictionary,* and *International Bible Commentary.* He is completing a manuscript on the Old Testament and African tradition for Orbis Books.

Madipoane Masenya (ngwan'a Mphahlele) (D.Lit. & Phil., Biblical Studies: OT specialization). Professor of Old Testament Studies and Chair of the Department of Old Testament and Ancient Near Eastern Studies, UNISA. Research interests include gender issues and the Hebrew Bible, and wisdom texts (both ancient Israel and African contexts). She has published widely on the Bosadi (womanhood) readings of biblical texts, with her seminal work being *How Worthy Is the Woman of Worth? Rereading Proverbs 31:10–31 in African-South Africa* (Peter Lang, 2004). Most recently she was associate editor of *The Africana Bible: Reading Israel's Scriptures in Israel and the African Diaspora* (Fortress, 2010).

Andrew M. Mbuvi (Ph.D.), Associate Professor, Biblical Studies and Hermeneutics at Shaw University Divinity School, High Point, North Carolina. He is a Kenyan New Testament scholar with wide-ranging research interests, including biblical and philosophical hermeneutics, African novels and literature, and postcolonial theory. Currently serves as cochair of the African Biblical Hermeneutics Section in the Society of Biblical Literature and has authored *Temple, Exile and Identity in 1 Peter* (T&T Clark, 2007) and contributed to *Encyclopedia of African Religions* (Sage, 2009).

Sarojini Nadar (Ph.D.), Associate Professor, School of Religion and Theology at University of KwaZulu-Natal, South Africa, and Director of its Gender and Religion Program. Current cochair of African Biblical Hermeneutics section of the Society of Biblical Literature and has published widely in the field of feminist biblical hermeneutics, with a special focus on HIV&AIDS, and gender-based violence. She is committed to transformative praxis and is always in search of ways to bridge the gap between the academy and civil society.

Elivered Nasambu-Mulongo (Ph.D. candidate) in Old Testament and Interpretation, Toronto School of Theology, University of Toronto. A Kenyan biblical scholar specializing in interpretation of the Hebrew Bible, African women's interpretations, postcolonial approaches, and Bible translation. Her unpublished MTS thesis was "Ordination of Women in Kenya: Talking from Experience." Her dissertation intends to explore how African women interpret the Bible.

Jeremy Punt (Ph.D.), New Testament Professor at Stellenbosch University, South

Africa. His publications on hermeneutics and critical theory in New Testament interpretation in Africa include "Paul and the Others: Insiders, Outsiders, and Animosity," in *Animosity, the Bible, and Us: Some European, North American, and South African Perspectives*, ed. J. T. Fitzgerald et al. (SBL, 2009), and "Postcolonial Theory as Academic Double Agent? Power, Ideology, and Postcolonial Biblical Hermeneutics," in *Postcolonial Interventions: Essays in Honor of R. S. Sugirtharajah*, ed. Tat-siong B. Liew (Sheffield Phoenix, 2009).

Gerrie F. Snyman (D.Th.), Old Testament Professor in the Department of Old Testament and Ancient Near Eastern Studies, University of South Africa. His research interests are in biblical hermeneutics and early Second Temple period texts. His publications include a recent book (in Afrikaans) on the ethics of interpretation in a South African context (*Om die Bybel anders te lees: 'n Etiek van Bybellees* [Pretoria: Griffel-Media, 2007]) and is currently working on "whiteness" as a heuristic key to understanding African hermeneutics' unease with what is known as Western hermeneutics.

Lovemore Togarasei (Ph.D.), Associate Professor, Biblical Studies, Department of Theology and Religious Studies at University of Botswana. A Zimbabwean biblical studies scholar with a special focus on New Testament, his other research interests include the Bible in African Christianity, HIV and AIDS, and pentecostalism. He has authored *The Bible in Context* (UOBamberg, 2009) and is currently working on a book to be titled *The New Testament for a New Africa*.

Maarman S. Tshehla (Ph.D.), Senior Lecturer, New Testament Studies, University of South Africa. Research interests include African biblical studies and Pauline studies. He is at present revising his Ph.D. thesis into a book, tentatively titled *God of the Book: Nineteenth Century Basotho and the Bible*, to be published by Cluster Publications.

Robert Wafawanaka (Ph.D.), Assistant Professor of Biblical Studies at The Samuel DeWitt Proctor School of Theology of Virginia Union University, Richmond, Virginia. A Zimbabwean Hebrew Bible scholar, his research interests included issues of land, poverty, and wealth in the Hebrew Bible.

Robert S. Wafula (ABD), Old Testament, Drew University, Madison, New Jersey. A Kenyan biblical studies scholar, his special focus is on postcolonialism, ethnicity studies, cultural hermeneutics, justice, representations, and inter-ethnic/racial reconciliations. He is currently working on his Ph.D. dissertation entitled "Biblical Representations of Moab: A Kenyan Postcolonial Reading."

Gerald West (Ph.D.) teaches Old Testament/Hebrew Bible and African Biblical Hermeneutics in the School of Religion and Theology, University of KwaZulu-

Natal, South Africa. He is also Director of the Ujamaa Centre for Community Development and Research, a project in which socially engaged biblical scholars and ordinary African readers of the Bible from poor, working-class, and marginalized communities collaborate for social transformation. He has published widely on the subject.

Alice Yafeh-Deigh (Ph.D.), Assistant Professor of Biblical Studies, Azusa Pacific University, School of Theology. A Cameroonian biblical studies scholar whose areas of interest, expertise, research, and teaching include New Testament exegesis, Greco-Roman sexual ethics, cultural hermeneutics, feminist hermeneutics, postcolonial hermeneutics, and literary and rhetorical methods of biblical interpretation.

Gosnell L. Yorke (Ph.D.), Lecturer in Greek and New Testament, University of KwaZulu-Natal, South Africa. He hails from the Caribbean (St. Kitts-Nevis) and, in 1987, earned his doctorate in New Testament Studies from McGill University, Canada. From 1996–2006 he served as a translation consultant with the United Bible Societies in Africa. He has also taught in North America and the Caribbean and has published principally in the areas of Bible translation, Afrocentrism and postcolonialism, the New Testament and orality, and the Bible in Africa and the diaspora.

Index of Ancient Sources

Index of Modern Authors

Lightning Source UK Ltd.
Milton Keynes UK
UKOW03f1851200814

237273UK00001B/87/P